NEW YORK CITY

AND
NEARBY ATTRACTIONS

FODOR'S MODERN GUIDES

are compiled, researched, and edited by an international team of travel writers, field correspondents, and editors. The series, which now almost covers the globe, was founded by Eugene Fodor.

OFFICES
New York & London

FODOR'S NEW YORK CITY:

Area Editors: MICHAEL IACHETTA, VIRGINIA PUZO
Editorial Contributors: DAVID FRANKEL, JENNIFER HARTIG, BETH IOGHA, JOHN MAXYMUK, DENNIS STARIN
Editorial Consultants: IRA MAYER, LEONORE FLEISCHER
Editor: ALAN TUCKER
Editorial Associate: JUDITH deRUBINI
Research: MARY ANN PALMER
Illustrations: SANDRA LANG, TED BURWELL
Maps and Plans: DYNO LOWENSTEIN

FODOR'S
NEW YORK CITY
AND NEARBY ATTRACTIONS
1982

FODOR'S MODERN GUIDES, INC.
Distributed by
DAVID McKAY COMPANY, INC.
New York

Copyright © 1982 by FODOR'S MODERN GUIDES, INC.
ISBN 0-679-00812-8 (David McKay edition)
ISBN 0-340-27868-4 (Hodder & Stoughton edition)
No part of this book may be reproduced in any form without permission in writing from the publisher.

All the following Guides are current (most of them also in the Hodder and Stoughton British edition).

CURRENT FODOR'S COUNTRY AND AREA TITLES:

AUSTRALIA, NEW ZEALAND
  AND SOUTH PACIFIC
AUSTRIA
BAJA CALIFORNIA
BELGIUM AND
  LUXEMBOURG
BERMUDA
BRAZIL
CANADA
CARIBBEAN AND BAHAMAS
CENTRAL AMERICA
EASTERN EUROPE
EGYPT
EUROPE
FRANCE
GERMANY
GREAT BRITAIN
GREECE
HOLLAND

INDIA & NEPAL
IRELAND
ISRAEL
ITALY
JAPAN AND KOREA
JORDAN AND HOLY LAND
MEXICO
NORTH AFRICA
PEOPLE'S REPUBLIC
  OF CHINA
PORTUGAL
SCANDINAVIA
SOUTH AMERICA
SOUTHEAST ASIA
SOVIET UNION
SPAIN
SWITZERLAND
TURKEY
YUGOSLAVIA

CITY GUIDES:

LONDON
NEW YORK CITY
PARIS

ROME
WASHINGTON, D.C.

FODOR'S BUDGET SERIES:

BUDGET BRITAIN
BUDGET CARIBBEAN
BUDGET EUROPE
BUDGET FRANCE
BUDGET GERMANY

BUDGET ITALY
BUDGET JAPAN
BUDGET MEXICO
BUDGET SPAIN
BUDGET TRAVEL IN AMERICA

USA GUIDES:

USA (in one volume)
ALASKA
CALIFORNIA
COLORADO
FAR WEST
FLORIDA
HAWAII

NEW ENGLAND
PENNSYLVANIA
SOUTH
SOUTHWEST
SUNBELT LEISURE
  GUIDE

SPECIAL INTEREST SERIES:

CIVIL WAR SITES

MANUFACTURED IN THE UNITED STATES OF AMERICA
10 9 8 7 6 5 4 3 2 1

Contents

Map of New York City viii-ix

FOREWORD xi

INTRODUCTION TO NEW YORK CITY 1
Points of Interest map 16–17

FACTS AT YOUR FINGERTIPS 19

When to Go; Planning Your Trip; Tips for British Visitors; Tourist Information; Packing; What to Do with the Pets; What Will It Cost; Hints to the Motorist; Hotels and Motels; Dining Out; Drinking Laws; Religious Worship; Business Hours and Local Time; Postage; Sports; Seasonal Events Outside New York City; Roughing It; Farm Vacations and Guest Ranches; Fishing and Hunting; Camping Out; State Parks; Tipping; Senior Citizen and Student Discounts; Hints to Handicapped Travelers; Metric Conversion; Emergency Telephone Numbers; Holidays; Climate.

NEW YORK CITY: A CONGREGATION OF NEIGHBORHOODS 41
Orientation map of Manhattan 44–45
Map of Lower Manhattan 57
Map of Chinatown-Little Italy-SoHo 67
Map of Greenwich Village 72
Map of Midtown Manhattan 84–85
Map of the United Nations 96
Map of Lincoln Center 102
Map of the Upper West Side 103
Map of the Upper East Side 107

SIGHTSEEING CHECKLIST 125

PRACTICAL INFORMATION FOR NEW YORK CITY 129

How to Get There 129
Hotels and Motels 130
Telephones 142
How to Get Around 142
Tourist Information Services and Recommended Reading 151, 152
Seasonal Events 153

CONTENTS

Free Events   156
Tours and Special-Interest Sightseeing   158
Parks   161
   Map of Central Park   162
Zoos   164
Gardens   165
Beaches   167
Babysitting Services   169
Children's Activities   169
Participant Sports   172
Spectator Sports   177
Lotteries   180
Historic Sites   180
Libraries   185
   Plan of the 42nd Street Library   186
Museums   189
   Plan of the American Museum of Natural History   191, 192
   Plan of the Cloisters   194
   Plan of the Frick Museum   196
   Plan of the Metropolitan Museum of Art   198–201
Movies   212
Music   214
Dance   218
Stage   220
Shopping   224
   Map of Fifth Avenue/Midtown shopping   228–9
   Map of Manhattan shopping   238–9
Restaurants   251
Desserts   304
Cafés   305
Night Life   306
Bars   318
   Map of Manhattan areas active at night   320–321

Attractions Near New York City

FIRE ISLAND AND THE HAMPTONS   331
   Map of Long Island resort areas   336–7

WESTCHESTER AND THE HUDSON VALLEY   358

CONTENTS

THE CATSKILLS — 379
Map of the Catskills 381

THE SARATOGA AREA — 395

THE ADIRONDACKS — 402
Map of the Adirondacks 405

THE THOUSAND ISLANDS — 421

THE NIAGARA FRONTIER — 426
Map of the Niagara Falls area 427

THE JERSEY SHORE AND ATLANTIC CITY — 439
Map of the Sandy Hook area 441
Map of the Jersey Shore beaches 443
Map of Atlantic City 446

Map of New York State 462–3

INDEX — 464–8

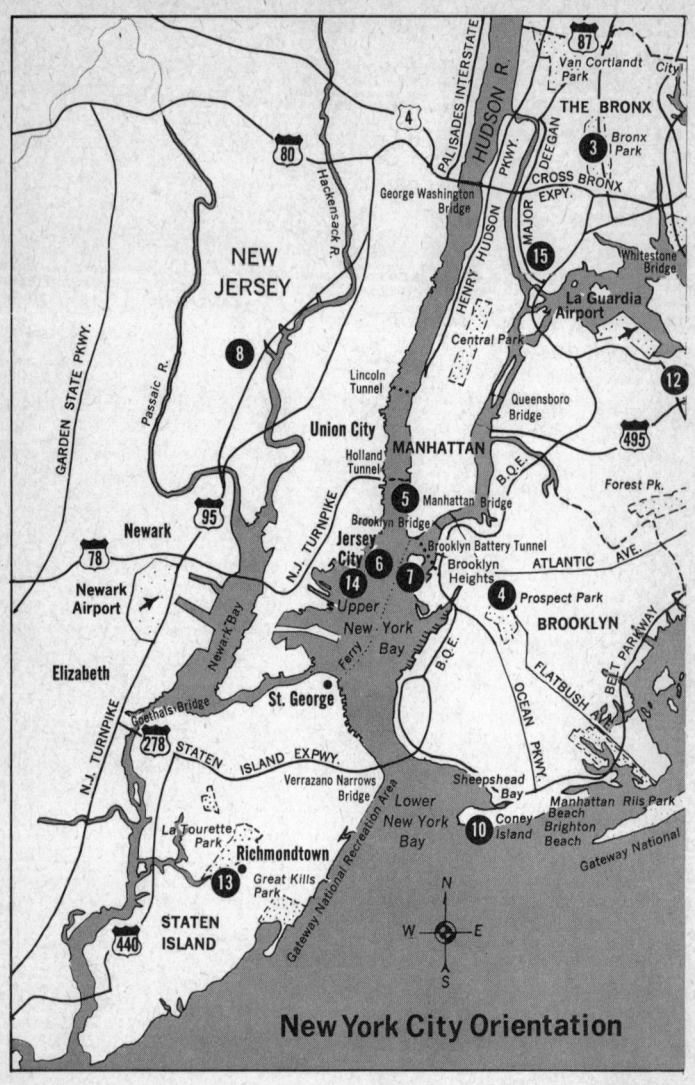

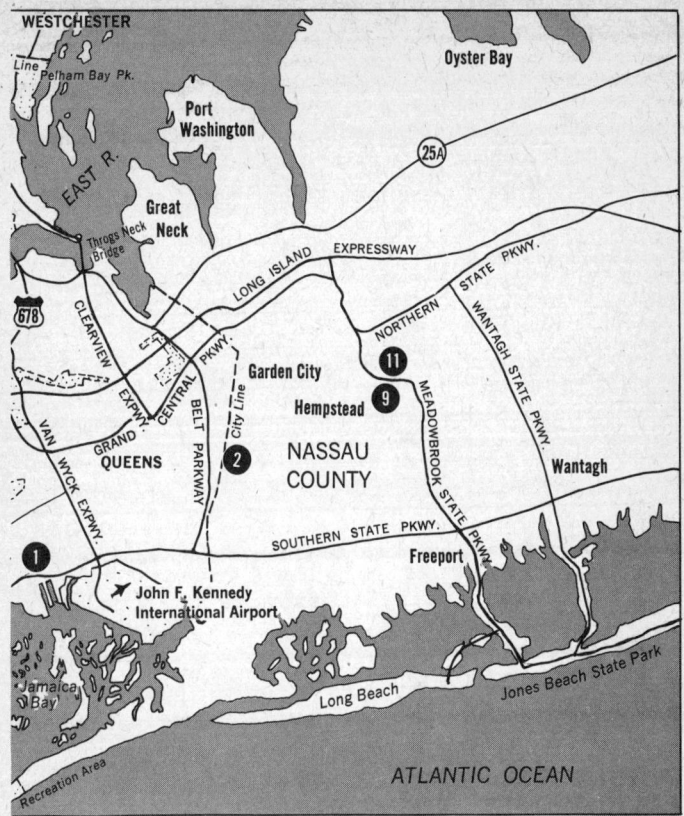

Points of Interest

1) Aqueduct Race Track
2) Belmont Park
3) Bronx Zoo & Botanical Garden
4) Brooklyn Museum & Botanical Garden
5) World Trade Center
6) Ellis Island
7) Governors Island
8) Meadowlands Sports Complex
9) Nassau Coliseum
10) New York Aquarium
11) Roosevelt Raceway
12) Shea Stadium
13) Staten Island Historic Museum
14) Statue of Liberty
15) Yankee Stadium

LANGUAGE/30
For the Business or Vacationing International Traveler

In 21 languages! A basic language course on 2 cassettes and a phrase book... Only $14.95 ea. + shipping

Nothing flatters people more than to hear visitors try to speak their language and LANGUAGE/30, used by thousands of satisfied travelers, gets you speaking the basics quickly and easily. Each LANGUAGE/30 course offers:

- up to 2 hours of guided practice in greetings, asking questions and general conversation
- special section on social customs and etiquette

Order yours today. Languages available:

ARABIC	GERMAN	JAPANESE	RUSSIAN
CHINESE	GREEK	KOREAN	SERBO-CROATIAN
DANISH	HEBREW	NORWEGIAN	SPANISH
DUTCH	INDONESIAN	PERSIAN	SWAHILI
FRENCH	ITALIAN	PORTUGUESE	TURKISH
	VIETNAMESE		

To order send $14.95 per course + shipping $1.50 1st course, $1 ea. add. course. In Canada $2 1st course, $1.50 ea. add. course. NY and CA residents add state sales tax. Outside USA and Canada $14.95 (U.S.) + air mail shipping: $6 for 1st course, $4 ea. add. course. Masterchage, VISA and Am. Express card users give brand, account number (all digits), expiration date and signature. SEND TO: FODOR, Dept. LC 760, 2 Park Ave., NY 10016, USA.

FOREWORD

New York City—one of if not, arguably, *the* top tourist and business-travel destination in the world—is loaded with attractions (and distractions). Everyone in the world, except perhaps a few older folks in the Ural Mountains, knows this.

Fodor's New York City is designed to describe and explain the city to you, and to help you decide, once you're there, what you want to do and where you want to go. The book is intended to be your tool for making some order out of a chaos of possibilities. We have therefore concentrated on giving you the broadest **range** of choices the city offers, and within that range to present **selections** that will be safe, solid, and of value to you. The descriptions we provide are just enough for you to make intelligent choices from among our selections, based on your own tastes and pocketbook.

All selections and comments in *Fodor's New York City* are based on the editors' and contributors' personal experience. We feel that our first responsibility is to inform and protect you, the reader. Errors are bound to creep into any travel guide, however. We go to press in the late fall of the year, and much change can and will occur in New York City even while we are on press and during the succeeding twelve months or so when this edition is on sale. We cannot, therefore, be responsible for the sudden closing of a restaurant, a change in a museum's days or hours, a shift of chefs (for the worse), and so forth. We sincerely welcome letters from readers on these changes, or from those whose opinions differ from ours, and we are ready to revise our entries for next year's edition when the facts warrant it.

Send your letters to the editors at **Fodor's Modern Guides, Inc., 2 Park Avenue, New York, NY 10016.** Continental readers may prefer to write to Fodor's Modern Guides, 1–11 John Adam Street, London WC2, England.

Finally, a word about the "nearby attractions": New York City is the major port of entry for the Northeast. This book would have to be published in several volumes if we tried to cover it all. Instead, we have selected only a few of the more popular nearby side trips a visitor might want to add to an itinerary after arriving in the city.

NEW YORK CITY'S ETHNIC MAKE-UP

New York City must be considered in the context of the urban, suburban, and so-called exurban areas that surround it and of which it is the working center; this area has an estimated population of about 17,000,000 people, and is the most populous urban area in the world. (Mexico City is second and Tokyo third.)

The population of the five boroughs of the city itself is a little over 7,000,000. Of these, two million are Jewish (not an ethnic category, to be sure), and about two and a half million black. The figure for blacks includes those with heritages from Haiti, Trinidad, and other places in the Caribbean area. There are about 1.6 million Hispanic-Americans (Puerto Rico, Cuba, Dominican Republic, South America, Mexico). It is now difficult to estimate the Italian-American population, but it is presumed to be something less than a million, as is the Irish-American community here, many having moved out to the suburbs. Other noticeable ethnic presences are Greek, Indian, Chinese, Japanese, Korean, German, Hungarian, and Russian.

Here are selected figures for registered *aliens* resident in the city:

Dominican Republic	75,000
Italy	46,000
China	43,000
Jamaica	38,000
USSR	20,000
India	15,000
England	14,000
Korea	14,000
Poland	9,000

The total of registered ("legal") aliens is 576,000, but the N.Y. City Planning Commission estimates that there are about 750,000 "undocumented" (illegal) aliens here, most of whom have not been included in any of the official population figures given above.

INTRODUCTION TO NEW YORK CITY

The Cosmopolitan Colossus

by MICHAEL IACHETTA

They call New York City "The Big Apple," and perhaps you wonder why.

The name was originally used in the 1920s and '30s by colorful people in the sports and entertainment world—particularly jazz musicians—as a way of saying, "I'm playing New York City; I've made it to the big time—the Big Apple." A variation on the same theme goes: "There are many apples on the tree, but when you pick New York City, you pick the Big Apple."

At least that's the explanation offered by Charles Gillett, president of the New York Convention and Visitors Bureau. He should know. Gillett is the sharpie who created and launched the Big Apple advertising campaign in 1971—a campaign that today lures approximately 17½ million visitors who spend over $2 billion annually in New York City.

The native New Yorker, whether born, bred, or transplanted here, thinks that the Big Apple is the greatest city in the world. And New Yorkers usually go out of their way to make sure visitors leave with the same impression.

With New York City attracting more visitors than any other city in the world, tourism is a major factor in its economy. The New York "attitude" may take some getting used to—that brusque, diffident manner that ignores everyone else on the street is basically a way to get a few extra moments of solitude—but most citizens in all five boroughs appreciate the never-ending parade of new friends who come here to explore the city's wealth of attractions. Don't let the few, overpublicized rotten apples spoil the barrel, so to speak.

Right from the start we'll admit that New York City *can* overwhelm you—with statistics alone: There are more than 100,000 hotel rooms in every price category; and over 350 theaters, 120 museums, 400 art galleries, and 37 single-spaced pages of restaurants in the New York telephone directory's business Yellow Pages. But statistics alone do not make up a city.

New York is, first and foremost, a gateway to America, and a swinging gateway at that—and has been almost since its birth. Endless succeeding generations continue New York City's tradition of ethnicity —from Chinatown to Little Italy, Yorkville, the West Side, all around the town. At its core, however, the Big Apple is much more than East Side chic and Madison Avenue slick, Brooklyn and Bronx street smarts and Queens and Staten Island middle-American open hearts. At the core of the Big Apple is the New Yorker, a very special breed, walking around to his or her personal version of "Lullabye of Broadway," no matter which borough they live in.

They may not go around humming "New York, New York, what a wonderful town" or singing that paean of praise to the Big Apple, "New York, New York" as Frank Sinatra does, but New Yorkers know that their city is a unique place. And a surprising number of our 8 million residents are anxious to help you get to know their city. Forget about the stereotype of the cold, blasé New Yorker. Are you in doubt about how to get from here to there? Is the subway map a maze of indecipherable colors, letters, and numbers? Just ask someone. But be prepared for the answer to come in any one of a variety of accents, depending on where you are.

INTRODUCTION

Indeed, the average New Yorker can be an endless font of information. He or she can tell you all about "The Met," be it the Metropolitan Opera House, the Metropolitan Museum of Art, or the Mets baseball team. Of the Opera House at Lincoln Center they'll tell you of the moment when the dazzling crystal chandeliers begin to rise, signaling the start of a world-class opera, ballet, classical, or pop concert. Of the museum they'll tell of the New American and Chinese wings, the costume department, or the grand staircase and foyer by which you enter the building from Fifth Avenue. Of the Mets, who play out at Queens' Shea Stadium—well, they'll cheer on the local underdog team even if they try to steer you to Yankee Stadium instead, where you can catch the "Bronx Bombers," as the Yankees are affectionately known.

In short, whatever your taste, the Big Apple has something—and more—to satisfy it. But don't be tempted to bite off more than you can chew, especially at first bite. In other words, don't try to see and do everything at once. Break down your visit into manageable parts. First take a quick look at *Fodor's New York City* and decide what your "must see" attractions are, and give these high priority on your list of things to do. The book is organized so that you can conveniently group certain visits together—for example, the Statue of Liberty in the morning, the Wall Street area (including Trinity Church, the New York Stock Exchange, and Fraunces Tavern) in midafternoon, and the World Trade Center as close to sunset as you can time it make a full day of glorious sightseeing.

You may also want to decide right away whether you'll limit your excursions to Manhattan Island—as most tourists do—or whether you'll "take" the Bronx and Staten Island, too (as the song goes), or even Brooklyn and Queens; or take your visit borough-by-borough, neighborhood-by-neighborhood. This will save you a great deal of travel time on subways and buses or in cabs and automobiles, and you'll be fresh for the "real" business at hand: sightseeing, shopping, eating, and otherwise exploring the city.

Here, then, is a quick look at what the five boroughs have to offer, an appetizer of sorts before the movable feast that is the city as a whole. (Additional attractions and more detailed listings about those mentioned below are given in the appropriate sections of this book.)

There are those who call Manhattan the most exciting city in the world. But just as New York City is not the United States, Manhattan is not New York City. Indeed, Manhattan Island—you can prove to yourself that it is an island by taking a Circle Line cruise around it—is the smallest of the city's five boroughs. It is 13.4 miles long and only 2.3 miles across at its widest point, but it contains the artistic, financial, fashion, architectural, creative, and gourmet capitals of the world. We'll detail Manhattan's myriad offerings later, but the point for the moment is that while Manhattan is probably where you'll want to spend the bulk of your time in New York, visits to the other boroughs will help fill out your impressions of the city.

Almost everyone knows, for example, that Manhattan is at the heart of the nation's theatrical and musical activities. But the Brooklyn Academy of Music, known as BAM, has been one of the city's busiest performing arts centers since 1859. It is also the nation's oldest such complex, housing an opera house, a theater, numerous rehearsal areas, and several "performance spaces" that are used for small theatrical presentations and especially intimate concerts. Sarah Bernhardt played Camille here; Edwin Booth portrayed Hamlet, Pavlova danced *Swan Lake,* Enrico Caruso gave recitals. And all of their latter-day counterparts continue the august Academy's grand traditions.

Brooklyn may no longer have its own baseball team (the Dodgers moved to Los Angeles in 1958), but it would still rank as the fourth largest city in the country—if it were a city unto itself. Known to some as the "Borough of Churches" because of the number of its religious institutions—many dating back to pre-Civil War days—Brooklyn's highlights also include:

- The world's largest collection of Victorian brownstones in such neighborhoods as Brooklyn Heights (where literary figures Walt Whitman, Hart Crane, Arthur Miller, and Norman Mailer have lived);
- The Brooklyn Museum, bested only by those in London and Cairo for its Egyptian art collection;
- The extensive Botanic Gardens, with its special herb garden designed for the sightless; the Fulton Ferry, where Robert Fulton established his steam-powered ferry route from Manhattan in 1814 (recently refurbished and brought back into service for special weekend events);
- An endless variety of ethnic enclaves, with the Middle Eastern fare along Atlantic Avenue a particular standout from a culinary point of view;
- The city's most popular beach and amusement park—Coney Island and Astroland, respectively, where more than a million and a half people are likely to congregate on a hot summer Sunday;
- And, of course, the beautiful Brooklyn Bridge, spanning the East River from lower Manhattan. (The bridge has a wonderful pedestrian lane above the roadway, but it is scheduled for repairs and may be closed for a season or two.)

If Brooklyn is a borough of contrasts between industrial and shipping interests on the one hand, and 500-acre parks, miles-long beaches and well-preserved "olde New York" settlements on the other, Staten Island is the city's most rural area.

INTRODUCTION

An island of low, fertile hills and valleys, the borough—alternately known as Richmond—includes a wildlife refuge as part of Gateway National Park (parts of which are also in Brooklyn, Queens, and New Jersey) and much recreational parkland. The 80-acre Snug Harbor Cultural Center constitutes the largest single restoration project going on in the U.S. Voorlezer's House—known as the original Little Red Schoolhouse and built in 1695—is the oldest elementary schoolhouse still standing in the nation. It is part of the Richmondtown Restoration, which features buildings, furnishings and crafts of the 17th, 18th, and 19th centuries . . . and more.

Would you believe, for example, that the highest point on the Atlantic Coast between Maine and Key West is on Staten Island? That's Todt Hill, almost 410 feet above sea level. And would you believe that despite its considerable historical legacy, Staten Island is probably most famous for its ferry ride—a five-mile excursion across New York Harbor to the southern tip of Manhattan. Almost 320 million people a year make the round trip (many of them commuting just as easily as others might by bus or subway), as beautiful a nautical experience as the Big Apple offers. The tab? Twenty-five cents—round trip!

Geographically, Queens is New York's biggest borough. Its 13 parks cover 6,000 acres of land. It contains nearly 300,000 homes, features two of the nation's most famous tennis stadiums, and two of its leading thoroughbred racetracks. It is home to the New York Jets and Mets, giving the borough both a pro football and pro baseball team. Queens also boasts New York City's two commercial airports—John F. Kennedy on the southern shore and La Guardia on the northern shore.

Although the two airports are less than ten miles apart, those shores provide 196 miles of waterfront, with fine Atlantic Ocean beaches offering a cool respite from summer heat and humidity. The Queens Museum's star attraction is the 15,000-square-foot model of New York City that was originally featured at the 1964 World's Fair. And both that museum and the Science Museum are located on the former fairgrounds site.

The Bronx is the northernmost borough of New York. It is known as the "Borough of Universities" because it has ten institutions of higher education—more than most countries in the world. Its 42 square miles (23 percent of which are parkland) include a veritable Zoo's-Who in the Bronx Zoo. World-renowned for its collection of more than 3,000 animals representing over 800 species, the Bronx Zoo is newly renovated with a monorail and a tramway, and with "cages" simulating the animals' natural habitats. Nearby is the borough's other main attraction, the New York Botanical Garden, whose 250-acre expanse includes the 40-acre wilderness Hemlock Forest beside the Bronx River Gorge.

INTRODUCTION

Because the Bronx is preeminently residential, many of its neighborhoods retain their original character. City Island, for instance, is a bit of seafaring New England tucked away on Long Island Sound—a nautical enclave of century-old houses and boatyards where America Cup-winning sailboats have been built. Other Bronx features:

- Mott Haven Historic District, with townhouses dating back to the Civil War era;
- Riverdale's fine country-style churches;
- The Van Cortlandt Mansion, dating back to before 1758, which served as headquarters for both American and British troops during the Revolution;
- And the wide avenue known as the Grand Concourse—a curving 4½-mile boulevard patterned after Paris' Champs Élysées, with the largest collection of Art Deco residences in the world.

For recreation-seekers the Bronx offers four 18-hole golf courses, the three-mile-long Orchard Beach, Pelham Bay Park, and an outdoor arena whose name tells all: Yankee Stadium.

By now you get the point that the Big Apple has more to offer than Manhattan's concrete canyons, skyscrapers, museums, theaters, nightclubs, restaurants, shipping districts, hotels, and pleasure palaces. If it is worth going beyond Manhattan's borders to sample what the rest of the city has to offer, there is still no denying that Manhattan is where most of the "action" really is.

Although most New Yorkers calmly ignore the fact, their hometown has been the political capital of the world for over a quarter of a century—ever since the United Nations set up headquarters here in 1952, on land that is international territory, donated by John D. Rockefeller for the purpose. But New York City is more than a political capital. It is the international marketplace of ideas, and the great catalyst of projects in publishing, advertising, entertainment, and finance.

Like Paris, London, and Rome, it is a capital of cosmopolitan thought with a large and diversified diplomatic corps whose members, many in colorful dress, add spice to the fashion parade. They also add glitter, excitement, sometimes mystery, to social functions and parties, and assure the reputation of the hostesses; their opinions and appearances add leaven to panel discussions on nationwide television broadcasts, and their thoughts often are recorded by energetic newsmen.

Even though it has only three major daily newspapers of its own, New York remains a world press center. Its columnists are read, via syndication, in papers all over America—and in some foreign countries. The faces and voices of television news personalities based in New York City are as familiar to Americans across the country as they are to viewers in the metropolitan area. The gossip that is generated by the comings and goings of people in the entertainment world is avidly read by newspaper readers all over the country. Who hasn't heard of Earl Wilson and his night-walking, night-stalking brethren? Similarly, and for less understandable reasons, the lives, loves, and leisure-time pursuits of New York area society, as minutely chronicled by an oversized corps of society writers, are of more moment to column readers in any town on the other side of the Hudson than is news of their own local school-board elections.

Equally important is the answer to the questions, what are the television, film, and Broadway stars and the international social leaders wearing this season . . . this month . . . this week? New York City is a world capital of fashion and glamour; *Women's Wear Daily* tells it first to the trade and the word spreads out from there.

It is true that the most beautiful women in the world can be seen strolling along Fifth and Madison Avenues, and that they will be dressed in the latest styles, some in quiet good taste, some in the bizarre fashions women's magazines contend "everyone" is wearing this year. (And a lot of New Yorkers are.) The Garment Center serves two masters: the average American woman—and the society leaders. The average American woman is the best-dressed "average" in the world because Seventh Avenue designers and manufacturers make it possible for her to dress smartly, even with chic, at budget costs. Helping the secretary, the department store clerks, the office worker dress well is the major burden of Seventh Avenue, for there are so many of these lovely women in the work force around the country, and their appearance—appealing, charming, attractive—has been a cause for comment by visiting foreigners. They are aided in their task, of course, by the cosmeticians, the hairdressers, milliners, furriers—and all the others who labor in the vineyard, the New York City vineyard, to make the American woman one of the best dressed in the world.

Society leaders insist on the innovations, the sometimes outlandish distinctive touches, that attract the cameras and columnists—and the designers serve them so well that it has now come to the point where women at a formal dress party may be wearing just about anything that seems new and different and still be dressed in style. And if some designs are shocking—what of it? It's grist for the fashion writer's mill, and likely to lead to a nationwide reputation for the designer.

As a shopping center, New York City is incomparable. To this market place, this giant bazaar, flow goods from all over the world, from a splendiferous new Rolls Royce to a carving set handcrafted by an artisan in a far-off village of Kashmir, from the latest Danish modern furniture to an antique candlestick holder from Yemen. New York City abounds in shops of every variety and size. There are the well-known department stores, such as Macy's and Gimbels, and the obscure grocery stores selling dried seaweed, bean curd, and other exotica essential to Japanese-style cookery. Almost anything that is available anywhere in the world can be found somewhere in New York City.

Start, for example, with the sidewalks of Manhattan's Fifth Avenue, from 34th to 59th Streets. Here, skyscrapers, traditional office buildings, and banks mix with the giant department stores and bookshops, jewelers, shoe stores, men's and women's haberdashers, specialists in crystal, porcelain, leatherware, tobacco products, toys, and more. Still more stores spread along the streets east and west of Fifth Avenue, especially on the main thoroughfares of 34th, 42nd, and 57th Streets. At Herald Square—where 34th Street meets Broadway and Avenue of the Americas (Sixth Avenue)—Macy's and Gimbels tower over opposite corners vying to bring shoppers the most of everything at the best of prices.

Due south of this famous intersection (which is the last stop on the Macy's Thanksgiving Day Parade route—an event televised all across the country) is the discount camera center. The prices here are so low that even Japanese tourists frequent the shops along West 32nd and 33rd Streets for "imported" bargains. To the north, on 47th Street between Fifth Avenue and Avenue of the Americas, is the diamond district. Eighty percent of the diamonds bought and sold in the U.S. are traded on this one block!

Still more shops stretch off Fifth Avenue from 49th to 51st Streets in the labyrinthine underground passages beneath Rockefeller Center's skyscrapers. West 57th Street is sprinkled with fabric shops and fashion boutiques and, as you head eastward, increasingly with art galleries and specialty shops. Second, Third, and Lexington Avenues, in the 50s and 60s, are for the *très chic,* what with Bloomingdale's—by far the city's most notoriously trendy department store—exclusive boutiques and haughty antique dealers.

Madison Avenue, also on the East Side, has its own shopping character from the mid-50s up to as far as 90th Street. The boutiques of leading international designers, galleries with the latest in contemporary art (as well as considerable pickings for more traditional tastes), and stylish houseware shops and restaurants fill to overflowing with the smart set.

Across town, on the Upper West Side along Columbus Avenue and Broadway (in both cases from about 66th to 79th Streets), tastes are a little less trendy. Returning down the West Side along Broadway or Seventh Avenue and into the 30s brings you to the garment district, where one third of all clothes worn in the U.S. are manufactured. A few more blocks south is the fur district, where some manufacturers sell retail as well as wholesale.

INTRODUCTION

In shopping terms, Greenwich Village has lost much of its former distinction as a center for unusual crafts, handmade goods, and specialty shops. Nonetheless, a handful of established book and antique dealers, and even the occasional craftsperson have withstood the change in the Village's character—the book and antique people mostly centered around Broadway between 9th and 13th streets, the craftspeople sprinkled throughout the East and West Villages.

Over the past decade the warehouses and factories of SoHo—the abbreviation stands for "South of Houston Street"—have been converted into artists' studios and loft apartments upstairs, and art galleries, craft shops, and clothing boutiques on the lower floors. East of SoHo is Little Italy, where the best pasta, salami, espresso coffee and, especially along Mulberry Street and its immediate offshoots, the best genuinely Italian restaurants are to be found. Canal Street, the southern boundary of Little Italy and SoHo, is the street for appliances, hardware, and all manner of supplies for the do-it-yourselfer.

Canal Street is also the dividing line between Little Italy and Chinatown. On Mott Street south of Canal, you'll discover some of the best—and often least expensive—Chinese food in town, or anywhere. The service may be indifferent (waiters don't always understand English, and there's nothing leisurely about the pace), and the surroundings only a step removed from basic coffee shop, but the experience and shops are alone worth the visit.

The Lower East Side, particularly along Orchard, Eldridge, and Grand Streets, is a bargain hunter's paradise. Designer clothes, men's furnishings, towels, sheets, lingerie, handbags, shoes, children's clothing, wallpaper, yarns, and fabric are among the "finds" in small, crowded shops where discounts usually run to 20 percent off uptown prices. This is a predominately Jewish area, and many of the shops are closed on Saturdays—the Jewish Sabbath—but open for a full day beginning bright and early Sunday mornings. It may not be wholesale, but the prices come about as close to that mark as you're likely to find anywhere.

In fact, "getting it wholesale" is one of many New Yorkers' favorite games—plants in the West 20s, lighting fixtures and restaurant/cooking supplies along the Bowery, Latin American foods on East 116th Street, Italian goods along Arthur Avenue in the Bronx, Middle Eastern specialties on Brooklyn's Atlantic Avenue. The New York City section in most local bookstores have several slim volumes with detailed information on Lower East Side and other discount/wholesale shopping areas.

But of all these things, clothing is the most important, and women from around the country, during visits, flock to the New York City stores and shops they have heard and read about in the national magazines.

And the crowds in New York's shops these days are being swelled by visitors from abroad who are discovering that the relative decline of the dollar has made the United States a vacation paradise—the phrase that used to be used so often for the benefit of dollar-bearing Americans traveling in foreign lands. Oriental and European commercial and financial institutions have set up shop, too, in New York City; and in midtown Manhattan today you can see as many Japanese as you used to see Americans in Tokyo wandering around the Ginza.

Besides all this, New York City is a center of maritime commerce—and in fact is the second busiest port in the world (after Rotterdam).

Financier to the Nation

Despite the recent and widely publicized miseries of its own fiscal administration, New York is still the financial center to much of the world (though the flood of foreign investment into America has captured attention of late); and its tradition for shrewd wheeling and dealing began in 1626, only seventeen years after Henry Hudson, an Englishman on a Dutch payroll, first explored it thoroughly. Peter Minuit, the first Dutch governor, thought he had put over a fast deal on the Manhattan Indians who had sold him the island for $24 worth of trinkets. But the Indians were the commercial ancestors of the sharpies who sold the Brooklyn Bridge to generations of credulous hayseeds—the friendly "First Americans" didn't even own the land they sold; their village was in Inwood, about twelve miles away, on the northern tip of the island.

Although the British first took the city as an act of war in 1664, they finally managed to hold onto it with the help of a shady deal involving the swap of New York for the Caribbean island of Curaçao, of all places. But while the Dutch had New York (it was Nieuw Amsterdam then, of course) they welcomed the first Jews to land in what is now the United States—twenty-three men, women, and children who were the forerunners of New York's present Jewish population of well over two million, the city's largest ethnic group.

New York got its first newspaper in 1725, and ten years later freedom of the press was established in North America when its publisher, John Zenger, was acquitted of a libel charge. New Yorkers were split in their allegiance during the Revolutionary War; the city was a battleground during part of it, and Nathan Hale, a young schoolteacher given a spy assignment by George Washington, was hanged by the British near the present site of Grand Central Station. It was a battleground, too, during the Civil War, but the fighting then was between the police and

INTRODUCTION

New Yorkers rioting in protest against the draft laws. They've been exerting their right to protest ever since. Union Square became the focal point of the antiwar demonstrations of the late 1960s and early '70s, just as it was the heart of the Communist May Day parades during the Depression-ridden Thirties.

The United States experienced its greatest period of growth after the Civil War, and so did New York. The huge waves of immigration began to sweep in from Europe, and most of the wealth resulting from the winning of the West seemed to flow through New York. This was the era of the great millionaires: J. P. Morgan, the banker; Andrew Carnegie and Henry C. Frick, the steel men; and the transportation magnate, Commodore Cornelius Vanderbilt, whose nautical title derived from his operation of the Staten Island ferry. It was also the time of the newspaper giants: Horace Greeley, of the New York *Tribune,* James Gordon Bennett of the *Herald,* Joseph Pulitzer of the *World,* and then William Randolph Hearst and his *Evening Journal.*

New York was a big city in the Nineties, with a population 1,500,000. But it really became a world metropolis on January 1, 1898, when Brooklyn, the Bronx, Queens, and Richmond (Staten Island) were combined with Manhattan to form Greater New York; in 1900, the expanded city's population neared 3,500,000.

In the early years of this century, the central city, trapped on Manhattan Island, found a new direction for growth—straight up. The skyscraper, architectural trademark of New York, started with the twenty-story Flatiron Building in 1902, and in 1913 the 60-story Woolworth Building became the tallest in the world. It held this title for seven years, until it was displaced by the 77-story Chrysler Building. The Chrysler's primacy lasted only eleven years, until 1931, when the 102-story Empire State Building became king. Even though a television tower brought its height up to 1,694 feet, it was surpassed in 1972 by the twin-tower 110-story World Trade Center in the downtown financial district. Sadly for New York though, it lost its world skyscraper championship in 1974, when the Sears Roebuck building was opened in Chicago.

The New York that draws and fascinates visitors is the city of gleaming skyscrapers and shining opportunity, and the way to come upon it is as the immigrants did it, from the sea. You can do this, no matter what part of the country you are driving from, by routing yourself into Elizabeth or Bayonne, New Jersey, crossing one of the bridges to Staten Island, and driving to the St. George car ferry, which crosses to the Battery. Then you'll come to Manhattan from the Upper Bay, with the Statue of Liberty and Ellis Island (where the immigrants were processed in the old days) on your left, and the military reservation of Governor's Island on your right. During the twenty-minute ride, the magnificent skyline of the downtown financial district will loom larger and larger directly in front of you, and you'll feel the full impact of this most dramatic city on earth.

Next best way to do it—and this takes more detailed arranging—is to fly into La Guardia airport (planes landing at John F. Kennedy airport generally do their circling too far away for a good view of the heart of the city) at twilight, when darkness creeps up from the city streets, and the lights go on in a million windows all over town.

These are the quickest ways to get a feeling for the glamorous and exciting New York—the New York of Broadway openings and experimental plays in Greenwich Village warehouses, of smart restaurants in the East Fifties, cooperative apartments on upper Fifth Avenue, and television production centers around Radio City; of advertising agencies and magazine offices on Madison Avenue; of Lincoln Center, Carnegie Hall and the art galleries along 57th Street; of all the power, wealth, energy and talent that, despite its faults and problems, still make The Big Apple the capital of the world.

The Visitor's New York

This is the New York of the visitor and of the eager, career-bound arrival—and of a relatively small proportion of the city's residents. But it is a city that millions of New Yorkers living in a thousand neighborhood communities in Upper Manhattan, Brooklyn, the Bronx, Queens, and Staten Island know little about. They still talk about "going to New York" when they're planning a visit to midtown Manhattan, and many do this only on such occasions as birthdays and wedding anniversaries. It's equally unfamiliar to the 400,000 commuters who come into the city five mornings a week and then return at night to hundreds of suburban "dormitory" communities in Long Island, northern New Jersey, New York's Westchester and Rockland counties, and southwestern Connecticut.

If Manhattan Island sounded small to begin with, the "New York" of the tourist and visitor is basically a smaller still rectangular piece of that land mass about a half-mile wide and about one and one-quarter miles long. Its boundaries are roughly 59th Street on the north, 33rd Street on the south, Third Avenue on the east, and Eighth Avenue on the west. Within this tight little area of less than a square mile are the two major railroad stations, all the airline offices, the bus terminal, all the major department stores and legitimate theaters, most of the nightclubs, almost all the well-known hotels, plus Times Square, Rockefeller Center, Carnegie Hall, Madison Square Garden, the New York Coliseum, and two of the tallest buildings on earth. Just outside its peripheries are Lincoln Center, Central Park, the United Nations

INTRODUCTION

headquarters, and the most expensive and elegant residential areas. Even though the visitor will make occasional forays to such outlying points as Chinatown and the financial district to the south, and the Metropolitan Museum of Art to the north, most of his New York will be in this one small section.

Unknown to him are the neighborhoods where New Yorkers live—the Inwoods and Yorkvilles, the Williamsburgs and Flatbushes, the Mott Havens and Morrisanias, the Flushings and the Ozone Parks, or the ghettos of East Harlem and Bedford Stuyvesant—which form the borderlands of the glamorous New York and which are the crucibles in which New Yorkers are created.

Because they are products of such crucibles, New Yorkers know how easy it is to get burnt here. So they are ever wary of the jostler, the pickpocket, the hustler, the hit-and-run thief, the modern-day equivalent of the conman out to sell you the Brooklyn Bridge. The sophisticated traveler, of course, is ever ready for some version of the hustle—and not just on the disco dance floor. So be careful. For, as we said, the Big Apple has its share of rotten apples.

Nonetheless, New York's problems somehow seem worse than those of other cities; perhaps because of the city's size, and the relatively small area in which so many people are concentrated, New York's ailments have the appearance of being seen through a magnifying glass. They are very real, however, and quite often affect even the casual visitor. The native New Yorker knows that taxis are almost unobtainable and surface traffic impassable at 5:30 at night, so he walks whenever possible, and when the distance is too great, he submits himself to the physical beating of rush-hour subway riding, knowing full well what he's getting into. The visitor, on the other hand, chews his cuticles loose while waiting for a cab to turn up; or he wanders into the subway and quickly pops out again with the unhinged look of a rear echelon soldier who strayed onto a field of machine-gun fire.

To understand New York, the visitor must understand the New Yorker, and what makes him the way he is. The New Yorker is a very special individual, created and molded by natural selection in the environment in which he lives. The individual who adjusts to the city becomes a New Yorker; those who don't become psychiatric patients, or they move away and become out-of-towners, the word New Yorkers use to describe inhabitants of all the rest of the world.

The New Yorker must surely be ranked among the most put-upon people on earth. Smoke gets in his eyes—not romantically, but literally. His ears are split by a fearsome cacophony of shrieking fire engines and ambulances, banging jackhammers, and the assorted roarings of the demolition and construction which go on unendingly, concurrently, and side by side. The most masterful assault against him is mounted by the buses whose fumey, Bronx-cheering exhausts offend his eyes, ears, nose, and throat, and insult him at the same time. The New Yorker has to be a heads-up individual—otherwise he will be brained by icicles and clots of snow falling from terraces and rooftops in the winter; and, in the summer, he will be spat upon by air conditioners and blasted by their heat exhausts. Occasionally, he must also be heads-down to avoid the dog droppings that litter the streets. But this problem is lessening somewhat. With tough fines imposed on heedless persons who refuse to "scoop up" after their dogs, more New Yorkers are changing their ways and are cooperating with the law.

All of which must certainly explain why the New Yorker joins the Parisian as one of the most irritable cusses on earth. But, like the Parisian, the New Yorker is embarrassed by his bad temper. If you're able to break through his shell and make him stop for a moment, he'll try to compensate by knocking himself out to help you. Let a good, juicy catastrophe hit—such as the transit strikes of 1966 and 1980, or the overnight power blackout of July 1977, or the crippling snowstorms of early 1978 and early 1979—and unsuspected reserves of kindness, cheerfulness, cooperation, and make-do ingenuity can be revealed.

Philosophic Cabdrivers

The cabdriver is a special kind of New Yorker. To all his other annoyances is added the crowning frustration of New York traffic, and his ego has been warped by having had too much written about him. The best of the cabdrivers are those who keep their mouths shut and just drive. Those who believe their own publicity, and decide that they are characters, are often smashing bores, pouring unsolicited comments (based on mountainous stores of misinformation) into the captive ears of their passengers.

In meeting and understanding native New Yorkers, the language barrier is not as formidable as it might at first seem to anyone whose impressions are based on having seen and heard New Yorkers in the movies. It must be recognized at the outset that the Jewish influence on the New Yorker is as important as the Irish on the Bostonian. New Yorkers are likely to look upon their lives with the wry, sardonic, humorous cynicism that has formed part of the Jew's protective armor down through the ages. Perhaps this is why some television comic material sometimes sounds strange to audiences in Kansas City. The New Yorker's speech, threaded with Yiddish words that now have entered the local vocabulary for good, is likely to carry a rising inflection. Public relations men hailing from the Midwest, and not of the Jewish faith, think nothing of hanging over the bar in P. J. Clarke's calling each other "schlemiel," or accusing a client of having "chutzpah," a marvelous guttural-sounding Yiddish word that means "gall" and sounds like it. Common among New Yorkers is the practice of answering a question with a question, or answering a question with a shrug that employs all the facial muscles, the arms and shoulders, and even some back muscles.

While there are some quaint grammatical variations in the New York language, it's the pronunciation, the slurring together, the elimination of vital vowels and letters, that confuse the out-of-town listener. These accents are getting more homogenized with each passing day, but they still exist to a surprising degree.

Learning Native Customs

Despite this seeming barbarity of speech, many New Yorkers achieve an advanced state of civilized development, and the visitor seeking to acclimatize himself to New York would do well to adapt suitable local customs to his own needs. For example, New Yorkers have learned how to live with the fact that their city is probably the only one in the world besides Tokyo that suffers from *pedestrian* traffic jams.

This means no stopping at high noon on the sunny side of Fifth Avenue to tie shoelaces, no bunching up at street corners to talk with friends, and no milling around in front of theaters after the performance has ended. Failure to observe these simple precautions could lead to a collision of bodies that would pile up and block all sidewalk traffic.

And beware of the push-boys. They are the men and boys who push the carts carrying clothes from one place to another in the Seventh Avenue garment district. They boldly thrust ahead, looking neither to right nor left, all the while shouting, "Watch it!" Jump when they come your way.

Visitors wishing to observe the quaint feeding habits of New Yorkers can watch them eat on the run at a hot dog stand or counter restaurant, or at their leisure in a swank place in the East 60s. New Yorkers eating their fast-food lunch indulge in none of the niceties of Continental dining. Typically, hundreds of people are served between noon and 2 P.M. in establishments that will have only counter stools and too few waiters or waitresses. This is accomplished by feeding each patron in an average time of 15 minutes.

Fancy eating, which we now call dining, takes up to 2½ hours, and at lunch time is indulged in by owners of companies, salesmen entertaining clients, public relations men, and well-to-do visitors. Headwaiters, captains, wine stewards, and just plain waiters hover around these guests brandishing huge menus offering delicacies from around the world. Dining well is one of the real pleasures of a New York City visit.

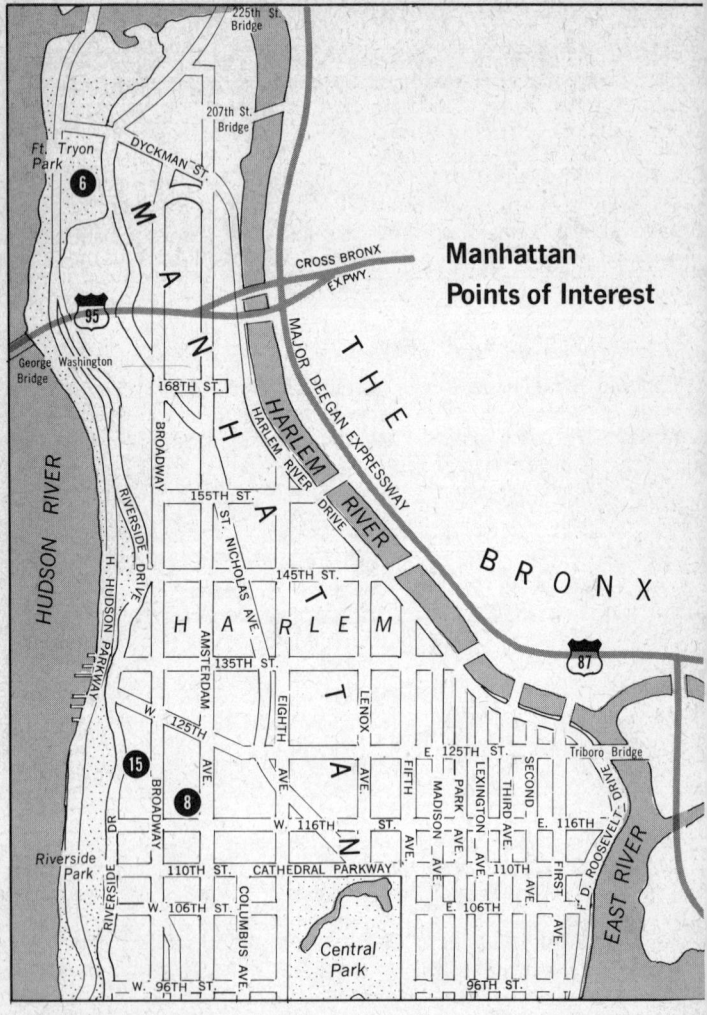

Points of Interest

1) Carnegie Hall
2) Central Park Zoo
3) Chinatown
4) Citicorp Center
5) City Hall
6) Cloisters
7) Coliseum
8) Columbia University
9) East Side Airlines Terminal
10) Empire State Building
11) Frick Museum
12) Gracie Mansion
13) Gramercy Park
14) Grand Central Station
15) Grant's Tomb
16) Guggenheim Museum

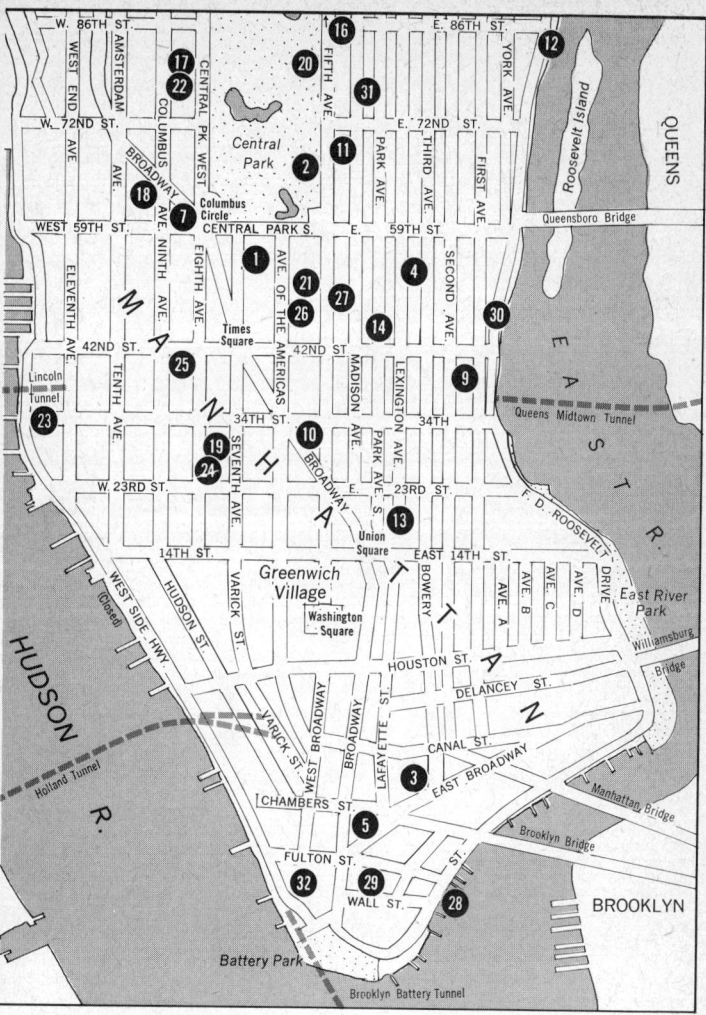

17) Hayden Planetarium
18) Lincoln Center
19) Madison Square Garden
20) Metropolitan Museum of Art
21) Museum of Modern Art
22) Museum of Natural History
23) N.Y. Convention Center (Constr.)
24) Pennsylvania Station
25) Port Authority Bus Terminal
26) Rockefeller Center
27) St. Patrick's Cathedral
28) South Street Seaport
29) N.Y. Stock Exchange
30) United Nations
31) Whitney Museum
32) World Trade Center

The City

This then is New York City; in population only the seventh largest city in the world (Shanghai is first), and even so splintered into its own little cities; always a pacesetter, yet in some ways unbearably provincial; city of opportunity for the ambitious, the eager and the talented from all over the country, yet a stern testing ground where many fall by the wayside in face of brutal competition; a gourmet's paradise—and at the same time a city of greasy spoon restaurants; art center of the world, a city of symphony, opera, drama—a city of television watchers and street-corner cowboys; magnet for the starry eyed—magnet for the drifter, the junkie, the criminal; a city whose skyscrapers of concrete and glass startle, assault, sometimes titillate the senses—a city of many dirty streets, shabby buildings, unbearable traffic. In short, despite the gripes and complaints, it is what every New Yorker—born or adopted—really feels about his hometown: New York *is* the greatest city in the world. It may often be subconscious or only secret, but somewhere, somehow, every New Yorker is really proud that his city, in great measure, entertains, educates, finances, and clothes the rest of the nation—and a not inconsiderable part of the rest of the world.

FACTS AT YOUR FINGERTIPS

WHEN TO GO. The four seasons are so clearly defined in New York and the state large enough and its geography varied enough that you can find almost anything you want there, sometime and somewhere. Sports, of course, vary according to the seasons: racing at Saratoga in August, skiing in the Adirondacks in winter, sailing on Long Island Sound in summer. A much more detailed breakdown is given in the *Practical Information* sections for the different regions later on in this book. Increasingly, however, the state's cultural life is year round. While the cream of the music, theater, dance and art life for the entire USA takes place in New York City between October and May, there is absolutely no form of entertainment and cultural activity (except, perhaps, grand opera) that is not fully available there throughout the summer months as well. And elsewhere, all over the state, a variety of local festivals and programs has grown up to meet the needs of both seasonal visitors and local residents. Mid-October is usually the best time for viewing the gorgeous fall foliage.

The answer to the question, When To Go, ultimately has to be—anytime. New York is basically *the* heartland of the entire northeastern part of the United States, and indirectly of the entire country. You will find more than you could possibly wish for going on there at any time of year. So unless you are in pursuit of a special interest, go whenever you can.

New York City residents are resigned to a few humid days of 95°-and-over temperatures each summer. The other extreme is the down-to-minus-15° winter climate in the Adirondacks. In autumn, the favorite areas for fall foliage viewing are the Catskill Mountains in the southeast and the Adirondacks in the north. The season is late September into early October, usually best around the Columbus Day holiday weekend. (the first or second in October). March and April are often the snowy and rainy months around New York. The upstate areas can get road-clogging snowfalls in winter, so if you plan to drive then, check with the State Police first.

You won't be alone when visiting New York City—in 1980 (last figures available) the Big Apple welcomed 17 million visitors, of whom 2.6 million were from overseas and 4.3 million were convention delegates.

PLANNING YOUR TRIP. A travel agent won't cost you a cent, except for specific charges like telegrams. He gets his fee from the hotel or carrier he books for you.

A travel agent can also be of help for those who would prefer to take their vacations on a "package tour"—thus keeping their own planning to a minimum. If you prefer the inconvenience of standardized accommodations, the various hotel and motel chains publish free directories of their members that enable you to plan and reserve everything ahead of time.

If you're planning to drive and you don't belong to an auto club, now is the time to join one. They can be very helpful about routings and providing emergency service on the road. Two such are: the *American Automobile Association*, 8111 Gatehouse Rd., Falls Church, VA 22047; and the *Amoco Motor Club*, 3700 Wake Forest Rd., Raleigh, NC 27609. The *Exxon Travel Club*, 800 Bell St., Houston TX 77002, provides information, low-cost insurance, and some legal service. The *National Travel Club*, Travel Building, Floral Park, NY 11001, offers information, insurance, and tours. Some of the major oil companies will send maps and mark preferred routes on them if you tell them what you have in mind. Try: *Exxon Touring Service*, Exxon Corporation, 1251 Avenue of the Americas, New York, NY 10020; *Texaco Travel Service*, 125 E. 42nd St., New York, NY 10017, or *Mobil Travel Service*, 150 E. 42nd St., New York, NY 10017. In addition, most states have their own maps, which pinpoint attractions, list historical sites, parks, etc. City chambers of commerce are also good sources of information. The tradition of free road maps at gasoline stations has almost totally disappeared.

Plan to board the pets, discontinue paper and milk deliveries, and tell your local police and fire departments when you'll be leaving, when you expect to return. Ask a kindly neighbor to keep an eye on your house or apartment; fully protect your swimming pool against intruders. Have a neighbor keep your mail, or have it temporarily held at the post office. Consider having your telephone temporarily disconnected, if you plan to be away more than a few weeks. Look into the purchase of trip insurance (including baggage), and make certain your auto, fire, and other policies are up-to-date. The *American Automobile Association* (AAA) offers both group personal accident insurance and bail bond protection as part of its annual membership. Today, most people who travel use credit cards for major expenses such as gas (although many stations accept only their own companies' cards—not bank or other commercial cards), repairs, lodgings, and some meals. Consider converting the greater portion of your trip money into travelers' checks. Arrange to have your lawn mowed at the usual times, and leave that kindly neighbor your itinerary (insofar as possible), car license number, and a key to your home (and tell police and firemen he has it). Since some hotel and motel chains give discounts (10–25%) to Senior Citizens, be sure to have some sort of identification along (Medicare, AARP, or NRTA cards) if you qualify. (See below at the end of the *Hotels and Motels* section.)

TIPS FOR BRITISH VISITORS

Passports. You will need a valid passport and a U.S. Visa (which can only be put in a passport of the 10-year kind). You can obtain the visa either through your travel agent, or directly from the *United States Embassy,* Visa and Immigration Department, 24 Grosvenor Sq., London W1 (tel. 01-499 3443).

No vaccinations are required for entry into the U.S.

FACTS AT YOUR FINGERTIPS 21

Customs. If you are 21 or over, you can take into the U.S.—200 cigarettes, 50 cigars or 3 lbs of tobacco; 1 U.S. liter of alcohol; duty-free gifts to a value of $100. Be careful not to try to take in meat or meat products, seeds, plants, fruits, etc. And avoid narcotics like the plague.

Insurance. We heartily recommend that you insure yourself to cover health and motoring mishaps, with *Europ Assistance,* 252 High St., Croydon CRO 1NF (tel. 01-680 1234). Their excellent service is all the more valuable when you consider the possible costs of health care in the U.S.

Tour Operators. The price battle that has raged over transatlantic fares has meant that most tour operators now offer excellent budget packages to the U.S. Among those you might consider as you plan your trip are—
American Express, 6 Haymarket, London SW1.
Thomas Cook Ltd., Thorpe Wood, Peterborough, PE 3 6SB.
Cosmos, Cosmos House, 1 Bromley Common, Bromley, Kent BR2 9LX.
Cunard, 8 Berkeley St., London W1.
Jetsave, Sussex House, London Rd., East Grinstead RH19 1LD.
Laker, 9 Grosvenor St., London W1.
Page and Moy, 136-138 London Rd., Leicester LE2 1EN.
Speedbird, 200 Buckingham Palace Rd., London SW1.

Air Fares. We suggest that you explore the current scene for budget flight possibilities. As well as the regular budget flights of *Laker,* all the main transatlantic carriers have stand-by tickets, available a short time before the flight only, as well as APEX and other fares at a considerable saving over the full price. Quite frankly, only business travelers who don't have to watch the price of their tickets fly full-price these days—and find themselves sitting right beside an APEX passenger!

Hotels. You may have need of a fast booking service to find a hotel room in New York. One of the very best ways to do this is to contact *HBI-HOTAC,* Globegate House, Pound Lane, London NW10 (tel. 01-451 2311). They book rooms for 58 individual hotels in New York and for most of the large chains (Holiday Inns, Hilton, Ramada etc.), so you can have a multiple choice with only one contact. HBI-HOTAC specialize in booking for business firms, but they also deal with the general public.

Information. One excellent source of information is the *State of New York Division of Tourism,* 35 Piccadilly, London W1 (tel. 01-734 7282). Although they are not open for personal callers, they will be happy to let you have brochures and other information to help you plan your trip.

FACTS AT YOUR FINGERTIPS

TOURIST INFORMATION. The New York State Division of Tourism is a well-staffed office devoted to promoting tourism within the Empire State, and it makes available to residents and nonresidents alike all sorts of information relevant to vacationing in New York State.

Among the publications are the *I Love New York Travel Guide to New York State*, the *I Love New York Travel Guide to New York City*, a special Tourism Map, and the *Guide to Outdoor Recreation in New York State*.

Other literature includes pamphlets and folders on camping, skiing, winter sports, fishing, hunting, historic sites, bicycle routes, children's camps, suggested tours of the state, and a seasonal calendar of events.

All literature of the New York State Division of Tourism is free, and can be obtained by writing to: New York State Division of Tourism, 99 Washington Ave., Albany, NY 12245. There are branch offices in: Binghamton, Buffalo, Elmira, Kingston, Jericho on Long Island, New York City, Ogdensburg, Rochester, Syracuse, and Utica. The state's toll-free Vacation Information telephone number is (800)-342-3810. In New York City, the Division of Tourism's office is at 230 Park Avenue, in the Helmsley Bldg., phone (212) 949-9300.

PACKING. *What to take, what to wear.* Make a packing list for each member of the family. Then check off items as you pack them. It will save time, reduce confusion.

Time-savers to carry along include extra photo film (plenty), suntan lotion, insect repellent, sufficient toothpaste, soap, etc. Always carry an extra pair of glasses, including sunglasses, particularly if they're prescription ones. A travel iron is always a good tote-along, as are some transparent plastic bags (small and large) for wet suits, socks, etc. They are also excellent, of course, for packing shoes, spillable cosmetics, and other easily damaged items.

Winter in New York can be *cold;* you'll need woolen clothes and an overcoat —but not thermal underwear, because the living spaces inside tend to be overheated. Spring and fall are very temperate, usually, but unpredictable, so take medium-weight outer garments, plus a raincoat. Winter begins promptly at the end of November, and summer at the end of May. Summers are usually hot and humid—but you'll still want to have lightweight "business" clothes for the better restaurants, etc.

Fun extras to carry include binoculars, and a magnifying glass—useful in reading those fine-print maps. Every member of the family should have a sturdy pair of shoes with non-slip soles.

Women will probably want to stick to one or two basic colors for their wardrobes, so that they can manage with one set of accessories. If possible, include one knit or jersey dress or pantsuit. The general consensus among well-traveled women is that a full-skirted traveling dress will show less wear and wrinkling. For dress-up evenings, take along a couple of "basic" dresses you can vary with a simple change of accessories. That way you can dress up or down to suit the occasion. An extra sweater is always a safe thing to pack, even if just

FACTS AT YOUR FINGERTIPS 23

to protect you from the air conditioning. Men will probably want a jacket along for dining out, and include a dress shirt and tie for the most formal occasions. Turtlenecks are now accepted almost everywhere and are a comfortable accessory. Don't forget extra slacks.

Remember, New York City can be a formal place, so bring dress clothes for the level and style of activities you have in mind.

WHAT TO DO WITH THE PETS. If you are going to New York City, leave them at home.

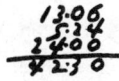

WHAT WILL IT COST? This is a crucial question and one of the most difficult. It is particularly difficult in the case of New York because costs can vary so much across the state. Small towns in the northern or western parts of the state will obviously be much cheaper than midtown Manhattan, for example. You can pay $35 for a double in a motel upstate and $70 for a double in a motel *of the same chain* in Manhattan. Moreover, within Manhattan itself, while a West Side "tourist" hotel in the 40s might charge around $35 a night for a single and $45 for a double, rates in the 50s would be $15 to $20 higher; and on Central Park South or Fifth Avenue a single could cost anywhere from $75 to over $120 per night. In Manhattan, you can be charged $10 to $15 in your hotel for a breakfast that might cost no more than $3 in a coffee shop just around the corner. For this reason the cost estimates are given with a range. Two people can travel in the surrounding New York region for $110.00 a day (not counting gasoline or other transportation costs), as you can see in the table below. For gasoline, figure about $10 for each 100 miles (at 15 miles to the gallon).

In some areas you can cut expenses by traveling off season, when hotel rates are usually lower. Major hotels in Manhattan, too, offer discounted weekend packages, some of which include theater tickets and/or a fancy brunch. The budget-minded traveler can also find bargain accommodations at tourist homes or family-style YMCAs and YWCAs. Some state and federal parks also provide inexpensive lodging. Another way to cut down on the cost of your trip is to look for out-of-the-way resorts. Travelers are frequently rewarded by discovering very attractive areas which haven't as yet begun to draw quantities of people.

The figures in the table reflect averages for the overall region and are obviously *lower than you should realistically budget for New York City itself.* If you're planning to visit the city exclusively, add about 15% to the figures shown. New York City offers an un-averageable range of accommodations, however, as you will see later in this guide, and daily expenses as below for two *can* be anywhere from $80.00 to $600.00.

If you are budgeting your trip, don't forget to set aside a realistic amount for the possible rental of sports equipment (perhaps including a boat or ice skates), entrance fees to amusement and historical sites, etc. Allow for tolls for bridges and superhighways (this can be a major item), extra film for cameras, and souvenirs.

Typical Expenses for Two People, Outside New York City

Room at *moderate* hotel or motel	$45.00
Breakfast, including tip	5.00
Lunch at *inexpensive* restaurant, including tip	12.00
Dinner at an *inexpensive* restaurant, including tip	25.00
Sightseeing tour	15.00
Evening drinks	4.00
Admission to museum or other historic site	5.00
	$111.00

After lodging, your biggest expense will be food, and here you can make great economies if you are willing to eat simply in your room or to picnic. It will save you time and money, and it will help you enjoy your trip more. That beautiful scenery does not have to whiz by at 55 miles per hour. New York State is well equipped with picnic and rest areas, often in scenic spots, even on highways and thruways, so finding a pleasant place to stop is usually not difficult. Before you leave home put together a picnic kit. Sturdy plastic plates and cups are cheaper in the long run than throw-away paper ones; and the same goes for permanent metal flatware rather than the throw-away plastic kind. Pack a small electric pot and two thermoses, one for water and one for tea or coffee. In other words, one cold and one hot. If you go by car, take along a small cooler. Bread, milk, cold cereal, jam, tea or instant coffee, bouillon cubes and instant soup packets, fruit, fresh vegetables that need no cooking (such as lettuce, cucumbers, carrots, tomatoes, and mushrooms), cold cuts, cheese, nuts, raisins, eggs (hard-boil them in the electric pot in your room the night before)—with only things like these you can eat conveniently, cheaply, and well.

Even in restaurants there are ways to cut costs. Always stop at the cash register and look over the menu before you sit down. Most New York City restaurants post a menu in the window. Have a few standard items like coffee, soup, side dishes, etc., to test the price range. Look around to see what other people are actually receiving. Are the portions big or small? Order a complete dinner; à la carte always adds up to more. If there is a salad bar or smorgasbord, you can fill up there and save on dessert and extras. Ask about smaller portions, at reduced prices, for children. Most places are providing them now. Go to a Chinese restaurant and order one less main dish than the number of people in your group. At fancier establishments try sharing an appetizer or dessert. You'll still come away pleasantly full. Ask for the Day's Special, House Special, Chef's Special, or whatever it's called. Chances are that it will be better and more abundant than the other things on the menu. Remember that in many restaurants lunch may be a better bargain than dinner. Insist on *no ice* in your beverages; you'll get 30%–50% more to drink. Drink half your coffee then ask for a refill; usually it won't be charged. Below, in the section on restaurants, we suggest some chains that offer good value for your money.

If you like a drink before dinner or bed, bring your own bottle. Most hotels and motels supply ice free or for very little, but the markup on alcoholic beverages in restaurants, bars, lounges, and dining rooms is enormous. And in any case, a good domestic dry white wine makes a fine aperitif and is much cheaper than a cocktail.

HINTS TO THE MOTORIST. New York State currently observes the 55 mph speed limit and shows reduced accident statistics to justify doing so. The state uses sophisticated speed detection devices, including radar and aircraft. So watch your speedometer!

Probably the first precaution you will take is to have your car thoroughly checked by your regular dealer or service station to make sure that everything is in good shape. Secondly, you may find it wise to join an auto club that can provide you with trip planning information, insurance coverage, and emergency and repair service along the way. Thirdly, if you must have your car serviced, look for a repair shop displaying the *National Institute for Automotive Service Excellence* seal. **NIASE** tests and certifies the competence of auto mechanics in about 10,000 repair shops nationwide.

Whether you are traveling through an empty wilderness or a heavily populated, well-serviced area, there are certain items of car equipment that you should have along: (1) spare tire, probably inflated, plus a jack, jack handle, wheel nut wrench, and two wooden blocks; (2) an empty one-gallon can and about five feet of hose, for getting gas; (3) a tool kit that includes an adjustable wrench, a knife, pliers, screwdrivers, and a tire pressure gauge; (4) extra sparkplugs and a fanbelt; (5) an extra can of oil; (6) jumper cables and gloves; (7) an extra set of keys (and a good place to hide them); (8) road flares and a flashlight; (9) a fire extinguisher; (10) the name and address of your insurance agent, and your car insurance policy number; (11) in winter, chains, an ice scraper, small shovel, carton of dry sand; (12) trash bag.

If you get stuck—on interstate, freeway, or country lane—use the universal rule of the road. Pull off the highway onto the shoulder, raise the hood, attach something white (a handkerchief, scarf, or a piece of tissue) to the door handle on the driver's side, and sit inside and wait. This is especially effective on limited-access highways, usually patrolled vigilantly by state highway officers. A special warning to women stalled at night: remain inside with the doors locked, and make sure the Good Samaritan is indeed what he seems. It is easier to find telephones along the major highways these days, since their locations are more frequently marked than they used to be. If you're an AAA member, call the nearest garage listed in your Emergency Road Service Directory. Or ask the operator for help.

New York's terrain shouldn't offer problems to a reasonably cautious driver. Unmarked side roads, especially in mountainous upstate, should be inquired about or explored on foot if at all: they may be private or long out of use, hence unfit for modern autos. Once off the thruways, roads upstate can be very curving, and local people, who know them better than you do, may drive faster than you can, or should. Play it safe for yourself.

Traveling by car with your pet dog or cat? Some motels will accept them but be sure to check ahead. This matter is usually specified in the free directories which the motel chains publish. If it's a first-time trip for your pet, accustom it to car travel by short trips in the neighborhood. And when you're packing, include its favorite food, bowls, and toys. Your dog may like to ride with its head out the window. Discourage this. Wind and dust particles can permanently damage its eyes. Dogs are especially susceptible to heatstroke. Don't leave your pet in a parked car on a hot day while you dawdle over lunch. Keep your pet's bowl handy for water during stops for gas; service station attendants are usually very cooperative about this. Make sure your pet exercises periodically; this is a good way for you and the kids to unwind from unbroken traveling too.

One tip for frequent motel stops along the road is to pack two suitcases—one for the final destination, and the other with items for overnight stops: pajamas, shaving gear, cosmetics, toothbrushes, fresh shirt or dress. Put the overnight luggage into the trunk last, so it can be pulled out first on overnight stops. A safety hint: Don't string your suits and dresses on hangers along a chain or rod stretched across the back seat. This obstructs vision and may cause an accident.

DRIVING LAWS

Traffic laws in general conform with those of other states, but may differ in two instances—driving age and insurance. The speed limit is 55 miles per hour unless otherwise posted.

Motorists must show proof that they have $10,000/$20,000/$5,000 liability insurance with a company that covers New York State. Check with your insurance agent.

Out-of-state drivers may drive in New York State if they are at least 16 years old. Drivers under 18, however, may not drive at any time in New York City or Nassau County, and may not drive between the hours of 8 P.M. and 5 A.M. unless accompanied by a parent or guardian.

Motorcyclists must wear a New York State-approved protective helmet, equipped with a chinstrap and at least four square inches of reflective materials on each side. They must also wear state-approved goggles or face shields. If the motorcycle has a windscreen, it must be a type approved by the Commissioner of the Department of Motor Vehicles. Motorcyclists may carry a passenger if there is a "buddy" seat provided behind the operator, complete with footrests and handgrips, and if the passenger is wearing a state-approved helmet.

CAMPERS AND TRAILER TIPS

Trailers and campers must not exceed 13½ feet in height, 8 feet in width, or a length of 35 feet for a single vehicle or 55 feet for a combination. Otherwise, a special hauling permit must be obtained from the Department of Operations,

New York State Thruway Authority, 200 Southern Blvd., Albany, NY 12201. Phone (518) 449-1750.

HOTELS AND MOTELS. *General Hints.* Don't take potluck for lodgings. You'll waste a lot of time hunting for a place and often you won't be happy with what you finally get. If you don't have reservations, begin looking early in the afternoon. If you have reservations, but expect to arrive later than five or six P.M., advise the hotel or motel in advance. Some places will not, unless advised, hold reservations after six P.M. And if you hope to get a room at the hotel's *minimum* rate be sure to reserve ahead or arrive very early.

If you are planning to stay in a popular resort region, at the height of the season, reserve well in advance. Include a deposit. Most chain or associated motels and hotels publish directories of their memberships and will make advance reservations for you at affiliated hostelries along your route.

A number of hotels and motels have one-day laundry and dry-cleaning services, and many motels have coin laundries. Most motels, but not all, have telephones in the rooms. If you want to be sure of room service, however, better stay at a hotel. Many motels have swimming pools, and even beachfront hotels frequently have a pool. Even some motels in the heart of large cities have pools. An advantage at motels is the free parking. There's seldom a charge for parking at country and resort hotels. Baby-sitter lists are always available in good hotels and motels, and cribs and cots are always on hand, usually at minimal cost. Better hotels and motels generally add a moderate charge for moving an extra single bed into a room.

Hotel and motel chains. In addition to the hundreds of excellent independent motels and hotels throughout the country, there are also many that belong to national or regional chains. A major advantage of the chains is the ease of making reservations en route, or at one fell swoop in advance. If you are a guest at a member hotel or motel, the management will be delighted to secure you a sure booking at one of his affiliated hotels for the coming evening—at no cost to you. Chains also usually have toll-free WATS (800) lines to assist you in making reservations on your own. This, of course, saves you time, worry, and money. The insistence on uniform standards of comfort, cleanliness, and amenities is more common in motel than in hotel chains. (Easy to understand when you realize that most hotel chains are formed by simply buying up older, established hotels, while most motel chains have control of their units from start to finish.) Some travelers, however, prefer independent motels and hotels because they are more likely to reflect the genuine character of the surrounding area.

Since the single biggest expense of your whole trip is lodging, you may well be discouraged and angry at the prices of some hotel and motel rooms, particularly when you know you are paying for things you neither need nor want, such as a heated swimming pool, wall-to-wall carpeting, a huge color TV set, two huge double beds for only two people, meeting rooms, a cocktail lounge, maybe even a putting green. Nationwide, motel prices for two people now average $40 a night; hotel prices start at $45, with the average around $65. This explains the recent rapid spread of a number of budget motel chains whose rates average $20 for a single and $25 for a double, an obvious advantage. Unfortunately, very few of these are in the Northeast; and those which are are sparsely represented.

Prices in the budget chains are fairly uniform, but this is not the case in chains such as Ramada, Quality, Holiday Inns, Howard Johnson's, and TraveLodge. Their prices vary widely by area, location and season. Thus, in New York State alone, two adults in one bed may pay $35 in a small town upstate and $70 in midtown Manhattan in motels *of the same chain*. Among the national non-budget motel chains, the upper price range is occupied by Hilton, Marriott, and Sheraton; the middle range includes Holiday Inns, Howard Johnson, Quality Inns, and TraveLodge; and the least expensive are usually Best Western, Ramada, and Rodeway (mostly in the South).

HOTEL AND MOTEL CATEGORIES OUTSIDE NEW YORK CITY

The New York City hotel and motel categories are discussed in the introduction to the city hotel listings. But our classifications for the selected hotels and motels in the *Nearby Attractions*—Long Island, the Catskills, Atlantic City, and the others—follow the categories used in the rest of the Fodor's guidebooks:

Deluxe: Minimum facilities must include bath and shower in all rooms, valet and laundry service, suites available, a well-appointed restaurant and a bar (where local law permits), room service, TV and telephone in room, air conditioning and/or heat, pleasing decor, an atmosphere of luxury and elegance, and ample and personalized service. In a deluxe *motel*, there may be less service rendered by employees and more by machine or automation (such as refrigerators and ice-making machines in your room), but there should be a minimum of do-it-yourself in a truly deluxe establishment.

Expensive: All rooms must have bath or shower, valet and laundry service, restaurant and bar (local law permitting), at least some room service, TV and telephone in room, attractive furnishings, heat and/or air conditioning. Although the decor may be as good as that in deluxe establishments, hotels and motels in this category are frequently designed for commercial travelers or for families in a hurry and are somewhat impersonal in terms of service. Valet and laundry service will probably be lacking; the units will be outstanding primarily for their convenient location and functional character, not for their attractive or comfortable qualities.

(*Note:* We often list top-notch ultra-modern hotels in this category, in spite of the fact that they have rates as high as deluxe hotels and motels. We do this because certain elements are missing in these hotels—usually, the missing element is service. In spite of automated devices such as ice-cube-making machines and message-signaling buzzers, service in these hotels is not up to the standard by which we judge deluxe establishments. Room service is incredibly slow in some of these places and the entire atmosphere is often one of expediency over comfort, economy of manpower and overhead taking precedence over attention to the desires of guests.)

Moderate: Each room should have an attached bath or shower, there should be a restaurant *or* coffee shop, TV available, telephone in room, heat and/or air conditioning, relatively convenient location, clean and comfortable rooms and public rooms. *Motels* in this category may not have attached bath or shower, may not have a restaurant or coffee shop (though one is usually nearby), and may have no public rooms.

Inexpensive: Nearby bath or shower, telephone available, clean rooms are the minimum.

Senior Citizens may in some cases receive special discounts on lodgings. The *Days Inn* chain offers various discounts to anyone 55 or older. *Holiday Inns* give a discount to members of the NRTA (write to National Retired Teachers Association, Membership Division, 401 Grand Ave., Ojai, CA 93023). *Howard Johnson's Motor Lodges, Marriott, Quality Inns, Ramada Inns, Rodeway Inns, Sheraton,* and *Treadway Inns* (a New England chain) have all offered varying discounts to members of the AARP, the NRTA, the National Association of Retired Persons, the Catholic Golden Age of the United Societies of U.S.A., and the Old Age Security Pensioners of Canada. However, the amounts and availability of these discounts vary, so check their latest status. *The National Council of Senior Citizens,* 925 15th Street NW, Washington, DC 20005, works especially to develop low-cost travel possibilities for its members.

Vacations and Senior Centers Association, 225 Park Ave. S., New York, NY 10003, is an affiliation of 17 social and religious agencies that arranges low-cost camping vacations for New Yorkers aged 55 to 90 at 17 sites in New York, New Jersey, and Connecticut at rates of $75 to $100 a week.

The closest thing America has to Europe's bed-and-breakfast is the private houses that go by the various names of tourist home, guest home, or guesthouse. These are often large, still fairly elegant old homes in quiet residential or semiresidential parts of larger towns or along secondary roads and the main streets of small towns and resorts. Styles and standards vary widely, of course; generally private baths are less common and rates are pleasingly low. In many small towns such guesthouses are excellent examples of the best a region has to offer of its own special atmosphere. Each one will be different, so that their advantage is precisely the opposite of that "no surprise" uniformity which motel chains pride themselves on. Few, if any, guesthouses have heated pools, wall-to-wall carpeting, or exposed styrofoam-wooden beams in the bar. Few if any even have bars. What you do get, in addition to economy, is the personal flavor of a family atmosphere in a private home. In popular tourist areas, state or local tourist information offices or chambers of commerce usually have lists of homes that let out spare rooms to paying guests, and such a listing usually means that the places on it have been inspected and meet some reliable standard of cleanliness, comfort, and reasonable pricing. Two specialized directories of such guesthouses are: *A Directory of Tourist Homes in the Eastern United States and Maritime Canada,* by Jon and Nancy Kugelman, published by McBride and Howe Books, 157 Sisson Ave., Hartford, CT 06105; and *Guide to Guest Houses and Tourist Homes USA,* published by Tourist House Associates of America,

Inc., P.O. Box 335-A, Greentown, PA 18426. (New York City itself does not offer guesthouses as a practical alternative for accommodations.)

In larger towns and cities a good bet for clean, plain, reliable lodging is a YMCA or YWCA. These buildings are usually centrally located, and their rates tend to run to less than half of those of hotels. Nonmembers are welcome but may pay slightly more than members. A few very large Ys may have accommodations for couples but usually sexes are segregated. Decor is spartan and the cafeteria fare plain and wholesome, but a definite advantage is the use of the building's pool, gym, reading room, information services, and other facilities. For a directory, write to National Council of the YMCA, 291 Broadway, New York NY 10007; and the National Board of YWCA, 600 Lexington Avenue, New York, NY 10022.

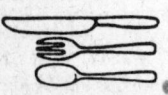

DINING OUT. For evening meals, the best advice is to make reservations in advance whenever possible. Most hotels have set dining hours. For motel-stayers, life is simpler if the motel has a restaurant. If it hasn't, try and stay at one that is near a restaurant.

Some restaurants are relatively fussy about customers' dress, particularly in the evening. For women, pants and pantsuits are now almost universally acceptable, but a number of the better Manhattan restaurants make exception to this, so it is best to check beforehand. For men, tie and jacket remains the standard, but turtleneck sweaters are becoming more and more common. Shorts are almost always frowned on for both men and women. Standards of dress are becoming progressively more relaxed, so a neatly dressed customer will usually experience no problem. If in doubt about accepted dress at a particular establishment, call ahead. If you're traveling with children, find out if a restaurant has a children's menu and commensurate prices (many do).

When figuring the tip on your check, base it on the total charges for the meal, not on the grand total, if that total includes a state sales tax. Don't tip on tax. In New York, figuring the tip is quite easy. Statewide, the sales tax on restaurant meals is 4%, so just multiply it by 4. In New York City the state and city sales taxes total 8¼%, so just multiply that by 2.

RESTAURANT CATEGORIES

Restaurants located in large metropolitan areas are categorized in this volume by type of cuisine: French, Chinese, Armenian, etc., with restaurants of a general nature listed as American-International. Restaurants in less populous areas are divided into price categories as follows: *super deluxe, deluxe, expensive, moderate,* and *inexpensive.* As a general rule, expect restaurants in metropolitan areas to be higher in price, although many restaurants that feature foreign cuisine are often surprisingly inexpensive.

We should also point out that limitations of space make it impossible to include every establishment. We have, therefore, included those which we consider the best within each price range.

FACTS AT YOUR FINGERTIPS

Although the names of the various restaurant categories are standard throughout this series, the prices listed under each category may vary from area to area. This variance is meant to reflect local price standards, and take into account the fact that what might be considered a *moderate* price in a large urban area might be quite *expensive* in a rural region. In every case, however, the dollar ranges for each category are clearly stated before each listing of establishments.

Super Deluxe: This category indicates an outstanding restaurant which is lavishly decorated, and which must have a superb wine list, excellent service, immaculate kitchen, and a large, well-trained staff.

Deluxe: Many a fine restaurant around the country falls into this category. It will have its own well-deserved reputation for excellence, perhaps a house specialty or two for which it is famous, and an atmosphere of elegance, attentive service, often unique decor. It will have a good wine list where the law permits, and will be considered the best in town by the inhabitants.

Expensive: In addition to the expected dishes, it will offer one or two house specialties, wine list, and cocktails (where law permits), air conditioning (unless locale makes it unnecessary), a general reputation for very good food and an adequate staff, an elegant decor and appropriately dressed clientele.

Moderate: Cocktails and/or beer where the law permits, air conditioning (locale not precluding), clean kitchen, adequate staff, better-than-average service. General reputation for good, wholesome food.

Inexpensive: The bargain place in town, it is clean, even if plain. It will have air conditioning (when necessary), tables (not a counter), clean kitchen and attempt to provide adequate service.

DRINKING LAWS. In New York State, the minimum age for the consumption of alcohol is 18; in New Jersey it is 19. Opening and closing hours for bars vary from county to county. The hours for New York City—which is actually five integrated counties—are described in the New York City section. Laws for the retail sale of bottled liquor and alcoholic beverages also vary, except that throughout New York State the liquor outlets are closed on Sunday by law. That means wine and the hard stuff. Beer may usually be obtained on Sundays, but even that varies. In New York City, no beer may be sold at markets and other such outlets—which may not by law sell wine or distilled spirits at any time, by the way—until noon on Sunday. In New Jersey, most counties allow retail sale of all bottled alcoholic beverages on Sundays.

RELIGIOUS WORSHIP. A listing of all of New York's religious institutions is subject for a book unto itself. The most comprehensive source of information is the Yellow Pages, which has separate listings for "Religious Organizations," "Churches" (broken down by denomination), "Synagogues," etc. For specific details about services in New York City, consult the Friday *New York Times.*

FACTS AT YOUR FINGERTIPS

BUSINESS HOURS AND LOCAL TIME. New York State, like the rest of America, is on Standard Time from the last Sunday in October until the last Sunday in April. In April the clock is advanced one hour, for Daylight Savings Time, and in October is turned back an hour. The entire state lies within the Eastern Time Zone, which is 5 hours earlier than Greenwich Mean Time on local standard (winter) time.

POSTAGE. At press time, rates for international mail from the United States are as follows: *Surface* letters to Canada and Mexico are at the U.S. domestic rate: 20¢ for 1 ounce or under, 37¢ for 2 ounces or under, but these rates actually get airmail carriage to those countries. Surface letters to other foreign destinations are 30¢ for the first ounce and 47¢ for up to 2 ounces. Airmail letters to foreign destinations other than to Canada, Mexico, and some Caribbean and South American countries are 40¢ ½ ounce, 80¢ 1 ounce, $1.20 1½ ounces, $1.60 2 ounces. Postcards (except for Canada and Mexico, which go airmail for 13¢) are 19¢ for surface mail and 28¢ for airmail to any foreign destination. Standard international aerogram letters, good for any foreign destination, are 30¢, but of course nothing may be enclosed in them. Postal rates are no exception in this period of inflation, so check before you mail, in case they have gone up since press time.

SPORTS. From the body-surfers at Jones Beach to the skiers at Lake Placid to the boccie players on Thompson Street in Little Italy, New York provides encyclopedic opportunities for sports enthusiasts. New York charges non-residents $10.25 for a week for fishing licenses, $52.50 to hunt big game, $32.50 to hunt small game. There's even an archery certificate for $4.25 if you're willing to give the animals a better chance.

SEASONAL EVENTS OUTSIDE NEW YORK CITY

January

Hovey Memorial Alpine Races. Adirondacks (Wilmington).

New York State Junior Ski Jumping Championships. Adirondacks (Lake Placid).

February

Winter Carnivals. Adirondacks (Lake Placid, Malone, Saranac Lake, Schroon Lake, Walton).

Winter Fishing Derby. Thousand Islands (Cape Vincent).

May

Sacandaga Wildwater Canoe Races. Adirondacks (Northville).

FACTS AT YOUR FINGERTIPS

June

Adirondack Championship Rodeo. Adirondacks (Lake Luzerne).
Belmont Stakes. Third leg of racing's Triple Crown. Long Island (Belmont Park).
Flat-Water 44-mile Canoe Marathon. From Long Lake to Tupper Lake. Adirondacks.
Shinnecock Swordfish Tournament. Hampton Bays (Long Island).
Spinning, weaving, and dyeing demonstrations. Hudson Valley (Van Cortlandt Manor, Croton-on-Hudson).
Water Carnival. Adirondacks (Tupper Lake).
White-Water Races on Esopus Creek. Catskills (Phoenicia).

Summer-long Events

Adirondacks: Concerts, plays, lectures, old movies, and art shows at the Lake Placid Center for Music, Drama and Art. Operas in English at the Lake George Opera Festival.

Niagara Falls: The Artpark, a 172-acre facility in the Niagara River Gorge at Lewiston, has a 2,400-seat outdoor theater that offers music, dance, and drama from the 4th of July to Labor Day weekend (early September).

July

French Festival. Thousand Islands (Cape Vincent).
German Alps Festival. Catskills (Hunter).
Summer Ski Jump. Adirondacks (Lake Placid).

August

Marlin Tournament. Hampton Bays (Long Island).
National Polka Festival. Catskills (Hunter).
Paint and Palette Festival. Adirondacks (Saranac Lake).
Stone and Gem Show. Thousand Islands (Cape Vincent).

September

Shaker Craft Show. Hudson Valley (Old Chatham).
U.S. Open Tennis Championships. Long Island (Flushing Meadows).
White Water Canoe and Kayak Slalom Race. Catskills (Unadilla).

October

Adirondack Hot Air Balloon Festival. Glens Falls (Adirondack Community College).
Chrysanthemum Festival. Hudson Valley (Seaman Park, Saugerties).

November

Eastern States Antiques Fair. Hudson Valley (White Plains).

December

Christmas Carnival and Festival. Hudson Valley (Bear Mountain State Park).

FACTS AT YOUR FINGERTIPS

ROUGHING IT. More, and improved, camping facilities are springing up each year across the country, in national parks, national forests, state parks, in private camping areas, and trailer parks, which by now have become national institutions.

Because of the great size of the United States and the distances involved, youth hostels have not developed in this country the way they have in Europe and Japan. In the entire 3½ million square miles of the U.S. there are upwards of 200 youth hostels, and because they are, in any case, designed primarily for people who are traveling under their own power, usually hiking or bicycling, rather than by car or commercial transportation, they tend to be away from towns and cities and in rural areas, near scenic spots. In the U.S. they are most frequent and practical in compact areas like New England; and in New York there are 20 youth hostels in the state as a whole. Although their members are mainly younger people, there is no age limit. You must be a member to use youth hostels; write to American Youth Hostels, Inc., 1332 I St. NW, Washington, DC 20005. There is also an office in New York City at 132 Spring St., 10012, in the SoHo area. A copy of the *Hostel Guide and Handbook* will be included in your membership. Accommodations are simple, dormitories are segregated by sex, common rooms and kitchen are shared, and everyone helps with the cleanup. Lights out 11 P.M. to 7 A.M., no alcohol or other drugs allowed. Membership fees: under 18—$7; 18 and over—$14; family—$21. Hostel rates vary; $1.50 to $3.50 per person per night is average. In season it is wise to reserve ahead; write or phone directly to the particular hostel you plan to stay in.

Useful Addresses: *National Parks Service,* U.S. Dept. of the Interior, Washington, DC 20025; *National Forest Service,* U.S. Dept of Agriculture, Washington, DC 20025. For information on state parks, write *Department of Parks and Recreation,* Empire State Plaza, Agency Building 1, Albany, NY 12238.

The *National Campers & Hikers Assoc.,* Box 451, Orange, NJ 07051. *Kampgrounds of America, Inc.,* P.O. Box 30558, Billings, MT 59114, is a very helpful commercial camping organization.

Vacations and Senior Centers Association, 225 Park Ave. So., New York, NY 10003, arranges camping vacations in the New York–New Jersey–Connecticut tri-state area for New Yorkers from 55 to 90 at rates of $75 to $100 a week.

FARM VACATIONS AND GUEST RANCHES. Farm vacations continue to gain adherents, especially among families with children. Some accommodations are quite deluxe, others extremely simple. For a directory of farms which take vacationers (including rates, accommodations—which may include fishing and riding facilities, as well as good home cooking—dates, etc.), write to *Adventure Guides, Inc.,* 36 E. 57th St., New York, NY 10022, for their 240-page booklet *Farm, Ranch, and Country Vacations.* A list of ranch resorts is also available, from the State Department of Commerce, 99 Washington Ave., Albany, NY 12245.

FACTS AT YOUR FINGERTIPS

FISHING AND HUNTING. Fishing licenses are required for freshwater fishing for all over 16 years old, and may be purchased at county clerk and town clerk offices, and at some sporting goods stores. No license is required for saltwater fishing.

Hunting licenses are required for all over 14 years old. All hunters using bow and arrow are required to obtain a special bow-hunting stamp. For information on seasons, license, and regulations, write to: New York State Department of Environmental Conservation, Division of Fish and Wildlife, Albany, NY 12233.

CAMPING OUT. Sixty-four state parks and two state forest preserves provide an endless variety of woodland campgrounds for the vacationer. The state maintains marked trails in the Adirondack and Catskill Forest Preserves. The backpacker may camp on any state-owned land in the Forest Preserve or State Reforestation Areas.

For maps and information contact the New York State Office of Parks and Recreation, Albany, NY 12238.

STATE PARKS. The state of New York has 148 state parks, forests, and recreation areas, many of which have excellent facilities for the camper. Usually there is a nominal fee for the use of a campsite; and in most places there are toilet and cooking facilities, complete with running water. There are some 400 camping areas in the state, more than 1,000 miles of hiking trails, 4,000 lakes, ponds and reservoirs, 2,000 mountain peaks to climb (48 of them over 4,000 feet), and 127 miles of Atlantic coastline. An *Empire Passport* offers unlimited, year-round entry to all New York State Parks and recreational facilities. At $20, it's one of the state's biggest bargains. Or check on the *Golden Park Pass*, which is free to any resident aged 62 or over, and provides lifetime free admission for day use of state parks (Mon.-Fri., except holidays). The *Passport* is on sale at all state parks, or by mail from Passports, State Parks, Albany, NY 12238. Below are listed some of the state parks, providing accommodations, as well as something extra.

Adirondack Forest Preserve is a gigantic area stretching from the Black River in the west across to the shores of Lake Champlain on the east. It comprises over two million acres for camping, picnicking, and nature study. Within its borders are over 30 different camping areas, some small, some large, but all excellent. There are many mountains to climb, while water enthusiasts will enjoy the hundreds of mirror lakes which dot the area. The entire preserve is crisscrossed with twisting hiking trails; and there are facilities for both tents and trailers. The only drawback may be that there is little in the way of electrical hookups.

Bear Mountain State Park has a year-round inn with an excellent cafeteria if you don't want to cook. The park cares for five different museums open to the public. Tennis courts and an archery range wrap up a quality park where you and the entire family will find many things to do.

Catskill Forest Preserve is located in the Catskill Mountains west of the Hudson River. Here the mountain laurel grows in profusion, and from the lookout atop *Slide Mountain* you can see a summer panorama of soft reds and white. Anglers will want to try their skill on the world-famous *Beaverkill,* while the rest of the family will enjoy hiking along the winding trails.

At *Harriman State Park,* several children's areas dot the camp area, while the white-sand beaches on some of the lakes afford the sun-worshipper a chance to get that summer tan.

Jones Beach State Park is probably the most famous of the state parks. This more-than-2,000-acre park on the Long Island shore offers something for the entire family: 6½ miles of sand, restaurant, cafeterias, picnic areas, boat rental, pitch and putt golf, outdoor dancing and an outdoor theater, summer concerts and roller skating, swimming and fishing are just some of the activities you may enjoy. Open year round.

Ogden Mills and Ruth Livingston Mills Memorial State Park is a small state park north of Poughkeepsie offering an unusual attraction for the visitor. For a slight admission fee you may see the museum dedicated to the Mills family, in which are displayed many different mementos of an earlier period, including rugs and tapestries, antiques and rare books, all collected by the former owner. While there are no campsites, you are invited to use the picnic tables provided. Also there are a golf course and a boat dock.

Palisades Interstate Park is situated on the New York–New Jersey border and includes the following State Parks: Bear Mountain, Harriman, Nyack Beach, Rockland Lake, Stony Point and Tallman Mountain. It follows the beautiful and sometimes awesomely high, rocky cliffs hanging over the western shore of the Hudson River from the Bear Mountain area down to the region across from New York City. Spectacular views from lookout and picnic spots, as well as an exciting drive that hugs the cliffside and takes you past rock formations, lush vegetation, and recreation areas along the river at the bottom of the Palisades.

TIPPING. Tipping is supposed to be a personal thing, your way of expressing appreciation of someone who has taken pleasure and pride in giving you attentive, efficient, and personal service. Because standards of personal service in the United States are highly uneven, you should, when you get genuinely good service, feel secure in rewarding it, and when you feel that the service you got was slovenly, indifferent, or surly, don't hesitate to show this by the size, or withholding, of your tip. Remember that in many places the help are paid very little and depend on tips for the better part of their income. This is supposed to give them incentive to serve you well. These days, the going rate on *restaurant* service is 15% on the amount *before* taxes. Tipping at counters is not universal, but many people leave at least 25¢, and 10% when it comes to anything over that. For *bellboys,* 25¢ per bag is usual. However, if you load him down with all manner of bag, hatboxes, cameras, coats, etc., you might consider giving an extra quarter or two. In many places the help rely on tips for a goodly portion of their income. For one-night stays in most *hotels* and *motels* you leave nothing. If you stay longer, at the end of your stay leave the maid $1.00–$1.25 per day, or $5.00 per person per week for multiple occupancy. If you are staying at an *American Plan* hostelry (meals included) $1.50 per day per person for the waiter or waitress is considered sufficient, and is left at the end of your stay. However, if you have been surrounded by an army of servants (one bringing relishes, another rolls, etc), add a few extra dollars and give the lump sum to the captain or *maître d'hôtel* when you leave, asking him to allocate it.

For the many other services you may encounter in a big hotel or resort, figure roughly as follows: doorman, 25¢ for taxi handling, 50¢ for help with baggage; bellhop, 25¢ per bag, more if you load him down with extras; parking attendant, 50¢; bartender, 15%; room service, 10–15% of that bill; laundry or valet service, 15%; pool attendant, 50¢ per day; snackbar waiter at pool, beach, or golf club, 50¢ per person per day, or $2.50 per week; golf caddies, $1–$2 per bag, or 15% of the greens fee for an 18-hole course, or $3 on a free course; barbers, 50¢; shoeshine attendants, 25¢; hairdressers, $1; manicurists, 50¢. Masseurs and masseuses in clubs and hotels get 20%.

Transportation: Taxi drivers in New York *expect 20%.* Limousine service, 20%. Car rental agencies, nothing. Bus porters are tipped 25¢ per bag, drivers nothing. On charters and package tours, conductors and drivers usually get $5–$10 per day from the group as a whole, but be sure to ask whether this has already been figured into the package cost. On short local sightseeing runs, the driver-guide may get 25¢ per person, more if you think he has been especially helpful or personable. Airport bus drivers, nothing. Redcaps, in resort areas, 35¢ per suitcase, elsewhere, 25¢. Tipping at curbside check-in is unofficial, but same as above. On the plane, no tipping.

Railroads suggest you leave 10–15% per meal for dining car waiters, but the steward who seats you is not tipped. Sleeping-car porters get about $1 per person per night. The 25¢ or 35¢ you pay a railway station baggage porter is not a tip but the set fee that he must hand in at the end of the day along with the ticket stubs he has used. Therefore his tip is anything you give him above that, 25–50¢ per bag, depending on how heavy your luggage is.

SENIOR CITIZEN AND STUDENT DISCOUNTS. Many attractions throughout New York City offer considerable discounts to Senior Citizens and students. Some may require special city-issued Senior-Citizen identification, but in most cases showing a driver's license, passport, or some other proof of age will suffice—"senior" generally being defined as 65 or over for men and 62 or over for women. Museums, first-run and neighborhood movie theaters and even some stores will often post special Senior-Citizen rates. Those places offering student discounts are generally somewhat more stringent in their proof requirements—a high school or college ID, international student traveler card, or evidence of age may be requested. Unfortunately, there is no uniformity on these matters.

HINTS TO HANDICAPPED TRAVELERS. Important sources of information in this field are: The *Travel Information Center,* Moss Rehabilitation Hospital, 12th St. and Tabor Road, Philadelphia, PA 19141. *Easter Seal Society for Crippled Children and Adults,* Director of Education and Information Service, 2023 W. Ogden Ave., Chicago, IL 60612. Many of the nation's national parks have special facilities for the handicapped. These are described in *National Park Guide for the Handicapped,* available from the U.S. Government Printing Office, Washington, DC 20402. TWA publishes a free 12-page pamphlet entitled *Consumer Information about Air Travel for the Handicapped* to explain available arrangements and how to get them. Other publications giving valuable information about facilities for the handicapped are: the book *Travel Ability,* by Lois Reamy, published by Macmillan; the book *Access to the World,* by Louise Weiss, published by Chatham Square Press; and the annually revised guide *The Wheelchair Traveler,* by Douglass R. Annand, Ball Hill Road, Milford, NH 03055.

METRIC CONVERSION.

CONVERTING METRIC TO U.S. MEASUREMENTS

Multiply:	by:	to find:
Length		
millimeters (mm)	.039	inches (in)
meters (m)	3.28	feet (ft)
meters	1.09	yards (yd)
kilometers (km)	.62	miles (mi)
Area		
hectare (ha)	2.47	acres
Capacity		
liters (L)	1.06	quarts (qt)
liters	.26	gallons (gal)
liters	2.11	pints (pt)
Weight		
gram (g)	.04	ounce (oz)
kilogram (kg)	2.20	pounds (lb)
metric ton (MT)	.98	tons (t)
Power		
kilowatt (kw)	1.34	horsepower (hp)
Temperature		
degrees Celsius	9/5 (then add 32)	degrees Fahrenheit

CONVERTING U.S. TO METRIC MEASUREMENTS

Multiply:	by	to find:
Length		
inches (in)	25.40	millimeters (mm)
feet (ft)	.30	meters (m)
yards (yd)	.91	meters
miles (mi)	1.61	kilometers (km)
Area		
acres	.40	hectares (ha)
Capacity		
pints (pt)	.47	liters (L)
quarts (qt)	.95	liters
gallons (gal)	3.79	liters
Weight		
ounces (oz)	28.35	grams (g)
pounds (lb)	.45	kilograms (kg)
tons (t)	1.11	metric tons (MT)
Power		
horsepower (hp)	.75	kilowatts
Temperature		
degrees Fahrenheit	5/9 (after subtracting 32)	degrees Celsius

EMERGENCY TELEPHONE NUMBERS. For police, fire, or ambulance, dial 911. The Manhattan fire department may also be reached on 628–2900; the fire department also possesses medical emergency equipment.

HOLIDAYS. Most businesses, banks and many restaurants will be closed the following holidays (the dates are for 1982): New Year's Day, Jan. 1; Washington's Birthday (observance), Feb. 15; Easter Sunday, April 11; Memorial Day (observance), May 31; Independence Day, July 4; Labor Day, Sept. 6; Thanksgiving Day, Nov. 25; and Christmas Day, Dec. 25.

In addition, banks and some businesses may be closed on Martin Luther King's Birthday, Jan. 15; Lincoln's Birthday, Feb. 12; Good Friday (from noon), April 8; Columbus Day (observance), Oct.11; Election Day (partially), Nov. 2; Veterans Day, Nov. 11.

The annual St. Patrick's Day Parade occurs on March 17; this means that Fifth Ave. is closed from 42nd St. to 86th St., the town is flooded with mobs of unruly, drugged or drunken young punks, and normal activity in midtown Manhattan all but comes to a halt.

New York City having more Jews than Tel Aviv, it is inevitable that the city slows down considerably on the important Jewish religious holidays: Passover, beginning April 8; Rosh Hashanah, Sept. 18; Yom Kippur, Sept. 27; Hanukkah, Dec. 11.

Subway, bus and train schedules will have less service on all official holidays and on some of the unofficial ones.

CLIMATE. In the New York City area, precipitation is moderate and distributed fairly evenly throughout the year. Precipitation averages in the vicinity of 3.5 inches per month, except in July and August, when it increases to about 4.25 inches per month. Most of the rainfall from May through October comes from thunderstorms.

There is a small chance of snow in November and in April, with a virtual certainty of snow (up to an average 8.8 inches in February) in December, January, February, and March.

Throughout the year, relative humidity averages about 60% at noontime. The average daily variation in temperature is rather small. Here are the average highs and lows by month, in degrees Fahrenheit:

Jan. 26–39	Jul. 68–85
Feb. 27–40	Aug. 66–83
Mar. 34–48	Sep. 60–77
Apr. 44–61	Oct. 51–67
May 53–71	Nov. 41–54
Jun. 63–81	Dec. 30–41

The winds in the winter months can be fierce, especially in the canyons of midtown Manhattan, and the wind-chill factor can lower the effective temperature a great deal.

NEW YORK CITY

A Congregation of Neighborhoods

by ROSELLEN CALLAHAN and MICHAEL IACHETTA

Rosellen Callahan, former travel editor of the Woman's Home Companion, *contributed to many national magazines and was a past president of the Society of American Travel Writers. Michael Iachetta, a syndicated travel writer with the New York* Daily News, *is also a member of the Society.*

The time of day and the portal you choose to reach Manhattan make a world of difference in your lasting impression of the city. If you approach it at dusk, driving along the rim of the precipitous Palisades on the New Jersey side of the Hudson River leading to the high span of the George Washington Bridge or through the Lincoln Tunnel, the

NEW YORK CITY

city is the most majestic, radiant, exciting sight you'll see in a lifetime of travel.

The jagged skyscrapers silhouetted against the dusky evening sky, their galaxy of lighted windows reflected in the rippled river, is indescribably overwhelming. The newcomer rarely completely recovers from this stunning introduction to the city. This is quite understandable when you consider that New Yorkers, and their New Jersey neighbors who live on the perimeter of Manhattan's skyline, have themselves never ceased to be awed by this magnificent vista.

If your route leads you by way of the under-river Holland Tunnel to New York—an unfortunate choice—you'll find yourself swept into a vortex of the city's tangled traffic and eddies of the bustling, jaywalking pedestrians bent on making the most of those seconds and split-seconds which stretch and stress their day. Coming upon the city this suddenly, your first impression could be a distracting combination of intensity, indifference, squalor, and splendor.

Seen from the vantage point of an airplane window, the city reveals itself as a cluster of odd-shaped islands tethered together by bridges. For New York is really a complex of boroughs: Manhattan, Brooklyn, Queens, the Bronx, and Richmond or, more commonly, Staten Island.

Yet, anyone who speaks of New York City means Manhattan. Even Brooklynites will say "we're going into the city," when in fact they live within the city limits.

Manhattan is only a little over twelve miles from tip to toe and less than three miles across at its widest point. Small in size, true—but you could spend a month exploring this island and never cover all the historic sites, hidden mews, jazz dens, restaurants, museums, ships, opera-concert houses, theaters, parks, and ethnic neighborhoods.

New York is a city that defies a pat description. Bustling, brash, complex, changeable, confusing—yes. Exciting, amusing, inspiring, rewarding—this, too. Unfriendly, indifferent, cold? Not really, if you spend time enough, give of yourself enough, in getting to know it.

It's been said that cities are one of the extraordinary creations of man and that New York is the master mold for the megalopolis. True or not, New York is without question the most magnetic city in the world, a unique blend of people of all races, religions, and cultures. "Melting pot" is the easy term once applied—but not everything melts.

What makes New York tick? Why is New York, well . . . New York? Why is there so much energy, in people in the arts as well as among the businessmen? To begin with, the major industries in New York that generate jobs and money are (in no order) finance, stock brokerage, consumer banking, commodities exchange, export-import, shipping, advertising, public relations, tourism, publishing, broadcasting, medicine, insurance, garment design and manufacture, printing—though the shops themselves have tended to move to New Jersey in recent years—and the performing arts, plus the services that have developed around these: lawyers by the platoon, designers, agents and their stables, messenger services, and so on. What makes New York tick? Simply, this is where deals are made. This is what the nervous energy, the seeming aggression stems from. This is why so many of the world's corporations have offices here, if not their headquarters. This is why the pop-music producers are coming *back* to the city after a wave of migration to Los Angeles. Office space and apartments are becoming harder and harder to come by here.

Some Americans, especially in the West and South, harbor fear of and dislike for New York City. This traces back to the Populism of the late 1800s that condemned "Wall Street" for crucifying "the toilers" on a cross of gold. In fact, the farm mortgages *were* largely held by Wall Street bankers, who *did* control the money supply to suit their needs, and who *did* control the railroads that *did* discriminate against farmers and ranchers. New York manipulated, and still does—and is seen by some still to be full of foreigners and loud-mouths as well.

New York's appeal has many facets. Good theater, great restaurants, exquisite shops, successful careers, financial gain, freedom, and privacy. It offers to each, whether visitor or resident, his own reward. It also demands much in return. The demands and rewards partly explain the frenetic pace of the city, the unremitting drive of the people, their seeming indifference to the stranger in their midst.

The Private Life of New Yorkers

To New Yorkers, privacy is precious and time is fleeting. Their ways of achieving privacy and hoarding minutes take many forms. For some it means learning to be oblivious to the suffocating crowds and ear-shattering noises around them by losing themselves in a private world of personal plans and thoughts. Best friends will pass each other by without a sign of recognition if they are late for appointments.

Next-door neighbors in apartment houses may mumble a reserved "good morning" or "good evening," but will rarely engage in conversation for fear it will open the way to impromptu visits at inconvenient times. Yet, if they meet each other a long way from home, they are likely to fall into each other's arms like long-lost friends. Crowds in a subway or on the street may sidestep a stranger who has been felled by a heart attack and hurry on their way, lest they be involved in the time-consuming business of appearing as a witness.

The heavy population density of New York City is one of the most important factors in shaping the character of New York and the New Yorkers. When there are up to 2,000 people living on *one block* you

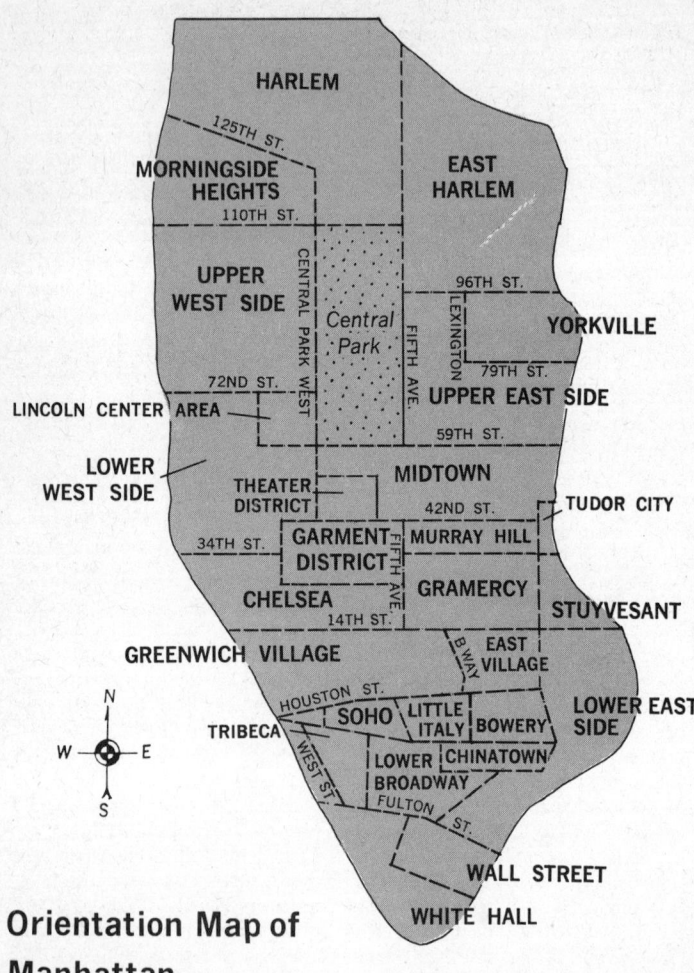

Orientation Map of Manhattan

Lower Broadway, Wall Street area, and **White Hall** area are what New Yorkers call "downtown," by which they mean the financial district. Almost no residential.

Chinatown: Life out on the streets or in restaurants in full force. Little night life, though, in the bar and night club sense. Heavily residential, but in tenement buildings.

NEW YORK CITY

Little Italy: Residential area like no other in city. Restaurants, Italian food shops, cafés, and street life in full measure among shabby tenement buildings.

SoHo: A strange mix of artists-in-residence and light manufacturing. Restaurants and street life here and there. **TriBeCa** is similar but with more manufacturing and less street life, fewer residents.

East Village: Mostly lower-income residential in tenements, but mixed with light commercial enterprises. East portion is redolent of Middle-European immigrants who settled here. Hippies were centered here in 60s and 70s.

Greenwich Village: Primarily residential, and often quite expensive housing. New York University a big presence in central area. Restaurants, bars, night life, and stay-up-late street life as overwhelming as ever. Attractive brownstone buildings.

Chelsea: An area in transition. Some artists' lofts and good housing, lots of not so good. Street scene is spotty and can be gamy.

Murray Hill: Predominately low-rise buildings, a mix of offices and residential housing, often quite good. The **Gramercy Park** area is similar but with more light manufacturing in loft buildings in the west—and artist and photographer lofts too. Restaurants and street life spotty, especially at night.

Garment District: Fascinating but hectic during the day, but not promising for ordinary visitors. Little residential, so deserted at night.

Theater District: Crowded with restaurants, too. Can be extra sinister late at night, after theater crowds have dispersed.

Midtown: *The* business district—but the east side of the area is heavily residential, with high-grade housing. Restaurants, night life, street life abound in spots throughout. Watch out for bicycles during the day. **Tudor City** is an almost entirely residential part of Midtown.

Upper East Side: On its west side, the most expensive living space in the country. Mostly cooperative or condominium apartments. Exquisite brownstone buildings on sidestreets. Posh galleries too. Profusion of restaurants and night life is mostly in residential eastern half of area, where rents are a bit lower, though still high.

Yorkville: Mix of expensive and inexpensive housing. Strong element of German and Central-European heritages.

Lincoln Center Area: Besides the Center, it is middle-class residential, with plenty of restaurants and street life revolving around the Center.

Upper West Side: The far west and far east zones are middle- and upper-class residential, good but not quite as high-rent as the Upper East Side. Lots of restaurants, night life, street life on the two sides, up Broadway and Columbus Avenue, where the apartment buildings are largely cooperatives or condominiums. The Amsterdam zone is still mostly low-income tenements, but the area is in the process of being upgraded.

Morningside Heights: Its west side is the Columbia University/Barnard area.

Harlem is Harlem. **East Harlem,** sometimes called Spanish Harlem, also has an Italian element in spots.

The other areas of Manhattan—**Lower East Side, Bowery, Lower West Side,** and the northern parts of Manhattan—have little or nothing to offer most visitors.

can expect to find people passing each other in the street without recognition. And when just one of them drops a newspaper like *The New York Times,* the wind will make any street look like the worst slum street in five minutes. Although a lot of the best things about the city stem from the density—the street life, the nightlife, the array of restaurants and cafés, the excitement—so do many of the worst aspects.

But come a common catastrophe, New Yorkers, native-born and ex-outlanders, will offer the shelter of their homes, their help and counsel without stint. They are a conundrum, and even they cannot explain themselves.

A Bit of History's Perspective

Knowing a bit of New York's history will help you to understand the circumstances and pressures which have tempered the character of the city and its citizens.

Unlike New England whose settlers came to the New World primarily to escape political and religious injustices, Nieuw Amsterdam, as New York was named first, was settled by Dutch families in the employ of the West India Company, a Netherlands trading combine whose sole interest was carrying on a profitable trade with the Indians. From the start, they fared well. In their first year, they realized a profit of 250 guilders from the skins of beavers and otters alone. Considering that their governor, Peter Minuit, paid only sixty guilders, or roughly $24, worth of trinkets to the Indians in exchange for the island of Manhattan, it was an exceptionally good year.

From its earliest days the community welcomed the stranger. It needed the brawn and skill of the newcomer's hands to help build the village, and it cared little about his race, color, or religious beliefs. A French Jesuit who passed through in 1643 reported home that "there may well be four or five hundred men of different sects and nations . . . there are men of eighteen different languages." Eight years later another sect was added when twenty-three Jewish men and women arrived to seek sanctuary. A Virginian, who paused on his way to the English colonies north, also complained: "The people seem not concerned what religion their neighbor is of, or whether he hath any or none." And so it has remained throughout the centuries.

New York's geographic location—an elongated island jutting into a huge protected harbor, with a mighty river at its side coming from deep within the country's interior of untapped riches—foreordained her supremacy as the greatest commercial city in America.

New York also straddled a strategic slice of the Atlantic coastline, separating the English colonies of New England from Virginia and cutting off the westward expansion of Connecticut and Massachusetts.

NEW YORK CITY

This, plus her commercial enterprise, nettled the British and in 1664, King Charles II presented his brother, the Duke of York, a little gift of "all the land from the west side of the Connecticut River to the east side of the De la Ware Bay," and sent a flotilla of warships to convince the Dutch colony's governor, Peter Stuyvesant, that surrender was preferable to annihilation. The practical, business-as-usual tradespeople urged the governor to surrender "in the speediest, best and most reputable manner." Nieuw Amsterdam passed into the hands of the British, was renamed New York, and the citizens went on about their business of trade and commerce.

The city learned early how to assimilate rather than be devoured. Long after the capitulation to the British, the Dutch clung to their traditions. The character of early New York became a composite of Dutch vigor and English tenacity. Trade remained the city's cachet, and has throughout the centuries. The ramifications of this have not been to everyone's taste; Emerson (from the vantage point of Boston) called New York "a sucked orange."

From the first, New York insisted upon and enjoyed a greater degree of religious liberty and political freedom than did most of the other colonies, and word of these special privileges spread abroad. The city's character reflected one bright new facet after another as wave after wave of political and religious refugees broke over its shores.

French and German Palatinates, fugitives from the religious persecutions of Louis XIV, sought sanctuary here in the early 18th century, followed by settlers from England, Ireland, and Scotland, who fled their homelands as the Stuart cause began to collapse.

Migrations ceased while New York suffered through seven bitter years of siege during the Revolutionary War. Again New Yorkers adjusted themselves to living under the threat of British guns, suffered a disastrous fire which destroyed the heart of the city, and played a waiting game, knowing that come what may, they would retain their individuality. By November, 1783, New York was part of the new Union and served as the nation's capital for the following six years.

"Loud, Fast, and Altogether"

Why didn't New York remain so? Its citizens may have decided that being the home of the national government would divert them from their historic role. A century and a half of history had tempered and forged New York into the nation's greatest city of commerce. Whatever the reason, New York passed the plum on to Philadelphia and got on with the business of becoming the "noisy, roaring, rumbling, tumbling, bustling, stormy, turbulent" city Walt Whitman found so disturbing.

In a way it always had been turbulent. Even in 1774, John Adams complained that "They talk very loud, very fast, and altogether. If they ask you a question before you can utter three words of your answer, they will break out upon you again, and talk away." There are grounds for complaint today in this respect.

It wasn't just rudeness, as John Adams felt, but rather exhilaration. The city has a way of stimulating the mind, crowding it with ideas, opinions, thoughts which refuse to be dammed up for long and come spilling out "loud, fast, and altogether." These are the very forces which have sent New York spiraling upward and outward.

The Erie Canal's completion in 1825 assured New York's monopoly of the nation's rich trade. Building burgeoned and the city's growth reached out to such scattered rural hamlets as Greenwich Village and absorbed them. By 1850 New York's population was well over a half-million and its real estate was valued at $400,000,000. Grand opera, concerts, and legitimate theater productions were adding the needed note of culture. Men were becoming millionaires and their wives were casting eyes abroad for titled mates for their daughters. Fifth Avenue soon would sprout with palatial residences and galas be given for visiting royalty. New York was, if ever there was, the pot of gold at the end of the rainbow.

Once again immigrants came to find it: Russian Jews fleeing the Tsarist pogroms; Italians escaping oppressive poverty; Irish Catholics who had coped with confiscation of their property and denial of religious freedom but could no longer battle starvation after the awful potato famine; and many more.

Their voyage often took ninety or more days. Jammed into the reeking holds of sailing ships with scarcely room enough to lie down, many succumbed to cholera. Those who survived the journey were often so weak they had to be carried off the ship. When steamships retired the last of these "floating coffins," more than 23,000,000 immigrants had come through this gateway over a forty-year period.

Many headed for neighborhoods where immigrants from their homeland had already settled. Here they were able to buy familiar foods, join their own societies, read the news in their own language. Few ever learned to speak English.

Politicians preyed on their ignorance and poverty, manipulated their votes or, if need be, bought them with picnic excursions and food baskets. They were crowded into slums on the lower East and West sides, not too many cuts above their steerage experiences. Sweatshops paid slave wages for a 60-or-more-hour week. Advertisements for domestic help at one period often read "No Irish need apply."

Yet the ideal of America never dimmed. The immigrants were free and their children were free. Free to learn, to pull themselves up by their bootstraps and become lawyers, doctors, merchants, financiers, patrons of the arts, and senators. The fabric of New York is shot

NEW YORK CITY

through with the sparkle, color, and tensile strength of these multitudinous ethnic-religious-political groups. They and their children and grandchildren have helped to make this city great.

In your wanderings throughout the city you will see remnants of these immigrant enclaves and find the imprint of their imagination on the skyscrapers of lower Manhattan, the elegant shops along Fifth Avenue, the bright lights of Broadway, the opera houses, concert halls, museums, and the home of the United Nations. The imprints of the Dutch and English are there, too. It is this pattern of people and events which has made New York the fascinating, cosmopolitan, polyglot city that it is.

Sailing Around Manhattan

The best introduction to New York City, weather and season permitting, is to take a three-hour Circle Line boat around Manhattan. The Circle Line operates from Pier 83 on the Hudson, at 43rd Street and 12th Avenue, from April 1 to November 15. Boats leave approximately every 45 minutes beginning in mid-morning. The cost for adults is $7.50, for children under 12 it is $3.75; for specific departure times call 563-3200.

As the boat pulls out of the dock, heading down the Hudson River, you pass Manhattan's lower West Side, which is undergoing fundamental—if controversial—changes and where the presently out-of-service West Side Highway is scheduled to be replaced. In any case, heavy construction is going on with the building of a convention and exposition center on 12th Avenue in the mid-30s and as the housing at Battery Park City (near the World Trade Center) gets under way. The ferry rounds the island's southern tip, giving a superb view of the Statue of Liberty and of the Wall Street skyline. Heading up the East River, you'll pass under three very different spans to Brooklyn: the Brooklyn, Manhattan, and Williamsburg bridges. A glimpse of fashionable Brooklyn Heights is available and you may see, a mile or so upriver, the old Brooklyn Navy Yard.

Looking back to the Manhattan side, you'll have passed Chinatown and the Lower East Side and now be closing in on the United Nations Building at 44th Street and 1st Avenue. On your right will be the sometimes dormant Delacorte Geyser and Roosevelt Island with its new housing developments. The bridge overhead is the stolid Queensboro or "59th Street," and right next to it, the tramway linking Roosevelt Island with Manhattan. Farther up, you'll catch a glimpse of the mayor's residence, Gracie Mansion, built in 1799 by Archibald of that name.

Then it's upstream under the Triboro Bridge (it links Manhattan to Queens and the Bronx). After several smaller spans, you'll see on the right refurbished Yankee Stadium and the nostalgic traveler may look on the Manhattan side to a cluster of red high-rises and recall the fabled Polo Grounds, scene of many dramatic sports moments, that once stood on the site.

About a mile onward, the Hall of Fame for Great Americans still looks out from a Bronx hillcrest, once part of New York University's uptown campus (the entire school is now located in Greenwich Village). Today this outdoor colonnade designed by Stanford White is on the campus of Bronx Community College. Then, rounding the northern tip of Manhattan through the Spuyten Duyvil cut, the cruise slips past Columbia University's boathouse, Inwood Hill Park, and the Henry Hudson Bridge. Once again, you're on the Hudson River flanked on the west by the towering Palisades of New Jersey. On the east you'll see The Cloisters and the heights of Fort Washington Park as you approach the George Washington Bridge, Grant's Tomb, Riverside Church, the Soldiers and Sailors Monument. The midtown towers come into view as you head back to the dock past the rebuilt luxury-liner piers between 54th and 45th Streets. It's a cruise you'll long remember.

Beginning at the Beginning

New York is an easy city to explore with the aid of a city map, which you can pick up at the New York Convention and Visitors Bureau at Columbus Circle, opposite the Coliseum. The bus systems and the more than 500 miles of subway tracks will take you to almost any sight you want to see. On occasion you may find a car more convenient for reaching widely separated attractions on fringes of the city, but for in-town touring a car is an expensive handicap. On-the-street parking is limited to very short periods and overtime parking can result in your car being towed away, costing $65 or more to recover. Garage parking is often difficult to find and can cost as much as $10 for two hours in midtown. You will find walking the most rewarding way to come to know the city and its people, to savor its flavor, and to make little discoveries of your own. In fact, New Yorkers themselves walk, and walk a great deal more than do the denizens of any other U.S. city. This is the key to the vitality of the city's amazing street life—and it continues to amaze even long-time New Yorkers. Here is what we have seen on the streets in the past few months (a selection): mimes, jugglers, magicians, flutists and violinists ("Music student needs help for tuition"), a team of "medical students" taking blood pressures, comedians, country-music groups, singers accompanied by music taped on a cassette player, trained dog acts, cats and monkeys dressed up in Victorian outfits, a man riding a bicycle and wearing a purple silk Musketeers suit and hat with purple feathers, bagpipers, blind beggars, crippled beggars, very healthy beggars, three-card monte conmen plying their three cards on cardboard boxes—this on Fifth Avenue!—and Renaissance troubadours—all of the above soliciting our money—and street vendors selling nuts and dried fruits, fresh-squeezed orange juice, parasols, handbags and gloves, luggage, bags of lavender, "solid gold diamond" rings (for $5.00!), tube socks ("For Mother's Day!"), real marijuana, phony marijuana, fruit, shish-kebab, Japanese dumplings and Chinese egg rolls, hot dogs (of course, with hot sauerkraut and/or onions), real New York egg creams, and giant inflatable vinyl frogs—with or without city peddler licenses.

The Battery Park area, where the city's history began, is an excellent starting point for a day's walking tour of lower Manhattan. The bus and subway systems converge here at Bowling Green, the little "Green before the fort" where early burghers bowled on summer evenings. Within a small radius are some of the city's most historic sites.

To appreciate the strategic geographical situation of the city, which gave it a commercial advantage over all other cities, walk along the esplanade of Battery Park. It is a salt breeze-swept stroll which tycoons from Wall Street often take to help clear heads and quiet nerves when they are faced with multi-million-dollar decisions. Here you can watch a parade of luxury cruise liners and freighters steaming out to sea, tugs herding strings of barges, and ships of all flags anchored in the bay.

Look down to a point called The Narrows, where the Lower Bay funnels into the Upper Bay, and you'll see the 4,260-foot main span of the Verrazano-Narrows Bridge cinching the waist of the water between Brooklyn and Staten Island. It was at this point in 1524 that the Florentine navigator Giovanni da Verrazano, seeking a passage to Asia at the behest of King Francis I of France, discovered what he described as "this very agreeable situation located within two small prominent hills, in the midst of which flowed to the sea a very giant river."

While history does credit Verrazano with the first sighting of this magnificent harbor, the mighty river was named for Henry Hudson, an Englishman in the employ of the Dutch East India Company, who arrived eighty-five years later on another mission to "seek a new route to the Indies by way of the North."

Despite a long campaign by the Italian Historical Society of New York to make the Verrazano name better known—first by having The Narrows, and the bridge spanning it, named Verrazano—the Florentine is still not reaping the just rewards for his discovery.

The Statue of Liberty

There is one ferry which, until recently, has never been threatened with extinction. It is the ferry from Battery Park to the Statue of Liberty, probably the most symbolic structure in the United States, and certainly the most symbolic of New York.

A visit to Liberty Island is more rewarding if one knows beforehand a bit about the forces of friendship which inspired the statue, the genius of its construction, and the long struggle to make it a reality. That it stands in New York harbor is as much a miracle as was its completion.

The idea of the monument was first discussed at a small dinner party given by French historian Édouard de Laboulaye at his home in Versailles, shortly after the close of the American Civil War. It was to be a gift from the people of France to the people of the United States to commemorate the long friendship between the two nations—a friendship which dated from the American Revolution, when French aid to General George Washington helped to turn the tide of victory to the side of the Colonies.

The guests were prominent men in politics, letters, and the arts. One was Frédéric Auguste Bartholdi, a young Alsatian sculptor. Some of the guests had reservations about the idea. They held that it was impossible for gratitude to exist for long. They doubted that in an emergency France could count on America to remember the aid France had given and return it in kind. The idea went into hibernation for some years. When the idea was revived, it was decided that if a statue were to be constructed, it would be with the proviso that the French people would give the statue proper if the people of the United States would build the pedestal.

Bartholdi was sent to America to discuss the project with prominent philanthropists. During the ocean voyage he roughed out several concepts for the monument. But it wasn't until he sailed into New York's magnificent harbor that he conceived the idea of a "mighty woman with a torch" lighting the way to freedom in the New World. The perfect site was New York, the gateway to that world.

In France, public fêtes and lotteries were held to raise funds to build the statue. Gounod, the famous composer, wrote a song about the statue and presented it at the Paris Opera. Because the statue was to be a gift from the people of France, the government was not approached for financial aid, and it was seven years before the needed $250,000 was finally subscribed.

On this side of the ocean the proposed site for the statue stirred up old embers of hostility. Why, some states demanded to know, should they be called upon to donate money to finance the construction of a pedestal for a "New York Lighthouse"?

Piece by piece, the statue was taking form in France, while Americans continued to hassle and withhold contributions. To help kindle enthusiasm for the project, the 42-foot right arm and torch was exhibited in 1876 at the Centennial Celebration of American Independence held in Philadelphia. Public apathy could not be overcome. It looked as though construction of the pedestal never would be completed, and that the generous gift could not be accepted.

Joseph Pulitzer Saves the Statue

Philadelphia, Boston, San Francisco, and Cleveland offered to pay all the cost of a pedestal if the statue were presented to them. It was at this point that Joseph Pulitzer of the *New York World* launched a campaign to "nationalize" the project. In editorials he stormed at New Yorkers who failed to contribute according to their means; assailed the provincial thinking of citizens in other states who refused assistance because the statue was to stand in New York Harbor; called upon everyone to avert the shame of rejecting the most generous gesture one nation had ever made to another. The public's conscience was pricked and the campaign became a crusade.

Benefit balls, sporting events, and theatrical performances were held. Schoolchildren deposited their pennies and nickels in classroom containers. Contributions poured in from distant states. Completion of the pedestal was assured and the statue was packed, piece by piece, in 214 cases and shipped to New York to be assembled and mounted. The Statue of Liberty Enlightening the World was dedicated October 28, 1886, with these words by President Grover Cleveland: "We will not forget that Liberty has here made her home; nor shall her chosen altar be neglected."

The 151-foot statue is a monument to the herculean genius of its sculptor. To achieve the correct proportions of this mighty woman, Bartholdi made a four-foot study model, then cast and recast it until it was thirty-six feet high. The statue then was divided into dozens of sections and each section enlarged four times. Liberty's eyes became two feet wide, her nose four feet long, her waist an ample thirty-five feet. On the mold of each section, copper sheets 3/32-inch thick were pressed and hammered into shape. Bartholdi had chosen copper for several reasons. It was light, easily worked, strong enough to withstand shipment, and impervious to the effect of New York's salty air.

The pedestal, one of the heaviest pieces of masonry in the world, towers eighty-nine feet above its foundation, the eleven-pointed star-shaped old Fort Wood. Alexandre Gustave Eiffel, the French engineer who constructed the famous Eiffel Tower in Paris, designed the framework which secures the statue to the foundation. Four huge iron posts run from the base of the statue to the top, forming a pylon which supports the weight of the whole structure. From this central tower a maze of small beams and iron straps were installed to support each section of the statue so that no piece bears the weight of the one above it. Thus, the statue is anchored to its pedestal, and the pedestal to the base in such a way that for a windstorm—and New York has severe ones—to overturn the monument, it would just about have to upend the whole island.

It is only a ten-minute ride from Battery Park to Liberty Island, and the ferry slowly skirts the monument so that you can take several closeup pictures. Once on the island, most visitors prefer to wander around on their own, and National Park Service guides are on hand to answer questions and provide you with a free souvenir pamphlet which details the history of the statue and the island.

In the base of the statue is the American Museum of Immigration. Circular in layout, the museum describes with multi-media exhibits such subjects as who settled this country, how they got here, what they brought with them (in addition to hopes and dreams), where they put down their roots, and how they fared.

Here, too, the poetic tribute written by Emma Lazarus is inscribed, its words making clear the symbolism of the Statue of Liberty:

> Not like the brazen giant of Greek fame,
> With conquering limbs astride from land to land;
> Here at our sea-washed, sunset gates shall stand
> A mighty woman with a torch, whose flame
> Is the imprisoned lightning, and her name
> Mother of Exiles. From her beacon-hand
> Glows world-wide welcome; her mild eyes command
> The air-bridged harbor that twin cities frame.
> "Keep ancient lands, your storied pomp!" cries she
> With silent lips. "Give me your tired, your poor,
> Your huddled masses yearning to breathe free,
> The wretched refuse of your teeming shore.
> Send these, the homeless, tempest-tossed to me:
> I lift my lamp beside the golden door!"

An elevator takes you up ten floors to the balcony which runs around the top of the pedestal. On each of the four sides you'll find a sketch and description of the view before you, which makes it easy to identify Staten Island, the Verrazano-Narrows Bridge, Fort Jay, Governors

Island, the Brooklyn, Manhattan, and Williamsburg bridges, Ellis Island, and the skyscrapers of lower Manhattan.

For the stout of heart and strong of limb there is a staircase which spirals up twelve more stories to Liberty's crown for a stratospheric view. You are not necessarily committed to go the whole way in one uninterrupted climb. Rest platforms are located every third of the way up, where you can also cross over and climb back down if you have a change of heart about making it all the way to the crown.

The Statue of Liberty Ferry leaves Battery Park daily every hour on the hour between 9 A.M. and 4 P.M. (5 P.M. on Sundays). The round trip costs $1.50 for adults, 50 cents for children 11 and under, which includes admission to the Museum of Immigration as well as the Statue itself. The elevator to the top is an extra 10 cents; the walk costs only the 12-flight effort. For further information: 732–1286.

Allow yourself at least two and a half hours for the ferry ride and tour of Liberty Island. It's worth the time.

Another historical site in the Upper Bay—and accessible by ferry from Battery Park (except in winter)—is Ellis Island. Its buildings were, from 1892 to 1954, the immigration processing entry point into the United States for over ten million people, primarily Europeans. The ferry operates between April 25 and November 1, leaving daily at 9:30 and 11:45 A.M. and 2:00 and 4:15 P.M. The price for adults is $1.50, for children under 11, 50 cents, and that includes a one-hour guided tour of the island. Phone: 732–1286.

Battery Park

On your return to Battery Park, you might find a circular stroll rewarding before continuing your tour of lower Manhattan. You'll discover statues tucked into bowers, and the handsome Marine Memorial is especially worthy of a few moments. Stand behind the memorial—an eagle on a black marble pedestal facing a corridor of huge granite slabs engraved with the names of those who gave their lives to the sea—and you will see the Statue of Liberty dramatically framed.

The Victorian-cupolaed gray building, with its gay red window-frames and bright green roof (near the park's exit), is the home of the city's fireboats. If you are lucky enough to be here on a day when a ship enters the harbor on her maiden voyage (admittedly a rare event), you'll see a fireboat or two saluting the liner with 200-foot plumes of spray.

The round brownstone building near the entrance to the park is Castle Clinton, built as a fort in 1811 to defend New York against any British attack. When the clouds of war cleared, the fort was ceded to

New York City, transformed into Castle Garden in 1823, and served as a theater and public center. Here Jenny Lind, "the Swedish Nightingale," performed for $1,000 a night, an extraordinary fee in those days. From 1855 to 1890 the castle was used as the nation's principal immigrant depot, more than 7,000,000 "tempest-tossed" souls passing through its gate into a bright new world. When Ellis Island became the new depot, the castle served as the New York City Aquarium until a modern one was built on Coney Island. Today, Castle Clinton is a National Monument, and plans are underway to restore it to its original appearance.

New York is rather poor in ancient landmarks as compared to Boston and Philadelphia. Disastrous fires in the latter part of the 18th century and beginning of the 19th century took their toll of many historical homes and buildings. During the city's rapid rise as the nation's major metropolis, many fine old buildings were demolished to make way for the new. It wasn't until 1918, when Trinity Corporation decided to tear down the century-old St. John's Chapel to make way for commerce, that New York's civic pride was finally kindled. Public feeling ran high and protests were long and loud. Commerce won, however—as is usual in New York City—and the chapel came down.

It was a boom time, a period of fierce rivalry between moguls, and big buildings became an expression of this rivalry. As each tried to top the other, the old gave way to the new. In 1908 the Singer Building (now known as the Paul Building) at 561 Broadway, between Spring and Prince Streets, soared up to a record forty-seven stories. By 1913 the Woolworth Building, 233 Broadway between Barclay Street and Park Place, topped it by thirteen floors. The Equitable Life Assurance Society, 120 Broadway between Pine and Cedar Streets, covered an entire city block with a 44-story straight-sided building. Its ugly functional form jarred the city fathers into action, and New York's first zoning law was enacted in 1916. Buildings, they decreed, must have setbacks, a style which became known as the "wedding cake." (By a stretch of the imagination, the progressive bottom-to-top setbacks do resemble the tiers of a wedding cake.)

In your stroll through lower Manhattan you'll find many architectural forms. Opposite Bowling Green, at the intersection of State, Whitehall, and Bridge Streets, is the Customs House, an ornate Maine granite edifice studded with statuary by Daniel Chester French, which reflects the sprawling rococo period of building at the turn of the century. It seems a doughty dowager compared to the debutante across the way, the sleek new skyscraper at No. 2 Broadway, where many of New York's foremost brokerage houses have offices.

You'll find the streets down here are narrow, cut-up, and squeezed awry by the confluence of the Hudson and East rivers. If there is one

NEW YORK CITY

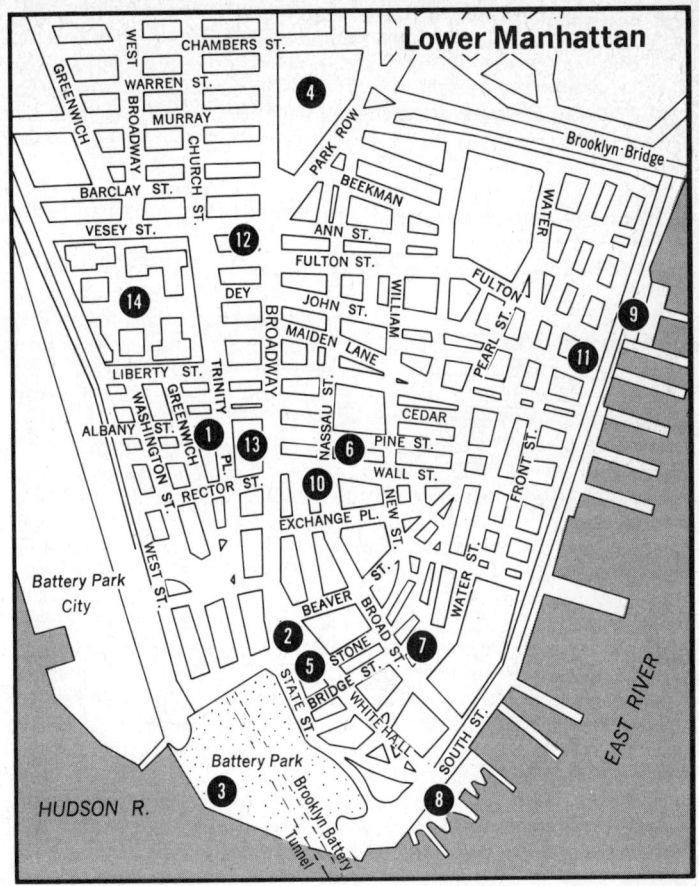

Points of Interest

1) American Stock Exchange
2) Bowling Green
3) Castle Clinton Nat. Monument
4) City Hall
5) Customs House
6) Federal Hall Memorial
7) Fraunces Tavern
8) Ferry to Staten Island
9) Fulton Fish Market
10) N.Y. Stock Exchange
11) South Street Seaport
12) St. Paul's Chapel
13) Trinity Church
14) World Trade Center

place you'll need a street map to guide you, it is here. Yet, it is this crazy-quilt street pattern laid out by the first settlers which makes the scrambled spires so spectacular when viewed from a distance. Tucked into this granite-chrome-glass jungle are a few historic buildings which have managed to escape destruction or have been cleverly reconstructed.

Fraunces Tavern

One is Fraunces Tavern, at 54 Pearl Street (425-1776), a block east of the Customs House. Erroneously called "the oldest building in Manhattan," it is in fact an excellent reconstruction dating from 1907. Its square proportions, hipped roof edged with a light balustrade, regular window spacing, and white portico are perfect examples of the Georgian Colonial style favored in the early 18th century. Built of brick—which likely saved it from going up in flames during the disastrous fires of the Revolution—and turned from a residence into a successful business building (which staved off demolition)—it has had a long, colorful history. The original building was erected in 1719 as a residence for Étienne de Lancy, a wealthy Huguenot. His grandson turned it into a store and warehouse in 1757, and in 1762 it was sold to Samuel Fraunces, a West Indian of French and Negro blood, who renovated it, making it the Queen's Head Tavern.

Taverns in those days were more than food and drink emporiums. Captains of commerce, politicians, army officers, and fraternal groups often used them as meeting halls. It was at Fraunces Tavern that the Chamber of Commerce of the State of New York was founded in 1768 to help press the fight against the Stamp Act and the tax on tea. Here, too, George Washington called his officers together in the tavern's Long Room to bid them farewell.

It was a heart-wrenching leave-taking, one officer writing in his diary: "Such a scene of sorrow and weeping I had never before witnessed, and I hope may never be called upon to witness again. It was indeed too affecting to be of long continuance—for tears of deep sensibility filled every eye—and the heart seemed so full that it was ready to burst from its wonted abode. Not a word was uttered to break the solemn silence that prevailed, or to interrupt the tenderness of the interesting scene. The simple thought that we were then about to part from the man who had conducted us through a long and bloody war, and under whose conduct the glory and independence of our country had been achieved, and that we should see his face no more in this world, seemed to me utterly insupportable ... he walked silently on to Whitehall, where a barge was in waiting ... as soon as he was seated,

NEW YORK CITY

the barge put off into the river, and when out in the stream, our great and beloved General waved his hat, and bid us a silent adieu."

Fraunces Tavern is still a popular meeting place. The Sons of the Revolution in the State of New York purchased the property in 1904, faithfully re-created the original building, and today use it as their headquarters. A restaurant and bar occupy the first floor, and here, perhaps, you may see leaders of industry discussing million-dollar deals over lunch. But note: luncheon and dinner meals are served here from Monday to Friday only.

On the floors above you can view the Long Room, where Washington made his adieus, and wander through a small museum of relics from the Revolutionary period, paintings and prints depicting historical events, and such questionable Washington memorabilia as a fragment of broken tooth and lock of hair. The museum, like the bar and restaurant, is closed on weekends.

South Street Seaport

New York City gained much of its prominence and wealth as a major seaport. A nonprofit organization with a membership of more than 25,000 people established the South Street Seaport Museum, covering a four-block area around the former Fulton Fish Market in lower Manhattan, in remembrance of the city's early seafaring days.

The museum gallery is located at 16 Fulton Street, a book shop is located nearby (at the corner of Fulton and Water Streets), and a model ship and print shop are located at 207 Water Street, a short walk north from Fulton Street.

The primary goal of the museum organization is to restore the historic buildings in the four-block area and several early vessels. Several such vessels are on view at any given time, such as the *Peking* or the *Wavertree,* a square-rigger built in 1885. Other vessels open to the public include the original *Ambrose Lightship,* built in 1904, and a hospital ship. To tour the ships is $3.00 for adults, $1.50 for children and students; Senior Citizens may board free. A covered Market Place features gift, craft and antique shops, and there is an assortment of food available—seafood as well as hamburgers served from different stalls. Table-and-chair eating also available. For general information relating to the Seaport and its activities, call 766–9020.

Also one of New York's oldest and best seafood restaurants, Sweets, is in the South Street Seaport complex on Fulton Street near South Street—serving customers on a first-come, first-served basis. Open 11:30 A.M.–8:30 P.M. daily. Closed in July. Phone: 825–9786.

Wall Street

Wall Street, which is only seven blocks long, has become an inclusive name. When one says "I work in Wall Street," he usually is referring to the financial district in general. His office might be on Pine, Broad, or Cedar streets. Or he might say "I work on the street," which translates into "I work for a brokerage house."

The street, which follows what once was the walled northern boundary of the original Dutch colony, became a financial center soon after the Revolutionary War. The new Republic was $80,000,000 in debt and the first Congress, which met in a hall at the corner of Broad and Wall Streets, voted to issue stock to help pay the costs of the war. Trading was a new catch-as-catch-can business carried on by auctioneers in coffee houses and so disorganized that people were reluctant to invest. There was no assurance, they complained, that they could sell their securities when they wanted to. To give trading some semblance of order, a group of twenty-four merchants and auctioneers decided to meet each day at regular hours to buy and sell securities. They chose as their meeting place a shady spot under an old buttonwood (sycamore) tree which stood in front of the present 68 Wall Street. They were the first members of the New York Stock Exchange.

Today the Exchange has over 1900 member firms, and an average 45 million shares are traded daily behind the ornate façade on Broad Street, around the corner from Wall Street. Visitors are welcome to the second-floor gallery (weekdays until about 3:30) where you can look down on the Exchange floor and listen to a recording describing what all the frantic business is about. Guides take you on a tour and in the course of an hour demonstrate how a sale is recorded on tape. If you stand up in front, they may choose your name to demonstrate how a sale is run through. At another area there is a sort of animated Punch and Judy demonstration of how a Californian who wants to sell his stock is able to find a buyer in Boston and have the order executed through the Exchange.

Around the corner from the Exchange is a handsome Greek Revival building, on the corner of Wall and Nassau Streets. It is the Federal Hall National Memorial, built in 1842 on the site of New York's first City Hall. It's quite an historic corner. Here, freedom of the press and freedom of speech were won by John Peter Zenger in 1735, the first Congress convened, and on April 30, 1789, General Washington inaugurated president. It was here that the Congress adopted the Bill of Rights.

The present structure served as customs house and subtreasury building and later housed the Federal Reserve Bank of New York. In

NEW YORK CITY

a way, the handsome building is an anomaly. If architecture is your forte, you will wonder why a circular rotunda was placed in a rectangular building (and well you should). But such were the vagaries of the period of Greek Revival. Originally the plan was to build a Roman dome over the rotunda, set squarely in the middle of this Greek temple. The dome was never built, but the handsome rotunda remains.

Administered by the National Park Service, Federal Hall Memorial Museum, 15 Pine Street (344–3830), is filled with permanent exhibits. These include displays of early historical documents (you can purchase duplicates of many of them, including the Constitution and Bill of Rights) and miniature replicas in glass cases of momentous civil liberty victories. Pick up one of the headphones, push the button, and you can even hear the proceedings of the John Peter Zenger trial.

The low marble building across the street at 23 Wall Street is the home of the powerful J. P. Morgan banking company. If you study its façade you'll find the faded scars of the bomb which, in anarchist days, was meant for his son John Pierpont Morgan, Jr., but which killed several unfortunate passersby instead.

At the head of Wall Street, fronting on Broadway, is one of New York's richest landlords, Trinity Church. Its holdings—a land grant Queen Anne of England made to it in 1705 and bequests of large farms by early settlers—once extended along the Hudson River from about St. Paul's Chapel at Fulton Street to Christopher Street in the Greenwich Village area.

A History-Making Church

The present church building, erected in 1846, is the third one to occupy this site. The graveyard dates from even before 1697; much history is written on its headstones. If the gate is open you can wander along its tree-shaded paths to seek out the final resting places of Alexander Hamilton, Robert Fulton, and others who figured in the city's early history.

The church also contains an admission-free exhibit room. The showings cover a wide range of subjects, and there is no set schedule. It is best, therefore, to check with the church to see what exhibits are planned (285–0872). If you visit Trinity around the lunch hour, you might also stop in at the Trinity Church Coffee House directly behind the church at 74 Trinity Place.

Were it not for a favorable decision in the courts, Trinity would be just another poor parish today. After the great fire of 1776 reduced Trinity to a smoldering heap, a group of American revolutionists challenged her right to rebuild. They held that the fidelity of two of the church rectors to the loyalist cause had discredited the church; that its special status as the established Church of England in America under a royal charter was no longer valid now that the city had become part of the newly created State of New York; that the lands no longer belonged to her. Through passage of the New York State Act of 1784, however, Trinity was enabled to build chapels throughout the city with the income derived from her vast properties. It is the rentals from her large landholdings which have made Trinity one of the world's wealthiest corporations today. Leasing the land instead of selling it, Trinity was able to amass a fortune, as have other great land-holding institutions, such as Columbia University, owner of the property on which Rockefeller Center stands.

North of Trinity Church at Broadway and Fulton Street is one of the city's few remaining examples of Colonial architecture, St. Paul's Chapel, one of many Trinity built throughout the city. When it was erected in 1766, it stood in a field outside the city. Townspeople complained that it was much too far to go to church; yet it is only a five-block walk from Trinity. St. Paul's Georgian-Classic revival style bears a distinct resemblance to St. Martin-in-the-Fields in London, probably for good reason, since its architect, Thomas McBean, was a pupil of Gibbs, who built St. Martin. There is much to hold you here. There is a light, cheerful air to the interior which is rare in Colonial churches. Fourteen priceless Waterford crystal chandeliers glisten in the azure-tinted nave and galleries, providing an unusually elegant, if somewhat controversial, embellishment. Ever since these gleaming candlelight fixtures—they are wired for electricity now—were installed in 1802, parishioners have had some reservations about their propriety. Mumblings are still to be heard about their making the church look like a ballroom.

On either outer aisle you will find a handsome box pew. One was the special preserve of the governors who worshipped here in the comfort of upholstered chairs and draft-deflecting canopies. The pew on the left was also used by George Washington. Original William and Mary chairs in bright red satin brocade give the pew an air of elegance seldom seen in churches. Duncan Phyfe, whose cabinet shop was around the corner from the chapel, fashioned the handsome sofa you can see in the rear of the church. The altar, its railing, and a great deal of the ornamentation in the church is the work of Major Pierre L'Enfant, the designer who later planned the city of Washington, D.C.

St. Paul's congregation is probably the most scattered in the city. People who once lived in the area and were displaced when housing gave way to office buildings still return for Sunday services. They drive in from as far away as Long Island, Westchester, and New Jersey. Weekdays, the chapel serves as a quiet haven for office workers, who

NEW YORK CITY

come to midday service or to sit on the secluded outdoor benches beside the peaceful cemetery.

Directly behind St. Paul's is the gigantic World Trade Center, operated by the Port Authority of New York and New Jersey. The Center takes up sixteen acres of lower Manhattan and stretches from Cortlandt Street on the east to West Street on the west and from Liberty Street on the south to Barclay and Vesey Streets on the north.

From top (107 floors up) to bottom, the World Trade Center has become a major sightseeing attraction—and part of the lure is the food as well as the view. Its various dining rooms, cocktail lounges, private rooms upstairs, and its concourse-level dining room, bar, and café below have to be seen to be believed. And so does the view of the city from perhaps the most famous of the Big Apple restaurants, Windows on the World, and its less expensive counterpart, the Hors d'Oeuverie, a cocktail lounge and grill that is another part of the restaurant complex. They share the same view from the top: roughly 50 miles of New York City sea, river, harbor, sky, bridges, ships, planes, skyscrapers, and more—especially when the stars start staging their own light show.

Windows on the World (we'll use the apt abbreviation WOW) has been compared to an immense spaceship, an ocean liner—you name it and pick your own superlatives—for decor, design, and view. WOW's entrance has you walking along a mirrored reception chamber lined by huge rocks that offer a naturalistic counterpoint to the plants and flowers that seem to be everywhere. You are seated in multi-tiered dining rooms made to seem even larger by mirrors—but it is still the skyline that is the real view, no matter what a people-watcher you may be. And the people in WOW are privileged, "beautiful people." The main dining room is a private club Monday through Friday until 3 P.M., becoming a regular restaurant thereafter. The food doesn't match the view—but what could.

You can nibble on the hors d'oeuvres, sample the grilled entrées, or have dessert at the Hors d'Oeuverie, on the same level as WOW, or come for Sunday brunch. It is a lot less costly than WOW, a good place for snacks and drinks—and the view is equally spectacular. And when the evening sun goes down the Hors d'Oeuverie becomes one of the most romantic nightspots in town for nightcaps, dancing to a trio or piano, or just star-gazing in the adjoining City Lights Bar. The phone number for these 107th floor wining and dining spots is 938–1100.

Other worthwhile (and less expensive) stops at the World Trade Center are the Observation Deck, open from 9:30 A.M. to 9:30 P.M., with sunset an especially spectacular time to be there; the Big Kitchen series of deli-style fast-food emporiums in the main concourse of Two WTC, where the crowds at lunch hour are a sight to behold; and the Skydive Café on the 44th floor of One WTC. The latter is an inexpensive-to-moderately priced luncheon cafeteria with a bar that is also open after work. The Observation Deck costs $2.50 for adults, $1.25 for children 6 to 12 years old, and is free for Senior Citizens; telephone 466-7377.

City Hall

Return to Broadway and stroll up to City Hall. Almost any day of the week you are likely to see the welcome mat being spread out for a foreign dignitary, a group of VIPs, a newly-crowned beauty queen, a DAR delegation, or an award-winning actress. Many come to greet the mayor in legitimate roles. Others come seeking publicity. To have their picture taken with the mayor of the world's largest city is an almost certain way to hit the headlines and the TV screens. It's been the plaint of many a mayor that acting as the world's greatest greeter cuts deeply into the day's work of handling affairs for the city.

City Hall is both a museum and a municipal capital. Architecturally it is considered one of the finest public buildings in America. During the period between 1803 and 1811, when it was being built, construction costs rose to $538,000—a shocking amount in those days. The Common Council members, pinching pennies wherever they could, decided considerable money could be saved by using marble on the front and sides only. Brownstone would be used to face the back. After all, they maintained, most of the city's population lived south of the park and it would be a waste to use marble when it seldom would be seen. The city, they believed, would never grow much beyond City Hall. When the building was renovated in 1956, at a cost of $2,000,000, the outside was faced in limestone on all four sides, to afford equal respect to the citizens of each point of the compass.

The mayor's office in the west wing overlooks the triangular park where Dutch burghers once bowled and where, a century later, spunky Revolutionists raised Liberty Poles and demonstrated against British rule. Even today it is not always a peaceful view. Demonstrators often congregate here to march and shout demands for a special action by the city fathers.

A handsome, curving double staircase leads to the Governor's Room on the second floor of City Hall. The elegant quarters, "appropriated as an office to His Excellency the Governor of the State," have been the scene of many gala, historic receptions. It had been traditional, even as far back as the Dutch and English rules, to set aside an area in City Hall for the governor's convenience. Today, New York's governor is not so honored. He is housed in an archaic monstrosity upstate in Albany with not one iota of the charm of the Governor's Room, which is now a showcase of antique furnishings and priceless portraits of early American heroes. One of the most notable items in the museum is

George Washington's desk. Open Monday to Friday, 10 A.M.–3 P.M. Free. 566-5700.

On leaving City Hall, walk around to its rear and over to the tall-towered Municipal Building. A passageway through its arch will bring you out on Park Row, near the approach to the Brooklyn Bridge, the city's oldest span. From here, it is only a five-minute walk north to Chinatown.

Chinatown, Their Chinatown

Chinatown may come as a bit of surprise or disappointment, depending on your preconceived picture of it. Many tourists are drawn to the area in hopes of glimpsing the seedy side of life they've seen in class B movies and read about in mystery-thrillers. They are due for disappointment.

Long gone are the bloody fratricidal tong wars, knifings in the night, and the stealthy slipping of dead victims into the black East River waters. Gone too are the opium dens, where men made the world take on a rosy glow after puffing a pipeful of poppy seed. The tongs have turned into modern civic and fraternal organizations and the dens of iniquity have disappeared, though gangs of juvenile thugs (mostly immigrants from Hong Kong) have gained some notoriety recently.

Today, Chinatown is a colorful pocket of Oriental shops and restaurants catering to Chinese who live in other parts of the city, to local government department heads, Park Avenue matrons, Broadway stars, and out-of-town visitors (in short, to all lovers of good Chinese cuisine).

Chinatown is tiny, encompassing something like a dozen or so square blocks. Thousands of Chinese are crowded into tenements lining the narrow, crooked streets. Here, somehow, the tenements seem almost proper to their surroundings. Perhaps it's because pseudo pagodas crown their roofs, bright banners garland the streets, and temple bells and the singsong talk of venerable elders crowd out sounds of the 20th century. There is a faint aura of China's ancient civilization all around: emporiums which have modern adding machines but prefer to do their bookkeeping with the beaded abacus; apothecary and herb shops where family medicinal formulas are compounded. Stalls and shopwindows are piled high with exotic displays of condiments and herbs, snow peas, bean curd, shark fins, duck eggs, dried fungi, squid, and other ingredients used in the delectable Chinese dishes. In keeping with the Oriental theme, even the sidewalk telephone booths have been designed as tiny pagodas.

The juncture of Worth and Mott Streets, across from Chatham Square, is the gateway to Chinatown. A Chinese Museum is located at 81 Mott Street, and for 75 cents weekdays or $1 weekends you can view exhibits of ancient Chinese coins, costumes, deities, and dragons. There are displays of flowers, fruits, chopsticks, and incense with explanations of their history and the symbolism attached to each. Push a button at the bottom of a musical instrument display case and a Chinese combo in native costume flashes on the screen to demonstrate how they sound. Youngsters especially enjoy the educational quiz, a game of thirty-eight questions along the lines of "Which city is farthest north, Peking or New York?" and "Who invented paper and printing, the Chinese or Egyptians?" You register your choice by pressing one of two buttons and by the end of the game you have a few nuggets of knowledge to confuse and confound your friends.

The museum also supplies you with a walking-tour map which is most helpful in identifying the Buddhist Temple, Christian churches, Chinese theaters, and other local attractions. Chinese characters and English appear on most signs. There are dozens of shops to browse through. Jade and ivory carvings, good-luck charms, slitted brocade dresses, tea sets, and sweets are to be had for generally lower prices than you can purchase them uptown. Open daily 10 A.M.–6 P.M. (964-1542).

You may hear little English spoken as you wander through Bayard, Pell, and Doyers Streets, though many of Chinatown's citizens can speak it if they please. Nor will you find them especially warm, restaurant owners and shopkeepers included. They maintain a cool dignity born of a culture which predates the Western by many centuries.

Dignity disappears when the Year of the Dragon (or Tiger, or any of the 12 in the Chinese horoscope) comes in, the whole town joining in the gay antics and colorful parades of fire-breathing monsters which mark the start of the lunar New Year. Firecrackers explode everywhere. Huge dragons, unicorns, and lions prowl through the streets to scare away evil spirits. Old and young dance along behind, shouting "Gun hay fat choy!" (Happy New Year with prosperity). Merchants offer gifts to the dragon and heads of lettuce sprouting dozens of dollars to be dispensed to the poor, for the dragon is an emblem of guardianship and generosity. It is a time when Chinatown is at its liveliest, most colorful best. Not even snow flurries can dampen the high spirits of the celebrants nor those from the outside who have come to watch and participate.

To the west of Chinatown is an emerging artist's neighborhood, christened TriBeCa ("Triangle Below Canal," bounded by the West Side waterfront—Greenwich Street—and West Broadway), which offers cheaper lofts for those driven out of SoHo by rising rents. There are a few not-run-of-the-mill bars, restaurants, and night spots here.

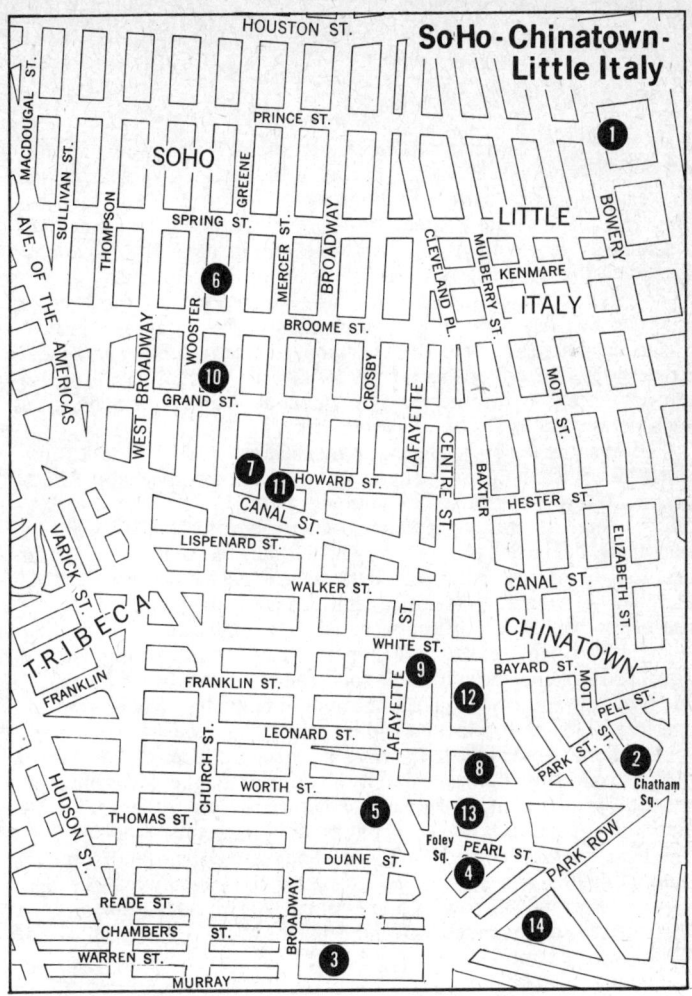

Points of Interest

1) Bowery Mission
2) Chinese Museum
3) City Hall
4) Federal Court
5) Federal Office Building
6) Museum of Colored Glass & Light
7) Museum of Holography
8) N.Y. State Office Building
9) N.Y. State Supreme Court
10) Performing Garage
11) SoHo Repertory Theatre
12) Criminal Court
13) N.Y. County Court
14) Police Headquarters

The Bouwerie, the Bowery

Just north of Chinatown, in the shadow of the Williamsburg Bridge, is the Bowery. Once an Indian trail used by Peter Stuyvesant to ride to his *bouwerie,* or "farm," the thoroughfare grew into a fashionable amusement and theater center in the early 19th century, then went into a decline as people moved uptown to new neighborhoods. For almost a century the Bowery has been the "street of forgotten men."

You'll see them curled up in doorways or sprawled on the street, a newspaper or hat cushioning their heads, sleeping off an ever-present hangover. There are beds in the flophouses above the gin mills and pawn shops, but the bed that used to cost 25¢ a night now goes for $1.45 or even more. The men here live by panhandling and on the charity of such organizations as the Salvation Army.

The Army began operating in the area before the turn of the century. Their lassies were not especially welcome when they invaded the Bowery in 1880 to "Go for souls—and go for the worst." Their work to reform derelicts and teach them to lead useful lives was fought by saloon and dance hall proprietors, who felt the preachings were bad for business. The Army had no church nor meeting place; so they preached and sang on street corners until a reformed Harry Hill offered them the use of his bawdy, gaudy music hall for the salvation of souls. The Army's historian recalls: "Alcoholics and prostitutes—the poor and downtrodden and discouraged—soon found new hope and comfort . . . Not only souls were saved, but minds and bodies. Roofs were put over the heads of people who had no other home on earth. Hundreds were fed and clothed by the Army's busy soup kitchens." The lassies marched on to other areas of the city and thence to other areas of public service. Despite their efforts and the efforts of many other charitable service institutions, however, derelicts still take refuge there.

Where do they come from? Just about everywhere and from all stations of life. Some were born to be bums. Others were, perhaps, successful businessmen with fine families who could no longer cope with the pressure, competition, and demands of the commercial world. Whatever their motivation, they have found a solace of sorts in the anonymity of Skid Row. The ranks of the rehabilitated are thin.

The Lower East Side

Housing projects and artist's lofts are encroaching on their Bowery haunts, and within a few years the derelicts may have to move on to other doorways. Some already have made the move. You'll see them

NEW YORK CITY

on the fringes of Greenwich Village and the East Village a little north of here.

Between the Bowery and the East River is probably New York's most integrated area. The entire city often has been called a "melting pot," but the mile-square east side area (bounded roughly on the south by Canal Street and on the north by Seventh Street) is, some observers feel, the most dramatic example of the blending of many races, religions, and cultures in the world.

Here, immigrants were crammed into ghettos and English was treated as a foreign language. Only those with the greatest stamina survived, and those with the greatest will succeeded in escaping from it. From here came Alfred E. Smith, a son of Irish immigrants, who became governor of New York State. Several sons of Jewish immigrants made the climb to success, too. Among them were Senator Jacob Javits, composers George and Ira Gershwin, comedian Eddie Cantor. A little Italian boy made it also—Jimmy Durante. The neighborhood also spawned its share of gangsters: a few are in jail, a few are living high.

While most shops all over the city are closed on Sunday, those on the Lower East Side bustle with activity. The Jewish Sabbath is observed on Saturday, while Sunday is a big shopping day down here. Grand Street, often called the "Street of Brides," is lined with one shopwindow after another of bridal gowns. The neighborhood now has a large Hispanic community, to add to the diversity.

The stalls on Orchard Street, a street so jammed with shoppers one can hardly wiggle through, display everything from clothing to kitchen wares. Bargaining is the way most transactions are handled, and customers should be wary to inspect merchandise—sometimes these stalls or shops deal in "seconds" in order to keep their prices low. Grand Street is for fine linens, the Bowery is for lamp stores, and Allen Street is the wholesale tie district—all featuring bargain prices.

Little Italy

Little Italy lies east of SoHo, just north of Chinatown, and south of Greenwich Village. Centered on Grand Street and its intersection with Mulberry and Mott Streets, Little Italy is the home of Ferrara's, (195 Grand Street, 226-6150), the city's foremost Italian coffee and sweet shop, as well as dozens of Italian restaurants, imported-food shops, cafés, and clam bars—including Umberto's Clam Bar, at Mulberry and Hester Streets, where Joey Gallo was shot to death. These clam bars feature a special hot and spicy tomato sauce with mussels, conch or squid, dishes unavailable anywhere else in the city.

South of Houston (SoHo)

SoHo, on West Broadway (part of which was renamed La Guardia Place a few years ago), between Canal and West Houston Streets, and off to the sides on Prince, Spring, and Broome Streets, is an area with which many native New Yorkers aren't familiar. It is only in the last 15 or so years that (at first) artists and writers began moving into the area, bringing their imaginations to bear on buildings formerly used as warehouses and for light industry. They came because they liked what were then inexpensive rents for the lofts—the lofts, often in need of plumbing and wiring but offering wide-open spaces—while gallery owners appreciated the high-ceilinged spaciousness of the old buildings, which allowed exhibit room to showcase the modern art and sculpture of today's genre. As rents rose, the area became fashionable among art patrons, jetsetters, and young professionals. So following the artists, writers, and galleries, a number of interesting and off-beat restaurants and bars came to be. Ironically, with few exceptions (the Bohemian Cupping Room Café on West Broadway, and O.G. Dining Room and Bakery on Thompson Street among them), most of SoHo's more unusual spots are far too expensive for the neighborhood's natives who work at art. On weekends and most weekday evenings West Broadway is thronged with people who come to SoHo to gallery-hop and browse at the poster shops and boutiques as well as to eat and drink.

Greenwich Village

Greenwich Village is not an entity but rather a collection of little villages. Its heart is Washington Square, at the end of Fifth Avenue, and its extremities reach out farther and farther each year. Roughly, it is bounded by Houston Street (pronounced "HOUSE-ton") on the south, 13th Street on the north, Hudson Street on the west—although much of the area between Hudson (the street) and Hudson (the river) has recently been restored and taken on a "village" look. Its eastern boundary now extends to Lafayette Street and the vague beginnings of the East Village, where most of the real latter-day Bohemians have migrated. If the Village has a "Main Street," it is 8th Street (and up onto Greenwich Avenue), centered on Village Square at Sixth Avenue.

Rents in Greenwich Village have soared out of the reach of poor poets and struggling artists. Today's Village residents are largely career people—business executives, lawyers, doctors, teachers, successful writers and artists—who have been drawn by its small-town neighborliness and convenient location to the city's business centers. Others, tired

NEW YORK CITY

of being bound by commuter train schedules, have come down from the suburbs and live in old houses they have renovated. You'll see little clusters of these tidy row houses on such tree-shaded side streets as Charles and Perry, Bedford and St. Luke's, their tiny rear gardens bright with blooms.

The Village is also home to a large segment of New York's Italian population. Their province south of Washington Square, really an extension of Little Italy, is a tangle of shops strung with tangy cheeses, breads, red peppers, garlic, bunches of oregano and rosemary. Housewives stream in from all parts of the Village to pinch the melons, poke through the tomatoes, and argue a bit about prices before making their selections.

In the early 20s the Village was a lively and bawdy place, a Montmartre in the midst of Manhattan. Painters and sculptors had discovered deserted lofts could be rented for a song. Poets and playwrights followed, crowding into the old buildings south of Washington Square, which became known as "Genius Row." They produced their plays in a theater converted from an old box factory, displayed their paintings in the park, scavenged for coal to heat their cold-water flats.

Since the turn of the century, it has been a center of creativity and intellectual curiosity that nurtured some of America's greatest writers and artists: Henry James, Edith Wharton, O. Henry, E. E. Cummings, Maxwell Bodenheim, Rockwell Kent, and many others. Their haunts —cellar speakeasies, chile con carne joints, hole-in-the-wall restaurants, murky nightclubs with tawdry epicene shows—drew the curious uptowners who wanted a taste of *la vie Bohème*.

Many of their haunts are long gone, victims of urban renewal. Others remain as shrines to their talent and genius. This bawdy phase, however, is but one of many the Village has passed through, for its history dates back to post-Revolutionary days.

The first settlers fled to the Village during the yellow fever plagues which raged through the lower city from 1791 to 1798. Founded in haste on the site of an old tobacco plantation, the little village grew haphazardly and the streets meandered off in unplanned directions. The crazy-quilt street pattern contributes to the Village a quaint charm but drives uninitiated taxi drivers to distraction. One street changes its name in mid-block; another circles back and crosses itself; West 4th wanders across West 10th, 11th, and 12th and runs into West 13th; Little West 12th is four blocks away from its larger namesake. To explore the area, a detailed map is mandatory. Even then, it is difficult to find your way without asking directions. You'll find the Villagers friendly and willing to help you out of the maze.

NEW YORK CITY

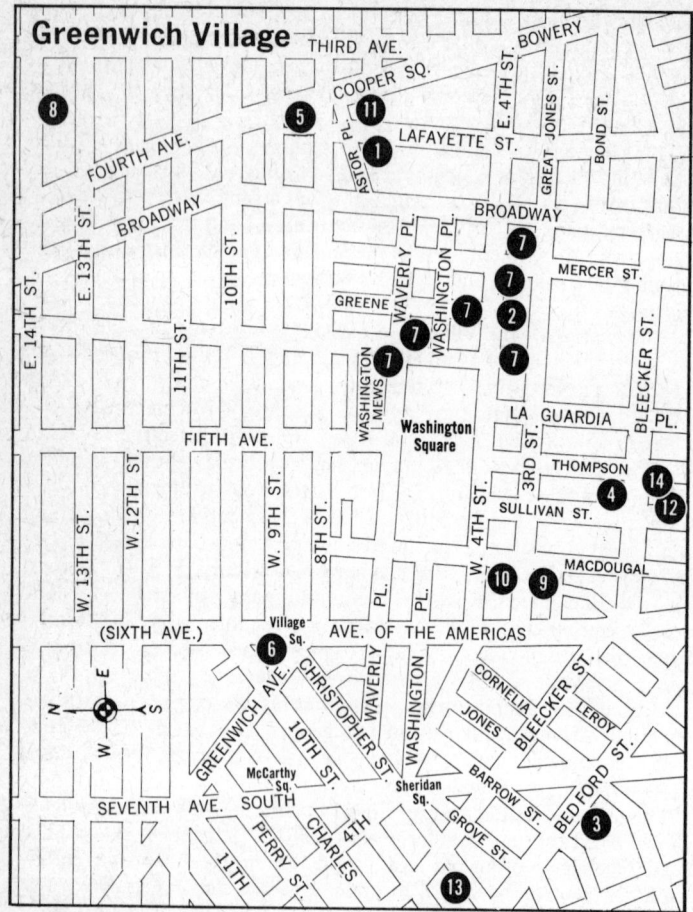

Points of Interest

1) Astor Place Theater
2) Bottom Line
3) Cherry Lane Theater
4) Circle in the Square Theater
5) Cooper Union
6) Jefferson Market Library
7) New York University
8) Palladium Theatre
9) Players Theater
10) Provincetown Playhouse
11) Public Theater (Papp)
12) Sullivan St. Playhouse
13) Theater De Lys
14) Village Gate

NEW YORK CITY

Focal Point of the Village

Washington Arch, at the foot of Fifth Avenue, is the best point to start a stroll through the most colorful and historic Village areas. It is easily reached by a Fifth Avenue bus marked "8th Street," by 6th and 8th Avenue subway to West 4th Street station, or the BMT to 8th Street and Broadway.

Washington Square served as a potter's field for plague victims and public place for executions in the late 1700s. By 1823 it had been filled with 10,000 victims of the plague and the gallows. It had served its purpose and it was time for a change, the city fathers decided; so the plot was turned into a drill ground for militia. Eventually it became known as Washington Square Park, although most of its former greenery has today been changed to concrete.

Should you choose a Sunday in spring, summer, or fall for your stroll, you'll be treated to one of the town's best known free entertainments. The fountain in the square is a meeting place for jazz and bluegrass musicians, guitar-players, and pluckers of homemade instruments. Within their ranks you may run into a recording artist who has come down to play a session with a group of unknown troubadours just for the sheer fun of it. Sunday strollers are apt to include young parents with toddlers, a multitude of dog-walkers, and arms-around-each-other couples of all ages; in all manner of dress.

The fountain is a good vantage point for viewing the red-brick, white-trimmed houses which line the north side of the square. Built around 1830, they remained a fashionable center of New York for a generation, sheltering members of old New York's aristocracy and a long-gone way of life so vividly described in Henry James's *Washington Square,* the novel which appeared on stage and in film under the title *The Heiress.*

Edith Wharton lived in the old Boorman house on the northeast corner of the square, a setting which inspired her novel *The Age of Innocence.* Down the street from her house, at No. 3, John Dos Passos wrote *Manhattan Transfer* and artist Norman Rockwell painted his own brand of "primitives." Rose Franken, author of *Claudia,* lived at No. 6 before this, while other, lovely patrician homes began to vanish.

Several, including the home of William Rhinelander Stewart, which stood on the northwest corner of Fifth Avenue, have been replaced by an apartment house. Fortunately, the building has been so constructed that it blends in with the remaining old houses. Only the building's first five floors are on the square and they are aligned with the roofs of the surviving houses. The red-brick facing and white trim of the new building blends with the old homes. The granite-colored upper floors are set back and front on Fifth Avenue, making that part of the structure seem completely divorced from the square. During construction of the apartment's foundation, workers found an underground stream. It was old Minetta Brook, which was buried by fill two centuries before. The brook surfaced and now bubbles up in a glass container in the apartment's lobby. It also spouts up in a fountain at No. 33, which is now a New York University residence hall.

The university, which has been here since the 1830s, owns and leases about four-fifths of the land around the square. In its original building, which stood at 100 Washington Square East, Professor Samuel F. B. Morse developed the telegraph and Samuel Colt invented the single-shot pistol.

When its student body began bursting the seams of the campus building on and around the square, the university reluctantly gave notice to the artists and writers along Genius Row. Loud outcries were to no avail, and the row of garrets has been replaced with the Georgian-style Law School at the southwest end of the square and the modern Roman Catholic Holy Trinity Chapel. Other modern N.Y.U. additions are the Hagop Kevorkian Center for Near Eastern Studies and the Bobst Library. Up the street, the tall brick-and-glass Loeb Student Center covers the site of Madame Blanchard's boardinghouse, whose boarders included Theodore Dreiser, Eugene O'Neill, Zona Gale, Frank Norris, O. Henry, and many other literary notables.

MacDougal Street Promenade

From here it's a short walk to MacDougal Street, which is called Washington Square West at this point. A few steps up MacDougal Street brings you to MacDougal Alley, one of the most charming back streets in the Village. Most of the little homes here were former stables and carriage houses of the elegant old homes on Washington Square North. Brightly painted, with doorways lit by gas lamps, they are among the most prized studios and apartments in all New York City. At the rear of the old homes on the east side of Fifth Avenue you'll find a similar cobbled street, lined by converted carriage houses, called Washington Mews.

Returning to the west side of Washington Square, passing the Law School, and walking on into the lower part of MacDougal Street, you will see the rebuilt Provincetown Playhouse, a pioneer off-Broadway theater made famous by the early works of Eugene O'Neill. This stretch of MacDougal Street is part of New York's "Little Italy," which has been invaded by a new breed of struggling artists who will sit you down on a campstool and paint your portrait, for a price, in short order. There are boutiques where you'll find witty, trendy, and ethnic clothes and jewelry; leather goods shops and fortune-reading ateliers; a few good restaurants; coffee houses (the latter now, alas, a Village rarity); and pizza and souvlaki eateries.

MacDougal Street leaves this mood behind as it crosses Bleecker Street, home of the Circle-in-the-Square Theater, which produced the early works of Tennessee Williams. The original theater group has now made the move uptown to Broadway and is operating at the Circle in the Square–Joseph E. Levine Theater, with an annual subscription season. Between Bleecker and Houston (a Dutch term meaning "house garden") is a row of well-kept, old brick houses where well-to-do professional people live. A similar row on Sullivan Street backs onto them and the private park between is shared by householders on both sides.

Turn back to Bleecker Street, head west across Sixth Avenue—officially known as the "Avenue of the Americas"—and you'll come to Father Demo Square and the Renaissance-style Church of Our Lady of Pompeii. Spend a minute or so in the church, for its lovely stained-glass windows and religious paintings are well worth the time. You are now at the beginning of the Italian shopping mart, which stretches from Sixth over to Seventh Avenue. The pushcarts have vanished from this colorful neighborhood, as have all but a very few produce stores. But the aromatic fish stores, bakeries with their mouth-watering Neapolitan cakes and pastries, meat and cheese and grocery shops make this one of New York's unique streets, with a character and flavor all its own.

The Village's meandering streets can really defeat you at this point, but find Leroy Street and follow its bend to St. Luke's Place. Here you'll come upon a poplar-lined street of handsome Anglo-Italian houses, almost as elegant as those of Washington Square. Built in 1880, they have housed many a New York celebrity. No. 6 was once the home of New York's dashing mayor, Jimmy Walker. At an earlier time, it was the residence of the French Consul, and if you look to the left of the doorway you can still see, set in the wall, a title bearing the arms of the French Republic.

At the end of the street, turn right on Hudson and explore the streets which twist and turn off it: Morton Street, with its attractive but seedy houses, and Bedford Street, where Edna St. Vincent Millay and John Barrymore lived (at different times) in New York's narrowest house. It is numbered 75½ and is only nine feet broad, having been built in the driveway of the old Cardoza farmhouse.

Three of the most contradictory houses in the Village are found at the corner of Grove and Bedford Streets. The house on the corner, a faded historic mansion, is backed up against a little doll house which is said to have been used for slave quarters a century ago. Next door, at 100 Bedford, is a gingerbread house known as "Twin Peaks." Local legend claims it was designed as a "dream house" by a Village artist, and that the sketches of his fairytale domicile caught the eye of financier Otto Kahn, who financed the dream. To many it is a nightmare.

Follow Grove Street to the point where it bends, and you will see the gate to Grove Court, a fenced-off cluster of small brick houses circling a shady garden. Grove Court was the home of O. Henry when he became affluent and it is the setting of his story *The Last Leaf.*

While you're following these winding streets, look for Commerce Street and the Cherry Lane Theater, the famous playhouse (converted from a box factory) which has given many a struggling playwright an opportunity to display his works. Follow Grove Street to St. Luke's Chapel on Hudson Street. St. Luke's was built by Trinity Church in 1822 and still maintains many of its old traditions. The church itself burned recently, but will be rebuilt. Wings of little brick houses jut out from St. Luke's. These old row houses also date from the 1820s and one was the boyhood home of Bret Harte.

Now, follow Grove in its eastward course, and before long you'll emerge into a nine-way intersection at Sheridan Square. The area around the square is studded with restaurants, shops, theaters, and cafés.

Meandering Mood

If you still are in the mood for meandering, pick up Waverly Place, and don't be startled when you find it meeting itself after awhile. Richard Harding Davis, who lived at No. 108, often walked in circles, too. Nearby is Gay Street, a crooked little path punctuated here and there with Greek Revival houses built in the 1820s. Ruth McKenney lived in the basement apartment of No. 14 with *My Sister Eileen.* A worthwhile detour, before you reach the square, is a walk along Bleecker Street, turning left from Grove and following it to where it comes to an end, at Bank Street and Eighth Avenue. This stretch of Bleecker, like much of the Village, is a designated landmark district, and most of the buildings along it date from the early 19th century. Some of the most attractive antique and gift shops in the city are along here. The White Horse Tavern, on Hudson Street, not too far from the end of Bleecker, was the favorite Manhattan drinking place of poet Dylan Thomas. Farther west, at West Street and Bank Street, on the waterfront, is Westbeth, the former Bell Labs building converted into an artist's community. A committee screens applicants so that only working people in the arts are offered apartments.

Follow Gay to Christopher, cross that street, and then follow it westward for a few blocks' worth of good window-shopping and brows-

NEW YORK CITY

ing. The entire length of Christopher Street is the center of New York's large homosexual community. This route will take you across the Sheridan Square intersection again.

Village Square

Back at the Gay-Christopher intersection, turn right into the intersection that takes in Greenwich Avenue, 8th Street, and Avenue of the Americas. This is Village Square, one of the crossroads of the Village. The open-fronted vegetable stand to the right was once Luke O'Connor's Columbian Gardens, where back in 1896 young John Masefield, the late Poet Laureate of England, hauled beer kegs and mopped floors. Across the square to the north is a block of some historic interest. Patchen Place, itself a small courtyard of great charm, off West 10th Street between the Avenue of the Americas and Greenwich Avenue, was the site of E. E. Cummings' apartment for many of the later years of his life. The iron-barred Women's House of Detention, across the street behind the Jefferson Market building, was demolished in late 1973. The property belongs to the city and there is doubt as to its ultimate destiny. Interested Village citizens have pushed for a semi-public park that would adjoin the neighboring Jefferson Market Courthouse, a cherished landmark since 1878. Its unusual Italian Gothic architecture is the work of Calvert de Vaux, one of the architects of Central Park, and Frederick Withers, who designed the picturesque gate of the Little Church Around the Corner. Its clock tower once served as the neighborhood fire lookout. Long unused, the Courthouse was refurbished inside and out and is now a branch of the New York Public Library.

Two major Village streets lead from this intersection in opposite directions. 8th Street between Fifth and Sixth Avenues changes personality yearly, it seems. Doorways and sidewalks are crowded and often trash-littered, especially on weekends, and shops, too, have changed radically over the years; garish snack shops and noisy record stores currently predominate. This single, busy block is still worth a visit—but a brief one. Going diagonally northwest between this intersection and Eighth Avenue is Greenwich Avenue, one of the more interesting promenades in the Village. Cafés, some good restaurants, eye-catching clothing shops (both trendy and classic), and interesting Villagers to look at make it a fun strolling route, and most of the neighborhood is out every weekend, bound on errands or the pursuit of pleasure. The farther northwest you go, the more conservative the shops and people seem. Greenwich Avenue is the Village in microcosm. The triangular vacant lot opposite St. Vincent's Hospital at Seventh Avenue and West

12th Street used to contain an apartment house inhabited by village characters, where Edmund Wilson made his first home in the city.

The East Village

East Village, the new Bohemia, is more or less bounded by 14th Street on the north, the Bowery on the west, Houston Street on the south, and the East River. The area has inherited many of Greenwich Village's ways of the '20s. Here, every day is Freedom Day, and you'll see it celebrated in a variety of ways. This enclave of the disciples of unconventional living centers around Tompkins Square, seven blocks east of Washington Square.

Cheap rents first drew the poor painters and poets. Rooms and lofts could be rented for as little as $20 a month. Included, of course, were squalor and a lot of do-it-yourself decorating and repairs. There were other attractions, too. The new crop of artists and writers found the atmosphere lacked prejudice. Many residents live communally, sharing the work and expenses of their room and board.

The area abounds with talent, though many artists have moved to SoHo or to TriBeCa. Most of the area's new poets' works are published in underground magazines, mimeographed and stapled in someone's cellar, and distributed to friends and colleagues. Many an avant garde theatrical production has been given a try-out at La Mama E.T.C., 74A Fourth Street just west of Second Avenue. This small coffee house-cum-stage is one of those theaters which is called not just Off-Broadway but Off-Off-Broadway.

St. Mark's Place is the main promenade for the East Village. It is a stretch between Third and First Avenues, the extension of East 8th Street, and along it you'll see one or two emporiums that frankly proclaim themselves "head shops," a reminder that just a few years ago the East Village was one of New York's major outposts of the drug culture. Hundreds of runaway teenagers flocked here to live in anonymity and self-imposed communal poverty until sheer desperation —or the police—sent them back to their parents. Some remainder of this subculture still exists, and this is another area of the city where old-time, immigrant-family citizens and the young, free-living newcomers are learning to coexist without too much antagonism.

On St. Mark's Place, there are also several clothing shops, mostly of the wildly informal variety; boutiques with jewelry and leather goods; record stores; and a popular movie house attracting buffs with its program of cinema classics, mostly the old musicals. Between Second and First, the architecture is considerably more attractive, and do note the charming edifice that is the First German Methodist Episcopal Church.

What was East Village before the invasion of the latter-day Bohemians? The square, named for one of New York's governors, Daniel B. Tompkins, was a nice, quiet neighborhood of mixed cultures, people of Ukrainian, Czech, German, Polish, Russian, Italian, Jewish, and, lately, Puerto Rican origins. Russian and Turkish baths, the special delicacies in delicatessen, meat, and produce stores reflect the heterogeneous ways of the neighborhood. Handsome churches of all faiths—among them, St. Nicholas Russo-Carpathian, St. Brigid's-on-the-Square, and St. Mark's Church-in-the-Bouwerie—have served generation after generation.

This is the area Dutch Governor Peter Stuyvesant retired to after he surrendered Nieuw Amsterdam to the British. It became a defense post against the British in 1812, later a parade ground, then a recruiting camp for Civil War soldiers and scene of draft riots, mass meetings, and hunger strikes. Its tumultuous background is reflected in the area's explosive temperament today.

The City Moves North

Fortunately there were enough parade grounds scattered around the city to break up the forward march of square block upon square block of brownstone houses. The city was lucky, too, in having a few imaginative builders.

One was Samuel Ruggles, who had bought a large tract of land between what is now 20th and 21st Streets, extending east of Park Avenue South and west of Third Avenue. It is now known as Gramercy Park, center of one of the nicer residential areas in the city. In the early 1800s, when Ruggles bought the property, the area was far north of the city. His contemporaries derided his dream of turning this woodland tract into an English-type residential square and dubbed it "Sam Ruggles' Vacant Lot." The men of little vision lived to eat their words.

Ruggles divided the tract, making a square of forty-two lots that he set aside for a park, and the bordering area, which was carved into sixty-six building lots. The elite of New York were attracted with the promise that only those who built houses around the square would have the use of the park. Two golden keys to unlock the gate of the fenced-in park were given to each homeowner. The snob appeal made the venture an instantaneous success.

Mrs. Stuyvesant Fish, leader of society's "400," became a resident and many others followed. They included Cyrus W. Field, who was responsible for the first Atlantic cable; the illustrious architect Stanford White, whose career came to a sudden end when Pittsburgh millionaire Harry K. Thaw shot him for flirting with his ladylove (showgirl Evelyn Nesbit); James W. Gerard, the pre-World War I American ambassador to Germany; and wealthy philanthropist Peter Cooper. Shakespearean star Edwin Booth's home at 16 Gramercy Park is now the headquarters of the Players' Club, and the National Arts Club is housed in the mansion at No. 15, which once had been the home of Samuel J. Tilden, the man who was almost elected president.

The social register tenants are gone and the homes have been broken up into apartments occupied by decorators, writers, business executives, and wealthy widows. You'll see the lucky keyholders sitting in the park on a sunny afternoon, reading or watching the youngsters play quiet games. It is an oasis of peace and solitude, for no dogs, bikes, or swings are permitted.

Theodore Roosevelt's birthplace (28 East 20th Street) is now a National Historic Site. It is a fine example of a typical well-to-do Victorian home. The furnishings, including the scratchy horsehair sofa which menaced a small boy in short pants, are just as they were described later by T.R. in his autobiography. The home, and the adjacent museum of the relics Roosevelt collected during his years of adventuring, are open weekdays.

Nearby, the stretch of Broadway south of 23rd St. is the center of the photographers' loft district. North, at 1 East 29th Street, is a little church with a legend, a symbol of how time has worn down prejudice. When it was built in 1849, it was named the Church of the Transfiguration, but it has been known as "the Little Church Around the Corner."

It is filled with memorials, the most famous of which is a window dedicated to Joseph Jefferson, in his role of Rip Van Winkle, leading his shroud-clad friend, George Holland, to the church. In the post-Civil War period actors were socially unacceptable. On the death of Holland, when Jefferson spoke to the pastor of the church of his choice about funeral arrangements for his friend, the pastor turned him away, suggesting that he make arrangements at the "little church around the corner, where they do that kind of thing." It is now the actors' favorite church, and many a Broadway and Hollywood star attends services here. Of course, it is a favorite with brides, too.

The church on the corner of 29th Street and Fifth Avenue is the Marble Collegiate Church, designed by Samuel A. Warner and built in 1854 during the first phase of the Romanesque Revival boom which spread throughout New York. Its pastor is Dr. Norman Vincent Peale, author of *The Power of Positive Thinking*.

New York's Own Chelsea

The Chelsea area, on the west side across town from Gramercy Park, has let many of its historic landmarks slip through its fingers. Yet many writers find the remnants of its past gentility and the unfrenetic pace of Chelsea to their liking and the recent proliferation of cozy contemporary bars, moderately priced restaurants, and brownstone renovations has made it one of the up-and-coming neighborhoods of the city's "far west" end. Still a living symbol of the area's attractiveness to literary figures, the Chelsea Hotel, at 222 West 23rd Street, has been home to many celebrated writers. Thomas Wolfe and Dylan Thomas lived here and Brendan Behan wrote his book on New York in one of its apartments. Composer Virgil Thomson still lives there, though of late it has become a popular haunt of touring rock and roll stars.

The hostelry, a Victorian Gothic edifice with wrought-iron balconies, turrets, and chimney stacks, has been designated by the Municipal Art Society as one of New York's architectural monuments which should be preserved at all costs. In 1978 it was named a National Historic Landmark. If you should step into the Chelsea note the teakwood fireplace in the lobby and the bas-relief mural over it. It is the work of resident Rene Shapshak and depicts the arts—painting, drama, music, dance, architecture, literature, and sculpture. Harry S. Truman stopped by here many times when Mr. Shapshak was working on a bust of the former president. To the right of the registration desk is a staircase. Walk up a flight and you can see the hotel's famous web of wrought-iron railing ascending flight after flight to the skylight.

Across the street is the McBurney YMCA, the oldest "Y" in the city. Over the years its membership has included Lowell Thomas, Dale Carnegie, Arthur Godfrey, James Michener and Brendan Behan.

Chelsea's Night Before Christmas

The most notable of all Chelsea's residents was Dr. Clement Clarke Moore, who penned in 1822 the poem *A Visit from St. Nicholas,* more familiarly known today as *'Twas The Night Before Christmas.* Moore grew up on his grandfather's farm here, a spread which bordered the Hudson River and ran from what is now 19th to 23rd Streets. The grandfather, Captain Thomas Clarke, had come to this country from England to fight in the French and Indian War. When his tour of duty was ended in 1750, he decided to remain, buy a farm, and build a mansion, which he nostalgically named "Chelsea" after the Chelsea Royal Hospital on the Thames, a charitable institution Nell Gwynne talked King Charles II into building for old, invalided soldiers. The lovely old mansion is gone; so, too, are Dr. Moore's house and the Grand Opera House where Josie Mansfield, Lily Langtry, and Edwin Booth performed.

The oldest building in Chelsea, which dates from 1785, is a two-and-one-half-story brick house with a steeply pitched roof and dormer windows at 183 Ninth Avenue, corner of 21st Street. Its ground floor now is occupied by a dairy store.

If you wander through 20th, 21st, and 22nd Streets between Eighth and Ninth Avenues, you will see evidence of Chelsea's struggle to maintain its gentility. Many of the old brownstones have been tinted a lively pink, yellow, or blue. Their intricate wrought-iron balustrades gleam and their tiny front gardens are well tended.

The General Theological Seminary, with an entrance at 175 Ninth Avenue between 20th and 21st Streets, stands on land which once was Captain Clarke's apple orchard. Dr. Clement Moore served on its staff as a professor of Hebrew. Its library, housed in a new building, is famous for its collection of rare theological books.

The rectory of St. Peter's Episcopal Church at 346 West 20th Street was built in 1831 on property donated by Dr. Moore. The adjoining Gothic Revival church was added in 1836; its parish house is a lively center of art festivals and dramatic productions. Visitors are always welcome.

This is the southern fringe of what was once "Hell's Kitchen"—20th to 50th Streets, west of Eighth Avenue—an area which spawned such notorious mobsters as Mad Dog Coll and Owney Madden. It was predominantly Irish for many years, but with the coming of better times for the Irish and urban renewal, the Irish have moved elsewhere. The area now has a Greek (and slightly Turkish) atmosphere. Little nightclubs feature beautiful belly dancers, their spangles and beaded brass shimmering as they weave and wiggle to the mysterious tempo of wailing flutes and tinkling finger cymbals. Glasses of anise-flavored *ouzo* cast their spell over members of the audience, and now and again one will rise and slowly take up the controlled movements of a Greek folk dance. But the number of these clubs is dwindling.

Midtown Manhattan

Midtown Manhattan, which ranges roughly from 34th Street (the Empire State Building on Fifth Avenue marks the southern boundary) to 59th Street (Central Park begins There) and river to river, is a center of superlatives. The biggest buildings, best restaurants, most art galleries, brightest lights, greatest concentration of big business, largest complex of theaters, best bargain basements, most exclusive department stores, and the most specialized services are all here.

Here you can have your dog psychoanalyzed, then hire a professional dogwalker to take him for a stroll. Pick up a glittery gown or mink stole for a pittance at thriftshops, where Broadway and TV stars leave them to be sold on consignment. Swim and sun high in the sky on a hotel

NEW YORK CITY

roof in the morning and ice skate in the afternoon at Rockefeller Center. Buy a blue wig or a sable trench coat, if you care to.

You can see more and better French Impressionist art in a day's tour of museums and galleries here than you could see in Paris in all of a week. You can make a world tour of cuisine. Name any dish and it's yours: Brazilian, Japanese, Greek, French, German, Italian, Indian, Armenian, Polynesian, Jewish, Hungarian, Chinese, Spanish, Swiss, Belgian, Irish, Mexican, regional American. You can have breakfast at 5 P.M. or 5 A.M., for New York never sleeps.

It has been said that the forest of commerce in Wall Street reflects the purpose and push of dour, determined men. If so, then uptown New York, with its elegance, culture, countless diversions, and green acres, reflects the fruits of the dour men's labors.

The midtown shopping area is without peer in America. The most elegant, extravagant, and rare fabrics, furs, jewels, and accessories are displayed in profusion. Modish copies are offered to those of modest budget. The uninitiated are hard-pressed to tell the difference between the black Dior original and genuine strand of Oriental pearls on the dowager and the "authentic" copy and simulated pearls worn by the young career woman. Seventh Avenue, as a result, is a girl's best friend. The world's great concentration of garment manufacturers is right at her doorstep. The "rag business," as the trade affectionately calls itself, is concentrated in the west 30s, along Seventh Avenue. Fortunes are made and lost here, depending on the consumer's whim. Those dress houses which guess wrong twice in a row go bankrupt. Often you can profit from their mistakes and buy the unpopular models (they might be exactly to your taste) for less than cost in one of the bargain basements or cut-rate specialty shops in the neighborhood. The wholesale millinery firms are here too. Many have retail salesrooms on 38th Street, where you can also buy all the trimmings for a do-it-yourself creation.

Festive Fifth Avenue

Fifth Avenue is a festival all year-round, with a continuous showing of spectaculars. Its pioneers have fought to maintain its prestige and preserve its *haute monde* image. As far back as 1907, they formed the Fifth Avenue Association to do battle with any element which might threaten its lustre. At Christmastime, the street features tinseled trees, twinkling lights, bright garlands, and jolly St. Nicks. In springtime, awnings and entrances bloom with artificial flowers and perfume wafts onto the street to entice you inside. At night, windows are kept lit, offering the stroller an incomparable window shopping tour.

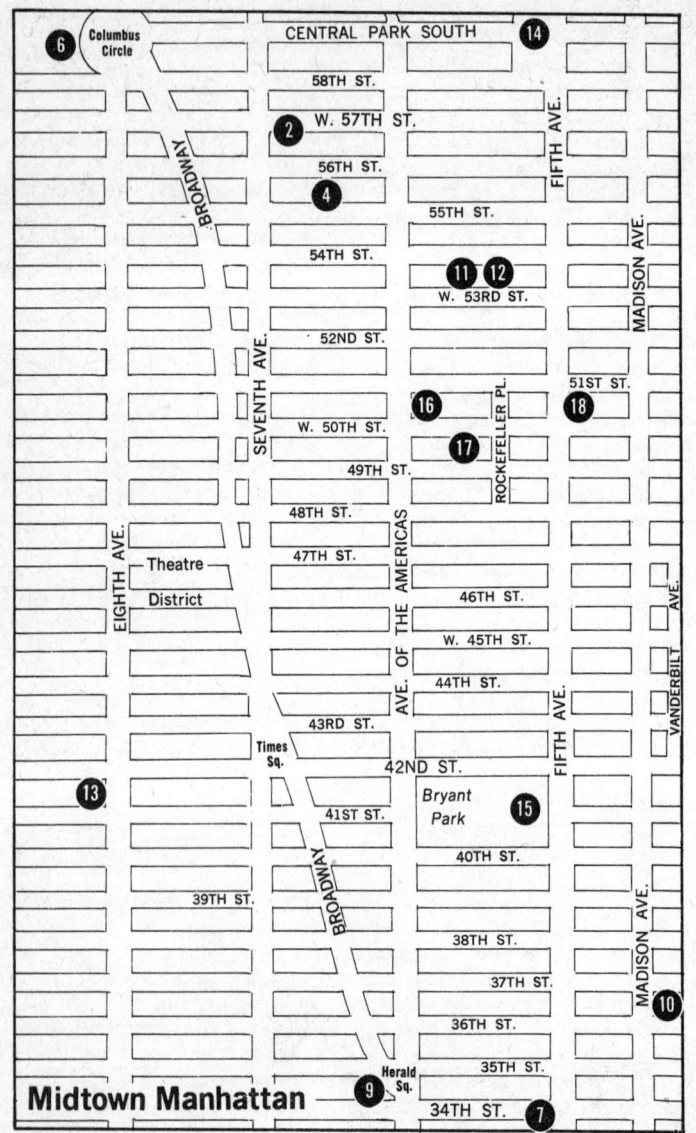

NEW YORK CITY

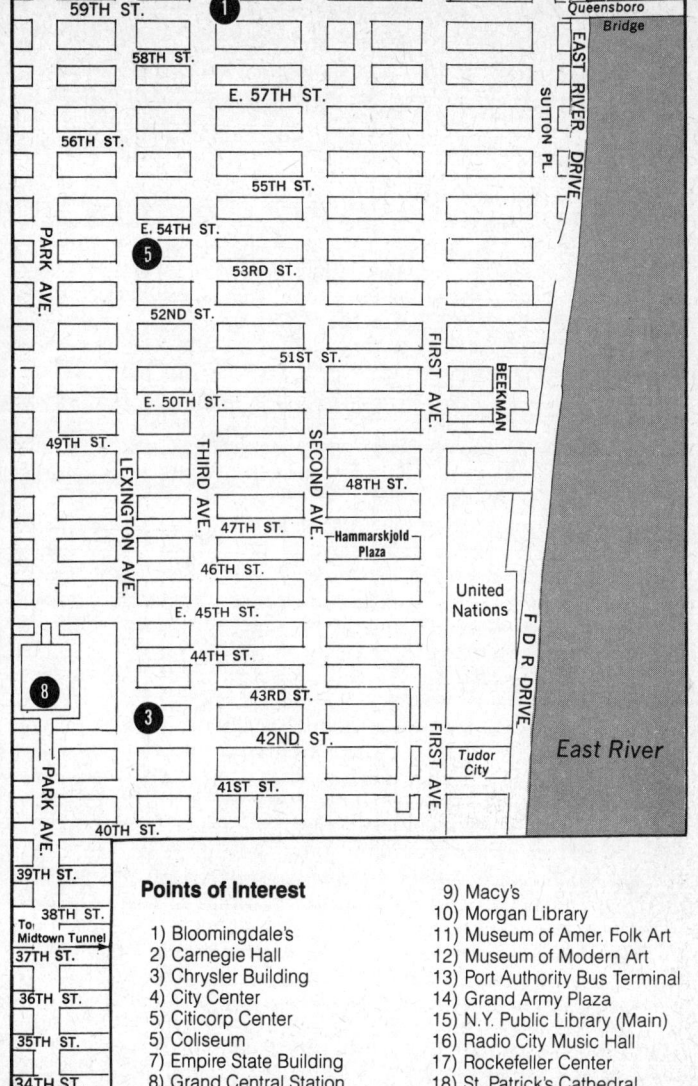

Points of Interest

1) Bloomingdale's
2) Carnegie Hall
3) Chrysler Building
4) City Center
5) Citicorp Center
5) Coliseum
7) Empire State Building
8) Grand Central Station
9) Macy's
10) Morgan Library
11) Museum of Amer. Folk Art
12) Museum of Modern Art
13) Port Authority Bus Terminal
14) Grand Army Plaza
15) N.Y. Public Library (Main)
16) Radio City Music Hall
17) Rockefeller Center
18) St. Patrick's Cathedral

NEW YORK CITY

No matter what the season, the Empire State Building, on Fifth Avenue at 34th Street, remains a favorite attraction for natives and visitors alike. Perhaps because it held the title of tallest building in the world for so long, perhaps because it has been immortalized in so many films (not the least of which is *King Kong*), and perhaps because it gave New York its state title—"The Empire State"—it has retained a special place in people's hearts despite the fact that the World Trade Center stands a full 100 feet taller. It opened in May 1931 (it took only a year and a half to construct). Some 15,000 people work in the building and more than a million and a half people still visit its observatory annually for what remains a spectacular panorama of New York and its surroundings. This observatory, incidentally, is open nightly until 11:30—two hours later than the one at the World Trade Center. Tickets cost $1.70 per person.

The merchants have done battle with the city fathers about parades on Fifth Avenue, which disrupted business. They won, up to a point. Today all parades except two—the Columbus Day and St. Patrick's Day parades—start at 60th Street, above the main shopping area. Despite their efforts to keep Fifth Avenue on the highest plateau, some interlopers have managed to open up tourist-trap linen-china-cameras-radios-gimcracks shops.

Midtown does not readily lend itself to cut-and-dried walking tours. It is an area to be explored according to one's whims and particular interests. There are museums which specialize in collections of modern art, contemporary crafts, folk art, costumes of all nations, re-runs of old silent movies, and lecture programs. There are scores of foreign tourist information centers and airline ticket offices with advice to inspire your next vacation. There are awesome views to be seen from observatories atop midtown's tallest buildings, a world to explore underground, a hundred little personal discoveries to be made if you venture off the beaten track. And, of course, there's the shopping. Virtually every one of New York's major department stores has a character of its own—a style that is manifested in the stores' own decor, in the merchandise they carry and in the people who shop at them. The accent is almost always on clothing—women's more so than men's, though Bloomingdale's gives equal if not preferential treatment to males—with furniture and household goods almost as an afterthought, something you might pick up "to complete the outfit" while passing through. Well, that may be an exaggeration, but here's a quick look at The Top Ten. Most, incidentally, have evening shopping hours on Thursdays throughout the year, and every night from the end of November through Christmas.

Altman's, at 34th St. at Fifth Ave., 689–7000, is where everyone's grandmother seemingly used to shop (back when Best & Co. was its

NEW YORK CITY

main competitor)—and still does. They're attempting to update the look and feel of the store, and the merchandise is generally of top quality, even if a little staid.

Bergdorf Goodman, on Fifth Ave. at 57th St., 753–7300, is as starchily traditional as Bloomingdale's is modishly outrageous. If you're looking for a pure silk-lined fur nose-warmer, this would be the place.

Bloomingdale's, at 59th St. and Lexington Ave., 223–3109, is the place for high tech, high fashion, and high prices. The pace is frantic, the aisles (at least on the main floor) crowded and the attitude haughtily exclusive whether you're looking for the latest designer originals or for a colander in the housewares department or for an Oriental rug. Worth a trip just to sightsee!

Bonwit Teller, on 57th St. between Fifth and Madison Aves., 764–2300, is the newest "old" member of the fraternity—recently reopened under a spectacular new roof (and behind gleaming glass and chrome) with four floors of the latest in women's fashion. Spacious and just a touch snobby, but with style.

Gimbels, across 34th St. and Broadway from Macy's, 736–5100, has the feel of a dingy bargain basement throughout, although the prices don't usually match the ambience.

Henri Bendel, on 57th St. between Fifth and Sixth Aves., 247–1100. Don't turn your nose up until after you've passed the chocolate counter —one of the best in the city. Thereafter he prepared to shop among the elite (and that means salespeople as well as customers).

Lord & Taylor, at 37th St. on Fifth Ave., 391–3344, has the best Christmas windows of any store in New York. Forever being renovated, the mood is nonetheless old-style but sophisticated.

Macy's, at 34 St. and Broadway (Herald Square), 971–6000, retains its title as the world's largest department store under one roof. It has been modernized bit by bit over the last few years, with the popular Cellar (for housewares and gourmet foods) setting the tone for the rest of the store. Probably still the best all-purpose department store in Manhattan.

Ohrbach's, at 34th St. between Fifth and Sixth Aves., 695–4000, is another bargain-basement-type store, but with a moderately contemporary feel and better than average merchandise (clothes).

Saks Fifth Avenue, at 50th St. and Fifth Ave., 753–4000, calls itself the "largest specialty shop in the world." It may well be, in its old-world, traditional way, a little dated, but it is always practical and reliable for the basics in clothing and other goods.

Three of the city's greatest attractions are in this midtown area: Times Square, where the Great White Way begins; Rockefeller Center; and the United Nations.

The Great White Way starts at Times Square, a point where meandering Broadway crosses 42nd Street and Seventh Avenue to form a tiny plaza which is anything but square in shape.

It is a monument to the vision and the gambling spirit of three men: Oscar Hammerstein I, an impresario who in 1894 sank a two-million-dollar fortune, and then some, into building the first theaters here; August Belmont, a financier who more than matched Hammerstein's gamble by extending the subway to bring the crowds uptown to the new theater district; and publisher Adolph S. Ochs, who built the Times Tower in 1904 as the new headquarters for his influential newspaper, *The New York Times,* and dedicated it with a night of revelry which has become a New Year's Eve tradition.

Theaters Move Uptown

Hammerstein's fellow impresarios knew a good thing when they saw it and moved their theaters uptown. With such a captive audience as Times Square offered, promoters of soft drinks, cigarettes, liquor, chewing gum, and two-trouser suits put up huge animated electric advertisements which outshone the sun.

Times Square became a symbol of facing life and making good. Dreams of becoming a dramatic star overnight, writing a musical hit, waxing a smash record, or marrying a millionaire swam in the heads of small town girls and small city boys who flocked to this street of dreams. For a special few, the dreams came true. Stars were born, fortunes were made, and millionaires wedded to their gold. Those who couldn't make the grade on Broadway took the ferry over to Fort Lee, New Jersey, and worked for the "flickers," a new form of entertainment legitimate actors deplored or ignored. The flicker performers made it big and went on to Hollywood, fame, and fortune.

The theater district has become tarnished quite a bit since the glamorous pre-Depression days when top-hatted stage-door Johnnies waited for their favorite Follies dollies, wined and dined them on the Ziegfeld Theater roof, and slipped a hundred-dollar bill under their plates for the privilege.

Broadway's Constant Lure

Times Square has taken on a midway bazaar-like look, with its soft drink and pizza stands, pinball and shooting galleries, racy lingerie and fake "fire sale" shops. Some of the old prestige theaters now feature X-rated movies and ladies of the evening roam the streets along with a hodgepodge of other derelicts and eccentrics. Within the radius of a few blocks in the 40s, however, there still remain numerous legitimate

NEW YORK CITY 89

theaters, surely the greatest concentration of dramatic and musical productions you will find anywhere in the world (with the possible exception of London's West End). This tight little center of entertainment offers a rare opportunity for last-minute shopping. If you've neglected to order theater tickets in advance, make a tour of the box offices just before curtain-time and you might just be lucky enough to pick up a pair of unclaimed seats at regular prices. Or check with the Times Square Ticket Service office (the sign reads "TKTS") at 47th Street and Broadway, where tickets for cultural events from concerts to legitimate theater are usually available and always to be had for half the box-office price plus a minimal service fee.

Incidentally, right near this ticket mecca in the small triangular-shaped Duffy Square is a city-run visitors information center where you can pick up advice. The TKTS booth is open daily from 3 to 8 P.M. for evening performances, noon to 2 P.M. for Wednesday and Saturday matinees, and noon to 8 P.M. for all Sunday shows. Lines for first choice of the evening selections begin to form in late morning, much earlier for matinees. Telephone 354–5800. (There is a second TKTS booth down in the Wall Street area at 100 William Street, which is open Monday through Friday from 11:30 A.M. to 5:30 P.M. and Saturday from 11 A.M. to 3 P.M.; the lines here are generally much shorter than those uptown, and you may well save time making the extra trip downtown. Take the No. 2 or 3 IRT subway to the Wall Street stop—it shouldn't take more than 15 to 20 minutes each way.)

Times Square is the object of what seems to New Yorkers like a never-ending battle for upgrading. One major example of what appears to be a successful move in this direction is the Manhattan Plaza apartment/restaurant complex along the north side of 42nd between Ninth and Tenth Avenues. The residential units are made available to performing artists only—primarily those involved with the nearby theater—who give a percentage of their income as rent. In response to the immediate filling up of the apartment building, a whole slew of restaurants sprang up in and around Manhattan Plaza, while the theaters on the south side of 42nd have been rehabilitated as legitimate Off-Broadway houses. As of press time, there was considerable controversy over another Times Square improvement plan known as the Portman Project. This would involve the razing of three of Broadway's oldest theaters in order to make way for a new midtown hotel. Still, however else one may object to the strip shows and triple-X-rated movie houses in the area, it can't be denied that their neon lights burning 24 hours a day add, shall we say, color and spectacle.

For passenger ships, a series of three piers at 48th, 50th, and 52nd Streets has been turned into a climate-controlled, modern terminal for cruise ships and the rare transatlantic liners. These piers provide not only more comfort and convenience for passengers but also excellent vantage points for tourists to watch the whole procedure of loading, unloading, and leave-taking.

The marble-and-glass building—formerly known as the Times Tower, then the Allied Chemical Building—located on the north side of 42nd Street between Broadway and Seventh Avenue, is still ushering in the New Year with a bright ball descending the flagpole on the building, reaching the bottom at the stroke of midnight.

The Avenue of the Americas

You might first like to stroll up Sixth Avenue, more accurately known as the Avenue of the Americas. Note the emblems of all the nations in North, Central, and South America hanging along the avenue. Like many areas of mid-Manhattan, it is changing as glittering new skyscrapers take the place of older edifices.

Bryant Park, located between 40th and 42nd Streets behind the New York City Public Library, is a green and relaxing spot to visit and rest, if the dope-pushers and occasional crazies don't annoy you. Named in 1884 for William Cullen Bryant, poet and journalist, it is a gathering place for impromptu public speakers and their eclectic sort of audience. A couple of booksellers have opened bookstalls there. The park is also an excellent vantage point from which to view one of the city's more unusual skyscrapers. Located between the Avenue of the Americas and Fifth Avenue, with entrances on 42nd and 43rd Streets and adjacent to the also intriguing new Graduate Center of CUNY, the Monsanto Building slopes gently upward, narrowing from its base to its towering roof, producing the rather uneasy effect of a hill carved from glass and stone. It was the city's first such structure and was designed by Gordon Bunshaft of the architectural firm of Skidmore, Owings & Merrill. A similar one curves inward from both 57th and 58th Streets, also between Fifth Avenue and the Avenue of the Americas. Incidentally, this same firm also designed Lever House in 1952 at 390 Park Avenue, along with many other notable city buildings.

Midtown is where the famous private men's clubs, portrayed so often in the *New Yorker* cartoons, are thickest on the ground. Look for them as you stroll; by and large they are understated and easy to miss. A representative selection (look, but you can't enter unless you are a member): University Club, at the corner of Fifth Avenue and 54th Street; the Century Club, favored by men in the business of publishing; next to it, on 43rd Street between Fifth and Sixth Avenues, is the Princeton Club, looking like a power substation; the Metropolitan Club, at Fifth Ave. and 60th Street, in a building designed by McKim, Mead & White; the Harvard Club, 44th Street between Fifth and Sixth

NEW YORK CITY

Avenues; the Racquet & Tennis Club, at 370 Park Avenue (53rd Street); and the Yale Club, across from the PanAm Building at Vanderbilt Avenue and 44th Street.

But back to Sixth Avenue. Walk north from 42nd Street and you'll see many other recently constructed buildings. At 1133, corner of 43rd Street, is the Kodak Exhibition Center, where you might stop in to see the exhibits in its downstairs gallery. Now a short detour east on 44th toward Fifth Avenue to the Algonquin Hotel and restaurant, still operating at No. 59. Behind its rather unimposing Renaissance façade many figures have wined, dined, and discussed the hours away: Dorothy Parker, Harold Ross, and Robert Benchley, among others. East on 45th Street is a concentration of the city's best hi-fi and electronics retail outlets. East on 46th Street, still off Sixth Avenue, is an array of Brazilian shops and restaurants. At 47th Street, you just might be tempted to take another detour east for a look at the block-long area known as the city's diamond center—it's obvious why when you see the countless glittering shop windows.

For the next three blocks on the west side of the avenue you'll be passing the three newest (early seventies) skyscraper members of the Rockefeller Center community. Between 47th and 48th Streets is the 45-story Celanese Building, which was completed in 1973. The next block north contains the 51-story McGraw-Hill building. Here you should plan to take an hour out to see *The New York Experience* in the building's plush Trans-Lux Experience Theater. The production is a multiple-screen entertainment that surrounds the audience with sights, sounds, and multi-sensory special effects utilizing thirty-seven projectors and fourteen screens and quadraphonic sound. Included as a part of the presentation is an exhibit of Little Old New York, re-creating local city life as it was in the late 19th century. On 48th Street, between Sixth and Seventh Avenues, are musical instrument retail shops. The next block, on Sixth Avenue, between 49th and 50th Streets, is the sleek 54-story corporate home of Exxon. This trio of buildings features open plazas and modern sculpture, where the weary sightseer can sit down with area office workers, especially at midday.

Radio City Music Hall, on the east side of the avenue at 50th Street, is a primary attraction, though its future is in doubt for financial reasons. It is the largest indoor theater in America, with a seating capacity of six thousand. When traditional seasonal pageants of the Nativity or the Glory of Easter are presented, the four blocks bounding the Music Hall are jammed with people who will wait for hours in sleet and rain to buy tickets for the presentation. If you want to take in one of these special pageants without waiting hours in line, it would be wise to write ahead for tickets. Two major television and radio network headquarters are located a couple of blocks beyond—CBS, between

52nd and 53rd Streets and designed by Eero Saarinen, and ABC at 54th Street. Both are on the east side of the avenue. (NBC's headquarters are a few blocks south, in Rockefeller Center.)

On 55th Street, turn left and walk almost to Seventh Avenue if you want to pick up a pair of tickets at the New York City Center, 131 West 55th Street, which usually features ballet. Now that you're this far, you might also want to continue two blocks north along Seventh Avenue, swing east around the corner of 57th Street, and check out coming concerts at Carnegie Hall. New Yorkers have been grateful ever since the last-minute decision was made not to tear down this hall in the early 1960s, when Philharmonic Hall in Lincoln Center was being built.

Those of you with an artistic bent should backtrack to 53rd Street and turn east toward Fifth Avenue. On this one block you'll find the handsome sculpture garden and avant-garde works of the Museum of Modern Art, at 11 West 53rd Street, the Museum of American Folk Art at 49, and the Museum of Contemporary Crafts at 29. Another art excursion—one which will require your traipsing several blocks to Columbus Circle at the southwest corner of Central Park—is to visit the statue at the corner of 59th Street and Broadway, Gaetano Russo's "Columbus," lending its name to Columbus Circle. On the park corner is architect H. Van Buren Magonigle's "Maine Memorial" with figures by sculptor Attilio Piccirilli. That massive building over to the northwest is the New York Coliseum, where public or trade exhibitions of varying interests are held.

Rockefeller Center

In our ramble up the Avenue of the Americas we've introduced you to several of the buildings that make up Rockefeller Center.

Rockefeller Center is a city-within-a-city; you could easily spend the whole day within its complex of twenty-one buildings. Many of its residents—it has a daytime population of 240,000—never leave its confines from their arrival in the morning until they go home. There is no need to, for the center has just about everything one could ask for. There are almost thirty restaurants, several shoe repair shops, drugstores, chiropodists, dentists, oculists, gift and clothing shops, bookstores, hairdressers, barbers, banks, a post office, movie theaters, schools, and subway transportation to all parts of the metropolis. Consulates of many foreign nations have offices in the center, as do airlines, railroad and steamship lines, and state and other travel information bureaus.

A shop-lined concourse, an underground passageway almost two miles long, ties together all its buildings and brings you almost to the doorstep of the Sheraton Centre and New York Hilton hotels. On rainy days, the concourse traffic is almost as thick as that of Times Square, but a lot drier.

It is the world's largest privately owned business and entertainment center and another monument to the courage and vision of the men who made New York City capital of the world. It was built because an opera house was not—a multimillion-dollar gamble on America's future during the height of the depression years.

In October 1928, just before the big stock market crash, John D. Rockefeller, Jr., headed a civic drive to give New York a new opera house, arranging to lease from Columbia University the land on which part of Rockefeller Center now stands. The new Metropolitan Opera Company was to occupy the center of the plot and the remainder of the land was to be leased to private builders for commercial development. Before the grand design could get started, the opera company, plagued by legal difficulties and depressed funds, abandoned its plans for a new home and withdrew from the project. It left Mr. Rockefeller holding a long-term lease which committed him to a $3,300,000 annual rental. He was faced with a difficult decision: whether to abandon the development or go it alone? He decided to build.

The site of the center has an historic past. Until the turn of the 19th century, the area was part of Manhattan's "common lands," which stretched from 23rd Street northward. In 1801, Dr. David Horsack transformed twenty acres of these pasturelands into his famed Elgin Botanic Gardens; garden club ladies for miles around made pilgrimages to pick up ideas for their own plantings. When rising costs made the venture impractical, Dr. Hosack sold the property to New York State and a few years later the State Legislature turned over the property to Columbia College as an aid-to-education grant. At the time, the land was worth about $125 an acre. Today Columbia University receives millions of dollars a year rental for just the ground; its lease to the center runs until 2069.

The center gave a new life to the down-at-the-heels midtown area, changing it from a sprawling low-rent residential area to a soaring business and entertainment complex far in advance of the times. It was a pioneering approach to urban design. Skyscrapers were planned in relation to one another and fifteen percent of the land was set aside for a promenade of plantings and a breeze-swept plaza.

The Channel Gardens—six formal beds running from Fifth Avenue to the Lower Plaza—with their ever-changing seasonal plantings, draw millions of visitors. Artists, designers, and sculptors work year-round to devise new and dramatic floral patterns for the ten seasonal displays. The showings run consecutively, starting with thousands of lilies at Easter; tulips, hyacinths, daffodils, and other flowering bulbs in the spring; an all-azalea show; such perennials as foxglove, delphinium, and stock; summer lilies and snapdragons; marigolds and evergreens; tropical palms and bougainvillaea; begonias and coxcomb; chrysanthemums of every size and hue; and ending with the greatest Christmas tree of all. Even the rooftops of many buildings are landscaped, giving upper-floor tenants a soul-satisfying view of green foliage and brilliant blooms below.

The Lower Plaza, where you can ice-skate from the end of September through April and dine alfresco in the warm weather, is a kind of ceremonial town square where distinguished visitors are greeted, occasional concerts given, and special events commemorated with colorful ceremonies.

The 70-story RCA building, at 30 Rockefeller Plaza, faces one of the city's few privately owned streets. The three-block-long street, which bisects the center from 49th to 51st Streets, is closed once a year (on one Sunday in July) to protect Columbia University's ownership of this passageway.

From the Observation Roof on top of the RCA building you can see as far as Connecticut on a clear day. Smog and haze, however, make this a rare occasion. Still, you'll be treated to a spectacular view. A visit to the observatory is included in a guided tour of Rockefeller Center's highlights, a hour-long educational stroll which takes you to a landscaped roof garden, the interior of the Music Hall, the famous murals and art works scattered throughout the center, and along the concourse of shops of all nations. Along the way you might bump into a TV star or two. Another guided tour takes you behind the scenes at NBC's radio and TV studios. Separate tours of Radio City Music Hall are also available. Call 246–4600 for details.

When in doubt about what to see and where it is, visit the center's information booth in the main lobby at 30 Rockefeller Plaza, where you can also pick up tickets to television-show tapings. You might also consider an evening visit (sunset is best) to the Rainbow Room bar, which opens at 5:30 P.M., Tuesday through Saturday, and at 11:30 A.M. on Sunday.

Across Fifth Avenue at 51st Street is the Gothic-styled St. Patrick's Cathedral. Based on the design of the Cologne Cathedral in Germany, work on the Roman Catholic St. Patrick's commenced in 1858, it opened as a house of worship in 1879, and was finally completed in 1906. Constructed of white marble and stone, the church's towers ascend 330 feet. Thirty-foot pillars support the cross-ribbed Gothic arches which rise 110 feet inside, where stained-glass windows from France light the nave.

The United Nations

New York City grew from a metropolis to a cosmopolis in 1952, when the United Nations moved into its elegant new home overlooking the East River between 42nd and 48th Streets.

The hand of John D. Rockefeller, Jr., is imprinted on this monument to peace and brotherhood, for it was his offer of a gift of the 18-acre site that figured in the final decision to choose New York as the permanent headquarters for the UN.

Before the coming of the United Nations, the district was a crumbling conglomeration of ex-slaughterhouses, junkyards, and tenements. Today the area around the UN is studded with elegant structures and has become a showcase of new architectural design.

A bit of parkland makes the UN grounds—which are not U.S. territory—a pleasant place to stroll and watch the busy river traffic of freighters, tankers, and pleasure boats plying the East River.

The visitors' entrance to the United Nations Headquarters is at the north end of the marble and limestone General Assembly Building, at 45th Street and First Avenue. There is a museum-like quality to the vast lobby with its free-form multiple galleries, soaring ceiling, and collection of art treasures contributed by member nations.

Visitors are welcome to attend most official meetings and admission is free. Tickets are issued in the lobby fifteen minutes before meetings are scheduled to start. Because there is no advance schedule of meetings for any given day and since they may be canceled or changed at the last minute, the majority of tickets available to individual visitors are issued on a first-come, first-served basis.

At most meetings, speeches are simultaneously interpreted in the official languages—Chinese, English, French, Russian, and Spanish—and there are earphones at each visitor's seat with a dial system which permits you to tune in the proceedings in the language of your choice.

The decor and color schemes of the meeting rooms—General Assembly Hall, the chambers of the Security Council, Trusteeship Council, Economic and Social Council—have been chosen for their soothing, subdued qualities. Sometimes they work this magic and other times they fail. At times, speeches by delegates become so impassioned that visitors may be tempted to rise and shout "bravo." Be forewarned: protocol demands that visitors remain silent throughout all the proceedings.

Taking the hour-long guided tour through the headquarters buildings is the most satisfactory way to see all the meeting rooms, to learn the aims, structure, and activities of this world body, and to appreciate fully the art works and exhibits displayed. Tours leave the main lobby

NEW YORK CITY

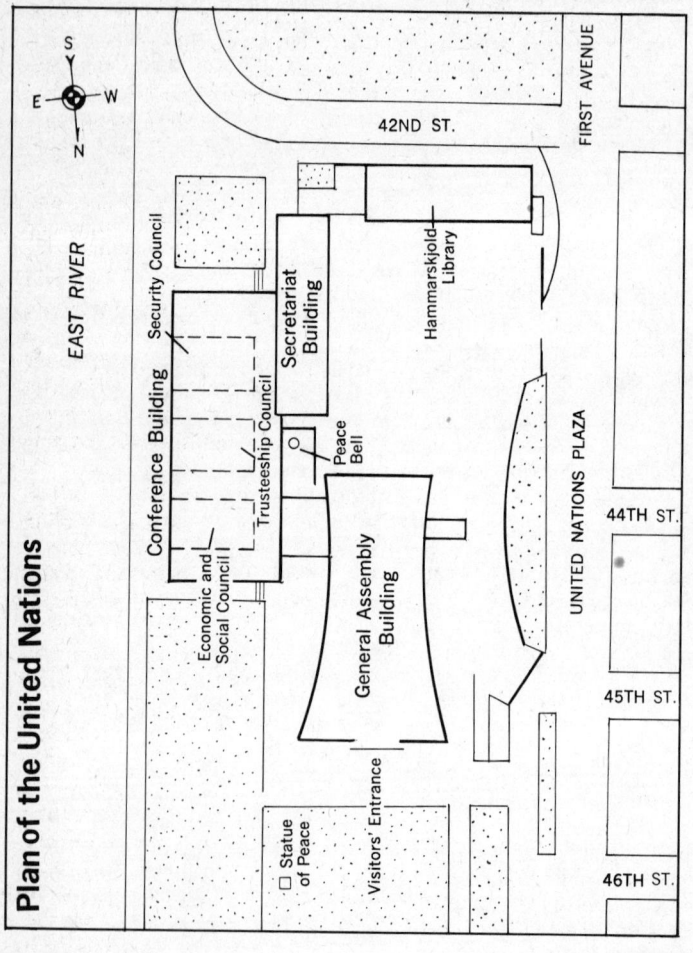

Plan of the United Nations

approximately every 15 minutes between 9:00 A.M. and 4:45 P.M., seven days a week. Most are in English, although you can request and reserve for other languages on the day you plan to tour. The cost is $2.50 for adults, $1.50 for students, and $1.00 for children. Phone: 754-7710.

If you would like to lunch with the delegates, stop by the information desk in the main lobby and ask about making a table reservation in the Delegates' Dining Room. Tables for visitors are in short supply and are assigned on a first-come basis. The earlier you make the reservation, the better.

On the lower concourse there is a coffee shop for a quick snack and lounges to rest your weary bones. Here, too, are several shops which offer the books, art, and handicraft products of the UN's member nations. Many a returning traveler shops here for some item he forgot or could not find while on a trip to Africa, Asia, Europe, or South America.

The sliver of land you see in the middle of the East River just to the north of the UN is Roosevelt Island (formerly Welfare Island) which once served as a prison stronghold. The riptides around the island acted as prison "walls," for not even the strongest swimmer could navigate the 700-foot crossing to the mainland.

If one had money and influence there was no need for such a foolhardy escape attempt. William Tweed, for instance, came and went as he pleased, though a prisoner. Tweed was the greedy political boss of New York who fleeced the city of $150,000,000 in the four years between 1867 and 1871. When reformers caught up with him and sent him off to a cell on Welfare Island, he arranged to live a life of ease. His ill-gotten gains bought him all the creature comforts. Gourmet meals were sent in from New York's finest restaurants. A masseur came in regularly to rub away his tensions. It's said he even had the prison bars replaced by a picture window. When life became too boring, Tweed managed to get a night off and a launch to take him over to the mainland for a round on the town. This kindly and loving care was enjoyed by Tweed and other moneyed mobsters and racketeers until the reformers once again bestirred themselves. The prison is gone now and in its place are two modern hospitals for the aged and chronically ill—plus the Delacorte Geyser, on the southern tip, which occasionally spouts a tall plume of an estimated 4,000 gallons worth of water per minute 400 feet into the air. There are also new housing units (many units are already occupied), reached from 59th Street and Second Avenue by a tramway over the East River (you may have seen it in Sylvester Stallone's movie *Nighthawks*).

Exploring Turtle Bay

As you leave the United Nations there are three general routes which you can follow, each one of which will lead you to fascinating aspects of the area extending roughly from 40th to 49th Streets and from Third Avenue to the East River. It is known as Turtle Bay, whose name comes from the mid-18th century Turtle Bay Farm tract which bordered on a little cove of that name.

You can return to 42nd Street and head west. If you look up between First and Second Avenues you'll see some of the apartment buildings and hotels of Tudor City. If you've time, you might walk up the stairs along 42nd Street and enjoy this rather private little city of Tudor-style buildings around a small park. Go back down the stairs and you'll surely notice the building with the huge glassed-in garden near Second Avenue. That's the Ford Foundation Building and its offices are arranged in an L around this pleasantly leafy 130-foot-high arboretum. In the next block between Second and Third Avenues is the Daily News Building, home of one of New York's three daily newspapers. Step into the lobby here if you want to scan the latest weather charts or watch the huge revolving globe. Continuing westward you'll come to the Chrysler Building at the northeast corner of 42nd Street and Lexington Avenue. When it was first built in 1930, its 1,048 feet made it the tallest building in the world. But it was soon topped by the completion of the Empire State Building in 1931. Now the twin World Trade Center towers are the highest in the city.

Westward again, between Lexington and Park Avenues on 42nd Street, is the new steel-and-glass Grand Hyatt Hotel, a glistening high-tech structure standing in the company of the beaux-arts classically styled Grand Central Terminal, the Art Deco Chrysler Building and other similarly spectacular delights. Grand Central was built from 1903 to 1913. If you go inside the always-busy train station, you'll be able to take escalators directly up to the lobby of the Pan Am Building, a 1963 office skyscraper addition to the terminal. At the time it was announced much protest was raised since it would—and does—effectively block the vista up and down Park Avenue.

We said you had three alternative routes through Turtle Bay from the UN. Another would be to head north along First Avenue—past the pleasant UN grounds and the posh twin 32-story apartment towers of the United Nations Plaza. Your destination on this route is Beekman Place, where the townhouses on the two blocks between First Avenue and Beekman Place on 50th Street and along Beekman Place itself between 50th and 51st Streets are gracious reminders of the 1920s. The roof of the Beekman Towers Hotel is also an excellent stop for a drink and a view of the Upper East Side.

The third jaunt is more circuitous and will serve to illustrate the dramatic juxtaposition of old townhouses and new office buildings that this city is capable of creating. Go north on First Avenue to 47th Street and turn left. Note the Holy Family Church and its pretty little courtyard on the north side of this divided street. This is where Pope Paul VI visited in 1965 in connection with a UN plea for peace. Next, a quick stop in the rock garden at Japan House (333 East 47th Street) is refreshingly tranquil. On the southeast corner of 47th Street and Second Avenue you might check out the current exhibit of alfresco, avant-garde sculpture in front of the rather conservative-looking office building. Continue on 47th Street to 747 Third Avenue, which is wonderfully imaginative with its undulating, multicolored brick walkways, circular outdoor phone booth, and benches and chairs. Look for the statue of a nude woman at the revolving doors.

Now turn right on Third Avenue, passing the Harcourt Brace Jovanovich building's uniquely designed bookstore, and cross Third Avenue on 48th Street to peek into the "citified" courtyard of the Buchanan apartment building. On the northwest corner of Lexington Avenue and 48th Street in the elegant Barclay Hotel is the Caswell-Massy Co. Ltd., reputedly America's oldest pharmacy (1752).

A bit farther up Third Avenue is the giant Citicorp Center headquarters of the New York-based international bank. Opened in 1978, the center features a pedestrian mall. It is a refreshing change from the plain glass boxes that dominate the rest of the avenue. Indeed, Citicorp is so refreshing especially because it includes The Market, a multilevel international bazaar of restaurants and retail food shops that delight the eye as well as the palate of New Yorkers and tourists alike. The Market surrounds a sky-lit atrium and gives a village-square ambiance. There are tables and chairs where you may just sit and people-watch or picnic by bringing your own sandwiches or buying some at one of the eateries. If you time it right, you may even enjoy free entertainment, on Saturday mornings for children and daily for adults, from chamber music ensembles to jazz to poetry readings. (Call 559–4259 for schedule.) And if alfresco dining (or almost) in a stone canyon isn't what you have in mind, you can choose from a bevy of international restaurants that includes: The Greek taverna that is Avgerninos, the Italian Alfredo's, the Auberge Suisse, Les Tournebroches, and Richoux of London, a British coffee shop that is veddy, veddy Edwardian (with costumed waitresses). For sandwiches and desserts, consider Slotnick Daughters and for Scandinavian gourmet goodies such as herrings, salads and pâtés, consider Nyborg and Nelson. For spiritual nourishment, there is also a church—St. Peter's—in the building, and that church has staged some excellent plays of off-Broadway caliber. All of which combines to make Citicorp a nice place to visit for business or pleasure.

Up in Central Park

Central Park, a vast oasis of rural beauty in the midst of a concrete jungle of midtown spires, runs from 59th Street to 110th Street and from Fifth Avenue to Central Park West (an extension of Eighth Avenue). Masterfully designed by Frederick Law Olmstead and Calvert de Vaux, the park was designated a National Historic Landmark in 1965.

Before venturing into the park you might want to pick up some pamphlets and advice from the New York Convention and Visitors Bureau at Columbus Circle, just directly across the street from the park's entrance and from the Coliseum.

New York can thank its good fortune that there were men of vision in 1850 who insisted that this 840-acre spread be earmarked as a park. It was none too soon, for real estate developers were gobbling up huge hunks of land just to the south and turning them into bleak stretches of look-alike brownstone residences.

A stroll through the park will reveal the woodland terrain of New York as it might have been in the days of the Dutch settlers, long before dredges and bulldozers leveled the surrounding hills and rocky outcroppings to erect a fence of luxury apartment houses.

If you take a drive down through the park from the north end at dusk, just as the lights begin to sparkle in the windows and the last rays of the sun silhouette the spires at the south end, you will be rewarded with a most strikingly beautiful sight. These roads, however, are frequently closed to traffic to allow for strollers, bicyclers and joggers.

Or hire a carriage—they park across the street from the Plaza Hotel at 59th Street and Fifth Avenue—and take an old-fashioned leisurely turn around the ponds, lakes and woodlands. Should your horse slow down to a walk in some secluded section, don't be concerned about his being too tired to make it back. New York horses have never lost their sense of romance, and they know the likeliest settings for it. Rates are $17 for the first half hour, $5 for each additional 15 minutes. (Do make sure to agree on the rate before leaving.)

At this same corner of the park—a lively and interesting part of the city for people-watching—there are bookstalls open on nice days.

The park is a many-splendored mélange of fountains and ponds, statues and monuments, promenades and wooded paths. Park benches are lined with nannies gossiping away while their young Park Avenue charges swing and slide in the playgrounds. Joggers run year round while looking over their shoulders at oncoming traffic. On warm weekdays, office workers find a favorite rock by the pond, spread out their lunches, and share them with the water birds. In the winter, they skate at Wollman Memorial Rink, currently being renovated. On Sundays, families come to picnic, play soft ball, pitch horseshoes, ride the merry-go-round, fly kites, row boats, ride bicycles on the curling, care-free drives, and absorb enough sun and fresh air to last them through another week of molelike living. The newest crazes in the park are skateboarding and roller-skating.

Off the 64th Street entrance on Fifth Avenue is a small zoo with a splendid collection of birds, wild animals, and a sea lion pond. The animals are terrific "hams" and at feeding time, especially, they put on shows that rival the circus. For the small fry, there is another little zoo populated with domestic animals which willingly allow children to pat their heads and smooth their fur. (Adults are granted admission here only if accompanied by a child.) Near the Conservatory Pond at 74th St. off Fifth Ave. are the statues of Hans Christian Andersen and Alice in Wonderland.

On summer evenings you can attend outdoor performances of plays at the Delacorte Shakespeare Theater. The theater accommodates around 2,000—but get there in the afternoon to get in line for first-come, first-served tickets. Enter from Central Park West or Fifth Avenue at 81st Street. Both the Metropolitan Opera and the New York Philharmonic perform free in the park each summer as well.

The park is fringed with some of the world's great art and history centers. You could spend a week on either side of the park and never go any higher than the ground floors of these buildings.

Lincoln Center

Lincoln Center for the Performing Arts is an elegant four-block cultural world, located between 62nd and 66th Streets west of Broadway (actually between Columbus and Amsterdam Avenues). Get acquainted with the buildings by taking one of the guided tours, or wander around the open plazas and parks on your own. Tours leave from Avery Fisher Hall every half hour between 10 A.M. and 5 P.M. daily. The cost for adults is $3.75; Senior Citizens and students, $3.25; and children $2.50. Call 877–1800. Standing on Broadway, the building you see to the left of the large central fountain plaza is the New York State Theater, home of the New York City Opera and the New York City Ballet. On the right is Avery Fisher Hall, home of the New York Philharmonic and the first of this $185 million complex to open (September 1962). Between the two is the Metropolitan Opera House, with its two colorful Marc Chagall murals depicting motifs and themes relating to music.

NEW YORK CITY

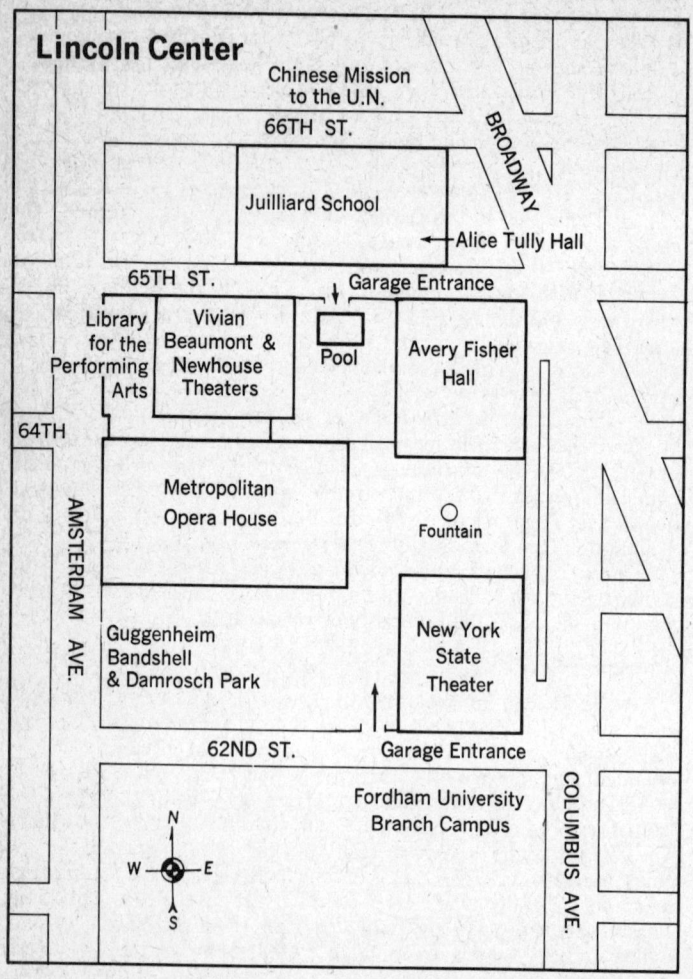

NEW YORK CITY

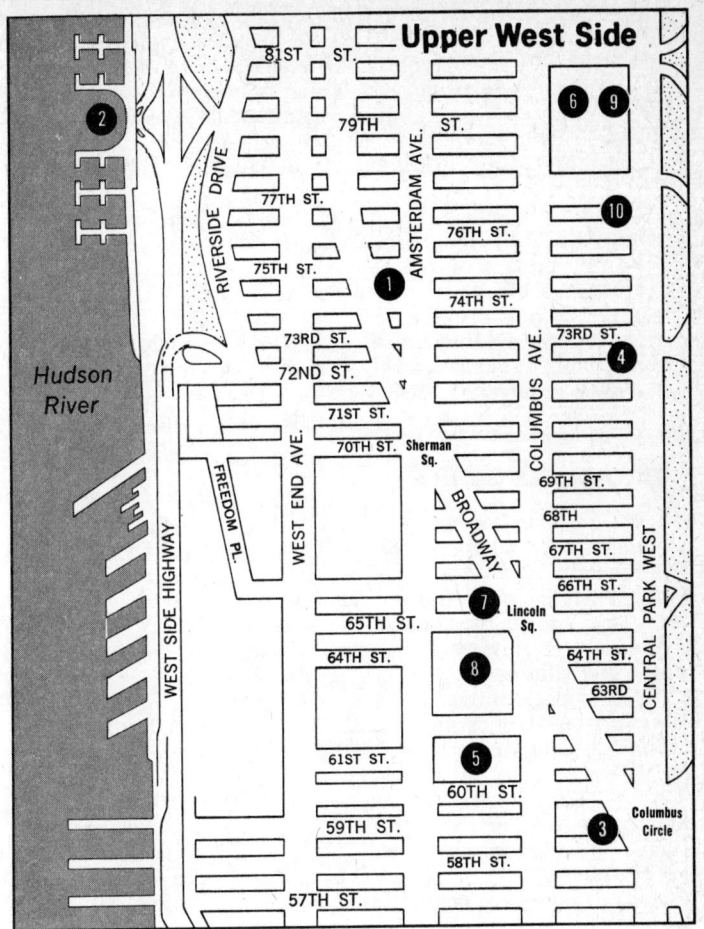

Points of Interest

1) Beacon Theater
2) Boat Basin
3) The Coliseum
4) The Dakota
5) Fordham University
6) Hayden Planetarium
7) Juilliard School
8) Lincoln Center for the Performing Arts
9) Museum of Natural History
10) New-York Historical Society

This is, of course, where The Metropolitan Opera company performs. It also has the Center's largest seating capacity: for over 3,700 people in its main auditorium. Tucked behind Avery Fisher Hall is the charming Eero Saarinen-designed Vivian Beaumont Theater. And in back, with an additional entrance on Amsterdam Avenue, is the Library and Museum of Performing Arts, a branch of the New York Public Library. Also on these grounds is the Guggenheim Bandshell for alfresco concerts.

Across 65th Street is the Juilliard School of Music campus, which includes Alice Tully Hall, a Lincoln Center facility noted especially for its chamber music presentations.

And, at the southern end of the Lincoln Center group is the midtown campus of Fordham University.

Columbus Avenue from 67th Street to 80th Street in the city's newest "scene," with restaurants, bars, food shops, boutiques, roller-skate rental shops, and the special New York blend of show-offs, street musicians and mimes, and with-it people.

The Historical Society

If you are interested in tracing the history and growth of New York, visit the New-York Historical Society's headquarters at 77th Street and Central Park West. Here, there are exhibits which trace the city's history from the Indian tribes which lived in the area before the white man came, through the stories of Giovanni da Verrazano, Henry Hudson, and Peter Stuyvesant. There are displays depicting the English period before the outbreak of the American Revolution; the periods of strife and struggle during the Revolutionary War; and New York when it was the capital of the new nation. There are rare collections of just about everything which shows how New York's earliest residents lived and fared.

Across 77th Street is the American Museum of Natural History, founded in 1869 "for the purpose of encouraging and developing the study of natural science, advancing the general knowledge of kindred subjects, and of furnishing popular instruction." It has been operating for over a century and houses tens of millions of zoological, geological, anthropological, and botanical specimens that are studied by scientists, students, and scholars from all over the world.

A week wouldn't be enough to see all the exhibits, which cover close to twelve acres of floor space. To make the most of your visit, pick up a guide book and check off the exhibits you want to see first. Two of the museum's greatest attractions are the 94-foot life-size model of a blue whale on the first floor and the two huge halls' worth of dinosaur fossils on the fourth floor. Other highlights include the 64-foot-long

NEW YORK CITY

Haida Canoe, made from the trunk of a single cedar tree; the Hall of the Biology of Man, which is devoted to the evolution, structure, and function of man as an organism; reconstruction of the extinct dodo; the exhibition of the Courtship of Birds; the collection of mammals; the Northwest Coast Indian Hall; the Hall of Man in Africa; and the demonstration-participation lectures in the People Center where onlookers are invited to try on costumes or play instruments, for example, of cultures around the world.

If your time is limited, you might find it worthwhile to rent an Acoustiguide, a one-hour tape-recorded lecture tour contained in a small portable case with ear plugs. The rental sets are available at the 77th Street entrance information desk.

A connecting passageway takes you to the Hayden Planetarium, at 81st Street and Central Park West, the department of astronomy of the American Museum of Natural History. Unless you have sailed the seas or lived in the unpopulated plains and mountaintops away from the bright lights of the city, you never have seen the heavens as they are shown in the planetarium.

The first part of the program is given in the circular Guggenheim Space Center, where a mechanized model of the solar system, forty-eight feet in diameter, is suspended from the ceiling. Here you learn about the motions of the planets and their moons.

The planetarium has numerous exhibits: murals of lunar landscapes, eclipses, and the aurora borealis; collections of meteorites (some weighing up to thirty-four tons); ancient Chinese, and German astronomical instruments. But the most popular exhibits of all are the five scales which register what your weight would be in outer space. A 130-pound person would weigh 113 pounds on Venus, but on the moon he would weigh 20 pounds, on Mars 47 pounds, on Jupiter 336 pounds, and on the sun 3,550 pounds. If you want to test your weight, count on waiting, for the lines are often long. Teenagers and young adults might also be interested in Laserium—the star show seen to the accompaniment of rock music. For information call 724–8700.

East Side Museums and Galleries

On the Fifth Avenue side of Central Park and on the side streets off Madison Avenue in the 60s and 70s is the city's greatest concentration of art galleries and museums. You might work your way up Fifth Avenue to 92nd Street, then over to Madison Avenue and down to the 60s.

A good starting point is the Frick Collection on Fifth Avenue at 70th Street, a splendid example of French classic architecture, formerly the home of Henry Clay Frick (who made millions in the steel industry).

The mansion enclosing a peaceful glass-roofed courtyard and the private collection of the fine paintings, ornaments, and furnishings will give you an idea of the scale of living enjoyed by New York society before the income tax. (No small children allowed.)

Now head east to Madison Avenue and up to the 70s, where New York's art gallery district is centered. Many of the galleries which once clustered around 57th Street have moved up to these quieter surroundings. Here you will find Sotheby Parke Bernet's main branch, whose auctioneers have run the price of art collections into the millions of dollars. Christie's is also on the East Side, over at 502 Park Avenue.

Also in this area are the Danenberg Galleries; the Graham Galleries, established in 1857 and reputedly the city's oldest; Perls Galleries, the distributor of Alexander Calder's works (he designed the cement and slate pavement in front); and the elegant Wildenstein Gallery, which presents important collections of Old Masters and French Impressionists. There are dozens of noted galleries, smaller and more intimate, besides these. In one afternoon you might be able to see more works of Renoir, Braque, Klee, Picasso, Redon, Chagall, Dufy, and Modigliani than you could in Paris.

In the midst of all this art is yet another great museum, the Whitney Museum of American Art, at Madison Avenue and 75th Street. The building itself was opened by Mrs. Flora Whitney Miller and Mrs. John F. Kennedy in September 1966, is at first startling. Given slightly less than one-third of an acre on which to build, architect Marcel Breuer was faced with the problem of creating ample exhibition and storage space for a vast collection of 20th-century American painting and sculpture which had completely outgrown the Whitney's old home on West 54th Street. (Its original home was on 8th Street in Greenwich Village.) Breuer's solution was to turn the traditional ziggurat (or "wedding cake") design upside down, with each of the second, third, and fourth floors projecting fourteen feet farther out over the street from the one below. New Yorkers' reactions were mixed, but the building has drawn students and architects from all over the world to study its design—more so, in fact, than did Frank Lloyd Wright's Guggenheim Museum.

Three blocks north and one west (on Fifth Avenue) is the Duke mansion, the former home of tobacco tycoon James Biddle Duke and his daughter Doris. Today it is the headquarters for the Institute of Fine Arts of New York University.

Across the way, facing Fifth Avenue between 80th and 84th Streets, is the Metropolitan Museum of Art. The neo-Renaissance design of this imposing structure infringing on the reaches of Central Park was taken from the Columbian Exposition (Chicago World's Fair) of 1893. The

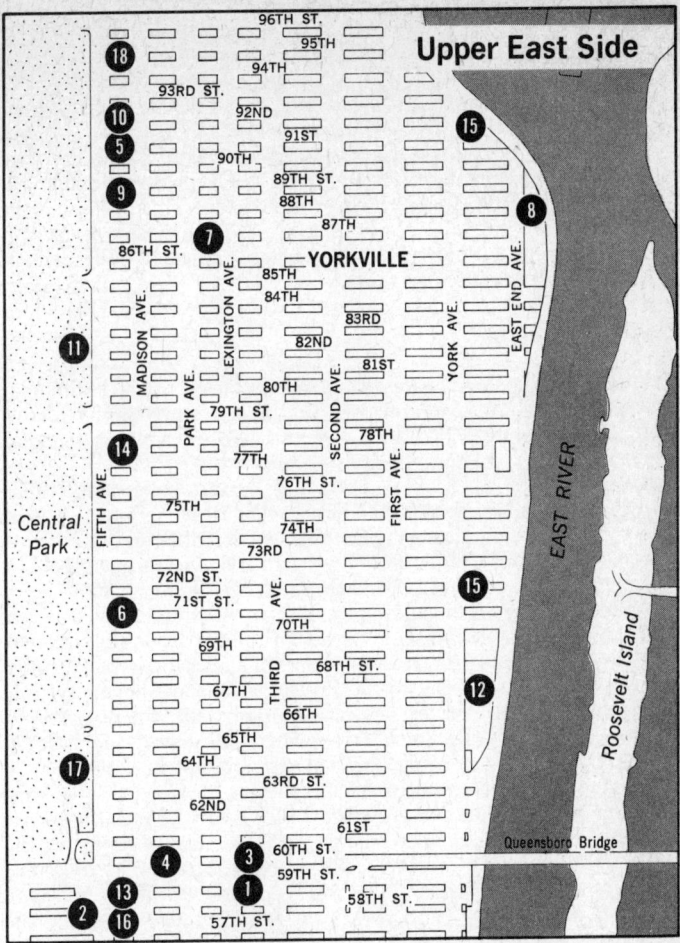

Points of Interest

1) Alexander's
2) Bergdorf Goodman
3) Bloomingdale's
4) Christie's
5) Cooper-Hewitt Museum
6) Frick Collection
7) Gimbels East
8) Gracie Mansion (Mayor's residence)
9) Guggenheim Museum
10) Jewish Museum
11) Metropolitan Museum of Art
12) Rockefeller University
13) F.A.O. Schwarz
14) Sotheby Parke Bernet
15) Sotheby's Decorative Arts
16) Tiffany
17) Central Park Zoo
18) International Center of Photography

museum houses one of the most comprehensive collections in the world. There are more than a million art treasures representing the work of fifty centuries. The whole of it cannot be enjoyed in one visit; so it would be best to study the floor plan and choose the galleries which hold the most interest for you. There are also Acoustiguides for rent here; the recorded tour takes approximately forty-five minutes. Its departments include Egyptian Art, Near Eastern Art, American painting, sculpture, furniture, armor, and arms. If you are interested in fashion, visit the Costume Institute, a favorite haunt of designers who come to study its period costumes.

Frank Lloyd Wright's Spiral

One of the most extraordinary buildings in New York is the Solomon R. Guggenheim Museum at 88th Street. The six-story spiral structure designed by the late Frank Lloyd Wright is worth a visit even if modern art doesn't interest you.

Eighty-sixth Street between Third and York Avenues is the center of old Yorkville, New York's German-American community, with restaurants and shops featuring German food, records, and other items. Nearby are lots of Czech- and Hungarian-style restaurants, too.

At 91st Street and Fifth Avenue is the former home of steel tycoon Andrew Carnegie. This handsome Georgian mansion is now occupied by the Cooper-Hewitt Museum for design and the decorative arts. One block north is the luxurious former home of banker Felix N. Warburg, whose widow presented it to the Jewish Theological Seminary to be used as a museum. The Jewish Museum has become the repository of the most extensive collection of Jewish ceremonial objects in the United States and also is one of the three most important in the world, the other two being in Jerusalem and Prague.

From here, even though it's a short hike north, your Fifth Avenue museum touring would not be complete without a visit to the fine Museum of the City of New York at 103rd Street. The museum's collections are extensive and cover a wide variety of fields, reflecting both the city of today and yesteryear. Its decorative arts collection includes outstanding examples of costumes, furniture, and silver. The print collection numbers over half a million items of paintings, prints, and photographs of New York City. A theater collection contains what is reputed to be the most complete history of the New York stage ever assembled, while the toy collection covers the whole fun world of playthings—with its dolls and dollhouses of particular note.

Incidentally, if you have children in tow you might plan to visit on Saturday when, during the school year, special activities are planned, including puppet shows and "please touch" demonstrations.

NEW YORK CITY

The Upper West Side Above 79th Street

The rocky ridge that begins in Central Park rises gradually as it travels uptown through Harlem and Morningside Heights to the precipitous lookout at Washington Heights. Here one of the big battles of the Revolutionary War was fought, and this upper end of Manhattan is rich in historic sites and lore.

One of the most scenic drives in the city is along Riverside Drive, which follows the Hudson River shoreline (inland of Riverside Park) from 72nd Street up to Inwood. The drive was another brilliant brainchild of Andrew Haswell Green, who was responsible for Central Park.

But Green, who had conservatively estimated the cost of the drive would run around $1,500,000, hadn't reckoned with Boss Tweed and his Forty Thieves. Tweed and boys liked the idea of building a park and drive; liked it so much that they made personal purchases of the land where the park was to be built and sold it to the city for a whopping profit. By the time the parkway was completed in 1885 the cost had zoomed up to $6 million.

At 79th Street, on the river, is the Boat Basin, a marina set alongside the Park promenade.

Along the route you will pass the boat basin where large yachts anchor. Next, at 89th Street, the Soldiers and Sailors Monument comes into view, a handsome Italian Carrara marble "silo" circled by twelve Corinthian columns. The 392-foot Gothic tower of the Riverside Church can be seen a mile to the north. Its 72-bell carillon is the largest in the United States and its range of tonal quality is superb. The largest bell, the *Bourdon,* weighs more than twenty tons, while the smallest weighs only ten pounds.

World's Largest Gothic Cathedral

Directly east, if you want to make a detour at this time, is the Church of St. John the Divine, on Morningside Heights (Amsterdam Avenue and 112th Street). Started in 1892, it will be the largest Gothic cathedral in the world when it is finally completed.

At Broadway and 116th Street is the main entrance to Columbia University; on the other side of Broadway nearby are Barnard College and the Union Theological Seminary.

General Grant's Tomb is at 123rd Street, and at about this point Riverside Drive begins to skirt Fort Washington Park. At 155th Street you might want to make another short detour east to Broadway to visit a unique cultural center which houses four special-interest museums. Here you'll find the Museum of the American Indian–Heye Foundation, which has an outstanding collection of Indian art and relics of North and South America. The Hispanic Society of America has a museum of ancient and modern Spanish culture. At the American Numismatic Society, you can see a vast collection of coins and medals, and the country's most comprehensive library on the subject. At the American Academy of Arts and Letters, you can view the memorabilia of many famous artists, writers, and musicians.

Continuing north and east to 160th Street and Edgecombe Avenue, you'll come to the Morris-Jumel Mansion, one of the city's few remaining examples of pre-Revolutionary Georgian architecture. Built in 1765 by Roger Morris and later occupied by Madame Jumel, a wealthy widow who married Aaron Burr in his old age, the home has many exquisite architectural details. It has recently been turned into a museum devoted to the Revolutionary War period.

Heading north and west, pick up Fort Washington Avenue and follow it to Fort Tryon Park. This is the brow of Manhattan; from this vantage point, you have an uninterrupted view of the magnificant sweep of the Hudson River up to the Tappan Zee Bridge, the precipitous Palisades shoreline of New Jersey, the graceful arc of George Washington Bridge, and the far reaches of the Bronx beyond Spuyten Duyvil.

The Cloisters

Set in the midst of this woodland park is The Cloisters, a structure of unusual form and grace assembled from many sections of medieval European monasteries. Five different cloisters have been connected by a charming colonnaded walk and merged with a French Romanesque chapel, a chapter house of the 12th century, and a Romanesque apse which is on loan from the Spanish government.

The museum's medieval art treasures were gathered by George Grey Barnard and acquired by the Metropolitan Museum with funds provided by John D. Rockefeller, Jr. (Admission, by contribution, can be made either at the Met or at the Cloisters, and is good at both locations on the same day.) Among the museum's most notable treasures are the *Hunt of the Unicorn* tapestries, which are considered to be among the world's greatest.

At the time Mr. Rockefeller arranged for the purchase of the Barnard collection, he also bought the woodland area of Fort Tryon as the site for The Cloisters. To ensure an uncluttered vista across the Hudson on the New Jersey side Mr. Rockefeller also purchased a 13-mile strip along the Palisades and gave it to the Palisades Interstate Park Commission.

NEW YORK CITY

On the lowlands at the northernmost tip of Manhattan is the "Great Maize Land" of the fertile Inwood Valley, where Henry Hudson came ashore and shared a feast of oysters proffered by the friendly Indian tribe which later sold its homeland to Peter Minuit for a trunkful of trinkets. This little gem of a park is the last vestige of natural woodlands which once covered all of Manhattan island. Today you still can see fragments of centuries-old oyster shells as you wander through the park's forest of giant trees and along the banks of Spuyten Duyvil.

During the days of discovery, Spuyten Duyvil was a narrow, unnavigable creek which trickled between the Harlem and Hudson Rivers, separating Marble Hill from Manhattan's mainland. In 1895 a canal was cut through these flatlands, shortening the water route between the Hudson River and Long Island Sound, thus obviating the necessity of sailing way down and around the Battery to reach a berth on the Hudson River.

Within a stone's throw of Inwood Park are Columbia University's athletic fields and boathouse. On nearly any spring day you'll see oarsmen out on the Spuyten Duyvil practicing for a regatta, and in the fall, Columbia's home football games are played at Baker Field.

While you're in the neighborhood, you might want to drive down to see the Dyckman House, a museum at 204th Street and Broadway. When it was built in 1783, the wealthy Dyckman family owned most of the Inwood area. Today the little 18th-century Dutch farmhouse is squeezed between clusters of seedy apartment houses and shops, a sorry setting for such an historic gem. It has been beautifully restored by the city, is furnished with authentic pieces of the mid-18th century, and has an enchanting garden. If you ignore the surroudings, you will find it a rewarding visit.

Manhattan is a civilization on the sea and of the sea and it is from the water one fully appreciates its size, shape, and style. The Circle Line is a three-hour boat excursion around the island which reveals many of the city's characteristics one cannot observe while exploring on foot.

Outside Manhattan

As far back as 1833 there was a movement afoot to consolidate the villages around Manhattan into one Greater New York. Brooklyn, the big brother of the outlying areas, had been incorporated as a village for some time and doing very nicely on its own. In turning down the proposal to come under the wing of the bustling, brash, flourishing city of New York, its spokesman General Jeremiah Johnson echoes the sentiments of most Brooklynites with the statement that "Between New York and Brooklyn there is nothing common—unless it be the waters that flow between them. And even these waters—however frequently passed, still form and must forever continue to form an unsurmountable obstacle to the Union."

A half century later Andrew Haswell Green, having finished his big Riverside Drive project, looked around for something else to keep him occupied and hit upon reviving the Greater New York concept. The Brooklyn Bridge had been completed in 1883 and Green decreed that the waters between New York and Brooklyn no longer constituted an "unsurmountable obstacle to the Union."

In 1889 he addressed the New York State Legislature and exhorted them to move on unification. By 1894 he had managed to place a referendum on unification before the voters of Manhattan, Brooklyn, Queens, Staten Island, and lower Westchester. The vote was a toss-up. The state legislature made up the voters' minds by enacting a bill for consolidation. On January 1, 1898, Brooklyn, Bronx, Queens, and Richmond (Staten Island) joined Manhattan to become Greater New York.

The Williamsburg and Queensboro Bridges, the Queens Midtown Tunnel, and miles of subway lines were built to bind the boroughs together, all save one: Staten Island, which could be reached by ferry only and remained a distant relative for fourscore years. Not until the Verrazano-Narrows Bridge was opened in 1964 was Staten Island brought fully into the fold.

The Rural Borough—Staten Island

Staten Island, the borough of Richmond, has always been the most rural area of New York City. Many of its families date back to the early 18th century, and its society is exclusive to the point of clannishness. One resident, whose family goes back to the 17th century, says that there was a time when the Vanderbilts were considered "common."

Cornelius Vanderbilt, who was born near Stapleton on Staten Island in 1794, was not to the manor born, to be sure, but he did have enterprise. At age twenty-three he started a ferry run over to the mainland and assumed the title "Commodore." Eventually he parlayed his ferry service into a railroad and hotel empire. His "rank" was given to the former Hotel Commodore on 42nd Street near Vanderbilt Avenue, which has reopened as a Hyatt hotel.

To this day Staten Island society is hard to crack, for the old families still have a tendency to stick together. Most of the old guard live up in the hills—Dongan, Emerson, Grymes Hills—in houses not exactly extravagant, but on property that has a long-time family background and a superb view of the Narrows. They are proud to point out that their Todt Hill, a 410-foot mound, is the highest point along the Atlantic coast between Main and Florida!

NEW YORK CITY

The island, an irregular triangle about fourteen miles long and seven miles wide, was given its name—"Staatenn Eylandt"—by Henry Hudson in 1609. It was a difficult piece of land to colonize for the original owners, the Unami Indians, were a wily lot. The Dutch started negotiating with the Unamis in 1630 and were repulsed with arrows and hatchets on three occasions before they finally were able to persuade the chieftain to sell the island. It wasn't long though before the Unamis were back to reclaim it. "They supposed that ye island by reason of ye war, by killing, burning and driving us off become theirs again," complained one colonist, Cornelius Melyn. The Dutch bought the island five times before they finally could call it their own.

When England took New Amsterdam in 1664, it appropriated Staten Island and made it a part of the province of New York. It was named Richmond County in honor of the Duke of Richmond, the son of King Charles II. Several disputes arose between the ducal proprietors from New Jersey and New York over which previous claims to the island's lush farmlands and timbered hills were still valid. It was a sticky decision to make.

The Duke of York, a man of great sporting spirit, chose a novel way of resolving the dispute. The property, he said, would be awarded to citizens who could circumnavigate the island in twenty-four hours. The first to accomplish the treacherous sail was Captain Christopher Billopp and in 1687 he was awarded the prize of 1,600 acres at the southernmost tip, which is now the village of Tottenville. The following year he built a fine mansion and it later became the scene of the famous conference Lord Howe called to determine the seriousness of American demands for independence. The Billopp Conference House at the foot of Hylan Boulevard has been restored and looks almost the same as when it first was built.

For more than a century and a half the island remained a farming area and preserve. In the 1830s fashionable bathing resorts sprang up on the north shore at Castleton, Stapleton, and New Brighton. New York socialites cruised over to spend the summer yachting, swimming, and picnicking on the beaches. Some were so taken with the bucolic atmosphere they built summer mansions and organized the Richmond Country Club, where they could meet for a stirrup cup and ride to the hounds.

For some reason Staten Island had a special appeal for Southerners, too. Many plantation owners spent their holidays here, and during the Civil War they sent their women and children to the safety of the isolated island.

The island's little scattered communities retained their rural, rustic atmosphere for almost a century more. Then came the dedication in 1964 of the Verrazano-Narrows Bridge, which opened the way from

Brooklyn to Staten Island. Real-estate developers moved in, bought up many acres of farmland, and converted them into look-alike housing developments. Brooklynites have discovered that the island's beaches are a lot roomier than theirs, and now are creating weekend traffic jams.

Yet there are still miles of farm-fringed country roads, secluded parks, hilltop lookouts with superb views of Upper and Lower New York Bays, historic houses, zoos, and museums, which make a whole day's excursion around Staten Island most worthwhile.

That Wonderful Ferry Ride

Bridges link the island to New Jersey and Brooklyn. The most delightful way to reach it from Manhattan is by ferry from the South Ferry terminal at the foot of Battery Park. The inexpensive ride—25 cents round trip!—is a miniature ocean voyage past Governors Island, the Statue of Liberty, and other harbor highlights during the 15-minute run to St. George. The ferry transports passenger cars too ($1.75), and having your own car (or renting one) makes it easier for you to see all that the island has to offer. Ferries depart every half hour in each direction; during the Kool Jazz Festival in late June/early July, there are special rides featuring old-time Dixieland bands.

Staten Island Restorations

From St. George head for Stapleton and pick up Richmond Road. Drive through the Dongan and Todt Hills' areas of old estates and past the Richmond County Country Club on to Richmond. This is historically and geographically the center of the island and the site of a fascinating restoration called Richmondtown.

Richmondtown was called Cocclestown when it first was settled in the late 1600s, prompted probably by the quantities of oyster and clam shells left behind by the Indians. By 1730 it had grown into a compact little village with a dozen dwellings, a courthouse, jail, taverns, the Church of St. Andrew, and the center of the island's government. When the island was merged with the other boroughs into Greater New York, the abandonment of Richmondtown as the county seat left it without the incentives for change or expansion. It was a blessing in disguise.

Historically minded Staten Islanders recognized it as "a perfect setting for a life-sized model of an American town that would tell the story of the growth of such a village better than any number of pictures, exhibition cases and dioramas." You'll see the town taking shape under the auspices of the Staten Island Historical Society and the city of New York. Little 17th- and 18th-century cottages, cooperage, and basket-

NEW YORK CITY

maker's shops, and other older buildings have been lifted off their foundations in villages around the island and brought here to form Richmondtown. The center of the settlement is the Museum of the Staten Island Historical Society, at Court and Center Streets, housed in a former county building built in 1848. The museum is small and its attendants—mostly volunteer workers—outdo themselves to make you feel welcome and show you around.

On display are assorted bits of Americana which show various aspects of how people worked and lived in centuries past. The community's 19th-century country general store is also popular. Ladies in bonnets and long gingham dresses tend store, selling old-fashioned licorice whips, horehound drops, taffy, and other delectables. The shelves are lined with ornate tea canisters and spice boxes. There are cracker barrels, old apothecary jars, a cigar store Indian, an old loom, and a spinning wheel. There is an assortment of irons that housewives warmed over a wood stove: small rounded ones for pressing ruffles, heavy cumbersome ones for bedsheets and workclothes. Behind an old barber chair you'll see an unusual collection of shaving mugs, each with its owner's name fired onto the ornate designs. A doctor's bleeding instrument is mixed in with a hodgepodge of other items usually found in the old general stores which served about every need of the community.

Ask one of the attendants for the brochure which gives the location and historic backgrounds of the various buildings clustered around the museum. There is the little clapboard Voorlezer's House, built about 1696 by the Dutch congregation as a church, schoolhouse, and a home for the *voorlezer* (church clerk). It is known as America's oldest remaining schoolhouse.

Treasure House, built by a tanner in 1700, is famous for the good fortune it bestowed on a later owner. About a hundred years ago when Patrick Highland took possession he found $7,000 in gold hidden in the walls. It's thought to be the cache of an overcautious or larcenous British paymaster.

The Guyon-Lake-Tysen House is one of the outstanding restorations. It was built about 1740 by Joseph Guyon and you can see his name marked in the mud coat over the dining room door. As each new owner took possession the house grew to meet his family's particular needs. You'll notice that the mantel in the dining room is of pre-Revolutionary design, while in the parlor, which was added later, the mantel is of the post-Revolutionary type.

If time permits, stop by the Jacques Marchais Center of Tibetan Art near the Lighthouse (338 Lighthouse Avenue), then pick up Amboy Road for a ride through a still somewhat rural area to the Conference House at Tottenville. On your return trip to St. George you can choose either Hylan Boulevard which skirts the shoreline or the inland Richmond Parkway which ultimately leads to the Victory Boulevard route to the ferry terminal.

The Indians Sold Brooklyn

Shortly after the West India Company settled Manhattan they sailed over to the "broken lands" southeast of the Battery to negotiate with the Indians for the purchase of the whole western end of Long Island.

Their first parcel in Brooklyn (Breuckelen—broken land) was acquired in 1636 and within a few years the company had brought over a number of Walloon families to settle along the Wall-boght (Wallabout Bay), the site of the Naval Shipyard.

Under the terms of "Provisional Regulations for Colonists," the company agreed to furnish them with "necessary supplies and clothes from the company's storehouses . . . at a reasonable price," which could be paid for in installments. The Colonists, in turn, were required to pledge that they would sell their farm produce and handicrafts to no one but the company's agents. They also were "bound to remain with their families for the space of six consecutive years at their destined place . . . and to faithfully fulfill their promises to the Indians and their other neighbors, whether in connection with trade or other matters."

The community grew and prospered quite separately from the earlier settlement of Nieuw Amsterdam. Brooklyn's colony burst the bounds of Wallabout Bay with the coming of Normans, French, and a group of English colonists from Massachusetts who had been excommunicated from the Puritan Church because they did not believe in the baptizing of babies. By 1643 the colonists had cleared and cultivated the lands as far as Gravesend Bay.

On Ilpetonga (high sandy bank) where the Canarsie Indians had lived in community houses (some of which were a quarter of a mile long), wealthy merchants built elegant homes. From the heights they could watch their clipper ships round Red Hook and berth at the waterside warehouses. To prevent the warehouses from marring their river view the merchant princes planted the roofs with lawns, flowering shrubs, and trees to form ingenious backyard gardens and shortcuts to the piers below. They called the area Clover Hill. Today it is known as Brooklyn Heights. With the coming of the Brooklyn Bridge and the subways, the patrician families fled the heights. Their homes have been partitioned into studios and apartments which are handsomely restored by artists, writers, and people who enjoy the Victorian atmosphere and one of the most exciting views in the world. This view alone makes a trip to Brooklyn worthwhile.

NEW YORK CITY 117

You can reach Brooklyn Heights by driving across Brooklyn Bridge and turning south, or by IRT Seventh Avenue subway to Clark Street. A stroll through the arboreal streets—Cranberry, Pineapple, Orange, Poplar, Willow—recalls a legend of old feuds. Before the Civil War these streets were named for prominent families. Local authorities were disturbed by the personality cult which wanted their names to go down in history by way of street signs. Overnight the family names were replaced with botanical street signs by the authorities. The families replaced their names and the battle of the street signs went on for weeks. Signs seesawed back and forth between families and fruit. The fruits and trees won in some cases and the families of Hicks, Montague, Pierrepont, and Remsen won in others. Miss Middagh, a supposedly staunch supporter of the fruit and tree campaign, also has a street named for her.

You'll find remains of Old World gentility in these streets. New Orleans-type wrought-iron balconies, stately pillared entrances, delicate scrollwork embellishments, ivy-covered brownstones, hidden mews of converted carriage houses similar to those of Washington Square make the 20th-century skyline across the river seem a mirage of the future.

Along Willow Street you'll pass a few of the older homes of the Heights. At 70 Willow Street is the van Sinderen House built in the Greek Revival style in the late 1830s. The three best examples of the Federal-style row houses of the early 19th century are found at 155–157–159.

An esplanade which extends from Remsem Street to Orange Street offers what photographic experts consider the most spectacular panoramic view of Manhattan. To the south, Wall Street's jungle of spires prick the clouds; parades of ferries, freighters, and barges ply between Buttermilk and East River Channels, often called the shipping crossroads of the world; the Statue of Liberty and the Verrazano-Narrows Bridge can be seen on the horizon. To the north, midtown's skyscrapers rise above the spidery spans of Brooklyn and Manhattan bridges.

Atlantic Avenue, nearby, is a center of Middle Eastern shops and restaurants toward its waterside end.

Fiery Sermons

Walking east from the esplanade you will come to the Plymouth Church of the Pilgrims on Orange Street, a severe, dark brick example of early Classic Revival architecture. Inside, its severity is softened with a series of memorial windows which trace the interesting history of Puritanism. It was here that the Abolitionist movement flared into a full-scale crusade.

Soon after the church was completed in 1849 Henry Ward Beecher began a series of fiery sermons and dramatic playlets on the evils of selling human souls on the auction block. William Lloyd Garrison, John Greenleaf Whittier, and other early Abolitionists also spoke from the pulpit. It was a bold program and one which inspired citizens throughout the country to raise their voices, even in cities where public discussions of slavery were not permitted. Abraham Lincoln worshipped here on two occasions in 1860 and took his stand against slavery in his historic speech at Cooper Institute.

Brooklyn—A City of Churches

Brooklyn was long known as the city of churches, and as you drive through the borough you will see spire after spire. It also has a fair share of institutions of higher learning, including Brooklyn College, Pratt Institute, Long Island University, and St. John's University. A half dozen parks, a world renowned museum, a botanic garden, and a huge aquarium offer a variety of diversions for all ages.

Flatbush Avenue, a few blocks from Brooklyn Heights, will lead you southeastward to the monumental Grand Army Plaza with its 80-foot-high memorial arch. A little beyond the Plaza to your left, onto Eastern Parkway and behind the Public Library, you'll come to Institute Park, where the huge Brooklyn Museum and the beautiful Botanic Garden are located.

The museum's collections of primitive and prehistoric art are world renowned: North and South American Indian handicrafts; works from Oceania, Indonesia, and Africa. There is a notable collection of American painting and sculpture from Colonial times to today. Its collection of Egyptian antiquities on the third floor is considered outstanding. One floor below is a fine collection of bronzes and porcelains from China, displayed in chronological order, as well as changing exhibitions from the museum's wealth of over thirty thousand prints and drawings. Up on the fourth floor the costume galleries and the series of American interiors from the 17th century to the present are also of special interest.

The 50-acre Botanic Garden behind the museum, with more than ten thousand trees and plants, is especially noted for its Garden of Fragrance, one of the relatively few gardens in the world planted and maintained for the blind. The plants were selected primarily for their fragrance and shape, so that the blind might enjoy nature's beauty by the sense of smell and touch. Signs in braille are posted at the edge of each bed to aid the blind in identifying the flowers and plants. It is noted, too, for its Japanese garden, and there are acres devoted to wild flowers, herbs, roses, tropical plants, and groves of flowering shrubs.

To the south of the Botanic Garden is Prospect Park, a 500-acre expanse of woods, meadows, footpaths, bridle trails, and tree-shaded drives. The project was designed by the same men who had collaborated on Central Park, Olmstead and de Vaux. Here you can visit the Lefferts Homestead, a Dutch Colonial farmhouse which was built in 1776 and originally stood at 563 Flatbush Avenue. When the Lefferts family bequeathed it to the city, the home was moved to the park as a museum.

The Italianate villa which serves as the Brooklyn Park Headquarters (Prospect Park West between 4th and 5th Streets) was once the home of railroad pioneer Edwin C. Litchfield. Built in 1857 from plans by Alexander Jackson Davis and called Ridgewood, it is said to have been one of the most elegant houses of its time and the center of Brooklyn social life.

A Day at a City Beach

Another summer day—make it a weekday when it's less crowded—can be spent in Coney Island. The island, which fronts on the Atlantic Ocean, once was a common pasture for early Dutch farmers. It became a fashionable beach resort in the mid-19th century when the enterprising Messrs. Eddy and Hart leased part of the island and built a pavilion. With the extension of the subway lines (BMT and IND), the island became accessible to all and now draws a half-billion people a year.

It was once a razzle-dazzle place with ferris wheels, carousels, roller coasters, tunnels of love, shooting galleries, penny arcades, sellers of pizza, hot dogs, saltwater taffy, and spun-sugar candy. Now Coney Island's number of amusements is diminishing, but it's still worth the excursion if only to get a taste of what the happy, gaudy, and thrilling heyday of this famous amusement park must have been like.

The New York Aquarium is here, too. Try to visit at feeding time: through portholes you can watch divers swim among the great white whales and feed them by hand; watch an attendant tickle an electric eel until it flashes and crackles a discharge of some 650 volts. You may see a pilot whale or seal which had gone astray and was given a home here. There are sea lions and seals, living coral, giant starfish, seahorses, octopi, and enough exhibits to keep you busy for half the day.

Another variation on the nautical theme is the fascinating Sheepshead Bay area. Take the Belt (also called Shore) Parkway east to Knapp St., head south a short way, then back west along Emmons Avenue. This mini-port for saltwater fishermen comes spectacularly alive in the predawn hours and again in late afternoon. The amazing bustle, in which you're welcome to take part, involves the all- or half-day chartering of party or private-charter fishing boats. Even if you don't want to test the Atlantic fishing in person, the returning catch—you can't get 'em any fresher—is for sale at reasonable prices.

Back to the Shore Parkway and farther east still, straddling the Brooklyn–Queens border, and you'll be passing New York City's largest park, the Jamaica Bay Wildlife Refuge. It encompasses more than eighteen square miles (remember that Manhattan comprises only 22 square miles) of underwater island and tidal marsh terrain with 257 species of native birds. A permit is required for access to the wildlife area here; write the city's Department of Parks, Recreation and Cultural affairs. However, saltwater fishing is permitted.

Queens

Queens, covering 121 square miles, abuts Brooklyn to the south and west and Long Island to the east. The lines of demarcation are very vague. Even the native hardly knows at what point he is in Queens, Brooklyn, or Long Island. (The position of Manhatten is quite clear. It's across the East River, either over it via the Queensboro Bridge or under it via the Queens Midtown Tunnel.)

Queens is a borough of beaches, baseball parks, airports, golf courses, racetracks, yacht basins, and expressways to Long Island's beach resorts and suburban communities. The borough also has thriving manufacturing areas—especially Long Island City on the western edge—and distinct neighborhoods. Some of the large ethnic groupings are the Italians of Maspeth and Ridgewood, the Irish of Woodside, the blacks of Hollis and Jamaica, the Greeks of Astoria, the Jews of Forest Hills, and the Puerto Ricans of Corona and Elmhurst.

Until well into the 20th century Queens was a rural area. Henry Hudson had nosed the *Half Moon* into Rockaway Inlet on the south shore for a short look-see, then continued on to the Upper Bay and then to Albany in search of the Northwest Passage. Three years later Adrian Block sailed through Long Island Sound and, while navigating the roaring currents of Hell Gate on the northern extremity of Queens, didn't dare give the area a second look. He, too, was heading for Manhattan.

After the West India Company had sewed up the Brooklyn area, it approached the Reckouwacky Indians about selling a piece of their domain, in what was to become Queens, so it could continue its expansion program. Once the deal was consummated, towns sprang up all over the virgin flatlands.

By 1643 Flushing was inhabited by a small band of English Quaker refugees under the leadership of John Bowne. The same year a band of Englishmen from Hemel Hempstead had settled Hempstead, which is across the borough line in Long Island. Jamaica was chartered as a

NEW YORK CITY

town by Governor Stuyvesant in 1656. They were followed by other English settlers and soon the area became known as Queens, in honor of Catherine Braganza, Queen of Charles II. It is not surprising, therefore, that during the Revolution, most of the people in Queens were British sympathizers.

Queens remained a loosely knit collection of small towns until the subway lines were extended to Jackson Heights, Flushing, and Jamaica. Today the borough has a population rivaling Brooklyn's, many of whom live in huge clusters of high-rise apartment houses.

There are only a few vestiges of its historic past. One is the Bowne House in Flushing (Bowne Street between 37th and 38th Avenues), which John Bowne built in 1661. For permitting Quaker meetings to be conducted in his home he was sent to Holland to be put on trial. His impassioned plea for religious tolerance won him a pardon and led to greater freedom of worship in the New World's settlements. His home is now a shrine to religious liberty.

Close by is the old Quaker Meeting House on Northern Boulevard between Main and Union Streets. It is one of the country's few remaining houses of worship dating from the 17th century. The meeting place was built in 1694 and has been in continuous use by the Society of Friends ever since, except for a time when it was occupied by the British forces during the Revolution.

Baseball, Tennis, and Racing

If horse racing, tennis, and baseball are your favorite sports, Queens is the place to head for. The National League's New York Mets (baseball) and the New York Jets (football) play at Shea Stadium in Flushing. The thoroughbreds run at Aqueduct in Jamaica. At the West Side Tennis Club in Forest Hills you can watch professional and amateur tennis tournaments.

For the less active pastime of strolling, sunning, and sightseeing, you might also plan on spending some time in Flushing Meadows–Corona Park in Corona. The site of both New York World's Fairs (1939–40 and 1964–65) with a few buildings of both expositions remaining, this area also contains a Hall of Science, a small zoo, a delightful aviary, a children's animal farm, and Louis Armstrong Stadium, site of the U.S. Open Tennis Championship.

The Bronx

It was a stroke of good fortune for New York City that The Bronx was slow in developing. When farsighted city officials began around 1870 to acquire lands to make Central and Prospect Parks they also turned their eyes northeastward across the Harlem River to the vast expanse of virgin forests and meadows of what was then called lower Westchester. They bought three parcels of land covering more than four thousand acres "to be held forever for the delight and well-being of the people of the city." In no other major city of the world has the country been kept this close to town (although at first glance the Bronx is hardly a "delight").

The history of the Bronx more or less parallels that of Queens. The Dutch West India Company purchased the area from the Indians in 1639 and two years later sold five hundred acres between the Harlem and Bronx rivers to a Scandinavian by the name of Jonas Bronck, later distorted to Bronx. He was joined by other colonists from New England and during the Revolution they, too, took the side of the Tories.

It wasn't until the mid-19th century that the area attracted any appreciable number of settlers. The Irish came in after the potato famine of 1840 to help build the Harlem and Hudson River Railroads. After the German Revolution of 1848 there was an influx of German farmers. They lived in small, independent settlements until 1874 when New York City enticed Kingsbridge, West Farms, and Morrisania to become wards of the city. Twenty years later they were followed into the fold by the townships of Westchester and parts of Pelham and Eastchester. Under the Greater New York Charter of 1898 these two annexations became the borough of the Bronx.

The lower Bronx is a cluster of unkempt neighborhoods and some are among the nation's most depressed areas. Its greatest claim to fame is Yankee Stadium; since its opening in 1923 it has been the home of the American League's Yankees and, from 1956 through 1972, of the football Giants.

Near the Stadium, under the Major Deegan Expressway, you can find the Bronx Terminal Market. A few years ago, it sold only to retail stores but that's changed. In one of those interesting experiments that makes living in New York a unique experience, groups of families began trying to save money by forming their own food co-ops and sending representatives to Bronx Terminal to buy wholesale lots of meat, fruit, and vegetables. Now these amateurs-turned-professionals compete with the Grand Union and A&P buyers for the best bargains.

The upper Bronx borders wealthy Westchester county and is a relatively open area with several college campuses—notably Fordham and Manhattan Universities—suburban communities, parklands, and parkways.

Those visitors to New York who say, "It's a nice place to visit but I wouldn't want to live there," probably never have crossed over the border of Manhattan into the primitive forests of Van Cortlandt Park, nor ventured up to Pelham Bay Park's breeze-swept beaches (marred somewhat in recent years by an unsightly landfill mound growing out of a garbage dump) or across the bridge to City Island and its wide views of Long Island Sound.

The parks can be reached by subway, but the pleasantest and quickest way to go is by car. The most scenic route to Van Cortlandt Park in the northwestern part of the Bronx is along Manhattan's Henry Hudson Parkway, an expressway which skirts the Hudson River just beyond Riverside Drive, crosses over Spuyten Duyvil, and leads you right into the park.

Van Cortlandt's 1,132 acres are primarily for play and relaxation. There are hiking trails through its rugged, heavily wooded terrain, playing fields, a golf course, bridle paths, tennis courts, a small lake where you can rent a rowboat in the summer and ice-skate in the winter.

Van Cortlandt House

This was George Washington country. Van Cortlandt House, at the southwest corner of the park just off Broadway, served as the General's headquarters in 1783 just before he launched his final and successful campaign to retake New York City from the British. The house was built in 1748 by Frederick Van Cortlandt, a descendant of one of the early and influential Dutch families, who managed his estate along the lines of an independent principality. Slaves tended his livestock and crops; women spun his flax, wove it into cloth, and turned the cloth into garments. A score of skilled artisans embellished his living quarters and fashioned his furniture. He was lord of all he surveyed and his word was law. It is one of the few historic houses which remained in the hands of the same family for generations. It wasn't until 1899 that Van Cortlandt's descendants sold the estate to the city, which maintains it as a museum. (The mansion is not to be confused with Van Cortlandt Manor, at Croton-on-Hudson in Westchester County, which is also a museum.)

The mansion's unpretentious square fieldstone exterior in no way prepares the first-time visitor for the elegance of its Georgian interior. The spacious rooms are furnished with handsome English, Dutch, and Colonial pieces. Its huge fireplace is framed with blue tiles. The heart of the house, the kitchen, speaks a volume on the self-sufficient way of life that was lived here: candlemakers, spinning wheel, loom, soapmakers, handwrought implements, and caldrons large enough to feed fifty.

Another historic house of note in the area is the Poe Cottage, a short drive southeast at Kingsbridge Road and Grand Concourse. The little farmhouse was built in 1816 by John Wheeler and was the home of poet Edgar Allan Poe and his wife, Virginia, from 1846 to 1849. Before she died here Poe wrote some of his finest works: *The Bells, Ulalume, Eureka,* and *Annabel Lee.*

Gardens and Zoos

From Van Cortlandt Park it is about 20 minutes' drive east to Southern Boulevard and 200th Street, and the New York Botanical Garden's flower displays, which spread over 230 rolling acres of the northern half of Bronx Park. In its center is a forest primeval of hemlocks. This dense stand of trees is one of the very few virgin tracts to have survived the ax in the East.

West of Hemlock Forest is a turn-of-the-century museum building which houses an herbarium, library, auditorium, and exhibition halls.

Across from the museum is a four-acre garden with hundreds of rock-loving plants. A short stroll will bring you to the Enid A. Haupt Conservatory, renovated and reopened in 1979: an elaborate complex of greenhouses where orchids, poinsettia, and other brilliant tropical plants give New Yorkers a taste of southern climes during long winter months. Behind the Conservatory, you'll come upon the vast Rose Garden, where several thousand plantings of more than 160 rose varieties are displayed in formal beds and country-style clusters.

The Bronx Zoo—the southern half of Bronx Park, at Fordham Road and Bronx River Parkway,—is built with moats rather than iron bars to give the illusion of a walk through the African Veldt while elephants, deer, lions, ostriches, peacocks, and other wild life roam around at will. The 252-acre zoo is one of America's largest, and, for the foot-weary, there's an aerial tramway that passes directly over the African Plains, the Great Apes House, and Goat Hill, as well as a tractor train and monorail.

But don't forget to get off and explore the windowless World of Darkness with its nocturnal and cave-dwelling inhabitants. Another outstanding addition is the World of Birds, a series of oval aviaries connected by ramps. These contain, for example, a spectacular rain forest with a hundred species that are common to such environments in the New World. There is a forty-foot waterfall and rainstorms are simulated from time to time. There are exhibits of swamp birds, species from arid scrublands and African jungles. In The Treetops, five regional groupings are viewable only from above. Explanatory placards and drawings by artist Carlene Meeker show other facets of this World, such as the diets of various birds.

The children's zoo, the first in the country, has pigs, sheep, goats, a working beehive, and a chicken hatchery. Adults may enter only if accompanied by a child. There are pony rides, and for the more adven-

SIGHTSEEING CHECKLIST

turous, there are even camels and llamas to ride. An outdoor restaurant and a dozen refreshment stands are spotted around the grounds.

Pelham Bay Park, a 2,000-acre jagged peninsula which juts into Long Island Sound, was part of the original 9,000-acre tract bought by English colonist Thomas Pell in 1654. Its rocky, rolling, wooded terrain is laced with bridle paths, picnic grounds, playfields, and the Pelham and Split Rock golf courses. On the sandy shores of the Sound is Orchard Beach, where you can rent bathing suits, towels, and a locker, roam the one mile crescent-shaped beach, picnic on 140 acres, visit the historic 215-acre Hunter and Twin Island Sites, or play paddleball or handball on the extensive recreational area fields. There are fishing facilities, too. Weekends bring out hordes of city dwellers, so it would be best to plan your excursion for a weekday.

The Bartow Mansion in the park is worth a visit. The handsome Greek Revival stone house was built in 1836, and today is the headquarters of the International Garden Club as well as a museum and landscape gardening exhibit.

A causeway connects the park with City Island, a busy center of boat building, rope and sail making, and pleasure boating. Fish fresh from the sea are served at the bustling waterside restaurants where you can watch sailboats get under way, their mainsails billowing before the wind as they head out to Long Island Sound.

In the beautiful residential section of Riverdale, in the West Bronx along the Hudson, is Wave Hill, at West 249th Street, whose spacious grounds—open to the public—include formal gardens, greenhouses, a herb garden, a beautiful and historic mansion house—Mark Twain, Theodore Roosevelt, and Arturo Toscanini have lived there—and a spectacular view of the Hudson and the Palisades.

Winding Up

New York is like a giant pastry shop. It offers hundreds of delectable delights, but they cannot be consumed all at once. One must return time and again to savor a dozen or so favorite selections each visit. Nor can each one be described in a guide if it is to be of a manageable size. These have been some of New York's pièces de résistance. You'll find many more listed in the New York City *Practical Information* section, which follows.

SIGHTSEEING CHECKLIST. No matter how you come to New York City, or how many times you've been here, your state of mind will determine the best approach for exploring the Big Apple. It is a world unto itself, and an incredible world at that. Even a recent Gallup Poll of typical

NEW YORK CITY

American travelers attested to the fact that New York is the nation's "top city," and is considered the "most interesting" city in the U.S. with the "best food" and the "best-looking women." Those quotes cover a lot of ground, territory we'll cover in the following pages with historical background and suggested walking tours. However, before we go—you should pardon the expression—Galluping off into helpful hints about how to get around the city, and what to look for, here is New York City's "Top Attractions Checklist" as compiled by the New York Convention and Visitors Bureau. We'll go into details later on, but for starters, this is the Bureau's list of must-sees:

(1) **The Statue of Liberty,** with an observation platform 22 stories above Liberty Island, offering a superb view of New York's bustling harbor. Don't miss the fascinating Museum of Immigration in the statue's base. Nearby is Ellis Island (open for tours, spring through fall) where millions of immigrants were processed.

(2) **The Empire State Building,** 1,472 feet high, is over 50 years old, but the sleek skyscraper of steel, limestone, and aluminum is as popular as ever. Each year millions of visitors enjoy the view from observation decks on the 86th and 102nd floors.

(3) **Rockefeller Center** is a city within a city, where you can ice-skate in winter and dine outdoors in summer. This midtown Manhattan landmark offers a superb guided tour to its varied delights. Nearby is the beautifully restored Radio City Music Hall Entertainment Center, where you can take in a musical extravaganza, Rockettes and all, in the world's biggest (6,000-seat) theater, a 1930s Art Deco marvel. A separate behind-the-scenes tour is available here, too. Also nearby, in the Center's McGraw-Hill Building, is a theater showing *The New York Experience,* a multi-media, multi-sensory show that helps put New York City into perspective.

(4) **Lincoln Center** is a vast performing-arts complex at 65th Street and Broadway that offers opera, symphony, dance, theater, films, a library—and a guided tour of the beautiful buildings that house them. From the Chagalls at the Metropolitan Opera House and the Henry Moore statuary seemingly climbing out of the reflecting pool outside the library to the Vivian Beaumont and Mitzi Newhouse Theaters, it is nothing short of a modern-day Acropolis minus the hills.

(5) **The World Trade Center** with its twin towers—each 110 stories tall—stands like a pair of soaring sentinels guarding New York's Harbor. On the rooftop "promenade" of the South Tower, you stand on the world's highest open-air observation deck (1,377 feet). On the top of the North Tower you can drink or dine at the elegant Windows on the World, the restaurant complex that offers New York's most spectacular view (although, not, alas, the city's most spectacular food). Down below, on the concourse level, you'll find The Big Kitchen (budget and gourmet foods) and the Market Dining Rooms.

(6) **The United Nations** offers new sights, services, and activities for visitors taking in the imposing glass building seemingly rising out of the East River. The official meetings are open to the public, there is a one-hour guided tour (even

SIGHTSEEING CHECKLIST

all-day tours for small groups) and several more interesting stop-off points, including the post office, gift shops, restaurants, and gardens.

(7) New York's neighborhoods:
- Chinatown
- Little Italy
- Yorkville (German, Middle European)
- Greenwich Village
- SoHo
- Upper East Side
- Upper West Side
- Brooklyn Heights
- Forest Hills
- Richmondtown
- Riverdale

You can literally tour the world in one city. But plan your excursions carefully.

(8) The Great Museums: The Metropolitan Museum of Art and the Msueum of Modern Art, the Frick Collection, the American Museum of Natural History, the Museum of the American Indian, the Museum of the City of New York, the New-York Historical Society, the Cooper-Hewitt, the Museum of Holography, the International Center of Photography, the Guggenheim, the Whitney, and the hundreds of galleries that make New York City the world's undisputed art center.

(9) Sports: The full gamut of sporting events can be observed at Madison Square Garden, Shea and Yankee Stadiums, the Flushing Meadows and Forest Hills tennis complexes, and the Belmont, Aqueduct, Roosevelt, and Yonkers racetracks. Baseball, boxing, hockey, soccer, football, tennis, track and field, horseracing—you name your game, New York City plays it.

(10) Times Square is the glittering "Great White Way" with its theaters, moviehouses, skyscrapers, and shops. If you can see only one play (make it *Amadeus*) one or musical (toss a coin between *Sophisticated Ladies, A Chorus Line* or *42nd Street*), your visit will be greatly enhanced.

(11) Houses of Worship offering food for the soul and impressive works of art and architecture include such landmarks as St. Patrick's Cathedral, the Cathedral of St. John the Divine (the world's largest Gothic cathedral), Temple Emanu-El, Riverside Church, Trinity Church and St. Paul's Chapel, and more than 2,500 other religious edifices.

(12) New York and American Stock Exchanges offer free tours during trading hours in the nation's marketplaces—the money capitals of the world. But beware of bulls and bears.

(13) South Street Seaport, an indoor-outdoor "museum" consisting of several blocks and three piers stretching along the East River waterfront at Fulton Street, near the site of the famous fishmarket. The entire area is being restored to its original appearance, as it was when South Street was one of the world's great ports for sailing ships. Among the attractions: a collection of historic ships, an old printing shop, a model-ships museum, the Fulton Market, the Titanic Memorial Lighthouse, and some of the best seafood restaurants in town.

That's a baker's dozen sightseeing attractions to give you something to think about while you're deciding where to eat, shop, stay, or be entertained. One way—perhaps the easiest and most relaxing way—to get your bearings is to take a sightseeing bus tour or a Circle Line three-hour sightseeing cruise around the island of Manhattan. Or maybe even a sightseeing helicopter trip. How to find these places, sights and sites? When in doubt, write or stop by the Bureau at 2 Columbus Circle (59th Street and Eighth Avenue in Manhattan), which will even supply you with free folders on all the city's boroughs. And, of course, read on.

PRACTICAL INFORMATION

FOR

NEW YORK CITY

HOW TO GET THERE. By air: Virtually every major (and most minor) airlines serve New York City. The three largest airports serving the city are *John F. Kennedy,* in southeastern Queens; *La Guardia,* in northern Queens; and *Newark,* in nearby New Jersey. A few private flights come in at *Teterboro,* in northeastern New Jersey. This choice of where your flight lands may be relevant, depending on where you are planning to stay in the metropolitan area.

By bus: The newly modernized Port Authority Building (8th Ave. at 41st St., 564–8484, Manhattan) is a fantastically busy place, with over 200 platforms where commuter and transcontinental buses alike load and unload. A few of the individual carriers who serve the region around New York City are: *Asbury Park-New York Transit; Garden State Coachways; Hudson Transit; Red and Tan Lines; Surburban Transit; Transport of New Jersey*—formerly known as *Public Service*— and *Lincoln Transit.* These all run from New Jersey.

From the Hudson Valley, try *Mohawk Coach Lines;* from Putnam and Dutchess Counties, call *Super Service.* The Berkshire area is connected to New York City by *Resort Bus Lines,* the Poconos by *Martz Trailways.* Of course, the busing giants, *Greyhound* and *Trailways,* have service to and from New York City from and to every region of the United States. Their passenger platforms are below street level in the terminal; those of the smaller lines are on the upper stories.

By car: The *Lincoln Tunnel* from New Jersey, and the *Midtown Tunnel* and *Queensboro Bridge* from Long Island, are the most direct arteries to mid-Manhattan. The *Holland Tunnel* from New Jersey, and the *Battery Tunnel* from Brooklyn, reach lower Manhattan. The *George Washington Bridge,* from New Jersey, and the *Triboro Bridge,* from Queens and the Bronx, give access to upper Manhattan.

The *Brooklyn-Queens Expressway,* from Queens and Long Island, and the *Verrazano-Narrows Bridge,* from Staten Island, will get you to Brooklyn. The expressway, of course, continues on through western Queens, which may also be reached from the north via the *Triboro Bridge.*

From upstate New York and New England, the city is accessible via many highways, both free and toll. The *New England Thruway* leads to the Bruckner Traffic Circle in the east Bronx, from which you may go to Queens *(Bronx Whitestone* or *Throgs Neck Bridges),* Manhattan *(Bruckner Expressway* and

Triboro Bridge) or the west Bronx and Manhattan *(Cross-Bronx Expressway)*. The *New York (Dewey) Thruway* extends via the *Major Deegan Expressway* (both I–87) to the south Bronx and Triboro Bridge. The bridge gives access to both Queens *(Grand Central Parkway)* and Manhattan *(Franklin D. Roosevelt Drive)*.

By train: Long-distance *Amtrak* routes reach New York from Chicago and the West, Washington, Florida and the South, plus Boston, Montreal, and Toronto, and all terminate in the city at either Grand Central Station (42nd to 46th Sts. on Park Avenue) or Penn Station (31st to 33rd Sts., 7th to 8th Avenues, 212–736–4545). Suburban lines stretch about 75 to 100 miles north *(ConRail's Harlem* and *Hudson Divisions,* 212–736–6000) and east *(New Haven* and *Long Island Railroads,* (212) 739–4200, operated by the Metropolitan Transportation Authority*)*. Both stations are quite good at giving out information; both have uncomfortable waiting areas. *Path Train Lines,* (201) 963–2558, service Jersey City, Newark, and Hoboken into Manhattan, terminating at the World Trade Center or Penn Station. All the commuter roads are notorious for their erratic service, lack of punctuality, and frequent equipment failure.

HOTELS AND MOTELS. Manhattan is an island literally filled with hotels, or so it seems when a visitor is trying to make up his or her mind where to stay. From the chic super-deluxe establishments to the modest, more reasonably priced ones, there is an incredibly wide range of accommodations available.

Those accustomed to the hotel situation in almost all other parts of the United States may be taken aback by (1) the paucity of motels in the city and (2) the lack of or limited parking areas at those that do exist. Motels by design were intended for motorists, and most everywhere but New York you can park in front of your motel room or in an open lot nearby. That is rarely the case in Manhattan, where space is at such a premium that monthly parking spots in some neighborhoods cost in excess of $200—the equivalent of rent for a studio or one-bedroom apartment in some other parts of the country.

Nor will you find the simple, inexpensive roadside stopover motels that are otherwise the norm in the U.S.—the $13.95–$21.95 double rooms complete with color TV, outdoor pool, etc. In other cities, or on the road, you can usually pull into one of these places in late afternoon and get a room for the night. As in so many other things, Manhattan is the exception. As for room rates, the $13.95–$21.95 range is about what you'd pay for a single at the YMCA or YWCA (details below); and no matter how much or how little you anticipate paying, it is always best to have a reservation ahead. That way you're assured of a room awaiting you upon arrival and that the rate will be confirmed. While you might be lucky once hitting town with no reservation and finding a suitable room, you might just as easily arrive simultaneously with five or six mammoth conventions—with not a room to be had.

HOTELS AND MOTELS

Another important suggestion in selecting a hotel or motel to suit your needs: If you have the luxury of planning ahead, consult a travel agent or, if you can get a copy ahead of time, the *Sunday New York Times Travel Section*. We've listed many hotels for you to choose from, including the range of rates for a *double* room—i.e., for two persons. Many of these hotels, however, offer special packages for visitors—particularly for non-expense-account sightseers. Most of these deals are built around weekend stays at reduced rates (when there are fewer businesspeople in town) and often include tickets to top Broadway shows, a bus tour, a bottle of wine or champagne on arrival, Sunday brunch (and the *Times*—a tradition among New Yorkers themselves) or other similar amenities.

Even if you have to pay a higher rate during the week, these weekend packages are definitely worth your consideration. In comparing them, however, be aware that in order to bring the numbers down to eye-catching appeal, some advertise the rate per person, based on double occupancy. Others give you the full weekend rate, all inclusive. Some are also available for one night, while others require longer stays. In other words, read the fine print carefully.

Because of the unique nature and diversity of New York City hotels and motels, we have tried to add a little extra detail to our general categories, and advise you to give consideration to geographic location as well as price and appointments. Getting around the city is time-consuming and expensive; thus a few extra dollars per night to be in the area in which you plan to spend most of your time (the theater district, lower Manhattan, the upper East Side, etc.) are probably well spent.

We've categorized our selection (it *is* only a selection) of New York's hotels based essentially on style, service, distinction of accommodations, and location. At the end of each individual listing we've included the range in price for a **double room for two people** as quoted at press time. You can expect that in most cases there will be very few rooms at the low end of the spectrum and many more at the higher end. In addition to these prices, there is also an occupancy tax charge included in your room rate (maximum $2), and the 8¼% New York City and State sales tax is added on to all hotel bills.

As a general guideline, our **super deluxe** category refers to the top hotels in Manhattan and, in fact, these few pinnacles of service and elegance rank with the finest hotels in the world. When the reality of the cost for such rarified atmosphere hits you—say, the $250 per night you'd have to spend for a double room overlooking Central Park at the Plaza—just remember that equivalent accommodations in London or Tokyo are almost double that price.

The **deluxe** hotels in our listing are only marginally less grand. The difference is one of history and tradition—either a slight fall from past glories or because they are so new and unproven—and is probably apparent only to those who cherish the nuance as much as the accommodation. These are all fine hotels and you can expect the maximum in service and comfort.

The **luxury** category is devoted to a select group of small- to medium-size hotels—most have 300 rooms or less—that aren't usually as centrally located as the super deluxe and deluxe establishments. Often they cater to business travelers, and their service therefore tends to be very personal. With few exceptions, the slight inconvenience of location (a plus for those who don't like being in the crush of things) is made up for by price and attention to detail. There are many excellent values in this grouping.

The hotels in our **first class** range include some more of the newer establishments and some of the convention-oriented "brand name" hotels that are also perfectly suitable for tourists. Their prices reflect the economy of today's world and while the accommodations are uniformly pleasant, they will often suffer from the sterile atmosphere that is so prevalent in contemporary large-scale hotels. This section also includes a few of the fine older hotels that have slipped from their former deluxe status. All hotels in this category will have a full range of services available, and such amenities as room service, television, and multiple in-hotel dining facilities are uniformly available.

The establishments include under **Motels, Chains** and **Simple But Practical** should be self-explanatory: serviceable places to rest your weary body at night but with little in the way of individuality or special services.

If you don't care where you sleep, the *New York Convention and Visitors Bureau* says there are always some rooms available somewhere, and they'll help you find one. Unfortunately the NYCVB closes at 6 P.M., so they are little help for late arrivals. And remember, prices quoted below are the range for a *double* room—one to be occupied by two people.

SUPER DELUXE

The Carlyle. 35 E. 76th St.; 744–1600. Located in one of New York's poshest residential areas, it is also handy to two of the city's best museums—the Metropolitan and the Whitney. All rooms are air-conditioned, suites have a pantry with refrigerator and some suites have private terraces and/or wood-burning fireplaces. The *Regency Room* offers elegant dining, and the *Bemelman's Bar* is decorated with murals by that whimsical artist himself. Bobby Short's piano often echoes in the Vertès-decorated Café Carlyle. There are 175 available rooms (the best are for full-time residents). Garage facilities. *$160–$185.*

Grand Hyatt New York. Park Ave. & 42nd St.; 883–1234. On the site of the old Commodore Hotel right next to Grand Central Station. This renovated masterpiece, done with lavish amounts of brass, glass, chrome and marble, features *nouvelle cuisine* at *Trumpet's* and a spectacular lounge overhanging 42nd St. Summer rates are available. *$110–$120.*

Helmsley Palace. 455 Madison Ave. at 50th St.; 888–1624. Constructed above and around the landmark Florentine Renaissance-styled Villard Mansions, originally built in 1855, the Helmsley is extravagantly rich-looking and in a location central to just about everything. Opened in late 1980 while construction was still going on, food and service are sadly still not up to the mark of the setting, the lushly appointed rooms or the locale. 875 rooms. *$115–$140.*

Marriott's Essex House. 160 Central Park South; 247–0300. Park Avenue has the reputation but Central Park South has the view, and is probably as attractive a location as can be found in the city. With 750 available rooms, the Essex House is one of the largest along this mini-hotel row, but it still manages to provide personal service along with its modern but Continental atmosphere. As is so for the other hotels along CPS, the Essex House is close to the Coliseum and Carnegie Hall, and not far from Lincoln Center or the theater district. *$110–$155*.

Park Lane. 36 Central Park South; 371–4000. A relatively new addition to the list of classic hotels on the southern boundary of Central Park, and one that quickly establishes itself as ranking right alongside them for dignity and service. There are views of the park, the skyline and, if you're high enough, the Hudson and East Rivers; a rooftop dining room; and a staff conversant in several languages. A favorite especially among knowledgeable foreign visitors. 640 rooms. *$110–$165*.

Pierre. 61st St. & Fifth Ave., opposite Central Park; 940–8100. This fine hotel, which opened in 1930, is primarily a residential hotel (cooperative apartments) and more than half of its 700 rooms are permanently occupied. Those which are not are available to transients, and these guests often occupy the highest echelons of society and celebrity. It's a favorite for entertaining, or you can be entertained in the *Café Pierre* or the *La Forêt* grill. *$165–$205*.

The Plaza. Fifth Ave. & 59th St.; 759–3000. The grandest hotel in the city has been on a major campaign to regain all its former glory, remodeling and touching up its public areas and redecorating rooms floor-by-floor. And even as the renovations have gone on, The Plaza has remained the most imposing and beautiful place to stay in New York. With Central Park on one side, and a small plaza complete with graceful fountain in front, this is New York's enclave of tradition and elegance in the European manner. None of the original 1907 flavor of this hotel has been lost. The 837 rooms are richly decorated, mostly in the French Provincial manner. Service is superb, the staff trained to the point of remembering guests' names—and using them. The Plaza's restaurants are famous in their own right, and include the staid *Oak Room*, the popular *Oyster Bar* (great for lunches and snacks), the *Palm Court* (where strolling musicians entertain during tea daily), the Hawaiian *Trader Vic's*, and the elegant *Edwardian Room*, where you dine by candlelight. *$125–$250*.

Regency. Park Ave. at 61st St.; 759–4100. French tapestries, Italian marble floors, gilt mirrors, guests such as Princess Grace, Audrey Hepburn, and Richard Burton (though the Beatles tried and never got in), and a garage ideally suited for 140 Rolls Royces—that's the level of elegance to be expected at the Regency. There are 500 rooms and suites, most decorated à la Louis XVI; telephones and scales in every bathroom; kitchenettes connected to many of the suites; the excellent *Le Restaurant*, offering Continental fare with French influence; and an exclusive bar and cocktail lounge. The Regency does not cater to such crass things as conventions; it does cater to the elite in business, society, and entertainment. *$135–$180*.

Sherry-Netherland. 781 Fifth Ave.; 355–2800. Though somewhat less well-known than its neighbors, the Plaza and the Pierre, the Sherry-Netherland is a distinguished hotel with an aura of grandeur all its own. The accent is unquestionably Continental and the atmosphere as sedate and elegant throughout the hotel as at the darkly graceful Sherry bar. The rooms are lovely and the location chic. 375 rooms. *$115–$175.*

DELUXE

Berkshire Place. 21 E. 52nd St.; 753–5800. Since it was refurbished in 1979, the Berkshire Place has become a most popular haunt, largely because of the *Rendezvous,* an attractive bar and restaurant on its main floor, and the bright garden-like atrium in the foyer. The rooms are simple and modern, the ambience young-and-on-the-go but with good attention to detail in the service. 420 rooms. *$125–$165.*

Harley. 214 E. 42nd St.; 490–8900. Another new Helmsley hotel, opened January 1981. Close to the United Nations but catering to the executive, the Harley is sleekly modern with such unusual touches as phone extensions in the bathrooms. 790 rooms. *$88–$112.*

Parker Meridien New York. 118 W. 57th St.; 245–5000. New (March 1981) and big (600 rooms), the Meridien is opened by Air France's hotel subsidiary. Unique features include a health club, rooftop pool, squash courts, jogging track, and that it is in walking distance from Carnegie Hall and the Russian Tea Room. The house restaurant, *Restaurant de France,* features *nouvelle cuisine. $110–$165.*

St. Moritz. 50 Central Park South; 755–5800. Another fine hotel on Central Park South, and although it is a little bit less expensive than the others, it doesn't sacrifice too much in the way of service or furnishings. Rooms are small but tastefully done, and the hotel is another favorite of foreign visitors. During the summer, the hotel sets up the *Café de la Paix* along the sidewalk. It may not be Paris, but the effect is still refreshing. 680 available units. *$85–$115.*

St. Regis-Sheraton. Fifth Ave. and 55th St.; 753–4500. The St. Regis represents the ultimate in Old World wealth and rococo elegance. John Jacob Astor IV built the place almost entirely of marble in 1904, intending it to be "not so much a hotel as a temporary home for those who are used to the best of everything, and who appreciate artistic surroundings." Although restoration of the hotel's full splendor is an on-going effort, many descendants of the famous "400," that original core of New York's social elite, still inhabit the St. Regis' 550 rooms. The hotel's luxury restaurants and bars are the *Oak Room,* the *King Cole Room* (which features excellent revues usually based on the work of Broadway songwriters), and *La Boîte. $79–$160.*

UN Plaza. 1 UN Plaza, at 44th St. and First Ave.; 355–3400. Facing the United Nations, this is an ultra-modern tower with great views from all rooms. Indoor pool, health club, indoor tennis, sauna, the works. The jazzy bar and restaurant is all-mirrored (which may lead to bumped noses as you enter), and typical of the sometimes garish decor of the rooms. Small lobby, comfortable rooms (some interesting duplex suites). 290 rooms. *$115–$135.*

Vista International. 3 World Trade Center; 938–9100. Opened July 1981. The first Hilton International property in the continental U.S., Vista provides every imaginable service from free shoeshines to a fitness center with pool and

HOTELS AND MOTELS

racquetball court to an executive business center (with secretarial help, Telex, library, and translation services) and four restaurants. 825 rooms. *$90–$115.*

Waldorf-Astoria. 301 Park Ave. at 50th St.; 355-3000. Some hotels seem to improve with age, and the Waldorf is in some ways a prime example. It is certainly the most renowned of American hotels, and the very mention of its name conjures up images of luxury. To a certain extent the reality lives up to the image. The Art Deco Park Avenue entrance is imposing, and the rooms are decorated in a gracious style, but it has lost much of its Old World charm. The neatly redone *Peacock Alley* is a popular jazz piano haunt, tucked away in the still-regal lobby, and the Waldorf is invariably host to countless distinguished guests. *$105–$185.*

LUXURY

Adams on the Park. 2 E. 86th St.; 744-1800. Right off Central Park, and a few blocks north of the Metropolitan Museum of Art, the feeling is European—borrowed from its eastward neighbors in the German-influenced Yorkville section. The large rooms have excellent views and are well kept if a little out-of-date. It is partially residential. 180 rooms. *$80–$86.*

Algonquin Hotel. 59 W. 44th St.; 840-6800. Long a favorite for its warm hospitality and literary history (its bar—and drinks are also served in the comfortable lobby lounge—and restaurant continue to be the watering hole and outpost of the *New Yorker* magazine staff), the Algonquin prides itself on the traditions of Europe's finest family-owned hotels. The modern comforts are here, the location absolutely perfect whatever your purpose in town, and the rates surprisingly reasonable. Steve Ross, a pianist specializing in Broadway show music, serenades the supper crowds. *$83–$85.*

Alrae. 37 E. 64th St.; 744-0200. A little-known luxury hotel just off Madison Ave., and in the prime of the high-fashion shopping zone. It is relatively small but gracious, and most of its guests live there on a long-term basis. Convenient, too, to uptown museums, galleries, and auction houses. 250 rooms. *$100.*

American Stanhope. Fifth Ave. at 81st St.; 288-5800. Its atmosphere is particularly gracious, and above all it features classic service. Shoes are polished if left outside the door at night; a baggagemaster will help guests arriving by ship clear their luggage through customs; and if the neighborhood—opposite the Metropolitan Museum of Art—seems a little out of the way, there's a free Rolls Royce shuttle service to 50th St. in the morning. Fine cuisine, elegant atmosphere in the *Saratoga Room*. And on a summer Sunday, having brunch outside at *The Terrace* as you watch the crowds amble to the Met is an experience you'll long remember. 275 rooms. *$90–$140.*

Doral Park Avenue. 70 Park Ave.; 687-7050. This hotel is a fairly recent addition to the ranks—an amalgam of a renovated hotel and a new building. The appointments are intended to be plush and there is definitely a predominance of luxury in all the rooms. It was decorated by Tom Lee, who was also responsible for the interiors of two sister hotels in Miami. Four blocks south of Grand Central Station. 200 rooms. *$90–$105.*

Dorset. 30 W. 54th St.; 247–7300. One of the lesser known of NYC's top stopping places, the Dorset is a very quiet, traditional hotel adjacent to the Museum of Modern Art and the corporate headquarters for such communications conglomerates as CBS, ABC, Capitol-EMI, and MGM. 190 available rooms. *$107–$140.*

Élysée. 60 E. 54th St.; 753–1066. This small hotel is elegantly tucked away between Madison and Park Avenues on 54th St. Its size permits the management to extend more than token service. Some individuality is maintained by assigning you a room having a name as well as a number, and the decor of each room varies. 110 units. *$95–$135.*

Gorham. 136 W. 55th St.; 245–1800. A small establishment very close to City Center, Carnegie Hall, the Museum of Modern Art and other midtown attractions. The accommodations aren't "luxurious," but they're relatively large, neat, and quiet. Most also have kitchenettes, and they're a bargain at the price. *$60.*

Gotham. 700 Fifth Ave. at 55th St.; 247–2200. Closed for renovations until mid-1982, but the new owners promise refurbished turn-of-the-century grace and elegance at this very central location.

Gramercy Park. 2 Lexington Ave.; 475–4320. Among the greatest beauties of London are its scattered parks and squares, forming oases in the city pattern. The namesake of this hotel is one of the few locations in the city that meets the London standard. The area is dignified and quiet. The hotel faces out on a small private park and is unpretentiously inviting. Yet many well-known rock groups stay here. Very comfortable bar. 500 rooms. *$65–$75.*

Kitano. 66 Park Ave. at 38th St.; 685–0022. New York's only Japanese owned and operated hotel, with half of its 80 rooms featuring Japanese decor. Good location, and a peaceful retreat with all the niceties of Oriental attention to detail. Excellent and beautifully done Japanese restaurant off the lobby on the second floor. *$80.*

Lombardy. 111 E. 56th St.; 753–8600. This ultra-smart hotel allows you a chance to stay in grand surroundings in a fine location. The rooms offer large distinguished accommodations, and Continental breakfast is included in the rates. Quite sumptuous, as is the outstanding French restaurant on the main floor, *Laurent.* 350 rooms. *$120.*

Mayflower. 15 Central Park West, at 61st St.; 265–0060. Unpretentious but most accommodating, this is the type of hotel New Yorkers wish they knew about to recommend for visiting friends. The views of Central Park are as good as from the south, and the feeling is simple friendliness. Close to Lincoln Center, Carnegie Hall, and the Coliseum but convenient via the Columbus Circle bus and train stations to just about everything. 240 available rooms. *$90–$105.*

Navarro. 112 Central Park South; 757–1900. All the advantages inherent in the address—good view of the park, proximity to Broadway, Fifth Avenue, and Lincoln Center, Upper East Side stores—and, because it is smaller than most of its neighbors, puts the accent on customized service. Elegant, with lovely, ample rooms. 135 rooms. *$102–$124.*

Sheraton-Russell. 45 Park Ave., at 37th St.; 685–7676. Located on Murray Hill and a little removed from the heart of the city, the Sheraton-Russell offers

HOTELS AND MOTELS

a calm dignity that contrasts well with the trials of city life. The hotel is used mainly by businesspeople, but its generous rooms, some with fireplaces, should appeal to other visitors. 170 rooms, parking facilities. *$79–$118.*

Shoreham. 33 W. 55th St.; 247–6700. A small hotel just off Fifth Ave., the Shoreham presents a dignified appearance and is splendidly located for shopping activities, the Museum of Modern Art, and Broadway. The rooms are modest but clean and each has its own pantry. 150 rooms. *$60–$70.*

Tudor. 304 E. 42nd St.; 986–8800. On the East Side of the city and a part of the Tudor City apartment complex, this hotel is near the UN and not far from Grand Central. The area is pleasant, quiet, and refined, and so are the accommodations, which have been recently refurbished. 475 rooms. *$66–$125.*

Tuscany. 120 E. 39th St., 686–1600. This is a smaller luxury hotel also just south of Grand Central. All of its rooms are studios, complete with service pantries and other extras, such as bathroom telephones and color televisions. It is residential and transient. 270 rooms. *$110–$115.*

Westbury. 840 Madison Ave. at 69th St.; 535–2000. In many ways this is one of the better hotels in the city. The neighborhood surroundings are unimpeachable (especially for high-fashion shoppers, museum buffs, and gallery browsers), and the dignified tone of the hotel is intended to complement them. The furnishings reflect a grand style and the rooms are tastefully comfortable. Farther uptown than most, this hotel's personal attention and ambience more than make up for any inconvenience. 325 rooms. *$130–$150.*

FIRST CLASS

Barbizon-Plaza. 106 Central Park South; 247–7000. With the advantages of a view overlooking the park and central location, this large hotel is a bargain in its neighborhood. It is often bustling with tours and conventions, but relief from these can be found in the generally bright rooms. 800 rooms, garage facilities. *$84–$95.*

Halloran House. Lexington Ave. & 49th St.; 755–4000. (Formerly the Shelton.) Opened in 1978 following extensive refurnishing. Excellent midtown location. Affiliated with Howard Johnson reservation service. First major NYC hotel with woman manager; also first with woman "doorperson" at entrance. 650 rooms. *$93–$108.*

Intercontinental New York. 111 E. 48th St.; 755–5900. (Formerly the Barclay.) Located half a block off Park Ave., one of this hotel's prime advantages is a degree of withdrawal from the bustle of the city while still being at the heart of the goings-on. This is an older, gracious hotel with pleasant, spacious atmosphere. Live birds frolic in the aviary in the lobby, restored to its original 1920s grandeur as part of a recent renovation. *The Barclay Restaurant* is quite nice. 770 rooms, garage facilities. *$113.*

Loew's Drake. 440 Park Ave.; 421–0900. The Drake underwent a major modernization and restoration program in 1979, and the rejuvenation has been effective and tasteful. In addition to having pleasant surroundings the hotel is well located, with telephone and loudspeaker in each of the new bathrooms.

There is also a lobby lounge, full concierge service and the new *Wellington Grill*. 640 rooms. *$115–$160.*

Loew's Summit. Lexington Ave. & 51st St.; 752-7000. The Summit has been completely redone in recent years. Ultra-modern guest rooms; lobby cocktail lounge; *Maude's* turn-of-the-century restaurant; Tower Suites; color televisions; refrigerators; phone in bathroom. ESP (Extra Special People) floor for those who want super-deluxe special services. Concierge. 770 rooms, garage. *$82–$97.*

Loew's Warwick. 65 W. 54th St.; 247-2700. The harried pace and uninspired lobby are misleading here. Once upstairs the rooms bespeak a simple, straight-forward elegance. The hotel attracts people in the communications, advertising, recording, and fashion industries, but it has all that is necessary to appeal to the average appreciative visitor. The rooms are large and generally handsome. *Sir Walter's Restaurant* has long been a favorite of show people. 500 rooms. *$100–$115.*

New York Hilton. 1335 Ave. of the Americas; 586-7000. The Hilton name is becoming synonymous with large, fancy, modern (and impersonal) hotels; this one is no exception. One of the biggest and most popular among conventioneers and tourists alike, the Hilton can offer such conveniences as extra-long beds and heated bathroom floors. Central to everything in midtown. There is also entertainment in the way of jazz combos at *Sybil's.* 2130 rooms. *$89–$129.*

New York Sheraton. Seventh Ave. & 56th St.; 247-8000. Standing in the lobby here is something akin to trying to meet somebody at the information booth in Penn Station. Tours are constantly arriving and leaving, the people who work at the hotel are rarely cognizant of which are which or who's who. Upstairs is as quiet as being in midtown ever gets and the rooms are attractive—some even luxurious. If you can get by without much in the way of service you'll be fine. 1600 rooms. *$57–$105.*

New York Statler. 401 Seventh Ave., at 33 St.; 736-5000. This is a huge (1700 rooms), busy hotel directly across from Penn Station and Madison Square Garden and practically in the heart of the garment center. Very popular among businesspeople trying to get in and out of the city quickly, and among those coming into town for concerts, sporting events, or trade shows being held at the Garden. The rooms are unspectacular but comfortable. *$74–$104.*

Roosevelt. 45 E. 45th St.; 661-9600. Its location on lower Madison Avenue near Grand Central Station is its most positive advantage. The accommodations give little hint of the hotel's once stately past. There is talk of its being closed and the building sold. 1075 rooms. *$71–$104.*

Sheraton Centre. 801 Seventh Ave. between 52nd & 53rd Sts.; 581-1000. Formerly the Americana. The new owners have done more than refurbish—they've essentially redesigned the lower public floors and meeting rooms in order to make them more attractive and more practical. With 50 floors, the Sheraton Centre lacks warmth and the rooms tend to be small, but many opt for it simply because it is situated so close to the theater district. There are five restaurants, including a disco. *$64–$145.*

Sheraton City Squire. 790 Seventh Ave.; 581-3300. In recent years a number of motels have been built in the city, mainly on the West Side. They are uniformly modern and attractive. The City Squire is one of the better ones, and closer to the city's activities than most. An indoor swimming pool is also open to the public for a fee. 700 rooms. *$57–$110.*

Southgate Towers. 371 Seventh Ave.; 563–1800. Opposite Penn Station on 31st St., this large hotel is somewhat removed from the main attractions and tends to attract people doing business in the garment center directly to the south. Accommodations are suitable to most ordinary demands. 1200 rooms, garage facilities. *$78.*

MOTELS, CHAINS, AND SIMPLE BUT PRACTICAL

Bedford. 118 E. 40th St.; 697–4800. A small, almost inconspicuous hotel two blocks south of Grand Central, the Bedford offers pleasant rooms, all with serving pantries. It attracts mostly businesspeople. *$79–$89.*

Best Western Skyline Motor Inn. 725 Tenth Ave. at 50th St.; 586–3400. One of the first real "motels" built in New York. Quite far west but comfortable and within walking distance to most theaters. That walk late at night, however, is not suggested. Indoor pool, free parking. *$64.*

Beverly. 125 E. 50th St.; 753–2700. Transient guests are usually business types, though tourists have found it increasingly well-suited to their needs. Some of the suites have pantries and terraces. Comfortable though not distinguished. *Kenny's Steak Pub* downstairs. 300 rooms. *$89.*

Blackstone. 50 E. 58th St.; 355–4200. A good midtown address, convenient to the best of the city's shops, theaters, and movies. 200 rooms. *$75.*

Chelsea. 222 W. 23rd St.; 243–3700. The Chelsea probably deserves a category unto itself—a study in contradictions, and totally unique among New York hotels. It was the first hotel in the city designated a historic and architectural landmark. It has a long history of sheltering creative talent—including the likes of Mark Twain, Thomas Wolfe, Dylan Thomas, Brendan Behan, Arthur Miller, Virgil Thomson, Ben Shahn, and Larry Rivers, to name a few. Some of the Chelsea's history is described in our *Walking Tours* section, and it is worth a brief visit even if you stay elsewhere. Today it is, shall we say, funky, attracting many rock stars who use it as home base when in New York. It is not for everyone. 400 rooms. *$45.*

Doral Inn. 541 Lexington Ave.; 755–1200. (Formerly the Belmont Plaza.) One of several commercial hotels along Lexington in the upper 40s. There is nothing impressive about it, but it is comfortable and centrally located. Frequented by airline personnel and often the site of labor negotiations. 700 rooms. *$82.*

Empire. 44 W. 63rd St. at Broadway; 265–7400. Located opposite Lincoln Center, you'd expect this once-flourishing hotel to be ritzy to the hilt. It is not. It is simple and modestly comfortable, popular for organized tours and among visiting musicians and performers. Weekly rates available. 600 rooms. *$60–$75.*

Executive. 237 Madison Ave.; 686–0300. More of a business person's hostelry, this is a small hotel for transients and residents a few blocks south of Grand

Central. The atmosphere is modest, the rooms plain. Continental breakfast. 110 rooms. *$68–$78.*

Holiday Inn–Coliseum. 440 W. 57th St., between Ninth and Tenth Aves.; 581–8100. A bit off the beaten track, but the location avoids a lot of traffic for those arriving via the Jersey approaches to the city. Decor and room appointments conform to the standards of the chain. Rooftop pool and kennel. 600 rooms. *$81.*

Howard Johnson's Motor Lodge. Eighth Ave. between 51st and 52nd Sts.; 581–4100. Right in the heart of the theater district and a few blocks from "Restaurant Row." Color televisions, radio, in-room movies. Free guest parking. Cocktail lounge and restaurant. 300 rooms. *$67–$77.*

Iroquois. 49 W. 44th St.; 840–3080. Right next door to the posher Algonquin, this is an adequately serviceable family favorite. Weekly rates are even more attractive than the daily ones. *$45.*

Lexington. 511 Lexington Ave.; 755–4400. This is a good hotel which was recently renovated. The rooms are more than adequate even if the decor is routine. If you care to trip the light fantastic Spanish-style, the *Chateau Madrid* supperclub is downstairs. 800 rooms. *$80–$250* (latter for a double suite).

Mansfield. 12 W. 44th St.; 944–6050. The location is good, just off Fifth Ave., and not far from Times Square. The Harvard and Princeton clubs are virtually next door. There are no pretensions and the quarters are agreeable. The staff is particularly good for a hotel in this price range. 200 rooms. *$44–$48.*

Murray Hill. 42 W. 35th St.; 947–0200. A small hotel offering quiet in a busy neighborhood. Pleasant, large rooms. Near *Altman's* and *Lord & Taylor,* but not in the Murray Hill district itself. 140 rooms. *$50.*

Picadilly. 227 W. 45th St.; 246–6600. One of the best hotels in its area, with warmth, charm, and comfortably adequate rooms. Directly in the heart of the theater district, across from Shubert Alley. 550 rooms. A theatergoers' delight. *$49–$52.*

Ramada Inn–Midtown. 790 Eighth Ave., between 48th & 49th Sts.; 581–7000. Center of the theater district. Color televisions, radio, in-room movies. Free guest parking. Cocktail lounge and rooftop restaurant. Rooftop pool (seasonal). 370 rooms. *$62–$77.*

Roger Smith. 501 Lexington Ave.; 755–1400. An unexceptional businessman's hotel near Grand Central. Its rooms are adequate and comfortable, though hardly distinguished. 200 rooms. *$60–$77.*

Rosoff's. 147 W. 43rd St.; 582–3200. A Times Square landmark since the turn of the century, you can easily miss this hotel because it shares an entrance with the restaurant of the same name. The gaudy entry belies the 45 simple rooms within. Good value for basic accommodations. *$40.*

Royalton. 44 W. 44th St.; 730–1344. This quiet, dignified hotel is situated near the Harvard Club and the Algonquin. A favorite with visiting British business people. Good value for the price. 175 rooms. *$58–$85.*

Seymour. 50 W. 45th St.; 840–3481. A pleasant, older hotel, somewhat modernized, with large rooms. 250 units. *$50.*

HOTELS AND MOTELS 141

Taft. Seventh Ave. and 50th St.; 247-4000. A very large old hotel a few blocks above Times Square and close to most theaters. The hotel is unpretentious—to be generous—and the rooms mostly modest. Its size makes it popular for meetings, conventions, and with travel groups. 1300 rooms. *$60–$65.*

Travel Inn Motor Hotel. 515 W. 42nd St.; 695-7171. Almost beside the Manhattan-side Lincoln Tunnel exit, the location is particularly convenient for those entering the city from the west. Off the mainstream but convenient to the 42nd St. crosstown bus. Pool. Parking. 250 rooms. *$54.*

Wales. 1295 Madison Ave.; 876-6000. The location on E. 92nd St. places guests in the heart of one of NYC's best neighborhoods, and close to the Metropolitan Museum of Art—though it is a mite uptown from the heart of the city. 100 clean and functional rooms, some with views of Central Park. *$32–$50.*

Wellington. 871 Seventh Ave.; 247-3900. Convenient to Carnegie Hall, the Coliseum, Broadway, and the Stage Deli. The rooms are contemporary but the hotel rundown. Provides most of the services of more expensive establishments to compensate. Used often by airline personnel. 700 rooms. *$54–$60.*

Windsor. 100 W. 58th St.; 265-2100. The accommodations here are considered good but plain. No attempt is made to transport you to another world, but rather to give you solid comfort. Close to the Coliseum, Carnegie Hall, and Fifth Ave. 300 rooms. *$80–$90* (year-round weekend rate: $40).

Wyndham. 42 W. 58th St.; 753-3500. Modest though undistinguished, the Wyndham is close to Carnegie Hall, Fifth Ave., and Central Park. Functional rooms, no room service. A favorite among theatrical and musical folk. 225 rooms. *$72–$76.*

ROCK BOTTOM AND LOWER

Although a handful of establishments in the *Motels, Chains, and Simple But Practical* category offer accommodations in the $50-and-under bracket, we would find it difficult to recommend most others without telling you to look at what you're getting before you make a reservation—not usually a practical way of doing things if you're trying to plan ahead. Many YMCAs and YWCAs, however, have rooms at very reasonable rates—beginning with singles at $13 a night. Sometimes they are limited to students and other young people, but check with the individual Y for specifics. Also, as with regular hotels, it is essential to make reservations well in advance for weekends, holidays, and other peak periods. Among the possibilities in Manhattan (see the Yellow Pages for those in the other boroughs):

Allerton House, 130 E. 57th St.; $20 and up single, women only. *Martha Washington Hotel,* 29 E. 29th St.; $20 single, women only. *William Sloane House YMCA,* 356 W. 34th St.; $15 single, $20 double; men and women. *West Side YMCA,* 5 W. 63rd St.; $18 single, men and a limited number of women. *Vanderbilt YMCA,* 224 E. 47th St.; $16 single, $22 double. Though they say they only accept men, they do also accept groups of women. *McBurney YMCA,* 215 W. 23rd St.; $13 single, men only. *International House of New York,* 500

Riverside Dr.; $75 per week, men and women. Accepts transient graduate students from May through August only.

THE OUTLYING BOROUGHS

Most of the hotels and motels outside Manhattan are grouped around two of the major metro airports—La Guardia and JFK, both of which are in Queens. Obviously the pace at these is going to be frantic, with guests constantly arriving and departing and with planes almost always buzzing overhead. Still, they are convenient for overnight stopovers, and those near JFK are also in close proximity to Aqueduct and Belmont racetracks. Prices indicated for the following generally reliable establishments are for doubles: **Hilton Inn at JFK,** 322–8700, *$71–$108;* **Holiday Inn of La Guardia,** 898–1225, *$80–$85;* **International TraveLodge at JFK,** 995–9000, *$65–$79;* **Howard Johnson's Kennedy Airport,** 659–6000, *$65;* **Sheraton Inn La Guardia,** 446–4800, *$90.*

Two other nearby possibilities in the Bronx bear mentioning for their close driving proximity to the city: **Capri Whitestone,** 555 Hutchinson River Parkway at the Bronx Whitestone Bridge tollgate, 597–0600; and **Van Cortlandt,** 6393 Broadway at 256th St., 549–7272. Both have doubles available for well under *$30.*

TELEPHONES: The area code for all five boroughs of New York City is 212. You do not need to dial the area code if it is the same as the one from which you are calling. Information (known as directory assistance) is 555–1212. When direct-dialing a long-distance number from within New York City, you must dial the number "1" (one) *before* you dial the area code and the number itself. An operator will assist you on person-to-person, credit-card, and collect calls if you dial "0" first. Pay telephones still start at 10 cents—one of the miracles of the modern world.

HOW TO GET AROUND. For those using public transportation, a handy number to keep in mind is the *New York City Transit Information* phone, (212) 330–1234. Open 24 hours a day, they'll give you the best route from wherever you are to wherever you're going. If calling from a phone booth, however, have a few extra nickels ready—the wait "on hold" can be a while.

By subway: The city's extraordinary subway system is your best bet for speed-thrift-convenience—usually. Late at night, when waits between trains are much longer, safety is a problem. When traveling at night, stay at or near the center of the train. Police patrol is spotty, so the volunteer Guardian Angels group (look for them in their white T-shirts and red berets) do their civic best to deter foul play on the trains. The weekday rush hours, usually cruelly overcrowded, are particularly oppressive on very hot summer days.

Of course, you'll want to know what stop is closest to your destination. A pocket atlas—obtainable at book stores and in the magazine kiosk on the Times

HOW TO GET AROUND 143

Square island (between 7th Ave. and Broadway, just north of 42nd St.)—superimposes subway routes onto the street maps. Once you've targeted the proper stop, check a map of the subway system—you can get one at any token booth or at the New York Convention and Visitors Bureau (at Columbus Circle). Subway maps also appear in the Yellow Pages for each borough. The map's main fault is that it is not drawn to scale. Rather, it enlarges areas such as downtown Brooklyn, mid-Manhattan and Jackson Heights, Queens, where many routes converge and mass changes from train to train occur at busy times. But it does help.

With the map you can utilize every stretch of track in the vast network. But remember to study it before you embark on a subway adventure. *Don't* grab a map as you rush to catch a train and expect to unfold and read it on a crowded platform en route. Use it patiently. You'll see, for example, that you can get from major terminals (Times Square; Roosevelt Ave.–Jackson Heights, Queens; Atlantic Ave.–downtown Brooklyn) to all but a few stops with no more than one change of train. And if you still have questions—about routes, schedules, rates—ask at a change booth or a conductor. Or call the Metropolitan Transit Authority, 330-1234.

A subway token costs 75 cents at press time. Reduced fares are offered Senior Citizens and the handicapped during certain hours. Note: You can use subway tokens on city buses, and get a free transfer, too.

Be cautious about using the subways after 7:00 P.M. If you must, stay on the platform in view of the entrance; on the train, travel in a middle car, near the conductor.

A trip to *Rockaway* (Queens) will cost an extra token each way south of *Broad Channel*. Staten Island has a surface train from the ferry at St. George to Tottenville.

Remember: Some trains have more than one route, depending on the time of day. It's all clearly explained on the map.

By automobile. While we urge all visitors not to attempt touring Manhattan by automobile, some people may wish to have a car at their disposal for trips to the outlying boroughs or for travel to other areas. It is worth noting that car-rental rates are considerably cheaper when you pick up a car at one of the airports than they are when renting from midtown locations operated by the same companies. Similarly, parking cars at centrally located midtown hotels is far more expensive than leaving them at lots and garages on the far west side of the island. Just make sure of the hours these garages are open so that you'll be able to retrieve your car when you want to. For short stays in the theater district, the Municipal Garage, which can be entered from 53rd and 54th Sts. between Broadway and Eighth Aves., is relatively inexpensive. In other garages, don't be surprised having to pay $8 to $10 for two hours' parking. Many restaurants (including Windows on the World at the World Trade Center) will "validate" your parking stub, entitling you to a discount or free parking at *designated* garages.

Trying to drive around in Manhattan can be an educational, if searing, experience. The main drawbacks: heavy traffic, scarcity of legal parking spots,

144　　　　　　　　　　　NEW YORK CITY

and very expensive garages—and unbelievable, car-wracking potholes. The police in Manhattan *will* quickly remove an illegally parked car from a zone marked "tow away," and it will cost at least $65 *in cash* to get it back. (You'll also get a parking violation ticket!) No excuse or plea sways the officers who man the West Side pier where cars are stored (these may be argued later in court), so prepare to pay. Better yet, don't drive or park illegally, or, best of all, forget about driving, except on weekends and holidays.

If you insist on driving, let's take the parkways first. *Manhattan's West Side Highway* is undergoing repairs south of 72nd St. and is closed south of 57th Street. Its future is uncertain. North of there, it parallels the Hudson and meets I–95 where the George Washington Bridge (to New Jersey) becomes the *Cross-Bronx Expressway* (to the Bronx and New England or to Long Island via the Triboro Bridge). The West Side Highway continues north, crossing the Harlem River into the West Bronx, where it is called the *Henry Hudson Parkway*. It leaves the city above Van Cortlandt Park and goes through Yonkers into Westchester.

On the east side of Manhattan, with access to the Brooklyn Bridge, the *Franklin D. Roosevelt Drive* (also called *East River Drive*) runs from the Battery to 125th St. and to the bridges to Queens (Triboro) and the Bronx (Willis Avenue). The road still continues beyond 125th St., however, along the east side of Manhattan, under the name *Harlem River Drive*. On it, you can get to upper Manhattan (Washington Heights and Inwood sections) or cut off to I–95 (George Washington Bridge west, Cross-Bronx Expressway east). The F.D.R. Drive, being rehabilitated one portion at a time, is old, twisting, subject to dense traffic and, in a heavy rain, flooding.

The *Bronx* has three big, relatively new roads. The *Cross-Bronx Expressway* (I–95) passes through the Bronx at about 174th St. and has exits onto almost every major north-south avenue. From west to east, it also gives access to the *Major Deegan Expressway* (I–87, the southern extension of the Thruway).

The *Bronx River Parkway* (to White Plains and central Westchester) terminates at the new Bruckner Traffic Circle. At that gigantic interchange, you can go to New England via I–95 or eastern Queens via the Whitestone or Throgs Neck Bridges.

The Bruckner Circle also leads to another major highway in the borough, the *Bruckner Expressway,* which runs southwest to the Triboro Bridge. Use the bridge to reach Manhattan or Queens. If you don't take the Triboro, the same road also loops around the southern tip of the Bronx and heads up the west shore of that borough as the Major Deegan Expressway (I–87). It has exits for Yankee Stadium and for the Cross-Bronx Expressway, and moves out of the Bronx as the New York State Thruway, later passing by Yonkers Raceway.

Queens is accessible from the west by two highways. From the Triboro Bridge, the *Grand Central Parkway* runs through the northwestern communities of Astoria and Jackson Heights, passing La Guardia Airport and Shea Stadium. After an interchange with the *Long Island Expressway* (I–495), it dips south,

HOW TO GET AROUND 145

touching Forest Hills and Kew Gardens, then bolts away to the northeast again, past Springfield Gardens and Queens Village. The Long Island Expressway runs fairly straight west to east from the Queens Midtown Tunnel (E. 36th St., Manhattan) as far as Rego Park (you'll see Lefrak City and other high-rise developments crowding in on both sides). Then it jogs northeast, connects via the *Grand Central Parkway* to Kennedy Airport and continues on to Nassau and Suffolk Counties. These two roads are the principal automotive corridors for commuters, shoppers and theatergoers from Long Island, and traffic is invariably formidable.

The main north-south highways in Queens are the *Brooklyn-Queens Expressway, Van Wyck Expressway,* and *Cross Island Parkway.* The first begins just east of the Triboro Bridge ("Brooklyn" exit from the Grand Central Parkway) and has interchanges with most major Queens thoroughfares as it passes over the mainly industrial western edge of that borough. The last exit in Queens is to the Long Island Expressway (L.I.E.).

The Van Wyck, important as the road to Kennedy Airport, connects with the *Southern State Parkway* for Nassau County. It intersects the Grand Central Parkway (which you must take to get onto the L.I.E.) and then becomes the Whitestone Expressway (I–678) through Whitestone and Bayside, Queens, on its way to the Bronx Whitestone Bridge. The Van Wyck is almost invariably— except, maybe, at 3:30 A.M.—snarled with traffic; leave early if you plan to use it.

The Cross Island starts in the north at the Whitestone Bridge and roughly parallels the north shore of Queens until it crosses Union Turnpike (a city street). Then it angles south past the Belmont Racetrack and traces the borough's eastern border until it is swallowed up by the Southern Parkway just east of Kennedy Airport. (Note: as your map will confirm, Southern and Southern *State* Parkways are not quite the same.)

Let's continue into *Brooklyn* with the Southern Parkway. Known as the Belt Parkway or Shore Road in Brooklyn, it girdles the entire borough along the southeast boundary around to the L.I.E. at the northwest. Major exits include Cross Bay Blvd. (to Rockaway), Flatbush Ave. (to Canarsie and eastern Flatbush), Ocean Parkway (to Sheepshead Bay) and Cropsey Ave. (to Coney Island and Bensonhurst). Along the way, you'll see signs for the Verrazano-Narrows Bridge to Staten Island. The Belt Parkway, after passing under that huge span, continues up the west shore past Bay Ridge (exit at 65th St.) and Borough Park (exit at Prospect Expressway). Finally, it reaches downtown Brooklyn and the three main routes to Manhattan (Battery Tunnel and the Brooklyn and Manhattan Bridges). Having now changed its name to the Brooklyn-Queens Expressway, the highway passes over Williamsburg and Greenpoint. If you're heading in the opposite direction—*from* Queens—you'll have a chance to cut over the Williamsburg Bridge onto Delancey Street in Manhattan.

NEW YORK CITY

CITY STREETS

Manhattan has probably the most regular and gridlike pattern, except that the *Lower East Side* and *Greenwich Village*, two of its most interesting and vital neighborhoods, lie outside the grid. (Another confusing area for out-of-town drivers: downtown—the *Wall Street* area.) Almost all the east-west streets and most of the north-south avenues are one-way. The two-way streets are spaced rather evenly from south to north: Canal, Houston, 14th, 23rd, 34th, 42nd, 57th, 72nd, 79th, 86th, 96th, 106th, 116th, 125th, 135th, and 145th. North of that, the island is considerably narrower and the last really wide one is 207th, just about a mile from the upper end of the borough.

All the north-south avenues are parallel except Broadway, whose traffic winds from northwest (the 225th Street Bridge to the Bronx) to southeast *(South Ferry)*. Traffic on Broadway is one-way southbound below 59th Street, two-way above there. An attractive parallel alternative to the West Side Highway (which is invariably under construction and snarled with traffic) is Riverside Drive from 72nd Street to the George Washington Bridge.

Central Park offers a lovely interior roadway. It is beautiful, especially at night, when thousands of distant skyscraper lights are framed by trees. This road is closed to motorists on weekends during the day and occasional summer evenings for the benefit of the city's many bike-riders.

The table on the next page will help you find your way around town.

Brooklyn is accessible from lower Manhattan via three bridges. The most northerly is the *Williamsburg*, from Delancey St., followed by the *Manhattan* (Canal St.) and the *Brooklyn* (Chambers St.). Broadway will take you to Canal St. or Chambers St., and for Delancey, take Bowery, which is just a continuation of 3rd Ave. below 9th St.

Brooklyn is often said to be impossible to navigate (perhaps Thomas Wolfe had this in mind when he wrote his famous short story, "Only the Dead Know Brooklyn"). But this reputation is undeserved. Most neighborhoods there are also grids; problems arise only because they meet one another at odd angles (note the half-left turns in the routes outlined below). Brooklyn's most famous street, Flatbush Ave., runs diagonally from northwest (at the Manhattan Bridge) to southeast *(Marine Park, Floyd Bennett Airfield* and the Belt Parkway). Along the way it passes through *Prospect Park* and very near the *Brooklyn Museum*. From the opposite direction, southwest, corner of Prospect Park, three wide and well-maintained roads run almost due south toward the Atlantic: Ocean Parkway, Ocean Ave. and Coney Island Ave. About two miles farther east, Utica and Ralph Avenues trace parallel paths through *Crown Heights, Brownsville,* and *Flatlands*.

Routes across the breadth of Brooklyn are more complicated. The only continuous one is Atlantic Ave., from the East River to the Queens border, on the north edge of the borough. In the center, take 39th St. (eastbound exit from the Belt Parkway) across *Borough Park* to McDonald Ave. Turn right, then quickly left on Ave. F, which you follow to Coney Island Ave. Turn right and

HOW TO GET AROUND 147

KEY TO MANHATTAN STREET NUMBERS

Here is a handy guide to finding most addresses in Manhattan. To get the cross street nearest to a building number, just cancel the last figure of the building's number. Divide remainder by two and add the key number below. Result is approximately the nearest cross street.

Ave. A, B, C, D 3	8th Ave. 9
1st Ave. 3	9th, 10th 13
2nd Ave. 3	11th Ave. 15
3rd Ave. 10	Amsterdam Ave. 59
4th Ave. 8	Columbus Ave. 59
5th Ave.	Lexington Ave. 22
1 to 200 13	Madison Avenue 27
201 to 400 16	Park Ave. 34
401 to 600 18	West End 59
601 to 775 20	Central Park West .... *
776 to 1286 .... *	Riverside Drive .... *
Avenue of the	Broadway
Americas .... Deduct 12	1 to 754 ... Below 8th St.
7th Ave.	754 to 858 ...... Deduct 29
1 to 1800 12	858 to 958 ...... Deduct 25
Above 1800 20	Above 1000 ...... Deduct 31

To find street numbers on cross streets commence as follows:

EAST SIDE	WEST SIDE
1 at 5th Avenue	1 at 5th Avenue
101 " Park Ave., Park Ave. South or 4th Avenue	101 " 6th Ave. (Ave. of Americas)
201 " 3rd Avenue	201 " 7th Avenue
301 " 2nd Avenue	301 " 8th Avenue
401 " 1st Avenue	401 " 9th Avenue
501 " York or Avenue A	501 " 10th Avenue
601 " Avenue B	601 " 11th Avenue

*Exceptions: Cancel last figure of house number and add or deduct key:

5th Avenue	Riverside Drive
775 to 1286 .... Deduct 18	1 to 567 .... Add 73
Central Park West .... Add 60	Above 567 .... Add 78

Example: 350 Park Ave. Cancel last figure (0), divide by 2, and add key number (34). **Answer: 51st Street.**

at Ave. J, turn left. This avenue runs block after block through the lovely and peaceful residential area of *Flatbush*. When you cross Utica Ave., start watching for Flatlands Ave., where you take a half-left. Flatlands keeps you on the crosstown route, becoming Fairfield in the *East New York* region. Follow on to Fountain, the border between Brooklyn and Queens. Take a left to Linden Blvd., then a right. In about a mile, Linden meets the Southern Parkway, west of *Kennedy Airport*. If you continue on Linden, you'll soon reach the *Aqueduct Racetrack*.

The southern tier of the borough contains the comparatively conservative communities of *Bay Ridge, Fort Hamilton, Bensonhurst, Sheepshead Bay,* and *Canarsie*. The route through here is, from the west, 86th St. to Stillwell Ave., where you take a half left onto Ave. U and follow it east to Flatbush Ave. near *Marine Park*.

It might be helpful to know about a few main streets in *Queens*. One route across the borough, west to east, begins with Metropolitan Ave. (exit from the southbound Brooklyn-Queens Expressway). It passes through a mostly industrial area at first, but soon becomes the main street in the *Ridgewood-Glendale* neighborhood you've probably seen in the opening of *All in the Family*. This is Archie Bunker "country." In *Forest Hills*, a block beyond 75th Ave., go left onto Union Turnpike, which angles northeast through *Kew Gardens, Flushing,* and *Bellerose*. It passes two of Queen's largest parks, *Cunningham* and *Alley*, before crossing into Nassau County.

The lower level of the Queensboro (59th St.) Bridge out of Manhattan lets the driver choose between the borough's two busiest roads, Queens Blvd. and Northern Blvd. The first runs east, connecting with Woodhaven Blvd. (to *Rockaway*), and the L.I.E., then curves south connecting with the Van Wyck Expressway (JFK Airport or the Bronx Whitestone Bridge) and leads onto Hillside Ave. (eastern Queens communities, *Hillside, Hollis,* and *Queens Village*.)

Northern Boulevard runs northeast past *La Guardia Airport,* the Grand Central Parkway-Van Wyck Expressway interchange, Shea Stadium and the *Flushing, Auburndale,* and *Bayside* areas. It is State Rte. 25A and continues into Nassau at *Great Neck*.

North-south through streets are scarce in Queens. In western Queens, use the Brooklyn-Queens Expressway; in east Queens, the Cross Island Parkway. In between, Woodhaven Blvd. runs from Queens Blvd. (at about 97th St.) south to *Rockaway*, becoming Cross Bay Blvd. en route. The Whitestone/Van Wyck Expressway combination goes from the Whitestone Bridge to Kennedy Airport at about 136th St. and thus serves *Whitestone, Murray Hill, Corona, Kew Gardens, Jamaica,* and *South Ozone Park*.

The Bronx is probably the most confusing of the four most populous boroughs. In the west Bronx, the main north-south roads are Jerome Ave. and Grand Concourse, the latter much broader and more attractive, but ending about 205th St. (The Grand Concourse serves as the east-west divider for the Bronx.) Jerome Ave. runs from *Yankee Stadium* all the way to Westchester, with driving made somewhat more "challenging" by the pillars of the IRT

HOW TO GET AROUND   149

elevated subway line. In the center of the borough, the Bronx River Parkway begins at the Bruckner Expressway, goes into Westchester at *Bronxville;* White Plains Road is parallel, about ½ mile to the east; it too has an "el" structure.

There are only a few east-west roads. Tremont Ave. begins just south of the 179th St. exit from the northbound Major Deegan Expressway (I–87) and runs through many different neighborhoods, rich and poor, eventually leading to the Throgs Neck Bridge. Fordham Rd., beginning at the bridge from 207th St., Manhattan, runs cross-borough at about 190th St., passing *Fordham University* and the *Bronx Zoo.* As US 1, it continues east under the name Pelham Parkway and ends with interchanges for the Hutchinson River Parkway and New England Thruway (both lead to Westchester).

The Staten Island Expressway crosses that borough's northern tier, directly off the Verrazano-Narrows Bridge from Brooklyn to the Goethals Bridge for New Jersey. Other limited access roads are planned around the perimeter, but, for now, Hyland Blvd. is the most reliable route to the more rural sections, like *Tottenville,* in Staten Island. It connects to the interchange with the recently completed West Shore Expressway which crosses south to the Outerbridge Bridge.

By bus: Of course, buses are slower than subways (during rush hour, they crawl along). But the routes are varied and, since there are almost always stops every two blocks, you can often get closer to your destination than on the subway. Midtown bookstores will sell you a large-print map and explanatory guide; it should make the subway look easy by comparison. In *Manhattan,* there are routes on all north-south avenues and major crosstown streets, as well as several trips that zigzag along a wandering path through (and sometimes out of) the borough. Look on the front of an approaching bus for a sign hinting at its destination. But to know *how* it gets there, you'll need to ask the driver or consult the map. Free maps are also available on some buses, but your best bet for a free map is the Convention and Visitors' Bureau, the MTA booths at Grand Central or Penn Stations, or the Yellow Pages.

Buses also cost 75 cents (to ride you need *exact* change, a token, or a transfer); Add-a-Ride tickets, which at press time are free, allow you to transfer from one route to a connecting line. Then there are the popular weekend Culture Bus Loops in Manhattan: Loop One (bus M41) and Lower Manhattan–Brooklyn Loop Two (bus B88). Each loop is routed from one likely tour site to another, and for $1.75 you can get on and off at as many of the loop stops as you like. Both lines run weekends and holidays from 10 A.M. to 6 P.M. You also get a free 44-page guidebook giving background information about each stop. The essentially self-guided loop routes, incidentally, can be an excellent, inexpensive way to get your bearings in the city, much as the London Transport tours are in that city. Staying on the bus, each ride runs approximately 2 to 2½ hours.

By ferry: The famous nickel ride from the Battery to *Staten Island* now costs 25¢ (round trip). It is most glorious at night when city lights create a spectacular show. The trip takes about half an hour each way, the boat moves swiftly, has a snack bar and room for cars, and passes close to the Statue of Liberty.

NEW YORK CITY

From the airports: Some hotels serve the airport terminals with their own limousines, so check when you make reservations. There are usually plenty of taxis available. The fare to Rockefeller Center, for example, will be about $12 from La Guardia, $25 (tip included) from Kennedy if traffic moves steadily. *JFK Express:* Subway-bus service, connecting points in Manhattan and Brooklyn with Kennedy International Airport, is available for $4, one way. Travelers can board a specially marked subway train (look for a white airplane on a blue background) at its starting point at 57th St. and Sixth Ave., or at seven other express stops: 47th–50th Sts. and Rockefeller Center; 42nd St. and 6th Ave.; 34th St. and Herald Square at 6th Ave.; W. Fourth St. and Washington Square at 6th Ave.; Chambers St. and World Trade Center; Broad and Nassau Sts.; Jay St. and Borough Hall in Brooklyn. The subway will terminate at the Howard Beach–JFK Airport station and passengers will be picked up by buses that will transport them to any of the airline terminals. Passengers leaving the airport can take the service into Manhattan for the same fare. The JFK Express operates at 20-minute intervals, seven days a week, from 6 A.M. to 11 P.M., from both terminals, and takes about one hour. *Helicopter* service into Manhattan is available, weather permitting, from all three major area airports. Heliports are located on the East River at Pier 6 in the Wall Street area, at 34th St., and at 60th St. Bell (943–5959) and Metropolitan (883–0999) both serve the Wall St. Heliport; Island (895–5372) goes to all three East River landing strips, and Helicopter Travel Inc. (888–6363) goes to 60th St. All are also available for sightseeing, with Metropolitan offering special camera mounts on its choppers. The fares vary from $28 to $49.50, one way. The Carey Bus Co. will bring you into Manhattan for $3.50 from La Guardia or $5.00 from JFK. The La Guardia bus makes stops at Grand Central Terminal (42nd St. and Park Ave., by the Grand Hyatt Hotel) and the East Side Airline Terminal (38th St. between First and Second Aves.); the JFK bus stops at the East Side Airline Terminal only. And of course the buses go back out to the airports—leaving from the East Side terminal—at the same fares, and stop at all terminals at the airports.

By taxi: The legendary garrulous New York cabbie is fast fading from the NYC scene. But there are still over 30,000 licensed cab drivers in New York: a complete cross-section of ages, races and education levels—and motoring skills and knowledge of city geography

Some will try to help you and save you money; others will want to take advantage of your inexperience in getting around the city or of the fact that the weather's nasty. If you carry an atlas, you can discuss the route of a long or complicated trip before you set out. The driver, by law, may not refuse to take any "orderly" passenger anywhere in the five boroughs, Nassau, Westchester, or to Newark Airport (the last three destinations entitle him to twice the fare shown on the meter). Neither may he charge each passenger separately when there is more than one passenger. These rules, along with the phone number of the city's Taxi and Limousine Commission, (212) 747–0930, are posted inside each cab. On the back of the roof-light, you'll find the vehicle's medallion (identification) number. Sharing of taxis is permitted between New York's

TOURIST INFORMATION SERVICES

airports and certain midtown Manhattan hotels. Inquire at the airport or at your hotel.

The fare is $1 for the first ninth of a mile, 10¢ for each subsequent ninth. You also pay for waiting time (including red lights and traffic jams). The driver expects, because he usually gets, about a 15 to 20% tip. A larger tip is appropriate if your destination is an area far from where he can reasonably expect to find a return-trip passenger. The rider pays bridge, tunnel and/or highway tolls. Currently, there is a 50 cents per ride surcharge between 8 P.M. and 6 A.M., and also all day on Sundays.

More and more fleets and independent drivers are using two-way radio equipment to handle telephone orders. There may be an extra charge for this service if reserved in advance; ask the dispatcher on the phone rather than waiting until the cab arrives and trying to work it out with the driver. Some of the better-known radio fleets are: *Minute Men,* 899-5600; *XYZ,* 685-3333; *Scull's Angels,* 457-7777; *Intra Boro,* 845-1100; *Ding-A-Ling,* 691-9191; and *UTOG,* 741-2000.

By limousine: If you really want to do it up right, there's only one way to go—chauffeur-driven car. *Carey Cadillacs* have a fixed price of $25 per hour or 95 cents per mile. A special airport fee system runs along these lines: from midtown to JFK is $40, and from JFK domestic terminals $45, international terminals $55, to midtown; all fees mentioned plus tips and tolls. *Fugazy Continental* has chauffeur-driven, six-passenger Lincolns with television and stereo for $26 per hour or $1.10 per mile, whichever is greater.

On foot: Several famous sections of Manhattan are easily seen on foot. They include, but are not limited to, Greenwich Village, Midtown, Wall Street, Lincoln Center, and the UN-Turtle Bay area.

TOURIST INFORMATION SERVICES. The *New York Convention and Visitors Bureau* at Columbus Circle (in the funny little skyscraper on the south side) has multilingual aides to assist you in making your sightseeing plans. At their headquarters, you can also obtain subway and bus maps, and information about hotels, motels, and restaurants, as well as seasonal listings of the city's special entertainment attractions. The Bureau is open Monday to Friday, 9 A.M. to 5 P.M.; call 397-8222.

For the Rockefeller Center area, there is a *Guided Tour and Information Desk* at 30 Rockefeller Plaza. Open daily except Christmas Day, this is the starting point for multilingual guided tours and a good source of brochures about the city in a variety of languages.

There is also the *Times Square Information Center,* 42nd Street and Broadway, 221-9869, open seven days from 9 A.M. to 6 P.M. Here you can find maps listing many of the city's attractions in French, German, Japanese, Portuguese, Russian, and Spanish, as well as in English. Also, the Times Square Ticket Center (TKTS) at Broadway and 47th Street (354-5800) and at 100 William Street in lower Manhattan (344-3340) sell Broadway and off-Broadway tickets at half-price on the day of performance.

NEW YORK CITY

New York magazine, published weekly and incorporating the listings sections from the old *Cue* magazine, does an excellent job of keeping a finger on the pulse of New York City. Weekly features include comprehensive information on cultural events, shopping, sports, street fairs, walking tours, museums and galleries, activities for children, and all manner of special events. *New York* also maintains a free ticket service information phone— 986–5872, Monday to Friday, 12:30 to 6:30 P.M.—which will advise you regarding ticket availability for theater, dance, and concerts.

New Yorker magazine, most famous for its literary efforts, also has excellent theater, music, dance and movie reviews, and listings (with brief, pithy commentary) of what's happening at art galleries, museums, nightclubs, opera, and ballet.

The city's daily papers—*The New York Times, New York Post* and *Daily News*—list current attractions, with the Friday weekend sections always geared to the most promising upcoming events. On Fridays, too, both the *Times* and the *News* list theater ticket availability through that Sunday. The huge Sunday *Times* is perhaps the best buy in town, though, with its "Arts and Leisure" and "Guide" sections overflowing with useful entertainment information and ads.

Of the city's varied weekly newspapers, the *Village Voice* is the one to consult for the latest on pop music, jazz, modern dance, and off- and off-off-Broadway theater.

Weather forecasts, time, traffic conditions, sports information, a jazz hotline, your daily horoscope, jokes . . . all can be obtained over the phone. For these and other numbers consult the White Pages of the telephone directory or dial 976–1000 for individual numbers.

RECOMMENDED READING. A selection of books for visitors with specialized interests:

The American Institute of Architects' *AIA Guide to New York City,* by Norval White and Elliot Willensky (Collier), is a comprehensive guide to city architecture and history. The Landmarks Preservation Committee of the City of New York published a booklet, *A Guide to New York City Landmarks,* that is sold at most city bookstores and cultural institutions, such as museums and libraries, usually for one dollar.

The Street Book, by Henry Moscow (Hagstrom), is, as its subtitle suggests, "an encyclopedia of Manhattan's street names and their origins" and a good source of city lore.

Manhattan Menus (Manhattan Menus Inc.), revised annually, is a compilation of approximately 175 menus from a representative cross-section of New York eateries, complete with prices and specialties of the house. For serious *gourmands,* there is Seymour Britchky's *The Restaurants of New York* (Random House) for an almost bite-by-bite account of meals at an equally wide variety of establishments.

The Lower East Side Shopping Guide, by Alan Teller and Sharon Greene (Shopping Experience, Inc.), is an oversize pamphlet-type publication that gives a store-by-store account of the wholesale/retail shops along Orchard, Grand,

SEASONAL EVENTS

and their surrounding streets. Other similar guides will lead to you warehouse and discount outlets throughout the metropolitan area.

The New York Walk Book (Doubleday) is the joint project of the New York–New Jersey Trail Conference and the American Geographical Society. It gives detailed information and maps for trails in all parts of the state, with a special section devoted to the five boroughs.

SEASONAL EVENTS. If New York City is normally overflowing with more exhibits, shows, and galleries than even its natives can take in, it is also home to numerous annual special events that range from car shows to ethnic food festivals, from the Ringling Bros., Barnum & Bailey Circus to the St. Patrick's Day Parade. As a general rule (of course there are exceptions), you can expect outdoor happenings to be free, although the temptation to purchase food or merchandise at most street fairs and carnivals will be high. Indoor events at the Coliseum (59th St. and Eighth Ave.), Madison Square Garden (32nd St. and Seventh Ave.), the Seventh Regiment Armory (66th St. and Park Ave.), and Lincoln Center (64th St. and Broadway) usually require the purchase of tickets. Phone numbers cited below are all in the 212 area code.

January. *The National Boat Show* and the *Greater New York Auto Show,* both open to trade and public, take over the Coliseum, showing off the latest, sleekest designs. Both are very popular, and the crowds on weekends especially can be overwhelming. Call 757–5000. . . . The *Winter Antiques Show* is resident at the Seventh Regiment Armory late in the month, featuring some of the nation's finest dealers and their latest acquisitions. Call 288–0200. . . . The spectacular *Ice Capades* glide and spin at Madison Square Garden for a two-week stint. Call 564–4400. . . . Rounding out the month is the explosive *Chinese New Year,* which arrives at the first full moon after January 21 (Tet, in the lunar calendar). Fireworks, food, and fun mark this 10-day celebration. Call 397–8222.

February. The two-day *Westminster Dog Show* finds hundreds of competitors strutting their stuff at Madison Square Garden. Call 682–6852. . . . *Black History Week* is marked at the American Museum of Natural History, Central Park West at 77th St., by way of films, exhibits and discussions. Call 873–1300. . . . The *Start Your Own Business Show* at the Coliseum attracts aspiring entrepreneurs of all kinds. Call 757–5000. . . . *White Sales*—offering huge savings on towels, linens, and other merchandise—fill the major department stores with bargain-seekers on Washington's and Lincoln's Birthday weekends.

March. The Coliseum hosts two popular events: The *Sport, Camping, Travel and Vacation Show,* where you can buy direct from the exhibitors; and for stay-at-homers, the *Antiques and Garden Show.* Call 757–5000. . . . You don't have to be Irish to tag along in the *St. Patrick's Day Parade* on the 17th. Just follow the green stripe down the middle of Fifth Avenue and join the politicians and tens of thousands of marchers all decked out in green. . . . If that's not enough of a three-ring circus for you, get your tickets for the *Ringling Bros., Barnum & Bailey Circus* at Madison Square Garden. The good seats at the kiddie matinees sell out first for performances through the end of May. Call 564-4400.

April. The *Easter Parade* (admittedly, sometimes in March) starts at St. Patrick's Cathedral, Fifth Ave. at 49th St., immediately following the morning services. Put on your Sunday best and stroll uptown with the rest of the crowd. ... For children, in the past there's been an *Easter Egg Rolling Contest* in Central Park, but the event has grown so popular, and the crush so bad, that its future is in question. Check the newspapers to be sure. ... When the New York Knicks are contenders, the *pro basketball playoffs* can be seen at Madison Square Garden. Tickets are very difficult to get so try to reserve early.

May. Parades abound: *Armed Forces Day, Brooklyn Bridge Day, Martin Luther King, Jr., Memorial Day* and *Norwegian Independence Day.* For dates and route information call 397-8222. ... The street festival season gets underway in earnest with the *Ninth Avenue International Festival,* a multi-ethnic feast (plus much free entertainment) that stretches along Ninth Ave. from 37th to 59th Sts. Call 581-7029. ... *The Park Avenue Antiques Show* is a week-long, nationally recognized display of American and European collectibles at the Seventh Regiment Armory. ... The *Washington Square Outdoor Art Exhibit* sprawls out covering lower Fifth Ave. at Washington Square Park, Broadway, University, and La Guardia Place for three weekends beginning the last weekend in May. There's *some* good art to be found here, but most is pedestrian and uninspired. ... *Memorial Day Weekend* is marked by parachute and acrobatic flying shows at Brooklyn's Coney Island. ... Little Italy comes alive for the *Feast of St. Anthony* on Mulberry St. for the last weekend of the month. You'll be overcome by the luscious smells of sizzling calzone (oversize cheese-filled dumplings, deep-fat fried), grilled sausages, and fresh shellfish. Rides, raffles, and games of chance and skill are also featured. Call 226-2978.

June. The *Feast of St. Anthony of Padua* continues the Italian festivities a wee bit north on Sullivan St. between Houston and Spring Sts. Call 777-2755. ... It's *Basically Bach* (with a few other well-tempered selections) at Lincoln Center's Avery Fisher Hall for six days—call 874-6770—while the free *Guggenheim Band Concerts* commence across the Lincoln Center Plaza in Damrosch Park. The latter run through August Wednesdays through Fridays, and Sundays, from 8 to 10 P.M. Call 867-8290. ... George Wein's *Kool Jazz Festival* brings a large congregation of jazz musicians and fans together for 10 days (through July 4th) of concerts all around the city—in concert halls, on the Staten Island ferry, and in the parks. Call 787-2020. ... The *New York Women's Jazz Festival* overlaps the Kool fête for eight days. Sponsored by the Universal Jazz Coalition, call 924-5026. ... *Shakespeare in the Park,* under the auspices of Joseph Papp's New York Shakespeare Festival Public Theater, brings the Bard free to the minions at the Delacorte Theater in Central Park (enter the park at 81st Street from either Central Park West or Fifth Ave.). The line for tickets, which are distributed on the day of performance only beginning at 6 P.M., forms early in the afternoon. Call 535-5630. ... The *Metropolitan Opera* also brings free concert performances of complete operas to various city parks during the month. No tickets necessary, but you might want to stake out your space

SEASONAL EVENTS

early, and bring a blanket and a picnic dinner. Call 755-4100. ... *Museum Mile* finds Fifth Ave. turned into a pedestrian mall as the ten museums between 82nd and 105th Sts. open their doors for a special midweek evening. ... The *Great Irish Fair* carries the spirit of St. Patrick into the summer with a two-day festival along the Brooklyn waterfront. ... Parades mark *Puerto Rican Day* and a *Salute to Israel.* Call 397-8222.

July. The *Fourth of July* is America's Independence Day and the fireworks literally begin at 9:15 P.M., sponsored by Macy's Department Store and most recently emanating from barges on the waters around the Statue of Liberty. Check newspapers for best vantage points and for details regarding the *Fourth of July Harbor Festival,* the *Old New York Festival,* and the parachutists and aerobatics shows at Brooklyn's Coney Island. ... It's *Mostly Mozart* at Avery Fisher Hall for the next six weeks, while Lincoln Center Plaza is given over to the *American Crafts Festival* for the first two weekends of the month. More than 300 craftsmakers sell their leather, furniture, glass, jewelry, and other wares with children's activities including mime, singing, magic and clowns. Call 677-4627. ... Joe DiMaggio usually shows up for *Old Timers' Day* at Yankee Stadium. Call 293-6000. ... More Italian-flavored street festivities are part of the nightly (for ten days) *Lady of Pompeii Feast* on Cornelia St. south of Bleecker St. in Greenwich Village. Call 989-6805.

August. The *New York Philharmonic* takes a portable stage to Central, Clove Lakes, Prospect, and other city parks for a series of alfresco performances. Blankets and picnics in order once again. Call 755-4100. ... *Lincoln Center Out-of-Doors,* at that cultural center's Plaza, is a three-week marathon of free shows drawn from all the performing arts. Call 877-1800. It's the Mets' turn for *Old Timers' Day* at Shea Stadium. Call 672-3000. ... The annual *Bluegrass Club of New York Amateur Band Contest* is held at the South Street Seaport Museum Pier. Call 687-9000. ... The *U.S. Open* at the National Tennis Center in Queens' Flushing Meadow Park features top international pros competing for top national honors. Call 592-8000.

September. The *San Gennaro Festival* on Mulberry and Grand Streets is yet another chance to fill up on Little Italy's best goodies—for 11 nights running! Call 226-9546. ... German-Americans celebrate *Steuben Day*—honoring one of the Europeans who aided the Colonists during the Revolutionary War—with a parade commencing on East 86th St. Call 397-8222. ... *New York Is Book Country* is the theme on Fifth Ave. from 47th to 57th Sts. for one Sunday this month, with major publishers setting up kiosks in order to tout their authors' latest literary efforts. Some authors are in attendance, there are some publishing demonstrations, and street performers line the route. Call 752-9880. ... The *New York Film Festival* previews art films as well as the latest soon-to-be-released Hollywood blockbusters for three weeks at Alice Tully Hall, Lincoln Center. Tickets are available—and often sold out—in advance. Call 362-1911. ... The *TAMA Country Fair* and *Festival of the Americas* street fairs, with about 800 booths each, get one Sunday apiece on Third and Sixth Avenues, respectively. For TAMA information, call 674-5094; for Festival of the Americas, call

921-8122. ... Brooklyn's Atlantic Avenue is turned into an *Atlantic Antic* for a celebration of Middle Eastern foods and crafts. Call 783-4469.

October. For walkers, parades: *Columbus Day, Pulaski Day, Hispanic Day,* and *Veterans Day* (for dates and routes call 397-8222); for runners, the 26-mile *New York City Marathon* begins on the Staten Island side of the Verrazano-Narrows Bridge and ends at Tavern-on-the-Green in Central Park. Hopefully, everyone starts and finishes on the last Sunday of the month. Call 758-6880. ... The fall foliage season is the perfect time for a hike through any of the city's parks, with the Cloisters up at the northern tip of Manhattan island perhaps the most spectacular of all. ... It's *United Nations Day* on the 24th, though there are no regular, official ceremonies. ... *Old Home Day* at the Richmond Restoration, 441 Clarke Ave., Staten Island, finds the doors open to period houses throughout the area. Call 351-1611.

November. The *International Ski and Winter Sports Show* stops at the Coliseum with the latest fashions for the slopes. Call 757-5000. ... *Macy's Thanksgiving Day Parade* is a thrill to see live as it wends its way down Central Park West (beginning about 8:30 from 77th St.), Broadway, and Seventh Ave. Everyone's wide-eyed as Snoopy, Bullwinkle, and other favorite cartoon characters march by as building-high balloons. Even Santa makes his first seasonal appearance! Call 397-8222. ... As of Thanksgiving weekend, the windows at *Lord & Taylor, Altman's,* and *F.A.O. Schwarz* are done up with spectacular, moving Christmas displays. Go at night, if possible, for the lines during the day at Lord & Taylor especially can be long and deep. ... The *National Horse Show* trots around Madison Square Garden for six days. Call 546-4400.

December. The annual Christmas tree lighting ceremony at *Rockefeller Center*, 47th Street between Fifth and Sixth Ave., is always an event. Call 489-2947. ... Tchaikovsky's *Nutcracker Suite Ballet* is the seasonal offering by the New York City Ballet at Lincoln Center's State Theater. The regular company is augmented by children from the School of American Ballet, and there are daily performances—which invariably sell out—for about three weeks. Call 870-5500. ... For crafty holiday shopping try the *American Crafts Holiday Festival* at NYU Loeb Student Center, La Guardia Place and Washington Square South. Plenty of jewelry, clothing, furniture, glass, leather, and other goods. Call 677-4627. ... And if you're lucky enough to be ringing out the old and ringing in the new in New York City, you can join the *New Year's Eve* revelry in Times Square as thousands watch an illuminated ball descend from the top of the Allied Chemical building at the stroke of midnight. Alternately, there are midnight celebrations (complete with fireworks and live music) in *Central* and *Prospect Parks*.

FREE EVENTS. Summer is especially full of outstanding free cultural offerings throughout New York City. Both the Metropolitan Opera (in late June and early July) and the New York Philharmonic (in late July and early August) travel the various city parks giving free performances—the Philharmonic concerts in Central and Prospect Parks usually augmented by fire-

FREE EVENTS

works accompanying the *1812 Overture* or some similarly suitable work. The Goldman Band concerts are held all summer long at the bandshell in Damrosch Park, in the southwest corner of Lincoln Center. Lincoln Center Plaza is also the scene of numerous free events, from the American Crafts Fair, held for two weekends beginning July 4th, to three weeks of daily performing-arts shows in August. A handful of Kool Jazz Festival concerts around the end of June are also free. At the Delacorte Theater in Central Park there are free Shakespeare productions, while the city's various other parks have extensive schedules of free dramatic, pop, jazz, classical, dance, and other offerings. (Call the individual parks or borough president's office for full listings.)

The Mall in Central Park south of the 72nd St. transverse and the area north around Bethesda Fountain are always overflowing with street entertainers—musicians, mimes, jugglers, magicians, and the like—who perform summer weekends and holidays from about noon to dusk. Most, though, do pass the hat.

Fireworks can be seen weekly throughout the summer at Coney Island on Tuesdays and at Rockaway's Playland on Wednesdays. On the Fourth of July, Macy's sponsors a spectacular half-hour-long fireworks display from different parts of New York Harbor. And on New Year's Eve, rain or snow or bone-chillingly cold, Central and Prospect Parks shine from the glimmer of overhead lightshows.

Beginning with the Ninth Ave. International Fair in mid-May, city streets are given over to carnivals, street fairs, and festivals right through to the end of September. Strolling and entertainment are always free at these extravaganzas (the Ninth Ave. fair attracts half a million people annually; other smaller ones a few thousand on a single block) although there's always food, rides, and merchandise to be bought. Call the Mayor's Office of Street Activities (566-2506).

Many of the attractions in the *Museums, Historic Sites,* and *Walking Tours* sections of this book are free—with some additional museums asking only a voluntary contribution. Others that usually have fees, such as the Guggenheim and the Whitney, are free Tuesday evenings. Tickets for television shows—live or taped—are always free, and available at the Convention and Visitors Bureau, or frequently from station personnel stationed outside the NBC and CBS buildings. All of the city's parks, zoos, and gardens are free, with the exception that there is a charge at the Bronx Zoo Fridays and weekends.

Floral displays begin with those at Rockefeller Center's Channel Gardens on Fifth Ave., but include Easter and Christmas displays in the Pan Am Building and a Spring Flower Show at One World Trade Center. At the Citicorp Center, there are daily (including weekend) popular and classical music programs in the Atrium, 153 E. 53rd St. Lincoln Center's Library of the Performing Arts, Amsterdam at 66th St., has free concerts on weekdays at 4:00, Saturdays at 2:30. Each Sunday at 5:00, there are jazz vespers at St. Peter's Church, 54th St. at Lexington Ave. Free outdoor art exhibits are common from spring to fall. Among the more famous are the Washington Square Outdoor Art Show, late May and early June, Greenwich Village; and the Brooklyn Heights Promenade Fine Arts Show, in May. The Canal Street Flea Market, 335 Canal St. (near

Chinatown), is open Saturday and Sunday. Also in lower Manhattan is a self-guided Heritage Trail, which you can pick up anywhere, though Trinity Church at the head of Wall Street is as good a place as any to begin. You can visit corporate New York in the guise of the J.C. Penney Co., 1301 Ave. of the Americas (52nd St.), where you can tour a testing center, the boardroom, etc. on weekdays at 9:30 and 2:00 (phone for reservations at 957–4840). The Manhattan Art & Antiques Center, 1050 Second Ave. (55th St.) has free admission to its complex of 72 shops, open every day. Up in Central Park, The Dairy (65th St., west of the zoo) has a free slide show every 30 min. from Tues. to Sun. There are also free guided park tours Wed., Sat., and Sun. at 12:30. Finally, you can tour a winery (the only one functioning in Manhattan) by calling at Schapiro's, 126 Rivington St., Sundays 10 to 6, every hour on hour. (Phone 674–4404 for weekday appointment.)

For other free tours, refer to the *Tours and Special-Interest Sightseeing* section, which follows.

TOURS AND SPECIAL-INTEREST SIGHTSEEING. Before you begin walking or busing around town, we urge you to take in *The New York Experience*, a multisensory film which will introduce you to the city and help you get your bearings. (Lower plaza, McGraw-Hill Building, 1221 Sixth Ave., between 48th and 49th Sts., 869–0345.) Admission charge.

General-interest bus tours are still available from midtown. *Gray Line of New York*, 900 Eighth Ave., 397–2600, offers 10 different tours covering uptown, downtown, and out-of-town. *Manhattan Sightseeing Bus Tours*, 150 W. 49th St., 245–6641, also has 10 tours. Reservations necessary. *Crossroads Sightseeing*, 701 Seventh Ave., 581–2828, covers many well-known Manhattan spots. *Short Line Sightseeing International*, 168 W. 46th St., (212) 246–5550, also has good touring choices. For the adventurous on a weekend, the biggest tour bargains of all—akin to the London Transport tours in that city—are the *New York Culture Bus Loops*, sponsored by the Metropolitan Transportation Authority (MTA).

There are two such touring loops, the M41 and the B88. Both emanate from Manhattan, although the second ventures into downtown Brooklyn. Each loop is routed from one likely tour site to another, and for $2.50 (in exact change — no bills), which includes a 44-page booklet describing each stop, you can get on and off at as many of the loop stops as you like. Both lines run weekends and holidays from 10:00 A.M. to 6:00 P.M. Staying on the bus, each ride runs approximately 2½ to 3 hours. To find the nearest starting point, call the N.Y.C. Transit Authority travel information number (a good one to have any time you wish to use public transportation): 330–1234.

If you want to skim the waters of the Big Apple, *Circle Line* cruises leave Pier 83 at the foot of W. 43rd St. and 12th Ave., 563–3200, approximately every 45 minutes beginning midmorning. Details of the sights en route are included in the introduction to the *Walking Tours* section, but it's a leisurely 2½- to 3-hour ride around the entire island. Adults, $7.50; children under 12, $3.75. April–November. Or you can take to the air via *Island Helicopter*, heliport at the foot

TOURS AND SIGHTSEEING 159

of E. 34th St. on the East River, 683-4575. Flights day or night, from $15.00 per person.

Still another unique perspective of Manhattan can be had by taking a hansom cab—horse-drawn carriage—through Central Park, down Fifth Ave., or wherever the spirit guides you. Carriages are always lined up at 59th St. and Fifth Ave., just outside the Plaza Hotel. The usual routes are a brief ramble through the park, or down Fifth Ave. for eight or ten blocks and back up Sixth Ave., but drivers will tailor a trip to your desires. It is not an inexpensive mode of travel, though, given the leisurely pace and the possibility of hitting traffic. Official rates are $17.00 for the first half hour, and $5.00 for each additional 15 minutes. And it is suggested to confirm the rate with the driver you choose before setting out.

Tours of some individual attractions in the city are also popular. These are described fully as part of the *Walking Tours* section but a brief reminder that they are available is in order. Among them: the *New York Stock Exchange*, 1 Wall St., 623-2065. Self-guided via automated narration and participant-activated exhibits. Mon.-Fri., 10:00 A.M.-4:00 P.M. Free; *United Nations*, First Ave. at 45th St., 754-7710. Hour-long tours are run daily, 9:00 A.M.-4:45 P.M. Adults $2.50, students $1.50, children $1.00; *Rockefeller Center* (enter 30 Rockefeller Plaza from 49th or 50th Sts. between Fifth and Sixth Aves.), (212) 489-2947. Tours include walk through NBC studios, Radio City Music Hall (when there's no performance) and general area, leaving the tour desk every 30 minutes from 9:30 A.M.-5:30 P.M. daily. $2.35 per person; *Radio City Music Hall*, 50th St. at Sixth Ave., 246-4600—call for schedule and prices; *Lincoln Center*, Broadway at 64th St., 877-1800—Avery Fisher Hall is the starting point every half hour between 10:00 A.M. and 5:00 P.M. daily, Adults $3.75, students and Senior Citizens $3.25, children $2.50.

For offbeat tours, contact *Adventure On A Shoestring, Inc.*, 300 W. 53rd St., 265-2663, and meet new people in unusual surroundings at budget-minded but imaginative events. You can visit clubs, restaurants, and theaters, escorted by the people at *Big Apple At Night*, 59 E. 54th St., 371-3455. *Discover New York* is a series of six Sunday-afternoon walking tours, sponsored by the *Municipal Art Society Tours*, 457 Madison Ave., 935-3969. Brooklyn Heights, Upper West Side, Upper Fifth Avenue are some of the areas on the itinerary; $5.00 per person. Other walking tours are listed regularly in the *Cue* section of *New York* magazine.

In addition to all of the above, and the museums, historic sites, and places to be seen on walking tours, all of which are described under those entries in this book, there are other fascinating places which don't fit into such convenient categories, yet deserve mention. Here are a select few:

Guinness World Records Exhibit Hall, Empire State Bldg., 34th St. and Fifth Ave., 947-2335. Over 200 exhibits, including moving light displays, replicas, etc., all from that wonderful book.

The city's police force is one of the best in America when it comes to human relations with the population they serve. You can look in on their training facility, the *Police Academy,* 235 E. 20th St., 477-9700, and also see a museum devoted to the history of the department.

Supreme Court of New York County and the *Criminal Court* are located at 60 and 100 Centre St., respectively. If a publicized trial interests you, or if you simply want to see the routine business of a court, they—and smaller courts—are open to the public.

The *Mormon Visitors Center,* Broadway & 65th St., 595-1825, features archeological exhibits in replica of artifacts from both Eastern and Western cultures. A diorama with talking mannequins relates the story of a contemporary Mormon family, a 19th-century pioneer family, and a *Book of Mormon* family of 2,000 years ago. Open seven days, 10:00 A.M.-8:00 P.M. Free.

You may not readily associate New York with the cotton crop, but it has the *Cotton Exchange,* 4 World Trade Center, 938-2650, one of the busiest futures markets in the world. If you call ahead, you can arrange for someone to meet you and briefly explain how the trading works.

If you're interested in—or puzzled by—our nation's fiscal and monetary policies, visit the New York *Federal Reserve Bank,* 33 Liberty St., 791-5000. You must call a week in advance to set up a tour, but they will then explain the Federal Reserve System and central banking, show you check processing and the gold vault.

Whether a new product on the market attains the Good Housekeeping Seal of Approval (*Good Housekeeping* being a major homemaking magazine) is determined at the *Good Housekeeping Institute,* 959 Eighth Ave., 262-6467. Morning and afternoon tours visit laboratories for appliances and chemicals, the needlework center, test kitchens and beauty clinic.

Gallery Passports, 1170 Broadway, 288-3578, organizes tours to artists' studios and lofts in the city and to other art attractions outside New York that can be seen in a day (Baltimore, Md., and Williamstown, Mass., for instance). Sept.-May.

The largest Black community in America is in upper Manhattan and the *Penny Sightseeing Company,* 303 W. 42nd St., 247-2860, offers a tour through Harlem. Ask especially about their special Saturday-night tours.

The largest theatrical community in America is in mid-Manhattan and you can glimpse its workings close up through *Backstage on Broadway,* 228 W. 47th St., 575-8065. The tour guides are professionals from all branches of the industry and the program draws praise from educators around the country.

Con Edison, New York's public utility for electricity, has installations all over the metropolitan area and several of these are visited by bus provided by the company. Con Ed's *Energy Museum,* 145 E. 14th St., 599-3434, displays the past, present, and future of electricity. Closed Sun. and Mon.

If you've never been in a transoceanic port before, the busy piers and luxury liners may prove fascinating indeed. The newspaper shipping pages list departure schedules, and if you call the line for its visiting policy (on ocean liners visitors are generally allowed about two hours before sailing), you'll be ready to stroll the decks while passengers board.

PARKS

PARKS. These cover nearly a sixth of the city's land and provide welcome contrasts to its concrete canyons and crowded sidewalks. Vandalism and inadequate maintenance have taken their toll, but a spirit of preservation and renewal is increasingly in evidence.

The parks may disappoint those seeking pure pastoral beauty and restful solitude. They *are* beautiful—there's something very special about looking at the skyscrapers of Manhattan from a snow-covered Central Park, where cross-country skiers wend their way across the Sheep Meadow; or getting a feel of New England during the fall foliage season in the Bronx's Van Cortlandt Park. But New York's parks have gradually evolved into recreational and cultural areas, especially in summer.

If there's a promenade for strollers you can rest assured that there'll be street entertainers—musicians, magicians, jugglers, and even comedians—all along the route. More formally, both the Metropolitan Opera and the New York Philharmonic offer series of free park concerts during the summer, travelling from one borough to the next. And it is not unusual for these concerts to draw several hundred thousand fans a night. (Take a blanket, a picnic dinner, and arrive late afternoon for an 8:30 performance if you want to plant yourself within view of the stage.)

There are marathons, walk-a-thons, and races for men, women, children and handicapped in the different parks. There are weekend festivals sponsored by various ethnic, civic, and commercial organizations. The *Parks Department* sponsors drama, film, poetry readings, music and dance throughout the boroughs, with schedules available in local newspapers and magazines (see *Tourist Information* section). And of course there are miles and miles of trails for leisurely walking (not recommended for night), lakes for boating, bicycle lanes for two-wheel enthusiasts . . . and more.

Unique among Metropolitan New York parks is Gateway National Recreation Area, a federally administered park that stretches through parts of Brooklyn (Floyd Bennett Field, a former navy airstrip, is where numerous special events are staged), Queens (the Jamaica Bay Wildlife Refuge on Cross Bay Blvd. is a lure to birdwatchers from all over, while Jacob Riis Park is one of the city's most popular—and cleanest—beaches), Staten Island, and New Jersey. Ranger-guided tours, hikes, and educational programs are offered regularly all year round. Call the Park Authority for dates and times at 474–5606.

We must also reluctantly note that, with the exception of nights when there are special planned events, most of New York's parks are not very safe strolling areas after dark.

MANHATTAN

Central Park has 840 acres which include lakes for rowing (you may rent a boat, at the Loeb Boat House), stable and trails for horseback riding, dozens of baseball diamonds and playfields, a bocci green, a zoo, and a skating rink. (The

NEW YORK CITY

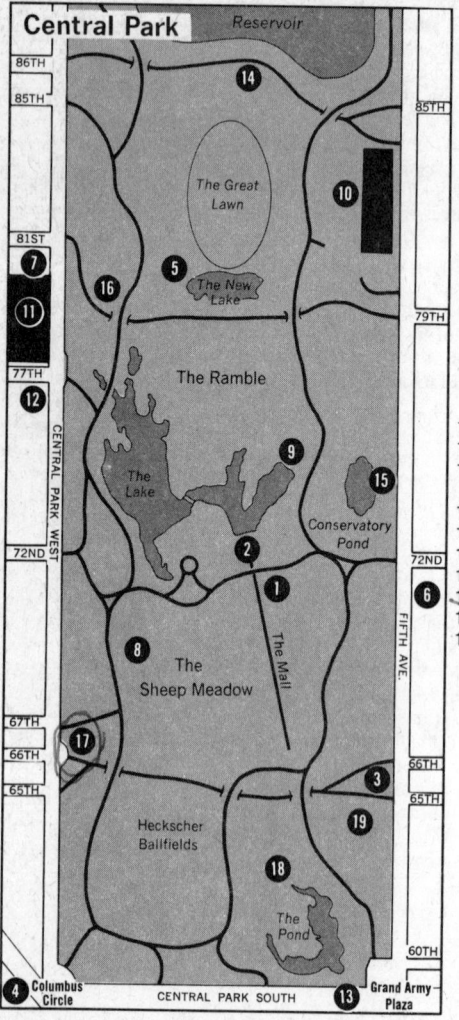

Points of Interest

1) Bandshell
2) Bethesda Fountain
3) Children's Zoo
4) Coliseum
5) Delacorte Theater
6) Frick Collection
7) Hayden Planetarium
8) Lawn Bowling Area
9) Loeb Boat House
10) Metropolitan Museum of Art
11) Museum of Natural History
12) New-York Historical Society
13) Plaza Hotel
14) Police Station
15) Sailboat Storage House
16) Shakespeare Garden
17) Tavern on the Green
18) Wollman Memorial Rink
19) Zoo

Wollman Skating Rink was being renovated as of this writing, with its scheduled date of completion not available.)

The New York Shakespeare Festival makes use of the Delacorte Theater near the 81st St. entrances (from either Central Park West or Fifth Ave.) for free performances of the classics. (Tickets are given out on a first-come, first-served basis beginning at 6 P.M. the night of the performance only; the line for tickets starts forming in early afternoon.)

The Goldman Band Shell is in the Mall midway between East and West 72nd Street, and has frequent free concerts. The Mall itself is where most of the park's regular street performers congregate (best times for a stroll are Saturday or Sunday afternoons from May to October, from noon to dusk). North of 72nd St. is the Bethesda Fountain (inoperative), another popular meeting place right by the edge of a lake. On nearby Conservatory Pond, you may see people maneuvering their battery-operated remote-controlled model sailboats in good weather; the boats are stored in a building to the east of the pond. A jogger's track and bridle trail circle the Reservoir in the 80s. The Metropolitan Museum of Art borders the park at Fifth Ave. and 82nd St.

Cars are banned from all park roads except the east-west transverses almost all but rush hours.

Riverside Park runs along the Hudson River beginning at 72nd St. and north through Harlem. Invariably less crowded than Central Park, Riverside is a neighborhood outpost, full of families and sunbathers. A favorite stroll is along the promenade by the 79th Street Boat Basin, where a number of yachts serve as full-time city residences.

Fort Tryon Park at the northern tip of Manhattan, high over the Hudson, runs south of the Cloisters. Besides the view of the Palisades across the river there is an attractive but somewhat wild garden area.

Battery and *Washington Square Parks* in lower Manhattan are small and don't even pretend to bring the country to the city. The latter, in fact, is mostly concrete. However, Battery Park gives a good harbor view and cooling breezes off the water in summer, while Washington Square is an active mingling ground for Greenwich Villagers. Some sing, play guitars, and smoke dope; some argue social issues, some play chess, and some romp with their children and pets. Washington Square is also the scene of a very New Orleans-like carnival every Halloween night (late in October).

BROOKLYN

Prospect Park's northeast corner is right at Brooklyn's Grand Army Plaza, near the Brooklyn Public Library, Brooklyn Museum and Botanic Gardens. The park itself is more than 500 acres, with lakes, boathouse, riding stables, a Quaker cemetery, the historic Lefferts Homestead and Litchfield Mansion (both open to the public) and a bandshell at 3rd St. and Prospect Park South that is used for small jazz, pop, and classical concerts during the summer.

Also of interest: *Marine Park,* with its 18-hole public golf course.

QUEENS

Flushing Meadows/Corona Park is partially on the site of the 1964 World's Fair grounds, near La Guardia Airport and Shea Stadium. Housed in what was formerly the New York State Pavilion are the Queens and Science Museums, and a few rides and mildly "glamorous" playgrounds also survive. Top of the Park is a restaurant overlooking the park and its immediate surroundings.

Cunningham and *Kissena Parks* are, as is Flushing Meadows, in the central part of the borough.

STATEN ISLAND

Clove Lake is the most popular of Staten Island's parks, with boating, fishing, horseback riding, and wooded paths. A short ride from the Staten Island Ferry terminal on a Victory Blvd. bus makes the park easily accessible to the visitor.

Although not actually a park, *Fort Wadsworth* is one of the quieter spaces in New York City. It is situated under the Staten Island end of the Verrazano-Narrows Bridge and commands an impressive view of New York harbor. To get there, take the Bay Street bus from the ferry terminal. On the grounds is the Fort Wadsworth Military Museum (closed Tues. and Wed.) which traces the history of the fort, which is still an active military post.

Other area parks include *Silver Lake, Latourette* and *Willow Brook*.

BRONX

The woods-and-flowers highlight of the Bronx is easily the *Botanical Garden*, with its 250 acres and thousands of trees, shrubs, and plants. Depending on the season, you'd want to look out for the rose, rhododendron, magnolia, or azalea gardens. (For further details see the *Gardens* section below.)

Pelham Bay Park is almost entirely surrounded by water and is the largest of the Bronx's public parks. Also especially scenic is *Van Cortlandt Park*, which includes the Van Cortlandt Mansion Museum—an 18th-century Colonial manor, furnished today just as it was when built in 1748.

ZOOS. New York has several zoological centers, but the *Bronx Zoo* (Fordham Road & Southern Blvd., Bronx; 220–5100) is something special. Over 250 acres, with more than 3500 animals, it is one of the largest in the world. It has recently been modernized and wherever possible the animals are not caged, which makes sections such as the African Plains most fascinating. A tractor train will allow for a quick survey, the Bengali Express monorail covers the Wild Asia area May through October, and a Skyfari cable car affords an overview of the entire zoo.

The Bronx Zoo is open 10:00 A.M. to 5:00 P.M. (5:30, Sundays and holidays; 4:30, November through January). Admission is free Tuesdays, Wednesdays, and Thursdays; $2.00 for adults, 75 cents for children, and Senior Citizens free at other times. There are nominal additional fees for the various rides. There is also a new children's zoo opposite the elephant house where admission is 80 cents for kids and 70 cents for adults! The Bronx Zoo can be reached via the IRT No. 2 or 5 trains to the East Tremont Ave. stop or by car at the intersection of the Pelham and Bronx River Parkways.

New York's other zoos can hardly rival the Bronx Zoo for size, in maintenance, or for educational value. Both the *Central Park Zoo* (including the *Children's Zoo*) (E. 64 St. & Fifth Ave.; 360–8213) and the *Prospect Park Zoo* (Empire Blvd. & Flatbush Ave., Brooklyn; 965–6587) are in the process of being rehabilitated. Also of possible interest are Staten Island's *Barrett Park Zoo* (614 Broadway; 266–8500) and Queens's *Flushing Meadow Zoo* (111 St. at 54 Ave.; 699–7239).

The *New York Aquarium* (Surf Ave. & W. 8th St., at Brooklyn's Coney Island; 266–8500) is filled with mammals, fish, and birds from the world's water environments. They are displayed and publicly fed to the delight of adults and children alike.

GARDENS. A youngster who grows up in New York City is sometimes called "a child of cement." As you have seen from our discussion of parks, it need not be so. And giving surprise to the visitor expects to see no green in New York at all are the New York and Brooklyn *Botanical Gardens,* each ranking among the world's most beautiful public gardens. They have horticultural displays all year round, are open daily, and admission is free.

New York Botanical Garden, directly north of the famed Bronx Zoo, has brought pleasure to New Yorkers since 1891. Its 250 rolling acres contain some 12,000 different species of plants, some of which bloom on such specialized sites as Rhododendron Slope, Daffodil Hill, Azalea Glen, and Magnolia Dell.

There is also a spectacular 40-acre Hemlock Forest, virgin land unchanged since the days the Indians camped out there. Ancient hemlock, maples, giant oak, poplar, beech, hickory, ash, and tulip trees shade the forest floor. The Bronx River slices through this forest primeval, cascading over a falls not far from *Snuff Mill.* There you will find a post-primeval restaurant, the *Lorillard Snuff Mill,* with dining terrace overlooking the river. There is a picnic area nearby.

The garden's 11 greenhouses feature a world of flowers: lush jungle blooms from Asia, desert plants from Africa, pineapple, oranges, and pomegranates from the tropics. There's also a plant sales area. Almost worth a trip to New York itself is the glass conservatory (inspired by London's Kew Gardens Conservatory).

The *Museum* (Italian Renaissance style) has displays explaining the evolution of plants and their use to man. The paleo-botanic exhibit has some 30,000 plant fossils, some of which date from the year 500 million B.C.

There are five acres of wild flowers, meadows, and rock gardens, and there is an herbarium with some 3,000,000 species. There are flower-bordered pools, 3 miles of roads, 15 miles of paths. There is an *Easter Show* in March, a *Rose*

Day in June, and a *Christmas Show* in December. Call 220–8777 for general information.

To get there: Take New York Central Harlem Division to Botanical Garden Station; or, 6th Ave. Concourse-205th St. (D) subway train to Bedford Pk. Blvd. Walk east 8 blocks. By car, Pelham Pkwy. west from New England Thruway and Hutchison River Parkway; Bronx River Parkway to Mosholu Pkwy. Use Mosholu Pkwy. from Henry Hudson Pkwy.

Japan House, at 333 E. 47th St., has both indoor and outdoor gardens. The gardens are a favorite relaxation spot for office workers on their lunch hour. There is also a library, art gallery, and auditorium here.

The 50-acre **Brooklyn Botanic Garden,** directly behind the Brooklyn Museum, features two of the most beautiful *Japanese gardens* in this hemisphere. The pond-and-hill garden, built in 1913 by Takeo Shiota, is a landscape of symbols. The pond takes the shape of the Japanese character for the word "heart." There is a tori, or gate, in the pond; a shrine on top of the hill. And there are caves which echo the delicate sound of five tiny waterfalls.

The second Japanese garden, which was opened in 1963, is an exact replica of the 15th-century Ryoanji (Buddhist) Temple of Kyoto, one of the most famous abstract gardens of contemplation in the Far East. There is a replica of the viewing wing of the ancient Ryoanji Temple. The tennis-court-size garden area is filled with swirling patterns of gravel, and fifteen stones (imported from Japan) arranged in five groups. The original purpose of the starkly simple design: to draw the minds of monks into meditation.

Another unique feature of the Brooklyn Botanic Garden is its *Fragrance Garden for the Blind.* The plants, raised in beds, are specially selected for identification by taste, touch, or smell. The plaques describing the flowers are in Braille.

There is also a *Shakespeare Garden* (with the various plants and flowers mentioned in the Bard's works), a wild flower garden, a rose garden, a range of greenhouses, and an abundance of cherry trees which burst into sudden bloom in late April, retain their pink glory through early May.

Hours vary according to season; open seven days a week. Call 622–4433 for information.

To get there: From the East Side, take Lexington Ave. IRT subway downtown express marked Utica Ave. or Atlantic Ave. to Nevins St. Change to B'way 7th Ave. train. Ride to Eastern Parkway, also called Brooklyn Museum Station. From the West Side, take B'way 7th Ave. IRT, downtown express marked New Lots Ave. or Flatbush Ave. Get off at Eastern Parkway. (Trip takes about 25 minutes from Grand Central Station.)

If you delight in strolling through quiet *formal gardens,* you'll be glad to learn that Gallery Passport, 1170 Broadway, 288–3578, often includes them in tours to spots in the city and the supporting areas, like *Boscobel* in Westchester. Bus transportation to the various attractions is included in the service.

Manhattan's own **Conservatory Gardens,** in Central Park near Fifth Ave. at 105th St., is just what the name suggests: a greenhouse featuring blooming plants, displays changing seasonally. It's about a 15-minute stroll uptown from the Guggenheim Museum.

The **Ford Foundation** at 320 E. 43rd St. has an indoor garden with a 160-foot ceiling. The garden is in the lobby on this impressive building and has all kinds of flowers, shrubs and vines. Open weekdays.

The **Queens Botanical Gardens,** 43–50 Main Street, Flushing, is a recent addition to the city's attractions. Noted for its summer rose garden and fall chrysanthemum show, the garden also offers a shop (reasonable prices) and popular horticultural programs. Environmentalists will be pleased to learn that this 30-acre Gardens is "planted" on a former garbage dump! *To get there:* IRT subway Flushing Line uptown to Main St. (the last stop); then take the Q44 bus, south on Main St., ask for the Botanical Gardens stop.

Also worth a visit is the **Wave Hill Center for Environmental Studies** in Riverdale, Bronx (West 249th St. and Independence Ave.). It offers an outdoor sculpture garden, greenhouses, and gardens (formal, "wild," aquatic, herb, rose), as well as concerts, lectures, etc. The view of the Hudson River and Palisades is spectacular. *To get there:* We recommend a cab or your car. The trip by subway-bus-foot is a trip itself (IRT Seventh Ave. subway, No. 1 train to 231st St. station; No. 10 or No. 100 City Line Bus from NW corner of 231st St. and Broadway to 252nd St.; cross Parkway Bridge, on foot; walk on 252nd St. to Independence Ave. The entrance to Wave Hill is a few blocks down the road—at 249th St.).

BEACHES. By far the most famous of New York City beaches is **Coney Island**—a 3½-mile stretch of Brooklyn facing out on the Atlantic Ocean. Upwards of a million and a half people will descend upon Coney Island's breezy shores on a hot summer day. Yet for all its continued popularity, this is a sadly rundown area, of which author Mario Puzo has written, "There was a time when every child in New York loved Coney Island, and so it breaks your heart to see what a slothful, bedraggled harridan it has become, endangered by the violence of its poor and hopeless people, as well as by the city planners who would improve it out of existence. If I were a wizard with one last magic trick in my bag, I would bring back the old Coney Island."

Coney Island is not quite that bleak; it retains a certain tacky charm, with the idle parachute jump at nearby *Astroland Amusement Park* towering above the beach and boardwalk—and with what invariably seem like the best frankfurters, French fries, and cotton candy in the world. Coney Island remains an experience, safe certainly by day, if only by dint of the massive crowds that include representatives of every racial group and ethnic community in the city.

In addition to Astroland, the *New York Aquarium* is also nearby, and the side streets are dotted with some of the best Italian restaurants in New York (*Gargiulo's* on W. 15th St. is a garish, 500-seat remnant of Coney Island's bygone glory days; it also consistently garners raves for outstanding food and service).

The B, D, F, M, N, and QB trains all converge at Stillwell Ave., Coney Island; it is also accessible by car via the Belt Parkway, heading east from lower Manhattan by way of the Brooklyn Battery Tunnel. Take the Ocean Parkway exit south about ½ mile until you reach the waterfront. The main beach area and other attractions will be to your right. There are also express buses that go to the Coney Island area, which you can pick up at designated stops between Wall St. and E. 34 or 50.

Almost as famous and easily as popular is **Jones Beach,** just beyond the city limits on Long Island. Jones Beach is more parklike than Coney Island, without Coney's array of distractions—with the noteworthy exception of the nearby *Jones Beach Marine Theater,* an outdoor arena where the stage floats in the water. (Evening performances only, always of big, brassy, well-known musicals.) The beach itself is usually very clean, despite the millions who come to bathe and swim there daily during the June to August season.

To get to Jones Beach by car, take either the Long Island Expressway or the Southern State Parkway to the Meadowbrook Parkway and follow the signs to the parking lots. Despite their size, these lots fill up quickly, and the area is then closed to further traffic. So if you're planning to make the one-hour trip (unmercifully longer on a hot Sunday), leave early in the morning.

Alternatively, leave from the Port Authority Bus Terminal (41st St. and 8th Ave. in Manhattan, 564–8484). There is continuous loading for this special service weekdays from 9:30 to 11:00 A.M. and weekends from 8:00 to 9:30 A.M. leaving for the beach. Return buses depart Jones Beach beginning at 5 P.M. weekdays and from 2:30 to 5:00 P.M. weekends. The fare is $4.00 each way. There is also a train-bus combination advertised for $6.00 round trip ($4.00 for children), involving the Long Island Railroad from Penn Station and a change to a bus at the Freeport Station.

Jacob Riis Park in Queens, named for the turn-of-the-century photographer and philanthropist, and recently incorporated into *Gateway National Park,* is another popular seaside resort. The beach and its waters are generally rated among the cleanest of any in the city and within the park's borders are an 18-hole pitch-and-putt golf course; numerous playgrounds for children of all ages; free tennis, shuffleboard, handball and squash courts; boardwalk; and some grassy, shaded picnic areas. It should be noted that the far eastern end of the beach has in recent years evolved into an unofficial nude sunbathing area popular especially among New York's homosexual community.

Riis Park has parking facilities for 10,000 cars, and is easily reached in about an hour via the Belt Parkway going east from Lower Manhattan. Take the Flatbush Ave. South exit and continue over the Marine Parkway Bridge onto the Rockaway Peninsula. Using public transportation, take the No. 2 or 3 IRT line to Flatbush Ave. in Brooklyn; at the Flatbush/Nostrand junction upstairs, take a bus marked Riis Park or Beach 116 St. (it's best to ask for the bus stop, as there are different lines running from every corner).

New York's beach lovers do run the risk of oil spills or shark alerts periodically closing their favorite haunts, but with the above, as well as *Orchard Beach* near City Island in the Bronx, and *Wolfe's Pond Park* in Staten Island, they're never at a loss for alternative sun-'n'-fun spots.

BABYSITTING SERVICES. For parents who may be hesitant to bring their children to the Big Apple, there should be comfort in the fact that there are a number of reliable sources for babysitters here. Perhaps the best known is *The Babysitters Guild,* 60 E. 42nd St., 682–0227. Their prices will be steep by the usual babysitting standards, but their reputation is impeccable. Rates start at $4.35 an hour, and escalate depending on the number and age of children, and where the sitter is to work; for example, the fee for two children aged 8 and 10 staying at the Plaza would be $5.25 an hour. In all cases there is a four-hour minimum and an additional fee for carfare: $3.00 round trip during the day and until midnight, $5.50 after midnight. Rates for infants up to six months are higher because the Guild uses only people trained as baby nurses for children that young. In contrast, you can work out your own deal with sitters recommended to you by *New York University,* 720 Main Building, 100 Washington Place, 598–2971. Other sitting sources include *Barnard College Babysitting Service,* 606 W. 120th St., 662–7676/280–2035; *Cornell Nursing School Babysitting Service,* 420 E. 70th St., 472–8393; *Part-Time Child Care,* 19 E. 69th St., 879–4343; and *Stern College For Women,* 245 Lexington Ave., 481–0562.

CHILDREN'S ACTIVITIES. Whether it's a trek to a zoo and rubbing shoulders with a gnu, soaking in art and history at a museum, or seeing the sights on foot, New York is a never-ending source of wonderment and adventure for children . . . as well as their parents. Indeed, many "adult" attractions in this city take on new meaning when considered from a family point of view. Broadway, for example, is thought of primarily as part of the grown-up world—but musicals such as *Annie* and *Barnum,* among others in recent years, play extra matinees to accommodate youngsters. Similarly, many of the places listed below are among New York's most popular all-around attractions, but ones with programs or exhibits geared especially to children.

MUSEUMS

American Museum of Natural History, Central Park West at 79th St., 873–4225. There's an endless supply of meteorites, rock samples from the moon, dinosaurs, invertebrates that will fascinate even the most difficult-to-please child. Lectures and movies also offered. Open daily, 10:00 A.M.–4:45 P.M., and to 8 P.M. on Wednesday evenings. Suggested contribution: adults, $2, children, $1.

The *Hayden Planetarium,* a separate division of the American Museum of Natural History, Central Park West at 81st St., 873–0404, presents its star-filled Sky Show. The special effects are astounding. Call for schedules. Adults (13

NEW YORK CITY

years and over), $2.75; students and Senior Citizens, $1.75; children (under 12), $1.35.

Brooklyn Children's Museum, 145 Brooklyn Ave., 735–4432, has over 50,000 objects highlighting the areas of geography, natural history, and anthropology. The museum encourages youngsters to participate in various projects. Special entertainments include story hours, science talks, and movies. Open Wednesday–Saturday, 10:00 A.M.–5:00 P.M.; Sunday, noon–5:00 P.M.; holidays, 1:00–5:00 P.M., closed Monday and Tuesday. Contribution.

Fire Department Museum, 104 Duane St., 570–4230, exhibits two centuries' worth of hand-pumps, fire engines, uniforms, and medals. Open Monday–Friday, 9:00 A.M.–4:00 P.M., closed Saturday, Sunday, and holidays. Free.

Junior Museum, Metropolitan Museum of Art, Fifth Ave. & 82nd St., 879–5500. A marvelous introduction to art for children ages 5 to 12. Children are encouraged to participate in discussions, workshops, and film and slide programs. Schedules vary, so call ahead. Contribution.

New York Hall of Science, 111th St. and 48th Ave., Flushing, Queens, 699–9400. Closed for renovation through 1983, plans for the exhibits were drafted with a hands-on approach in mind.

South Street Seaport Museum, 16 Fulton St., 766–9020, has tall ships at Pier 16, a printing museum and printshop, nautical toy and game shop for children, and a book and chart store. Activities include tours, concerts, square dances, street festivals, workshops, and harbor sailings. Open every day, 11:00 A.M.–6:00 P.M., closed holidays. Admission for exhibit vessels only: adults, $1.50; students, 75 cents; children under 6 and Senior Citizens, free.

Staten Island Children's Museum, 15 Beach St., Stapleton, Staten Island, 273–2060, changes its exhibits periodically. Emphasis is on arts and sciences. Open Tuesday–Friday, 3:00–5:00 P.M.; Saturday, Sunday, and school holidays, 1:00–5:00 P.M. Adults, 50 cents; children, 25 cents.

For other facilities, see *Museums.*

FUN AND GAMES

Two stores offer puppet shows, free. *Barnes & Noble Sales Annex,* Fifth Ave. at 18th St., 675–5500, every Sunday at 11:00 A.M. and 12:30 P.M. Uptown, *F.A.O. Schwarz,* Fifth Ave. and 58th St., 644–9400, Monday–Friday, 2:30 P.M.

Puppet shows presented by independent companies include: *Alice May Puppets,* Origami Center, 31 Union Sq., 255–0469, November–May, Sunday at 2:00 P.M.; *Lea Wallace Puppets,* First Moravian Church, 154 Lexington Ave., 254–9074, Saturday, 2:00 P.M.; *Nicolo Marionettes,* New York Stage Works, 15 W. 18th St., 242–3967, September–mid-May, Saturday, 1:00 P.M. and Sunday, 1:00 and 3:00 P.M.; *Penny Jones & Company Puppets,* Greenwich House Music School, 46 Barrow St., 924–4589, October–April, Saturday and Sunday, 3:30 P.M.; *Puppet Store,* 477 Atlantic Ave., Brooklyn, 625–3983, shows on weekends, 1:00 P.M., also sells puppets and books.; *Museum of the City of New York,* 1220 Fifth Ave., 534–1672, changes show every week, early November–April, Saturday, 1:30 P.M. Reservations for these and for the magic and other live perfor-

CHILDRENS ACTIVITIES

mance shows listed below are always advisable and often necessary a few weeks ahead.

Magic Town House, 1026 Third Ave., 752–1165, features hour-long magic shows on Saturday, Sunday, and school holidays, 1:00, 2:30 and 4:00 P.M. (Shows for adolescents are held Saturday evenings.) *Mostly Magic,* 53 Carmine St., 924–1472 combines magic and comedy with audience participation, Saturdays at 3:00 P.M.

Original plays, fairy tales, and musicals are given at the following theaters: *Courtyard Playhouse,* 39 Grove St., 765–9540, Saturday and Sunday, Labor Day to June, 1:30 and 3:00 P.M.; *Henry Street Family Theater,* 466 Grand St., 766–9334, October–mid-April, Saturday and Sunday, 3:00 P.M.; *Off-Center Theater Company,* 436 W. 18th St., 929–8299, September–May, Tuesday, Wednesday, Thursday, and Sunday.; *Onstage Children Company,* 413 W. 46th St., 246–9872, mid-September–May, Saturday, 1:30 and 3:00 P.M.; *Thirteenth Street Theater,* 50 W. 13th St., 741–9282, Saturday, 1:00 and 3:00 P.M. Also check the Friday editions of the *New York Times* and the *Post* for extensive listings for that weekend.

ZOOS

Bronx Zoo, Fordham Road and Southern Blvd., 220–5100. There is a brand-new children's zoo opposite the elephant house where children are thrilled to discover that admission is 80 cents for kids and 70 cents for adults! As for the main zoo—also recently renovated—rides include the Bengali Express monorail through the spectacular Wild Asia exhibit (where the animals roam free), a tractor train, and a Skyfari cable car. Open 10:00 A.M. to 5:00 P.M. (5:30, Sundays and holidays; 4:30, November–January). Admission is free Tuesdays, Wednesdays, and Thursdays, $2.00 for adults, 75 cents for children, and Senior Citizens free at other times. There are nominal additional fees for the various rides.

Central Park Zoo, Central Park, E. 64th St. and Fifth Ave., 360–8213. Most of the animals are in buildings. It's a pleasant place to spend an hour or two, ride around in a pony cart, and have lunch at the outdoor cafeteria. Open every day, 11:00 A.M.–5:00 P.M. Free.

New York Aquarium, Surf Ave. & W. 8th St., Coney Island, Brooklyn, 266–8500. Over 3,000 varieties of marine life are shown in outdoor and indoor exhibits. The whale and dolphin show is very popular with children. Open every day, 10:00 A.M.–5:00 P.M. Admission.

Other good animal facilities include: *Jamaica Bay Wildlife Refuge,* Cross Bay Blvd., between Howard Beach and Broad Channel, Queens, 474–0613, open every day, 8:00 A.M.–6:00 P.M., free; *Prospect Park Zoo,* Empire Blvd. and Flatbush Ave., Brooklyn, 965–6587, open late June–Labor Day, 10:00 A.M.–4:00 P.M., free; *Staten Island Zoological Park,* 614 Broadway, Staten Island, 442–3100, open every day, 10:00 A.M.–4:45 P.M., admission.

SIGHTSEEING

There is also, of course, the *Statue of Liberty,* which is reached by ferry from the South Ferry subway stop of both the IRT 7th Avenue and IRT Lexington Avenue lines. Children love to climb up the narrow, circular ramp to the statue's crown. An elevator can take you up to the first 10 stories, the last 12 stories are on foot.

The 102-story *Empire State Building* on Fifth Ave. between 33rd and 34th Sts. is always popular. From the terraces of the 86th floor one can rent binoculars and look out across the whole city—and simply being in one of the world's tallest buildings is an unforgettable experience for a child. And don't forget the *World Trade Center!*

Nostalgia Special, IND Subway, W. 57th St. and Ave. of the Americas, The B Line, 330–3060. A vintage subway train takes its passengers to the New York Public Transit Exhibit in Brooklyn and on to Rockaway Beach. Open Saturday, Sunday, and holidays, from Memorial Day weekend to Thanksgiving weekend. Admission.

Between Memorial Day and Labor Day, the city opens many outdoor pools for *swimming.* Van Cortlandt Park has one in the Bronx, Greenwich Village (Clarkson St. and 7th Ave.) in Manhattan, Flushing Meadows in Queens and Bedford-Stuyvesant (Kosciusko St. and Marcy Ave.) in Brooklyn— but the area is rough. An indoor pool open all year is at 342 E. 54th St., Manhattan.

Several plots in the city have been protected from development and preserved as *nature areas.* Most notable are Wave Hill's 28 acres in the Bronx (675 W. 252nd St.) and the larger High Rock Conservation Center on Staten Island (Nevada Ave.). Central Park's *Ramble* is a favorite for bird watchers; hilly and wooded, it lies just north of the 72nd St. lake and can be reached on foot in 10 minutes from the Museum of Natural History.

Toys and hobbies galore can be seen—or bought—at F.A.O. Schwarz (58th St. and 5th Ave.) and Polk's Hobby Shop (32nd St. and 5th Ave.), and Central Park has plenty of space, on weekdays, to fly kites or model airplanes.

Many of the listings under *Walking Tours, Historic Sites,* and *Museums* will likely also prove exciting and memorable for children. And you might want to check the daily papers for such special events as the holiday pageants at Radio City Music Hall and the regularly touring circus, ice, Disney and Sesame Street shows that play Madison Square Garden.

PARTICIPANT SPORTS. The sports most participated in by New Yorkers are probably **jogging** and **bicycling**. Statistics bear this out, as do two major events created by interest in these two sports—the annual New York City Marathon (run through all five boroughs and a great way to sightsee on foot if you're up to covering 26 miles, 385 yards) and the 50-kilometer (31-mile) Bicycle Challenge 'round and 'round and 'round, etc.) Central Park. For the latter, participants are free to cycle one six-mile loop around the park

SPORTS

or to go for as many as they can right up to the end. Both events draw international fields and are as much a circusy party as athletic competition.

The reasons for the popularity of jogging and bicycling are fairly obvious: They are relatively inexpensive, require no in-place equipment (just some park space), and their exercise and health value are intensified in the city environment, where the air is never better than "kind of pure" and so many people work inside sitting down. The reasons for the popularity of the New York City Marathon are not so obvious—but it must have something going for it because the cut-off number for participants is 16,000—and the waiting list to get into the run is usually over 20,000! In any event, the marathon is always held on the third Sunday in October when the weather is usually fall crisp, cool, and clear. And the guiding spirit behind the race is the New York Road Runners Club, headquartered at the International Running Center, 9 East 89th St., New York, NY 10028, 860–4455.

Indeed, the Road Runners Club is a treasure trove of Big Apple running information for joggers of every speed. They can tell you about races scheduled while you are in town, or of the city's best running routes. These routes range from the obvious—such as the reservoir loop in Central Park or the scenic strip along the East River Drive leading to Randall's Island—to the not so obvious, such as the "Museum Mile" from 82nd to 104th Sts. passing ten museums along Manhattan's Fifth Avenue, or another lake loop in Flushing Meadows Park. The club even has a book filled with mapped running routes all around the city, yours for a nominal fee. For further information about running around the Big Apple, and for Marathon entry forms, write the Road Runners Club, P.O. Box 881, F.D.R. Station, New York, NY 10150. And if you are interested in running the Marathon, make sure to write early and to follow the instructions regarding earliest acceptable postmark.

The 50-kilometer cross-country tour drew 3,000 international cyclists, including a French exhibition team, for its first running in 1981. The number is expected to grow for the annual event, scheduled for the second week in July. For further information, contact the City of New York Department of Parks and Recreation, 360–8111.

Central Park in Manhattan and Prospect Park in Brooklyn have automobile roadways that are reserved for walkers, runners, and pedalers during daylight hours on weekends and often during non-rush hours weekdays. You can find plenty of places to rent a bike on the nearby side streets and avenues—check the Yellow Pages—or you can rent in Central Park at the Loeb Boathouse near the 72nd Street lake. You must bring some identification and at least $10.00–$25.00 or a major credit card as a security deposit. The bikes cost about $2.50 per hour, with special rates for the day, and a couple of brisk circuits of the park are certainly worth it for the activity and the view of the city and its citizens at leisure. Central Park is especially interesting for the various ad hoc music parties that fill the air in summertime, while Prospect Park is more of a family and community park.

There are plenty of informal participatory sports such as **softball, volleyball, soccer, rugby, frisbee,** or **pushball** in all the city's parks, and even the more formal league teams often look for "pick-up" players to substitute for their own absentees. In winter, cross-country **skiing** and **tobogganing** are popular in Central Park, while spring brings the **roller-skaters** out en masse. In good weather, there are a number of vans set up along Columbus Ave. in the 70s for renting skates, and on good days there is a shop near the corner of Columbus and 75th St. that rents skates also. In Central Park, most of the team games are played in the 60s and 70s, although there are many playing fields farther uptown as well. If you are brave enough to play rugby with total strangers, bring your own ambulance!

For general park information, call 360–8196; for free events information call 755–4100.

For a variety of inexpensive sports choices, from **handball** and **paddleball** to **swimming** and **jogging/exercise classes,** consider the "Y" 's way—a $5 daily guest membership offered by various YM-YWCAs and YM-YWHAs around town. Call the Y general information number (564–1300) for the address of the Y nearest you so you can check what they have to offer. Two handy Ys to keep in mind because of their location and facilities are the West Side Y at 5 West 63rd St. (787–4400) and the Vanderbilt (a k a Grand Central) Y, 224 East 47th St. (755–2410). The former has an indoor track, one of the best-organized running clubs in town, locker and shower facilities and pool, and is almost directly across the street from Lincoln Center and from Central Park. The Vanderbilt offers paddleball, handball, volleyball, sauna, swimming, and a convenient Grand Central Station area location close to the East River and the United Nations.

Increasingly, you'll also come across Y-like health clubs and spas throughout the city, some with tennis and racquetball courts, pools, and extensive exercise rooms. Access to these is almost always by membership only, although you may be able to purchase a day-pass if you have a friend who belongs to one or another of the clubs. If on business, you might also be able to gain admittance through a company membership.

Chess and backgammon, and sometimes Go, are not exactly participant sports, but this is what is available at Chess Mart, 240 Sullivan St. at 3rd St., and the Chess Shop, 230 Thompson St. near 3rd St., both in the Village. These places, and the Game Room, 2130 Broadway at 75th St., stay open way into the evening.

There are plenty of **bowling alleys:** in lower Manhattan, Bowlmor (110 University Pl.); in midtown, Times Square Lanes (1482 Broadway); check the Yellow Pages for other lanes.

Billiard Academies—or, if you prefer, pool halls—are similarly numerous. McGirr's, 709 8th Ave., is probably the most atmospheric, fully complemented by cigar smoke and colorful characters. Its location, near the theater district, bus station, and the former site of Madison Square Garden, might be responsible. Elsewhere in Manhattan, you can cue up, in Inwood, near the Cloisters, at Guys and Gals (500 W. 207th St.). Brooklyn offers: in Flatbush, Action (2168 Albemarle Rd.); in Sheepshead Bay, near the charter fishing boat piers, Sheepshead Billiards (1710 Sheepshead Bay Rd.); in Bay Ridge, near the Verrazano-

SPORTS

Narrows Bridge, Skytop Cue Club (512 86th St.) Queens locations include: in Little Neck, The Little Neck Recreation Center (250-21 Northern Blvd., Little Neck); in Forest Hills, Jacy's (96-42 Queens Blvd., Forest Hills). In Staten Island, you may play or take a lesson at Golden Cue (135 Canal St., Stapleton).

The city's numerous public **golf courses** are playable for a weekday green fee of $5.00, $7.00 on weekends. Phone ahead to get a "best guess" on how long a wait you'll have before teeing off. In Brooklyn, play at Dyker Beach (86th St. and 6th Ave.; 836-9722) or Marine Park (2880 Flatbush Ave.; 338-7113). In Queens, there's the Clearview in Bayside (202-12 Willets Point Blvd.; 229-2570), Douglaston Park in Douglaston (Commonwealth Blvd. & Marathon Parkway; 224-6566), Forest Park in Ridgewood (Interboro Parkway and Main Drive; 296-2442), and Kissena Park in Flushing (N. Hempstead Turnpike and Fresh Meadows Rd.; 445-3388). Staten Island's courses are Silver Lake (Victory Blvd. and Park Rd.; 447-5686), South Shore (Huguenot Ave.; 984-0108), and LaTourette (Forest Hill Rd.; 351-1889). The Bronx offers Mosholu-Booth (Jerome Ave. and Holly Lane; 822-4845), Van Cortlandt (Broadway near 242nd St.; 543-4595), and Pelham-Split Rock (City Island and Pelham Bay Park W.; 885-0838). There are two courses at the latter, and Split Rock may be the toughest challenge within the five boroughs. If a driving range would content you, Golf City in Whitestone, Queens, has over 100 tees and a battery of sport and game attractions suitable for a family outing. Golf City is at 140-15 20th Ave., reached via the 20th Ave. exit of the Whitestone Expressway, between Shea Stadium and the Whitestone Bridge; 746-4800. There are also large driving ranges and miniature golf layouts near the City Island Causeway in the Bronx and across from Floyd Bennett Field (near Gateway National Park and the Rockaways) in Brooklyn.

Ice-skating is popular, even fashionable, at the famous Rockefeller Center rink and the Wollman Memorial Rink (under renovation at press time) near 59th St. in Central Park. Other city locations are Sky Rink (450 W. 33rd St. in Manhattan, where the New York Rangers work out), Riverdale (236th St. and Broadway in the Bronx) and another Wollman Memorial, this one in Brooklyn's Prospect Park.

Roller-skaters gather in Central Park on a mall at about 70th St. due east of Central Park West—follow the skaters or the sound of blaring radios and tape players to find them. The most glamorous of New York's roller discos is Manhattan's Roxy (515 W. 18th St.; 691-3113), while the only banked rink is in Brooklyn at Sweet Ruby's (Wyckoff and Myrtle Aves.; 456-3300). When not occupied for rock concerts or flea markets, Skate Pier 84 (44th St. and 12th Ave., Manhattan; 244-4270) keeps you outdoors at the edge of the Hudson. Beginners flock to Greenwich Village's Village Skating (15 Waverly Pl.; 677-9690), while only the most experienced venture out to Brooklyn for the standard-bearing roller rink of them all, the Empire (200 Empire Blvd.; 462-1570). Check the Yellow Pages for additional neighborhood locales.

Fishermen can rent or charter boats to try their luck in the waters surrounding New York. Favorite launching points are City Island in the Bronx (Jack's Bait and Tackle) and the Sheepshead Bay area of Brooklyn (Bay End Dock Co.

or Canarsie-Jamaica Marine at the Canarsie Recreation Pier, east of Sheepshead Bay). There are numerous other fishing excursions at both these locations.

Tennis courts maintained by the Parks Department are used by city residents, who purchase a season permit, valid from early April to the end of October, for $27.00; but visitors may buy individual $4.00 passes at the Central Park Courts (93rd and Central Park). These passes entitle the player to one hour of tennis on any of the city-run courts, a list of which may be obtained from the Parks Department. The Central Park courts are very popular, and players often have to wait an hour or two after signing in for a court, but at other locations, though they are sometimes tricky to find and not as well maintained, one can often sign in and walk right on to the court. For privately owned courts, rates vary considerably from summer to winter, often running as much as $10.00 an hour higher in the winter. The rates also vary according to the time-slot required: the hours before work, 7–9; lunch hours, 12–2; and the evening hours from 6–10, being generally most in demand and therefore most expensive. Prices per hour range from a low of $16 to a top of $25 for inexpensive courts, to a low of $27 to a high of $58 for the most expensive. (And many courts will be raising their prices soon.)

Courts in *Manhattan,* starting south and working uptown: *Wall Street Racquet Club,* foot of Wall St. at East River (952–0760); free parking; 9 new indoor Har-tru courts; low weekday rates. *Village Tennis Courts,* 110 University Place (989–2300); Acrycushion 6 surface courts; ball-machine practice courts; moderate. *Gramercy Tennis and Racquet Club,* 708 Sixth Ave. near 23rd St. (691–0110); new Elastraturf courts; moderate; major credit cards. *Midtown Tennis Club,* 341 Eighth Ave., corner 27th St. (989–8572); 8 Har-tru tournament courts; indoor and outdoor courts; limited back line space; moderate. *Tennis Club, Grand Central Terminal,* 15 Vanderbilt Ave. (687–3841); 2 Elastraturf courts; very expensive but luxurious. *Manhattan Plaza Racquet Club,* 450 W. 43rd St. (594–0554); new Elastraturf courts; excellent tennis pros; expensive. *Sutton East Tennis Club,* 488 E. 60th St. at York Ave. (751–3452); 8 clay courts; cramped space; moderate to expensive; open Oct. 26th to Apr. 5th. *Tower Tennis Courts,* 1725 York Ave. between 88th and 89th Sts. (860–2464); deco-turf indoor courts, limited side lines; expensive.

In the boroughs outside Manhattan the price range is considerably lower, being as low as $4.00 for open-air courts in the summer, and in the winter ranging from a low of $8.00 to a high of $23.00.

Brooklyn: Brooklyn Racquet Club, 2781 Shell Rd. (769–5167); 14 indoor and outdoor clay courts; free parking and babysitting; inexpensive. Parade Grounds Tennis, 305 Coney Island Ave. (633–5400); Har-tru surface courts; moderate to inexpensive. *The Bronx:* Stadium Tennis, 11 E. 162nd St. (293–2386); only open to transients in the winter, in the summer it reverts to a city court; 8 unevenly laid, rubberized cork surface courts; moderate to inexpensive. *Staten Island:* Richmond Racquet Club, 2282 Forest Ave. (727–6787); Har-tru surface courts; open year round; $12 flat rate or 5-hour coupon book for $35. *Queens:* Sterling Tennis, 40–15 126th St, Corona. (446–5619); Har-tru courts; open-air in summer; inexpensive. Boulevard Gardens, 51–26 Broadway, Woodside (545–

SPORTS

7774); indoor and outdoor clay courts; moderate to inexpensive. U.S.T.A. National Tennis Center, Flushing Meadows Park, Flushing (592–8000); this is the tennis complex where the U.S. Open Championships are played—there are 9 indoor and 24 outdoor courts, all in excellent condition; surfaces are Deco II; moderate to inexpensive.

Squash courts are available at the following Manhattan locations: Fifth Avenue Racquet Club (405 Fifth Ave.), Manhattan Squash Club (41 W. 42nd St.), Park Avenue Squash and Racquet Club (3 Park Ave.), Town Squash (151 E. 86th St.), and the Turtle Bay Racquet Club (541 Lexington Ave.). Manhattan's only platform tennis courts are at the Apple Platform Tennis Club, 215 E. 24th St. Because racquetball courts come and go as quickly as the ball flies off the wall at you, the Yellow Pages are your best source of information. Fees are generally somewhat lower than for tennis.

Some of the larger city parks maintain bridle paths for **horseback riding.** Near Forest Park, along the Brooklyn–Queens border, the nearest riding stable is Stanley's in Forest Hills (88–03 70th Rd.); in Staten Island, riding horses and horse-drawn hayrides are available at Clove Lake Stables (1025 Clove Rd.); the Bronx has the Van Cortlandt Park Riding Academy, in the northern tip of the park (Broadway and 254th St.); in Manhattan, the Claremont Stable (175 W. 89th St.) is right near Central Park; in Brooklyn, there are Prospect Park Riding Stables (51 Caton Place, off Prospect Park West) and Jamaica Bay Riding Academy (7000 Shore Parkway). All the stables listed also offer instruction. You can expect to pay $15–18 per hour, without instruction, but usually including a trail guide.

Some other sports opportunities in New York center around schools. Consult, according to your special interests, Offshore Sailing School, Aqua-Lung School of New York, Rohde's Academy of Fencing, A&L Scooter and Motorcycle, or Parachutes Incorporated.

SPECTATOR SPORTS. Baseball season, April through October, features the Yankees and Mets, and each schedules about 75 home dates, of which nearly half are night games. The Mets' ballpark is Shea Stadium, in Flushing, Queens (672–3000), while the Yankees play at their famous stadium in the Bronx, "the house that Ruth built" (293–6000). Tickets are available at many Ticketron outlets throughout the metropolitan area and a fairly good seat is usually not too hard to find unless the team is involved in crucial, late-season action. Caution: Shea Stadium can be uncomfortably chilly on spring and autumn nights. And the Yankee Stadium area isn't the safest place in the world, so don't linger too long after the game.

Pro football is a furious business, but New York's two pro football teams, the Jets and the Giants, are less furious than most and have been having more ups and downs than opposing linemen in recent seasons. Therefore general admission tickets to their Sunday National Football League games are usually readily available at Ticketron outlets and at the respective stadiums, even through both teams have hordes of regular season-ticket holders. The Jets share

Shea Stadium with the aforementioned Mets—the result being they never play any home games until the Mets have finished their baseball schedule. Jets reserved seat tickets cost $9 and if you think it can get cold nights during baseball season, wait until the winter winds come howling in across Flushing Bay. Bring blankets, anti-freeze, hats, gloves—you name it, because, Baby, it gets cold outside when you root, root, root for the home team Jets. For ticket and game information call the stadium or 421-6600.

The pro Giants left Yankee Stadium for the greener pastures of the nearby New Jersey Meadowlands sports complex in East Rutherford, New Jersey. Tickets for games at Giants Stadium are also $9; phone (201) 935-8222. The season runs from September through January.

Yankee Stadium is most readily accessible via the IRT No. 4, and the IND D and CC subway lines to the 161 St. stop. Shea Stadium can be reached by way of the No. 7 Flushing line to the Willets Point–Shea Stadium station. The Shea parking lot (follow the signs from the Van Wyck Expressway or Grand Central Parkway) accommodates thousands of automobiles, though the traffic on both of these highways is always great. To get to the Meadowlands, see information in the *Jersey Shore* section below.

Basketball and **hockey** are the major attractions at Madison Square Garden, which stands above Penn Station at 32 St. and Seventh Ave. Known simply as "The Garden" to generations of athletes and sports fans, this 20,000-seat arena hasn't grown a real winner in recent seasons in either the Knicks—New York's pro basketball entry in the National Basketball Association—or the Rangers, the Big Apple's National Hockey League representative from Manhattan. Again, the result is that tickets are readily available on any given night, at prices ranging from $6 to $14 for Knicks games and $5 to $15 for Rangers games.

Both teams play a regular season that runs from early October to early April, excluding post-season playoffs that may go another six weeks. The regular season involves about 40 home dates. To find out who's battling either of these home teams call 563-8000. Parking near the Garden is difficult and expensive, so try using the IRT 1, 2, or 3 trains, or the IND A, CC, or E lines to Penn Station.

Diehard sports fans can catch more pro basketball action by venturing out of Manhattan to the Meadowlands to see the scrappy New Jersey Nets play their version of NBA ball (201-935-8888), while New York's best brand of hockey is played at the Nassau Coliseum on nearby Long Island, where the Islanders—1980 and '81 Stanley Cup champions—skate through their NHL season (516-794-4100).

The Garden used to be famous for its **boxing** matches but has fallen on hard times of late for a variety of reasons. The *Daily News* still sponsors the exciting Golden Gloves programs each spring; the very lack of polish and ring experience guarantees action galore. And Madison Square Garden is still home for the final rounds of its post-season collegiate National Invitational Basketball Tournament, offering a Holiday Festival over the Christmas semester break that brings in excellent college teams and is occasional home court for such exciting local college squads as St. John's, Fordham, Manhattan, and Seton Hall. The Garden

SPORTS

also hosts some prizefights, indoor pro tennis, prestigious track and field events such as the Millrose Games and entertainment events such as ice shows, the circus, rodeos, wrestling, horse shows, and even rock 'n' roll headliners who play the main arena (564-4400) as well as the smaller Felt Forum (563-8000).

Flat and harness tracks draw millions of **horse racing** enthusiasts each year. Thoroughbred racing takes place at Aqueduct Racetrack in Ozone Park, Queens, and Belmont Racetrack in Elmont, on nearby Long Island, with the season running from October through April at Aqueduct and from May through October at Belmont. Aqueduct is the largest thoroughbred racing track in the U.S., while Belmont is where the third and final leg of the "Triple Crown," the Belmont Stakes, is run to determine the nation's best three-year-old racehorse. Since post times vary seasonally it's best to check first with the New York Racing Association (212-641-4700) before heading out to the tracks. Working folks benefit from the night-time programs of standardbred harness races at Yonkers in Westchester County (914-968-4200; just over the New York City border at the edge of the Bronx), Roosevelt Raceway in Westbury (516-222-2000; on nearby Long Island), and the Meadowlands (from January through August), new home of the Hambletonian, in East Rutherford, New Jersey (201-935-8500). The Meadowlands also runs thoroughbred horses *at night* from September through December.

The New York City Off-Track Betting Corporation (OTB) is the nation's first government-run off-track betting operation. OTB offers betting programs from some of the best thoroughbred and harness tracks in America. It is a source of entertainment and sport for thousands of New Yorkers and visitors who want to get a bet down or just study the Damon Runyan characters who frequent OTB. There are over 150 branch offices throughout the city's five boroughs, many open seven days a week. Free admission. For further information, the New York City OTB phone number is 221-5624.

Tennis reaches its peak here in early September when the U.S. Open Tennis Championships are played at the USTA National Tennis Center, Flushing Meadows, Queens (212-592-8000). This is one of four titles which enjoys supreme status worldwide, and although tickets for the finals are scarce, you can catch most of the big names as they work their way through the early rounds. The prestigious tournament was recently moved from the West Side Tennis in Forest Hills (212-268-2300) which is still synonymous with the best tennis in the world. Forest Hills stages its own major pro tennis event in the early fall.

Golf tournaments are proliferating so fast that almost any area is a candidate for the next one, although the annual Westchester Classic in early June at the Westchester Country Club in Rye (914-967-6000) is one of the major steps on the Pro Golfers Association Tour (and really just a short drive away from one of the area's great amusement parks, Rye Playland).

You're probably aware of the sudden burst of interest in **soccer** in the U.S. This area's championship team, the Cosmos, are led by highly paid imported stars. The Cosmos play from April through August at Giants Stadium in the Meadowlands. Tickets cost $7 and $12 for adults, $4 for children, and information is available in New York at 265-8600.

College football, basketball, and **baseball** can provide some exciting moments on a highly skilled amateur level—as well as the opportunity to see some of the Big Apple's most beautiful campuses. Columbia University, for example, plays football against Ivy League rivals such as Harvard, Yale, and Princeton at antiquated Baker Field, Broadway at 218th St. in the colorful Inwood section of upper Manhattan. St. John's in Brooklyn, Manhattan in the Riverdale section of the Bronx, and Fordham in the Little Italy section off Fordham Road in the Bronx, play a very competitive brand of club- and small-college-division-level football, as does Wagner on rural Staten Island, Iona in Westchester, and Seton Hall in nearby New Jersey, where Rutgers plays the closest thing to a big-time football schedule in the metropolitan area.

All of the above-named colleges and universities have top basketball, baseball, and track and field programs and compete actively in such relatively minor sports as soccer, lacrosse, crew, and swimming. Indeed, Columbia is a perennial Ivy League soccer powerhouse. Most field women's teams in major sports as well. In fact, Fordham has become a national power in women's basketball.

LOTTERIES. At any given time, New York State will have several lotteries going, all benefiting local school districts across the state. Bets range from 50 cents up, with prizes as high as $1,000 a week for life. As of press time there are four regular lotteries being conducted: *Instant Winners, New York Numbers, Win 4* and *Lotto*. The "games" for each vary, ranging from scratch-and-match-the-pictures to genuine lotteries whereby individuals choose a series of digits and compare their number to one drawn at random. Tickets can be purchased at thousands of newsstands and candy stores, but winners for each game are drawn on a different basis. For example, for the lotteries mentioned above, winning numbers for New York Numbers and Lotto are drawn live on television—on Channel 5 in New York City at about 8:30 P.M. nightly for Numbers and Tuesday and Thursday for Win 4 and at about 10:15 P.M. on Saturdays for Lotto; Instant Winners tells you immediately after purchase what you have won in the preliminary rounds, with winners eligible for a grand prize drawing. Each day's or week's numbers are reported in the daily papers as well. Even if you don't win anything, you'll have an interesting souvenir—and you'll have helped the state's school system.

HISTORIC SITES. Wall Street Area and the Harbor: If you are conducting your own walking tour of historical sites and sights, you might do well to start out where the city did—at the harbor. Henry Hudson, an Englishman employed by the Dutch East India Company, sailed his ship, the *Half Moon,* into the harbor in 1609 and the area's inclusion in what Europeans called the "New World" dates from then.

Battery Park. Time your explorations to arrive Tuesday at noon (from the end of June to early September) and your explorations can be accompanied by the brassy beat of a Battery Park Band Concert. A few of the historic sites of note (walking clockwise):

HISTORIC SITES

Shrine of Saint Elizabeth Ann Seton, 7 State St. Canonized in 1975, the first American-born saint, she once lived at 8 State St.

Jewish Immigrant Memorial. In front of the Staten Island Ferry Terminal, it commemorates the 23 Jewish men and women who arrived in Nieuw Amsterdam (then chiefly inhabited by Mana-hatta Indians) in 1654, and stayed to found several of America's most distinguished families.

Verrazano Statue. Honors the Florentine navigator who pre-dated Henry Hudson, entering the harbor in 1524. Despite the fact that he boldly took possession of "this island-bay, river, and all countries, rivers, lakes and streams contiguous and adjacent thereunto," his employer, Francis I of France, did nothing further about it, and the island, therefore, never was colonized by France.

Castle Clinton National Monument. Originally built as a harbor fort in 1811, it has been substantially restored as such. It has also served as the Castle Garden amusement center, where P. T. Barnum staged the musical "event of the century" by presenting Jenny Lind. Those who could not obtain tickets formed rowboat parties and listened to the Swedish Nightingale from the river. From 1855 to 1890 the ex-fort played host to some 7,000,000 "new Americans" as the country's chief immigrant entrance station. After that it served as a station for fishes—the city's aquarium—until 1941.

Bowling Green. This is the site, many believe, where Peter Minuit bought the island Manhattan from the native Algonquins. A century later, it was indeed a lawn where sportsmen played bowls. The original 1771 fence around the green is intact today.

U.S. Custom House. It was built by Cass Gilbert in 1907, when America was newly conscious of its central position on the world stage. This may account for the themes of the white marble sculpture: the great continents and commercial cities of the globe.

Fraunces Tavern (corner of Broad and Pearl Sts.). One of the few remaining restored Colonial buildings in the city. Built in 1719 as a handsome private house for Etienne de Lancey, it was bought in 1762 by a Frenchman, Samuel Fraunces, otherwise known as "Black Sam." He ran it as the Queen Charlotte, or Queen's Head Tavern, and it was there, in the second-floor dining room, that General Washington gave the farewell dinner to his officers. Souvenirs of the occasion can be seen in the third floor *Museum of the Revolution.* The ground-floor restaurant open for lunch and dinner weekdays, Washington's birthday. The Tavern once offered "first-class regular dinner for 25 cents, for gentlemen only." The prices are now somewhat more elevated. The entire Tavern is closed weekends. The Museum is open Monday–Friday, 10:00 A.M.–4:00 P.M. Free.

To reach Battery Park, take East or West Side IRT (local) to South Ferry.

While at Battery Park you will no doubt want to visit the *Statue of Liberty.* The 151-foot-high lady, the world's best-known symbolic monument, may be visited via the special ferry which leaves from Battery Park every hour on the hour from 9:00 A.M. to 4:00 P.M. daily, with additional sailings Saturdays, Sundays, and holidays, April through October round trip fares for adults, $1.50; all children (11 years and under) 50 cents. For further information, call 248–8097.

The boat trip takes 20 minutes; allow two hours for round trip plus inspection of the Statue. Refreshments and souvenirs available on boats. The Statue has been raising her torch over New York Harbor since 1886.

There is also a ferry from Battery Park to *Ellis Island,* the former immigrant-processing center, through which the ancestors of many, many Americans reached the New World. The ferry leaves the park 4 times a day (9:30 A.M., 11:45 A.M., 2:00 P.M., and 4:45 P.M.) 7 days a week. The cost is $1.50 for adults and 50¢ for children under 12. The price includes a guided tour of the island, which takes about 2 hours and includes the old buildings.

Lower Manhattan

A few old streets: Stone Street was the first cobbled under the orders of Nieuw Amsterdam's governor, irascible peg-legged Peter Stuyvesant, who also built a wall along the north edge of the settlement in 1658 as protection against the Indians.

Wall Street follows the course of that original wall. Several years later the first road was built (1668), linking the first colony to a suburban village called Nieuw Haarlem. The road was called Broadway. At 45 Broadway there is a tablet at the site of the first house built on Manhattan in 1613. Nearby is the historic *Trinity Church,* reputed to be the wealthiest single church in the world. In 1705, Queen Anne gave Trinity Parish a grant of land covering a substantial chunk of lower Manhattan; the church still owns much of it. Alexander Hamilton and Robert Fulton are buried in the graveyard. The church (built in 1845, the third on the site) and graveyard are open daily from 7:00 A.M. to 6:00 P.M. The Trinity Museum is open Monday–Saturday, 10:30 A.M.–3:30 P.M., Sunday, 12:30 P.M.–3:30 P.M. Admission to all is free.

Nearby is the *Federal Hall National Memorial,* on the site of the country's first capital, where our first President took his first oath of office. A statue of Washington stands on the spot today. The museum includes the Zenger Room, with documents relating to John Peter Zenger's fight for freedom of the press. Call for schedule of weekly concerts 264–8711.

In the busy City Hall-financial district stands *St. Paul's Chapel,* where Washington worshipped. You can see his pew in the north aisle. The church was also the site of a special service after Washington's inauguration. This handsome church was built in 1761–66, and is the oldest public building in Manhattan. It fills the block between Broadway, Vesey, Church, and Fulton Streets.

Some other Historic Sites in Lower Manhattan: St. Mark's-in-the-Bouwerie, at 10th St. at intersection of Stuyvesant St. and Second Ave., was consecrated in 1799. It stands on the site of a chapel originally built on the edge of Peter Stuyvesant's 300-acre farm (or—in Dutch—Stuyvesant's *bouwerie*). You can see Stuyvesant's grave, and a statue of him, in nearby Stuyvesant Park. Nearby Stuyvesant Town, a "city" within a city—35,000 call this middle-income development "home"—covers part of his river-front farm.

At the east end of Fulton Street is the *South Street Seaport,* an area undergoing restoration. Pier 16 has several tall ships, some of which the public may

HISTORIC SITES

board and view; a museum with displays and folklore about the history of the Port of New York; and several shops in restored 18th- and 19th-century buildings with goods and services in the manner of the era.

Have lunch at nearby *Sweets* (corner of Fulton and South Street), one of the world's finest seafood restaurants, little changed in style or excellence since it was founded in 1845. To reach Sweets and/or the Fulton Fish Market, take IRT or BMT line, or Broadway bus to Fulton St. and walk east.

Civic Center

City Hall. The present structure was opened in 1812, restored in 1956. In 1824, Lafayette, the great French ally of the colonists during the Revolutionary War, was officially entertained here. You may sometimes see ceremonies on the steps in honor of a person or group that has performed a good deed. Also of interest is *The Governor's Room,* where period furniture and portraits of George Washington, Alexander Hamilton, and John Jay, among others, are on view. Open to the public, Monday–Friday, 10:00 A.M.–3:00 P.M. Free.

Nathan Hale Statue. West of City Hall, but still within the surrounding park, a statue commemorates the patriot whom the British hanged as a spy in 1776. As he prepared to ascend the gallows, he uttered his historic farewell, "I regret that I have but one life to give for my country."

Greenwich Village

The Village was the city's first residential suburb, started in the late 1730s when people fled "north" to escape the plague. *Washington Square* was designated as a potter's field and public execution ground. By 1826, when it became a drill ground for militia, some 10,000 bodies, victims of the plague or the gallows, had been buried there. Around this time the Square's redbrick, white-trimmed houses were built. The old *Boorman House* on the northeast corner was the home of Edith Wharton, William Dean Howells and Henry James.

Washington Arch, at the foot of Fifth Ave., was first built in 1889 when the city celebrated the centenary of Washington's inaugural. The present version was designed by the famous Stanford White, and built in 1895.

Two blocks over from the Square, at the corner of 6th and Greenwich Ave., is the *Jefferson Market Courthouse,* built in 1877 and more recently saved from the wrecker's ball and turned into a branch of the N.Y. Public Library.

There are many other historic houses in the Village—for example, *The narrowest house in the city* at 75½ Bedford St., whose tenants included Edna St. Vincent Millay and John Barrymore. But the only house in the district which you can visit is *The Old Merchant's House,* 29 E. 4th St., 777-1089. The house was built in 1830, was lived in by the same family, the Tredwells, from 1835 to 1933 when the last of the Tredwell sisters died, in her nineties. The house was bought by a grandnephew and presented to the city. Sundays, 1:00–4:00 P.M., group tours by appointment. Adults, $2.00; students and Senior Citizens, $1.00.

To get there: take Third Ave. bus to 4th St.; or IRT Lexington local to Astor Place.

Another noteworthy old house not far from the Village is the *Theodore Roosevelt Mansion,* 28 E. 20th St. 260-1616. The Rough Rider was born and grew up in this typical upper-middle-class brownstone which is well kept up, and open to visitors. Daily 9:00 A.M.–5:00 P.M., except Monday–Tuesday, October–May. Adults, 50¢; children and Senior Citizens, free.

Midtown and Uptown

The Abigail Adams Smith Museum at 421 E. 61st St. 838-6878. One of Manhattan's last 18th-century buildings. Originally the carriage house for the home the then Vice-President John Adams had built for his daughter Abigail. A gem kept in perfect condition by the Colonial Dames of America. Guide on duty. Monday–Friday, 10 A.M.–4:00 P.M. Adults, $1.00; Senior Citizens, 50 cents.

Far Uptown: *Morris-Jumel Mansion,* W. 161st St. and Edgecombe Ave. This Georgian Colonial hilltop house was built in 1765. A year later, George Washington slept here for a night. His camp bed may still be seen. Here too Aaron Burr married the wealthy Mme. Jumel, then in her sixties, and soon divorced her. *To get there:* Fifth Ave. bus 2 or 3 to 162nd St.; or IND Eighth Ave. subway to 163rd St. (AA local). Tuesday–Sunday, 10:00 A.M. to 4:00 P.M. Adults, $1.00; students and Senior Citizens, 50 cents.

The Dyckman House, 204th St. and Broadway, was built in 1783, and was the farm residence of the wealthy Dyckman family, which once owned most of northern Manhattan. The only remaining Dutch farmhouse in New York City. *To get there:* IND (Eighth Ave.) subway (A) to 204th St. Tuesday–Sunday, 11:00 A.M.–5:00 P.M. Free.

General Grant National Memorial, Riverside Dr. and 122nd St., 666-1640. The Civil War general and two-term president is buried in the crypt, with photo and other exhibits also housed in the tomb. Open daily, 9:00 A.M.–5:00 P.M.; closed Monday and Tuesday, October–May.

The Other Boroughs

Brooklyn: *Brooklyn Heights,* a picturesque neighborhood of brownstone, brick, and old wooden houses high on a bluff overlooking New York Harbor, was designated New York's first "historic district." The New York Landmarks Commission calls the Heights "by far the finest remaining microcosm of our city as it was more than 100 years ago." Once a year the Brooklyn Historical Society conducts walking tours of some of the private homes, but even at other times you may wish to wander through the streets and trace the evolution of the New York townhouse: wooden and brick Federal style, Greek Revival, Gothic Revival (which came into style in the 1840s). Romanesque Revival, and Renaissance Revival. The Heights' *Lady of Lebanon Church* is the first Romanesque Revival building in the U.S. An esplanade reached by way of Montague Street, the residential area's primary shopping block, affords a spectacular view of the lower Manhattan Skyline and the New York Harbor.

Lefferts Homestead, Prospect Park, 965-6560. A homestead built in Dutch Colonial days. Call for schedule.

Bronx: *Van Cortlandt Mansion Museum* 543-3344. Built in 1748, this house, now run by the Colonial Dames, has furnishings and household goods which reflect both its Dutch and British owners. Tuesday–Saturday, 10:00 A.M.–4:45 P.M.; Sunday, 2:00–4:45 P.M. Adults, 75 cents, children, free. *To get there:* IRT Broadway subway to Van Cortlandt Park (end of line).

Poe Cottage, Poe Park, Kingsbridge Road, 881-8900. Edgar Allan Poe wrote many of his works (including *Annabelle Lee*) in this small cottage, which has barely been preserved as it was in the poet's day.

Queens: *Bowne House,* 37-01 Bowne St., Flushing 359-0528. The Society of Friends assembled in this old house. Built in 1661, it is today a shrine commemorating the struggle for religious freedom. Tuesday, Saturday, Sunday, 2:30 P.M.–4:30 P.M. Adults, $1.00; children 25 cents.

Staten Island: *Billou-Stillwell-Perine House,* 1476 Richmond Rd., Dongan Hills. Original section of this house was built prior to 1675, later additions date up through 1830.

Conference House, south end of Hylan Blvd., Tottenville 984-2086. Built in 1680. The only peace conference during the Revolutionary War was held here. Wednesday–Sunday, 1:00 P.M.–5:00 P.M. Adults, 50 cents; children, free.

LIBRARIES. The *New York Public Library* consists of two branch networks, the first covering Manhattan, the Bronx, and Staten Island, and the second taking care of Brooklyn and Queens. Although beset by severe financial difficulties in recent years, the system includes a number of outstanding individual branches, some of which will be detailed below. The library operates an excellent home reference information service: 790-6161. There is also a "readers' advisor" service:

The crown jewel of the system, on Fifth Avenue from 40th to 42nd Streets, is, ironically, a private library open to the public—funded originally by the Samuel J. Tilden Trust and the Astor and Lenox libraries of the 1890s. The city contributed to its founding by donating the site and constructing the $9 million building that was to house the collections.

The *Main Branch*'s two-block-long Beaux-Arts façade, with twin lions perched alongside the steps leading to the entrance, is a symbol of New Yorkers' quest for knowledge. With a public card catalog containing 10 million entries, and more than half an acre of reading rooms, it includes resources for virtually every field of endeavor. Only the Library of Congress and Harvard's Widener Library are larger.

The 42nd St. library, however, is something of a museum as well as a research center. Sixteen years under construction, it opened in 1911, christened at the time by President Taft. The expansive marble foyer bespeaks extravagance in a way that is rarely seen in New York. In addition there are several galleries

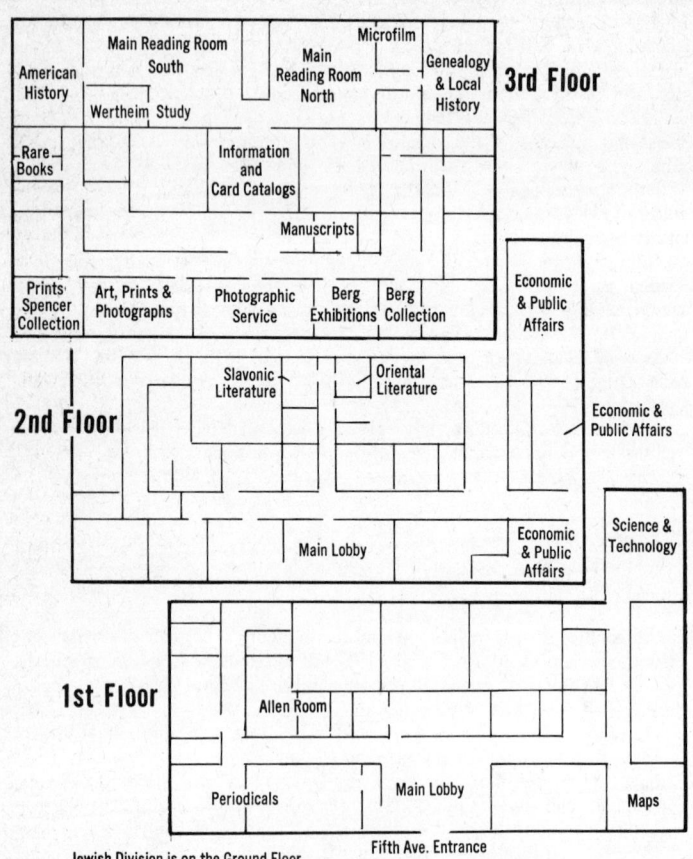

New York Public Library at 42nd Street

LIBRARIES

throughout the building, and such specialty reference rooms as the Manuscript, Art, Print, Oriental Language, Technology, and American History Rooms. Most of these are open to the public; for some, including the Manuscript Room, a special pass is needed. There are always two or three special exhibitions at the library—prints, books, or manuscripts—as well as "mini-exhibits" of such things as Walt Whitman matter (from the Oscar Lion Collection) and the Berg Collection, which has large exhibits that change twice a year or so. The Berg specializes in literature, and, except for the exhibit area, is open to qualified scholars and researchers only.

Several other midtown Manhattan branches are of particular interest, and worth noting here. These include the *Mid-Manhattan Library* (sometimes known as the Annex to the Main Building, at 40th St. and Fifth Ave.; Whereas the 42nd St. Main Branch is purely a reference and research facility, the Mid-Manhattan Library is a less comprehensive research and reference collection—specializing in science, education, and business, though in the near future it will include history and sociology too—with some circulating titles); the *Library and Musuem of Performing Arts* at Lincoln Center (111 Amsterdam Ave.; there are really two libraries here: one, open to the public, for records, printed music, dance, film and drama books, and the other, open to qualified researchers by permission. This branch also has regular exhibits of performing arts materials such as set models, designers' sketches, music manuscripts, etc.); the *Donnell Library* (20 W. 53rd St., also strong on performing and fine arts and popular books in foreign languages); and the *Library for the Blind and Physically Handicapped* (166 Avenue of the Americas).

The number of other branches and the hours they are open have dwindled during the course of New York's various fiscal crises, so it is best to check with individual branches when planning a visit.

SPECIAL-INTEREST LIBRARIES

New York has numerous specialized libraries on almost all subjects. Some, listed below alphabetically by subject area, are open to the public. Others may be found by consulting the *Special Libraries Directory of Greater New York*, available at the Mid-Manhattan Library, 8 E. 40th St. If the library you are interested in is not open to the public, you may know someone in a professional association who is allowed in. In all cases, we suggest you call before going.

Advertising and marketing. *Batten, Barton, Durstine & Osborne Information Retrieval Center*, 383 Madison Ave., 355–5800, and *NBC Information Services*, 30 Rockefeller Plaza, 664–4444. It's best to identify yourself as a student.

Architecture, crafts, and design. *Fashion Institute of Technology Library*, 227 W. 27th St., 760–7695, and *American Craft Council*, 22 W. 55th St., 397–0600.

Banking. *C.I.T. Library*, currently 650 Madison Ave., but may move; 572–6500, and *New York Stock Exchange*, 11 Wall St., 623–3000, where an appointment is necessary.

Behaviorial sciences. *American Society for Psychical Research,* 5 W. 73rd St., 799–5050, and *Kristine Mann Library,* 28 E. 39th St., 697–7877, the latter specializing in the work of Carl Jung.

Biblical studies. *American Bible Society,* 581–7400, where Bibles can be found in more than 100 languages.

Broadcasting. *ABC General Library,* 1926 Broadway, 887–7777, and *Museum of Broadcasting,* 1 E. 53rd St., 752–7684. The latter includes a large videotape collection of historic TV broadcasts.

Business subjects. *American Institute of CPA Library,* 1211 Avenue of the Americas, 575–6200, and the *Brooklyn Public Library,* 280 Cadman Plaza W. An appointment is needed at the 80,000-volume library of the *NYU Graduate School of Business Administration,* 100 Trinity Pl., 285–6000.

Chemistry. *Chemists' Club Library,* 52 E. 42nd St., 679–6383.

Civil liberties. *ACLU,* 132 W. 43rd St., 944–9800.

Economics and commerce. *Dun and Bradstreet,* 99 Church St., 285–7000 asks that you call ahead for an appointment. The same is true for *The Black Economic Research Center,* 112 W. 120th St., 666–0345. Also, *U.S. Department of Commerce,* 26 Federal Plaza, 264–3860.

Education. *Manhattan Community College,* 134 W. 51st St., 267–3527, has an extensive collection of non-white materials. *Children's Book Council,* 67 Irving Pl., 254–2666, is self-explanatory. If you're thinking of studying abroad, exchange programs are evaluated at the *Information and Reference Division of the Institute of International Education,* 809 UN Plaza, 883–8470.

Engineering. *Cooper Union,* on Cooper Square at E. 8th St. and Third Ave., 254–6300.

Flowers and plants. *Horitcultural Society of New York,* 128 W. 58th St., 757–0915.

Geography. *American Geographical Society,* Broadway and 156th St., 234–8100, and *Explorers Club,* 46 E. 70th St., 628–8383. An appointment is essential to the latter.

History and Genealogy. *New York Genealogical and Biographical Society,* 122 E. 58th St., 755–8532.

Industry and labor. *American Arbitration Association,* 140 W. 51st St., 484–4000. Data, laws, and court decisions in this field are at *Worker's Compensation Board,* 2 World Trade Center, 488–4141 and the *U.S. Department of Labor,* 1515 Broadway, 944–3435.

Insurance. *College of Insurance,* 123 William St., 962–4111.

Journalism. *NYU Bobst Library,* W. 4th St. at La Guardia Pl., 598–2450, has the morgue of the late *Herald Tribune.* Scholars preferred.

Medicine. *New York Academy of Medicine,* 2 E. 103rd St., 876–8200.

Music. in addition to the previously mentioned Lincoln Center and Donnell Branches of the Public Library, the *Wallace Library,* 799–5000, at Juilliard's Lincoln Center building requires advance arrangements. Also see the *Metropolitan Opera Association Archives* at Lincoln Center, 799–3100.

MUSEUMS

Public administration. *John Jay College of Criminal Justice,* 444 W. 56th St., 489–5183, has special collections on police work. *New York City Housing Library,* 218 W. 64th St., 581–4855, has literature on urban planning.

Publishing. *Oxford University Press Library,* 200 Madison Ave., 679–7300.

MUSEUMS. Examples of everything beautiful that man has fashioned with his hands throughout the ages are on view in New York, much of it housed in buildings which are of great architectural interest themselves.

The fine arts lead, and such museums as the Metropolitan and the Museum of Modern Art are among the best in the world, but if the Old (or New) Masters don't move you, stimulation can be found in other museums. There are studies of nature and the stars, of man's history on earth, and more particularly, of his life in New York City. Smaller museums, or portions of larger ones, are devoted to coins, musical instruments, rare books, crafts and folk art, ships, interior decoration, clothing, textiles, medicine, historical figures—the list is endless. Once a year, usually in mid-June, the stretch of upper Fifth Ave. known as "Museum Mile" becomes a pedestrian mall between 6:00 and 9:00 P.M. From 82nd to 105th Sts., strollers are free to come and go at ten of the city's best-known museums, including the Metropolitan, the Museum of the City of New York, the Jewish Museum, and the Cooper-Hewitt. Admission to all is free that night, with street musicians, mimes, and clown troupes entertaining the walkers outside.

Lastly there often are exhibitions sponsored by banks, oil companies, and large industrial corporations, usually in the lobbies of their office buildings; or you may find a display of anything literally from soup to nuts squirreled away in some corner of a school, church, YMCA, or firehouse—you name it. Nothing is impossible in the Big Apple.

The following New York City museums are all in Manhattan unless otherwise noted.

Abigail Adams Smith Museum. 421 E. 61st St., 838–6878. Built in 1799 as a coachhouse and stable on a 23-acre estate, the structure has gone through many phases, functioning at various times as a country inn, a private home, and an office building. Abigail Adams, daughter of President John Adams, lived on the estate with her husband, William Stephens Smith, an aide to George Washington. As a museum its Greek Revival interior includes parlors, bedrooms, ballroom, library, music room, dining room, and kitchen, with authentic appointments from the early 1800s. The museum shop sells items from the Adams-Smith period. Open Monday–Friday, 10:00 A.M.–4:00 P.M. Closed holidays and August. Children under 12, free; adults, $1.00; Senior Citizens, 50 cents.

American Academy and Institute of Arts and Letters. 633 W. 155th St. 368–5900. Works by and about members, which include paintings, music, sculpture, and graphics. Research facilities open to accredited scholars, by appointment. Open Tuesday–Sunday, 1:00–4:00 P.M. Closed Mondays and holidays. Free.

NEW YORK CITY

American Museum of Immigration. Liberty Island, 732-1236. Sponsored by the National Park Service, the permanent exhibit contains photographs, artifacts, and films depicting the history of American immigration. A comprehensive library also houses books and documents, and photographs from the collection of Augustus F. Sherman. By appointment; contact the librarian. Museum shop; handicap facilities. Open daily from 9:30 A.M.–5:00 P.M. Free.

American Museum of Natural History. Central Park West at 79th St., 873-4225. Perhaps the largest museum of its kind in the world, where everything involving animal, vegetable, and mineral is dramatically highlighted. The newest permanent treasure is the Garner Stout Hall of Asian Peoples, focusing on the rich cultures of Asia with 3,000 artifacts and artworks from the dawn of civilization to the present, many of which have never been shown to the public. It's a fascinating trip back into time, from 600,000 years ago when Peking Man inhabited China to the late 19th century when Western technology began changing traditional ways of life. Explore the Arab world, the Indian Subcontinent, the Himalayan Mountains, the Mongolian steppes; and be dazzled by the peerless Chinese jades, rare Tibetan religious tapestries, and exquisite Japanese ivory carvings. Also new is the permanent Arthur Ross Hall of Meteorites, which showcases a wide variety of meteorites, rock samples from the moon, an audiovisual program showing the impact of meteorites, and a series of exhibits examining the origin and significance of meteorites. In other parts of the museum are exhibits on minerals and gems, birds, dinosaurs, fishes, invertebrates, reptiles and amphibians, shells, forests, ecology, mammals, and man. There are frequent lectures and movies, a graduate-study program, three theaters, library (325,000 volumes represent one of the largest and most valuable research collection on natural history on this continent), laboratories, and cafeteria. Open daily, 10:00 A.M.–4:45 P.M., and to 8:00 P.M. on Wednesday evenings. Closed Thanksgiving and Christmas days. Suggested contribution: adults, $2; children, $1.

Hayden Planetarium. a separate division of the American Museum of Natural History, at 81st St. and Central Park West, 873-0404, presents its ever-popular Sky Show. A huge, star-filled dome brings the heavens to life via a Zeiss Projector and other dazzling special-effects techniques. A lecture tour precedes the show. Schedules vary, so call ahead. Adults and children over 13 years, $2.75; students and Senior Citizens, $1.75; children under 13 years, $1.35.

American Numismatic Society. Broadway at 155th St., 234-3130. The society advances numismatic knowledge as it applies to history, art, archeology, and economics. Exhibits include a large collection of coins and commemorative medals. Special emphasis is on the United States collection. Lectures on numismatic research are open to the public. Library, museum shop. Open Tuesday–Saturday, 9:00 A.M.–4:30 P.M., Sunday, 1:00–4:00 P.M. Free.

Asia Society. 725 Park Ave. at 71st St., 288-6400. A $16.6-million, eight-story, red-granite building, designed by Edward Larrabee Barnes, is the new headquarters for this nonprofit educational group which concentrates on Asian affairs. Although not exactly a museum, the facility offers permanent exhibits which accent Far Eastern art. *The Mr. and Mrs. John D. Rockefeller 3rd Gallery* comprises three sections: an installation of South Asian stone and bronze sculp-

MUSEUMS

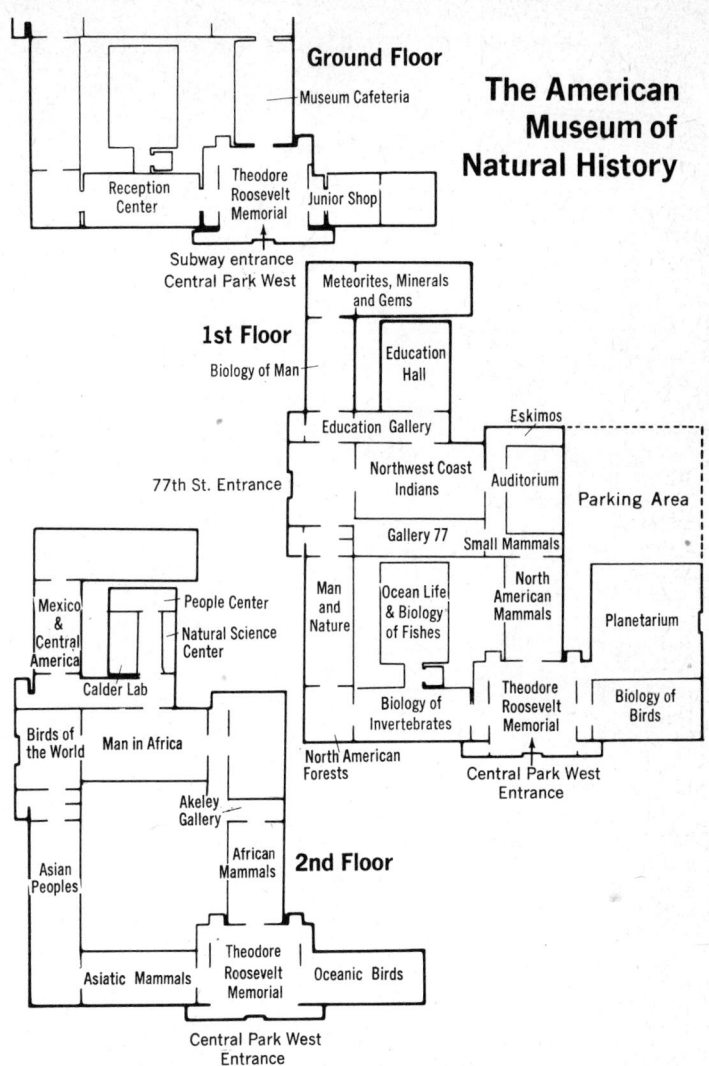

The American Museum of Natural History

The American Museum of Natural History

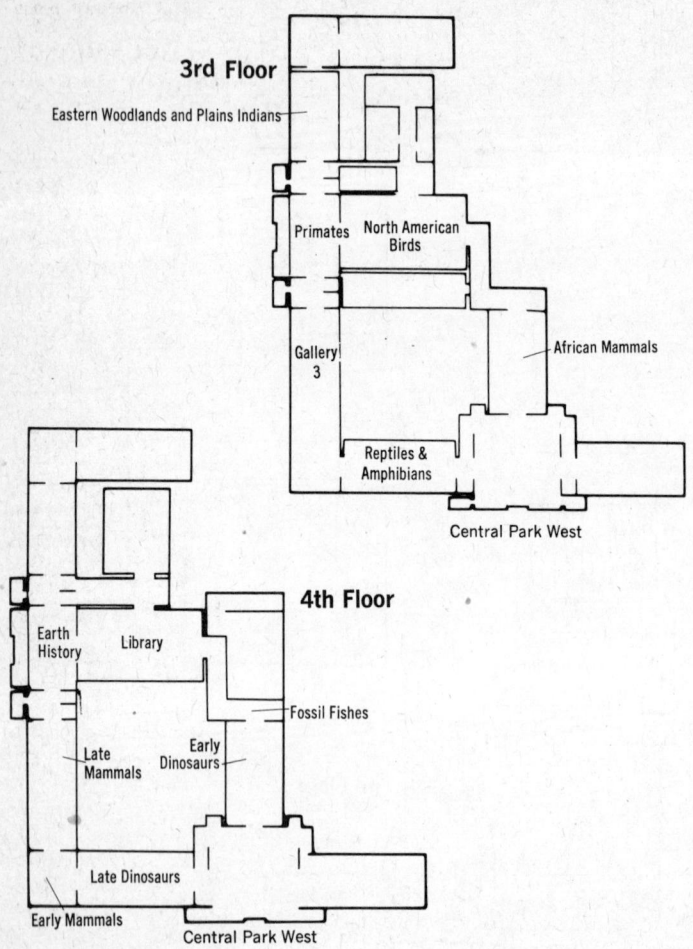

tures, including art from India, Nepal, Pakistan, and Afghanistan; the Chinese section, displaying ritual bronze vessels, ceramics, sculptures, and paintings, along with a small group of Korean ceramics; and the Japan section, which houses ceramics, paintings, and wood sculptures. The second exhibit is the *John Ross Gallery*, which features Southeast Asian art—a group of important stone and bronze sculptures from Cambodia, Thailand, Burma, and Indonesia. Temporary and traveling exhibits will be presented in the *C. V. Starr Gallery*, a gift of the Starr Foundation. Open Tuesday, Wednesday, and Friday, 10:00 A.M.–5:00 P.M., Thursday, 10:00 A.M.–8:30 P.M., Saturday, 10:00 A.M.–5:00 P.M., and Sunday, noon to 5:00 P.M. $2.00.

China House Gallery. 125 E. 65th St., 744-8181. Classical Chinese art is exhibited at this facility operated by the China Institute in America, Inc. Open Monday–Friday, 10:00 A.M.–5:00 P.M., Saturday, 11 A.M.–5:00 P.M., and Sunday, 2:00–5:00 P.M. Free.

The Cloisters. Fort Tryon Park, 923-3700. A branch of the Metropolitan Museum of Art, this medieval art complex is perched on a hill overlooking the George Washington Bridge and the Hudson River. Constructed from the ruins of five French cloisters, some of the highlights include: 12th- and 13th-century Spanish frescoes; the extraordinary Unicorn tapestries; Romanesque apse; a complete 12th-century architectural ensemble from a ruined abbey of Gascony; Romanesque wooden figure of the Enthroned Virgin and Child; the Bury Saint Edmunds Cross; stained-glass lancets from the Carmelite Church of Boppard-am-Rhein; early Christian chalice of Antioch; an arcade from a Benedictine priory of Froville in eastern France; and scores of other priceless objects. It's well worth the trip uptown to this very peaceful retreat. Can be reached on the M4 bus, which goes up Madison Ave. in midtown. Open Tuesday–Saturday, 10:00 A.M.–4:45 P.M.; Sundays and holidays, 1:00 P.M.–4:45 P.M., Sundays, from May to September, 12:00 P.M.–4:45 P.M.; closed Mondays. Suggested contribution: adults, $3; Senior Citizens and students, $1.50; members and children with parents, free.

Cooper-Hewitt Museum. 2 E. 91st St., 860-6868. Part of the Smithsonian Institution, and housed in the former mansion home of Andrew Carnegie, the collection's accent is on decorative arts of all periods and countries including architecture and ornament drawings, prints, textiles, ceramics, wallpapers, metalworks, woodworks, and specialized materials. Open Tuesday, 10:00 A.M.–9:00 P.M., Wednesday–Saturday, 10:00 A.M.–5:00 P.M., Sunday, noon–5 P.M. Closed Mondays and holidays. Admission, $1.50; free on Tuesday evenings, 5:00–9:00 P.M.

Federal Hall National Memorial. 26 Wall St., 264-8711. It was near this site that George Washington delivered the first inaugural address of an American president. In the room bearing his name are miniature paintings, snuffboxes, and documents. In the Bill of Rights Room a diorama depicts the debate over that famous document. The John Peter Zenger Room honors the journalist-printer who founded the *New-York Weekly Journal*. Open September to May, Sunday–Friday, 9:00 A.M.–4:30 P.M.; daily in summer. Closed major holidays. Free.

Plan of the Cloisters

Upper level

- Books and Reproductions
- Upper Driveway
- Froville Arcade
- Entrance Hall
- Late Gothic Hall
- Campin Room
- Boppard Room
- Tapestries
- Fuentidueña Chapel
- St. Guilhem Cloister
- Romanesque Hall
- Cuxa Cloister
- Tapestry Room
- Hall of the Unicorn Tapestries
- West Terrace
- Langon Chapel
- Pontaut Chapter House
- Early Gothic Hall
- Gothic Chapel

Lower level

- Entrance
- Lower Driveway
- Treasury
- Glass Gallery
- Bonnefont Cloister
- Trie Cloister
- Gothic Chapel

MUSEUMS

Frick Collection. 1 E. 70th St., 288-0700. This lovely collection is housed in the former residence of Henry Clay Frick, the Pittsburgh coke and steel industrialist. The works on permanent exhibit represent Mr. Frick's collection over a period of 40 years. The elegant interior is appointed in French, English, and Renaissance pieces which reflect Mr. Frick's lifestyle while he was in residence. Some highlights: South Hall—Renoir's *Mother and Children,* Vermeer's *Officer and Laughing Girl* and *Girl Interrupted at Her Music;* Boucher Room—Eight panels showing the *Arts and Sciences* painted by Boucher for Madame de Pompadour; Dining Room—18th-century British paintings of Hogarth's *Miss Mary Edwards,* Gainsborough's *Mall in St. James's Park;* Fragonard Room—Fragonard's *The Progress of Love,* 18th-century French furniture, including pieces by Riesener, Lacroix, Gouthière, Dupré, and Carlin, and Sèvres porcelains; Living Hall—Titian's *A Man in a Red Cap* and *Pietro Aretino,* El Greco's *Saint Jerome;* Library—British portraits and landscapes by Gainsborough, Reynolds, Lawrence, Romney, and Turner. Don't miss the great portrait of Robert de Montesquiou by Whistler. Other rooms contain works by Van Dyck, Goya, Bellini, Ingres, Constable, Degas, and many more great masters. Open September–May, Tuesday–Saturday, 10:00 A.M.–6:00 P.M., closed Mondays; June–August, Wednesday–Saturday, 10:00 A.M.–6:00 P.M., Sunday, 1:00–6:00 P.M., closed Monday and Tuesday. Adults, $1.00; students and Senior Citizens, 50 cents. Children under 10 not admitted; those under 16 must be accompanied by an adult.

Solomon R. Guggenheim Museum. 1071 Fifth Ave. at 88th St. 960-1313. The ultramodern façade and interior created by Frank Lloyd Wright is the centerprice for the modern works on display. The *Justin K. Thannhauser Collection* consists mainly of French works from the Impressionist and Post-Impressionist eras: Pissaro, Manet, Renoir, Cézanne, van Gogh, Gauguin, Toulouse-Lautrec, and Degas, and heavily emphasizing works by Picasso. *Pioneers of 20th-century Art* is a new gallery containing a selection of 40 of the finest and most famous paintings of Picasso, Braque, Léger, Chagall, and many others. Artists represented in the *Peggy Guggenheim Collection* include Klee, Ernst, de Kooning, Gorky, Kandinsky and Pollack, among others. The main, spiral gallery is used exclusively for the temporary exhibits for which the Guggenheim is famous; check the newspapers or *New York* and *New Yorker* magazines. Special events include concerts, poetry readings, and lectures.

During 1982 there will be a number of major special exhibitions at the Guggenheim, the most important probably being "Kandinsky in Munich," the first of a three-part exhibition stretching into 1986. Kandinsky in Munich will include some of his teachers' works as well as a selection of his own works up to 1914. In February (9th to 14th) there will be performances of his rarely seen stage composition *The Yellow Sound* at the Marymount Manhattan Theater. The exhibition is January 12 to March 21. Other exhibitions are: Art of the Avant-Garde in Russia, through January 3, 1982; Giorgio Morandi, through January 17; Jack Tworkov, January 29 to April 3; Italian Art Now, April 2 to June 20; Selections from the Guggenheim's Collection, April 9 to June 20 and July 1 to August 22; and Scandinavia Today: Jorn, Fahlstrom, and Young

The Frick Collection

MUSEUMS

Talent, September 14 to November 2. Exhibitions beyond that have not been scheduled as of presstime. Open Tuesday, 11:00 A.M.–8:00 P.M., Wednesday–Sunday and holidays, 11:00 A.M.–5:00 P.M., closed Mondays. Admission: $2.00; students and adults over 62, $1.25; children under seven, free; Tuesday evenings, 5:00–8:00 P.M., free.

Hispanic Society of America. Broadway and 155th St., 690-0743. The famous Spanish masters, El Greco, Velasquez, and Goya are elegantly displayed here, along with collections of jewelry, sculpture, pottery, tiles, and textiles that reflect the history and culture of Hispanic people. Open Tuesday–Saturday, 10:00 A.M.–4:30 P.M., Sunday, 1:00–4:00 P.M. Closed Monday and holidays. Free, but contributions are appreciated.

International Center of Photography. 1130 Fifth Ave., 860-1777. The only museum in New York City devoted exclusively to photography. Formed in 1974, the galleries display continuous, changing exhibits of works by Lewis W. Hine, Gordon Parks, Ernst Haas, and others, and of younger photographers whose works have never before been shown. The museum shop sells books, postcards, posters, and limited-edition prints. Also offered are lecturers, courses, and workshops. Open Tuesday–Sunday, 11:00 A.M.–5:00 P.M., closed Monday. Adults, $1; students, 50 cents; Senior Citizens and members, free.

Japan House Gallery. 333 E. 47th St., 832-1155. Headquarters for the Japan Society, the gallery features exhibits from well-known Japanese and American museums and private collections of Japanese art. Special events include movies, lectures, audiovisual presentations, concerts, and drama. Open daily, 11:00 A.M.–5:00 P.M., Fridays to 7:30 P.M. Free.

Jewish Museum. 1109 Fifth Ave., 860-1888. The museum boasts the most comprehensive collection of Jewish ceremonial pieces and artifacts in the nation. Permanent exhibits feature "The Book and the Spade: Archeology and the Bible," and "A Celebration of Jewish Life." Events accenting Jewish themes include concerts, lectures, films, and workshops. Open Sunday, 11:00 A.M.–6:00 P.M., Monday–Thursday, noon–5:00 P.M., closed Friday, Saturday, major Jewish holidays, and some legal holidays. Adults, $1.75; children, 6–16 and students, $1.00; Senior Citizens, a contribution.

Metropolitan Museum of Art. Fifth Ave. and 82nd St., 879-5500. At the top of the grand staircase on the second floor of this venerable institution is a stunning eighteen-foot mural by the 18th-century Italian painter Tiepolo, whose masterpiece heralds the newly installed *European Paintings Gallery*, devoted exclusively to European paintings from the 15th century to the first half of the 19th century. All the great masters in the museum's general collection are now housed in this one section, whereas once they were scattered throughout the museum. Some representative works include El Greco's "The Miracle of Christ Healing the Blind," Vermeer's "Portrait of a Young Woman," Rubens's "Self-Portrait with Helena Fourment," Rembrandt's "Aristotle with a Bust of Homer." (See the accompanying *Plan of the Museum* for a more detailed breakdown of this gallery.)

The *Robert Lehman Wing* contains a special collection, primarily European old master paintings and drawings from the 15th to the 18th centuries, but some

The Metropolitan Museum of Art

Ground Floor

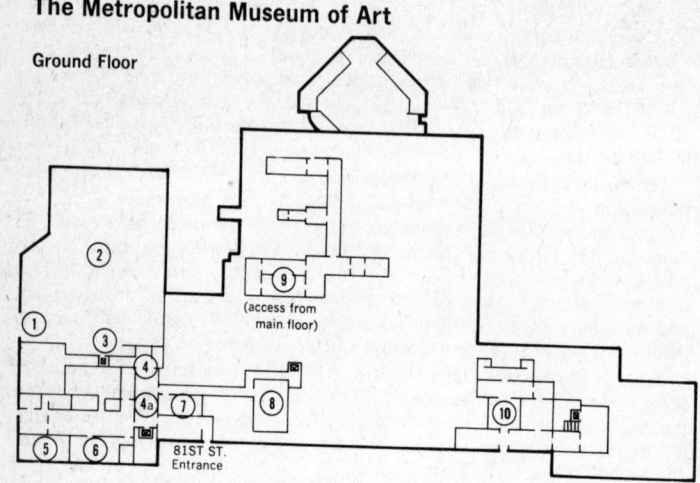

1) Auto Entrance
2) Public Garage
3) Elevator to Garage
4) To Garage
4a) Orientation Center (to open late 1982)
5) Junior Museum Library
6) Junior Museum Auditorium
7) Photography Sales
8) Slide Library
9) European Decorative Arts
10) Costume Institute

The Metropolitan Museum of Art

Main Floor

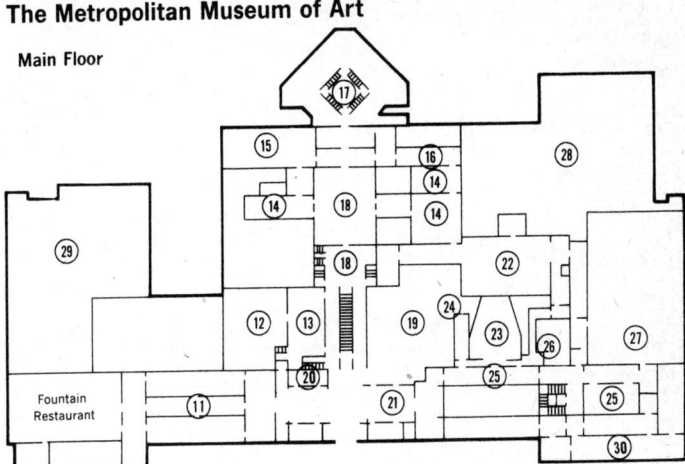

FIFTH AVE.

11) Greek and Roman Art
12) Library
13) Blumenthal Patio
14) European Sculpture and Decorative Arts
15) French Period Rooms
16) English Period Rooms
17) The Robert Lehman Collection
18) Medieval Art
19) Art and Book Shop
20) Gift Shop
21) Great Hall (the lobby)
22) Arms and Armor
23) Grace Rainey Rogers Auditorium
24) Membership Office
25) Egyptian Art
26) Concerts and Lectures Box Office
27) Sackler Wing/Temple of Dendur
28) The American Wing (At press time, the Federal Galleries, Shaker Room, and Folk Art Gallery are scheduled to open at the end of 1981.)
29) Michael C. Rockefeller Collection of the Art of Oceania, Africa and the Americas (Primitive Art), to open late January, 1982
30) Portions of the Egyptian Galleries to reopen in 1983

The Metropolitan Museum of Art
2nd Floor

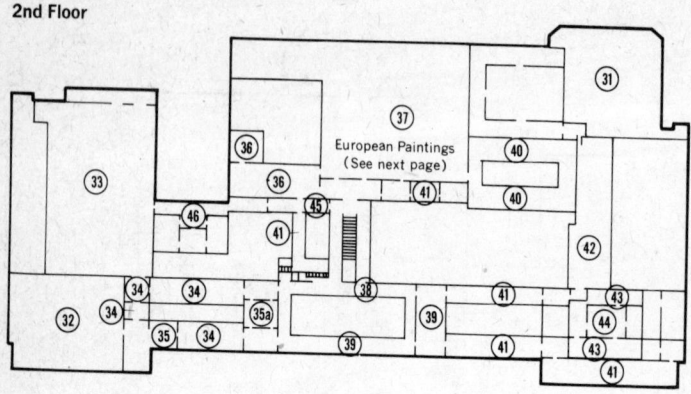

31) The American Wing
32) Islamic Art
33) The Andre Meyer Galleries
34) Greek and Roman Art
35) Ancient Near Eastern Art
35a) Assyrian Gallery
36) 20th Century Art
37) European Paintings
38) Great Hall Balcony
39) Far Eastern Art
40) Musical Instruments
41) Special Exhibition Areas
42) Sackler Exhibition Hall
43) Douglas Dillon Galleries for Chinese Painting
44) Astor Garden Court and Ming Furniture Room (access from main floor)
45) Acquisitions Gallery
46) Galleries for Drawings, Prints and Photographs

MUSEUMS

The Metropolitan Museum of Art
European Paintings Galleries

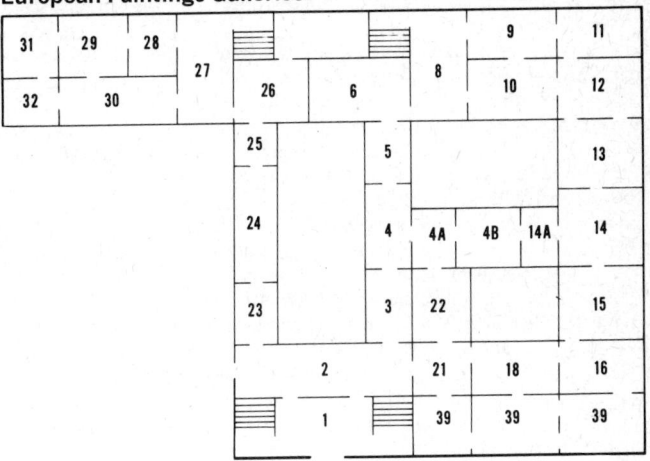

(This area is No. 37 at the top of the main staircase on the 2nd floor.)

1) Tiepolo
2) Reynolds, Gainsborough, Pannini
3) Giotto, di Paolo, Sassetta
4) Italian secular painting
4A) Pinturicchio
4B) Botticelli, Mantegna
5) Bellini, Mantegna, Tura
6) Botticelli, Lippi, di Cosimo
8) Titian, Tintoretto, Veronese
9) Moretto, Moroni, Correggio
10) Claude, Poussin
11) La Tour
12) Vermeer, De Hooch, Steen
13) Ruisdael, Cuyp, Van Goyen, Hobbema
14) Rembrandt, Hals, Vermeer
14A) Memling, Dürer
15) Rembrandt, Hals
16) Lawrence, Raeburn
18) Greuze, Chardin, Robert
21) Watteau, Boucher, Fragonard
22) Guardi, Hogarth, D. Tiepolo
23) Van Eyck, Van der Weyden
24) G. David, Bosch
25) Holbein, Cranach, Clouet
26) Bruegel, Cranach, Patinir
27) Rubens, Van Dyck, Jordaens
28) Van Dyck, Jordaens
29) El Greco
30) Caravaggio, Carracci, Reni, Rosa
31) Velazquez
32) Murillo, Zurbaran
39) Special Exhibitions

19th and 20th. The *André Meyer Galleries* are an extremely effective mounting of the Museum's later 19th-century European paintings: from Goya and Delacroix through the Impressionists—and that is where these galleries are at their best—to the Post-Impressionists.

The fairly new *American Wing*, which still has a few sections unopened, is arguably the most impressively mounted of the Museum's permanent exhibits. It has room settings from the 17th to 19th centuries as well as painting, sculpture, and all sorts of other objects.

Even newer are the *Astor Garden Court* and *Ming Furniture Room* and the *Douglas Dillon Galleries for Chinese Painting*, marking the first phase in the permanent reinstallation of the museum's collections of Far Eastern art. The Astor Garden Court alone is worth a visit to the museum; it is a reconstruction of an actual 19th-century Chinese scholar's garden. It is on the second floor but can be reached only from below on the first floor.

The north wing houses the *Egyptian Galleries*, including the Temple of Dendur, a gift of the government of Egypt to the Met, brought over disassembled and then reassembled on the present site. In 1982 the Egyptian Galleries will be only partly open, because the exhibit is being redone.

Other galleries and collections are: *Islamic Art; Ancient Greek, Roman* and *Near Eastern Art; Twentieth-Century Art; Prints and Drawings; Far Eastern Art*—especially ceramics and sculpture; *Musical Instruments of the Past and of Non-European Cultures; European Sculpture and Decorative Arts; the Costume Institute; French and English Period Rooms; Medieval Art* (in impressive churchlike settings); *Arms and Armor;* and, of course, usually, two or three featured temporary exhibitions.

Scheduled to open early in 1982 is the mammoth *Michael C. Rockefeller Collection of the Art of Oceania, Africa, and the Americas* (translation: primitive art).

Major special exhibits scheduled at the Met during 1982 are (tentatively): Forms and Emotions in Photographs, February 16 to May 9; Central Asian Treasures from Berlin (stucco, embroidery, weavings, and other Nomadic art from the Central Asian people of the Early Christian Era), late March to the end of June; France in the Golden Age, from May 26 to September 6; In Search of Alexander, October 27 to January 6.

The *Junior Museum*, on the ground floor, has a snack bar of its own. The *Thomas J. Watson Library*, for research, has more than 155,000 art books and 1,000 periodical items. In the southern wing of the museum, on the main floor, there is a restaurant (serving so-so food) laid out around a fountain and pool, indoors. The museum also provides free lectures and films from time to time, plus subscription concerts and lecture courses on art.

In a way, the museum is also a sort of art supermarket, with these shops: A reproductions shop, for pendants, other jewelry, sculpture, and so forth, up to and including solid-silver reproductions of Early American silverware; a Christmas card shop; a children's shop; a regular—and very extensive—bookshop; and a poster shop.

MUSEUMS

Call or write for the museum's monthly calendar of events. Floor plans, friendly staff members, and special services are available.

Open Tuesday, 10:00 A.M. TO 8:45 P.M.; Wednesday–Saturday, 10:00 A.M. to 4:45 P.M.; Sunday and holidays, 11:00 A.M. to 4:45 P.M.; closed Mondays, including Monday holidays. Suggested admission: $3.00 for adults, $1.50 for students and Senior Citizens. Members and children under 12 with an adult are free.

(In good weather and especially on weekends, there is almost always some sort of street theater going on for the tired museumgoers sitting on the steps outside the main entrance, usually mimes or magicians, plus, say, a brass quintet playing Gabrieli, and lots of hot-dog vendors.)

Pierpont Morgan Library. 29 E. 36th St., 685–0008. A Renaissance palazzo built in 1906 to house the already-burgeoning collection of medieval and Renaissance manuscripts, Old Master drawings, and rare books amassed by financier J. Pierpont Morgan, this dwelling in the heart of midtown Manhattan has become one of the city's classic landmarks. The library covers manuscripts from the 6th to the 16th centuries, and many books date from their original printing. A scholar's reading room is open for study and research; accreditation is necessary, and the library asks visitors to abide by its very strict rules when using the material. The walls in the West Room are clad in a vivid red-silk damask that provides the dramatic setting for the paintings, sculpture, stained-glass windows, and furniture that adorn the room. The exhibits, usually on a chosen theme, are changed from time to time. The East Room houses three tiers of bookcases, from floor to ceiling, and all technological precautions have been taken to protect the literary gems contained therein (you can read the titles through the case doors). The old mansion, which is set apart from the library by a garden, is on Madison and 37th St. It is Victorian in style and has 45 rooms. Open: Tuesday–Saturday, 10:30 A.M.–5:00 P.M., Sunday (except July), 1:00–5:00 P.M., closed Monday, holidays, and August. Contribution $1.50.

Museum of American Folk Art. 49 W. 53rd St., 581–2474. Weathervanes, whirligig toys that moved with the wind, paintings of people and landscapes, steamboats, gravestone rubbings and carvings are found in the museum's collection of 450 pieces representing the nation's folk art heritage. The museum shop offers handmade items, postcards, and books on folk art. Open Tuesday–Sunday, 10:30 A.M.–5:30 P.M., Thursday, 10:30 A.M.–8:00 P.M., closed Monday. Adults, $1.00; students and Senior Citizens, 50 cents; children under 12 free. Thursday 5:30–8:00 P.M., free.

Museum of the American Indian—Heye Foundation. Broadway at 155th St. Indians from North, South, and Central America are represented here with artifacts of hides and feathers, masks, totempoles, pottery, stone, jade and turquoise, and painted wooden sculptures. Children will gravitate to this exhibit. Open Tuesday–Saturday, 10:00 A.M.–5:00 P.M., Sunday, 1:00–5:00 P.M., closed Monday and holidays. Adults, $1.00; students and Senior Citizens, 50 cents.

Museum of the City of New York. Fifth Ave. at 103rd St., 534–1672. A fascinating exhibit highlighting the history and culture of New York City—from a small Dutch town into the "Big Apple." Formidable portraits of New York's founding fathers look down on dioramas of historic scenes; a small-scale model shows the island of Manhattan when the "town" was walled off from the "country." There is a Fire Gallery with 18th- and 19th-century firefighting equipment, a turn-of-the-century streetcar, a history of the Stock Exchange, silver made by early craftsmen, ship models, period costumes, antiques, and six fully furnished rooms. The Dutch Galleries show a life-size reconstructed portion of Fort Amsterdam, and a multimedia show called "The Big Apple" is presented. From October to April, the museum's popular Sunday walking tours give visitors a chance to explore New York neighborhoods. Children's events include puppet shows, concerts, a "Please Touch" exhibit. Open Tuesday–Saturday, 10:00 A.M.–5:00 P.M., Sunday and holidays, 1:00–5:00 P.M., closed Monday. Free.

Museum of Holography. 11 Mercer St. in SoHo, 925-0526. This museum, which was founded in 1976, is the first of its kind anywhere in the world. Holograms, which are pictures developed by laser light, create three-dimensional images. A permanent exhibit focuses on the history of the medium and its current state. A film called *An Introduction to Holography* is shown continuously in the 75-seat theater. Holographic portraits of people such as Andy Warhol, Joseph Papp, and William Buckley are on view in the New York Holofame. Open Wednesday–Sunday, noon–6:00 P.M., Thursday, noon–9:00 P.M. Adults, $2.00; children and Senior Citizens, $1.00.

Museum of Modern Art. 11 W. 53rd St., 956-6100. The museum (affectionately nicknamed MOMA) is currently engaged in a major expansion and renovation project that will significantly increase its gallery space—will in fact almost double it—and provide new services for its visitors and members. Because of the construction, the galleries as they had been set up over the past many years have largely been closed. During most of 1982 the entrance will be from what used to be the "back" of the museum, on 54th St. Only two relatively small spaces will be open to the public, one for special exhibits and one for a sort of highly selective "best of" the museum's collection. This will be in the new West Wing, the one currently under construction at press time. During 1982 the rest of the new West Wing galleries will be under construction, and meanwhile the old main building and its North and Garden Wings will be renovated and enlarged. The museum portion of the expansion should be completed by the spring of 1983. As it is presently planned, at no time during 1982 will the entire museum be closed to the public—but be warned that what you will get to see, though among the very best of modern art, will not be very extensive.

When completed, the new configuration will include four public floors with permanent exhibits, and one public floor for temporary exhibits, to total, as we have said, about twice the old gallery areas. The key to the new plan is the Garden Hall, a four-story steel-and-glass structure that will house a new system of escalators that will be a vast improvement over having to trudge up and down the old gloomy stairwells. There will also be a new restaurant for visitors—but this time on the other side of the Sculpture Garden. Next year's edition of *Fodor's New York City*, of course, will include complete floor plans of the completed project.

THE MUSEUM OF MODERN ART IN 1982

During most of 1982, while full-scale construction and renovation of the museum's existing facilities are underway, the museum's public program will take place in completed portions of its new West Wing. A selection of key works from its collections of Painting and Sculpture, Architecture and Design, and Photography will be on view on the Mezzanine and a program of major temporary exhibitions will be displayed in new Ground Floor galleries.

NEW YORK CITY

The Museum of Modern Art was founded in 1929 for the purpose of introducing to the public works of modern art—an area not then being covered at all by the Met. In acquiring works for the Museum, Alfred H. Barr, Jr., the first director, acted on the belief that art was not limited to painting and sculpture, drawings and prints, and extended the scope of the collections to include films, photographs, architecture and design.

The museum's collections now include masterpieces of modern art from about 1880 to the present. In the new configuration the painting and sculpture collection will still be arranged more or less in chronological order, giving a sense of history and continuity to the art. The great movements of the late nineteenth century and the twentieth are all represented with outstanding, first-rate examples: Post-Impressionism, Cubism, Dada, Surrealism, Expressionism, Futurism, Constructivism, Abstract Expressionism, and more. Some of the most famous pieces of easel art on exhibit—though we can't guarantee you'll see these during 1982—are van Gogh's "The Starry Night," Matisse's "Dance," Picasso's "Les Demoiselles d'Avigon," Andrew Wyeth's "Christina's World," and Jackson Pollock's "One (Number 31, 1950)." The architecture, design and photography collections are now probably the best in the world, including architectural models from Le Corbusier's studio, Edward Steichen photographs, Tiffany glass, posters, and so much more. Classic films have usually been shown at least once a day at the museum; the new setup will include not one but two auditoriums.

During the summers the Abby Aldrich Rockefeller Sculpture Garden has been used for delightful evening concerts; whether this will be the case in the summer of 1982 is not known to us at press time.

The tentative schedule (at press time) for the special exhibits in the temporary exhibition space during 1982 is as follows: January–March: drawings from the collection; March 31–June 29: Giorgio de Chirico; July 14–September 14: new work on paper II; July 21–October 12: Richard Neutra; September 29–November 30: the work of Atget—Old Paris; November 3–February 8: Louise Bourgois; December 15–February 8: Frank Lloyd Wright's Johnson Wax Building.

There are also gallery talks, possibly some lectures and other events, and a bookshop. Open daily, except Wednesdays, 11:00 A.M. to 6:00 P.M.; Thursday, 11:00 A.M. to 9:00 P.M. Adults, $1.50, children and Senior Citizens, 75 cents. Tuesdays pay what you wish.

New York Fire Department Museum. 104 Duane St., near City Hall, 570-4230. Authentic firefighting equipment used during the 19th and early 20th centuries. Hand-drawn pumpers, engines, sliding poles, uniforms, and fireboat equipment are scattered throughout the museum. Children will love touring this old firehouse. Open Monday–Friday, 9:00 A.M.–4:00 P.M., closed Saturday, Sunday, and holidays. Free.

New-York Historical Society. 170 Central Park W. at 77th St., 873-3400. Founded in 1804, the museum showcases American history and art, with emphasis on the city's and state's contributions. The exhibits are dotted with Colonial rooms, early American toys, 18th- and 19th-century fine arts, early photographs of New York City, and original watercolors by John James Audubon. It also has one of the finest reference libraries of American history in this nation, housing over 500,000 volumes. Open Tuesday–Friday, 11:00 A.M.–5:00 P.M., Saturday, 10:00 A.M.–5:00 P.M., Sunday, 1:00–5:00 P.M., closed Monday. Adults, $1.50; children, 75 cents.

New York Public Library. Fifth Ave. and 42nd St., 790–6262. Stored at the library are treasures such as a Gutenberg Bible, early Shakespeare folios, the manuscript of Washington's Farewell Address, Currier & Ives prints, and other rare books, prints, and manuscripts. Frequently-changed exhibits display selected portions of the library's holdings; otherwise, only accredited scholars can gain access to them. There are special exhibits: the Berg Collection (rare literary materials), the Oscar Lion Collection (Walt Whitman), and others. Open daily except Thursday and Sunday, 10:00 A.M.—6:00 P.M. Free.

South Street Seaport Museum. 203 Front St., 766–9020. New York's historic waterfront has undergone dramatic restoration, and the museum, with its collection of ships models and maritime folklore, is the centerpiece of activity. You can tour several old ships that are moored at the South Street pier, and climb aboard the 378-foot, four-masted, square-rigged, oceangoing *Peking*. Many shops, operating in structures styled from the 19th century, offer merchandise that was popular during that time. The Book and Chart Store, Model Shop and Gallery, and Browne and Co. Stationers are good representations of that bygone era. The museum shop sells navigation charts and instruments, stationery, boat kits, and souvenirs. Concerts and square dances are held on the pier throughout the summer. Open daily, 11:00 A.M.–6:00 P.M., closed major holidays. Admission for vessels: adults, $1.50; students, 75 cents; children under six, Senior Citizens, and members, free.

Studio Museum in Harlem. 2033 Fifth Ave. at 125th St., 427–5959. Hailed as the principal center for the study of Black art in America, the museum exhibits works by local and international Black artists, African jewelry, and small artifacts, some of which are for sale. Special events include children's workshops, concerts, films, lectures, poetry readings. Open Wednesday, 10:00 A.M.–9:00 P.M., Tuesday, Thursday, and Friday, 10:00 A.M.–6:00 P.M., Saturday and Sunday, 1:00–6:00 P.M., closed Monday. Free.

Theodore Roosevelt House. 28 E. 20th St., 260–1616. Here is where our 26th President was born and lived during his formative years. The Greek Revival house contains memorabilia and historical items highlighting the Rough Rider's life. Such items include personal diaries, eyeglasses, relics of World War I, campaign buttons. Open daily, 9:00 A.M.–4:30 P.M., closed Monday and Tuesday. Adults, 50 cents; children under 16, free.

Whitney Museum of American Art. 945 Madison Ave. at 75th St., 794–0600. This museum contains the world's most comprehensive collection of 20th-century American art, with special emphasis on the work of current artists. Marcel Breuer's architectural structure contains a sunken sculpture garden, lobby floor, three cantilevered gallery floors, and office space. There's a restaurant, and the museum shop sells catalogs, posters, and postcards on American art and artists. Weekend lectures are popular. Major special exhibitions scheduled at the Whitney for 1982 are: American Prints, through January 24; Ceramic Sculpture, through February 7; Selected Works Acquired Since 1978,

February 4 to April 4; Katherine Schmidt, same dates; Robert Smithson Sculpture, February 18 to April 18; Aspects of the New Aesthetics, April 15 to June 20; Nam June Paik, April 29 to June 27; Ed Ruscha, July 8 to September 5; Milton Avery, September 16 to December 5; Ellsworth Kelly, December 16 to February 27, 1983. Starting March 9, 1983, will be the 1983 Biennial Exhibition. Open Tuesday, 11:00 A.M.–9:00 P.M., Wednesday–Saturday, 11:00 A.M.–6:00 P.M., Sunday, noon–6:00 P.M., closed Monday. Adults, $1.50; Senior Citizens and children under 12 with an adult, free.

A SELECTION OF OTHER MUSEUMS
(All are located in Manhattan.)

African-American Institute. 833 United Nations Plaza, 949–5666. Changing exhibits of contemporary and traditional African art. Monday–Friday, 9:00 A.M.–5:00 P.M.; Saturday, 11:00 A.M.–5:00 P.M. Free.

Afro-Arts Cultural Centre, Inc. 2191 Adam Clayton Powell, Jr., Blvd., at 139th St., (212) 831–3922. Artifacts from East and West Africa. Daily, 9:00 A.M.–6:00 P.M., for groups only. Adults, $1.75; children, $1.25.

Alternative Museum. 17 White St., below Canal St., 966–4444. Mixed-media works by known and unknown artists, mostly of avant-garde nature. Wednesday–Saturday, 11:00 A.M.–6:00 P.M. Contribution requested.

American Craft Museum I. 44 W. 53rd St., 397–0630; **American Craft Museum II.** 77 W. 45th St., same phone number. Single shows spotlighting various craft media are divided between the two locations. Monday–Friday 11:00 A.M.–7:00 P.M. Adults, $1.50; students, children under 16, Senior Citizens, 75 cents; covers entry to both buildings. Museum II opens in May, 1982.

American Institute of Graphic Arts. 1059 Third Ave. at 62nd St., 752–0813. Competitive graphic design exhibits of both commercial and noncommercial origins. Monday–Friday, 9:30 A.M.–4:30 P.M. Free.

Aunt Len's Doll and Toy Museum. 6 Hamilton Terrace at 141st St., 926–4172. Over 3,000 dolls and accessories, plus wind-up, mechanical, and tin toys. Tuesday–Sunday, by appointment only. Adults, $2.00, children, $1.00.

Bible House. 1865 Broadway at 60th St., 581–7400. Among 38,000 volumes: two leaves from the Gutenberg Bible, fragments from the Dead Sea Scrolls, an 18-volume Braille Bible. Monday–Friday, 9:00 A.M.–4:30 P.M. Free.

Cathedral Museum. 1047 Amsterdam Ave. at 112th St., 678–6913. Thirteenth- to 19th-century holdings from the collection of the Cathedral of St. John the Divine (the Cathedral itself well worth exploring). Monday–Friday, 11:00 A.M.–4:00 P.M., Saturday–Sunday, 1:00–4:00 P.M. Free.

Center for Inter-American Relations. 680 Park Ave. at 68th St., 249–8950. Exhibits concerned with the Western Hemisphere, from pre-Columbian to contemporary times. Tuesday–Sunday, noon–6:00 P.M. Free.

Drawing Center. 137 Greene St. near Houston Sts., 982–5266. Group shows by promising unknown artists, and thematic shows by established figures, all based on work done on paper. Schedule varies seasonally. Free.

Fashion Institute of Technology. 227 W. 27th St., 760–7760. Historic and contemporary displays of European and American fashions, textiles, furnish-

MUSEUMS

ings, fashion illustrations, and photographs. Tuesday, 10:00 A.M.–9 P.M., Wednesday–Saturday, to 4 P.M. Free.

Firefighting Museum. 59 Maiden Lane near Nassau St., 530–6800. Equipment, costumes, and assorted paraphernalia plus an extensive library that includes a photo file of old fire engines. Monday–Friday, 10:00 A.M.–4:00 P.M. Free.

French Cultural Service. 972 Fifth Ave. at 79th St., 570–4400. Month-long shows by French photographers on view in the lobby of the former Payne Whitney family mansion. Monday–Friday, 10:00 A.M.–5:00 P.M. Free.

Goethe House New York–German Cultural Center. 1014 Fifth Ave. at 83rd St., 744–8310. Various cultural and educational programs are held on the premises; book, periodical, and recorded disk libraries. Tuesday and Thursday, 11:00 A.M.–7:00 P.M., Wednesday, Friday, Saturday, noon–5:00 P.M. Free. Special events at other times, entry usually by ticket.

Grey Art Gallery. 33 Washington Pl., 598–7603. A New York University gallery regularly given over to shows of mostly 20th-century fine arts; also, the Ben and Abby Grey Foundation Collection of Contemporary Asian and Middle Eastern Art. Hours vary. Free.

Grolier Club of N.Y. 47 E. 60th St., 838–6690. Rare books, manuscripts, and prints. Monday–Friday, 10:00 A.M.–5:00 P.M., Saturday to 3:00 P.M. October to June only. Free.

Institute for Architecture and Urban Studies. 8 W. 40th St., 398–9474. Exhibits explore architecture in the context of the culture at large. Monday–Friday and some Saturdays, 9:00 A.M.–5:00 P.M. Free.

Interchurch Center. 475 Riverside Dr. at 120th St., 870–2932. Displays pertaining to interfaith concerns. Monday–Friday, 9:00 A.M.–4:30 P.M. Free.

J. M. Mossman Collection of Locks. 20 W. 44th St., 840–1840. Historic survey of security instruments. Monday–Friday, 10:00 A.M.–4:00 P.M. Free.

Kitchen. 484 Broome St., SoHo, 925–3615. Continuous showings of new video and mixed-media works with the accent on the avant-garde. Tuesday–Saturday, 1:00–6:00 P.M. September–May only. Free.

Library and Museum of Performing Arts. 111 Amsterdam Ave. (Lincoln Center), 799–2200. Both the gallery areas and the book, record, and film archives focus on the performing arts, with frequent special programs for children and adults. Hours vary. Free.

El Museo Del Barrio. 1230 Fifth Ave. at 105th St., 831–7272. Puerto Rican and Latin American fine arts. Tuesday–Friday, 10:30 A.M.–4:30 P.M., Saturday–Sunday, 11:00 A.M.–4:00 P.M. Voluntary contribution.

Museum of American Illustration. 128 E. 63rd St., 838–2560. Contemporary, historical, solo, group, and theme shows drawn from the Society of Illustrators' 800-piece collection. Monday–Friday, 10:00 A.M.–5:00 P.M. Closed in August. Free.

Museum of Broadcasting. 1 E. 53rd St., 752–7684. Enormously popular for its ever-growing library of classic and contemporary radio and television programs, all available for individual screening. Tuesday–Saturday, noon–5:00 P.M. Suggested contribution: adults, $2.00, children under 14, $1.00.

National Academy of Design. 1083 Fifth Ave. at 89th St., 369–4880. Small but select and carefully focussed changing exhibits of both old and contemporary graphics. Tuesday–Sunday, 1:00–5:00 P.M. $1.50.

New Museum. 65 Fifth Ave. at 14th St., 741-8962. Housed in a building of the New School for Social Research, but not a part of the school, this truly new museum—founded in 1981—shows art of the last ten years by young artists who have had little exhibition exposure elsewhere. Noon to 6:00 P.M., 8:00 P.M. Wed. Closed Sun. Contr.

Pen and Brush. 16 E. 10th St., 475–3669. Painting, sculpture, and graphic arts exhibits sponsored by the oldest professional women's creative arts organization in New York. Monday–Friday, noon–4 P.M. October to June only. Free.

Puerto Rican Museum for the Arts. 3755 Broadway at 155th St., 222–2966. Puerto Rican and Latin American fine arts on the campus of Boricua College. Monday–Friday, 9:00 A.M.–9:00 P.M. Voluntary contribution.

Schomburg Center for Research in Black Culture. 515 Lenox Ave. at 135th St., 862–4000. The largest museum and multimedia library in the world documenting the history, literature, and arts of Black people. Hours vary. Free.

Songwriters Hall of Fame. 1 Times Square, 221–1252. Pop music memorabilia ranging from Fred Astaire's hat and cane to the latest in electric guitars. Monday–Saturday, 11:00 A.M.–3:00 P.M. Free.

Urban Center. 457 Madison Ave. at 50th St., 935–3960. Architectural exhibits housed in the historic Villard Houses—now part of the Helmsley Palace Hotel! Hours vary. Free.

Bronx. *Bartow-Pell Mansion Museum and Garden,* Pelham Bay Park, 885–1461. The mansion, built in 1842, is a Greek revival restoration with sunken gardens, period furnishings, paintings, and a 200-volume library containing books on architecture, gardening, and herbs. Open Tuesday, Friday, and Sunday, 1:00–5:00 P.M. Contribution requested; children under 12 with adult, free.

Bronx Museum of the Arts, 851 Grand Concourse, 681–6000. This museum, founded in 1971, has a collection of Roman sculpture, decorative ironwork, and murals. Open Monday–Friday, 9:00 A.M.–5:00 P.M., Sunday, 12:30–4:30 P.M.

Hall of Fame for Great Americans, W. 181st St. and University Ave., 220–6187. Original bronzes of 94 prominent Americans on display in the turn-of-the-century Stanford White edifice located on an important Revoluntionary War site. This site is now on the campus of the Bronx Community College. (Call ahead to be sure of access). Open Monday–Saturday, 9:00 A.M.–5:00 P.M. Free.

Valentine-Varian House Museum of Bronx History, 3266 Bainbridge Ave., 881–8900. Isaac L. Varian, mayor of New York City from 1839–1841, was born in this house, which was built in 1756 and was later the site of a Revolutionary War skirmish. Indian and military artifacts, natural history displays, paintings, and prints and photographs tracing the history of the Bronx. Open Sat., 10:00 A.M.–4:00 P.M., Sunday, 1:00–5:00 P.M. Contribution; children under 12, free.

Brooklyn. *Brooklyn Museum,* Eastern Parkway and Washington Ave., 638–5000, has an outstanding collection of ancient Egyptian art; in addition there

MUSEUMS

are galleries devoted to the primitive arts of Africa, Japan, and Indonesia. The *Hall of the Americas* has exhibits of American primitive art. Also on view are the arts of India and the Orient, American painting and sculpture, prints, drawings and watercolors (many by Homer and Sargent), costume collections, pewter, silver, ceramics, glass, and 28 completely furnished American period rooms—from Colonial days through the 19th century. The museum has concerts, films, and lectures (write or call for a schedule), and there is a cafeteria in the building. The *Gallery Shop* sells folk art and handicrafts from over 65 countries. Open Wednesday–Saturday, 10:00 A.M.–5:00 P.M., Sunday, noon–5:00 P.M., holidays, 1:00–5:00 P.M., closed Monday and Tuesday. Contribution.

Brooklyn Children's Museum, 145 Brooklyn Ave. at St. Mark's Ave., 735-4400. A natural history museum designed especially for children with exhibits showing American Indian and other prehistoric cultures, fossils, mounted mammals, tame live animals, and a planetarium. Open Sunday, Monday, and Wednesday–Friday, 1:00–5:00 P.M., Saturday, 10:00 A.M.–5:00 P.M., closed Tuesday. Free.

Lefferts Homestead, Prospect Park, Flatbush Ave. near Willink Gate, 965-6560. The homestead was build in 1776 and contains costumes, textiles, and period furnishings. Open Wednesday–Sunday, 1:00–4:00 P.M. Free.

Long Island Historical Society, 128 Pierrepont St., 624–0890. If your ancestors come from any of the four counties that make up Long Island (Kings, Queens, Nassau, or Suffolk), you might be interested in spending time in the reading room of this museum, which has 125,000 volumes pertaining to local history and genealogy. The museum also has a collection of paintings, graphics, and costumes. Closed during August. Open Tuesday–Saturday, 9:00 A.M.–5:00 P.M. Admission $1.00.

Queens. *Bowne House Historical Society,* 37–01 Bowne St., 359–0528. Known for the *Flushing Remonstrance.* John Bowne, advocate of religious freedom when New York was still Nieuw Amsterdam, lived in this house built in 1661. It contains 17th-century furnishings, a pewter collection, and Bowne family memorabilia. Open Tuesday, Saturday, and Sunday, 2:30–4:30 P.M. Admission.

Hall of Science of the City of New York, Flushing Meadow Park, 699–9400. Close for renovation through 1983. Children almost always enjoy museums of science and technology; this one has a children's museum, cafeteria, and scientific toys for sale. The museum has a planetarium and an amateur radio station as well as collections explaining atomic energy, space science, and the environment. Open Wednesday–Friday, 10:00 A.M.–4:00 P.M., Saturday, 10:00 A.M.–5:00 P.M., Sunday, 11:00 A.M.–5:00 P.M. Suggested donation: adults, $1; Senior Citizens and students, 50 cents.

Queens Museum, NYC Bldg., Flushing Meadow, Corona Park, 592–2405, on site of 1964 World's Fair. This is the home of the Panorama, a scale model of New York City, among other exhibits, many changed every month or two. Open Tues.–Sat., 10:00 A.M.–5:00 P.M., Sun., 1:00–5:00 P.M., closed Mon. Free.

The Store Front Museum, 162–02 Liberty Ave., 523–5199. Founded in 1970, this Black art and history museum has a collection of paintings, drawings, and sculpture by Black artists in the United States and abroad, including tribal art from Africa. A cultural center presents lectures, films, concerts and dance recitals. Open Tuesday–Friday, 9:30 A.M.–4:30 P.M. Free.

Staten Island. *Staten Island Museum* (formerly Staten Island Institute of Arts and Sciences), 75 Stuyvesant Pl., 727-1135. The science and ecology exhibits show plants, animals and insects typical of Staten Island. The arts part of the museum contains paintings, graphics, and decorative arts. Open Tuesday–Saturday, 10:00 A.M.–5:00 P.M., Sunday, 2–5:00 P.M., closed Monday. Free.

Conference House Association, Conference House Park (7455 Hylan Blvd.), 984-2086. The only peace conference during the Revolution was held September 11, 1776, in a house constructed in 1690 known as the Conference House, or Billopp House, which now may be seen by guided tour. Open daily, 1:00–5:00 P.M., closed Monday. Admission 50 cents.

Jacques Marchais Center of Tibetan Arts, 338 Lighthouse Ave., 987-3478. Here you may view examples of Tibetan and Buddhist art, study Eastern religions and philosophy in the 20,000-volume library, and meditate in one of the gardens. Closed November through March. Open Saturday and Sunday, 1:00–5:00 P.M. Admission $1.00.

Richmondtown Restoration, Richmond and Arthur Kill Roads, 352-1611. Approximately 31 buildings, including the 1695 Voorlezer House, a Cooper's Shop, Stephens House and General Store, and St. Andrew's Episcopal Church have been reconstructed on this several block site. Open Saturday, 10:00 A.M. –5:00 P.M., Sunday, noon–5:00 P.M. Contribution.

Staten Island Historical Society Museum, 302 Center Street, 351-1611. houses military artifacts, china, lithographs, and an excellent collection of tools. Information about buildings open to the public, the ongoing work of restoration, and—in the summer—student tour guides, is available here. Open Tuesday–Saturday, 10:00 A.M.–5:00 P.M., Sunday, 2:00–5:00 P.M., closed Monday. Adults and children, 50 cents.

MOVIES. Since 1963, the Film Society of Lincoln Center has produced what many regard as the most important film event in the country, the New York Film Festival, where many of the most innovative and critically acclaimed American and foreign films receive their first New York showing. It is the Big Apple's answer to Cannes, usually runs around two weeks from late September to mid-October at Lincoln Center and includes a "New Directors/New Films" annual series co-sponsored with the Museum of Modern Art. Tickets range from $4 to $6, opening and closing night are at Avery Fisher Hall, all other performances at Alice Tully Hall.

But New York is a year-around film festival. You'll hear many New Yorkers referring to movies as *films, flicks,* or *cinema,* and this art form is taken very seriously by fans, aspiring filmmakers, and professional critics. If two weeks pass and you haven't read about a W. C. Fields, Humphrey Bogart, or Marx Brothers Festival, better check to see if you're really in New York.

MOVIES

Movies are advertised daily in all the papers, but for complete listing (and usually showing times) look to *New Yorker* and *New York/Cue* magazines, or to the Friday and Sunday *New York Times.*

There are at least five common formats for the presentation of movies here. First come the expensive ($5 or more) and prestigious East Side houses like the *Coronet* (993 3rd Ave. at 59th St.) or the *Beekman,* Second Ave. at 66th St.

Multi-screen neighborhood houses like *Loew's 83rd Street* (at Broadway) show features that have gained enough critical acclaim and made enough money in their first-run engagements to justify wide dissemination. They also host premieres of action-packed, star-studded "flicks."

Ten years ago, art film houses were known for foreign movies. Since film has come to be regarded as a kind of literature that can be experienced more than once, the situation has changed. Venerable theaters like *80 St. Marks* (8th St. and 2nd Ave.), the *Regency* (Broadway at 67th St.), and the *Bleecker St. Cinema* (Bleecker and La Guardia) have done well with old foreign and American classics and more recent works whose true values have surfaced since they first (sometimes unsuccessfully) came out. Some houses also have special midnight showings, on the weekend, of strange and often offensive cult films; read the listings carefully for these as they are frequently not advertised.

A fourth category includes museums, libraries, and churches that show films, often seldom-seen ones, in the course of retrospective examinations of great careers in the industry. Admissions are usually modest and the setting interesting beyond the film itself (such as the *Museum of Modern Art,* 53rd St. between 5th and 6th Aves., or the *Whitney Museum* on Madison Ave. at 75th St).

Finally, filmmakers not yet established in the big time want their work seen and occasionally have showings in out-of-the-way lofts or college buildings. They sometimes exhibit individually, sometimes band together in "collectives." Since they have little money for publicity, the best way to learn about a showing is to keep your eyes open for handbills and posters in Greenwich Village and near campuses around the city. Read the *SoHo News* and *Village Voice* for news of offbeat films.

Although ambitious plans for the facelifting of the Times Square area of Broadway are underway, some of its theaters are currently given over to X-rated films (this is true of W. 42nd St. and 8th Ave. as well). Those which are not, like the *National, Loew's State I* and *II,* show first-run action features—sure moneymakers. But colorful though the area may be, beware of the low lifes that infest some of the movie houses on this neon-lit strip.

There are some movie houses, however, that are as interesting as the movies they show because of their locale. The *Paris,* for example, at 4 W. 58th St., shows first-run foreign and art films right across the street from the venerable Plaza Hotel and Central Park. The *Harold Clurman,* 412 W. 42nd St., opens late in the afternoon, Mondays through Fridays, to show film retrospectives in a renovated theater in the heart of a new off-Broadway theater row on the spruced up West Side. The *Little Theatre,* in Joe Papp's Public Theatre complex at 425 Lafayette St., opens late in the afternoon to show old art films, giving one the opportunity to catch an off-Broadway play in the same building that evening.

The *Carnegie Hall Cinema,* 7th Ave. at 57th St., is an excellent art-film showcase for foreign as well as American films—and is right around the corner from Carnegie Hall, the classical music mecca. The *Thalia,* Broadway at 95th St., shows oldies but goodies and is an upper West Side institution, a liberal dowager of art-film houses, while the *Anthology Film Archives,* 80 Wooster St., way downtown, digs into its treasure trove to delight film buffs seeking the unusual. And smack in the middle, on the fashionable East Side from the 50s into the 80s is a veritable Hollywood movie belt of first-run films in "piggy back" theaters, with as many as five different films playing in different showcases in the same complex.

MUSIC. Manhattan is beyond serious dispute the most active musical city in the world, and the one with the largest population of professional musicians. (Most of them live and/or perform on the Upper West Side near Lincoln Center, where you will see many people carrying violins, cellos, and the like to and from lessons, rehearsals, and performances, and where it is not uncommon to hear tenors practicing scales as they do their grocery shopping.) Your only real problem is which performance to choose. In their daily entertainment sections, *The New York Times* and other daily papers list all the day's musical events—and Friday's papers include the entire weekend's goings-on, including church performances. The Sunday *Times* has the week's list.

Lincoln Center, Broadway at 64th St., is the musical heart of New York City, with *Carnegie Hall* (247-7459) its soul. Within the less-than-20-year-old Lincoln Center complex are *Avery Fisher Hall* (home of the New York Philharmonic, American Philharmonic Orchestra, the Mostly Mozart festival, and many visitng orchestra performances—874-2424); the *New York State Theater* (home of the New York City Opera—877-4727); the *Metropolitan Opera House* (base for that company as well as for many visiting ballet troupes—799-3100); *Alice Tully Hall* (probably the most acoustically perfect of the halls, and site of numerous chamber music recitals—362-1911); the *Juilliard School of Music* (799-5000)—one of the world's most respective such institutions; and the *Guggenheim Bandshell* in the outdoor *Damrosch Park* (765-5100). Also part of the complex are the *Library and Museum of Performing Arts* (where some concerts and recitals are also held, especially for children—799-2200); and the *Vivian Beaumont* and *Mitzi Newhouse Theaters* (765-5100). The plaza at Lincoln Center is also the base for dozens of free concerts daily throughout the summer.

The various buildings opened one at a time, beginning with Avery Fisher Hall in 1964—then called Philharmonic Hall, but renamed after a donor contributed $5 million to have the acoustics adjusted. Interestingly, attractive as all the buildings at Lincoln Center are—the Met with its Chagall murals lighting up the plaza, the Calder sculpture that adorns Damrosch Park—designed by such recognized architects as Max Abramovitz (Avery Fisher) and Philip Johnson (State Theater, and later overseer of the reconstruction of Avery Fisher), they have almost all been beset by acoustical and structural problems. Avery Fisher and the Beaumont/Newhouse theaters have all undergone serious reconstructions, and the New York State Theater is next on the list. Indeed, in Avery Fisher Hall, only the outside façade and general shape of the auditorium remain as originally constructed.

Thus New Yorkers, and musicians and fans around the world, were especially appreciative of the efforts to save Carnegie Hall (154 W. 57th St.) from destruction following the completion of Lincoln Center. It took such great musicians as Isaac Stern to spearhead the campaign to save Carnegie when it was threatened with demolition in order to make way for yet another midtown office building. Opened in 1891 with a concert conducted by Tchaikovsky, it remains an acoustical marvel and leaves New York's musical heart and soul intact.

They say New York's longest running musical hit is the New York Philharmonic. The oldest symphony orchestra in the U.S., it is nearly 150 years old yet incredibly vital under music director and conductor Zubin Mehta, who gets the best out of the 106 extraordinarily gifted musicians in the orchestra. The Philharmonic season runs September 10 through May 12 at Avery Fisher Hall. Tickets cost from $5.00 to $17.50. The orchestra, of course, attracts outstanding guest soloists and conductors. And Avery Fisher Hall is the home of the Mostly Mozart Summer Music Festival, New York City's version of Tanglewood, with more than 40 low-cost concerts (about $8.00 for a reserved seat) from mid-July through late August. Basically Bach, another low-cost music festival, spills over from Carnegie Hall to Avery Fisher Hall and various churches in early June.

As it approaches its century mark, the Metropolitan Opera Company performs at the Metropolitan Opera House from September 21 through April 11. Tickets range from $10.00 to $60.00. Partial-view seats are available from $5.00 to $25.00.

Across the Lincoln Center Plaza, in the New York State Theater, the New York City Opera approaches its 40th year with new vim, vigor, and vitality under artistic director Beverly Sills—its prima diva not too long ago. Its seasons run from February 25 through May 2 and from September 2 through November 14. Its tickets range from $3.50 to around $25.00, with side views in the $20.00 category.

The reasons for the difference in price between the Met and the New York City Opera (NYCO) vary. Stated briefly, the differences are: Established in 1944, the NYCO is the country's leading opera company in presenting American artists, commissioning new American works, and staging innovative productions. Its leading performers usually look as good as they sing—sometimes better—and are eminently believable when cast in romantic roles. Indeed, some of the performances resemble stylish musicals on Broadway; the arias are clearly understood because the NYCO stresses diction and acting ability as well as singing, and several performances are sung in English. Performers are usually on their way up—so costs are down. The Met, of course, presents stars of international stature (in more ways than one)—names such as Carreras, Domingo, Horne, Milnes, Nilsson, Pavarotti, Price, Scotto, Stratas, Troyanos, and Verrett. And if some don't look the part when they hit the high Cs—indeed, some look as though they could swallow the high seas—the opera is the thing here, and nobody does it better than the Met. The aria the better, with costly, opulent productions to match.

Alice Tully Hall in the Juilliard Building is small, intimate, and perhaps the best acoustical building in the complex—a suitable home for the Chamber Music Society of Lincoln Center, which has commissioned over 30 compositions and has given 13 New York or American premieres since its inception in 1969. Also attracts outstanding performers, from pianists to vocal groups, as well as stages (usually free) performances by Juilliard students.

Many guest artists, composers, and visiting orchestras perform at various times at each of these Lincoln Center auditoriums and theaters. For information on performances and prices write for the Lincoln Center Calendar, Lincoln Center, 1865 Broadway, New York 10023. Tickets are also available by mail, but they should be ordered a month in advance. In the city, tickets are obtainable through Lincoln Center or at Bloomingdale's at Third Ave. and East 59th St., or through most Ticketron outlets. There are also occasional free outdoor performances at Lincoln Center, either on the plaza or at the Guggenheim Bandshell, in the summer.

For sheer musical variety and artistry, Carnegie Hall is hard to beat with instrumental recitals by the likes of Horowitz, Stern, and Rudolf Serkin, visits by orchestras such as the mighty Chicago under Solti, the Detroit under Dorati, the Philadelphia under Muti, the Boston under Ozawa, and an atlas of other famed orchestras as well as vocal recitals by world greats, from Nilsson to Pavarotti. Performances go on virtually year round. Tickets vary, from around $5.00 to $15.00.

The off-Broadway equivalent in the Big Apple music world may well be the 92nd St. YM-YWHA, 1395 Lexington Ave., which offers major chamber music and orchestral series as well as performances by individual artists of international stature and a fun series featuring Broadway tunesmiths performing and speaking about their work. Colleges such as Hunter and the College of the City of New York (CCNY) also offer programs featuring major musicians, as does Abraham Goodman House, 129 W. 67th St., sort of the off-off-Broadway of the music world.

Here are some other possibilities:

Amato Opera Theatre, Inc., 319 Bowery. 228–8200. Two generations of Amatos have produced this showcase company for student and young professional singers.

The *Bel Canto Opera Company* is an amateur opera company performing at the Madison Avenue Baptist Church at 30 East 31st St. 535–5231.

The *Light Opera Company of Manhattan* (affectionately known as "LOOM") presents excellent Gilbert and Sullivan operettas throughout the year at their small theater at 351 E. 74th St. 535–6310.

The Manhattan and other borough parks have an extensive free concert series June through August. The New York Philharmonic performs twice each summer in the Sheep Meadow at Central Park and at least once in a park in every borough. So does the Met.

MUSIC

Free concerts are also offered at the *Greenwich House Music School* (IRT 7th Ave. subway to Christopher St. stop; ask for directions to 46 Barrow St.); *The Museum of the City of New York* (5th Ave. bet. 103rd and 104th St.; Sunday, October–May) and *The New-York Historical Society* (107 Central Park West, near 77th St., Sunday, November–April).

Check the listings in the music section of *The New York Times* Sundays for news of frequent concerts at the Metropolitan Museum of Art, the Guggenheim, the Nicholas Roerich Museum, the Brooklyn Museum, the Frick Museum, the concerts of live or recorded music on certain Sundays in the medieval splendors of The Cloisters (which are part of the Metropolitan Museum of Art but located uptown in Fort Tyron Park), and, usually, many other fine professional performances and recitals, each and every day.

The sound of music—usually free—fills some of the city's great churches. Some suggestions: St. Bartholomew's Episcopal Church, Park Ave. at 51st St., presents mixed choir concerts Sundays at 4:00 P.M. The beautiful Riverside Church, Riverside Drive at 122nd St., presents carillon concerts at noon Saturdays and 2:00 P.M. Sundays. St. Peter's Lutheran Church, in the Citicorp Center at 54th St. and Lexington Ave., has Jazz Vespers Sundays at 5:00 P.M. as well as interesting theater performances. And Trinity Church, at Broadway and Wall St., presents organ recitals on weekdays. (For more complete information, call the churches.)

The Library and Museum of the Performing Arts at Lincoln Center also showcases outstanding young concert artists, as do other branches of the New York Public Library. Check the Events Calendar of the New York Public Library, free at all branches. And don't overlook the Brooklyn Academy of Music (BAM), 30 Lafayette St., Brooklyn, the nation's oldest performing arts center, with its various chamber and orchestral series as well as performances by internationally acclaimed guest artists in its four theaters (where dance, theater, films, and children's programs are also staged). The BAM season usually runs from October through June. Tickets range from around $3 to $15.

POPULAR MUSIC

Pop and rock concerts are presented all over town all year long. The *Dr Pepper Festival* comes to various places around town during July and August, while some of the old-style former movie houses like the *Palladium* on E. 14th St. and the *Ritz,* a former ballroom, on E. 11th St., draw young people from the suburbs as well as the neighborhood and Manhattan. The biggest attractions, such as Bruce Springsteen or The Grateful Dead, can fill *Madison Square Garden, Radio City Music Hall,* or the *Savoy Cabaret,* 141 W. 44th St., for several nights. Other halls that play big-name pop, rock, or jazz headliners are Carnegie Hall, Avery Fisher Hall (Lincoln Center), and sometimes even Alice Tully Hall, also at Lincoln Center.

The *South Street Seaport,* Pier 16 at Fulton St. on the East River, presents pop and jazz Sunday evenings, and Save-Our-Ships concerts, on the waterfront from June through August in one of New York's more unusual but pleasant settings.

The *Kool Jazz Festival,* from around June 26 to July 5, percolates in Carnegie Hall, Avery Fisher Hall, and other places around town.

For events, dates, and times while you are in town, check the daily papers, or *New York* magazine, or the *Village Voice* or *SoHo News.*

For information on other nonclassical music, that performed in club settings where drinks or meals are served, refer to the *Night Life* section later in the book.

DANCE. New York is now the dance capital of the world, and the Metropolitan Opera House is perhaps the largest and most important impresario of ballet, with the entire Lincoln Center complex the vital nerve center that keeps the Big Apple on its toes. (You will see students of the ballet around Carnegie Hall on 57th St. and Broadway in the 60s, 70s and 80s, going to and from the many ballet schools there.) Three Russians help New York maintain its dance excellence: George Balanchine, Rudolf Nureyev, and Mikhail Baryshnikov.

It is Balanchine, of course, who built the *New York City Ballet* (NYCB) into one of the great ballet companies in the world, his dancers whirling through abstract geometrical patterns choreographed by Balanchine in plotless ballets whose very simplicity reflects the lines in the NYCB's home, the New York State Theater in Lincoln Center. With 110 dancers, the NYCB is the largest dance organization in the Western world. And it is Balanchine who has brought the proud traditions of Russian Imperial ballet to the New World and put them to work in creating the sleek, neoclassical, and decidedly American NYCB. Balanchine and the NYCB's other principal choreographer, Jerome Robbins, have created more than 160 ballets. These ballets are now regarded as *the* classic repertoire of the 20th century. The 1982 season will be the NYCB's 75th. The fall dates are November 11 through February 15. December is reserved for Balanchine's Christmas classic, *The Nutcracker.* Tickets from $4.00 to $20.00.

Across the Lincoln Center Plaza, at the Metropolitan Opera House, the *American Ballet Theatre* (ABT) usually stages its fall season from October through November and its summer season from mid-April through June. ABT has made its reputation by becoming America's prime repertory company. They perform the great 19th-century classics as well as important works of the early 20th century and a regular crop of story and contemporary ballets.

While NYCB prides itself on being a "starless" company where dance is the true star under the first of America's great balletic émigrés from Russia, the legendary Balanchine, the ABT is nonetheless the Big Apple's—and America's —"star" ballet. The ABT is now under the leadership of its talented superstar, Mikhail (Misha) Baryshnikov, the latest of the dance defectors from Russia's brilliant Kirov Ballet, noted for its soft, lyrical style and its brilliant interpretations of story ballets. The dashing Misha and one of his leading ladies, Natalia

DANCE

Makarova, another defector from the Kirov, have managed to inject the Russian spirit into the American dance tradition that makes the ABT so special. Misha choreographs, too, a budding Balanchine. ABT tickets vary, from around $5.00 to $35.00 and climbing.

It was, of course, Nureyev, the first of the great Russian dancers to defect from the Kirov, who, with his superstar quality slowly dimming over the years, gave ballet its mass appeal in America. And it was the box office power of Nureyev's name that helped fill the Met when Rudi danced as visiting guest star with some of the world's best troupes—troupes first imported to America by another Russian great, the late impresario Sol Hurok. Hurok's death left a void. And the Met stepped into that void, acting as its own impresario to keep its house full during the summer months. But it is names like Balanchine, Nureyev, and Baryshnikov that bring the crowds in.

It is their popularity that helps keep both the State and Met filled with visiting dance companies when the NYCB and ABT aren't performing, and when the respective house opera companies aren't doing their thing. So it is possible for a dance aficionado to look forward to seeing, say, the athleticism of Russia's *Bolshoi*, the lyricism and story ballets of Germany's *Stuttgart*, the stateliness of the *National Ballet of Canada*, the pageantry of Britain's *Royal Ballet*, and the avant-garde leanings of the *Netherlands Dance Theater*—to name just a few of the great troupes that have come to the Big Apple in recent seasons.

But the troupers go beyond the classical greats. The City Center Theater at 131 W. 55th St., for example, is home for such world-class companies as the *Alvin Ailey* (with its haunting blend of spiritual, modern jazz and story ballet rising out of the Black experience), the up-and-coming *Harlem Dance Theater*, and the mod, hip, with-it *Joffrey Ballet* that dances classics as well as rock-inspired pieces. *Paul Taylor* and his company fuse the classics with modern dance, humor and a marvelous athleticism; so do *Twyla Tharp*, *Murray Louis*, and *Alwin Nikolais* (who uses more lights than the hippest disco).

The Brooklyn Academy of Music draws all kinds of dance companies, too. Indeed, its *Ballet America* series is a national celebration of dance paced from October to June. Companies from Los Angeles, San Francisco, Pennsylvania, Cleveland, and Utah are among the visitors. In addition, *Martha Graham* and *José Limon* bring their respective companies here regularly.

The entertainment pages of the Sunday *Times* and the *Village Voice* are always full of dance events, ranging from those mentioned above to smaller presentations given in lofts, on college campuses, at churches and elsewhere, and ranging from avant-gardists such as *Merce Cunningham* to folk troupes from Senegal and the Ukraine. In fact, a directory of Big Apple dance troupes lists over 140 companies in all!

Some things to keep in mind when buying tickets for performances at some of the more expensive houses: Dance has become very, very popular in recent years. The major companies sell out regularly, and in advance. If you can, write for your tickets ahead, or call and charge them to a major credit card to ensure seats for the performance you want. If you're planning to be here during Christmas season and want to take the kids to see *The Nutcracker* at the State

Theater, write as far ahead of time as possible. Despite a month of daily performances, *The Nutcracker* is invariably a hot ticket.

The best seats for dance at the State Theater are in the first ring, where you can look down and see the dancers' feet. Because there are no aisles down the center of the sprawling auditorium, you may get tired of climbing over people and vice versa if you sit in the center, so consider aisle seats at the ends of the row, or seats as near the aisle as possible. They cost less, too.

Because the acoustics are so bad at the Uris, dance home of many a visiting troupe, you may want to sit further back, in a lesser-priced seat that still affords a good view of the dancers. And because the glitterati sit up front at the Met doesn't mean you have to; dance and music critics have found the viewing and hearing is actually better farther back in the orchestra rows. The Dress Circle seats offer an excellent vantage point at considerable savings over an orchestra seat—an important consideration in these days when ballet tickets at the major houses are edging into the $40.00 and up category. Substantial savings can be made by purchasing an obstructed-view seat at the Met or State theaters.

Lastly, don't overlook the fact that discount ballet (as well as theater, symphony and opera) tickets go on sale the same day as the performance at TKTS booths (see the *Stage* section, below). If you have the time to wait in line, the savings are substantial—and you may hear dance fans discussing their own version of the who's on first theme—whether the NYCB's Peter Martins and Helgi Tomasson are better than ABT's "Misha" (Baryshnikov) and Fernando Bujones, or whether Natasha (Natalia Makarova) and Gelsey (Kirkland) of ABT are better than Suzanne (Farrell) and Pattie (Patricia McBride) of the NYCB. They used to compare the Yankees' Mantle, the Giants' Mays and the Dodgers' Snyder the same way in the old days. That's how big dance is in the Big Apple nowadays.

STAGE. Broadway's 43 theaters sold over 10.5 million tickets in 1980—the latest year for which figures are available. That's more than $175 million—or an average of $16.57 per ticket, according to the New York League of Theatre Owners and Producers.

The 1980–81 season, by all accounts, was even bigger. Despite the recessionary economy here, more tickets were sold at higher prices than at any other time in Broadway history. And with 36 percent of the ticket buyers from outside the New York metropolitan area (11 percent were foreigners), all those numbers add up to Broadway being New York City's number one tourist attraction. And that's not even counting the tickets sold at the nearly 15 Off-Broadway theaters in the Greenwich Village area and the more than 230 Off-Off-Broadway showcases found everywhere from SoHo to the Upper West Side, from Chelsea to the Bowery. As Ethel Merman sings it, there's no business like show business—and theatrical show business is obviously big business here.

At least part of Broadway's renaissance can be attributed to a combination of promotion and marketing campaigns undertaken by the League, the city and the state. Most prominent among these is the effort to simplify ticket buying and,

STAGE

indeed, it is easier to buy Broadway tickets today than it ever has been. You can phone for reservations for a particular show from virtually anywhere in the world, charge the tickets to a major credit card, and have them waiting for you at the box office the night of the show. In the metropolitan area (and sometimes throughout the Northeast) you can purchase theater tickets and seats for other performing arts events at computerized Ticketron outlets (call 977–9020 for the location nearest you) up until the day before a performance. On the day of the performance, you can pick up last-minute seats to many plays, musicals, and other attractions for half price (plus a small service charge) at one of two TKTS booths—the first at Broadway and 47th St., the second at 100 William St., a few blocks north of Wall St. And, of course, you can always go directly to the box office of the show you want to see and get tickets there.

Some facts and hints: The Times Square TKTS booth is open from 3:00 to 8:00 P.M. daily for evening performances, from noon to 2:00 P.M. for Wednesday and Saturday matinees, and from noon to 8:00 P.M. for both matinees and evening performances on Sunday. On William St. the hours are 11:30 A.M. to 5:30 P.M. weekdays for evening performances only, and from 11 A.M. to 3:00 P.M. on Saturdays, again for evening shows only. Lines at the Times Square booth can be very, very long. If you have very specific preferences you'd probably want to be on line by 10:30 or 11 in the morning for matinee tickets, by 2:30 or so for evening performances. Unless you happen to be touring the Wall St. area the same day you're planning to attend the theater, you're not likely to be near the William St. booth; nonetheless, it is often worth a little extra subway time to travel down there. The lines and wait (except at lunchtime) are shorter, and the selection just as good as uptown. On Saturdays especially, the William St. booth usually has no line. The TKTS booths, however, accept cash only—no credit cards, no checks. They handle many opera, ballet, concert, and off-Broadway attractions as well as those on the Great White Way.

You should also look into "twofers"—tickets that entitle you to buy two tickets for the price of one when presented at the box office for specified performances. Twofers are usually available at hotel desks, at restaurant cashier booths, and at the offices of the New York Visitors and Convention Bureau, 2 Columbus Circle. Sometimes they are even distributed while you're waiting on line at the TKTS booth. Or write in advance to Hit Shows, 303 W. 42nd St., New York, NY 10036, and enclose a self-addressed, stamped envelope.

The emphasis here on half-price tickets is simple: Broadway prices have skyrocketed in recent years, and although tickets for equivalent presentations elsewhere—in Las Vegas or Tokyo or London—are often even more expensive than full price in New York, the $35 top-price seat for a Broadway musical is increasingly the norm, while one show imported from England during the 1981–'82 season had a $100 top-ticket (the "cheap" seats were to be $70) for a two-part, eight-hour show. Thus it is easy to understand why more than 20 percent of all theater tickets in New York are sold through the TKTS booths.

The best advice for getting in to see the biggest hits on Friday and Saturday nights is to write well in advance to the box office, or to phone a reservation via credit card. If you're writing, send a certified check or money order for the exact amount, give several alternate dates and enclose a stamped, self-addressed envelope. Tickets for these same hits are usually easier to get for weekday evenings and matinees, though the sooner you make your decision as to what you want to see and when you want to see it, the better chance you have of getting your first choice. For sold-out shows, you might try waiting at the box office around 6:00 P.M. the night *before* you want to see that show. That's when unused "house seats" (a handful of the best seats held by the management for VIPs) are put on sale. This is admittedly a risky bet. Many shows also sell standing room—usually on the day of the performance, at prices ranging from about $5 to $8. And if there's only one "must see" sold-out show for you, try a ticket broker. Brokers charge full price plus a commission, the latter *legally* limited to $2.50 per ticket, and all too often the hottest tickets go only to favored customers. Golden and LeBlang Theatre Ticket Services, 207 W. 45th St., 757–2300 "since 1894, the largest theatre ticket agency in the U.S.A.," is one creditable such service. Others are located at major hotels.

Picking a new show is as easy as ABC. Study the classified listings on the theater pages of the daily newspapers or in the *New Yorker* or *New York/Cue* magazines (the latter include concise capsule reviews of all offerings), where you'll find casts, telephone numbers, prices, curtain times, and theater addresses. Ticket-availability boxes appear in the amusement pages of the *New York Times* and *Daily News* on Fridays. Hint to reading between the lines: When the availability chart says "all sections, all performances" or even "most sections," chances are you can get tickets to that show at the TKTS booth. For quick suggestions, scan the ads for major Tony Award winners—Broadway's equivalent of Hollywood's Oscars. Among recent winners that should be playing through the '81–'82 season: *Amadeus* (musings about Mozart), a stage remake of *42nd Street*, the burlesque revue *Sugar Babies* (starring Mickey Rooney and Ann Miller), the Duke Ellington-inspired *Sophisticated Ladies*, the Lauren Bacall star-vehicle *Woman of the Year*, and the seemingly perennial pleasers *Annie* and *A Chorus Line*.

A recent trend on Broadway has been toward short-run one-man or one-woman shows featuring young talents such as Liza Minnelli, Neil Diamond, Bette Midler, Gilda Radner, and Peter Allen, and older standbys such as Lena Horne, Tony Bennett, and Andy Williams. Horne, in fact, began what was to be a six-week limited engagement at the end of the '80–'81 season—a run that was extended again and again until, as of press time, she is scheduled to be knocking 'em dead at least through the beginning of 1982.

Many of the city's theaters themselves are handsome, steeped in theatrical history and designated city landmarks. Indeed, no visitor should bypass *Shubert Alley*, a narrow private walkway (open to the public) between 44th and 45th Sts. west of Broadway. It is named for the three famous producing and theater-owning brothers of the early part of the century, Sam, Lee and J.J. Shubert. Both the *Shubert Theater* and the *Booth* are on the alley (along with an "I Love New York" souvenir shop, restaurant, and ticket agency). At the foot of Shubert Alley on 44th St. is also *Sardi's*, famous theatrical hangout and site of numerous opening-night parties. Its walls are lined with caricatures of the famous Broad-

STAGE

way personalities who have wined and dined there—though neither the food nor the service seems as pleasing to non-regulars as to those who are instantly recognized.

Broadway means different things to different people. To most, it means the New York City theater district situated around the bright lights of Broadway. But to theater people, it means a geographic entity of 36 square blocks bounded by Sixth and Ninth Aves. and 41st and 53rd Sts. In the theaters on those blocks are tried-and-true dramas and musicals and British imports on the main featuring the best talent money can buy. Since it costs around $1 million to stage a musical and about half that for a straight play, Broadway doesn't take chances and leaves the risk-taking on new and unproven plays to Off-Broadway (OB) and Off-Off-Broadway (OOB).

There are many differences between Broadway, OB, and OOB. For openers, Broadway performers work under an Equity (actors' union) contract for a basic minimum pay. The OB minimum is a lot less because the theaters are a lot smaller, the cost of mounting a play a lot less because of relaxed union regulations. And the OOB performers may be working for the experience, exposure, and contributions in everything from SoHo lofts to church basements to showcases in Queens short on scenery but long on desire.

OOB is, as the Off-Off-Broadway Alliance (OOBA) describes it, "alternative theatre—a place for testing potential, for experimentation and the discovery of new talent . . . the research and development division of the American Theatre. Pulitzer Prize winners *A Chorus Line, No Place to Be Somebody, Talley's Folly* and *Buried Child* are among the many works introduced in this arena for emerging artists." For information about OOB performances, read the *Village Voice* or *SoHo News* or contact OOBA, 162 W. 56th St. 757–4473. Keep your eyes open as you walk around, too. There are lots of theater endeavors not advertised on a regular basis, but you'll see posters or signs—such as the 78th Street Theater Lab's "BYOB Cabaret" (*literally* off Broadway). Churches frequently host such theater.

OB was born in much the same way when it started in the 1930s in Greenwich Village around the time when the *Provincetown Playhouse* on MacDougal St. began showcasing playwright Eugene O'Neill there. Bette Davis and Henry Fonda worked OB, so did Geraldine Page, Jason Robards, George C. Scott, and Coleen Dewhurst, and so did—and do—Meryl Streep, Dustin Hoffman and Al Pacino. Edward Albee and Lanford Wilson got their playwriting start there, Jose Quintero became an OB legend for his direction of O'Neill works there, and Brecht, Weill, Ionesco and Beckett got some of their first important U.S. exposure there. Indeed, Joe Papp's Public Theater complex there is a veritable supermarket of lively theater choices.

In brief, some of the best theater in America was—and is—presented OB in Greenwich Village theaters such as the *Cherry Lane, Circle-In-the-Square* (downtown), *Theatre de Lys, Roundabout, Public, The Negro Ensemble,* and *Circle Repertory* at less than half of Broadway prices. America's longest running show, *The Fantasticks,* has been playing for over 20 years at the *Sullivan St. Theater.* And the *Circle Rep, Manhattan Theater Club,* and *Hudson Guild*—all

NEW YORK CITY

uptown—keep turning out hit after hit that move from OB proving grounds to Broadway. Newest members of this OB community—right on the fringe of Broadway itself—are the nine theaters of *42nd Street Theater Row*, between Ninth and Tenth Aves., across from Manhattan Plaza. Sadly, despite their relatively consistent quality and quest for innovation, just about all of these theaters and companies are in constant financial trouble, struggling from one production to the next, forever hoping to hit upon that one huge Broadway possibility—as *Chorus Line* and *Pirates of Penzance* were for *Joseph Papp's New York Shakespeare Festival Public Theater*—whose proceeds will finance other endeavors. Tickets for OB shows are usually about half the price of Broadway seats, and often less. They are even cheaper OOB.

Papp's theater complex on Lafayette St., near Astor Place, generates some of the most exciting theatrical events in the city. The various theaters play host to young playwrights honing their craft in workshop situations, to experienced actors and directors needing the feedback of a small intimately housed audience, to short-lived experimental works, jazz concerts, dance series, film retrospectives and anything related to the performing arts. Other reliable sources of interesting theater are the internationlly famed *LaMama Experimental Theater Club* (74A E. 4th St.), *Playwrights Horizons* (416 W. 42nd St.), the *American Place Theater* (111 W. 46th St.), *CSC Repertory* (136 E. 13th St.), *Jean Cocteau Repertory* (330 Bowery), and *New Federal Theater Group* (446 Grant St.). OB may also mean a trek even farther uptown—to the *Master Theater*, 103rd St. at Riverside Drive, or to the *Riverside Church*, 112th St. at Riverside Drive, where the *Equity Theater* presents dramatic and musical classics, or to the *Phoenix* at Marymount Manhattan College, 221 E. 71st St.

Central Park's *Delacorte Theater* continues to be home to summertime Shakespeare productions co-sponsored by the city and Joseph Papp's Public Theater. Tickets to these generally first-rate outdoor productions are free, distributed beginning at 6:00 P.M. on the night of performance. The line for tickets, however, begins forming early in the afternoon, so take a blanket, a book, and maybe a picnic for before the show. There are usually two productions each summer, running about a month each. The theater is set beside a rock-bounded lagoon near W. 81st St., and is accessible via the 81st St. entrances to the park from Central Park West or Fifth Ave.

Sitting in the Delacorte listening to Shakespeare's words will make you feel far removed from the pass-the-hat informality of OOB, from the OB of Greenwich Village, or the bright lights of the Great White Way. But it's all there for the taking, and all part of New York's great theatrical life. After all, the theater in Manhattan has to strain to outdo the everyday theater of the streets.

 **SHOPPING.** Whether or not you came to New York for the shopping, you probably won't be able to resist it while you're here. The city offers such a variety of stores, goods and services that, even if you don't buy, a shopping expedition can be exciting and fascinating.

SHOPPING

First, though, you should know where to look for what you do want. The telephone book Yellow Pages are valuable guides (there is one volume for Consumers, another for Businesses). Or check the local newspapers and magazines for ads or articles on current sales. If you're not looking for something too esoteric, the major department stores (Macy's, Gimbels, Bloomingdale's) may surprise you with the completeness of their stock. Although a specialty store might have a collection that more exactly matches your tastes, the department stores have at least a little bit of almost everything, and after seeing some particular sections—both Macy's and Bloomingdale's for example, have lavish cookware departments—you may feel no need to look further.

Nonetheless, it's fun to explore. Most of New York's serious shopping is done in the midtown area, between 34th St. and 60th or so—this corresponds to the "downtown" of other American cities. But other areas have valuable resources too. On the residential Upper West Side, from 72nd to 86th Sts. for instance, there's a concentration of quieter, neighborhood-type stores along Broadway, and the southern parts of Amsterdam and Columbus Aves. are now arcades of new, trendy shops and restaurants. This part of town has traditionally been the middle-class area of Manhattan, and though it's rapidly becoming fancier and more expensive, you'll still find some very civilized browsing there in the way of books, foodstuffs, antiques, and so on. The more fashionable Upper East Side, from the 60s through the 80s, is terrain for the serious collector of antiques and art (the auction houses are here, and the galleries of Madison Ave.) and for lovers of handsome boutiques. For bargains you really go downtown. For apparel, for example, a long stretch of Orchard Street from Houston Street south is the nearest the city comes to an old-fashioned marketplace. Don't go on Saturday, when many businesses shut for the Sabbath—though they do open Sunday—and don't be deterred by the countless small, poky stores—there are good buys here for those with the patience to look. *A. Altman,* for example, at 182 Orchard, is renowned for women's fashion.

But if shopping is at all a tourist attraction in New York—and we believe it is—there are two stores that ought to be on everyone's "must-see" list: Bloomingdale's and Macy's.

Bloomingdale's, taking up the square block from 59th to 60th Sts. and between Lexington and Third Aves., is nothing less than a fashion showplace whether you're looking at designer dresses, Oriental goods (much of them imported from the People's Republic of China), or sheets and pillowcases. The main floor, with its walls upon walls of mirrors and stark lighting, is a chic open bazaar half given over to makeup, perfume, and fast-buy women's items, the other half a complete men's haberdashery. Informal and cheaper clothing is on the below-street-level floors, while the rest of the store features pretty much the kind of general merchandise you'd expect any well-stocked department store to have—only extravagantly displayed and with prices to match. Perhaps most interesting of all is how difficult it is to actually purchase anything here: The salespeople invariably act as though they're doing you a favor to answer a question or write up a sales receipt. Obviously they must have better things to do.

Macy's, also a full block square from 34th to 35th Sts. between Seventh Ave. and Broadway, is more the everyman's department store. At Macy's the brand names and merchandise are familiar; it's not so much what the store carries as the depth of stock in virtually everything. The basement-level Cellar is the most popular part of the store, overflowing with housewares in what has been designed as a series of integrated boutiques. The Cellar also has a wonderful cheese counter (relatively reasonably priced) and a full stock of tinned, bottled, and otherwise prepared gourmet items (not so reasonably priced, though you can't beat the selection), and a small grocery with first-rate produce (very highly priced, but you won't find a rotten apple, or mushroom, in the barrel). The children's floors are indeed a wonderland from Thanksgiving through the New Year, with free shows and a spectacular decorating job. And the store is eminently reliable as far as shipping and/or delivering whatever you may purchase —from coffeemakers to carpets, parkas to pianos. The store also has one of the finest soda fountains in the city on the fifth floor.

Moving essentially from downtown north:

May's, at 14th St. and Union Square (Broadway), provides a huge assortment of inexpensive merchandise. Certain items such as housewares, sheets, and such are at bargain prices, but the clothing is a mixed bag. A string of odd clothing and miscellaneous stores stretching along 14th Street to the west of May's are for the intrepid shopper only. Do not buy casette tapes, pantyhose or other merchandise in sealed wrappers; they may be irregulars.

On 34th St. between Fifth and Sixth Aves. there are a large number of shoe stores, plus *Gimbels,* (noted for bargain values), *Ohrbach's* (known for its low-priced copies of high-priced women's clothing), and one of the outlets of the chain called *The Gap,* selling men's and women's jeans and jeans-style fashions. Finally, at Fifth Ave., *B. Altman* is the last of 34th Street's department stores. This is a favorite of the middle-income shopper—respectable, always-acceptable merchandise is sold here; there is a fully stocked menswear department, along with excellent furniture, china, and glassware sections and fine foods. Altman also has one of the best of the department-store dining rooms.

Fifth Ave. between 34th St. and 59th St. has long been known as a mecca for shoppers, although in recent years some of its more illustrious residents have folded their tents and been succeeded by less refined tenants. It is well to be suspicious, in fact, of several stores in this stretch selling cameras, electronics, carved "ivory," and such. But Fifth Ave. still offers an unusual number of fine shops of every description, and it remains a top attraction for visting shoppers.

The traditional Fifth Ave. tour begins at 38th St., at *Lord & Taylor.* Here the Christmas-window decorations are a special treat, while the store itself is known for its fine clothing. At 50th Street, *Saks Fifth Avenue* has long been a beacon of fashion and accessories. As you walk north along Fifth in the 40s and 50s, you'll notice that this is where many of the airlines have their offices, and also that this is good bookshop country (*Scribner's* and *Rizzoli,* both near 49th, are the most handsome).

Henri Bendel (pronounced BEN-del by those in the know) on 57th Street just west of Fifth Avenue, is a small pearl of a store—set up in aisles of boutiques—

known for its trend-setting women's fashions and for its always beautifully designed displays and windows. Just opposite it, on the corner of 57th St. and Fifth Ave., is *Bergdorf Goodman,* chic and expensive; and a little farther east on 57th St. is the new *Bonwit Teller,* reopened after an absence and much reduced in size.

While in the neighborhood, consider *Alexander's,* one block south of Bloomingdale's. This is another store noted for inexpensive clothing of all kinds, some of it very stylish; while it's somewhat chaotic and noisy, the values are good, offering special purchases and close-outs, some with famous labels, and Alexander's has a reputation for decent quality.

Some of the stores we've named have branches scattered in other parts of the city. Shopping in midtown deserves some strategic thinking: Try to avoid the hours between noon and 2:00 P.M. (when office workers descend *en masse* to get their errands done) and weekends. Also crowded are the late-opening nights—usually Thursdays, when many of these stores will close at 9:00 P.M. If you prefer to avoid the midtown rush, find out if a branch is more convenient by calling the main office, or checking the ads in the newspapers, although stock and selection at the branches is rarely as good as at the flagship stores.

SPECIAL SHOPPING NOTES

As enticing as the larger stores are the hundreds of specialty stores that are the signature of the city. The list below is partial, and concentrates on relatively "stable" stores that have been in business for some time. A further guide, as mentioned, is the Yellow Pages. If these fail, try calling a free service called Cityphone, 675-0900. Tell them what you're looking for—they'll try to find a source.

As you walk through the city, you may see some stores with the notation "To the Trade" on the door or window. Such stores sell goods at wholesale prices to business clients, and often do not accommodate the general public. However, some of them do occasionally open their doors for a special sale. Check the "Living" sections of the daily and Sunday papers or the "Sales & Bargains" column of *New York* magazine for announcements of the latter.

Sales tax in New York City at press time is 8¼%.

WOMEN'S CLOTHING

All of the well-known department stores previously mentioned dedicate much or all of their floor space and counters to wooing women. Competition is fierce; there are frequent sales and special offers, which are widely advertised in the local papers.

Generally speaking, the largest array of merchandise, and therefore the greatest range of choices, will be found in the larger department and specialty stores. *B. Altman's,* on Fifth Ave. at 34th St., is best known for conservative styles, though it also offers fine traditional sport clothes. Very reasonable (and moderately modish) items are on the sixth floor. *Lord & Taylor* has a range of

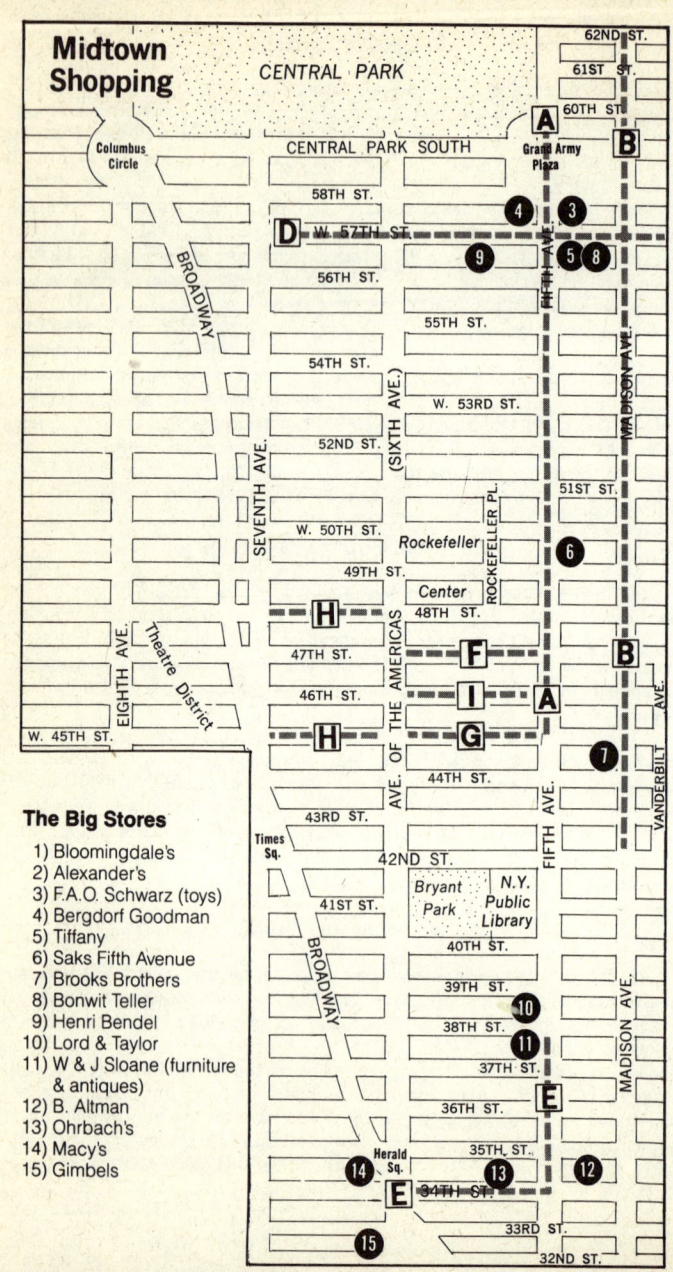

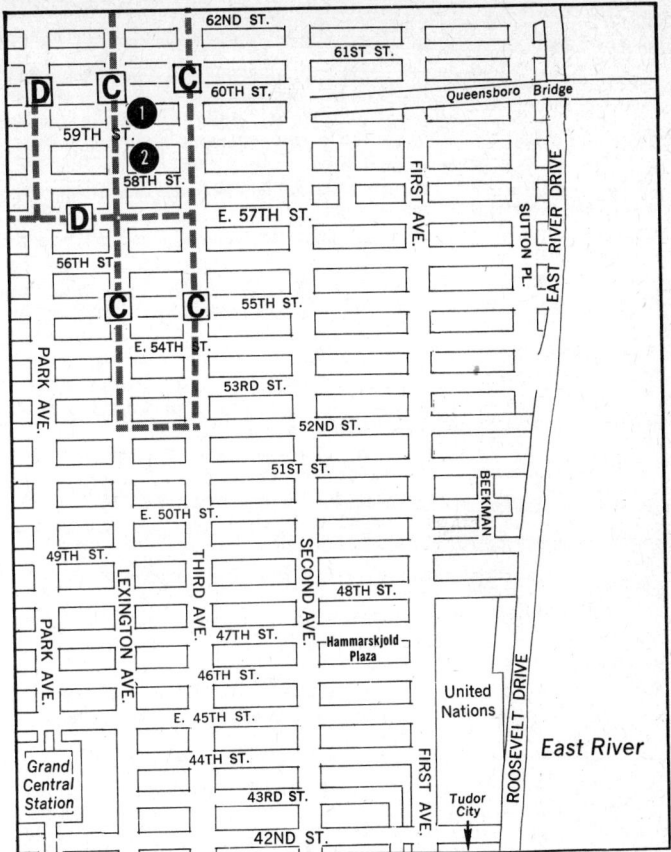

The Areas

A Fifth Avenue: clothing, accessories, jewelry, silver, design, luggage & leather, bookstores—all, except tourist-trap electronics and camera shops, are very up-market in both quality and price.

B Madison Avenue: boutiques of all description, men's clothes, leather & luggage—like Fifth Ave., all up-market. Also on some sidestreets. Art galleries above 57th St.

C Lexington & Third Avenues: boutiques and shops, but less prestigious than those of Fifth and Madison Avenues. Some antique stores on Third.

D 57th Street: boutiques, art galleries, antique specialists—most quite prestigious and expensive.

E 34th Street Area: clothing shops, but distinctly non-posh.

F Gems and jewelry.

G Hi-Fi.

H Musical instruments.

I Brazilian imports.

traditionally styled fashion which appeals to women of every age, including the young contemporary customer, male as well as female.

Saks Fifth Avenue (on Fifth Ave. and 50th St.) still touts the best in "carriage trade" fashion. It isn't cheap, but the labels are famous, and the store has a reputation for accessories. *Bergdorf Goodman* (on Fifth Ave. at 57th St.) is indispensable for those who can afford its outstanding collection. It appeals to the young—and to their grandmothers.

It is only natural to center your shopping attention on the bigger stores; but you should also sample the fantastic range of boutiques around the city. Try walking along Madison Ave. between 60 and 78th Sts. or so, for a dazzling array of high-fashion shops nestled amid the galleries and salons. *Veneziano,* near 68th St. is a favorite of the members of the best-dressed list (prices are steep, as is to be expected in this area). Just south is *Halston,* one of the more famous names in the current pantheon. And at Madison and 65th St. you'll find *Betsey Bunky Nini,* for a younger look—the Betsey in the store's name is designer Betsey Johnson, though she is no longer affiliated with the place.

Right nearby, near 69th St., is *Jaeger International Shop,* where the tailored look finds its finest expression in some stunning sportswear. (Another Jaeger outlet is to be found just opposite Bergdorf Goodman, in the I. Miller store on 57th St. near Fifth Ave.) And near 71st St. you'll find *Saint Laurent Rive Gauche,* for the best Paris has to offer.

Back a little farther downtown, though still on the subject of Paris, the *Courrèges* shop is on 57th St. just off Madison Ave.; or for a change in manner, look at the sweetly English printed fabrics, clothing, and home accessories of *Laura Ashley,* on Madison near 63rd St. Finally, a midtown shopping expedition is not complete without a stop at *Martha Inc.* and at *Evelyn Byrnes,* two of the proudest and oldest names in New York fashion. The two stores are directly across from each other, at 58th St. and Park Ave.; an ample pocketbook is a necessity.

There are plenty of worthwhile places to visit besides the above shops, less mainstream both in style and in locale. On the Upper West Side try *Charivari for Women,* at Broadway and 84th St., for Italian and American clothes in the latest modes—very modern but also very handsome. *Charivari Sport,* one block north, offers once again very modern stylings; these, however, are more informal in nature, and the prices are relatively modest. Women in larger sizes will find beautiful clothes in natural fabrics at *Ashanti Bazaar,* 872 Lexington Ave. at 65th St.; also a good selection at the *Forgotten Woman* at 880 Lexington Ave. at 65 St. To see what the young of New York are wearing, this is a good place to stop, as is *Reminiscence,* in Greenwich Village on MacDougal St. near 8th St. This shop carries a range of now-fashionable "antique" clothing, as well as up-to-date stuff under its own label. And for the truly young-at-heart (or those prepared to be a little outrageous), *Fiorucci* is truly entertaining; at 125 East 59th St.

Accessories and such. For shoes, *Gucci* might be your first stop; it offers high-styled, high-priced shoes and other accessories and leather goods, and

SHOPPING

there is a branch on Fifth Ave. (Gucci follows the maddening Italian tradition of closing between noon and 2:00 P.M., when most New Yorkers are up and doing. Because Gucci items are great status symbols in Japan, and cost a good deal more there, you will often see clusters of Japanese visitors crowding the sidewalk outside the shop, waiting for the store to reopen after lunch.) *Charles Jourdan,* nearby at 55th St. and Fifth, can't be beaten for the latest Parisian shoe and boot designs—once again at astronomical prices. For more modest budgets, there's *Chandler's,* across the street, and *I. Miller,* at 57th Street and Fifth Avenue. Though its name may be less well known than the Fifth Ave. stores, *Maud Frizon USA,* at 210 E. 60th St., is a true competitor, both in styling and in prices; for fine shoes at low prices, a good place to look is *Etiquette,* at 28 W. 38th St.

Handbags, gloves, scarves, and the like can well be bought at the department stores that cater to women, for example Bonwit Teller or Saks. But one downtown handbag outlet is worth knowing about—*Fine & Klein,* at 119 Orchard St. The price range of the wide selection of bags here ranges from very low to very high, but even the very high items are substantially discounted. *Lederer,* at 613 Madison Ave. near 58th St., also has a huge selection, and though these satisfy the most discriminating tastes, the prices are mostly within reach. Purchasers of hats may enjoy *Whittall and Javits,* at 65 W. 37th St., or *I.J. Herman,* 15 W. 38th St., one of the last establishments left that do hat blocking.

Henri Bendel has a small but luxurious fur section, but the fur district proper is on Seventh Avenue, where *Varriale* is one of the more widely known names (call for an appointment). When buying furs you should comparison shop as far as possible, since you're probably making a sizable investment; in the same stretch of Seventh Ave. as Varriale, in the high 20s and low 30s, you'll find several more furriers, including *Balencia,* at 333 Seventh near 29th St., and *Aronowicz,* at 345 Seventh. Crossing town to the East Side, the *Fur Vault at Alexander's,* on Third Ave. and 58th St., is widely advertised and popular; the *Ritz Thrift Shop,* at 107 W. 57th St., offers fine used furs.

Bargain Shopping. Finally, there is the indescribable thrill of bargain shopping. Not just for a marked-down item (which can be a very good value at special season sales), but also for the designer dress you saw yesterday at an expensive midtown store and which you now find at a 50% to 75% reduction at a manufacturers' outlet.

Such shopping takes time and research. The advantage of an outlet, however, is that reductions occur at the very beginning of a fashion season. Often labels are cut out, but tags have code numbers veterans can identify as concealing a famous designer's handiwork. Stock can vary, and it may take several trips before you find precisely what you want. There may be slight irregularities in the stock, but *Loehmann's* (at Fordham Road and Jerome Ave. in the Bronx) and *Bolton's* (on Madison at 86th St., and at several other locations) are fascinating because you never know what they'll have next. Loehmann's, the grandmother of all the popular discounters, also has branches in Queens and Brooklyn.

Resale stores carry "gently used" things culled from the best private wardrobes—some of their merchandise may never have been worn. One well-known shop is *Resale Associates,* on Madison Ave. near 80th St. In a slightly different category *Damages—Mr. Martin,* at 169 E. 61st St., offers irregular pieces, samples, and the like at good prices. *Trishop,* on Third Ave. at 92nd St., and *Repeat Performance,* farther south on Third near 84th St., are two charity shops which regularly receive donations of fashionable clothes (some good-quality seconds, some perfect); this is not secondhand stuff, but comes direct from the department stores—you should look the clothing over before buying, but there is little here that is unsatisfactory. *Pushcart Trading Company,* 37th St. and Fifth Ave., has close-outs, special purchases, discontinued merchandise, household items, shoes, clothing, perfumes, toiletries, toys—the items change from week to week. Finally, *New Store,* at 289 Seventh Ave., near 27th St., has a large collection of designer lines at heavy discounts.

MEN'S CLOTHING

Barney's, Seventh Ave. and 17th St., calls itself the largest men's store in the world, and it's hard to see how it could have any competition. This is *the* center for menswear in the city—if only because so many different elements of gentlemen's garb are found here under one roof. Conservative styles, high-fashion tailoring, and the most modern fashions are all available, and in an enormous range of sizes. In addition, Barney's has occasional sales—very popular ones, and widely advertised. Very early on the first morning of a sale, the line of well-dressed men waiting for the store to open circles the block.

Brooks Bros. has been offering its wares to conservative New Yorkers since the beginning of the 19th century, and is still going strong at Madison Ave. and 44th St. The first floor contains an ocean of button-down shirts and striped ties, and the store is famous for its dignified high-quality suits; but you'll also find hats, haberdashery, sport clothes, and much else too. Still in the conservative vein are a series of stores in the same neighborhood, including *Chipp, Inc.,* at 14 E. 44th St., and the well-known name *Paul Stuart* (on Madison at 45th St.), for the slightly more adventurous. *F. R. Tripler,* on Madison Ave. at 46th St., is another long-established and reliable store.

Of course, all the major department stores have extensive men's sections.

In recent years, there has been a marked trend away from the stylish stores; the so-called "discount" men's outlet shops have taken a lot of the traffic away from their more impressive brethren. On Fifth Ave., in the area between 14th and 23rd Sts., you'll find a number of such places, of which perhaps the best known is *Harry Rothman,* on the corner of 18th St. The store has a good range of discounted suits, as well as sweaters, sport jackets, coats, and more. *Hampshire International,* nearby at 85 Fifth Ave., has similar stock at similar prices.

Part of the trend away from tradition has been toward stylish Italian clothes, such as those available at *Madonna* at 223 E. 60th St. *Charivari for Men,* 2339 Broadway at 85th St., also offers very handsome modern men's fashions. On the less formal side, jeans, workshirts, and western wear are an increasingly important element in men's fashion these days, and for that matter in women's too. Both sexes are catered to at *The Gap*, where the selection of jeans and related accessories is among the most complete in the city. There are several branches, the largest of which is at 86th St. and Third Ave. Downtown, *Hudson's* (105 Third Ave. near 14th St.) is the granddaddy of the so-called Army & Navy stores, though the merchandise here encompasses a far wider range than just military surplus. *Canal Jean*, at 304 Canal St. and on Broadway near Spring St., and *Unique Clothing Warehouse*, on Broadway near 8th St., both offer wilder, funkier, more diverse variants of jeans-style fashions. Both are city institutions, for inexpensive, trendy clothes.

While on the subject of Western-style clothing, let's talk shoes—or, rather, boots. *To Boot*, at 72nd St. and Columbus Ave., has a large selection of very fine cowboy boots, ranging from the straightforward to the ornate, and to be sold to both men and women; unfortunately, while the denims and shirtings of Western stylings may be bought relatively inexpensively, the same cannot be said of the footwear. To Boot also sells Western clothing.

More usual types of shoes may be bought all over the city, at branches of such chains as *Florsheim* or *Thom McAnn*. For distinctive stylings, try *Church's Shoes*, on Madison Ave. at 49th St.; this is a branch of the famous London bootmakers and offers elegant traditional footwear, but the price you pay for these traditional, but *very* durable and handsome, items is high. *Susan Bennis/Warren Edwards*, at 122 E. 55th St., offers unusual and fine-quality shoes for men and women, as does *Maud Frizon*, at 210 E. 60th St.; and *Barney's*, that great capital of menswear, has not one but two shoe departments. Lastly, *McReedy and Schreiber*, at 37 W. 46th St., is another popular shop.

A few expensive shops still specialize in what is popularly known as men's furnishings, and you had best visit these establishments with a thick wallet. Underwear, hosiery, ties, and shirts combine with sweaters, robes, and miscellaneous sportwear of the highest quality. *A. Sulka*, at 711 Fifth Ave. at 56th St., *Countess Mara*, at 110 E. 57th St., and *Alexander Shields*, at Park Ave. and 59th St., are good examples of this kind of store.

In New York City, men don't take a back seat even when it comes to the matter of haute couture. Designer fashions for men exist in virtually every major department and specialty store, and there are also high-fashion boutiques solely for men. Famous among these are *St. Laurent for Men*, at 543 Madison Ave. near 55th St., and *Pierre Balmain*, at 795 Madison near 68th St. St. Laurent in particular has fine shirts. And finally, of course virtually every men's department in the big stores such as *Bloomingdale's* or *Saks* is highly rewarding.

For renting good-quality, conservative, traditional formal wear, *Baldwin Formals*, 40 W. 56th St., and *A. T. Harris*, 419 Lexington Ave., near 44th St., should be satisfactory.

CHILDREN'S CLOTHES

All of the major department stores have children's sections that reflect their positions on the adult fashion ladder. Thus *Bergdorf Goodman* has elegant clothes in both the ready-to-wear and made-to-order categories. *Saks Fifth Avenue's* children's section is only slightly less posh. *Bloomingdale's* has very interesting clothes in a wide assortment, and *Alexander's* is the inexpensive (though good) end of the spectrum. Of all these stores, however, *Macy's* rates as the top choice, if only because of the size of its selection.

A great many boutique-style stores specialize in nothing but children's apparel, and they too cover the full spectrum of prices and styles. *Stone Free* alone carries a wide variety in its two children's stores, one on W. 72nd St. near Columbus and the other at 1086 Madison Avenue near 82nd St.; not surprisingly, the Madison Ave. branch is the more chic of the two, but both are unusual and appealing. (If these clothes appeal to you as you steer your children through Stone Free for Kids on 72nd St., there's an adult version of the store just opposite.) *Slithy Toves,* on W. 72nd between CPW and Columbus, features much unusual and handmade apparel for kids. *Cerutti,* at Madison and 68th St., received a measure of publicity from the patronage of Jackie Onassis, who reportedly purchased some of Caroline and John-John's gear there; the clientele is that affluent, and the prices reflect it. *Wendy's Store* is a delightful source of infant and toddler wear and toys, at 1046 Madison Ave., 80th St. For bargains, *Goldman & Ostrow,* at 315 Grand St. on the Lower East Side, is the real McCoy, or you could go a few steps down the block to *Rice and Breskin* (323 Grand). Or cross the river to Brooklyn and visit *Natan Borlam,* at 157 Havemeyer St. At this discount shop name brands are available at very low prices; open only Sunday through Thursday.

JEWELRY

Eye-catching, ready-to-wear, and conveniently centralized, high-fashion jewelry in New York clusters around 55th St. and Fifth Ave. Within a ten-minute walk, the shopper encounters Van Cleef and Arpels (at Bergdorf Goodman), the highly esteemed Tiffany & Co., Buccellati, Fortunoff, Harry Winston, and Cartier. Along with the dazzling adornments that have earned them reputations as dazzlingly expensive, these stores also sell attractive items everyone can afford.

Tiffany's, at Fifth Ave. and 57th St., is almost as elegant as the reputation that precedes it, though there really isn't anywhere here to have breakfast. Even more elegant is the fabled *Cartier's,* at Fifth and 52nd St., where the mantle of wealth and privilege hangs heavy over its gilt and plush decor, but even Cartier takes a backseat in high prices to *Harry Winston's,* at 718 Fifth Ave. *Fortunoff,* a relative newcomer, has been very successfully advertised by Lauren Bacall, and prides itself on discounting brand-name items and stocking a vast array of not-too-expensive trinkets that make very welcome gifts. *H. Stern,* across 51st St. from St. Patrick's, has beautiful precious and semi-precious stones, and jewelry.

If you could use a change from Fifth Avenue's typically cool and sophisticated sales transactions, shopping for jewelry can give you a great chance to do so. West 47th St., between Fifth and Sixth Aves., has been described more than once

SHOPPING

as the closest thing to a Middle Eastern bazaar to be found in New York—haggling included. This block is known as "the diamond district," and in shops packed with merchandise, where no time or expense has been wasted on decor, you can bargain over gems, gold, silver, and all kinds of semiprecious stones. Investigate *Bill Schifrin,* reputedly the world's largest purveyor of wedding rings, at Booth 86 of the National Jewelers Exchange. The whole block has an element of theater to it, and is well worth a visit, though the procedure of buying a stone here can be intimidating and chancy. It's best to go with a friend who knows diamonds.

LEATHER AND LUGGAGE

You will see any number of luggage shops tucked into the various corners of the city, and these are generally the best places to find bargains. *Innovation Luggage,* for example, has several branches, one of them at 42nd St. and Second Ave.; a walk down Orchard Street will furnish you with various displays of luggage, with *Altman's* (no relation to the department store), at 135 Orchard, among the better known. Sticking to the beaten path will involve higher prices, but willing buyers are apparently available in sufficient numbers to enable the more glamorous names to survive. *Gucci,* on Fifth Ave. at 54th St., has a worldwide reputation for its fine products, with prices to match. *Mark Cross,* just south of Gucci at Fifth and 51st St., is in the same class, as is *T. Anthony,* at Madison and 66th St. *Crouch and Fitzgerald,* at Madison and 48th St., is a handsome store that handles its own line of luggage, as well as *Louis Vuitton* bags (Vuitton also has its own outlet, on 57th Street near Madison); and *Dinoffer,* at 24 W. 57th St., is another of the city's reputable old names.

COSMETICS, PERFUMES, AND TOILETRIES

One of New York's finest toiletry shops is *Caswell-Massey,* on Lexington Ave. at 48th St. This is a place that combines a certain modern flair with extremely long-established quality (the store dates back to the eighteenth century); the variety of soaps and all kinds of other liniments and miscellany is a delight. Ask for a catalog; it's wonderful reading. *Il Makiage,* at 521 Park Ave. (60th St.), is a cosmetics boutique with a fashionable Upper East Side air. Down in Greenwich Village, *the Soap Opera,* at 51 Grove Street, and the *Bath Stop* on Thompson St. have a wide range of soaps—as also, of course, do the relevant sections of the major department stores. The department stores are also where most New York women go to buy perfumes. Yet *Pushcart,* at Fifth Ave. and 37th St., has many famous toiletries on sale at all times, although stock may vary from week to week.

BEAUTY SALONS

There are a few establishments that can't be neglected—*Georgette Klinger,* for example, with its beautiful engraved doors at 501 Madison Ave. near 53rd St., is known for facials and skin care, as is *Christine Valmy,* at 767 Fifth Ave. (near

58th St.). *Cinandre,* at 11 E. 57th Street, is as fashionable for skin and hair as its neighborhood implies, and of course there are both men and women who will go nowhere else but *Vidal Sassoon,* at 767 Fifth Ave. (58th St.) for their hair. Many of the department stores, including *Bloomingdale's* and *Saks,* have their own salons. And a less famous, but well-liked, salon is *Monique of the Waldorf,* at 301 Park Ave., at 49th St.

TOYS

The magnet for the majority of young and young at heart would have to be *F.A.O. Schwarz,* at Fifth Ave. and 58th St. Here, stuffed animals of a size that one would think would terrify a small person are instead immediate objects of delight; and every other conceivable game, toy, or member of a menagerie is available in some part of the store.

At least as famous is the toy department of *Macy's,* where most of the present crop of middle-aged, middle-class New Yorkers originally whet their acquistional appetites. Shelf upon shelf, counter upon counter—while most of the other department stores have representative departments devoted to toys, this has got to be the definitive department.

There are many dollhouse-and-miniature furniture retail stores in Manhattan; one is *Dollhouse Antics* on Madison Ave. near 92nd St.

Go Fly a Kite, at 1434 Third Avenue, is devoted to kites—from very simple ones to very expensive ones that one can't imagine being flown. Several stores specialize in model trains, including *Madison Hardware,* at 105 E. 23rd St., the *Train Shop,* at 23 W. 45th St., and the *Roundhouse,* at 14 W 45th St. *Polk's,* Fifth Ave. near 32rd St., features trains, plus boats and cars, models, radio-control equipment, and so forth.

Brentano's and *Barnes & Noble's* main stores also have interesting collections of toys and games for both youngsters and adults.

GOURMET FOODS AND EQUIPMENT

Whatever tastes in foodstuffs the visitor to New York may have, he can sate them here, and if he's not careful he'll develop a whole range of new ones too.

Probably New York's favorite delicatessen, and certainly its most often discussed, is *Zabar's.* This establishment occupies three storefronts, on Broadway at 80th St. On Saturday nights the store is open until midnight, and is jammed with New Yorkers who have picked up the bulky Sunday *New York Times*—on sale around 9:00 P.M. Saturday—and are now waiting in line to buy the fixings for a luxurious Sunday breakfast of smoked fish, bagels, cheese, and croissants, all sold here. Zabar's also has fine kitchen equipment, often at the best prices anywhere. They have sold their Cuisinarts at such a low price that for a time the company refused to sell them any. The fish counter—for whitefish, smoked salmon, sable, sturgeon, etc.—is usually especially crowded, and you must "take a number," but you'll also find meats, a slew of canned and packaged delicacies, coffees, fresh pasta, and much more. While you're on the Upper West Side, *Murray's,* at 2429 Broadway near 90th St., and *Barney Greengrass,* at 541

SHOPPING

Amsterdam Avenue, near 86th St., are also renowned for sturgeon, lox, and the like. On the Upper East Side, *Caviarteria,* unsurprisingly, specializes in caviar (at 29 E. 60th St.), and more diversified stores include *Fay & Allen's Foodworks,* at 1241 Third Avenue near 72nd St., and *E.A.T.,* at 1064 Madison near 81st St. While you're looking at galleries in SoHo, take a peak at *Dean & DeLuca's,* 121 Prince Street. This place isn't cheap, but you'll find a range of high-quality pastries, cheeses, pâtés, olive oils, sausages, and you-name-it, as well as impressive-looking kitchen equipment. *SoHo Charcuterie,* at Sullivan and Spring Streets, is another must. Another such place in the Village is *Balducci's,* at Sixth Avenue and 9th Street, which in addition to all the exotica also stocks fine fruits and vegetables, meats, fish, and so on.

Ninth Avenue is the city's grocery store, and by walking down it between, say, 40th and 50th Sts., you'll find all kinds of good-quality meats, vegetables, pasta, and ethnic specialties. *Molinari Bros.,* at 776 Ninth Ave. at 52nd St., is a place to go for excellent meat as well as homemade sausage, salami, pâté's, etc. This place supplies many of the city's fine restaurants and hotel dining rooms—it's not cheap but the quality and the service are first-class. Italian foods are best located by strolling through Little Italy, in the area of Mulberry and Grand Sts., and stopping at any of several stores of which the *Italian Food Center,* at 186 Grand, is an example. Also, *Ferrara's* is nearby: for pastry and coffees. Farther north, *Todaro's,* at 555 Second Ave. near 30th Street, has a mail-order business in Italian foods and is justly respected. *Tanaka,* at 326 Amsterdam Ave. at 74th St., will provide you with Japanese foodstuffs; for Chinese, try any of the curious-looking stores on Mott Street or Mulberry Street south of Canal Street, in Chinatown. For Hungarian provisions, try *Paprikas Weiss,* at 1546 Second Ave. at 78th St., which not only has spices, jams, jellies, and imported candies, but can also provide such esoteric items as ready-to-use strudel dough. *Mrs. Herbst's Strudels,* Third Ave, between 81st and 82nd Sts., also has delicious jams and the like, and you can also try her pastries at tables in the back of the shop, with coffee or tea. Indian spices can be found at a number of shops in "Little India," along Lexington Avenue between 26th and 30th Sts. In the way of coffee and teas, Zabar's has a famous name, and a very old but youthful-looking and expanding store is *Gillies 1840,* at Third Ave. and 84th St., plus other locations. In the Village at 109 Christopher St. near Bleecker, *McNulty's* has a wide range of teas and coffees too, as does *Cofféa,* Broadway near 86th St. The gourmet shops at *Bloomingdale's* and *Macy's* are also prime choices for fine and unusual spices, and their housewares departments are great places to find all kinds of cooking equipment. In cold meats, the store to measure all others by is *Schaller and Weber,* at 1654 Second Ave., near 86th St. Nearby, at 218 E. 86th St., is *Bremen House,* specializing in German foods. A good place for kitchenware is the *Cellar* in Macy's basement; alternatives are the chain of stores called the *Pottery Barn,* at several locations, which is noted for its good prices on a range of cooking equipment, and *Conran's,* at 54th St. and Third Ave. This last is an interesting place—downstairs is a range of modern furniture, while on the second floor are fabrics, rugs, and such, and pots, pans, earthen-

NEW YORK CITY

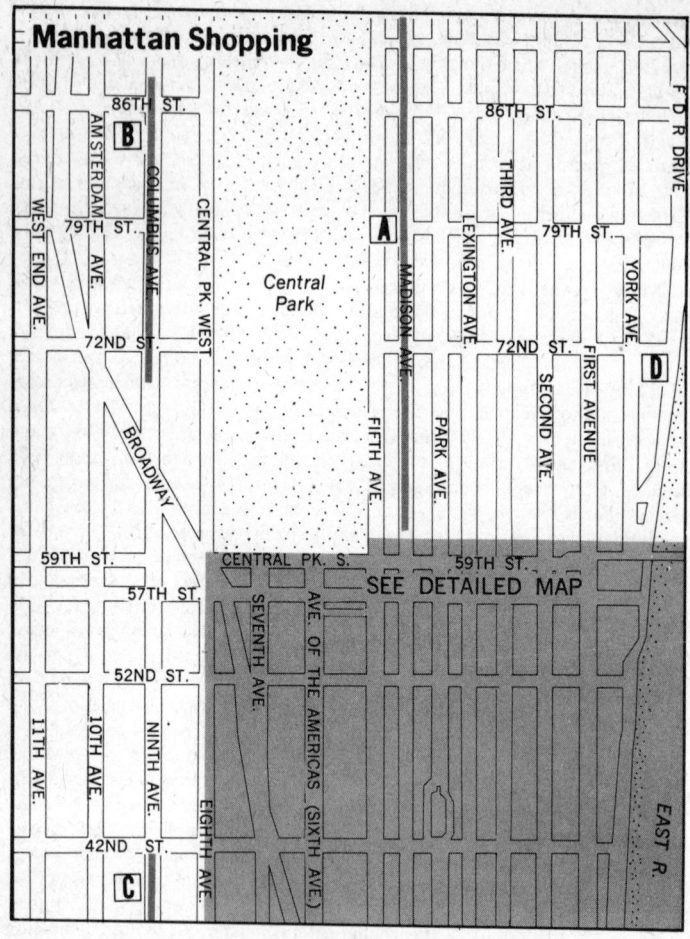

A Art galleries, swank boutiques, fine antiques, antiquities.
B Boutiques, ordinary antiques.
C Foreign food specialties.
D Sotheby Parke Bernet Decorative Arts Gallery.
E Second-hand books, antiques, auction galleries.
F Discount stores (clothes, accessories).
G Antiques, boutiques.

SHOPPING

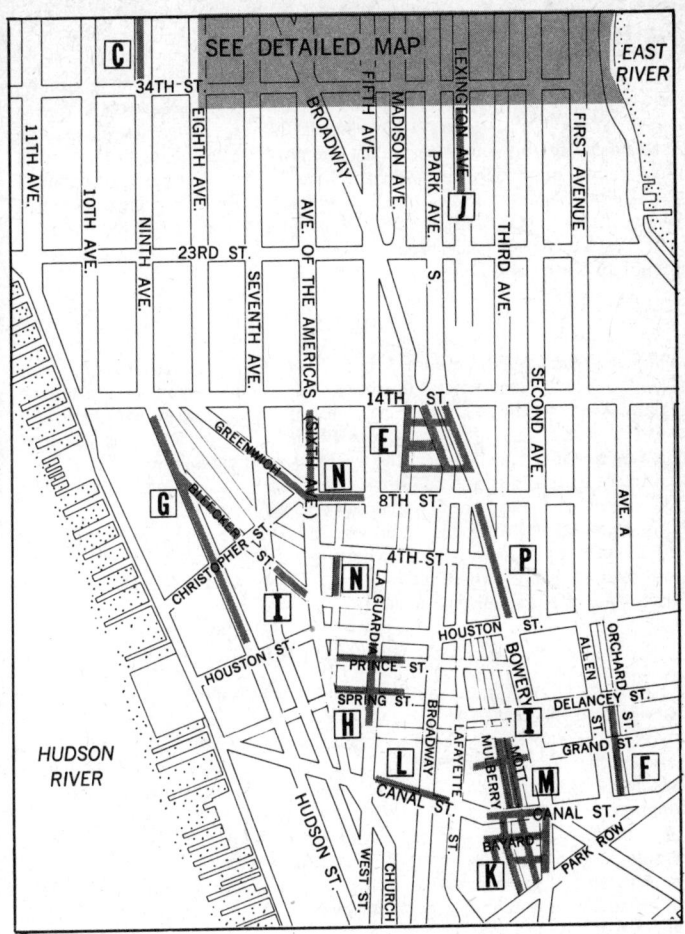

H Art galleries (contemporary), posters, boutiques.
I Italian specialties.
J Indian specialties.
K Chinese specialties.
L Tools and machinery.
M Jewelry.
N Clothing (trendy, funky, or casual).
P Restaurant equipment.

ware in unusual shapes, utensils, spices, serving ware, and all kinds of other things unexpected in this sleek, modern setting.

There is, of course, much more to explore, but lastly, for those with a sweet tooth... *Godiva*, at 701 Fifth Ave. near 55th St., makes well-known, beautifully packaged (and expensive) chocolate; *Kron Chocolatier*, 764 Madison Ave. near 66th St., and at 506 Madison Ave. at 53rd St., is where many New Yorkers go for this indispensable substance. Or try the pâtisserie at *Dumas*, on Lexington near 88th St. For a snack, the best of the several chains of stores selling cookies is generally considered to be *David's Cookies*, at several locations, including Zabar's. *Delices La Côte Basque*, at 1032 Lexington Ave. near 74th St., is famous for its pastries. Try the cheesecake at *Eileen's*, at 17 Cleveland Place (near the junction of Spring and Lafayette Sts.). And enjoy.

TOBACCO

Village Cigars, at 110 Seventh Avenue South, is a crowded little shop that has been around a long time at this busy Greenwich Village corner (Sheridan Square). *Nat Sherman*, at 711 Fifth Ave. near 55th St., is celebrated as "tobacconist to the world," and offers every conceivable type of tobacco. *J. R. Tobacco*, at 108 West 45th St., calls itself "the world's largest cigar store"—nobody has been heard to argue, and in addition to the merits of the selection, the prices are reasonable too. And one of the most respected names in the tobacco world, *Alfred Dunhill of London*, has a store at 620 Fifth Ave. in Rockefeller Center.

For pipes, two places are recommended—*Barclay Rex*, at 7 Maiden Lane, downtown, and midtown, *Connoisseur*, at 51 W. 46th St. Both have large assortments of pipes and pipe tobaccos.

ART AND GALLERIES

There is really no easy way to compile a useful guide to New York's art galleries. You will have to do what New Yorkers do: once you've checked these listings in the *N.Y. Times*, *New York* magazine, or the *New Yorker* and marked the ones that seem most interesting at the moment, you start walking, either down Madison Avenue from 86th St. or across 57th St. and up Madison to 86th, stopping as you go.

But in recent years New York has developed another art center downtown, for balance. This is SoHo, an area of beautiful cast-iron architecture that was once a manufacturing and warehousing district. As industry moved out over the last decade, leaving behind large "loft" spaces with huge windows for plenty of light, artists began to move in; and it wasn't long before galleries followed them.

SoHo is now fashionable, handsome, and diverse, but the galleries are still there in quantity. In just one building, 420 West Broadway, you'll find five, including *Mary Boone*, *Leo Castelli*, and *Sonnabend*. Castelli alone has been associated with such modern figures as Jasper Johns, Robert Rauschenberg, Roy Lichtenstein, Andy Warhol, and Cy Twombly. Other galleries within these crowded few blocks include *O.K. Harris*, at 383 West Broadway, *Holly Solomon*, at 392 West Broadway, and *Vorpal*, at 465 West Broadway (Vorpal is known for its representation of prints by M. C. Escher, that proponent of visual paradox); but there is too much here, in the way of painting, sculpture, and other forms harder to find names for (but most of it super-modern), to list, and the best thing to do is simply explore this quite small, concentrated area.

Uptown, of course, the scene remains as strong as ever, and here too we can only name a few of the best known galleries. For contemporary art, for example, *Tibor De Nagy,* at 29 W. 57th St., *Marlborough,* at 40 W. 57th St., *Sidney Janis,* at 110 W. 57th St., and *Betty Parsons,* at 24 W. 57th St., all have worthy reputations; they specialize in painting, but usually handle sculpture too. For older art (interspersed with recent work), try *Knoedler,* at 21 E. 70th St., or *Wildenstein,* at 19 E. 64th St., among many others. If you're interested in a somewhat newer art form, try the *International Center of Photography,* at 1130 Fifth Avenue, or *Photograph,* 724 Fifth Ave., between 56th and 57th Sts.

For those less interested in investing, but looking for something nice for their walls, the major museums, such as the Guggenheim, the Museum of Modern Art, the Metropolitan, and so on, all have fine in-house shops offering reproductions of works in their galleries. For the Metropolitan, particularly, this is big business, and the stock runs not just to posters, but also to pottery, jewelry, and so forth. *Poster Originals* is a well-stocked poster shop that, cannily, has two branches: one on the Upper East Side, at 924 Madison Ave. near 73rd St., and one in SoHo, at 386 West Broadway. Not all the stuff here is cheap, but all is handsome.

Off the beaten track, the *Aaron Faber Galleries* at 666 Fifth Ave. (53rd St.) has an impressive collection of artists' hand-crafted contemporary jewelry in limited editions. There is usually an exhibition by one of the artisans on the second floor.

Contemporary prints (and some old prints), are the only offering at *Associated American Artists, Inc.,* 663 Fifth Ave. near 52nd St. For older prints, etchings, and illustrated books you might try, among many others, *Lucien Goldschmidt,* 1117 Madison Ave. at 83rd St., for the old-fashioned appeal of the shop if for nothing else.

ANTIQUES

New York sports a huge variety of antique shops, and a lot of people spend a lot of time poring over a lot of objects, seeking finds. A word of warning: Prices in the city are usually higher than those offered in places farther outside the city; there are antiquers who make a point of not buying here, hoping to find better values elsewhere. But for both the serious collector and the amateur, there's simply so much in New York that browsing is worthwhile, and there's always the chance of a bargain.

The first place to start is at the auction houses. These are exciting, particularly if you've never been to one, and there's a rapid turnover of stock. Auction houses have sales on most days of the week, except Sunday. Check The *New York Times* for listings. As a general rule, Monday and Tuesday are exhibition days for midweek sales and Thursday for Saturday sales. No item, no matter how small, should ever be bought on the block without an examination at the exhibition. You may think you are getting a bargain on the silver vase from 40 feet away, but if on closer scrutiny you find an inscription from some sporting society on the other side, you have only yourself to blame, for there is ample time to examine each lot carefully. If you are bidding for the first time, don't hesitate to ask a staffer for advice.

Sotheby's is probably the most well known of the auction houses. A rapidly expanding business with worldwide branches, its three halls, at 980 Madison Avenue between 76th and 77th Sts. (fine arts and jewelry), at 1334 York Ave. (decorative arts) and at 171 E. 84th St. (books, stamps and coins), retain their prestigious air. *Christie's*, at 502 Park Ave. (59th St.), is claimed by many to be as good. They have a branch for Americana and other specialties at 219 E. 67th St., and are planning to open a "contemporary art" showroom. Smaller houses are *Phillips*, at two Upper East Side locations, and *William Doyle*, at 175 E. 87th St., among others. Goods on display at these establishments fall into varied categories, which at any one time may include fine art, jewelry, all sorts of furniture, porcelain, antique toys, and much more.

Having tackled the auctions, explore a few specific areas. Most of the best (and most expensive) shops are along 57th St. east of Fifth Ave., and on Madison Avenue in the 50s, 60s, and 70s. Smaller and less fancy shops are scattered all over, but the general concentration is on Third Avenue between 45th and 70th Sts. and the surrounding streets; Second and First Aves. within the same boundaries can also prove rewarding. Another antiques area is the area bounded by Broadway and University Place and 8th and 14th Sts. in the northern part of the Village. For example, *Ace Galleries* on University Place near 11th St. is an active auction house—a step down from Sotheby's, to be sure, but fun and less costly. Go—and you'll be sure to buy *something*. Other such auction houses—and there are many more—are *Tepper* at 110 E. 25th St., *Lubin*, 30 W. 26th St., and *Manhattan Galleries*, 1415 Third Ave at 80th St.

The Consumer Yellow Pages has a lengthy list of antique shops broken down into specific categories, and this is worth consulting before you start exploring an area which is quite widely dispersed.

There are, in fact, antique shops all over the city. Greenwich Village has a large concentration of stores—try walking down Bleecker Street between Christopher Street and Hudson, or look at oak furniture on Hudson Street between Bleecker and Christopher (those street names are accurate; they all criss-cross the area!). Second Ave. also has a lot of oak furniture, for several blocks south of 26th St. A store that seems to have a wide range of period furniture—English, Oriental, French—is *Gramercy Galleries*, at 52 E. 13th St. Provincial French furniture is well served in the city by *Pierre Deux*, at 369 Bleecker, *Le Vieux Monde*, nearby at 94 Charles St., and *Howard Kaplan*, at 400 Bleecker St. *Pat Sales* at 390 Bleecker offers American country antiques. And *Inglenook*, at 529 Hudson Street, offers antique American furniture, with a particular emphasis on wicker.

James Robinson, at 15 E. 57th St., has a worldwide name for antique silver; another source is *Wyler*, at 713 Madison near 63rd St. Try *Carol Ferranti*, at

888 Madison near 72nd St., for glassware and pottery, or *Leo Kaplan,* nearby at 910 Madison. *Second Childhood,* at 283 Bleecker St., is much loved for its collection of antique toys, which may include multi-shaped coin banks, dolls, hoops, books for children, and toy trains at any one time. Look for toy soldiers there, too. *The Antique Doll Hospital of New York*'s name is a bit misleading: they also buy, sell and appraise dolls, at 787 Lexington Ave. near 61st St. On the more serious side of the scale, *André Emmerich,* at 41 E. 57th Street, offers very high-quality pre-Columbian objects and such (there are also exhibits of modern paintings here) while the *Asian Gallery,* at 1049 Madison near 80th St., offers Far Eastern art and antiquities. *Atikoth* (16 E. 71st St.) and *Moriah* (28 W. 46th St.) trade in antique Judaica. For collectible clocks and watches, two establishments under the same roof are a best bet: *William Scolnick,* and *Joseph Fanelli's Clocks and Things,* both at 1001 Second Ave. at 53rd St. (This is a difficult and unusual field: "Not many people need ulcers," said the owner of one store that recently closed down its antique-watch operation.) The oldest autograph business in New York, at 25 E. 77th St., is *Charles Hamilton;* surprisingly, department-store *B. Altman* also has a reputable autograph section.

Griffin & Howe have both new and used hunting arms as well as antique firearms; 589 Broadway near Houston. *Centre Firearms,* 51 W. 46th St., is another such place. Specializing in antique firearms is *Robert Brooks,* 235 E. 53rd St. *The Soldier Shop,* 1013 Madison Ave., has antique firearms as well as books on the military and antique miniature soldiers. *Hunting World,* 16 E. 53rd, has every imaginable accessory for the hunter—as well as prints, etc.

There are many places for antique clothing—some of it tatty, some very fine. *Reminiscence,* on MacDougal Street near 8th St., and *Trash & Vaudeville,* at 4 Saint Marks Place, both sell old clothes (and new, too) in as-new condition, to fit with younger fashions. *Unique Clothing Warehouse,* 718 Broadway, is another source. Leaving the Village for the more sedate Upper East Side, pay a visit to *The Best of Everything,* at 242 E 77th St., for clothing, jewelry, and accessories from the 20s through the 50s. On the Upper West Side, there are several possibilities on Columbus Avenue in the 70s and low 80s—a good place to browse, since there are also a number of pleasant antique furniture and memorabilia shops here (along with an increasing number of interesting places to stop for lunch).

Jacques Carcanagues, at 119 Spring Street in SoHo, offers beautiful Middle Eastern kilim rugs, and *Alexander,* at 410 Columbus Avenue, is good for Orientals.

B. Harris & Sons, at 25 E. 61st St., is one of several reputable jewelers where you can find both antique and contemporary stuff on and around Madison Ave., from the 40s through the 70s. Another stop in the area might be *Macklowe Gallery,* on Madison near 76th; alternatively, you could visit the precious-stone and jewelry district along 47th St. between Fifth and Sixth Aves., where much antique gold, rings, and such are sold (although quality can vary widely).

You'll have to go through the Yellow Pages to find the shops that specialize in first-day covers, etc., but there are many good general stamp dealers, such as the long-established *J. & H. Stolow* at 915 Broadway (21st St.) and, rather rarified, *Stanley Gibbons* at 645 Fifth Ave. near 51st St. *Harmer*, 6 W. 48th St., conducts auction sales. And there are dozens of dealers grouped together downtown on Nassau St. *Stack's*, 123 W. 57th St., and *Harmer-Rooke*, 3 E. 57th St., are well-known dealers in coins (numismatics). *Macy's* at Herald Square (34th St.) has a good numismatic department; don't forget the auctioneers *Sotheby Park Bernet*, either, at 980 Madison Ave., 76th St.

One more recommendation before leaving the subject of antiques—the *Old Print Shop*, at 150 Lexington Avenue, near 30th St., for a fine display of collectible prints, maps, and other visual Americana. And a word of warning—some art and antique galleries limit their hours or close altogether during the summer months, so if you're visiting at that time it's wise to check ahead. And good hunting.

BOOKS

New York is the capital of American publishing, and is blessed with an apposite number of bookstores. The chains—Dalton's, Waldenbooks—are represented here, but there are also countless more specialized establishments, some of them quite large; and even in the marketing of bestsellers, the chains have good competition.

An early stop for any book buyer should be *Barnes & Noble*, on both sides of Fifth Avenue at 18th St. The main branch, on the east side of the avenue, is known for its vast array of scientific and technical material, college textbooks, and general reference stuff, though you'll also find more entertaining matter here. Across the road, the Sale Annex has a huge selection of low-price remaindered stock in many categories; here, too, the current bestseller list is sold well below list prices. (Barnes & Noble branches throughout the city also offer this feature.) If the college books you wanted aren't at Barnes & Noble, try browsing through the several bookstores on Broadway in the area of 116th Street, near Columbia University.

Another good browsing place is Fifth Avenue from 47th St. to 57th St. Here you'll find not only branches of *Barnes & Noble* (discount) and *B. Dalton*, but also *Brentano's*, *Doubleday* (two branches), *Rizzoli*, the *Antiquarian Booksellers' Center*, *Scribner's* (the most elegant shop), and more. Turn west on 47th St. and you'll come to the *Gotham Book Mart*, a store with a long and prestigious history, and still a favorite of New Yorkers in search of poetry, modern thought and literature, and the unexpected. *Coliseum Books*, Broadway and 57th St., and *Books & Co.*, 939 Madison Ave., both also have good selections of new and in-print titles. The *McGraw-Hill Bookstore*, in the McGraw-Hill Building plaza at Sixth Ave. and 49th St., has a wide selection of technical and business books. Medical books may be found at the stores associated with the city's large medical schools (Cornell, Mt. Sinai, New York University), and also at *General Medical Book Co.*, 310 E. 26th St., and *Julius Levin*, 1391 Madison Ave. at 96th St.

A real clue to the importance of books in the life of the city is the number of bookstores devoted to seemingly limiting specialties; these are some of New

SHOPPING

York's great pleasures. For example, the *Drama Book Shop,* at 150 W. 52nd St., for theater books; the *Ballet Shop,* near Lincoln Center at Broadway and 64th St., for coverage of dance—plus memorabilia; or *Quinion,* at 541 Hudson St., for two subjects that go surprisingly well together; theater and cookery. *Murder Ink,* at 271 West 87th St., specializes in mysteries; *Eeyore's,* at 2252 Broadway, is a children's bookstore; *Womanbooks,* 201 W. 92nd St., sells books by, about or for ... women. For the military buff, the *Military Bookman* is at 29 E. 93rd St. The moviegoer might go to *Cinemabilia,* at 10 W. 13th St. For books on music, try *Schirmer's* (two branches) or *Patelson's* (see *Music*).

There are a number of art bookshops, the best known of which are probably *Hacker,* at 54 W. 57th St., *Jaap Rietman,* 167 Spring St. in SoHo, *E. Weyhe* on Lexington Ave. near 62nd St., and *Wittenborn* at Madison Ave. near 80th St. The museum stores are also worth trying for this specialty, as is *Rizzoli* on Fifth Ave. near 56th St.; Rizzoli is also good for foreign-language material. The *Librairie de France* and the *Libreria Hispanica,* in Rockefeller Center at Fifth Ave. (and also downtown on Fifth, near the 18th St. Barnes & Noble) are probably the best sources for French and Spanish books.

For maps, globes, books on maps, nautical and navigation books, and charts: *Hammond,* 12 E. 41st St., and *Rand McNally,* 10 E. 53rd St. *Argosy,* at 116 E. 59th St., has antique maps (as well as a general selection of used books and sets). *Weitz,* Lexington Ave. near 91st St., also carries sets and fine bindings. New York has a very fine selection of occult bookstores, among them *Mason's* at 789 Lexington Ave. (61st St.) and *Weiser's,* Broadway near 8th St. in the Village. The *New York Astrology Center,* 127 Madison Ave. at 30th St., has books. See the Consumer Yellow Pages under "Book Dealers—New" for a complete guide to specialty bookstores by category.

Finally, older books. The *Antiquarian Booksellers' Center,* on Rockefeller Plaza, is a good place for the serious collector of rare books and first editions (or for the reader who would *like* to be a serious collector; some items here are quite expensive). See the Consumer Yellow Pages under "Book Dealers—Used & Rare" for a listing of other dealers and their specialties. At a less exalted level, but a very rewarding one: The hub of the used-book market is along Fourth Ave. between 9th and 14th Sts.—though it is shrinking. The best of them all, and not shrinking, is *Strand,* at Broadway and 12th St.; books here include, besides some rare books and the over one million used books, mint-condition reviewers' copies (at half price) and remainders, including art books at much-reduced prices.

Several shops carry large stocks of back-issue periodicals; two are *Jay-Bee Magazines,* 143 W. 29th St., and *A & S Book Co.,* 274 W. 43rd St. Some of the shops also carry celebrity photographs and old movie posters; check the Yellow Pages. *West Side Comix,* 107 W. 86th St., and *East Side Comix,* a branch at 302 E. 82nd St., have new, back-issue and rare comic books, as does *Supersnipe* at 84th St. and Second Ave.

The Complete Traveler, Madison Ave. at the corner of 35th St., specializes in travel guides and books about travel.

RECORDS

Immensely large selections from all major labels are the rule in New York City; two places where this is an understatement are *King Karol* and *Sam Goody*, both of them with various locations. The branch of King Karol at 126 W. 42nd is particularly vast—rock, folk, classical, jazz, it's all here. If your needs are current releases—cheaper in the U.S. than just about anywhere else in the Western world—try *Discomat* or *J&R Music* (at several locations), which sells its stock at well below list prices—it's better for popular music than for classical, and most of what you'll find here is fairly current. Also for discounted current LP's and out-of-print recordings. Walk along 8th St. between Sixth Ave. and Broadway; this is "L.P. Alley," and there's good browsing at any of the several stores along here, especially for domestic and imported classical recordings. *The Record Hunter*, at 507 Fifth Ave., near 43rd St., also concentrates on classical music and foreign labels.

If old Beatles singles and pop esoterica strike your fancy, chances are that the *House of Oldies*, at 267 Bleecker, or *Bleecker Bob's* on MacDougal at 8th St., will too. *Dayton's*, at Broadway and 12th St. (across the street from Strand Bookstore), has a stock of reviewers' copies of records in mint condition, at low prices, and also of out-of-print records, at collectors' prices. Most of the stock is popular; for hard-to-get classical stuff, try *Darton*, at 160 W. 56th St. Other secondhand disk shops are *Free Being*, 129 Second Ave., *Gryphon Bookshop*, 89th St. off Broadway, *Hall's*, 41 E. 7th St., *Golden Disk Records*, 239 Bleecker St., and *Ludus Tonalis*, 24 Eighth Ave. And if you're looking for a record that even the original issuing company doesn't have in its warehouse, try *The Record Exchange*, on Seventh Avenue at 55th St., but be prepared to pay what a serious collector would. For imported records, try *Discophile*, on 8th St. near Fifth Ave.

MUSIC AND MUSICAL INSTRUMENTS

First, walk along the section of 48th St. east of Seventh Ave., for about half a block. In this somewhat raffish environment, you'll find enough musical instruments, spread out over several shops, to equip dozens of orchestra—although the stock tends more toward brass instruments, electronic keyboards, guitars (both electric and acoustic), and the other necessities for rock and jazz than toward violins and cellos. They are here, too, though—specifically, at *Sam Ash*, 160 W. 48th St., one of the most well known and longest-established of these shops. Secondhand items are available on this street, but even the prices of the new pieces are often good, and Sam Ash and other leading stores such as *Manny's*, at 156 W. 48th St., and *Terminal Music*, at No. 166, advertise their discounts. Terminal also carries recorders (flutes) and recorder music. *Hargail*, at 51 E. 12th St., specializes in recorders and recorder music.

Down a couple of blocks, the *Professional Percussion Center*, at 151 W. 46th St., exists to service the drum community. *Charles Ponte*, at 142 W. 46th St., specializes in wind instruments, and has an amazing assortment of reeds and

SHOPPING

tools for same, including the classical wind instruments (one of the staff is even a retired bassoonist).

In pianos (many people travel to Manhattan just to pick one out, and have it shipped home), the great name is, of course, *Steinway*; the company's imposing showroom is at 109 W. 57th St. The saleshelp is friendly even to browsers, though, since there's a two year wait for many of their models. *Baldwin* is at 922 Seventh Ave., and Yamaha is at *Ostrovsky*, 154 W. 56th St., next to Patelson's; Ostrovsky also has used and reconditioned pianos of all makes and ages. *A & C Pianocraft,* 149 Wooster St. in SoHo, is among the best for rebuilt Steinways. Call 254–1840 for an appointment—and be forewarned: the entrance is hard to find. *Jack Kahn,* at 158 West 55th St., has a variety of brands of pianos, including the Bosendorfer, and runs frequent sales. For harpsichords, visit *Hugh Gough* at 80 Fifth Ave.; *Zuckermann* is at 160 Sixth Ave., also in the Village. *Schirmer* on Fifth Ave. has some harpsichords.

Try *Havivi,* at 140 W. 57th St., for classical string instruments; *Jacques Français* also deals in (rather up-market) violins, violas, cellos, at the same address. For organs, the famous *Hammond Company* has an outlet at 55 W. 44th St. For brass and woodwind instruments, *Giardinelli,* 151 West 46th St.—same building as the Professional Percussion Center—has a wide assortment, including lots of brass mouthpieces. Fine acoustic or "classical" guitars are sold at many specialist shops or workshops, among them *Juan Orozco,* Sixth Ave. and Spring St., *Noah Wulfe,* 115 W. 57th St. (also lutes), and *Matt Umanov* at 276 Bleecker St. An unusual assortment of foreign and folk music instruments is to be found at *Music Inn* on W. 4th St. near Sixth Ave. in the Village; they have records too.

Having the instrument, you also need music to play on it. One of the most popular sheet-music shops is *Joseph Patelson's,* at 160 W. 56th St.—all their music and books on music are discounted 10%. Many serious musicians stop in here (it is right behind Carnegie Hall). *Frank Music Co.,* on an upper floor of a very arts-and-show-business-centered building at 43 W. 61st St., has a wide selection of classical scores and parts, but there is no browsing and you must know what you want. Then, of course, there is also *Schirmer,* in Brentano's at Fifth Avenue near 47th St., and another branch at 40 W. 62nd St. near Lincoln Center: both stock the sheet music of most of the classical-music publishers, and both have books too. For up-to-the-minute rock stuff, there are the sheet-music departments of the various branches of *Sam Goody;* Schirmer has pop and some rock, too.

PHOTOGRAPHIC EQUIPMENT

A tip on buying cameras—buy the Sunday *New York Times,* and turn to the back few pages of the "Arts and Leisure" section. A number of discount camera stores regularly advertise here, and it's a simple matter to find where you can get the camera you want most cheaply—prices are included in the advertisements. Make sure, however, that you're not comparing apples and oranges—

that the camera advertised at a certain price also comes with the lens you want, and so forth.

There are many discount shops—so many, in fact, that it seems almost criminal to pay list price for a camera. Not all the stores are reputable, however, so shop carefully. One absolutely solid name is *Willoughby's,* at 110 W. 32nd St. This large, long-established shop has good—if not the best—prices, and a great deal of varied stock. Some equipment is also available on a rental basis. For many New Yorkers, Willoughby's is New York's photographic best bet. Another popular store is *Grand Central Camera,* near Grand Central Station at 420 Lexington Ave., and this too offers good discounts.

Hirsch Photo, at 699 Third Avenue at 44th St., discounts heavily and does a lot of developing work. *Fotomat,* with branches all over the city, is also popular for developing. *7 Hour Photo,* again with several branches, guarantees speed, whether it's color or black-and-white film to be processed. While on the subject of optics, *Dell & Dell,* at 19 W. 44th St., is an authorized dealer for Zeiss, Bausch & Lomb, and other fine makes of binoculars. Several manufacturers have showrooms, such as *Nikon's* in the "Channel" at Rockefeller Center.

SPORTING GOODS

A small number of New York stores will satisfy a large chunk of your sporting needs. Go to *Paragon* first. This store, at Broadway and 18th St., advertises itself as supplying equipment for tennis, hockey, camping, archery, squash, diving, golf, darts, skiing, skating (roller and ice), Ping-Pong, and more besides; the place is noisy and crowded, but that's only because it's popular, and because as a rule, the values are good. *Spiegel's,* at 105 Nassau St., and *Herman's World of Sporting Goods,* nearby at 110 Nassau and at various other locations such as 42nd St. between Sixth Ave. and Times Square, come similarly well equipped.

Try these stores before going to the more specialized places. *The Athlete's Foot,* with a number of branches around town, has a large variety of running and other sport shoes, as well as various sweatshirts and pants, shorts, and such. Fencers can resort to *Frederick Rohde's,* at 169 E. 86th St., or *George Santelli,* at 412 Sixth Ave. near 9th St. in the Village; a nice shop for fishermen is *Angler's Roost,* at 141 E. 44th St. If Paragon doesn't have all the camping gear you need, *Hudson's,* at 105 Third Avenue (13th St.), probably will, and *Kreeger,* at 16 W. 46th St., is another good source for backpackers; similarly, golfers may need to look no farther than Paragaon, but if they do they could try *Al Lieber's World of Golf,* at 147 E. 47th St. or *Richard Metz,* 35 E. 50th St. There are two important stores for riding equipment, quite close to each other—*H. Kauffman & Sons,* at 139 E. 24th St., and *Miller's,* at 123 E. 24th St.; both offer English and Western wear, saddles, books, and all the necessary apparel. The *Scandinavian Ski Shop,* at 40 W. 57th St., is long established, and keep selling skis all summer. *Peck & Goodie,* 919 Eighth Ave. near 55th St., have a superior line of ice skates and roller skates—and sell nothing else. *Goldberg's Marine* is the best-known of the city's suppliers of nautical and marine equipment for yachts-

SHOPPING

men: 12 W. 46th St. Besides general sporting shops (such as Paragon) which have diving equipment (scuba), there are a few specialists, among them *Richards Aqua Lung Center*, at 233 W. 42nd St. and *Scubaplus*, 201 E. 34th St.

ART AND CRAFT SUPPLIES

This is another field where much of your needs can be supplied at a few places. Go first to *Pearl Paint*, at 308 Canal Street. This five-story shop offers everything for the artist—canvasses, brushes, paper, pens, frames, easels, tables, stretchers, mats, and much more, including, of course, lots and lots of paint. The prices are good, and it's an interesting place to wander through, seeing the different kinds of people in the New York art community. Less exciting, perhaps, but equally good in their ways are such stores as *Sam Flax*, with several branches, *Arthur Brown*, at 2 W. 46th St. (this store advertises itself as having "New York's largest stock of artist materials"), *Lee's Art Shop*, at 220 W. 57th St., and *Charrette*, at 212 E. 54th St. and other branches (Charrette aims particularly toward the architect or professional draftsman).

Joseph Torch, at 29 W. 15th St., handles handmade papers. *David Davis*, at 539 La Guardia Place, is also recommended for its variety of pigments and quality papers; *Fezandie & Sperrie*, 111 Eighth Ave., is a treasure house of pure powdered pigments. *Baldwin Pottery*, nearby at 540 La Guardia, should have all you need for ceramic work. For those whose hobby is jewelry-making (or whose business this is, for that matter), a well-known name is *Allcraft Tool & Supply*—the main office is in Hicksville, Long Island, but the showroom is at 22 W. 48th St. Knitters will find yarns at any of several stores, including *Coulter Studios*, at 118 E. 59th St.; Coulter also stocks equipment for a number of fabric-related activities, such as weaving, needlepoint, and such. *Ladies Hobby Shop*, at 2350 Broadway near 85th St., is a small and friendly Upper West Side yarn store; *Design Point*, at 15 Christopher St., is a Greenwich Village equivalent specializing in needlepoint. *Alice Maynard*, 133 E. 65th St., *Erica Wilson*, 717 Madison Ave. near 64th St., and *Woolworth's*, 838 Madison near 70th St., all sell supplies for the knitter or needlepoint worker. And finally, for glass-workers, the best game in town is probably *Glassmasters Guild*, 621 Ave. of the Americas near 19th St. selling not only glass and the tools to work it, but also some rather nice finished pieces.

AND EVERYTHING ELSE

Finally, there's the large category of things that don't fit into any of our previous categories. A good entry to this field is *Hammacher Schlemmer*, at 145 E. 57th St. It's hard to describe this shop beyond saying that it sells gadgets—everything from the obviously useful to the intriguingly peculiar, from the clever corkscrew to the motor-powered surfboard. If anyone ever invents a better mousetrap, you'll find it at Hammacher Schlemmer.

While you're in the neighborhood, you might think about crystal. Both *Baccarat* and *Carole Stupell Ltd.* are on E. 57th St., at 55 and 61 respectively, and *Steuben* too is nearby at Fifth Ave. and 56th St., near *Tiffany* (which, in addition to its famous jewelry, also stocks crystal and gorgeous chinaware). At the more humble end of the china and glass scale, but still quite handsome and popular among New Yorkers for their good values, are the dinner services and barware stocked by the *Pottery Barn* chain, in several locations around town. There are regular sales, and the branch at 23rd St. and Tenth Ave. almost always has closeouts of good merchandise. *Stuppell China Outlet,* among others, carries discontinued chinaware patterns: 29 E. 22nd St. Discontinued silver flatware patterns are available at many places in the city; try *Golden Cockerel* at 82 Christopher St. (the Village), *S. Wyler,* 713 Madison Ave. at 63rd St., or *Panken & Thorn Antiques,* 207 E. 84th St.

New York has many shops selling unusual collectibles, such as beautiful and interesting mineralogical and fossil specimens (try *Astro Minerals,* 155 E. 34th St.; *Crystal Resources,* 130 E. 65th St.), and seashells (*Collector's Cabinet*—they also sell butterflies—153 E. 57th St.; *Seashells Unlimited,* 590 Third Ave.; *Captain Hook's* at 10 Fulton St.; *Glory of the Sea* at 124 MacDougal St. in the Village).

In addition to a whole range of gift ideas in the way of jewelry, china, and such, *Fortunoff* also stocks silverware (as, of course, does *Tiffany*). You could go somewhere expensive for your linen, towels, sheets, drapes, and such, but why, when you can go to the famous *Ezra Cohen,* at 307 Grand Street on the Lower East Side? Many New Yorkers shop nowhere else for these goods. *Liberty of London,* at 229 E. 60th St., is the New York outlet for the famous English fabrics, scarves and accessories, and *Tender Buttons,* with a large collection of antique and modern buttons, buckles, and cufflinks, is a good source for the trimmings. The millinery district, 38th and 39th Sts. between Fifth Ave. and Ave. of the Americas, has lots of outlets for wonderful ribbonry, silk flowers, beads, veils, trimming, and, of course, hats. *Sheru* on W. 38th St. (No. 49) is a good source of beads and crafts materials from around the world. *Simon's Hardware,* Third Ave. between 29th and 30th Sts., has one of the largest selections of decorative hardware in the country—so look here for those handles or hinges you can't find anywhere. There are good hardware stores all along Canal St. west of Chinatown; good selections of tools also at *Lilien Hardware,* 490 W. Broadway near Houston.

Not in the city, but in nearby New Jersey, is one of the nation's leading makers of astronomical telescopes: *Edmund Scientific,* 101 E. Gloucester Pike, Barrington.

Try *Capezio,* at several locations, for dance equipment. The best-known cutlery store is probably *Hoffritz,* with various branches, including one at 203 W. 57th St.; this establishment also sells barware, gadgets, and such. There are plenty of pet stores, but it seems a shame not to take a kitten or puppy off the hands of *Bide-A-Wee,* at 410 E. 38th St.; this is an animal shelter, not a business, and the prices are token, and tax-deductible. For classier dogs, try *Pedigree Pups,* at 969 First Avenue (they have cats, too). *Fabulous Felines* sells rare and unusual breeds: 133 Lexington Ave. And if you're not too far from home, you might be able to take away some tropical fish for your tanks at home; see *Fish Town USA,* Third Ave. near 34th St., and *Aquarium Stock Co.,* 31 Warren St., downtown, near City Hall. *Exotic Aquatics,* 272 Bleecker St. in the Village, also has snakes, lizards, and other animals not known to us! The flower district of the city is a few blocks of Sixth Avenue in the upper 20s—visit *Treemania* for unusual plants, or *Bonsai Dynasty* for those tiny trees in pots. (Visitors from outside the U.S. should consider the Customs regulations they may face on their trip home before buying plants or animals.)

There are several chess emporia in Greenwich Village; one of them is simply called the *Chess Shop,* at 230 Thompson St. near Bleecker. For a clock, go to *Tourneau,* at 500 Madison Ave. near 52nd St. *Bikes and Things,* at 377 East 23rd St., is an extremely well-equipped bicycle shop. A good, safe bet for stereo equipment is *Tech HiFi,* with several branches; there are a number of reputable hi-fi and advanced electronics shops, along with Tech, on 45th St. between Fifth and Sixth Aves. *Crazy Eddie* claims he will not be undersold, and if you can cope with the hustle and bustle atmosphere, you can find good buys in home electronic gear at his branch at 405 Sixth Ave. But you have to know the competition's prices before you go in. A better bet is *Uncle Steve's* at 343 Canal St. To keep you healthy through all this, *Brownies* was a health food store before there was health food—it's at 91 Fifth Ave. near Barnes & Noble.

New York has a considerable number of places selling herbs, herbal teas, and herbal preparations: *Aphrodisia,* 28 Carmine St. in the Village (they also have books, as does *Samuel Weiser* at 740 Broadway); *Caswell-Massey* at 575 Lexington Ave.; *Good Earth* at Second Ave. and 72nd St.; *Kiehl Pharmacy,* 109 Third Ave.; *McNulty's* and *Paprikas Weiss,* (see *Gourmet Foods* for addresses).

Finally, books, prints, drawings, photographs, and more are to be found at *Cityana,* 16 E. 53rd St., on the everfascinating subject of New York City.

There's obviously an enormous amount that we haven't been able to touch, and that every visitor will discover for him or herself. But you'll find that no matter how well you know New York, there's always more to see. That makes the city tantalizing, but also somehow reassuring.

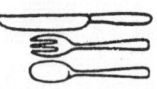

RESTAURANTS. There is really no single comment that can effectively describe the phenomenon of eating out in New York City. As the gastronomic capital of the United States—and by virtue of the international breadth of its offerings, of the world—it has by far more fine and distinguished restaurants than anywhere else in the country. Put at its simplest, there is a dining experience in the Big Apple to satisfy any palate (no matter how exotic one's tastes) and any budget.

No national nor ethnic cuisine is left out. Indeed, there are restaurants in New York offering various types of cooking not likely to be found anywhere else in the country—and we fervently suggest that you sample some culinary delight you may never before have had the opportunity to try. Such daring may well turn out to be a high point of your visit, though it may on the other hand engender a bit of future frustration as you contemplate the possibility of getting like preparations—say, a Thai whoefish with green chilies and onion—upon your return home.

NEW YORK CITY

You can cover the globe gastronomically in New York, spending as much or as little as you like. You can feast on steaks at the *Palm* or *Christ Cella*, paying dearly for every succulent bite, or you can opt for a reasonable facsimile at *Farnie's* or the *Blue Mill Tavern* for far less money. You can be transported to the far reaches of India at the delicately appointed *Raga* or *Shezan*, or you can head over to East 6th St. between First and Second Aves. where about a dozen friendly, inexpensive family-run eateries offer outstanding curries and tandoori specialties.

Most of the best restaurants in New York City center in Manhattan, and most of these are south of 86th St., so the bulk of our attention is focused on that area, although we have picked a few notables in the outlying boroughs for your additional consideration. Public transportation makes any corner of Manhattan Island, and most of the other boroughs, accessible, and the trip is frequently worthwhile. Enthusiasts of Middle Eastern cooking, for example, will do well to take a ride to Brooklyn's Atlantic Avenue section where there is a host of very good, modestly priced Lebanese restaurants (most owned by the Almontaser family, with the best of the lot, bearing the family name, at 218 Court St.; 624–9267). Similarly, many long-time natives swear that the *real* Little Italy of New York, with the best food at the cheapest prices, is on and around Arthur Avenue in the Bronx—at *Mario's*, *Stella D'Oro's*, *Il Boschetto*, and *Amerigo's* —not on Manhattan's Mulberry Street. The partisans battle on forever.

Time was, in fact, when you *had* to go way downtown to Chinatown or Manhattan's Little Italy for a good Chinese or Italian meal. Not any more. There are those who tell you the East Side svelte belt (starting aroung the Grand Central Station area off Second Ave. and heading uptown) has the city's best Chinese cooking, with rivals for the best of the best including *Uncle Tai's*, *David K's*, the *Sichuan Pavilion*, *Peng Teng's*, *Chef Ho's Hunan Manor*, and *Hunam*. True, they are expensive, which is why Chinatown still has its supporters. (By Chinatown they mean the six to eight cluttered blocks bordered by Canal St. on the north and the Bowery on the east with the boundaries spilling over into Manhattan's Little Italy itself.)

You name the style of Chinese cooking you want and New York has it, be it Cantonese, Shanghai, Peking, Hunan, Szechuan, Fukien, Taiwanese, or Mongolian. The same holds true for Italian cooking, whether you're looking for the staples of southern Italian Neapolitan cooking or the delicate flavorings of Florentine or Roman chefs. And again you have a choice of the more expensive restaurants (with the East Side's *Romeo Salta* or *Giambelli's* considered among the best of this breed), the tourist traps (such as *Mama Leone's*), or the moderately priced best of Little Italy (the *Grotta Azzura* taking top honors on that count for a savory balance between the quality of cuisine and price).

Indeed, the city is filled with ethnic pockets, and its restaurants spill over with the flavor of the Old World, Asia, the Orient. The far east 70s and 80s of Manhattan are known as the Yorkville area, and offer Slavic and German eateries galore. Greek and Thai restaurants have found a home north of the skin-flick houses on Eighth Ave. from 48th to 56th Sts. West 46th St. has taken on a decidedly Brazilian flavor, and mid-Manhattan looks like Tokyo East, with the smell of sushi and tempura coming out of just about every other doorway. Astoria, Queens, is Greek restaurant heaven; so is Greektown around W. 27th St., with its bazoukis and belly dancers.

By now you get the point that we have eschewed the normal geographic divisions of Manhattan in favor of trying to whet your appetite with some suggestions that you might otherwise miss—especially if you were concentrating only on those restaurants in the immediate vicinity of your hotel—for that is the best way to get a real taste of the Big Apple. But there are a number of places worth singling out because they afford a spectacular view to go along with that taste of the Big Apple.

Most prominent among these is *Windows on the World,* the restaurant complex on the 107th floor of the World Trade Center (the eponymous restaurant offers expensive à la carte dining and a northerly view; the *Hors d'Oeuverie* has the southern exposure and serves only drinks and snacks). Others to consider for views from on high: the *Rainbow Room* at Rockefeller Center, *Top of the Sixes, Top of the Park* and *Nirvana* (both overlooking Central Park), and *The Terrace* at Columbia University. For the reverse view and a totally unique dining experience, journey to Brooklyn's *River Café,* at the foot of the Brooklyn Bridge, where you dine on a barge moored in the East River while drinking in the Manhattan skyline towering above you just across the water. The food at all of these restaurants, alas, can hardly compete with the view—and rarely does, although the River Café, on its better days, comes closest to the mark. You also pay dearly for what you see, even on cloudy days.

The vote for the most imaginative decor and cuisine might well go to the *Four Seasons,* where the decorations and menus change with—that's right—the seasons. The most expensive and sumptuous restaurant in a town filled with expensive and sumptuous restaurants would probably be *The Palace,* where meals come in three prices: $50, $95, and $150 per person. The *Coach House* draws consistent raves as one of the best for American-International cuisine. The arguments still rage between steak-and-chop lovers as to whether the East Side's aforementioned *Christ Cella* is better than *The Palm,* or whether *Gage & Tollner* and *Peter Luger* are better than either of them, even if it means crossing the East River to Brooklyn to get to them.

The range in price is as great as the variety of New York restaurant offerings —accounted for in matters of service, presentation, location, and decor as well as in who the chef is and what his or her capabilities are. This is so be the cuisine Chinese, Continental (that ill-defined hybrid of European and American influences), French, Indian, Italian, or otherwise. While a fine meal at an elegant restaurant can (and often does) extract a sultan's ransom from wealthy gourmandizers, it is also possible to have a nearly duplicate meal, served in more humble surroundings (and without a platoon of liveried attendants), at literally half the tariff.

In addition, there are a number of ways to dine at even the most expensive establishments without necessarily going bankrupt in the process. Many of the city's finest restaurants—and the Four Seasons heads the list!—offer special pre-theater dinners at prices that are a third to half less than the same meal ordered during prime serving periods. The menu selections are generally a little more limited, and you must usually be seated between 5:00 and 6:00 P.M., but service, preparation and surroundings are at the same high standards for which these restaurants are noted.

Then, too, lunches are often 10 to 20 percent cheaper than the same dinners would be, so having a big midday meal at *Lutèce*, for instance, at a prix fixe for approximately $16.75, affords the opportunity to dine at what is generally considered the finest classical French restaurant in the city at a fraction of what a similar three-course meal would cost à la carte in the evening. Another suggestion: Nowhere is it written that you must order courses as suggested on the menu at luncheon or dinner. If you are two or three people, for example, there is no reason why you can't order a selection of appetizers (which in at least some cases are scaled down portions of entrées), a salad, and a dessert—all to be shared. You get to sample several different items and the check—even if there is a "plate charge"—is within reason.

Increasingly popular all around the city is the leisurely weekend brunch—a late morning/early afternoon repast that is more extravagant than the usual breakfast but not quite as heavy as a European-style lunch. This, again, can be a good way to try some of the fancier restaurants at moderate cost; many offer special prix fixe brunches featuring classic omelettes and other egg dishes, as well as more exotic fare, with your choice of alcoholic beverage and tea or coffee included.

Remember that New York eats late; the better restaurants (except those near theaters or concert halls) don't get busy until 8 P.M., if then. If you insist on eating dinner as the second hand sweeps past six, you may be the only person in the place. Don't worry about going for dinner at 11:00 P.M.; lots of places will still serve. We've listed some that stay open much later.

In preparing the following lists of suggested restaurants, we've sought to provide a wide enough range of choices to fit every traveler's tastes and budget. And our listings do represent a *selection*, not a complete survey by any means, of places that will—we hope—enhance your visit to New York.

We regret, as you do, the prices that any meal costs everywhere these days, and the toll in New York is probably higher than anywhere else in the nation. But the following categories are the facts of life in today's dining out world, and we can only suggest that you mitigate each foray to some expensive temple of gastronomy with a sojourn to at least one or more modest sub-temple. As a rule of thumb, the higher the price, the more necessary reservations become. Dress codes vary, so check when making a reservation.

The price categories we use are approximate; figure for an average three-course meal (appetizer, main course with vegetable, dessert) at a given establishment, per person. This does not take into account the suggestions offered above for lessening the blow to the pocketbook, **nor does it include wine or drinks, taxes or gratuities.** As of this writing, meals are taxed at 8¼ percent of the total bill; for average service, most New Yorkers simply double the tax as a tip. For outstanding service you may wish to tip 20 percent, with another five percent for the maitre'd if he or she has been especially helpful.

RESTAURANTS

Super Deluxe restaurants will cost $40 and up. **Deluxe** establishments will generally fit into the $35 range. **Expensive** dinners will usually cost about $25. **Moderate** meals should run about $15. A tab at an **Inexpensive** restaurant will cost an average of $10. Do not be misled, however, by traditional notions of super deluxe or deluxe. We have grouped the restaurants primarily by price category, and some very expensive places—particularly the *nouvelle cuisine* restaurants, and many establishments on otherwise abandoned SoHo streets—will hardly have the type of elegance one usually associates with such prices.

Today, credit cards, "plastic money," are a very acceptable commodity. Most—although not all—restaurants accept credit cards. These are indicated by the following abbreviations which appear at the end of the upcoming restaurant listings:

AE - American Express
CB - Carte Blanche
DC - Diners Club
MC - MasterCard
V - Visa

Where a listing says, for example, "No CB," that means that the restaurant in question accepts all credit cards except Carte Blanche. Because of the cost involved in processing credit card charges, some establishments offer a cash discount of 5 to 10 percent for cash-paying customers; others may request that you tip in cash.

During the summer, many restaurants are closed for vacation for as much as a month; call ahead to check.

We have arranged the restaurants according to general stylistic categories first (American-International, Steakhouses, Seafood, etc.) and then by national or ethnic cuisine rather than geographically, although we have endeavored to make specific references if a particular place is especially convenient to, say, the theater district or Lincoln Center. And we have broken down the sections within each cuisine by price category with entries in alphabetical order. This should simplify your comparisons as well as facilitate looking up information about a restaurant whose name you may know. But before we go to the formal listings, here are a few notes on additional places that don't fit the regular categories.

Fast food. Such internationally renowned operations as *McDonald's, Arthur Treacher's Fish and Chips,* and *Burger King* are alive and thriving all around New York City. *Kentucky Fried Chicken* is similarly well entrenched, with listings in the White or Yellow Pages of the telephone directory the best way to find the locations nearest you. When the budget is hurting, these are possible alternatives. *La Potagerie* (554 Fifth Ave. near 46th St.) doesn't quite qualify as fast food, but its large bowls of various savory soups constitute meals unto themselves.

Pizza seems to be a major staple of New York eating habits. *John's Pizzeria,* 278 Bleecker St. near Seventh Ave. in Greenwich Village, has what many insist is the best pizza in New York. They sell whole pies only, and there is almost always a wait for a table—they take no reservations. Wine and beer, however, are available. *Amalfi Pizza* nearby at Bleecker on Seventh Ave. So., does sell slices, as does *Ray's* at 11th St. and Sixth Ave.—another favorite among the cognoscenti. Every New Yorker has a different "best," it seems; we say, try Sicilian style for a change.

Middle Eastern. Another very inexpensive and hearty fast-food alternative unique to New York is *Amy's,* again with branches all around town, serving Middle Eastern sandwiches and salads in bright, well-kept surroundings. You can bring your own wine or beer to most branches after 6:00 P.M. Street vendors also sell barbecued shish kebab that is usually pungent from a tenderizing marinade.

Chains. Other chain-style operations with uniform outlets around the city include *Chock Full O' Nuts* (mostly in midtown office districts), *Zum Zum* (specializing in German *wursts* and beer), *Steak and Brew, B.O.S.S.,* and *Roast Beef and Brew.* The last three offer free all-you-can-eat salads with the modest price of a meal and represent a good value for the money when you need a quick bite.

Cafeterias. Try *Dubrow's* (38th and Seventh Ave.) in the heart of the garment district. *Horn & Hardart* has one remaining coin-in-the-slot "automated" cafeteria at 200 E. 42nd St.

24-hour stops. People in New York do seem to be hungry at all hours of the day and night, and the selection among available offerings is only slightly less limited than normal if the time happens to be 4:30 A.M. or so. There are three reliable places on Second Ave. between 4th and 6th Sts.: *Kiev* (117 Second Ave.; 674–4040), an outstanding coffee shop great for hearty soups, blintzes, and fruit-filled pancakes that are almost like fritters; *103 Second Restaurant* (533–0769), which feels as though it were transplanted from SoHo, serving spicy, chunky chili, Continental meals and sandwiches, and breakfast at all hours; and the *Binibon,* at the corner of 5th St. (no phone), where you'll find inexpensive oversize salads the best bet. The *Empire Diner* (210 Tenth Ave., at W. 22nd St.; 243–2736) is a glorified candlelit boxcar with eggs and pasta and salads at any time—and with the crowd worth the trip particularly in the wee hours. Among the places included in the listings below, the *Stage Deli* in the midtown theater district and Chinatown's *Hong Fat* are always open. Both *Palsson's* (158 W. 72nd St., 362–2590) and the *Riviera* (225 W. 4th St.—Sheridan Square, in Greenwich Village, 242–8732) serve until 4:00 A.M.

Dessert. Finally, if you turn to the last page of these listings, you'll discover our suggestions for desserts. These include notable ice cream parlors and pastry shops that just may lure you into forgetting lunch or dinner altogether.

AMERICAN-INTERNATIONAL

Super Deluxe

The Four Seasons. 99 E. 52nd St.; 754–9494. One of New York's most beautiful, ambitious, and interesting restaurants. As seasons change, so do menus and decor. The main dining room is dominated by a large, shimmering reflecting pool. Art work includes a Picasso, and changing floral displays constitute a veritable botanical garden. But the heart of the restaurant revolves around a series of gastronomic "events," featuring famous chefs from around the world preparing their most famous creations. Best seats are thought to be near the pool in the formal dining room, where prices can reach the stratosphere. The outside Grill Room is a little less fancy and a lot less expensive. Knowledgeable New Yorkers who don't mind eating early take advantage of less expensive pre-theater dinner ($22.50 prix fixe as of this writing) from 5:00 to 7:00 P.M. Entrée choices are staggering in each case, as is the selection from one of America's most complete wine cellars. If the chocolate velvet for dessert is a once-in-a-lifetime experience, so is the restaurant itself. Closed Sundays. All major credit cards.

Windows on the World. 1 World Trade Center; 938–1111. A stunning and lavish restaurant with a wraparound view of city that is suggestive of a ship's dining room—providing the ship is the *QE2* and she is perched atop the world's second tallest building, 107 floors up, where only the daringest crow would nest. Unfortunately, food doesn't always match the view—what could?—or the decor, which includes a rock-lined, mirrored reception chamber, a multi-tiered, multi-mirrored main dining room, a veritable acre of glass encompassing various dining rooms, cocktail lounges and private rooms, lavish touches of brass, wood, plants and fresh flowers, and waiters resplendent in white uniforms with gold epaulets. The neighboring **Hors d'Oeuverie,** on the same floor and run by the same management, is an internationally minded cocktail lounge and grill that can be inexpensive if you eat and drink lightly while enjoying the sights and listening to the piano music. Reservations way in advance for Windows; not required for Hors D'Oeuverie, although there is often a wait at the latter for seats. All major credit cards.

Deluxe

Christ Cella. 160 E. 46th St.; 697–2479. Perhaps the largest piece of roast beef around, ditto the steaks, and everything else is similarly served in oversized portions. Decor on two floors is simple, but who cares, for this is generally considered the best steak and roast-beef house in town, although supporters of The Palm will give you an argument there—and have for years in a rivalry reminiscent of the Yanks and Dodgers. Closed Saturday/Sunday during July and August. All major credit cards.

The Coach House. 110 Waverly Place (the Village); 777–0303. A glowingly handsome English inn setting, where the best American dishes are served along with European classics in what many galloping gourmets consider the best all-around restaurant in the Big Apple, even though it does not exert itself for new customers. Open at 5:30 P.M. on Saturday, 4:30 P.M. on Sunday, closed Monday. No V.

Rainbow Room. 30 Rockefeller Plaza (Rockefeller Center); 757–9090. Classic Art Deco room dripping chandeliers, chrome, tables on multi-levels, and spectacular view of city from 65th floor of the RCA building. It also features name bands for dinner dancing—but food doesn't match mood, view or ambiance. The adjacent **Rainbow Grill** offers dinner, disco, and a mediocre imitation Vegas-Paris cabaret show with some nudity. All major credit cards.

Expensive

The Conservatory. 15 Central Park West at 61st St.; 581-1293. A relaxed, attractive spot for the Lincoln Center crowd. Diversified menu includes Mongolian lamb chops, shrimp scampi, and breast of capon piccata. All credit cards.

The Ginger Man. 51 W. 64th St.; 399-2358. Another favorite dinner locale among those attending performances at Lincoln Center. A well-decorated, pub-style establishment that is noted for its spinach salad and steaks. Check for musical entertainment. All major credit cards.

Greene Street. 101-103 Greene St. between Prince and Spring (SoHo); 925-2415. Good but not great food in a delightful setting—plants, catwalks, lots of space—in the interesting SoHo area. AE, MC, V.

Hurley's Steak & Seafood. 49th St. and Sixth Ave.; 765-8981. Jammed at lunchtime. Very popular with broadcasting and advertising folks—the NBC headquarters and studios are about thirty feet away. Major credit cards.

The Leopard. 253 E. 50th St., near Second Ave.; 759-3735. A fine, spacious dining room, with tables comfortably far apart, overlooking a plastic garden. Prix-fixe meals include all the wine you wish—and the wines are surprisingly good. The Continental-style food is not four-star, but neither are the prices. AE, DC.

Maxwell's Plum. 1181 First Ave. at 64th St.; 628-2100. The bar is the mecca for NYC's single-and-mingle crowd. You can dine elegantly in the art nouveau, Tiffany-lighted dining area at the rear, where the menu is ambitious and interesting. The consummate New York City scene. All credit cards.

P. J. Moriarty's. 1034 Third Ave near 61st St.; 838-2438. A congenial place noted for the hearty American and international viands. The menu has new specialties each day, but the corned beef and cabbage is super special. All major credit cards.

One Fifth. 1 Fifth Ave. in the Village; 260-3434. You won't get seasick in this first-class dining salon, a restoration of the *Caronia's* dining room. Continental cuisine, clam bar, piano music. Modern jazz in the front room late evenings. All major credit cards.

One If by Land, Two If by Sea. 17 Barrow St., between W. 4th St. and Seventh Ave.; 255-8649. In what was once a stable, this charming restaurant is a favorite more for its ambience and unusual layout than for its food—land is meat, sea is fish, get it?—though the food is all right if you stick to basics. There is no sign outside the place, so look for the street number. Not terribly casual in dress. All major credit cards.

Proof of the Pudding. 1165 First Ave. near 64th St.; 421-5440. On the singles axis at 64th St. No menu; waiters recite choice—sometimes they sing them. Would you believe veal Alaska? Music. No CB.

Restaurant Leslie. 18 Cornelia St. (in the Village); 675-1255. Small understated Greenwich Village storefront featuring European-American food inspired by *nouvelle cuisine* chefs—*très* interesting. Dinner only. Closed Sunday. No credit cards.

Tavern-on-the-Green. Central Park West at 67th St. (just inside Central

RESTAURANTS

Park); 873-3200. This long-time New York landmark has three beautifully appointed rooms with views of the park, and outdoor dining when weather permits. Specialties: salads, veal and beef dishes. Attentive service, so-so food, and be sure to have a reservation lest you be sneered away at the door. Live band for dancing on some nights. All major credit cards.

Moderate

Joe Allen's. 326 W. 46th St., in the theater district; 581-6464. A long-time theatrical hangout which means you probably won't get a table at prime time unless you're recognized at the door. Casual place, casual-style food and a good value if you can get in. MC, AE, V.

Billy's. 948 First Ave. near 52nd St.; 355-8920. A neighborhood favorite among residents of the fashionable Beekman Place area. Has all the ambience of a Yukon saloon. Known for steaks and lamb chops. AE, CB, DC.

Café Loup. 18 E. 13th St.; 255-4746. A small, casual bistro in an unusual location, staffed by pleasant young people. The menu, chalked on blackboards, is more or less French—and the food is good. Major credit cards.

P. J. Clarke's. 915 Third Ave. at 55th St.; 759-1650. The most chic hamburger joint in town. A legend that is the special province of NYC's advertising and publishing set, though there's a branch for shoppers in Macy's Cellar. Good chili served in the bar area. No credit cards.

Crawdaddy. 45 E. 45th St.; 687-1860. New Orleans in New York: Creole dishes, gumbos, cheerful decor, live music evenings. Closed Saturday/Sunday. No CB.

Gardenia Club. 482 W. 43rd St.; 594-8402. In Manhattan Plaza, the artist/show business apartment complex. A rather romantic hideway, overlooking a pool. Chicken, simply prepared, is the specialty. Closed Mondays. Major credit cards.

Gottlieb's. 343 Bleecker St. near W. 10th St. in the Village; 929-7800. A very relaxed and comfortable place, and the food somehow matches. No DC.

Lion's Rock. 316 E. 77th St.; 988-3610. Very good Continental-type food in a casual atmosphere, with an attractive open garden at the rear. Dinner only, but brunch on Sunday. Major credit cards.

Ma Bell's. 218 W. 45th St.; 869-0110. Fronts on famed Shubert Alley. You can order your choices via the phone at your table. Good for pre- or post-theater dining. Closed Sunday. All major credit cards.

Martell's. 1469 Third Ave. st 84th St.; 861-6110. French farmer's sandwich is a specialty at this Upper East Side boite, which advertises its "spirituous liquors." Sidewalk café in good weather. Good bar scene. All major credit cards.

Jim McMullen's. 1341 Third Ave. near 77th St.; 861-4700. Natural brick walls, no reservations or credit cards. A hangout for models—Jim was one himself—the beautiful people and the sports crowd. Good seafood, first-class steaks.

J. G. Melon. 1291 Third Ave. at 74th St.; 744-0585. This is fast food for the Beautiful People. The bar is a regular meeting place for New York's informal chic set. Hamburgers are fine, as are the Monte Cristo sandwiches. Also a West Side branch at Amsterdam Ave. and 76th St. (874-8291). No credit cards.

Village Green. 531 Hudson St. in the Village; 255–1650. An interesting menu leaning toward French, the restaurant an extremely pleasant brownstone, with eating on two levels and a piano bar upstairs. AE, MC, V.

Inexpensive

Maestro Café. 58 W. 65th St. near Lincoln Center; 787–5990. Attractive decor, good "American-Continental" cuisine, lively service. Good for pre- or post-concert dining. No CB.

Ye Waverly Inn. 16 Bank St.; 929–4377. A Village landmark with three low-ceilinged, candlelit dining rooms—two with fireplaces—and a backyard garden. Down-to-earth American cookery that's been tired in recent years, though the pies and cakes are still homemade. No CB.

STEAKHOUSES

Super Deluxe

Joe & Rose. 747 Third Ave. near 46th St.; 980–3985. They built an entire skyscraper around this humble-looking eatery. Food is hardly humble, though, and the steaks and corned beef and cabbage are specials. Like The Palm and Pietro's, this is a New York phenomenon, where the service and surroundings belie the prices—but the food doesn't. No menu. AE.

The Palm. 837 Second Ave. near 45th St.; 687–2953. For the roughly two hundred ten million Americans who've been weaned on "New York cut" steaks, it's going to come as a rude awakening to discover that such a description has no meaning in N.Y.C. But if you are looking for just about the best piece of sirloin in town, this is the place. You should know that it's a madhouse at the prime dinner hours, and because of a non-reservation policy, an hour's wait is not the least unusual. We should also mention that the noise level is high and that the walls are decorated in a way that can only be described as vintage graffiti and that the waiters will do their best to antagonize you and get you in and out quickly. Yet beef lovers queue up gladly, and the double sirloin is a total delight. The cottage-fried potatoes and crisp onion rings are unequaled in the city, and the double lobster (carrying a tariff that may require payment in 30-, 60-, and 90-day notes) is simply splendid. A branch called **Palm Too,** 697–5198, directly across the street and serving the same food, tries to handle the overflow. Closed Sunday. All major credit cards.

Pen & Pencil. 205 E. 45th St.; 682–8660. Another steakhouse with an established (and highly vocal) group of supporters among the journalistic and entertainment crowd. In addition to grilled steaks and chops, a few Italian specialties can be ordered. All major credit cards.

The Post House. 28 E. 63rd St.; 935–2888. One of New York's newest and most elegant steak houses. All major credit cards.

Smith and Wollensky. 201 E. 49th St.; 753–1530. Steaks, chops, roast beef, and lobsters are the basic items, and flank steak surrounded by vegetables is a feature. All major credit cards.

RESTAURANTS

United States Steakhouse Company. 120 W. 51st St.; 757–8800. Owned by a friend of Mayor Koch, who may be seen here occasionally. Excellent steaks, chops, the works. Closed Sunday. All major credit cards.

Wally's Restaurant. 224 W. 49th St.; 582–0460. No frills in decor but excellent steaks, lobster, and some surprisingly good Italian dishes. Closed Sunday. Dinner only Saturday, MC, DC, V.

Expensive

Broadway Joe's Steak House. 315 W. 46th St.; 246–6513 or 974–9832. This well-known old-timer has an open kitchen. Waiters recite the menu. Closed Sunday. No CB.

Downey's Steak House. 705 Eighth Ave. near 44th St.; 757–0186. In the heart of the theater district and a good choice for after-theater dining among performers and theatergoers alike. Particularly good Irish coffee. Closed Sunday. All major credit cards.

Elmer's. 1034 Second Ave. near 55th St.; 751–8020. With a name like that, it has to be good—and it is. All major credit cards.

Frankie & Johnnie's. 269 W. 45th St. off Eighth Ave.; 245–9717. Well worth the short climb to the second-floor dining room. Great steaks and potatoes served—but open until midnight for dinner only. All major credit cards.

Gallagher's Steak House. 228 W. 52nd St.; 245–5336. Near the theaters, it has a rugged, comfortable air, red-checkered tablecloths in the several dining rooms, and a large bar. Uncomfortably noticeable preferential treatment for regulars. All credit cards.

Kenny's Steak Pub. 565 Lexington Ave. near 51st St.; 355–0666. Favorite of the NYC professional footballer, who appreciates the generous portions of steak and prime ribs. The noise can sometimes sound like a stadium. Banana layer cake a treat. Dinner only Saturday/Sunday from 5:00 P.M. All major credit cards.

Le Steak. 1089 Second Ave. near 58th St.; 421–9072. Red meat prepared lusciously in the French style. Steak sautéed in garlic butter is indescribably good. A unique steakhouse open for dinner only. No CB.

McCarthy's Famous Steak House. 839 Second Ave. near 45th St.; 687–6131. A favorite of newsmen and sports figures, as well as of those who just love good steaks and chops. Pleasant surroundings for pleasant eating. Closed Saturday/Sunday. All major credit cards.

Old Homestead Steak House. 56 Ninth Ave. near 14th St.; 242–9040. The oldest steakhouse in NYC, established 1865, in the heart of the wholseale meat market. If you're especially lucky, you may hit them on the day each year when they roll back prices to those offered on the date of founding. Oversize steaks and lobster, and home-fried potatoes are the specialties. Hot shrimp balls are an unusual appetizer. All major credit cards.

Slate Steak House. 852 Tenth Ave.; 581–6340. Near the Coliseum. Big with the TV crowd. All major credit cards.

NEW YORK CITY

Moderate

Blue Mill Tavern. 50 Commerce St. in the Village; 243-7114. Tucked away amidst century old buildings, and within walking distance of many Off-Broadway Village theaters. The management is Portuguese, and the food is good. All major credit cards.

Cheers. 120 W. 41st St.; 840-8810. Superb roast beef and more than ample portions. On the fringe of the garment and theater districts. All major credit cards.

Farnie's Second Avenue Steak Parlour. 311 Second Ave. near 18th St.; 228-9280. An unassuming neighborhood-type steakhouse that does its best to compete with its better-known and more expensive brethren. All major credit cards.

Inexpensive

Beefsteak Charlie's. Various midtown locations. Singled out mostly because of its low prices and "Small Fry" meals, which mean bargain prices for the kiddie korps.

SEAFOOD

Super Deluxe

Gloucester House. 37 E. 50th St.; 755-7394. Among the most extensive (and expensive) seafood menus in New York. Fabulous homemade biscuits. If you have an expense account this place will use it up for a month. All major credit cards.

Deluxe

Oyster Bar of the Plaza. Plaza Hotel, Fifth Ave. at 59th St.; 759-3000. If you want to combine Edwardian elegance with excellent seafood, this is the place. Full-course dinners will run high, but you can snack heartily very reasonably at the bar, as many New Yorkers do at lunch and after work. All major credit cards.

Expensive

Goodale's. 986 Second Ave. near 52nd St.; 755-7317. New England-style preparation is the signature of this owner-operated spot. Oyster stews and chowders are specialties. All major credit cards.

Joe's Pier 52. 144 W. 52nd St.; 245-6652. Huge, sprawling; music in lounge; city showcase for Broadway impresario Joe Kipness, who indulges his taste in seafood by pouring half the ocean's denizens onto the menu, which is not only extensive but satisfying. All major credit cards.

King Crab. 871 Eighth Ave. at 52nd St.; 765-4393. Gas lamps, track-lighting, young plants, old furniture and fresh fish, crabs, and interesting seafood combination. Open 7 days a week, dinner only Saturday/Sunday. AE, DC.

Oscar's Salt of the Sea. 1155 Third Ave. near 67th St.; 879-1199. Stuffed lobsters are a particular specialty of this exceptional seafood restaurant, and virtually everything on the extensive menu is prepared perfectly. The only discordant note is the inevitable wait (often quite long) for a table. AE, DC.

Pesca. 23 E. 22nd St.; 533–2293. A beautiful, simply appointed restaurant with an open feeling. Some very unusual seafood dishes. The preparation tends to Latin-style—Italian and Portuguese. AE.

Sea Fare of the Aegean. 25 W. 56th St.; 581–0540. The decor is Mediterranean, and the food first-rate. Shrimp Santorini is a specialty, and the striped bass is also out of the ordinary. All major credit cards.

Sweet's. 2 Fulton St., downtown; 825–9786 or 344–9189. A landmark from the old clipper-ship days. Exceptional fish prepared in the traditional manner and considered best seafood place in town—even though it takes no reservations and is usually crowded. It's in the Fulton Fish Market area and seems to get its fish fresh off the hook. Closed Saturdays, Sundays, holidays, and July. No credit cards.

Moderate

Broadway Bay. ("B'Way Bay" on the sign). Corner Broadway and 77th St.; 362–5234. Italian seafood specialties in a very casual Upper West Side atmosphere. The bar is especially comfortable—unprepossessing would be an understatement. No CB.

The Captain's Table. 410 Sixth Ave. near W. 9th St.; 473–0670; 860 Second Ave. near 47th St., 697–9538. Selections are broad and simple and the fish is fresh. Sixth Ave.—closed Monday, Second Ave.—closed Sunday AE, MC, V.

Dobson's. Columbus Ave. at 76th St.; 362–0100. This very large and understated restaurant is representative of the newly stylish Upper West Side, a dozen blocks north of Lincoln Center. The fish is fresh, the atmosphere casual—but not overly so. AE, MC, V.

Fisherman's Net. 493 Third Ave. near 33rd St.; 532–1683. Very reasonable. Daily specials with soup, salad, dessert—just like the old days. The wine list is poor. Look for the poem Ogden Nash wrote to and for the restaurant. All major credit cards.

Jane Street Seafood Café. 31 Eighth Ave. 2 blocks south of 14th St.; 243–9237. Narrow, intimate West Village setting with exposed brick and natural wood—and a gourmet touch in the kitchen. Slow service. AE, MC, V.

Oyster Bar. Inside Grand Central Station, off 42nd St. at Park Ave., 490–6650. After being closed for several years, this shrine of good seafood is back again, with a booming business in its vaulted main room, in the quieter Saloon (532–1358) and the first-come, first-served sit-down counter. Several kinds of oysters, clams, and crabs at any given time, plus specials that include fish not seen often enough in New York. Main room is noisy but exhilarating. Closed Saturday/Sunday. All major credit cards.

Inexpensive

Paddy's Clam House. 215 W. 34th St.; 244–9123. A glorified clam bar that is a favorite with downtown shoppers and Madison Square Garden habitues. Good food served quickly but sloppily. Daily full-course meal specials. AE, MC, V.

Sloppy Louie's. 92 South St. downtown; 952–9657. Looks like a slum from the outside, but frequented by the button-down Wall Street crowd. Brokers sit at long tables to enjoy the fish landed across the street at the Fulton Fish Market. Also across from the South Street Seaport Museum. Tables are usually for six, so dining is a communal experience. No reservations. Closed Saturday/Sunday. No credit cards.

DAIRY

Inexpensive

B & H Dairy Restaurant. 127 Second Ave.; near St. Mark's Place (8th St.); 777–1930. Tiny coffee-shop-style place for good eggs, cheese, blintzes, pancakes. No credit cards.

Farm Foods. 142 W. 49th St.; 586–9369. The soups, blintzes, and fish are uniformly excellent. Centrally located for Broadway theaters, Radio City, Rockefeller Center. No credit cards.

Ratner's Dairy Restaurant. 138 Delancey St., near Essex; 677–5588. A legend in its own time on the Lower East Side for East European Jewish dairy cooking. No credit cards.

DELICATESSEN

Deli connotes sandwiches of modest cost to most people, but New York delis are a class unto themselves—quite different from, say, an ordinary coffee or sandwich shop. Try as they may, from Los Angeles to Tokyo, no one can imitate a New York deli accurately. The best corned beef or pastrami on rye in midtown will run an easy $4.50, while special triple-decker combination numbers go for $7.00 and up. That may be "inexpensive" in that it falls under $10.00—but it is admittedly not cheap by most standards for a sandwich. Still, no one should be allowed to leave the city without sampling at least one of the delis listed below.

Expensive

Kaplan's at the Delmonico. 59 E. 59th St.; 755–5959. Classiest of the lot, with fantastic deli sandwiches. AE, DC.

Inexpensive

Carnegie Delicatessen. 854 Seventh Ave. near 55th St.; 757–2245. Great for concertgoers, deli-noshers. Open 6:30 A.M. to 4:00 A.M. No credit cards.

Fine & Schapiro. 138 W. 72nd St.; 877–2874. An easy walk to and from Lincoln Center—especially worthwhile on matinee days. Also Kosher Chinese delicacies.

Katz's Delicatessen. 205 E. Houston St.; 254–2246. A Lower East Side institution—cafeteria-style self-service that's a perfect treat after bargain-hunting on Orchard St. downtown.

Madison. 1175 Madison Ave. at 86th St.; 369–6670. Convenient to Upper East Side museums, this large, informal delicatessen restaurant offers a variety

RESTAURANTS

of sandwiches as well as appetizers, soups, smoked fish, dairy dishes, hot main courses, and Danish pastries. No credit cards.

Nathan's Famous. Broadway at 43rd St.; 594-7455. Having acquired fame and reputation at Coney Island, Nathan's in Manhattan now dispenses the same clams, scallops, oysters, pizza, barbequed beef sandwiches, and chow mein on a bun as at the original (still open) location. But Nathan's earned its nickname—"Famous"—with great hot dogs; and that's still its most popular item. Eat at stand-up counters, cafeteria-style at communal tables, or downstairs in the dining room. No credit cards upstairs; AE in the dining room only. Other branches now open—check the Yellow Pages.

Pastrami & Things. 297 Third Ave. at 23rd St.; 683-7185. Another Jewish delicatessen with a dining room and counter. The pastrami sandwiches are unsurpassed, and were chosen by *New York* magazine as the best in the city. Popular and crowded. No credit cards.

Reuben's. 244 Madison Ave. near 38th St., 867-7800; 770 Second Ave., 883-1193. "From a sandwich to an institution" is its boast, and justly so. No credit cards.

Second Ave. Kosher Delicatessen. 156 Second Ave. at 10th St.; 677-0606. Real kosher-style deli with all the trimmings—free pickles, cole slaw, waiters who invariably know what you want better than you do—and the unique offer of half sandwiches at half price. Easily among the best of the lot, and a bargain because of its out-of-the-way location. No credit cards.

Stage. 834 Seventh Ave. near 54th St.; 245-7850. This restaurant attracts a large after-theater crowd, but is nearly always bustling and noisy. Their sandwiches are packed with meat, the rye bread is superb, their appetizers tantalizing, and there is a variety of hot dishes, salads, and fish platters. Tables are for four, so if you're a couple expect company and surly-at-best service. Open 24 hours. No credit cards.

HEALTH FOOD

Inexpensive

Arnold's Turtle. 51 Bank St. in the West Village; 242-5623. Very popular small, informal Greenwich Village spot for fresh salads and simple vegetarian casserole dishes. No credit cards.

Grass. 1445 First Ave. at 75th St.; 737-3328. An alternative to hamburgers along singles-bar row. All major credit cards.

Great American Health Bar. 35 W. 57th St.; 355-5177; **II**, 15 E 40th St. 532-3232. Popular among diet-conscious shoppers stalking the exclusive women's department stores (Bendel, Bergdorf, Bonwit Teller) in the area. No credit cards.

Greener Pastures. 117 E. 60th St.; 832-3212. The salads and platters are a little more original than is usually the case, and the location is perfect when shopping at Bloomingdale's or catching an Upper East Side movie. No credit cards.

Healthworks! 153 E. 53rd St.; 838–6221. Flagship branch in Citicorp Center features salads galore plus yogurts, quiches and other light, interestingly prepared dishes. Also take-out. Other branches: 12 E. 36th St. (686–0401); 148 E. 57th St. (838–8370); 1345 Sixth Ave. at 55th St. (586–1980); 804 Madison Ave. at 68th St. (472–9300). No credit cards.

Vim & Vigor. 157 W. 57th St.; 247–8059. Expensive for what you get, but convenient to Carnegie Hall. No credit cards.

Zucchini. 1336 First Ave. at 72nd St.; 249–0559. Salads, soups, home-baked goods in a cheery Upper East Side setting. AE, MC, V.

SOUTHERN

Moderate

The Cotton Patch. 1068 Second Ave. near 56th St.; 688–6595. Old country-barn decor, with fried chicken, ribs, and steak. All major credit cards.

Jack's Nest. 310 Third Ave. (23rd St.); 260–7110. Soul food in immaculate setting, featuring hot cornbread, barbecued ribs, chitterlings, Southern fried pork chops, AE, MC, V.

Inexpensive

Sylvia's. 328 Lenox Ave., 534–9414. In the heart of Harlem, and not recommended unless you can drive up and park in front of the door. Nonetheless, you'll find what is unquestionably the finest soul food in the city. A luncheonette with but a few counter seats and a handful of booths, Syvia's Southern-fried chicken and stuffed pork chops (both under $4.00 including two fresh vegetables and cornbread) will be long remembered.

West Boondock. 114 Tenth Ave. near 16th St.; 929–9645. Sawdust on floor, down-home cooking, good live jazz thrown in for free. Saturday/Sunday dinner only. AE, CB, MC.

CUISINE BY NATIONALITY

AUSTRIAN

Expensive

Vienna '79. 320 E. 79th St.; 734–4700. The dining room is long, narrow, serene, decorated in non-Austrian motifs, and the food is what might best be termed *nouvelle* Austrian—from the Viennese fried chicken, veal goulash, and *Zwiebelrostbraten* (medium-size steak covered with deep-fried crisp onions) to the Wiener schnitzel, crêpes, and cream strudel. Dinner only. (An even newer sister restaurant, **Vienna Park,** is of equally high quality, located at 33 E. 60th St.; 758–1051.) All major credit cards.

BRAZILIAN

Deluxe

Casa Brasil. 406 E. 85th St.; 288–5284. On Wednesday this charming place serves *feijoada*, the Brazilian national dish. It includes rice, beans, many different kinds of meat, vegetables, fruit and several condiments. The rest of the week the kitchen turns out creditable Continental food; beef Wellington, purée of broccoli, tapioca with wine flavor. Bring your own wine and reserve at least a day in advance. There are two sittings per night, 7:30 and 9:30. The restaurant is small, popular, and closed Sundays. Cash or check, no credit cards.

Moderate

Brazilian Pavilion. 141 E. 52nd St.; 758–8129. Although the setting is modern, the interesting cuisine is traditional Brazilian with steaks Portuguesa (garlic!), shrimp Paulista, and Portuguese fish stew. The black bean soup is excellent; so is the dried codfish. Closed Sunday. AE, MC, V.

Via Brasil. 34 W. 46th St.; 997–1158. On Manhattan's Brazilian street. The decor is a touch off-beat, but the grilled meats, especially the Brazilian-style marinated steaks, are superb. Major credit cards.

Inexpensive

Brazilian Coffee Restaurant. 45 W. 46th St.; 719–2105. In the heart of the theater district. *Feijoada* is on the menu every Wed. & Sat. Excellent Latin American specialties are available at all times. Appetizers may dissappoint but shrimp dishes and codfish are good. So is the guava compote with white cheese. The service is as informal as the ambience. Expect to see many Brazilians eating here at lunch. Closed Sun. All major credit cards.

Cabana Carioca. 123 W. 45th St.; 581–8088. Pleasant, friendly, and anything but elegant, but the food is relatively good and cheap by today's standards—especially the *caldo verde* (vegetable and potato soup) and shrimp dishes. Open 7 days a week for lunch and dinner. Service can be erratic. DC, MC, V.

Chateau Bahia. 861 First Ave. at 48th St.; 753–2960. An attractive bar, a glass-enclosed section, and a large dining area in the rear. But the real attraction here is the seafood stew and the fish and shellfish dishes. It is open for lunch and dinner Monday through Friday, dinner only on Saturday, and closed Sunday. No CB.

Rio de Janeiro. 41 W. 57th St.; 935–1232. The dining area is dark, the decor somewhat barren, but the fish, shellfish, or chicken dishes can be interesting. *Feijoada* is served Wednesday and Saturday. Complimentary Brazilian-style appetizers are served with drinks. Closed Sunday. AE, MC, V.

BRITISH

Deluxe

Bull and Bear. Lexington Ave. and 49th St.; 872–4900. It's in the Waldorf-Astoria so expect it to be expensive. Everything is à la carte at both lunch and dinner, but the menu is large and so are the portions. Specializes in steaks, chops, and seafood. Open seven days a week for lunch and dinner. All major credit cards.

Cheshire Cheese. 319 W. 52st St.; 765–0616. Owned by two chaps from England, who also decorated their small pub most attractively. Small, candlelit dining room, jolly bar. Steak and kidney pie, roast beef with Yorkshire pudding, and imported Dover sole are headliners. À la carte. Closed Sunday, Monday, July, August, all major holidays, and Christmas through New Year's Day. Convenient to theater district. Excellent service. AE, DC.

Expensive

Charlie Brown's Ale & Chophouse. At 45th St. and Vanderbilt Ave. inside the lobby of the Pan Am Building; 661–2520. This pleasant pub, named after an old English inn, is handsome and has steak and kidney pie, mutton chops, Dover sole. Try a yard of ale here. Lunch, dinner, and after-theater à la carte. Lunch only on Saturday. Closed Sun. All major credit cards.

Ye Olde Chop House. 111 Broadway, near Wall St.; 732–6119. Much as it was in 1800, this restaurant is popular at lunch with Wall Street businessmen. Mutton chops, genuine Smithfield ham, seafood, and game in season are amply served up for hearty eating. Closed Saturday, Sunday and after 7:30 P.M., although they serve you if you arrive before closing. Also closed most major holidays. All major credit cards.

Moderate

Charley O's. 33 W. 48th St.; 582–7141. As much Dublin pub as London Tavern on an immense scale, it is one of the best restaurants in the Rockefeller Center area. The stand-up bar serves sandwiches, clams, oysters. The main dining area offers immense portions of ham, steaks, roast beef, pigs' knuckles, and more. It is closed Sunday, serves brunch on Saturday. (There's another branch at 9 Pennsylvania Plaza above Penn Station, entrance on 33rd St.; 947–0222.) No CB.

Friar Tuck. 914 Third Ave. at 55th St.; 688–4725. Romantic English pub with rooms on two different floors, lit by candlelight. Plain grilled meat dishes—such as lamb, mutton chops and roast beef—are good. Open seven days a week. All major credit cards.

Inexpensive

English Pub. 900 Seventh Ave. at 57th St.; 265–4360. Shepherd's pie and burgers in a simple, dark setting directly across the street from Carnegie Hall. Popular among music-industry types. No CB.

CHILEAN

Inexpensive

Chacareros. 76 W. 3rd St.; 473–8903. Typical and simple. House specialty: *empanadas,* what else? AE, DC, CB.

RESTAURANTS

CHINESE

Super Deluxe to Expensive

David Kay's Chung Kuo Yuan. 1115 Third Ave., 65th St.; 371–9090. Perhaps New York's most luxurious Chinese restaurant, with a piano bar/aquarium upstairs and a flower-drenched main dining area downstairs. The food matches the ambience, from the pork with pancakes and the spicy beef in orange sauce to the Peking duck and back again to the squab soup. There's even a glass-enclosed private garden looking out on the street. Open seven days a week. Szechuan-style available upon request. AE, DC.

Pearl's Chinese Restaurant. 38 W. 48th St.; 586–1060. Fairly small, with simple decor, it is a media favorite, especially with the publishing and broadcasting crowd who slurp up selections from 12 soups (The soup is almost a meal in itself). Best bets include the braised fish in sweet and sour sauce, the *moo shu* pork, and a variety of those steamed dumplings called *dim sum*. The food is filled with Cantonese nuances, from lemon chicken to pike. Closed Saturday, open for dinner only Sunday. No credit cards.

Shun Lee Dynasty. 900 Second Ave, at 48th St.; 755–3900. Many consider this one of the city's finest Chinese restaurants. The seasoning of these Mandarin and Szechuan dishes has been toned down somewhat, evidently in concession to American palates, but hot sauce is willingly served on the side. The sliced sautéed chicken, lobster ding, pan-fried noodles, or fried prawns are delicious specialties, but the menu includes many unusual and delectable items. The decor is colorful, with gold streamer room dividers and wood chimes overhead. Open seven days a week. AE, CB, DC.

Shun Lee Palace. 155 E. 55th St.; 371–8844. Decorated in what might be called Chinese Chippendale, the main room is a quietly lit and subdued Chinese/Hollywood set made up of alcoves, quiet corners, and large spaces, with a choice of tables or banquettes. The food is cross-China, a delicately tasty amalgam of Mandarin, Szechuan, Hunan, and Shanghai dishes. Indeed, all the Chinese classics are cooked here with finesse, from Peking duck through fried dumplings to baby spareribs. The chef will even produce Cantonese favorites on request, or any other you may request. This branch of the Shun Lee chain is open seven days a week. CB, AE, DC. The latest branch—**Shun Lee West**—recently opened at 43 W. 65th St., opposite Lincoln Center; 595–8845. AE.

Uncle Tai's Hunan Yuan. 1059 Third Ave. near 63rd St.; 838–0850. Adorned with hanging plants to resemble a garden (*yuan*), this handsome Hunan restaurant serves exciting and unusual Hunanese/Szechuan fare including venison in garlic sauce, sea bass in black bean sauce, and lamb in white sauce—all excellently prepared. Offerings here are often piquant and sometimes infernally spicy, sometimes sweet and sugary. It's a good idea to tell your waiter how you want your dishes cooked. Consider such specialties as vegetable pie wrapped in a pancake, the dry sautéed beef, the orange-flavored beef, carp, or fried noodles. Open seven days a week. AE, DC.

Moderate

Bill Chan's Gold Coin. 835 Second Ave. near 45th St.; 697-1515. Stunning dining rooms, a handsome bar and cocktail lounge. Both Mandarin and Cantonese cuisine is served. Tiny deep-fried frogs' legs are a delightful appetizer. Everything cooked to order, but most dishes tend to be bland and Westernized, although of top quality. Open seven days a week. Closed Thanksgiving, Christmas. No CB.

Chef Ho's Hunan Manor. 1464 Second Ave. near 77th St.; 570-6700. Chef Ho started at Uncle Tai's, helped open David K's, and went to Fortune Garden —three of the city's better Chinese restaurants—before branching out on his own, with two partners. There are some 100 choices on the mainly Hunan and Szechuan menu that is almost uniformly excellent in this comfortable, carpeted, somewhat dressy storefront, where most of the attention goes into the food. Money is well spent here with the dishes mild to searingly hot—you specify— lightly sauced and beautifully presented. Open seven days a week. All major credit cards.

China Pavillion. 200 W. 57th St. near Carnegie Hall; 765-4340. Paintings, fresh flowers, fine food. All major credit cards.

Foo Chow. 1278 Third Ave. at 74th St.; 861-4350. This Upper East Side Mandarin restaurant offers over 100 entries, but try the *muk hsu*, a delicious dish of shrimp, meat, bamboo shoots, and vegetables wrapped in a kind of pancake. Peking duck is available with 24-hour notice. All major credit cards.

Fortune Garden. 1160 Third Ave. at 68th St.; 744-1212. Divided into two sections, a cheerful front half and a squarish second half, the restaurant has captains take orders and the chef carries them out quite successfully, usually in the Cantonese-style, although the dishes can be spiced up Szechuan-style upon request. The kitchen is usually successful with beef and steak dishes, turns out interesting fish dishes—especially the whole sea bass in ginger sauce—and an excellent pork and pickled soup. The spring rolls and spareribs are exceptional. Open seven days a week. All major credit cards.

HSF (for Hee Seung Fung). 578 Second Ave. at 31st St.; 689-6969. The best-decorated of New York's smaller Chinese restaurants, HSF is a branch of an older Chinatown operation. Excellent *dim sum* (assorted dumplings which you choose from a succession of trolleys) for lunch. The room is oblong, the decor uncharacteristic of China, but the food goes a long way to make up for the lack of atmosphere. All major credit cards.

Hunam. 845 Second Ave. near 45th St.; 687-7471. The Hunam is generally acknowledged to be the progenitor of the cuisine of China's Hunan Province. (No one knows why they spell the restaurant's name with an "m.") It is also one of the city's best Chinese restaurants. Devilishly spicy items on the menu are thoughtfully marked, and the most important operative words for a first-time patron are "mild, please." Anyone whose Chinese eating experience has been limited to only traditional Cantonese cooking is in for a rare treat. AE, DC, CB.

Peng Teng's. 219 E. 44th St.; 682-8050. Owned by C. K. Peng and Philip Chiang, it features hard-to-find specialties from the cuisines of Peking, Szech-

RESTAURANTS

uan, and Hunan. Mr. Peng, who owns six restaurants in Taiwan, is the guiding genius, with two dishes named after him (squid with hot pepper sauce and a special beef). Mr. Teng is the new head chef recently imported. Minced squab and water chestnuts steamed in a bamboo container for six hours is just one reason to go—the very popular "Dragon and Phoenix" (lobster and chicken) is another. On Saturday and Sunday, *dim sum* at lunch can be inexpensive as well as satisfying both to body and soul. The two main rooms can be noisy, but there are glass-enclosed private rooms to help mute the sound for large parties. Uncle Peng is the onetime chef of Chiang Kai-Shek, and who cares about the noise. AE, DC, CB.

Sichuan Pavilion. 322 E. 44th St.; 986-3775. Two spacious rooms, well-spaced tables, pleasant decor with pandas painted on the wall, and located right off the UN, the restaurant has numerous chefs specially brought over from China to make up one of the most interesting menus in New York—bar none. Of course, the menu lists in red (a New York Chinese-restaurant convention) the spicy items. One of the rarities is the numerous rabbit dishes. This is one of the city's newer Chinese restaurants—and certainly one of the better ones. The captains will help you with your ordering if you feel like experimenting off the menu. Open seven days a week. No CB.

Szechuan East. 1584 Second Ave. at 82nd St.; 535-4921. Moderate-sized, moderately priced, but there's nothing moderate about the food—it is authentic, imaginative and spicy, with the captain or waiter available to help cool the cooking down. But don't. It's an adventure. Open seven days a week. AE, DC.

Inexpensive

Most of the restaurants listed below do not have liquor licenses, so you are welcome to bring your own wine or beer. However, it is advisable to call ahead to make sure this is the case, because the situation changes as pending licenses are granted.

Bo Bo. 20½ Pell St.; 962-9458. In Chinatown, tiny and unpretentious, but has a very good reputation for its authentic Chinese fare. Try the "house" dinner. No menu. No credit cards.

Chi-Mer. 11-12 Chatham Square; 267-4565. Excellent food, typically Chinatown atmosphere. One of the few places where you can get Peking duck without calling up in advance. All major credit cards.

China Bowl. 152 W. 44th St.; 582-3358. Serves most of the well-known Cantonese dishes and has moderately priced family dinners. Also American food. Pleasant surroundings and handy for theater-goers. AE, DC.

Empire Szechuan Gourmet. 2574 Broadway at 97th St.; 663-6980. Exotic Chinese food cooked Szechuan and Hunan style in what is basically a storefront with red wallpaper, minimal decor, and a glass-enclosed alcove that extends onto the sidewalk. But the food—especially the shrimp, pork and chicken dishes—make this a great favorite with both the Columbia crowd and Upper West Siders. No credit cards.

Foo Joy. 13 Division St. off Chatham Square in Chinatown; 431-4931. For a delightful change from the popular Cantonese cooking, try their specialties from Fukien Province (adjacent to Canton). Fukien pork chops, steam-fried flounder, lemon chicken, or garlic spareribs are savory departures from the traditional. No credit cards.

Hong Fat. 63 Mott St.; 962-9588. This little Chinatown hole-in-the-wall specializes in noodles in many different forms. Many consider this New York's best Cantonese restaurant. Open 24 hours. No credit cards.

Hunan House. 45 Mott St., Chinatown; 962-0010. Subterranean but with two dining rooms and excellent pan-fried dumplings, orange-flavor chicken (not the usual sweet-and-sour concoction) and similar fare. You must emphasize if you want your dishes hot, though. AE.

Hwa Yuan Szechuan Inn. 40 E. Broadway; 966-5534. Slightly away from the main Chinatown district, in a large informal room almost without decoration, you can get some of the best Szechuan food in town. Known for its excellent soups, carp with brown sauce, double-sautéed pork, fried noodles with shredded pork and bean curd, home-style, it is well worth getting to know better because it keeps getting better. No CB.

Nom Wah Tea Parlor. 13 Doyers St. off Pell St., Chinatown; 962-8650. Open only from 11:00 A.M. to 3:00 P.M. Trays of many different types of dumplings (*dim sum*), puffed vegetable rolls, and other tidbits are brought to your table. Choose what you want. They figure your bill from counting the number of empty plates on the tables when you are finished. A unique place. No credit cards.

Peking Duck House Restaurant. 22 Mott St. in Chinatown; 962-8208. The house specialty—Peking duck—doesn't have to be ordered 24 hours in advance as at most places. It is priced around $20—a relative bargain because it compares favorably with the same dish at higher-priced restaurants. And it can be almost a meal in itself for a party of four. AE.

Say Eng Look. 5 E. Broadway; 732-0796. Our Peking (Mandarin) choice is a particular favorite with those who know their way around NYC's Chinatown. The name means "4, 5, 6" and refers to a particularly fine hand in Mah Jong. You'll notice that most of the patrons are Oriental, and we consider that an expert recommendation. It is also a favorite of NYC Mayor Ed Koch. Again, the decor is unimposing, the overall space small, and the atmosphere on the noisy side. But no lack of ambience can really detract from the *moo shoo* pork, Tai-Chi Chicken, or the deep-fried fish wrapped in bean curd or seaweed. There's also a whole pork joint in an incredible brown anise sauce. The specials are the dishes to go for here. So popular has this restaurant become that they've opened a branch across the street—*1-2-3*—to handle the overflow. Tell your waiter if you want your meal served in courses, however, or all selections will arrive simultaneously. Beer and wine available. No credit cards.

Szechuan Cuisine. 33 Irving Place near Union Square (15th St., a block from Park Ave.); 982-5678. Gutsy, spicy food, where two can have a fiery meal for under $12, with choices including dried sautéed beef, kidney, ginger shrimp, and bean curd. No credit cards.

Szechuan Taste. 23 Chatham Square, Chinatown; 267-0672. Floor seemingly slants downhill but that doesn't tilt the menu, which is one of the city's

RESTAURANTS

best—and the lines to get in attest to its popularity. You may want to go easy on the hot stuff here. No CB.

Szechuan West. 2656 Broadway near 101st St.; 663-9280. One of the original Empire chefs has branched out on his own—and very well. His crispy fried flounder tops a list of virtually untoppable hot dishes at bargain-basement prices, in a simple storefront where the grandeur is in the food. No credit cards.

Ying. 220 Columbus Ave. at 70th St.; 724-2031. Outstandingly spicy Szechuan food of unusual variety and taste—and resaonably priced. Often crowded. Near Lincoln Center. AE.

CZECHOSLAVAKIAN

Moderate

Czechoslovak Praha. 1358 First Ave. at 73rd St.; 988-3505. An excellent restaurant whose specialties include *svickova* (a marinated beef dish similar to sauerbraten), goulash, goose, and duckling. For dessert, *palacinky*—a thin pancake stuffed with prune or apricot jam—is excellent. In the heart of the city's "Little Czechoslovakia" district. No CB.

Ruc. 312 E. 72nd St.; 650-1611. Long established, so it must be doing something right, although its kitchen has a tendency to be uneven. The duck, roast pork, and goulash portions tend to be substantial and filling, and the price is right. Ruc serves dinner only from 4:00 P.M. on weekdays, and from noon on Saturday and Sunday. AE, DC, V.

Vasata. 339 E. 75th St.; 650-1686. Owned by the Vasata family (which has a famous restaurant in Prague), it has a devoted following for the crisp roast duck, chicken paprikash, and game in season. Neat, pleasant dining room and small bar. Imported wines. Complete à la carte dinner starting from 5:00 P.M. seven days a week from Monday through Saturday and from noon on Sunday. No DC.

FRENCH

Super Deluxe

La Caravelle. 33 W. 55th St.; 586-4252. At the highest rank of New York restaurants, and among the top two or three French establishments in the entire city. A favorite with the social set at lunch. Very fashionable clientele in the evening, too. Elegant decor, top-notch wine cellar, attentive service, the latter especially so if you are known. This is one of those restaurants where the unrecognized diner can be treated rather cavalierly. (Tables near the entrance are considered the favored ones here.) Closed Sunday and the month of August. All major credit cards.

La Côte Basque. 5 E. 55th St.; 688-6525. Its reputation was made by its late founder, Henri Soulé, once also of the now legendary and defunct Le Pavillon. Stunning Bernard Lamotte murals enhance a totally handsome dining room. The cuisine is classic and can be superb. The service is a model of perfection. Closed Sunday. AE.

La Grenouille. 3 E. 52nd St.; 752–1495. A sublimely beautiful setting that complements a superb kitchen. The "in" place for lunch for expense-account diners. Often crowded, with the impact of the large number of diners accented by the proximity of one table to another. Classic French food as good as it exists in the city. Closed Sunday and holidays. AE.

Le Chantilly. 106 E. 57th St.; 751–2931. Large, stately, classical, and pretentious, but you can tell *toute le monde* it delivers when it comes to fish, lamb, veal, and desserts. Indeed, from soup to nuts, it is hard to beat—but at those prices, it should be. Open Monday to Friday for lunch and dinner, dinner only on Saturday, closed Sunday. No CB.

Le Cirque. 58 E. 65th St.; 794–9292. Plush, haute cuisine restaurant with animals painted as humans in interesting circusy mural. Offers excellent service and meals to match from a menu that draws the beautiful people. The cognoscenti order a traditional yet offbeat specialty (traditionally not listed on the menu) of spaghetti primavera—one of the city's better versions of this trendy dish. The restaurant is located in the Mayfair Hotel. It is closed Sun. AE, DC, CB.

Le Cygne. 53 E. 54th St.; 759–5941. This is the best of the newer restaurants spawned by La Caravelle. Its imaginative and well-executed dishes include an unusual appetizer of mussels in mustard sauce and whole braised pigeon. The desserts, too, are excellent. The atmosphere can be somewhat stuffy. Closed Sunday and month of August. No CB.

Le Madrigal. 216 E. 53rd St.; 355–0322. A favorite with the publishing crowd, this is one of New York's finest restaurants. Murals of 18th-century troubadours add a musical touch to this small restaurant. Closed Sunday; dinner only Saturday. AE.

Lutèce. 249 E. 50th St.; 752–2225. Probably the most ambitious and elaborate French food served in the United States. And almost as important, the pinnacle of perfection that has been achieved has not engendered the sort of pompous rudeness that is so much a part of the scene at other New York restaurants of this genre. The staff is almost uniformly pleasant, and aids immeasurably the consummate enjoyment of a unique dinner. The setting, in a former townhouse, is intimate and exquisite. If you only have the time (or budget) for one foray into fine French gastronomy, let us recommend Lutèce. Closed Saturday during the summer, closed Sunday throughout the year. AE.

Quo Vadis. 26 E. 63rd St.; 838–0590. Another superb restaurant of a singular standard. Gets its share of socialites who like the relaxed atmosphere in the two resplendent dining rooms decked with fresh flowers. Clams, oysters, eels in a special green sauce, and filet of beef in pastry crust are good samples of the haute cuisine. Fine wines and superb service. Steak and rack of lamb rank with the best around. Closed Sunday. All major credit cards.

Restaurant Raphael. 33 W. 54th St.; 582–8993. Considered by many to be the best argument for the *nouvelle cuisine*, Raphael hides behind elegantly understated doors, and is strictly by reservation only. Closed Saturday for lunch, and Sunday. Also closed the month of August. AE, DC.

Deluxe

Brussels. 115 E. 54th St.; 758-0457. Turn-of-the-century townhouse with walnut paneling, heavy chandeliers, and soft lights turning on to Old World ambience make Brussels *très haute,* posh, and perhaps a bit self-important. Belgian specialties—what else?—are features on a menu that also includes French haute cuisine and selected lofty Italian dishes. The food is first-rate, the atmosphere is rich and plush and the prices match. Superb wine list. Closed Sunday. All major credit cards.

Café Argenteuil. 253 E. 52nd St.; 753-9273. Notable are *quiche Lorraine, canard aux pêches,* and *bouillabaisse.* Fine wine cellar. One of the best purveyors of haute cuisine in the city. Don't miss the chocolate mousse in this small, très French bistro. Closed Sunday, dinner. No CB.

Café Nicholson. 323 E. 58th St.; 355-6769. An unusual restaurant in an unusual locale under the Queensboro (59th St.) Bridge. Prix fixe dinner includes wine. Superlative chocolate soufflé. Added attraction is the Rolls Royce that whisks you back to your hotel. Tips included on your check. Ceiling fans, potted palms, and turn-of-the-century antiques help take your mind off the price. Open for dinner Tuesday through Friday. AE, CB, DC.

Chanterelle. 89 Grand St. in SoHo; 966-6960. Don't let the location—a seemingly deserted warehouse corner in SoHo—scare you off, because Chantarelle is celebrated as one of the most adventurous and interesting of *nouvelle cuisine* haunts—even if some of the more experimental taste combinations don't always work. Meals are served in a spare, spacious dining room under a tin ceiling in a landmark building. The staff is haughty but knowledgeable and the ambience the new chic. Dinner Monday through Saturday. AE, MC, V.

Claude's. 205 E. 81st St.; 472-0487. Deep-red panels, bright metal and glass provide a handsome setting in this elaborate restaurant located in two remodeled brownstones. Everything is à la carte and worth ordering, especially the beef, veal, and lamb dishes. Closed for vacation in July. Dinner Tuesday through Saturday in August, Monday through Saturday thereafter. AE.

Clos Normand. 42 E. 52nd St.; 753-3348. Has beautiful murals and tiles by Jean Pages to spark the handsome provincial decor of the dining rooms. The atmosphere is pure Normandy. *Canard* (duck) served with figs, and a classic crab quiche, are the specialties. You might also care to try the Norman cider. Closed Sunday. No MC.

La Cocotte. 147 E. 60th St.; 832-8972. A charming and unpretentious restaurant opposite Bloomingdale's. An excellent pâté is served, and there are also some very good veal dishes among 24 specialties offered. Closed Sunday. All major cards.

La Colombe d'Or. 134 E. 26th St.; 689-0666. Informal country atmosphere in a small establishment featuring *bouillabaisse, cassoulet,* and other Provençal specialties. Dinner only Saturday and Sunday. Closed Sunday in the summer. AE, DC, MC, V.

La Petite Ferme. Lexington Ave. at 70th St.; 249-3272. The owner/chef is the scion of Burgundian restaurateurs and hoteliers, and the food is simple and well-prepared Reserve well ahead for a table at what looks like a prosperous farmhouse with a garden to boot. Closed Sunday. AE, MC.

La Rôtisserie Française. 153 E. 52nd St.; 759-1685. Good French food cooked fast on a spit, with partitions making a large room look more attractive than it is. But at relatively reasonable prices, who's looking too hard. Open for lunch and dinner Monday through Saturday with dinner only served Sunday after 5:00 P.M. AE, MC, CB, V.

La Tulipe. 104 W. 13th St.; 691-8860. Housed in the street level of a brownstone on a tree-lined Greenwich Village block overflowing with Continental restaurants. This rather small, trendy place, however, surprises with its emphasis on good *nouvelle cuisine*. Dinner Tuesday through Sunday. AE, MC, DC, V.

Laurent. 111 E. 56th St.; 753-2729. Grand food in the grand French style of haute cuisine, with prices to match. Closed Sunday. AE, DC.

Le Chanteclair. 18 E. 49th St.; 355-8998. Authentic French cuisine is the hallmark of this small, cozy restaurant whose mural of La Place de La Concorde gives the feeling of a Paris café. Owned by the Dreyfus brothers, who dominated French auto racing in the 1930s. The veal and beef dishes are particularly good. Closed Sunday. All major credit cards.

Le Lavandou. 134 E. 61st St.; 838-7987. Because the restaurant is small, and the tables close together, it can get pleasantly hectic when crowded—and it usually is because the food is up to the best around. Closed Sunday. AE.

Le Manoir. 120 E. 56th St.; 753-1447. The elegant French provincial decor complements a superb kitchen whose dishes, though unpretentious, are often outstanding. The poached bass and chicken in red wine are excellent, and there is an interesting offering of desserts to go along with the ten main courses. Closed Sun. All major credit cards.

Le Périgord. 405 E. 52nd St.; 755-6244. One of the finest midtown restaurants. *Gratin de langoustines*—crayfish in a cheese sauce—is one of the specialties on the varied menu. Closed Sunday, dinner only Sat. (Sister restaurant, **Le Périgord-Park** at 575 Park Ave.; 752-0050.) All major credit cards.

Le Petite Marmite. 5 Mitchell Pl. off First Ave. at 49th St.; 826-1084. Intimate and pleasantly appointed. Its location makes it a favorite of diplomatic laborers at the UN. Closed Sunday. All major credit cards.

Expensive

Cafe des Artistes. 1 W. 67th St.; 877-3500. Amusing 1930s decor and famous Howard Chandler Christie murals on the wall may transport you to another time and place, though the food is at its best when most simply prepared. Try the duckling with pear, the gravlax, or the desserts bearing not too-fancy names. Reserve days ahead for dinner, but this restaurant has lots of regulars, so don't be surprised if even then you don't get a good table. However, no one will raise so much as an eyebrow if all you want is an appetizer and a salad—which often suffices here—or if you'd care to eat at the small but cozy back-room bar. Open seven days a week, with brunch on weekends. All major credit cards.

Château Richelieu. 48 E. 52nd St.; 751-6565. Elegant and friendly reception for newcomers as well as regulars. Excellent fish dishes as well as usual haute cuisine favorites. Traditional atmosphere and the kind of courteous service that used to be common in all superior establishments. Closed Sunday, most holidays, the month of August. All major credit cards.

French Shack. 65 W. 55th St.; 246–5126. One of the finest French establishments in the city at this price, with food that is far above average. The only objections are the crowds and the occasionally slow service. All major credit cards.

La Bibliothèque. 341 E. 43rd St.; 661–5757. French provincial food, but the best part is the place itself, with books on the walls—of course—and a magnificent view of the UN. Great for a midafternoon drink or snack. Outdoor dining in good weather. Closed Sunday. All major credit cards.

La Grillade. 845 Eighth Ave. near 51st St.; 265–1610. Its owners are all from Brittany, assuring authenticity in their many Breton dishes. The duck, as well as the roast lamb with flageolets, are especially good. Friendly service. Lunch and dinner Monday through Friday, dinner only Saturday/Sunday. AE, DC, MC, V.

Le Petite Auberge. 116 Lexington Ave. at 28th St.; 689–5003. Pleasant inn-like surroundings. *Blanquette de veau* at lunch on Wednesday or Thursday sometimes; ask for it. The management came from the nearby Mon Paris. AE.

Le Cheval Blanc. 145 E. 45th St.; 599–8886. The food is excellent at this family-run restaurant, and its bargain status at lunch generates quite a crowd. It's best, therefore, to sample the fare at odd hours. Must reserve. Be prompt, with no one missing from your party. Not so much of a bargain at dinner. Closed Sunday, most holidays. No CB.

Le Moal. 942 Third Ave. near 56th St.; 688–8860. A long-time favorite, has pleasantly decorated dining rooms downstairs and upstairs. The family personally supervise the kitchen and the service. Provincial French cuisine has Breton overtones. The *moules marinière* are justifiably renowned. All major credit cards.

Le Paris Bistro. 48 Barrow St. in the Village; 989–5460. Next to the Greenwich House Music School, the restaurant is very comfortable, with garden dining in the back in season. *Steak au poivre* is a good bet. Dinner only. All major credit cards.

Le Vert Galant. 109 W. 46th St.; 582–7989. Very friendly, unhurried service in an elegant setting. Divine cheesecake, tender veal *piccata* and other house specials. Trio in lounge Wednesday through Saturday. Closed Sunday. AE, DC.

Les Pyrénées. 251 W. 51st St.; 246–0044. Has a pleasant Gallic atmosphere and serves provincial French food. Though the menu is familiar, *quiche Lorraine* and ham in aspic are worth trying. A good choice for theater-goers. Closed Sunday. No CB.

L'Olivier. 248 E. 49th St. near Second Ave.; 355–1810. In a converted brownstone, with cozy bar and tables downstairs (enclosed garden room in back in season), and a high-ceilinged room upstairs. Chef is owner. Try the *cassoulet maison*. Upper expensive range. Closed Saturday/Sunday. No CB.

Mon Paris. 111 E. 29th St.; 683–4255. Small, unpretentious, and popular. Serves that relative rarity these days: unabashed *cuisine bourgeoise*. Closed Sunday in summer.

Raoul's. 180 Prince St. in SoHo; 966–3518. The spirit of a genuine French bistro despite the neon beer signs in the window and the falling-apart-at-the-seams decor (that contrasts sharply with the high prices). Friendly place where you can eat at the bar or at tables. Dinner only. MC, V, AE.

The Terrace. 119th St. and Morningside Drive; 666–9490. On the top of Columbia University's Butler Hall, very good view of New York skyline, with good food and (usually) live chamber music. Good place for a romantic dinner. Dinner only, closed Mondays. Major credit cards.

Moderate

Crêpe Suzette. 313 W. 46th St.; 581–9717 or 974–9002. A little bistro that couldn't be plainer, but the food is well-prepared and portions ample. Breton crêpes are a specialty. Tiny bar, small wine list. Closed Sunday. AE.

Le Biarritz. 325 W. 57th St.; 245–9467. An unprepossessing restaurant with copper cookware on the walls and fresh flowers at each table, and where the kitchen turns out excellent peasant soups and seafood. The seafood-stuffed crêpe Biarritz is superb. Open seven days but for dinner only Saturday/Sunday from 5:00 P.M. AE, DC, V.

Le Bistro. 827 Third Ave. near 50th St.; 759–5933. Small and informal, provincial in spirit. A blackboard menu lists specialties of the day. Closed Sunday, dinner only Saturday. All major credit cards.

Madame Romaine De Lyon. 32 E. 61st St.; 758–2422. Would you believe 500 different kinds of omelettes? Also fine salads and fresh croissants. Open only for lunch Monday through Saturday, 11:00 A.M. to 3:30 P.M. Closed Sunday, most holidays and month of August. No credit cards.

Pierre Au Tunnel. 250 W. 47th St.; 582–2166. Has unusual decor resembling an actual tunnel. It's small and unpretentious, and has the familiar French menu with different specialties added each day. Good choice when heading to the theater. Closed Sunday. AE.

Inexpensive

La Crêpe. Various locations around the city, one most convenient to midtown at 57 W. 56th St., 247–1136; another near Lincoln Center on Broadway at 67th St., 874–6900. Menu of 100 different kinds of crêpes is offered. Excellent place for an inexpensive lunch, a quickie dinner or after-theater snack. AE, DC.

GERMAN

Moderate

Café Geiger. 206 E. 86th St.; 734–4428. A retail bakery in front, Continental-style café and restaurant in back. All major credit cards.

Kleine Konditorei. 234 E. 86th St.; 737–7130. Simple, homey dinner with everything from steak smothered in fried onions to different veal schnitzels ordered à la carte or as a dinner. Huge portions come adorned with several side dishes; friendly, informal service. AE, DC.

Inexpensive

Bavarian Inn. 232 E. 86th St.; 650–1056. Besides all the good, solid German fare and plentiful portions that you would expect from a *gemütlich* bar and restaurant (the restaurant rooms are open to the bar but raised above it), there is live zither music in the evenings. Major credit cards.

Ideal Lunch and Bar. 238 E. 86th St.; 650–1632. While this place looks like a shoe-repair shop converted to a lunch counter. it is by far the best food bargain on the Upper East Side. No credit cards.

GREEK

Moderate

Estia. 308 E. 68th St.; 628–9100. Fresh and simple Greek food, live music at 10:30 or so. All major credit cards.

Idra. 166 W. 4th St. in the Village; 691–5667. The atmosphere here is decidedly Greek taverna on both floors, enhanced by live entertainment. The menu features traditional Greek fare well-prepared and pleasantly served. No CB.

Molfetas. 307 W. 47th St.; 840–9594. Combination cafeteria-restaurant with simple decor, informal service, many lamb dishes and several simple fish dishes broiled with oil and lemon. Stock up on the Greek "caviar" (*taramasalata*) —tasty stuffed grapevine leaves.

Pantheon. 689 Eighth Ave. near 44th St.; 664–8294. Lemon soup and macaroni-based dishes are good in this popular gathering place close to the theater district. Lamb dishes are plentiful but tend to be overcooked, so consider the homemade yogurt, fit for the dieting gods. No CB.

Sirocco. 29 E. 29th St.; 683–9409. Greek-Israeli restaurant with musical revue, Mediterranean dishes. $6.00 minimum except Saturday when it is $10.00. Closed Monday. No CB.

Inexpensive

Acropolis. 767 Eighth Ave. near 47th St.; 581–2733. Fish dishes good, lamb dishes ample, stuffed grape leaves abound and the price—cheap—is right if you are in the theater district. DC.

Z. 117 E. 15th St.; 254–0960. Price not even withstanding, Z is often hailed as the best Greek food stop in the city. You might begin with the cheese-and-spinach appetizer—*spanakopita*—which is excellent at this pleasant, unassuming Greek restaurant where everything is served à la carte. The salads are superbly fresh and the lamb typically well prepared. Sandwiches, too, are offered and, weather permitting, there is dining in the garden. It happens also to be a favorite among budget-watching gourmands. Closed Monday. No credit cards.

HAWAIIAN
Moderate

Hawaii-Kai. 1638 Broadway near 50th St.; 757–0900. Polynesian, Chinese, American cuisine in touristy South Sea setting. All major credit cards.

Trader Vic's. Plaza Hotel, Fifth Ave. at 59th St.; 355–5185. Touristy but respectable, as befits the Plaza. All major credit cards.

HUNGARIAN
Moderate

Csarda. 1477 Second Ave. near 77th St.; 472–2892. Bright, clean, uncluttered, with good food served tavern-style. Dinner only. AE.

Green Tree. 1034 Amsterdam Ave. at 111th St.; 864–9106. Hungarian food with a Columbian accent—Columbia University, that is—is served at this family-style place where the decor is virtually nonexistent but the meals are substantial. If you are looking for home-style chicken *paprikàs*, stuffed cabbage, or noodles stop by—but never on Sunday, when it is closed. No credit cards.

Jacques' Tik Tak. 210 E. 58th St.; 753–5513. Goulash, stuffed cabbage or chicken paprikash, excellent *palacsintas* for dessert. The real specialty is the veal shank. Continental touches on the menu can be surprisingly good, service is attentive, and the trio fiddling away on Hungarian instruments can be downright romantic. All major credit cards.

Red Tulip. 439 E. 75th St.; 734–4893. Small, simply decorated, crowded, and offering live music with dinner, this is a good spot for stuffed cabbage, chicken, varied paprika dishes and strudel. Closed Monday and Tuesday. AE.

Inexpensive

Magic Pan. 149 E. 57th St.; 371–3266. Both Hungarian and French crêpes served. Soup, salad, and steak kebab is also available. Lunch is liable to be crowded but the dinner hour is much quieter. AE, MC, V.

Tip Top. 1489 Second Ave. (between 77th and 78th Sts.); 650–0723. This small, family restaurant is an outstanding value—complete home-cooked meals can be had for $4.00 or less. Stuffed cabbage or goulash and noodles can be topped off with *palacsinta*, thin Hungarian pancakes filled with fruit.

INDIAN/BENGALI
Expensive

Gaylord's. 50 E. 58th St.; 759–1710. This stunning restaurant serves Indian food unlike any you've ever tasted. It is one of the few U.S. restaurants we know of with a real tandoori oven from which emerge succulent baked delights and a marvelous bread called *nan*. Among the individual delectables are lamb in spinach sauce, chicken with a yogurt curry, mint chutney and, most surprising, a dessert tray full of Indian goodies. Dinner is served seven days a week; lunch Monday through Friday. All major credit cards.

RESTAURANTS

Nirvana. 30 Central Park South; 752-0270. The view from this penthouse restaurant overlooking Central Park is nothing short of spectacular. The window tables are romantic beyond belief but all are set beneath *shamianas*, multicolored tents, where you can feast on Indo-Bengali delights including tandoori and curries. The fare is likely to be no less spicy than the place is colorful so beware if yours is a tender palate. Unfortunately, spicy or not, the food is not up to the surroundings. No credit cards.

Raga. 57 W. 48th St.; 757-3450. One of the most beautifully decorated Indian restaurants in America, occupying the site of the old Forum of the Twelve Caesars. Most well-known Indian specialties, including a superb assortment of breads, stuffed or otherwise. Ancient musical intruments are part of the decorative charm. Live Indian music some evenings. Closed Sunday. All major credit cards.

Shezan. 8 W. 58th St.; 371-1414. Lots of mirrors, chrome, glass bricks, and carpeted walls (from the designers who created the Four Seasons) meet you when you descend a flight of steps at the New York address for this famed London and Indian mini-chain. The food is uneven—too often prepared ahead and heated upon your arrival—but if you make your wishes known the Pakistani-Indian cuisine will come out first-rate. Waiters will also gladly oblige to help you order and share the likes of the shrimp and vegetable curries, tandoori chicken and lamb kebabs. Closed Sunday. Dinner only on Saturday. All major credit cards.

Tandoor India. 40 E. 49th St.; 752-3334. One of the most beautiful and best Indian restaurants in the city—even though the curries are toned down to suit the American taste. Try the tandoori chicken, Indian breads, *pakhoras* (vegetable fritters), and *samosas* (sweetened pastries). Sometimes a more economical buffet. Closed Sunday. All major credit cards.

Moderate

Akbar India. 475 Park Ave. at 58th St.; 838-1717. Tandoor (clay-oven) items are featured at this attractive restaurant serving food from the northern part of the country. They tone down the spiciness to suit the American palate but will spice the dishes up upon request. A mixed plate offers opportunity to sample a little of everything. Open seven days a week, dinner only on Sunday. No CB.

Bombay Palace. 30 W. 52nd St.; 541-7777. A large midtown restaurant quite popular with Indian businesspeople. There is a buffet lunch available as well as à la carte dishes. All major credit cards.

Madras Woodlands. 310 E. 44th St.; 986-0620. Indian food, southern-style, which means lots of vegetable dishes, with delicious breads and good pancakes. All major credit cards.

Mahal. 119 Lexington Ave. at 28th St.; 689-5150. Restaurant of very contemporary design, on two floors with a waterfall running through both, serves authentic and rather out-of-ordinary dishes. The chicken Moghlai is a good middle-of-the-road choice on a first visit. There is a "businessman's buffet" at lunch. All major credit cards.

Shalimar of India. 39 E. 29th St.; 889-1977. A wide selection of Indian cuisine ranges from hot curries (*vindaloo*) to mild cream-style curry (*murghum* *masala*), from *mulligatawny,* a spiced lentil soup, to a delicately flavored coconut soup. And the Indian breads are excellent. All major credit cards.

Inexpensive

Ceylon India Inn. 148 W. 49th St.; 730–9293. Has been deservedly popular for over forty years and noted for its curries and Indian specialties. Quiet, exotic setting in the upstairs restaurant. Special complete dinners at fixed prices and à la carte. AE, DC.

Kashmir. 10 W. 46th St.; 730–9201. Though plain, this is a pleasant place for Indian and Pakistani cuisine. Curries and tandoori chicken are among the specialties prepared by the owner-chef. Complete lunches and dinners as well as à la carte. But be prepared for some of the spicier food around. All major credit cards.

Mitali. 334 E. 6th St.; 533–2508. One of about a dozen small, family-run Indian restaurants on the block (there are many more on First and Second Aves.), with excellent curries, typically ethnic decor and recorded music, and friendly, attentive service. AE.

There are a number of very inexpensive but—for the price—quite good Indian fast-food shops on or around Lexington Ave. from 26th St. to 29th St., in "Little India." While some of them are quite shabby-looking, don't be put off, as they offer some of the best food bargains in Manhattan, among them **Shaheen Sweets** at 99 Lexington Ave. at 27th St.

IRISH

Moderate

Eamonn Doran. 988 Second Ave. near 53rd St.; 752–8088. Muzaked and carpeted, an Irish pub gone Continental. Exhaustive list of imported beers, pleasant food, good service. All major credit cards.

Irish Pavilion. 130 E. 57th St.; 759–9040. In addition to the authentically Irish fare of Irish smoked salmon, Galway ham, or Dublin Bay prawns, Irish products—woolens, rugs, linens—are displayed and sold. The menu is à la carte and other savory entrées include generous chicken, beef, and lamb pies. No CB.

Landmark Tavern. 626 Eleventh Ave. near 47th St.; 757–8595. With a pot-bellied stove and mahogany bar, this century-old tavern offers charm and an unpretentious bill of fare. Dine heartily on homemade soda bread, shepherd's pie, and Irish potato soup. No credit cards.

Inexpensive

Costello's. 225 E. 44th St.; 599–9614. Renowned with the newspaper crowd for good food, conversation. (This is a new location for the famous old joint with the Thurber murals.)

Limerick's. 573 Second Ave. near 32nd St.; 683–4686. Brick walls and decor that might best be described as Irish miscellaneous make this an American idea of a typical Irish pub. But they do feature corned beef and cabbage and authentic Irish soda bread. Closed Saturday during the summer and on holiday weekends. No lunch Saturday. All major credit cards.

RESTAURANTS

Londonderry Pub. 134 W. 51st St.; 974–9077. Hearty pub atmosphere. All major credit cards.

McBell's. 359 Sixth Ave. near W. 4th St., in the Village; 675–6260. Red-checkered tableclothes, brick walls and antique lights make this not quite Dublin but more than just another Irish pub, especially if you stick to the simple fare such as Irish ham and bacon and stew served in a congenial atmosphere. No credit cards.

Rosie O'Grady's. 151 W. 51st St.; 582–2975. Irish and Continental specialties with kitchen open 'til 2:00 A.M., music seven nights. All major credit cards.

ITALIAN

Deluxe

Alfredo. 240 Central Park South (which is 59th St. across from the park); 246–7050. Northern Italian specialties that naturally begin with fettucine Alfredo. The location is relatively new, but its reputation for high quality is long standing—even if the reality does not often live up to that mark. Closed Sun. All major credit cards.

Antolotti's. 337 E. 49th St.; 688–6767. A conventional northern Italian menu, with items exceedingly well prepared. Service is first-rate, and the specialties are the veal and pasta dishes. No lunch served Saturday/Sunday. All major credit cards.

Barbetta. 321 W. 46th St. in the theater district; 246–9171. The most luxurious of the Italian restaurants, with its 18th-century furnishings and gorgeous crystal chandelier. Northern Italian cuisine, sometimes indifferently prepared, anf the best of wines are featured—and have been for over 75 years. Beautiful cocktail lounge and bar. Outdoor garden dining in season, but ask for seating downstairs when reserving indoors. Many romantic triangles are cemented here. Closed Sun. No DC.

Giambelli Albert. 238 Madison Ave. near 36th St.; 685–8727. The food is Northern Italian, delicate, refined, cooked with butter instead of olive oil, and light on garlic and tomatoes. The result is excellent pastas. Closed Sunday, and during the summer months, Sat. as well. All major credit cards.

Giambelli Fiftieth. 46 E. 50th St.; 688–2760. Good veal, fish, and pastas—but as expensive as the restaurant is ornate. Yet this Giambelli's is big with visiting Italian dignitaries and brass from Italy's tourism office, so they must be doing something right. Closed Sun. No DC.

Girafe. 208 E. 58th St.; 752–3054. On two levels, connected by a long, thin spiral staircase so it resembles its namesake, this restaurant provides a supper-club setting for savory pastas, especially the fettucine and carbonara. Closed Sunday. No CB.

Mercurio. 53 W. 53rd St.; 586–4370. A very popular establishment with excellent service—and food that is only slightly less so. The veal kidney and the fettucine Alfredo are good bets. closed Sunday all of July, Saturday in August. All major credit cards.

Nanni Il Valletto. 133 E. 61st St.; 838-3939. An offshot of the excellent original Nanni's on 46th St. (697-4161), and somehow Nanni manages to keep on top of both places—but Il Valletto is much the posher of the two and less noisy (and with less character). Closed Sunday. All major credit cards.

Orsini's. 41 W. 56th St.; 757-1698. Presents northern Italian and Roman cuisine in an elegant atmosphere. The back room is most romantic, with love seats and candlelight. This restaurant has a very stylish following and many executives take their protegés here for a discreet late dinner. Closed Sunday. All major credit cards.

Pietro's. 201 E. 45th St.; 682-9760. The steaks here are as good as in any house and the Italian dishes also rank with the best. Housed in two crowded floors of a former speakeasy. The New York atmosphere here is not to everyone's taste. No credit cards.

Romeo Salta. 30 W. 56th St.; 246-5772. This remarkable restaurant in a spacious former mansion is handsomely decorated. The extraordinary pastas are conscientiously prepared and the veal Villa d'Este with eggplant is outstanding. A large menu offers a wide choice of carefully prepared and attentively served dishes. Closed Sunday. All major credit cards.

San Marco. 36 W. 52nd St.; 246-5340. Northern Italian cuisine in a small, smart room decorated with a display of wines. Veal and chicken dishes and made-at-the-table *zabaglione* are special, as are the sweetbreads in white wine. Closed Sunday. AE, CB, DC.

SPQR. 133 Mulberry St.; 431-7610. Elegant but hardly understated turn-of-the-century dining room in the heart of Little Italy, where classic Northern and Southern Italian cuisine is served for lunch and dinner. Initials stand for *Senatus Populus Que Romanus* (the senate and people of Rome). Upstairs night club features dancing and name entertainment. Valet parking for dinner. All major credit cards.

Tre Scalini. 230 E. 58th St.; 688-6888. The mural of the Piazza Navona makes you feel as though you were in Rome, the pastas make you think you *are* there. It is a flashy modern dining room for Northern Italian cuisine that could hold its own on the Via Veneto. Closed Sun. All major credit cards.

Expensive

Bruno. 240 E. 58th St.; 688-4190. Simple modern dining room with a country atmosphere—and outstanding pastas, from linguine matriciana with tomato sauce, prosciutto and onion, to trenette in pesto (basil) sauce. Closed Saturday, dinner only on Sunday. All major credit cards.

Capriccio Ristorante. 11 W. 56th St.; 757-7795. On one of New York's busiest restaurant thoroughfares. Family operated, featuring fuzi Angela—a flat pasta that is chief among the many pasta specialties. Closed Sunday. All major credit cards.

DaSilvano. 260 Sixth Ave. south of Bleecker in the Village; 982-0090. Smartly trim storefront with excellent pasta dishes, from quill-cut penne in a Bolognese sauce to tortellini with a spicy meat filling. Very small place; must reserve. Dining out front in good weather. No credit cards.

RESTAURANTS

Gian Marino. 221 E. 58th St.; 752–1696. Fair food from six provinces of Italy; popular among show-business folk. Closed Monday. All major credit cards.

Il Monello. 1460 Second Ave. near 77th St.; 535–9310. A restful setting for some of the best pasta on the East Side, especially the green lasagne, tortellini, and thin pasta strands in a Bolognese meat sauce. Closed Sun. All major credit cards.

Il Nido. 251 E. 53rd St.; 753–8450. A stylish and currently very fashionable restaurant with provincial overtones—and some of the best ravioli and fettucine this side of Tuscany. The back room is noisy. Closed Sunday. AE, DC, V.

Isle of Capri. 1028 Third Ave. near 61st St.; 223–9430. Generally acknowledged as one of the best Italian restaurants in the city, though it can be very uneven. A "trattoria"-style operation where the food's the thing. Sidewalk café. Closed Sunday. AE, DC, V.

Italian Pavilion. 24 W. 55th St.; 586–5950. Owned by the same people who run Quo Vadis and in the same league. Closed Sunday. All major credit cards.

La Strada East. 274 Third Ave. near 22nd St.; 473–3760. Friendly, informal atmosphere where you may enjoy well-prepared food that includes all manner of pastas, veal, beef, and some unusual dishes. Closed Sunday, dinner only on Saturday. AE, CB, DC.

Monsignore II, 61 E. 55th St.; 355–2070. Strolling guitarist, romantic ambience, good food. Closed Sunday. All major credit cards.

Nanni's. 146 E. 46th St.; 697–4161. Excellent Northern Italian cuisine that reaches its highest standards in the tortellini and chicken Valdostana. The same owner runs Nanni Al Valletto. Closed Sunday. All major credit cards.

Patsy's. 236 W. 56th St.; 247–3491. Noted for its Neapolitan food and friendly atmosphere. Simple, cheerful surroundings. Many different pastas, but the stuffed shells are unusual in this bright, two-story restaurant that offers choice of 35 main courses. Closed Monday. AE, DC.

Per Bacco. 140 E. 27th St.; 532–8699. Possibly because it is a bit out of the way, this Northern Italian restaurant (the Trieste region) is one of the unsung stars of dining out in New York; but the daily specialties are the thing. Major credit cards.

Piccolo Mondo. 1269 First Ave. near 69th St., on the Upper East Side; 249–3141. Very good Northern Italian fare. The scampi here is among the best in the city. Overdecorated, though, and loud. Closed Mon. No V.

Poletti's. 2315 Broadway at 84th St.; 580–1200. If there is such a thing as an Upper West Side style, this restaurant—along with Teacher's—exemplifies it. Pastas are made on the premises, and the pastas are what you should go for here—rather than the overpriced main dishes. All major credit cards.

Roma di Notte. 137 E. 55th St.; 832–1128. Appeals to the eye. Stunning Roman decor in bar and cocktail lounge and dimly lit dining room. Dazzling array of appetizers, chicken Nero, rollatine of veal, fettucine are among many choices. They do a lot of cooking over a flaming rotisserie—none of which is terribly distinguished. No credit cards.

Sal Anthony's. 55 Irving Place near 17th St.; 982–9030. Go up a few stairs into a large, spacious, well-decorated room and you enter a restaurant that serves as delicate a tomato sauce as can be found this side of Florence. Excellent pastas and eggplant. All major credit cards.

Salta in Bocca. 179 Madison Ave. near 33rd St.; 684–1757. A pleasant if undistinguished-looking dining room, where the excellent pasta is what catches your attention, especially the green-and-white fettucine casalinga. Very noisy, with tables close together. Closed Sun. All major credit cards.

37th Street Hideaway. 32 W. 37th St.; 947–8940. Italian-American specialties in John D. Barrymore's former townhouse, After-theater suppers until midnight. Closed Sunday. No V.

Trastevere. 309 E. 83rd St.; 734-6343. Small, intimate, rushed, named for a section of Rome renowned for its restaurants—and lives up to its name. AE.

Moderate

Alfredo the Original of Rome. Citicorp Center, 54th St. at Third Ave.; 371–3367. The name tells the whole story, but surprisingly, the pasta is excellent. Slightly hectic service at lunch, so try in evening. All major credit cards.

Amalfi. 16 E. 48th St.; 758–5110. Established 1927 and as Italian as the Amalfi Drive. All major credit cards.

Angelina's. 41 Greenwich Ave. in the Village; 929–1255. A homey sort of place, unpretentious as far as decor and menu. The same à la carte menu is used for lunch and dinner. Veal parmigiana, shrimp marinara, and breaded pork chops are popular entrées. AE, DC.

Angelo of Mulberry Street; 146 Mulberry St.; 226–8527. Deep in the heart of "Little Italy." The pastas are a specialty, as is fish stew called *zuppa di pesce*. No credit cards.

Antolotti's. 337 E. 48th St.; 688–6767. Established in 1950 and improving with age. No V.

Caffè da Alfredo. 17 Perry St., just off Seventh Ave. in the Village; 989–7028. Roman and Northern Italian dishes. The service is casual, in the spirit of the restaurant in general, but friendly and efficient. The special pastas, changed daily, are among the best in the city, and these should be prime among your choices. Reservations must be made a few days in advance, and you must be punctual. Bring your own wine. Jackets and/or ties are unnecessary. Closed Mon. AE. (This is a better bet than the **Trattoria da Alfredo** of the same ownership, at 90 Bank St., 929–4400, which is closed Tuesdays and requires reservations weeks ahead. There is also the **Tavola Calda da Alfredo,** 285 Bleecker St. near Seventh Ave., 924–4789, which does serve wine.)

Eleonora Ristorante. 117 W. 58th St.; 765–1427. Northern Italian cuisine in a lavish theatrical setting celebrating the great Duse. After-theater suppers a specialty. Closed Sunday. All major credit cards.

Forlini's. 93 Baxter St. in the vicinity of Canal St.; 349–6779. Red sauce cooking with finesse. No V.

Gino's. 780 Lexington Ave. near 61st St.; 223–9658. The food is good, though hardly extraordinary, yet this restaurant is very fashionable for models, fashion buyers, photographers, and their camp followers. Being seen is obviously more important than the quality of the cuisine. AE, MC, V.

Il Gattopardo. 45 W. 56th St; 586–3978. Just as you'd expect a restaurant in Milan or Turin to look. Excellent service, very good food. Closed Sunday. All major credit cards.

Marchi's. 251 E. 31st St.; 679–2494. In an old brownstone, has a long-time reputation for its many-course dinner at fixed price. You eat whatever the host has selected for the day. Reservations recommended. Closed for lunch and on Sunday. AE.

Mona Lisa. 936 Second Ave. (50th St.); 421–4497. Dine in a skylight garden, with hearty cuisine, very good service. Closed Sun. AE, DC, CB.

Parioli Romanissimo. 1466 First Ave. near 76th St.; 288–2391. Small, gaudy, but terrific cannelloni and tortellini. Closed Sunday and Monday. AE, DC, CB.

Parma. 1404 Third Ave. at 80th St.; 535–3520. With its plain piperack decor, Parma sets an informal mood that lets one get down to the serious business of wrestling with some of the best pasta this side of, well, Parma. Dinner only, daily.

Patrissy's. 98 Kenmare St. in Little Italy; 226–8509. Friendly, informal, long-established Neapolitan restaurant, where everything is à la carte and you need a cart to carry off what you can't finish from their first-rate pastas. No CB.

Pete's Tavern. 129 E. 18th St.; 473–7676. The manicotti is the best thing on the menu, the tomato sauce not the most subtle. This is the tavern made famous by O. Henry. Very simple setting, with outdoor café in summer. Wonderful old-fashioned bar. All major credit cards.

Primavera Ristorante. 1570 First Ave., 81st St.; 861–8608. One of the best of the First Ave. storefront restaurants, especially the tortellini and fish dishes. Closed Sun. AE, DC, V.

Pronto Ristorante. Two branches: 801 Second Ave. at 43rd St., 687–4940; and 30 E. 60th St., 421–8151. Pasta made in front of your eyes; ultra-modern restaurant design and good Northern Italian dishes. No CB.

Rao's. 455 E. 114th St.; 534–9625. So tiny there were only six tables at last count, so out-of-the-way it is located in one of the city's most broken-down neighborhoods, but so "in" that the cognoscenti make the trip by car for some of the city's best homemade pastas. Dinner only. No credit cards.

Rocco. 181 Thompson St. in the Village; 677–0590. Neapolitan food, and very good—though the restaurant itself doesn't look very promising at first glance. Go here if you want the flavor of the Little Italy of times gone by. Major credit cards.

Trattoria. In the Pan Am Building. 45th St. between Vanderbilt and Lexington Aves.; 661–3090. Informal, though strikingly decorated with Italy's colors and posters. Outdoor dining—but on the least tranquil sidestreet in New York. Closed Saturday/Sunday. All major credit cards.

Vesuvio. 163 W. 48th St.; 245–6138. An excellent Italian restaurant in the Broadway theater district. Muraled walls and background music provide a relaxed setting for sampling the tasteful and imaginative fare. Seafood and fish are especially commendable. Some à la carte entrées may be more expensive. Closed Sunday. No MC.

Via Margutta. 24 Minetta Lane in the Village; 254–7630. North Italian cuisine in neat, cozy quarters. The varied menu offers excellent shellfish, veal Margutta, and cannelloni Via Margutta. Wine served in attractive glass carafes. Complete lunches and dinners or à la carte. No CB.

Inexpensive

Bleecker Luncheonette. Corner Bleecker and Cornelia; no phone. Literally a luncheonette with counter seats and a handful of tables. The menu is limited to equally few items, but everything is prepared to order and with a careful hand. The pesto is outstanding when in season, the meatballs the best around and the manicotti is heavenly. Yet to eat $10.00 worth here is a challenge; given the quality it would be a bargain at twice the price. Closes at 7:00 P.M., but if you're on line at 6:59 they'll still seat and serve you with a smile. No credit cards.

Guido's. 511 Ninth Ave., at 39th St.; 244–9314. Hidden behind the storefront Supreme Macaroni Company (where you can indeed buy freshly made pasta), this is family-style southern Italian cooking—festive, well-prepared and served with a friendliness that is rare indeed. Don't be misled by the minimum $8.00 charge at dinner, because you'd really have to stuff yourself to surpass it by much. Great before theater, but be sure to have a reservation. No credit cards.

Manganaro's. 492 Ninth Ave. near 38th St.; 947–7325. The best place in New York for overstuffed Italian hero sandwiches—eggplant parmigiana, mixed cold cuts, sausage and peppers. Bustling at lunch and closes at 7:00 P.M., but always worth the trip. Closed Sun. No credit cards.

Monte's. 97 MacDougal St. in the Village; 674–9456. Down half a flight of steps from street level, this restaurant has provided good, solid, bountiful, and unpretentious Southern Italian fare to the local Italian-Americans, New York University faculty and plenty of other New Yorkers for a long time—and at better than reasonable prices. Closed Tuesday. No credit cards.

Perretti. 270 Columbus Ave., at 72nd St.; 362–3939. Bright, glass-enclosed neon-lit dining room popular among neighborhood denizens and those headed to Lincoln Center. No reservations, so be prepared to wait. Pizza also served. AE, MC, V.

Puglia's. 189 Hester St. in Little Italy; 226–8912. This is a place for partying. Seating is at long, camp-style tables, the homemade wine served by the bottle (beer by the pitcher), the hearty Southern fare a mite greasy at times—but once the little old lady begins her sing-along routines (weekends only) you won't even notice. No credit cards.

Umberto's Clam House. 129 Mulberry St. in Little Italy; 431–7545. Site of the infamous Joey Gallo underworld murder but a favorite fresh seafood place. Very informal, with sidewalk tables in summer and open very late. No credit cards.

Vincent's Clam Bar. 119 Mott St. in Little Italy; 226–8133. The home of hot and spicy tomato sauce. Try your spaghetti with it, with scungilli or calamari—and you get one roll. Informal. No credit cards.

JAMAICAN

Moderate

Jamaican Seafood Restaurant. 432 Sixth Ave. near 10th St. in the Village; 982-3260. What you might expect, featuring a kind of Jamaican bouillabaisse, and all the trimmings, including plantains. No CB.

JAPANESE

Expensive

Benihana of Tokyo. East: 120 E. 56th St.; 593-1627. Also **West:** 47 W. 56th St.; 581-0930 and **Palace:** 15 W. 44th St.; 682-7120. The show is what counts here, with a chef attending to every party (though parties are often grouped together) chopping, seasoning, and stir-frying over an open gas-heated grill. There's certainly better and more seriously traditional Japanese food around, but the spectacle involved is entertaining. All major credit cards.

Gibbon. 24 E. 80th St.; 861-4001. Combination of French and Japanese cuisines in a remodeled private house, with some dining on street level, but the main dining area is one flight up. Features good fish dishes. Open for lunch Monday through Friday, dinner seven days a week. No CB.

Hakubai. 66 Park Ave. at 38th St. (entrance on side street); 686-3770. In New York's only avowed Japanese hotel, the Kitano. Very comfortable, uses very best raw materials for all dishes (the key to Japanese cuisine); everything is good here. All major credit cards.

Inagiku. 111 E. 49th St. in the Waldorf Astoria; 355-0440. Excellent, authentic food in handsome restaurant, decorated in Japanese style—though a bit overstated. Same dishes available in three different areas—a special bar, grill room, and main dining room, with prices escalating accordingly. *Tempura, sukiyaki,* and seafood do Japan proud. Closed Sunday, dinner only on Saturday. All major credit cards.

Kabuki. 115 Broadway, downtown; 962-4677. This financial district restaurant typically attracts large Wall Street crowds for lunch, but the dinner is quiet, almost intimate. There are tatami rooms along one wall and regular Western tables in the center. Special banquet-style dinners and *donburi* lunches are offered. Serves lunch and dinner Monday through Friday. All major credit cards.

Kitcho of New York. 22 W. 46th St.; 575-8880. A favorite of the Japanese themselves. In addition to the usual *sukiyaki* and *tempura* fare so popular with Americans, there are a number of unusually prepared delicacies. Southern Japanese cuisine. Gentle, attentive service. Closed Saturday. Open 5:00 P.M. Sunday. AE, DC.

Nippon. 145 E. 52nd St.; 355-9020. Probably New York's most famous Japanese restaurant. Like a Japanese garden, complete with a stream. Tatami rooms are regular tables in an attractive setting. Unusual Japanese dishes are featured along with familiar *sukiyaki.* Cosy bar and cocktail lounge. *Tempura* and *sushi* bar for light meals. Closed Sunday. Dinner only on Saturday. All major credit cards.

Robata. 30 E. 61st St., 688–8120; and **SoHo Robata,** 143 Spring St. in SoHo, 431–3993. Waterwheel, hanging plants, walls covered with reeds, and interesting Japanese murals approximate a Japanese farmhouse. *Robata* means "open fire." They broil fish over an open fire after you make your selection from the counter. Meat, too. No CB.

Shinbashi. 280 Park Ave. at 48th St.; 661–3915. Tatami rooms where you sit on the floor, kimono-wearing waitresses, and Western-style items to go along with good Japanese beef or seafood grilled with vegetables make this large, somewhat austere place an interesting choice. Closed Sunday, dinner only on Saturday. All major credit cards.

Moderate

Hatsuhana. 17 E. 48th St.; 355–3345. Small, very busy, specializing in raw-fish preparation and seafood. Totally authentic. Closed Sun. All major credit cards.

Hisae's Lobster House. 13 E. 37th St.; 889–9820. Japanese-style fish restaurant that is popular with devotees of seafood and the new low-calorie vegetable style of cooking. Good red snapper and sea bass make you forget about the noise. Art Deco tiles on the long bar near the entrance, and glass-topped tables that have never seen Tokyo, let alone Kyoto. Closed Sunday. AE, MC, V.

Kamehachi. 14 E. 47th St.; 765–4737. Decor is not a feature of this restaurant, but good Japanese food is. There is a bar for sushi—raw fish on vinegar rice—and a complete selection of traditional specialties, including broiled eel and *tempura*. Closed Sunday. AE, DC.

Lenge. 202 Columbus Ave., a bit north of Lincoln Center at 69th St.; 874–8278. Enclosed sidewalk café, *sushi* bar, tatami mat area. Good *tempura*, passable raw fish, unexceptional *sukiyaki.* AE, DC.

Miyokawa. 23 W. 56th St.; 586–6899. A delightful restaurant that is usually crowded with Japanese businessmen. Excellent *sushi* bar, *tempura*, and other specialties. Tatami (mats on the floor) dining is available. All major cards.

Nakagawa. 7 W. 44th St.; 869–8077. Authentic in decor and atmosphere. Divided into two sections, with a *sushi* counter and small tables up front and, down a few steps, more tables—but slightly larger. The food is authentic Japanese. AE, MC, V.

Rock Garden of Tokyo. 34 W. 56th St.; 245–7936. Kimono-clad waitresses cook your meals at tables with gas-flamed grills in the center. You can try your hand at it, too, in a food-preparation style called "Yakiniku." No CB.

Saito. 305 E. 46th St.; 759–8897. A baker's dozen of main courses offered in three places—a *tempura* bar, a section where you can eat on the floor Japanese style, or one for dining at Western-size tables in *teriyaki, sukiyaki,* or *yakitori.* Closed Sunday, dinner only Saturday. No CB.

Take-Zushi. 11 E. 48th St.; 755–6534. Look for the green awning, and go up stairs to the second floor. Rates up there with the best *sushi* in New York. Need we say any more? Crowded at lunchtime. No CB.

RESTAURANTS

Inexpensive

Bizen. 171 Spring St. in SoHo; 966-0963. The combination of art gallery (featuring works by Japanese artists), naturally woody setting, imaginative food preparation and unlikely music (usually Mozart or jazz) all at very reasonable prices is what SoHo as a residential neighborhood can be at its best. Relaxed and most pleasant. AE.

Dan Tempura House. 2018 Broadway, at 71st St.; 877-4969. From the outside it looks like a tacky Japanese coffee shop, but inside is a consistently satisfying restaurant most popular for its (obviously) *tempura* and seafood casserole-type dishes. For dessert: deep-fried ice cream—and it's wonderful, not just a gimmick. Convenient to Lincoln Center. AE, MC, V.

Dosanko Larmen. 423 Madison Ave. at 47th St., 688-8575; 10 E. 52nd St., 759-6361; 341 Lexington Ave. at 39th St., 683-4740; 135 E. 45th St., 697-2967; 19 Murray St. near City Hall, 964-9696. Noodles in hot broth, with various trimmings, light and healthful. Super cheap. No credit cards.

Genroku Sushi. 366 Fifth Ave. near 34th St.; 947-7940. Sit around an enormous counter and pick your dishes off a perpetually moving conveyor belt. In addition to *sushi,* you can choose Japanese curry noodle and rice dishes, *tempura, sashimi, gyoza,* fried chicken, even soups and desserts. You are charged by the number of plates you take. Open seven days. Very cheap. No credit cards.

Mikado. 21 W. 39th St.; 840-7636. Small, attractive, specializes in *domburi* dishes, which consist of hot bowls of rice covered with various mixtures such as vegetables, shrimp, or chicken. Closed Saturday/Sunday. No CB.

Sushi Ginza East. 4 E. 46th St.; 687-4717. Specializes in—what else?—*sushi* (seasoned rice topped with raw fish), but also serves sautéed beef and vegetables *(sukiyaki)* and good *tempura* (fried fish and vegetables). AE.

Taro. 20 E. 57th St.; 986-7170. A kind of Japanese McDonald's with noodles, filling the need for simple, tasty, low-priced meals served at round counters. It follows the concept of hundreds of similar restaurants in Japan, and serves *larmen* (noodle dishes) that come in soup, in fried dishes, or broiled with fish, chicken, or meat. Closed Saturday/Sunday. No credit cards.

JEWISH/KOSHER

Expensive

Lindy's. 50th St. at Sixth Ave.; 586-8986. The one-and-only, gone for a while, now revived and doing well. You come here for the cheesecake and the atmosphere—the rest of the food is carelessly prepared and overpriced. Not Kosher. All major credit cards.

Lou G. Siegel. 209 W. 38th St.; 921-4433. Serves authentic Jewish food under rabbinical supervision. The menu has *lungen* and *miltz* stew, stuffed derma, stuffed cabbage, meats, and poultry. Separate bar. No smoking after sundown Friday, closed Saturday. All major credit cards.

Moshe Peking. 40 W. 37th St.; 594–6500. A handsome restaurant only New York could spawn, featuring Kosher Chinese cuisine, including Peking duck, beef and veal. Closed Fri. sundown to Sat. sundown. All major credit cards.

Sammy's Roumanian Restaurant. 157 Chrystie St. on the Lower East Side; 673–0330. The waiters think they're comedians, but from the bowls of pickles and roast peppers on every table to the delicious chicken soup, blintzes, *karnatzlach* (a very garlicky sausage), and potted steak the food is not a joke. An experience, to put it mildly. No credit cards.

Inexpensive

Ratner's. 138 Delancey St. on the Lower East Side; 677–5588. Strictly Kosher dairy (and listed under that heading, too). Sunday breakfast is the best time for a visit. A great place to take the kids. No credit cards.

KOREAN

Moderate

Arirang House. 28 W. 56th St.; 581–9698. If you like spicy grilled beef and the sourest of pickles, this is the place for you. Best example of Korean cooking in the city, but the atmosphere within is darkly mysterious. All major credit cards.

Myong Dong. 42 W. 35th St.; 695–6622. Long bar, semicircular banquettes, and all kinds of banquets, from soups, *sirhas mandoo gook,* to *jeyook kooi* (slices of pork). Closed Sunday. All major credit cards.

Woo Lae Oak of Seoul. 77 W. 46th St.; 869–0058. Real Seoul food, with perhaps the largest menu of all the city's Korean restaurants. *Bool koki*—strips of marinated beef cooked over small fire—pork ribs, baked short ribs, noodles, and all kinds of fish swim up at you from the menu's printed page, inviting you to take the plunge. No CB.

Inexpensive

Ho Shim. 120 W. 44th St.; 575–9774. Screens, artifacts, waitresses in Korean national costumes. A theater district location where you can get good noodles, *yakitori* (broiled chicken), marinated strips of beef, and fried fish. No CB.

MIDDLE EASTERN

Moderate

Ararat. 4 E. 36th St.; 686–4622. Beautifully decorated establishment specializing in Armenian cuisine to match. Closed Sat., July and August. All major credit cards.

Balkan Armenian. 129 E. 27th St.; 689–7925. One of the oldest and most popular Armenian restaurants, offering such typical fare as stuffed grape leaves, egg-lemon soup, and a most unusual mushroom kebab. Short on frills. Closed Sun. No CB.

Bosphorus East. 121 Lexington Ave. at 28th St.; 679–8370. The former owner and performer in a famous Istanbul restaurant and nightclub brought his knowledge of Turkish cuisine with him to New York and serves samples in a small, pleasant little place. Dinner only seven days a week. All major credit cards.

Cedars of Lebanon. 39 E. 30th St.; 725–9251. A variety of interesting and absolutely authentic Lebanese dishes in cavernous and poorly decorated surroundings. All major credit cards.

Dardanelles. 86 University Pl. 3 blocks south of 14th St.; 242–8990. Authentic Armenian cuisine in soft-lit quiet Village setting. Shish kebab, yogurt soup, stuffed mussels, and Oriental pastries are a few headliners. Greek wines are also available, Dinner only Saturday/Sunday. All major credit cards.

NORTH AFRICAN–MIDDLE EASTERN

Moderate

Keneret. 296 Bleecker St. at Seventh Ave.; 243–0866. Archetype Village atmosphere with very good couscous, moussaka. Dinner only. All major credit cards.

PERUVIAN

Inexpensive

Peruvian Restaurant. 370 W. 51st St.; 974–9099. Small menu in a small restaurant, with *ceviche, escabeche de pescado,* and other goodies. No credit cards.

PHILIPPINE

Moderate

Philippine Garden. 455 Second Ave. at 26th St.; 684–9625. A pleasant change from almost any other type of cuisine, with fried fish in sweet-and-sour sauce, or chicken and pork with cabbage, scallions, bananas, sausages, and onions, real treats for the gastronomically curious. Atmosphere is relaxed and service quietly unobtrusive. Dinner seven days a week, lunch Wednesday through Friday. No CB.

POLISH

Inexpensive

Baltyk. 12 First Ave. one block north of Houston St.; 260–4809. Borscht, kielbasa with sauerkraut, pigs' feet, everything to delight a Slavic heart. No credit cards.

RUSSIAN

Deluxe

Russian Tea Room. 150 W. 57th St.; 265-0947. A landmark right next to Carnegie Hall, and a favorite among musicians, dancers, movie celebrities, and other show-biz folk. Perhaps the city's richest food, and Christmas decorations all year long. Borscht, *blini* (pancakes with caviar), chicken Kiev, and (on Wednesday only) the legendary Siberian *pelmeny*. Russian cream for dessert if you can handle it. Watch out for the lethal concoctions brewed by the "Cossack" bartenders. All major credit cards.

Moderate

Russian Bear. 139 E. 56th St.; 355-9080. Unexciting versions of chicken Kiev, beef Stroganoff, etc. All major credit cards.

SCANDINAVIAN

Expensive

Copenhagen. 68 W. 58th St.; 688-3690. Danish specialties include open-faced sandwiches, a sumptuous *koldtbord* buffet with 100 hot and cold delicacies to choose from, including 26 kinds of herring. Aquavit and elephant beer to wash it all down—and the best coffee in town. All major credit cards.

SPANISH-MEXICAN

Expensive

Fonda La Paloma. 256 E. 49th St.; 421-5495. Hot and spicy Mexican dishes here are all prepared to order and courteously served in a pleasant atmosphere. The guacamole is withour peer. Open seven days but only from 5:00 P.M. on Saturday/Sunday. All major credit cards.

Plaza España. 130 W. 58th St,; 757-6434. Authentic dishes in traditional surroundings. Try the garlic chicken. Closed Sunday, open for dinner only Saturday. AE, MC, V.

Victor's Café. 240 Columbus Ave. at 71st St.; 575-8599. The place to go for the finest Cuban food in the city. The soups are excellent, fried beef with garlic and onions, and rice with seafood or chicken are equally delicious. Unusual on Sunday are Cuban hero sandwiches and roast suckling pig. Victor's is so popular it now has a theater district offshoot called **Victor's Café 52**, 236 W. 52nd St., 586-7714. All major credit cards.

Moderate

Cantina. 221 Columbus Ave. at 70th St.; 873-2606. Not slavishly authentic food, but a very popular Upper West Side hangout. Try the Mexican kitchen casserole if you are very hungry. All major credit cards.

El Coyote. 774 Broadway, 9th St.; 677-4291. Mexican cantina decor and best-selling combination platters. After 7:00 P.M. there can be a considerable wait at the bar. All major credit cards.

RESTAURANTS

El Parador. 325 E. 34th St.; 679–6812. Small, plain restaurant that is so popular they leave you waiting for tables even when plenty are available. But the Mexican and Spanish cuisine are hailed by Latins. Try a Marguerita during the inevitable wait at the bar (that's the purpose, of course), which is a low-key singles scene in and of itself. Spanish wines and Mexican beers. Dinner only, à la carte. Closed Sunday. No credit cards.

Fonda Los Milagros. 70 E. 55th St.; 752–6640. Exciting Mexican dishes are served to the accompaniment of mariachi music. Try the *chiles rellenos* and *flautas de carne*. There are pre-theater and after-theater à la carte dinners. Closed Sunday. Dinner only Saturday. AE CB, DC.

Los Panchos. 71 W. 71st St. east of Columbus; 864–9378. Very accommodating neighborhood restaurant with outdoor garden for summer dining and a life-size burro at the bar. Food is simple but well prepared. All major credit cards.

Pamplona. 822 Avenue of the Americas near 29th St.; 683–4242. This bright, unimposing restaurant is among the best of those serving Spanish cuisine. Black bean soup is delectable, chicken dishes also commendable. Closed Sunday. No V.

Xochitl. 146 W. 46th St.; 757–1325. Not all the Mexican restaurants in New York are owned and staffed by Mexican-Americans, but this one definitely is. The decor is Brutally Plain, but the food is excellent and authentic. Warm tortillas served with all meals. AE.

Zapata's. 330 E. 53rd St.; 223–9408. Narrow, dim, dominated by a portrait of the revolutionary but Viva the good, heaping food portions that are reasonably well-seasoned. All major credit cards.

Inexpensive

Anita's Chili Parlor. 287 Columbus Ave. at W. 74th St.; 595–4091. Tex-Mex food inside, or at sidewalk tables to watch the Columbus Avenue madness. Service indifferent at best. No credit cards.

El Charro. 4 Charles St. in the Village.; 242–9547. Full selection of spicy Mexican fare available in this homey restaurant. The combination plates let you sample the usual variety of dishes such as *tortillas, tostadas, enchiladas,* and *tacos.* All major credit cards.

El Cortijo. 128 W. Houston St. between the Village and SoHo; 674–4080. A neighborhood restaurant whose Spanish fare consists of both meat and fish dishes. The *paella*, saffron-flavored rice with seafood and/or chicken and sausage, is good. AE.

El Faro. 823 Greenwich St., Horatio St. in the West Village; 929–8210. Don't be put off by the unappetizing exterior—or by the small, dark interior for that matter—for this is absolutely NYC's finest Spanish kitchen. Besides the obligatory *paellas*, there is a raft of other shellfish dishes called *mariscadas*. The sangría is the genuine article, and *natilla* is a special treat for dessert. Again, no reservations can mean a lengthy wait. (It has an uptown branch—**El Faro 72**—at 40 W. 72nd St. between Central Park West and Columbus Ave.; 362–2050.) All major credit cards.

El Tenampa. 304 W. 46th St.; 840-9398. Small, unpretentious, near theaters —and good. Closed Sunday. DC.

Rincón de España. 226 Thompson St. in the Village; 260-4950. Dinner only. No credit cards. And at **Rincón de España II,** 82 Beaver St., 344-5228, dress is as informal as food, which is good. Beaver St. closed Saturday/Sunday.

Tío Pepe. 168 W. 4th St.; 242-9338. From your vantage point on the sidewalk of this pleasant café you can watch the Village denizens while enjoying creditable Spanish fare and the music of a flamenco guitarist. Or choose the more intimate candlelit dining inside. AE, DC, MC.

SWISS

Expensive

Chalet Suisse. 6 E. 48th St.; 355-0855. A pleasing place for the famous Swiss cheese fondue or fondue bourguignonne (cubes of beef you cook yourself in hot oil at the table). Other specials: onion and cheese pie, veal dishes, and roesti potatoes. Complete dinners and à la carte. All major credit cards.

Swiss Pavilion. 4 W. 49th St.; 247-6545. Opened when the 1939 World's Fair closed. Inviting atmosphere and serves many Swiss specialties, including veal and snails, as well as cheese fondue and fondue bourguignonne. Not the best value in town. Complete lunch and dinner. Closed Sunday. Bar. On a lower level, there is the **Fondue Pot,** which is more informal, noisier and somewhat less costly for basically the same food. All major credit cards.

Inexpensive

La Fondue. 43 W. 55th St.; 581-0820. As the name suggests, cheese and cheese dishes, and fondue in particular, are featured here. For those who demand meatier fare there is filet mignon. A charming, casual atmosphere, but luncheon eating is liable to be crowded and rushed. All major credit cards.

THAI

Moderate

Thai Palace. 261 W. 54th St. No phone. Portions are small, like the restaurant, but a little bit goes a long way when the cooking is good—and it is better than that here. All major credit cards.

Siam Inn. 916 Eighth Ave. near 55th St.; 489-5237. Dozens of beguiling Thai specialties are skillfully presented by a shyly gracious and efficient staff in a cheerful modern dining room with decorative Thai accents. Close to the theater district, Columbus Circle, and Carnegie Hall—and gets very crowded during the pre-theater hours. AE, DC.

Inexpensive

Bangkok Cuisine. 885 Eighth Ave. near 53rd St.; 581-6370. Rice with duck, pork with pepper, fish with curry. The usual mixtures which make Thai cusine so delicious, yet hard to define, as though it were simply a mixture of Chinese and Southeast Asian (yet it is more than that). AE, MC, DC.

Pongsri Thailand. 244 W. 48th St., unlisted telephone. Within a month of opening became one of the most popular of Thai restaurants because of its spaciousness, gracious staff, modern theater-district setting and, especially, its seafood offerings. All major credit cards.

Thailand. 106 Bayard St. in Chinatown; 349-3132. The best of the lot, and one of the cheapest. Nobody does it better than they do here—but you'd better specify how hot you want your food done. Curries are authentic, fried fish and crab dishes outstanding, but the looks of this small, unpretentious restaurant leave a lot to be desired. Reservations a must. Closed Mon.

UKRAINIAN

Inexpensive

Odessa. 21 E. 7th St.; 245-1956. You come here for blintzes or pirogi, and if these are your idea of paradise, why let heaven wait? Set among various Ukrainian social clubs and churches in what can be a gamy Lower East Side neighborhood in the evening. No credit cards.

VIETNAMESE

Inexpensive

Griffin. 313 E. 46th St.; 371-4542 Vietnamese ownership who did better when this was run as a French restaurant. Still, the locale makes it especially popular with UN personnel at lunch. All major credit cards.

YUGOSLAVIAN

Moderate

Dubrovnik. 88 Madison Ave. near 29th St.; 689-7565. Named for the resort town on Yugoslavia's Dalmatian coast, this pleasant restaurant offers an interesting though limited selection of Yugoslavian specialties such as *brudet* (a sort of chowder), and *cevapcici* (flavorful ground meat sausages). American and Continental dishes fill out the menu. Closed Sunday, dinner only Saturday. All major credit cards.

Portoroz. 340 Lexington Ave. near 39th St.; 687-8195. Rough brick areas, white walls. The restaurant is named for a resort area, looks like a country inn—near Grand Central Station—and serves good *sarma* (stuffed cabbage), interesting ground beef and pork dishes, and even some Italian main courses. Closed Sun. All major credit cards.

FAMOUS FOR EVERYTHING BUT THE FOOD

"Most Expensive Restaurant in the World"

The Palace. 420 E. 59th St.; 355-5150. One of the most opulent restaurants in the U.S.—which, not uninterestingly, went bankrupt once a few years back. The imaginative multi-course dinners feature such delicacies as Scotch salmon stuffed with caviar, and the pastries are made on the premises. As one would expect, there is an extensive wine cellar. Service impeccable. Very, very expensive ($50, $95 or $150—take your pick—per person prix fixe; drinks extra; dinner only; there is a service charge of 20%), but perhaps worth it if you want something to talk about back home, and if you're prepared for the splurge of a lifetime. Reservations necessary. Staff of almost 30 serves about 40 guests. Gold-rimmed plates, cut crystal, brocaded silk chairs, silver pots filled with flowers, and fine if not spectacular food. Closed Sun. No CB.

Super Deluxe

Sign of the Dove. 1110 Third Ave. at 65th St.; 861–8080. A complete townhouse with terraces and a winter garden. The Sanctum Sanctorum is upstairs. Pretentious, and the food never measures up to the setting. No lunch Monday. All major credit cards.

"21". 21 W. 52nd St.; 582–7200. Great social cachet among high-class fixers, celebrity-chasers of all ranks, and slightly aging "beautiful people," and therefore in a category of its own. Somewhat difficult to enter unless you have reservations. Frequented by businessmen at lunch and "society" at night. Handsomely furnished dining rooms, a well-packed, convivial bar. Most-sought-after tables are downstairs, along the left wall. Located in several former townhouses, decorated with turn-of-the-century elegance, more a place to see and be seen—although food is good. Excellent wine cellar. All major credit cards.

Deluxe

Sardi's. 234 W. 44th St.; 221–8440. The place to see theater world celebrities, sometimes. The game here is to figure out why the personnel think the restaurant is any longer a special place, entitling them to treat ordinary customers in an offhand manner. Large dining room with convivial atmosphere has caricatures of the well-known as decoration. Best tables are thought to be those downstairs, near the entrance. Cannelloni alla Sardi is a special, for some reason. À la carte. Some 40 or so choices make for varied possibilities, but keep it simple. All major credit cards.

Top of the Park. Central Park West at 60th St. atop the Gulf & Western Bldg.; 333–3800. Dinner only. The view is terrific if you get a window table in the restaurant or the bar—the latter frequently noisy, ill-kept, overcrowded, and smokey. The food is not memorable because many of the items seem to be prepared in advance. Suitable if you want to look, eat, and run over to Lincoln Center. Dinner only. Closed Sunday. All major credit cards.

Expensive

Elaine's. 1703 Second Ave. at 88th St.; 534–8103. The only legitimate reason for trying this restaurant, unless you know the proprietress, is to try to catch a glimpse of the large number of publishing and journalistic notables or non-notables who call it home. The food's ordinary at best, and mere mortals are treated shabbily, if not worse. A club, however, for the likes of Woody Allen, Gay Talese (who?), and visiting Hollywood pretty faces. Primarily Italian menu, some American dishes in what is more like a renovated saloon than a celebrity haunt. AE.

RESTAURANTS

O. Henry's. 345 Sixth Ave. at W. 4th St.; 242-2000. Takes one back into the past with its Tiffany-style chandeliers, chopping block for tables, and waiters in butcher's coats and straw hats. Charcoal-broiled steaks and chops, plus a casual attitude toward food and guests equally, are the features of this Greenwich Village landmark. All major credit cards.

Toots Shor. 233 W. 33rd St. at Penn Plaza; 279-8150. A famous watering hole for New York's sporting fraternity, moved from its old midtown location to this relatively new spot opposite Madison Square Garden. Standard steak and chops fare, lively atmosphere. Closed weekends unless there are events of importance at the Garden. "Last of the Great Saloon Keepers" is no longer alive, but Toots' spirit lives. All major credit cards.

Top of the Sixes. 666 Fifth Ave. at 53rd St.; 757-8020. Provides a view of the city from its dining room and candlelit cocktail lounge. The menu is diversified with Continental overtones, but it is hardly haute cuisine. (In fact, most of the food tastes as though it were defrosted right from the Stouffer's freezer—which is the company that runs the restaurant.) No CB.

Uzie's. 1442 Third Ave. near 82nd St.; 744-8020. Giancarlo Uzielli holds forth for pasta-eating beautiful people. All major credit cards.

Moderate

Asti. 13 E. 12th St.; 741-9105. A sing-along place, with waiters and customers getting into the act, whether opera or musicals. Also features a "Flying Pizza" act. Italian-style cuisine, but who's to notice? Closed Monday, July and August. All major credit cards.

Bianchi and Margherita. 186 W. 4th St. in the Village; 242-2756. If you enjoy music, especially opera, and don't care too much about its quality, you'll love this place, where waiter, proprietor, bartender, and customer join together (with luck) to sing duos, trios, quartets, sextets, even solos. The food is like the music—enjoy it and stop fussing. Closed Sun. All major credit cards.

The Cattleman. 5 E. 45th St.; 661-1200. Has to be seen to be disbelieved. A jam-packed bar, one room with an 1890 dining-car interior, another looking like a very elegant Crazy Horse Saloon, and so-so steaks, prime ribs, and tenderloin brochettes. All this, and a stagecoach to take you to the theater after dinner! Miss Grimble's cheesecake. Bring appetite because portions are enormous. But quantity has little to do with quality. No CB.

Fraunces Tavern. 54 Pearl St., downtown; 269-0144. Original building dates from Revolutionary days (the present one only to the 1930s). Behind the white portico there's a restaurant for lunch and dinner and a museum filled with Early American memorabilia. It was here that George Washington feted his officers prior to assuming the first presidency. Quite convenient to Wall St. and for George. But, while history was made here, few gourmet meals are. And swallowing the past can be tough. Closed Saturday during summer.

Luchow's. 110 E 14th St.; 477-4860. A landmark since 1882, and one of the most renowned. The extensive menu has all of the German dishes one expects as well as game in season, but most are indifferently prepared. Topnotch wines and imported beers. Oompah band alternates with schmaltzy Viennese waltzes.

Many come to see the beautifully decorated Christmas tree. Eat the famous apple or lingonberry pancakes. All major credit cards.

Mama Leone's. 239 W. 48th St.; 586–5151. Known far and wide for the quantity, not quality, of food served in the complete dinners. Though the restaurant is large, the waiting line is usually larger, so make a reservation. The food isn't anything like it was when the original mama started cooking there in 1906. But strolling entertainers make up for the cafeteria-cum-trattoria style. All major credit cards.

Shah Jahan. 980 Eighth Ave. midway between Carnegie Hall and Lincoln Center; 586–4180. A touch of authentic Indian cuisine—tandoori, kebab, and curry—but just a touch. All major credit cards.

Inexpensive

McSorley's Old Ale House. 15 E. Seventh St. near Third Ave.; 473–8800. One of New York's oldest landmarks, a drinking and dining institution for over 125 years. These last few years women have be permitted to enter. No credit cards.

OTHER BOROUGHS

BRONX

Expensive

Thwaite's Inn. 536 City Island Ave.; 885–1023. This old eatery dates from the Gilded Age, and is doing a roaring trade nowadays since New Yorkers are once again getting curious, then proud about the diverse neighborhoods that make up their city. In this case, City Island, jutting into L.I. Sound from the extreme northeast Bronx, is being rediscovered as a tiny, relaxed fishing "village." Thwaite's helps its own cause by turning out superb dinners, with lobster the logical and palate-pleasing specialty on this island that is a little bit of Cape Cod in the Bronx. All major credit cards.

Lobster Box. 34 City Island Ave.; 885–1952. A little "inland" from Thwaite's, this is also a focal point for City Island day-trippers. After all, who else but Lobster Box is going to offer a choice between fifteen or more preparations of lobster or shrimp? The baking is their own. If you can find a table on the terrace, a view of Long Island Sound is yours along with a scrumptious meal, although the nearby honky-tonk atmosphere of fast-food restaurants, custard stands, and an arcade gives the area a bit of Coney Island atmosphere. All major credit cards.

Anna's Harbor Restaurant. 565 City Island Ave.; 885–1373. A large restaurant, with Italian seafood specialties such as lobster fra diavolo (hot and spicy). AE, MC, V.

RESTAURANTS

Between Thwaite's, near the beginning of City Island, and the Lobster Box, virtually at the farthest tip, are several seafood restaurants of slightly lesser quality—and slightly less expensive. These include the **Sea Shore** (885–0300) and the **Crab Shanty** (885–1810), both on the same main street from end-to-end of the island. All major credit cards except CB.

Moderate

Amerigo's. 3587 E. Tremont Ave.; 824–7766. Began life as a pizzeria nearly half a century ago, now boasts two dining areas—one decorated in a Roman motif, the other with a back wall that becomes a waterfall. But it is the sauce, soups, pastas, and veal that make it Amerigo the beautiful—and one of the best in the North Bronx. All major credit cards.

Il Boschetto. 1660 E. Gun Hill Rd.; 379–9335. Unpretentious, small white building just off the New England Thruway—but as close to haute cuisine, Neapolitan-style, as you can get in the Bronx—especially the fish and veal dishes. Favorite of Bronx politicians noshing pasta. No CB.

Jackson's. Fordham Rd. at Sedgwick Ave.; 298–0055. Their loyal clientele and your own good taste will agree: this is the borough's best steakhouse. An added inducement is that they stay open quite late, well after midnight. The location is great, about three blocks east of I–87 on Fordham Road, and there's music every night. Convenient to the Hall of Fame, Yankee Stadium, and the Bronx Zoo.

Mario's. 2342 Arthur Ave.; 584–1188. First-rate, unpretentious and adventurous Neapolitan cookery served up by the Migliucci family since 1919 in a style that has become famous throughout the Little Italy section of the Bronx and beyond. A favorite of *Times* gourmet writer Craig Claiborne. Octopus salad, *spiedini* (deep-fried mozzarella appetizers), striped bass, and beef and veal scaloppine among best dishes. Pizza may be the best in town, right up there with John's of Bleecker St. Ornate Bronx Renaissance decor. All major credit cards. Valet parking.

Within roughly 100 yards of Mario's, in the famed Arthur Ave. Italian shopping district, are three of the area's best Neapolitan restaurants—**Dom's** (no reservations, noisy, really little more than a bar but with a veal Française dish and a spaghetti and shrimp concoction that has regulars lining up from all over the city), the **Full Moon** (scungilli, calamari, pastas in what looks like a fast-food pizzeria), and **Ann and Tony's**, a family-style trattoria. No credit cards at any of these three restaurants—but good eating. And all within easy walking distance of the Bronz Zoo.

Stella d'Oro. 5806 Broadway near 238th St.; 548–2245. Family dinners Italian-style, with spaghetti à la Stella d'Oro the masterpiece, are graced with homemade pastas. The aromas from their nearby bakery may entice you to try some of their well-known egg biscuits. The restaurant is very near Van Cortlandt Park, so a visit to the area could also include a mansion tour, a Gaelic Football match, or some horseback riding. All major credit cards.

BROOKLYN

Super-Deluxe

Peter Luger. 178 Broadway, near Bedford Ave.; 387–7400. Many insist Luger, lying in the shadow of the Williamsburg Bridge, convenient to Manhattan and the Brooklyn-Queens Expressway, is the city's most venerable steakhouse. There's no menu, and the waiter recites the day's offerings—but given the neighborhood, you should arrive by car or cab only, and have one called for the ride back. No credit cards except their own house account.

River Café. One Water St.; 522–5200. Astronomically priced American-International cuisine in a glorified barge sitting under the Brooklyn Bridge. Spectacular waterfront view, less than spectacular food and service. Noisy. AE, DC, V.

Deluxe

Gage and Tollner. 374 Fulton St.; 875–5181. The unhurried pace of Brooklyn, before it surrendered its independence to New York City, is preserved here. The menu changes with the seasons, and you can expect delightful specials that follow nature's calendar. Try the Crab Meat Virginia. The owners have preserved the 1879 landmark building's original decor, too. No CB.

Lisanne. 488 Atlantic Ave.; 237–2271. French classic and *nouvelle cuisine* surprisingly well-prepared in an attractive, skillful restaurant that features a changing menu and extraordinary desserts. Closed Mon. Bring your own wine. MC, V.

Expensive

Jimmy's. 36 Joralemon St.; 858–3018. Good but not outstanding northern Italian fare in a gracious setting for which the service is a hair too overbearing. Still, pleasant dining in Brooklyn Heights near the Esplanade—which is a good place to walk off your meal. No credit cards.

Moderate

Bamonte's. 32 Withers St. in Greenpoint section; 384–8831. In business over 80 years, so whither thou goest, this is one of the city's best Italian neighborhood restaurants. MC, V.

Bay Ridge Seafood Center. 8618 Fourth Ave.; 748–2070. Where the men and women who work at the Fulton St. Fish Market go for seafood. Need more endorsement? Just be prepared for a wait despite the restaurant's size. AE.

Charlie's. 348 Flatbush Ave.; 857–4585. Victorian charm and simple American-Continental food. A favorite for Sunday brunch. AE, MC, V.

Della Rocco's Pier 69. 18 Bay Ridge Ave.; 745–9384. In business since 1894, so despite a mixed-bag decor, they must be doing something right—especially with the veal dishes, and the delicious fresh fish. AE, DC, V.

Henry's End. 44 Henry St.; 834–1776. Popular Brooklyn Heights spot with solidly prepared Continental dishes as well as better-than-usual hamburgers and salads, and excellent desserts. AE.

RESTAURANTS

Gargiulo's. 2911 W. 15th St.; 266–0906. A wide, spacious setting for some of the city's best Neapolitan cooking—it is a favorite of *Times* food critic Mimi Sheraton—in which pasta in the noodle category is homemade. Ravioli and fettucine dishes are classics, veal is good. Italian politicians love it as much as votes. Great atmosphere for kids, too. All major credit cards.

La Villa Storica. 225 9th St.; 788–5883. Restored 1840s Victorian mansion converted into an intimate restaurant, with five dining rooms and Corsican cuisine. Once seated, the table is yours for the night to savor a six-course prix fixe dinner ($12–$14).

Raintree. Prospect Park W. at 9th St.; 768–3723. A bit of SoHo comes to Park Slope by way of the restoration of a one-time soda fountain—the marble fountain counter has been converted to a bar—into a casually elegant Continental eatery. Piano music weekend evenings. AE.

Inexpensive

Brooklyn's Atlantic Ave. and Court St. (the two cross each other) have a big concentration of Middle Eastern restaurants, most owned by the Almontaser family and its various offshoots. Among the best, all serving essentially similar menus heavy on lamb and curry dishes, are: **Almontaser,** 218 Court St., 624–9267; **Adnan,** 129 Atlantic Ave., 625–8697; **Near East,** 136 Court St., 522–4188; and, a mite more expensive than the others, **Sinbad,** 172 Atlantic Ave., 624–9105, where there is live belly dancing Friday and Saturday nights.

QUEENS

Moderate

Cognoscenti consider it a toss between **Caesar's** (97–12 63rd Rd., 459–2828, major credit cards) and **La Stella** (102–11 Queens Blvd., 459–9511, closed Monday, AE, DC) as to which is the borough's best Italian restaurant. Flip a coin, but don't rule out **Manducati's** (13–27 Jackson Ave., 729–4602, no credit cards), a Long Island City neighborhood restaurant that is as good as most Neapolitan trattorias—and reason enough to consider making a culinary pilgrimage to Queens.

Jahn's. 17–03. Hillside Ave.; 847–2800. In the residential Richmond Hill area not far from Kennedy Airport or Forest Hills tennis, this beloved landmark is famous for old-fashioned ice-cream desserts. Every sweet tooth in Queens is enthralled by it, and you get a free ice cream soda on your birthday, no matter what your age. No credit cards.

Steinway Brauhall. 28–26 Steinway Ave.; 728–9780. Hearty German food served up off Northern Blvd., near the Steinway piano factory. Closed Monday. No credit cards.

STATEN ISLAND

Inexpensive

Jade Island. 2845 Richmond Ave.; 761–8080. Don't let the shopping-center location fool you: the food's excellent and invitingly served. There's a smorgas-

 **DESSERTS.** Perhaps inevitably, the best ice cream sundaes in New York are the biggest nuisance to obtain, and the prices are equal to those for a meal. Nonetheless, who can resist when the craving strikes? **Dave's Luncheonette** at Canal St. and Broadway downtown is an oversize coffee shop known near and wide for the best egg creams in the world. An egg cream, you ask? Nothing more than flavored syrup, milk, and seltzer, but legend has it Dave's knows the secret of the spoon. Very reasonable, very good and pretty much out-of-the-way.

Among the chain operations, there are a number of **Howard Johnson's** scattered throughout the city (two in Times Square) but we'd be less than candid if we didn't mention that they've been completely eclipsed by the burgeoning **Baskin/Robbins, Haagan Dazs, Seduttos,** and **Bassetts** specialty shops, while the California **Swenson's** chain has an outlet on 65th and Second Ave. (expensive, and the service is deplorable). It's getting so you can't go around the corner in New York without tripping over one or more of these ice-cream supermarkets, and the choice of flavors is mind-boggling. For a rather different—and possibly overpowering—treat, try **Copenhagen** at Broadway and 81st St. for take-out cone concoctions in giant cones made to order.

Agora. 87th St. and 3rd Ave.; 369–6983 is an old-fashioned ice cream parlor in elaborately Art Deco setting that is attached to a clothing boutique. Sundaes and ice cream sodas are especially good, served with mounds of real whipped cream. The "Flat Iron Building" is a specialty—pound cake, chocolate ice cream, hot fudge, and whipped cream prepared in the shape of its namesake. Other food is available, but why bother? All major credit cards except CB.

Hick's. 16 E. 49th St.; 688–5552. A lovely emporium where there are still good sodas and ice cream to be found. A popular luncheon place for shoppers at the nearby stores, but the prices are relatively high. Specialize in extravagant "Bon Voyage" baskets. No credit cards.

Macy's. 34th St. and Seventh Ave.; 695–4400. Yes, the world's largest department store happens to have one of the best ice-cream parlors in the city on the fifth floor. Beautiful green-and-white patio setting and great sodas. AE.

Rumpelmayer's. 50 Central Park South in the St. Moritz; 755–5800. More of a tradition than a good ice-cream parlor, the stuffed animals and bright setting are always pleasing for kids. All major credit cards.

Serendipity. 225 E. 60th St., 838–3531. A celebrity ice-cream-parlor-cum-boutique, where you're likely to encounter Barbra Streisand or Cher slurping and splurging. Expensive even by New York standards (a banana split for $5.00!), but most preparations are enough for two or three.

COFFEEHOUSES

In the boroughs, look for **Jahn's** various branches in Brooklyn and Queens; **Once Upon a Sundae,** 7702 Third Ave., 680-6532 (with original 1890s set-up) in Brooklyn; and **Hoft's,** 3200 White Plains Road, 654-5291, in the Bronx.

Moving briskly from ice cream to pastry, first and foremost is **Ferrara's,** the bastion of Italian sweets nestled at 195 Grand Street (226-6150) in the middle of "Little Italy." All sorts of specialties are available (most served with piping-hot cups of espresso or cappucino), and there are some nifty items to take away with you. The line for tables is long on weekends, but the setting is uniquely festive. Also strikingly attractive with brick and glass walls, marble counter and enclosed garden, and with outstanding cheesecake, is **Café Biondo,** 141 Mulberry St., 226-9285, around the corner from Ferrara's.

Another, more imaginative, way to enjoy great desserts in a civilized manner is to go to some of the best restaurants—**Four Seasons,** for example—later in the evening, such as after a concert or the theater, and tell the maître d'hôtel that you want only dessert. If their service is tapering off, they'll be happy to oblige. **Slotnick's Daughter,** 153 E. 53rd St. in the Market at Citicorp Center; (935-1744) offers the opportunity for people-watching while sipping a variety of imported coffees, ice-cream drinks, or sampling pastries and sandwiches. **Eclair,** 141 W. 72nd St. (873-7700) is part restaurant, but the real lure is the outstanding Austrian pastries. Similarly, **Cakemasters** at Third Ave. and 65th and at 122 W. 72nd St. is a bakery-cum-café. Up by Columbia University (diagonally across from the Cathedral of St. John the Divine) is the **Hungarian Pastry Shop,** 1030 Amsterdam Ave. (866-4230), with excellent pastries and breads at prices catering to the predominantly student clientele.

COFFEEHOUSES (CAFÉS). One of the pleasures of touring the Village is to stop into one of the numerous Italian-style coffeehouses for a cup of just about any sort of coffee or tea—in cooler weather—or some Italian ices in the summer. In the Continental tradition, these are places where you can sit ... and sit ... and sit. You will probably stumble onto your own favorite, but just in case, here are a few good ones: **Café Reggio,** 119 MacDougal St.; **Le Figaro Café** at the corner of MacDougal and Bleecker Sts. (one of the best known, closed for a while and reopened a few years ago); **Caffè Borgia,** across the street from Le Figaro; **Caffè Dante,** south of Bleecker St. on MacDougal; **Café Lucca,** at 228 Bleecker St. at Sixth Ave.; and **Café Sandolino,** on Barrow St. between W. 4th St. and Seventh Ave. (more of a student/seedy poet place, with light food). **Pane e Cioccolato,** Waverly Place at Mercer St., is a hangout for New York University students (the university is all around it).

Cafe de la Paix (—a bar in the St. Moritz Hotel at Sixth Ave. and Central Park South—59th St.) is probably the nicest midtown people-viewing spot, though you may get tired of looking at the double-parked limousines.

On the Upper East Side near Yorkville, and for a complete change of ethnic direction, there is **Mrs. Herbst's Strudels,** Third Ave. between 81st and 82nd Sts., where wonderful pastries and jams may be consumed, with coffee or tea, at tables; like Ferrara's, Mrs. Herbst's also sells its goodies retail. Also on the Upper East Side, on Fifth Ave. and 81st St. across from the Metropolitan Museum, there is the **Terrace Café** (actually a restaurant/bar) in the American Stanhope Hotel—fun when the museum is open, not so much fun when it isn't.

NIGHT LIFE. When a Broadway baby says good night, it's usually early in the morning, as the song says. And there are plenty of ways to make it through the night in New York City, with bars and lounges permitted to stay open and serve liquor until 4:00 A.M. every night except Saturday, when closing time is 3:00 A.M. Increasingly, too, the big-name discos stay open considerably past that hour—consider that many don't even open until 11:00 P.M. or midnight —and during the last year there has been a revival of semi-legal after-hours clubs. The latter either require an actual membership fee that can be used repeatedly, or *call* their fee at the door a membership fee, thus attempting to convince the authorities that they are private clubs (for which there are no restrictions on how late they can serve). The after-hours places actually do sometimes advertise discreetly in the *Village Voice* and *SoHo Weekly News,* catering to a young, high-paying, jet-setting crowd. And then there are the night-life happenings you just come upon, such as recently at an unlikely spot, "Rose," a Thai restaurant-cafe near 77th St. on First Ave., where four young professionals were doing a concert version of *Oklahoma!*

But most New York night life is of a more traditional nature, even if the styles and venues have changed and the hours have gotten later. The classy old hotel nightclubs are gone—the Persian Room at the Plaza, the Empire Room at the Waldorf, the Maisonette at the St. Regis—as are the big, flashy comics-and-kickline places such as the Latin Quarter and the Copacabana (though the Copa has been reincarnated as a disco). The accent today is on discos, hip cabarets, trendy rock and roll clubs, and country-in-the-city real or fake honky-tonks. And while you can still find quality entertainment at a handful of hotels and other fashionably appointed addresses, most of New York's night life seems to be housed in converted theaters and moviehouses, spruced up Art Deco ballrooms, one-time warehouses—even a former men's clothing store in the heart of Times Square that has a dance floor big enough to hold more than 2,000 people comfortably!

The rules as far as dress (and everything else—but we'll get to the rest in a moment) are concerned are probably what you'd expect—jackets and ties for men at the more traditionally-minded establishments, glitter and everything you've got at the big name discos, and casual-but-neat just about everywhere else. Admissions, cover charges and/or minimums, and show times vary from place to place, and sometimes from night to night at a given club depending on whether or not there is a live performer and on who that performer is. Call to check, and to find out what the policy is for reservations; some places will accept phone reservations, for others you may have to purchase tickets ahead. Such uncertainty is typical of the current night-life scene, where the in spot one

NIGHT LIFE

moment is closed the next; where the hot spot to see and be seen one night is forgotten by morning. Many clubs have a bar from which you can watch or at least hear the act without paying a cover or minimum; check.

Some places stand out as the ones to go to if you have only a few nights on the town. We'll single them out first and then provide a longer but still *selective* list broken down into various categories—jazz, pop/rock, cabaret, disco/dancing, country, floor shows, hotel rooms and piano bars, comedy/magic. Once in town, consult the *New Yorker* for comprehensive capsule listings of who's appearing where, and the *Village Voice* for the most complete advertising section devoted to night life. While the outlying boroughs have their share of popular bars and entertainment, all the serious night-life spots are centered in Manhattan; even for Brooklynites, a big night out involves a trip into "The City."

Key to credit card information following each listing:

AE = American Express
CB = Carte Blanche
DC = Diners Club
MC = MasterCard
V = Visa

CRÈME DE LA CRÈME

King Cole Room. At the St. Regis Sheraton, Fifth Ave. and 55th St.; 753-4500. The only remaining old-style hotel-room nightclub with name entertainment in the city, the King Cole Room offers revues of Broadway showtunes by the likes of Rodgers and Hart, Gershwin and Porter, sung by performers of the caliber of Mimi Hines and Larry Kert. Consistently high-caliber, small-scale productions in a smartly gracious setting. All major credit cards. Food available.

Café Carlyle. At the Carlyle Hotel, Madison Ave. and 76th St.; 744-1600. Bobby Short, considered the piano man's piano man for his mastery of the Broadway classics, alternates in six-month stretches with the jazzier Marion McPartland—and either way you are transported to a quieter, more humane world. All major credit cards. Food available.

Rainbow Room. 30 Rockefeller Plaza; 757-9090. Dance atop the RCA Building to name big bands under the direction of Bobby Rosengarden or Panama Francis, among others. The Art Deco splendor drips chandeliers and plush red walls and floors—and a spectacular 65th-floor view of the New York skyline. The food has slipped, although the kitchen still comes up with respectable American-International fare. (Entertainment at the **Rainbow Grill** across the hall has sunk to imitation Vegas-Parisian revues with some nudity.) All major credit cards.

Hors d'Oeuverie. 1 World Trade Center; 938-1111. More intimate for dancing than the Rainbow Room, and with an even more breath-taking view, the Hors d'Oeuverie features a light jazz trio that alternates with a solo pianist beginning at 7:30 P.M. You *can* be entertained cheaply here—the cover charge is a mere $2.50, and you can limit yourself to one drink ($3.00 to 4.00), but the temptation is to partake of the hors d'oeuvres, for which you are charged by the small plateful. Also, on weekends and during holiday seasons, get there early or you'll be subject to a long wait just to get into the elevator—a 107-story climb. No CB.

Xenon. 125 W. 43rd St., 221-2690. The "innest" of the "in" discos as of this writing, though **Studio 54** did finally reopen under new management in the fall of 1981. Yes, you are likely to spy Mick Jagger or Tennessee Williams or Diana Ross or Cher on the dance floor, picking up the beat from a $100,000 sound system with bizarre lighting effects to match. They're catty at the door—that's part of the mystique—and if you happen to arrive for one of the club's frequent special "theme party" nights the admission will zoom from the regular $12.00 to $25.00 or more. Drinks start at $4.00. No credit cards.

Savoy. 141 W. 44th St.; 921-9490. The newest of the large-scale rock clubs is housed in a renovated (to the tune of $1.5 million) historic (1903) Broadway theater, complete with original Tiffany glass ceiling in the foyer, boxes with mosaic glass borders, antique marble walls and trim, and outstanding sound and light facilities. The acts change nightly except for a handful of the biggest names, and range from the latest hard-rockers to the more generally esteemed James Taylor, Peter Allen, and Kris Kristofferson. Dancing when the act calls for it, otherwise 1,000 seats. You can charge tickets through TeleCharge, but no credit cards at the box office. AE inside for drinks.

Greene Street. 101 Greene St.; 925-2415. Greene Street will give you a taste of contemporary SoHo chic—a restaurant and cabaret two stories high, giving a rare New York feel for spaciousness. Its soaring walls, 10 skylights, fieldstone bar, tropical trees, pink and green mural, and tiered dining tables are a perfect setting for just about any kind of music—and the entertainment policy indeed runs from jazz to a cappella oldies groups. AE, MC, V.

For jazz aficionados it's more difficult to pinpoint one outstanding place. Details will follow in the listings, but consider **Eddie Condon's** or **Jimmy Ryan's** for Dixieland and mainstream sounds uptown on W. 54th St., or the **Village Vanguard, Sweet Basil,** or **Seventh Ave. South** for all styles in Greenwich Village. The **Blue Note** has reopened, on W. 3rd St.

Here then is a broader but still selective look at some of the better night spots in the Big Apple, broken down by category. "Inexpensive" refers to places where the cover and/or minimum total less that $5.00; elsewhere, figure on $10.00 *or more* per person.

JAZZ

At jazz clubs in particular you can often sit at the bar and still have a full view of the stage; this can be a big saving when there are cover and/or minimum charges at the tables.

Abingdon Square. 577 Hudson St.; 255-2788. Contemporary feel, brick walls, fireplace, very friendly Village crowd. Duos and trios, mostly contemporary and mainstream. Food. Inexpensive. All major credit cards.

NIGHT LIFE

Angry Squire. 216 Seventh Ave. near 23rd St.; 242–9066. Pleasant nautical setting with small intimate booths. Duos and trios with a modern edge. Music weekends only. Food. Inexpensive. No credit cards.

Bechet's. 1319 Third Ave. near 75th St.; 879–1001. Fancy Upper East Side supper club, with mainstream name ensembles and French-American fare. AE.

Bradleys. 70 University Pl.; 228–6440. Smoky and always crowded, it's the typical jazz bar, with the emphasis on reflective piano-bass combinations. Inexpensive. AE, DC.

Cookery. 21 University Pl.; 674–4450. Loud and boisterous, the restaurant seems an excuse to bring back oldtimers such as Helen Humes and Alberta Hunter. No credit cards.

Crawdaddy. Vanderbilt and 45th St.; 687–1860. Music to go along with the New Orleans decor and food, with name artists always in residence. All major credit cards.

Eddie Condon's. 144 W. 54th St.; 265–8277. Small-band jazz with a '40s ambience and decent food—part of the latter-day "swing street" (transplanted from the 52nd St. of old). AE, DC, MC.

Fat Tuesday's. 190 Third Ave. at 17th St.; 533–7902. Popular singles hangout (especially the bar and the street-level restaurant) with mainstream and contemporary artists downstairs. Dining. Closed Mon. AE, MC, V.

Ginger Man. 51 W. 64th St.; 399–2358. Harlem-oriented rhythm-and-blues across the way from Lincoln Center. No CB.

Gregory's. 1149 Third Ave. at 67th St.; 371–2220. Low-key jazz as background to friendly conversation. Stride piano Sundays from 5. Inexpensive. All major credit cards.

Hanratty's. 1754 Second Ave. at 91st St.; 289–3200. Stride, bebop, and singers of surprisingly good quality (including the occasional familiar name). The sister club of the same name on the Upper West Side sometimes also has music. Inexpensive. AE.

Jazz Forum. 648 Broadway near Bleecker St.; 477–2655. Loft popular among moderately "outside" players. Inexpensive. No credit cards.

Jazzmania. 40 W. 27th St.; 532–7666. Jam sessions with name participants are the constant order weekends only. No credit cards.

Jimmy Ryan's. 154 W. 54th St.; 664–9700. Dixie, swing, and bebop on the street popular for same. Inexpensive. AE.

Jimmy Weston's. 131 E. 54th St.; 838–8384. The restaurant is a popular hangout for sports celebrities, the bandstand in the far corner given over primarily to piano mainstream trios. All major credit cards.

Knickerbocker Saloon. 33 University Pl.; 228–8490. The spirit of old Charlie Knickerbocker lives in atmospheric dining room where jazz wafts in from the bar. Noisy but comfortable with simple American fare. AE, MC, V.

Marty's. 1265 Third Ave. near 73rd St.; 249–4100. Mel Tormé is a regular at this stylish supper club, and that should say it all. Food. Expensive. AE, MC, V.

Michael's Pub. 211 E. 55th St. at Third Ave.; 758–2272. Atmospheric olde English roome with solid mainstream jazz and occasional jazz-based revues. Continental food. Expensive. All major credit cards.

Mikell's. 760 Columbus Ave. at 97th St.; 864–8832. Neighborhood supper club featuring pop-oriented rhythm-and-bluesers. MC.

Other End. 149 Bleecker St. in the Village; 673–7030. Rock usually, but appearances by the likes of Stephane Grappelli and others with some frequency. No credit cards.

Peacock Alley. Waldorf-Astoria, Park Ave. at 50th St.; 355–3000. A cozy piano (and sometimes duo/trio) hideaway where the music plays from 6:00 P.M. to 2:00 A.M. All major credit cards.

Red Blazer, Too. 1576 Third Ave. at 89th St.; 876–0440. Some say the big-band revival such as it is emanated from here thanks to regular weekday stands featuring Stan Rubin's and Sol Yaged's ensembles. It may be true. Large and always busy with a slightly touristy flavor, and Dixieland on weekends. AE.

Seventh Ave. South. 21 Seventh Ave. S., above Houston St. in the Village; 242–4694. Easy-going upstairs room (no cover at the bar downstairs) owned by the sax- and trumpet-playing Brecker Brothers, and popular among their pop-funk-jazz friends. MC, V.

Star & Garter. 105 W. 13th St.; 242–3166. Light, airy room that's intimate and friendly. Mostly mainstream combos accompany moderately priced Continental meals. AE.

Storytowne. 41 E. 58th St.; 755–1640. Not quite Bourbon St., but big and brassy in the Dixieland fashion. All major credit cards.

Sweet Basil. 88 Seventh Ave. S. just south of Christopher St. in the Village; 242–1785. Knotty pine walls adorned with jazz memorabilia and a wide range of mainstream and contemporary musicians make this one of the most consistently pleasing establishments around. Sunday brunches feature trumpeter Doc Cheatham. AE, MC, V.

Village Gate. 160 Bleecker St. in the Village; 475–5120. Once a mainstay on the jazz circuit, the concerts are only intermittent these days, but always featuring name players. No credit cards.

Village Vanguard. 178 Seventh Ave. S. in the Village; 255–4037. The prototype jazz club—downstairs, smoky, with lousy sound system and cramped quarters. And everyone loves it just as it has been for 40 years. Proprietor Max Gordon can usually be spied napping at a center table. No credit cards.

West Boondock. 114 Tenth Ave. at 17th St.; 929–9645. Out of the way—take a cab to get here—but a staple for soulful music and inexpensive soul food. The music's free and always high quality even though the names are rarely known. AE, CB, MC.

West End. 2911 Broadway at 111th St.; 666–8750. If you first discovered jazz while in college, you'll feel perfectly at home at this haunt frequented by Columbia and Barnard University students. Inexpensive. AE.

NIGHT LIFE

POP/ROCK

Bottom Line. 15 W. 4th St.; 228–7880. A 400-seat showcase club that headlines name as well as up-and-coming acts, and occasionally stretches out for a classical, dance, or theater event. Two shows nightly, with admission varying from $7.50 to $10.00, depending on the performer. Best and most consistent club in the Village, especially popular among collegians. Snacks available. No credit cards.

CBGB & OMFUG. 315 Bowery near 3rd St.; 982–4052. New York punkers and new wavers from Blondie to Talking Heads to whoever-the-rage-is-today all served their apprenticeship here. Loud, long, and narrow—and the going can get a mite tough. Always call for set times—but don't necessarily believe what they say. No credit cards.

Eagle Tavern. 355 W. 14th St.; 924–0275. Bluegrass, old-timey string band and folk music brewed here Wednesdays and weekends. Very inexpensive. No credit cards.

Folk City. 130 W. 3rd St.; 254–8449. Once the spawning ground for the folk-protest movement of the '60s, the glory days are clearly over—though some of the old-timers occasionally return for old time's sake. Inexpensive. No credit cards.

Great Gildersleeves. 331 Bowery at 3rd St.; 533–3940. New, hard-rocking outfits come in for one night at a time, playing in a tacky, cavernous environment. Inexpensive. No credit cards.

Home. 1748 Second Ave. at 91st St.; 876–0744. A neighborhood bar where the back room is given over to studio musicians and other pros who are working out new, mostly rock-oriented acts. MC, V.

J.P.'s. 1471 First Ave. at 76th St.; 288–1022. Popular record-business hangout with a handful of performers appearing on a rotating basis—and with major name concert acts dropping in after their shows to jam. No CB.

Kenny's Castaways. 157 Bleecker St. in the Village; 473–9870. Folk-based rockers and old-time blues shouters are the mainstay with owner Pat Kenny's ever-jovial presence the place's biggest asset. No credit cards.

Max's Kansas City. 213 Park Ave. South at 17th St., 777–7871. Once the exclusive domain of the rock underground, Max's is forever undergoing changes in direction—none to the better in recent years, as it has tried to keep up with the new wave times. No CB.

Mudd Club. 77 White St. in TriBeCa; 227–7777. A disco with live bands, but nothing gets going until 1:00 A.M. at the earliest. Then again, the audience is really the show. No credit cards, and they're selective about whom they admit—lest the crowd get "too straight."

Other End. 149 Bleecker St., in the Village; 673–7030. Formerly the Bitter End, and home to many a '60s folk singer, at least some of whom continue to return to the brick-walled, cozy club. Also still noted for its share of "discoveries"—most recently Steve Forbert. No credit cards.

Ritz. 119 E. 11th St.; 254–2800. A 1935 ballroom (in an 1889 building) restored to its original Art Deco glamour and, as of this writing, the most popular rock club in town. Video (on a 30' x 30' screen) and dance music entertain before and after shows—the latter featuring everything from rockabilly to jazz, new wave to reggae. Downstairs is all dance floor (only a few banquettes along the walls provide seating), and the balcony is usually reserved for visiting VIPs, so be prepared to stand. No credit cards.

Savoy. See *Crème de la Crème* above.

Tramps. 125 E. 15th St.; 777–5077. The one spot in the city regularly featuring traditional blues artists such as Otis Rush and Big Joe Turner. AE, MC, V.

Trax. 100 W. 72nd St.; 799–1448. Same owner as J.P.'s and same description fits. No CB.

CABARET

Applause. 360 Lexington Ave. near 40th St.; 687–7267. Singing waiters and waitresses later take their turns on stage. All major credit cards.

The Duplex. 55 Grove St. near Seventh Ave. in the Village; 243–9306. A split-level West Village club popular among latter-day torch singers who try to turn their sets into mini-revues. No credit cards.

Freddy's. 308 E. 49th St.; 888–1633. Christine Jorgensen made a "comeback" here, and that sort of explains the tone of the place. No CB.

Greene St. See *Crème de la Crème* above.

Les Mouches. 260 Eleventh Ave. near 28th St.; 695–5190. Many a Broadway star comes in after the final curtain to try his or her hand at a solo act—and the names have been known to include Chita Rivera, Eartha Kitt, and Jaye P. Morgan among others. Disco dancing too. No V.

Mickey's. 44 W. 54th St.; 247–2979. Everything from *angst*-ridden singer/songwriters to supper clubby country bands and serious Dixie stompers. All major credit cards.

Onstage. 349 W. 46th St.; 265–3800. Mostly singers and small combos for the after-theater crowd. Hopping until 4:00 A.M., with kitchen open until 2:00. All major credit cards.

Once Upon A Stove. 325 Third Ave. near 25th St.; 683–0044. Skits and revues in the upstairs room. No CB.

Palsson's. 158 W. 72nd St.; 362–2590. Attractive second-floor room that seats about 50 people, with some additional space at the bar. Revues change every few weeks, and the kitchen stays open until last call at 4:00 A.M. All major credit cards.

Playboy Club. 5 E. 59th St.; 752–3100. Various lounges and show rooms, some with name entertainment, others strictly for conversation and/or dancing. For keyholders only, but keys can be purchased at the door. All major credit cards.

S.N.A.F.U. 676 Sixth Ave. near 21st St.; 691–3535. Ever on the lookout for unusual entertainers—from civil servant Quentin Crisp to torch singers and rock bands with a visual and/or comic twist. No CB.

NIGHT LIFE

SPQR. 133 Mulberry St. in Little Italy; 431-7610. Attractive upstairs nightclub in one of Little Italy's fancier restaurants, catering to the adult audience with crooners such as Julius LaRosa, Enzo Stuarti, Bobby Vinton. Dance floor, and dancing between sets. All major credit cards.

Sweetwater's. 168 Amsterdam Ave. near 67th St., north of Lincoln Center; 873-4100. Mostly singers—and a pleasant stop-off following Lincoln Center performances. No CB.

FLOOR SHOWS

The days of extravagant Las Vegas and Parisian-style floor shows in New York, once available at the Latin Quarter and Copacabana, are gone. The few that remain are not very good attempts at scaled-down versions of these lavish spectacles, and cater almost exclusively to tourists. For those who insist, we list them herewith, but given the prices most such establishments charge, we suggest that Broadway's *Sugar Babies* and *42nd Street*, both offering the old-style entertainment, are far better buys for your money.

Bianchi & Margherita. 186 W. 4th St., Village; 242-2756. Not the usual type of floor show at all—instead, you get live opera while you savor your veal piccata. The food's only fair, but the experience is fun. All major credit cards.

Chateau Madrid. 48th St. and Lexington Ave.; 752-8080. Continental and Spanish cuisine in this Hotel Lexington nightspot. Energetic Latin American shows with resident chorines and flamenco dancers. Nightly at 9:30 P.M. and midnight, except Saturday (8:30 and 11:30 P.M., 1:45 A.M.). **Flamenco Suite** offers dancers, singers, and guitarists from 10:30 P.M. Closed Monday. All major credit cards.

Club Ibis. 151 E. 50th St.; 753-3471. Continental restaurant with exotic decor—but you can't eat decor. The 9:30 and 11:30 P.M. shows (Saturday: 8:45 and 11:30 P.M., 1:30 A.M.) help take your mind off the food when the Ibis girls are in good form. Upstairs room features belly dancers, Middle Eastern musicians, etc., from 10:30 P.M. All major credit cards.

El Avram. 80 Grove St. near Sheridan Square in the Village; 243-9961. New York's only long-running Kosher nightclub is housed in a Spanish-designed room that offers belly dancers, singers, comedians, and dancing. Except for the mixing of national influences (Israeli, Spanish, Italian, and Greek) this is the stereotypical nightclub you'd expect to find anywhere but in New York. No DC.

Ipanema. 240 W. 52nd St.; 765-8025. Brazilian nightclub that tries none too successfully to transform Manhattan into Rio. Jazz on Wednesday, disco othernights. Closed Tuesday. All major credit cards.

La Chansonette. 890 Second Ave. near 48th St.; 753-7320. Singer Rita Dimitri re-creates the world of Piaf, Brel, and Aznavour to the accompaniment of guitarist/husband/real-estate person Stanley Brilliant. Pleasant French restaurant features trio for dancing Tuesday–Saturday, and Russian gypsy music Monday. All major credit cards.

Riverboat. 350 Fifth Ave. (Empire State Bldg.); 736-6210. Dance bands and American cuisine, with an "all you can drink" package including steak, dancing and show (such as it is) for about $25.00. Closed Monday. All major credit cards.

Sagapo. 15 E. 48 St.; 935-1107. Singers, belly dancers, bouzoukis, *etc.*, provide two floor shows nightly except Sunday from 9:30 P.M. (10 on Saturday). All major credit cards.

Sirocco. 29 E. 29th St.; 683-9409. Israeli songs, belly dancers, bouzoukis, and revues with Middle Eastern food to match. Shows at 10:00 P.M. and 1:00 A.M. except Monday. AE, CB, DC.

DISCO/DANCING

Adam's Apple. 1117 First Ave. near 61st St.; 371-8650. Two floors for dining and dancing. American cuisine, bar, lounge, sidewalk café, open seven days till 4:00 A.M. All major credit cards.

Bond's. 1526 Broadway, Times Square; 944-5880. Disco dancing in what was once a men's clothing store. Multi-tiered, occasionally books top rockpop entertainers. No credit cards.

Cachaca. 403 E. 62nd St.; 688-8501. Jazz sambas of Brazil alternate with recorded Brazilian and American disco music between sets featuring authentic Brazilian pop music with singer and trio. A supper club that really goes for south-of-the-border atmosphere. Disco swings into high gear after 11:00, open nightly except Monday from 8:00 P.M. to 4:00 A.M. All major credit cards.

Copacabana. 10 E. 60th St; 755-6010. Minus chorus girls but retaining some of its old glamour. The Copa is making a comeback at its original site, with upstairs cabaret shows and disco downstairs from 10:00 to 4:00. Closed Tues. All major credit cards.

Electric Circus. 100 Fifth Ave. at 16th St.; 989-7457. Light show, bands, disco on three action-packed levels that include carousel with steeplechase horses, antique fire engine, glass-enclosed VIP lounge, outstanding sound system, and 22,000 square feet waiting to be filled with dancing feet. AE.

La Folie. 21 E. 61st St.,; 765-1400. Small, elegant French restaurant with disco from 10:30 on ($5.00), or have dinner (four courses for around $40.00) and have disco charge waived. Closed Sunday. All major credit cards.

Le Cocu Discotheque Francaise. 152 E. 55th St.; 371-1559. Light show to turn on to reflected off stainless-steel dance floor from 10:00 to 4:00 nightly except Monday. MC, V.

Les Mouches. See *Cabarets.*

New York, New York. 33 W. 52nd St.; 245-2400. Laser lights, smoke machine, living theater in multi-level complex open seven nights from 10:00 for dancing to disco and rock. AE, DC.

Onde's. 160 E. 48th St.; 752-0200. Split-level supper club with good international food and a solid trio playing for listening/dancing from 8:00 nightly except Sunday. A pianist performs in the lounge. No CB.

One's. 111 Hudson St., in TriBeCa; 925-0111. Tuesdays are for live reggae, the rest of the week for the latest in recorded soul and rock-based dance music. Weekend afternoons there's a special kiddie disco (adults must be accompanied

NIGHT LIFE

by children) that's as popular among single parents as it is among the 12 and under set. No credit cards.

Rainbow Room and Grill. See *Crème de la Crème*.

Régine's. 502 Park Ave. at 59th St.; 826–0990. Mirrors reflect subdued lighting in this playpen for beautiful people with a good (if overpriced) restaurant open Monday/Saturday 8:00 to midnight. Disco action from 10:30 P.M. to 4:00 A.M. Closed Sunday. All major credit cards.

Roma di Notte. 137 E. 55th St., 832–1128. Dine on Italian food in a private cave, dance to music of toga-clad musicians on marble floor from 7:30 to 1:30. Closed Sunday. All major credit cards.

Roseland. 239 W. 52nd St.; 247–0200. New York's largest dance hall features two live orchestras for continuous dancing nightly Wednesday to Sunday, with matinees Thursday/Saturday/Sunday and disco nightly from midnight Wednesday to Saturday. Has 700-seat restaurant-bar, featuring American cuisine. Admission varies from $5.00 to $7.00. AE, V.

37th St. Hideaway. 32 W. 37th St.; 947–8940. Dining-dancing from 7:30 in actor John Drew's former townhouse, with performers usually including singer, trio. All major credit cards.

Wednesdays. 210 E. 86th St.; 535–8500. Disco/bar/restaurant complex that resembles underground European street festival in the form of a block-long underground village with sidewalk cafés, bistros, wine-and-cheese shops, gaslights, trees, huge drinks, American food and all kinds of night-life entertainment. Closed Monday. Cover charge from $4.00 to $6.00 depending on night. No CB.

COUNTRY

City Limits. 125 Seventh Ave. S. at 10th St.; 243–2242. An enormously friendly place to party western-style to live bands. Just make sure you have your dancing boots on and save room for some chili. The action begins at 10:00 P.M. nightly, and be forewarned: This is a big place but *very* popular. No credit cards.

Cody's. 16th St. and Sixth Ave.; 620–0377. Modern two-tiered singles bar (plus food) with strong country influence via live bands from 9:30 on.

Lone Star Café. 61 Fifth Ave. at 13th St.; 242–1664. The official Texas embassy in New York City, though the bands veer to blues and rock as often as to country. Still, the food and ambience are as close to Southern-fried as two New York owners are ever likely to make it. Great chili, ribs, and salads, too. No V.

O'Lunney's. 915 Second Ave. at 48th St.; 751–5470. The first New York country bar has the most genuinely Western feel to it—the sort of place where women in beehive hairdos and men in ten-gallon hats feel right at home. Live music that's always good for dancing from 9:00 P.M. nightly—sometimes on two floors. No CB.

Rodeo. 407 E. 70th St.; 535–2400. The live singers and bands aren't terribly consistent, but the ribs are possibly the best in town and the atmosphere downhome all the way. AE, MC, V.

Also check **Bottom Line**, **Other End**, and **Ritz** under *Pop/Rock* and **Savoy** under *Crème de la Crème*. All sometimes present name country acts.

COMEDY/MAGIC

Catch A Rising Star. 1487 First Ave. near 78th St.; 794-1906. See young new comedians the same time Johnny Carson's talent scouts do—with big-name graduates frequently dropping in to test new material. Some singers change the pace, with the festivities beginning about 10:00 P.M. and the cream of the crop usually going on between 11 and 1. Always a fun night, no matter how bad the acts get. AE, MC.

Comic Strip. 1568 Second Ave. near 82nd St.; 861-9386. Essentially same format as Catch—nonstop parade of up-and-comers—and frequently with the same acts shuttling between these clubs and the West Side's Improvisation. The fun begins about 9:30 P.M. No credit cards.

Dangerfield's. 1118 First Ave. near 61st St.; 593-1650. The "Can't get no respect" man does a stint himself several months out of the year, but mostly the stage is given over to promising newcomers—and Dangerfield has demonstrated a good ear for laugh-provoking talent over the years. Showtimes 9:30 and 11:15 P.M. Monday to Friday, 9:00 P.M. and midnight Saturday. Special Sunday showcase at 9:30 P.M. All major credit cards.

Improvisation. 358 W. 44th St.; 765-8268. Before there was Catch or the Comic Strip, the Improv, as it was fondly known, was giving birth to the careers of Richard Pryor, Robert Klein, David Steinberg, and others. They all return to see who the latest finds are as well as to tell their latest stories. Still the most Bohemian of the comedy rooms, and popular for after-theater entertainment and snacking. No credit cards.

Magic Town House. 1026 Third Ave., 61st St.; 752-1165. Matinee performances for children and teenagers, evening buffet shows (bring your own bottle) for drinking age teens and young adults. Reservations a must. No credit cards.

Mostly Magic. 53 Carmine St. in the Village; 924-1472. Magic and comedy are paired with audience participation Saturdays at 3:00 P.M. for children, with periodic special programs for adults. Reservations necessary. No credit cards.

HOTEL ROOMS AND PIANO BARS

Algonquin Oak Room. 59 W. 44th St.; 840-6800. Pianist Steve Ross holds forth, recreating the spirit of the '30s, '40s, and '50s from 9:00 P.M. Wednesday to Saturday and from 5:30 P.M. Sunday. Especially popular for after-theater supper buffet. Reservations suggested. No V.

Backstage. 318 W. 45th St.; 571-8447. Ted Hook's marvelous theater-crowd hangout features a pianist from 10:15 until closing, lampshades signed by the celebs who've dined there (most of Broadway), lunch, supper, and good burgers after midnight. No CB.

Beekman Towers. 3 Mitchell Place at 49th St. and First Ave.; 355-7300. Great East River and UN views, and sweepingly gentle piano music to go with them. No cover, no minimum, no hurry. AE, CB, DC.

NIGHT LIFE

Bemelman's Bar. Hotel Carlyle, Madison Ave. at 76th St.; 744-1600. Romantically private, usually featuring Barbara Carroll's equally intimate piano playing. All major credit cards.

Café Carlyle. See *Crème de la Crème*.

Carnegie Tavern. 165 W. 56th St., directly behind Carnegie Hall; 757-9522. Dark-brown walls that have a coppery glow and a glassed-in sidewalk café are especially special when the likes of Ellis Larkin is at the piano. Monday to Saturday, 8:00 P.M. to midnight. No CB.

Conservatory. 15 Central Park W. at 61st St.; 581-0896. Very pleasing, relaxed café/restaurant in the Hotel Mayflower, with singer/pianists nightly from 8:30. Convenient to Lincoln Center and the Coliseum. All major credit cards.

David K's. 1115 Third Ave. at 65th St.; 371-9090. While most people come here for gourmet Chinese food of the first order, some also stop by regularly for pianist Hugh Shannon, who inhabits the lounge Tuesday to Saturday from 9:00 P.M. AE.

Downey's. 705 Eighth Ave. at 44th St.; 757-0186. Steakhouse with name pianists in the bar area. No CB.

Front Row. One Times Square at 42nd St. and Broadway; 695-1880. This is the cocktail lounge of the Act I restaurant overlooking the lights of the Great White Way. Piano music from 7:00 P.M. to midnight. Closed Sunday. All major credit cards.

Hilton Hotel. 53rd St. and Sixth Ave.; 586-7000. Light jazzy fare trios and quartets at **Sybil's**, quieter piano music in the **Kismet Lounge**. All major credit cards.

Le Vert Galant. 109 W. 46th St.; 582-7989. Excellent French restaurant with pianist-singer in the lounge Wednesday to Saturday from 7:30 P.M. All major credit cards.

Monkey Bar. 60 E. 54th St. in the Hotel Élysée; 753-1066. Johnny Andrews has been at the piano here Monday to Saturday from 5:30 to 7:30 P.M. since 1941. Enough said. All major credit cards.

New York Sheraton. 870 Seventh Ave., 55th St.; 247-8000. Dancing from 9:30 P.M. to 1:00 A.M. at **Sally's** turn-of-the-century cabaret, which is sometimes given over to hour-long revues. Pianist in the **Falstaff Room** (No Shakespeare) from 5:00 P.M. to 1:00 A.M. All major credit cards.

Piano Bar. Broadway and 68th St.; 787-2501. Pleasant after-Lincoln-Center haunt in spacious, friendly quarters. No CB.

Pierre Hotel. Fifth Ave. at 61st St.; 940-8185. Class acts such as Bucky Pizarelli's trio inhabit the **Café Pierre** for listening, dining, drinking, and dancing from 8:00 P.M. on. All major credit cards.

Plaza Hotel. Fifth Ave. at 59th St.; 759-3000. The Grand Dame of New York hotels has a trio for dancing in the stately **Edwardian Room** Tuesday to Sunday from 6:00 P.M. to 12:30 A.M., and piano and violin in the classic **Palm Court** from 5:30 to 11:30 P.M. All major credit cards.

NEW YORK CITY

Polo Bar. Westbury Hotel, Madison Ave. at 69th St.; 535-2000. Quietly elegant piano music Monday to Saturday 5:30 to 11:30 P.M. All major credit cards.

Regency Bar. Regency Hotel, Park Ave. at 61st St.; 759-4100. A bit stuffy, perhaps, but intimate and with international overtones in the repertoire of the alternating pianists. Nightly from 6:00 P.M. All major credit cards.

St. Moritz Hotel. 50 Central Park South; 755-5800. Piano music at both **Café de la Paix** (Tuesday to Saturday from 5:30 P.M.) and **Harry's Bar** (nightly from 6:00 P.M.). No CB.

St. Regis-Sheraton. 2 E. 55th St.; 753-4500. **King Cole Room**, see *Crème de la Crème*. Also, quartet for dancing in **Astor's** from 9:00 P.M. to 1:00 A.M. Tuesday to Thursday, to 2:00 A.M. Friday and Saturday. All major credit cards.

Sheraton Centre. 52nd St. and Seventh Ave.; 581-1000. New Orleans atmosphere and dancing nightly in the **French Quarter**, piano in **Caffè Fontana** (Continental restaurant), another piano in the posh eatery **Rainier's**, and a cabaret with dance music in **La Ronde**. All major credit cards.

Sherry Netherland. 781 Fifth Ave. at 59th St.; 355-2800. A pianist plays in the **Petit Restaurant**. AE, DC, MC.

Sign of the Dove. 1110 Third Ave. at 65th St., 861-8080. Show tunes from pianist Lynn Mulinax are far more worthwhile than the food at this overpriced and underqualified Continental restaurant. All major credit cards.

Spindletop. 254 W. 47th St.; 245-7326. Broadway-area restaurant serving Continental food and background piano music from 5:00 P.M. No CB.

UN Plaza. 44th St. and First Ave.; 355-3400. Various pianists play from 6:00 P.M. to midnight in a greenhouse with muted lights called—what else?—the **Ambassador Lounge**. All major credit cards.

Village Green. 531 Hudson St. at Charles St. in the West Village; 255-1650. Piano music in the upstairs bar/lounge—the second floor of a tastefully appointed Greenwich Village restaurant. AE, MC, V.

Village Corner. Bleecker St. at La Guardia Pl.; 473-9762. Interesting, intimate Village spot where the entertainment is nowhere near as tacky as the surroundings might suggest. AE, MC, V.

Waldorf-Astoria. Park Ave. and 50th St.; 355-3000. **Peacock Alley**: see *Jazz*. Also, piano bar in the **Hideaway** from 8:30 P.M. All major credit cards

BARS. No one yet seems to have been able to drink at every one of Manhattan's bars—even in the pre-Revolutionary days. What we now offer the visitor to New York City is a *selection* of Manhattan bars, with an attempt to differentiate them by their qualities and their locations.

But we can take no responsibility for the results. Bars, even more than restaurants, are a very personal matter—especially to New Yorkers. Two seemingly similar bars, side by side, will each have its regular customers who will express disdain for the other place. Our descriptions, too, must be subjective to a great degree; "lively," for example, may mean different things to a football player than to a librarian.

BARS

Those who like well-appointed drinking places, where most of the clientele are well dressed, behave in a dignified manner, and have generally arrived at a comfortable station (or age) in life, would be well off at the good midtown hotel bars, many of which have been mentioned in the *Night Life* section, above. These are in the Plaza Hotel *Oak Bar* class. Piano bars, which tend to be restrained, are covered there, too. At the (almost) other end of the scale are the neighborhood bars, with names like Dottie's Pub and McGowan's Tavern. These are where the doormen and cab drivers drink, and where you will be 100 percent certain of getting into a conversation, whether you want to or not. In this group are the chains—*Martin's, Blarney Stone,* and others—where you will also find quite good and *cheap* food counters, with hot pastrami and the like.

That leaves all the rest in the middle. With the exception of a few ethnic bars, we have chosen to cover our selection of bars by geographical area, and to give you some idea of where each place fits in the spectrum.

Now to the subject of Manhattan's famous (infamous?) singles bars. Whereas it is possible for man and woman to meet in, say, a commuter bar in Grand Central Station, the phrase "singles bar" seems to belong to mysteriously designated places where everyone knows he or she is in a singles bar. Beyond that we can say nothing more definite, and can only mention which ones are clearly "singles"—though there are numerous borderline bars. By far the majority of the purely "singles" bars are on the Upper East Side. And in some parts of town the night of the week is important; Monday is usually the slackest day—but, well, not always. Peak hours vary, too, much too irregularly to be given here. Also, the character of the clientele may change radically from, say, early evening to the late evening. There is a belief in some quarters that singles bars wax and wane like mushrooms. Not true. Most of the places we'll mention here have been body exchanges for over a decade.

New York bars may stay open, legally, until 4:00 A.M. every night except Saturday (Sunday morning), when they must close at 3:00 A.M. Many places, however, close earlier; ask. At some places, when there is a particularly enjoyable crowd at closing time, the bartender will lock the doors and keep serving.

For a little amusement, ask any New York bartender about what happens here when the moon is full.

Enjoy some or all of the emporia below, but a word on New York street sense: Don't steam unsteadily out of a bar late at night and stroll off into a quiet side street; you'll make yourself a mark. And don't think there is necessarily safety in numbers, unless the numbers are in the vicinity of double digit. Better take a cab and be safe, until you develop your own street sense.

Tipping the bartender has unfortunately become an established custom here at most middle- and upper-class bars, so leave something in some proportion to all your drinks, but not necessarily 15 percent.

Visitors from Great Britain or Europe should keep in mind that American spirits are distilled to a higher proof than in the Old World. In other words, the booze here is stronger. On top of that, most New York bartenders put a lot more than the standard Continental shot (measure) into their concoctions, often serving what would be a double or even a triple.

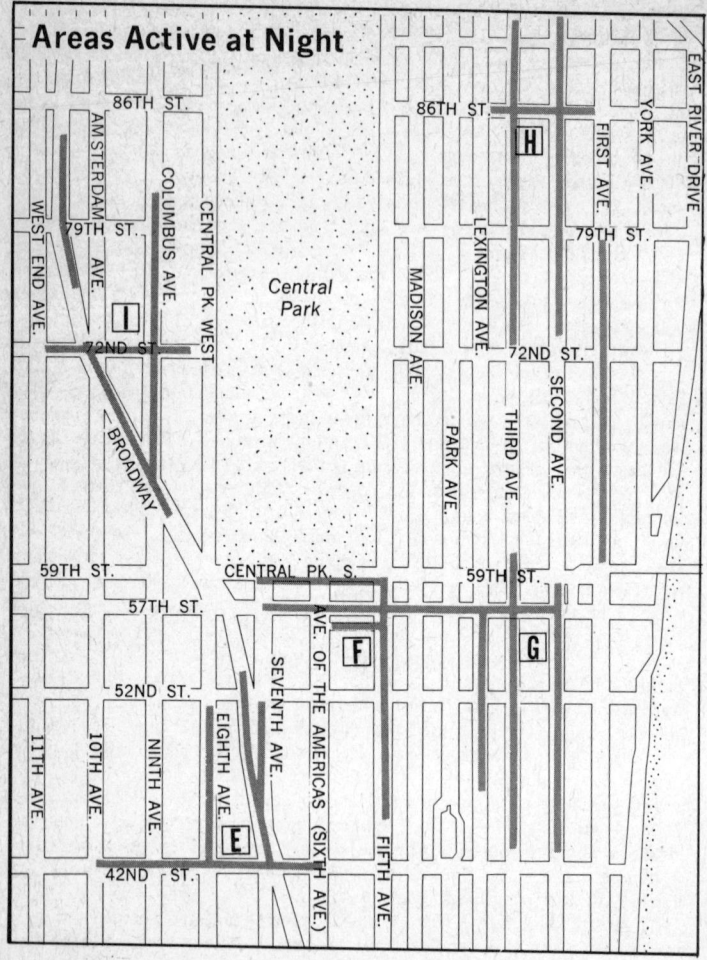

A **Chinatown.** Few bars and clubs, lots of restaurants.
B **Little Italy.** Some bars, lots of cafes and restaurants.
C **SoHo.** Bars, restaurants, cafes, street happenings.
D **Greenwich Village.** You name it, they've got it here, on and off the streets.
E **Times Square Area.** Theaters, movie houses, both straight and porn; bars, restaurants; drug sales on the street. Sleazy and dangerous, especially along 42nd St. and after theaters close.
F **Midtown.** Centered on Fifth Ave. and 57th and 59th Streets. A place for strolling in the early and middle evening; look at shop windows and the other

BARS

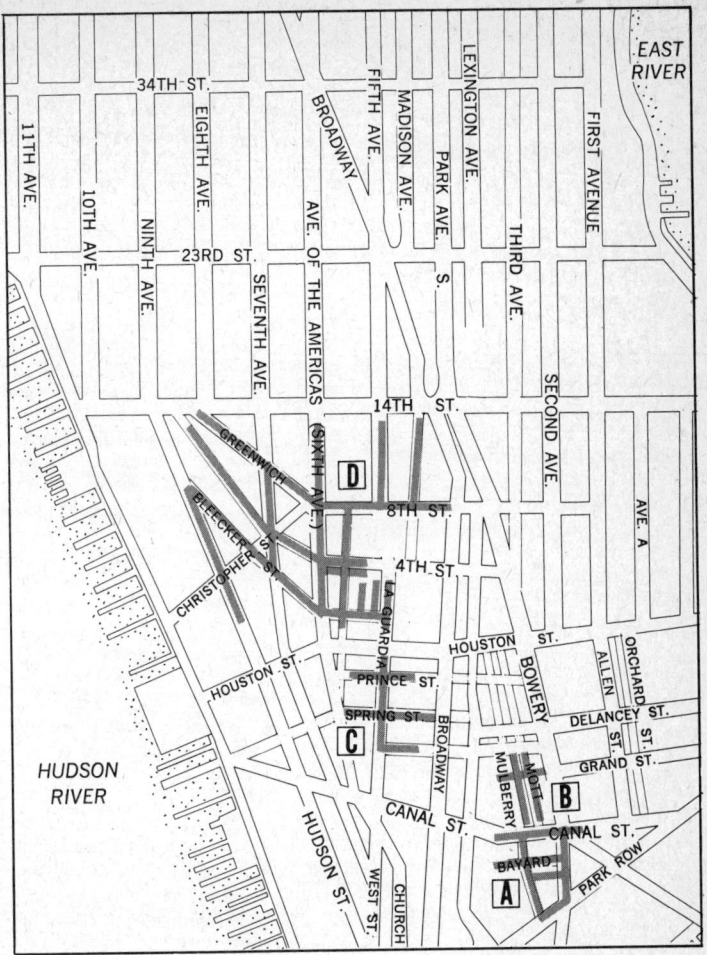

people. A fairly well-heeled group of strollers. 56th St. between Fifth and Sixth Aves. is "Restaurant Row." Some bars, lots of restaurants in entire area. Some street activity.

G **Midtown.** Second, Third and Lexington Aves. Lots of restaurants. Lots and lots of bars. Nightclubs here, too, and discos.

H **Upper East Side.** The three singles streets: First, Second and Third Aves. Restaurants, bars, clubs, discos.

I **Lincoln Center.** Also part of the Upper West Side. Bars, restaurants, clubs, discos. Lots of street life and mummery.

In almost all of the bars below you can also eat, if not London broil, at least hamburgers and sandwiches. If the food is of special note, we'll say so. Remember, too, that New York likes to eat *late*.

WALL STREET AREA

This area pretty much empties out of people after work hours—but not entirely. Some stay to drink and socialize. *Harry's at Hanover Square,* 1 Hanover Square (a block south off Wall and Pearl Streets) gets a very big crowd after work. *Pig 'n' Whistle South,* at 15 Trinity Place, is another crowded spot, as are *Rosie O'Grady's South,* at 211 Pearl St., and *Jim Brady's,* 75 Maiden Lane. The latter two may have Irish music later in the evening.

TRIBECA / SOHO

TriBeCa (TRIangle BElow CAnal St.) comes as close as any area south of 110th St. to being Manhattan's *terra incognito,* though if things take their usual course the artists who now enjoy the lower rents and large loft spaces here will soon be displaced by well-heeled dilettantes seeking an artsy ambience. Things usually don't happen till well after 9:00 A.M., but during the summer months you may come a little earlier to *Mickey's Place,* 283 Greenwich St. near Warren St. (take the West Side IRT subway to Chambers St.), where you can watch the sun set over the abandoned West Side Highway. Mickey's is very noisy, so you may not be able to hear the golden oldies with which the jukebox is loaded. *Morgan's Bar & Restaurant,* Hudson and Reade Sts., has more real TriBeCans than does Mickey's; so does *Barnabus* at 155 Duane St. But if there is a pool game going on at Barnabus and you don't have a seat at the bar, you may find yourself doing a lot of moving to keep out of the shooting line. (Nearby on West Broadway is Teddy's Restaurant, an Italian-style steakhouse, looking like a set from "Kojak," sitting improbably among the warehouse buildings.) Continuing north more or less along the Hudson St. axis—which will eventually bring you right up into SoHo—you come to *Puffy's,* 81 Hudson St., a place a great deal like Mickey's. You'll pass an excellent disco, *Ones,* at 111 Hudson St. *Magoo's,* a restaurant as well as a bar, is at the northern edge of TriBeCa, 21 Sixth Ave. at Beach St. near Canal St.

Cross Canal St. and you are in SoHo, which, with its tight concentration of lofts, restaurants, bars, clubs, and art galleries, is much more on the beaten path, and many of the folks you see will be daytrippers from New Jersey, but persevere, because when the sun goes down in SoHo, especially on the weekdays when the locals have the place more to themselves, the bars here can be interesting. The new-ish *Grand Street Bar,* east of West Broadway, has live country and Western music evenings. The *Broome Street Bar,* at the corner of West Broadway and Broome, is probably the best-known SoHo bar, with the most diverse clientele. Other recommended stops are *Berry's,* 180 Spring St.; *Central Falls,* 478 West Broadway; *Spring Street Restaurant,* 162 Spring; the *Wine Bar,* 422 West Broadway; and the place with the roomiest bar of all, *Mama Siltka's,* 468 West Broadway. Most of these bars have a special SoHo feeling that comes mostly from the architecture of the old commercial buildings that house them. This is not true, however, of *Frank Dowd's Rozinante Tavern,* corner of Sullivan and Spring Sts., which is more of a mix between the new SoHo and the old Little Italy. (Across the intersection from Dowd's is an excellent pizzeria, *Napoli Pizza,* which has tables outside for eating and drinking in better weather.)

GREENWICH VILLAGE/CHELSEA

Whereas SoHo's bars seem centered on one relatively small stretch of one street, West Broadway, the Village bars are nicely spread out, both in geography and in the type of clientele. The oldest is probably *McSorley's Old Ale House,* 15 E. 7th St., which until a few years ago banned women from its seedy delights. Go here, if for no other reason than to see what saloons looked like in New York a hundred years ago. This used to be a hangout for Village wise men; there was even a book written just about this joint. Nearby, opposite the Public Theater (the old Astor Library) is *Lady Astor's.* The decor here is of interest, the building being formerly an Astor family townhouse (mansion) property.

More in the middle of the Village, we recommend a stop at *Kettle of Fish,* 114 MacDougal St.—if you are an anthropologist. *Knickerbocker Saloon,* University Place at 9th St., has an older crowd, with jazz combo evenings. *Kiplings,* 1 University Place, caters to N.Y. University students. *One Fifth Avenue's* bar (actually two bars) at 8th St. east of Fifth features conversation that seems to have been written by Woody Allen. The food here is somewhat more pretentious than at most places in the neighborhood; live music in the front room later in the evening. *Feather's* is a traditional bar, very cozy inside, with a glassed-in porch outside for people watching, in the corner of the Fifth Avenue Hotel, at the corner of 9th St. A prime hangout for neighborhood lip artists is the *Cedar Tavern,* 82 University Place. (The Cedar used to be a real artist's hangout when it existed in a couple of other locations to the west.) At Fifth Ave. and 13th St., now minus the hideous giant iguana sculpture that used to stand on the roof before neighborhood killjoys forced its removal, endures the *Lone Star Café* ("Too Much Ain't Enough," says the banner across the façade), Texas' challenge to Manhattan. But we hear the reptillian eyesore is soon to be renovated and reinstalled.

Moving toward the so-called West Village: At 331 W. 4th St. is *Julius,* probably New York's oldest overt gay bar. At or near Sheridan Square (Seventh Ave. at Christopher and W. 4th Sts.) are the *Lion's Head,* 59 Christopher, and the nearby *55 Christopher Street;* both are dingy outposts of the local Literati. *The Riviera Café,* right across from Sheridan Square, is a good place for people-watching. A block or so south on Seventh Ave., on the east side of the street, resides the *Buffalo Roadhouse,* with scarcely a sign to identify it. You can eat and drink outside in good weather. Many of the outrageously dressed characters here seem to be off-duty stockbrokers, but it's still a nice place to elbow into. Across the street and down Barrow St., near the corner of Bedford St., is a wooden-slatted door that gives into a little courtyard. At the other side of the yard is a door with a little barred window in it. This is the back entrance to

Chumley's, an old Village hangout, and, on Sundays, often the site of poetry readings.

If you liked the Cedar Tavern, the Lion's Head, and Kettle of Fish, try the *Corner Bistro*, at 331 W. 4th St., near Abingdon Square, where Eighth Ave. starts off Hudson St. On Hudson St., at 11th St., is the *White Horse Tavern*, one of Dylan Thomas' favorite saloons. Going into Chelsea, we recommend a stop at the *Chelsea Place Restaurant*, 147 Eighth Ave. near 17th St. There is what seems to be a junkshop in front, but in the back is a busy bar and restaurant. Also north of 14th St., but not in Chelsea, is the rather dingy *Max's Kansas City*, which features music but has a congenial (more or less) bar scene; Park Ave. South near 17th St.

MIDTOWN

The midtown area has the widest variety of bars of any one part of the city; our review simply starts at the south and works north.

Pete's Tavern, Irving Place at 18th St., was probably one of O. Henry's drinking spots. The bar itself is a work of art; tables outside in good weather. *Caliban's*, Third Avenue near 25th St., is a comfortable brick-wall sort of neighborhood bar—and the neighborhood in question is an interesting mix of types. *The Back Porch*, Third Ave. at 33rd St., has tables outside in good weather for drinking or dining. *Guardsman II*, 34th St. between First and Second Aves., and *El Parador*—a fine Mexican restaurant on 34th St. east of First Ave.—are both something of singles bars, and are close to a group of first-run moviehouses on 34th St. So is *Brew's*, a sawdust-on-the-floor emporium on 34th St. between Lexington and Third Aves. *Kitty Hawk's*, at 565 Third Ave. near 37th St., is something of a singles bar, too, though in a low-keyed way. The big thing here seems to be the Space Invaders games.

We have mentioned the very good hotel bars. One of the coziest is the little bar just inside the entrance to the *Algonquin Hotel*, around to the right. Throughout the midtown area, you will find that bars near the big companies' offices will be filled with—surprise!—people from those companies. For example, find the bars nearest the CBS building on Sixth Avenue and you'll find broadcasting people. Some bars attract all sorts of hotshots, though, such as *Charley O's* at 33 W. 48th St. (plus good eats), or, for the slightly lower-ranked: *The Office Pub* on 55th St. east of Sixth Ave.; *Paul Revere's Tavern*, Lexington Ave. near 48th St. (mature advertising folks; very convivial at night, with piano music); *Maude's*, Lexington Ave. at 51st St. (a slightly younger ad crowd); *Molly Mog's*, 65 East 55th Street; and the king of them all, *P. J. Clarke's*, 915 Third Avenue at 55th St.

Charlie Brown's, in the Pan Am Building at the top of the escalators from Grand Central, has some singles action after work (all ages, it seems). *Goose & Gherkin Ale House*, 50th St., west of Second Ave., and *Knicker's* and *Tipton's*, both on Second Ave., near 49th St., are agreeable places; Knicker's features facilities for chess and backgammon, all comers. *John Barleycorn*, 209 E. 45th St., has, as you might imagine, an Irish atmosphere. *The Landmark Tavern*,

BARS

Eleventh Ave. at the corner of 46th St., is in a somewhat grim neighborhood, but the bar is, in fact, a landmark, is well kept up, and is fun. Try it for Sunday brunch if you aren't otherwise adventuresome. *Mimi's*, 984 Second Ave. at 54th St., is probably the best place in town for grown-up folks to mingle and have a good time. It's even busy on Mondays, with a sing-along piano bar. *The Autopub*, at Fifth Ave. between 58th and 59th Sts. in what used to be the General Motors Building (at press time it is up for sale), has some very unconventional decor: autos. *O'Neal's at 57th Street* is a very comfortable place; the bar sometimes sees discreet single action. Nearby, the *Carnegie Tavern*, in and behind Carnegie Hall at Seventh Avenue and 56th St., is a very pleasant place for a pre- or post-concert toddy; live music, too.

LINCOLN CENTER AREA

O'Neals Baloon is right across the street from Lincoln Center at 63rd St. The drinks are expensive but the place is busy and interesting. The name was originally to have been O'Neal's Saloon, but some city department objected, so to save money—and annoy the city—the owners merely exchanged a *B* for the offending *S*. Now there are lots of "saloons," such as *The Saloon* at Broadway and 64th St., a barn of a place. The bar has all the character of a baggage pick-up area in an airport. *The Ginger Man*, a serious bar in a serious restaurant, is around the corner a few steps east on 64th St.

Going up Columbus Avenue from Lincoln Center, the bars come fast and usually furious. To single out just a few: *Stephen's West Side Wine Bar*, 103 W. 70th St., and *Vintages*, Columbus and W. 70th St. (why two nearly identical wine bars need to face each other is another question); *T. J. W. Gleason's*, Columbus between 71st and 72nd Sts., a very comfortable neighborhood bar; *Palsson's*, 72nd St. between Broadway and Columbus—nice restaurant at back, too, as well as a modest cabaret upstairs; *O'Neal Brothers* (the ubiquitous), Columbus between 72nd and 73rd Sts., another neighborhood spot; *Nanny Rose*, Columbus at 74th St., a quiet bar scene, but here you can draw on the paper coverings on the tables, crayons being provided; *Ruelles*, newly expanded and a bigger circus than ever, at the corner of Columbus and 75th St., open to the street at two sides, with tables on the sidewalk; the infamous *Tap-a-Keg*, which advertises in neon over the front, "A Hell of a Joint"—and it is (the intergalactic bar in *Star Wars* was modeled after this place); the *Museum Café*, at Columbus and 77th St., is well situated, being across the street from the Museum of Natural History grounds, but it is less fun than it seems.

UPPER WEST SIDE

The *All-State*, on 72nd St. just east of West End Ave., is a dive, but very friendly and very cheap, patronized by the younger working people of the neighborhood. Almost next to Zabar's Delicatessen, on Broadway between 73rd and 74th Sts., is *Teacher's*, a very well designed and comfortable bar and restaurant (with mediocre food). *Café Central*, Amsterdam at 75th St., is a compact gathering and meeting place for the relaxed set, who may draw on the paper table covers as at Nanny Rose. The tiny partitioned bar area is frequently jammed with "singles." One block up is the relatively tranquil West Side branch of *J. G. Melon,* in a nice old-style bar setting. *Shelter,* at Broadway and 77th St., looks and feels like a singles bar, and, with Café Central and Ruelles, is maybe the closest the Upper West Side can come to a singles bar. *Marvin Gardens,* on Broadway between 81st and 82nd Sts., typifies the Upper West Side's ability to mix races, creeds, religions, ages, and anything else. *Hanratty's,* Amsterdam and 95th St., is on a less-than-good block, but somehow its pleasant character attracts Upper West Side literary folks. *The Abbey Tavern,* off Broadway on 105th St., is a long-time spot for Columbia hangers-on; and the *West End,* 2911 Broadway almost opposite Columbia University, is the headquarters for the college's drinking class.

UPPER EAST SIDE

Now we are in Singles Country. The bars that are pure-and-simple meeting places we will label as such, but up here the singles are really where you find them. Many of the latest "in" singles spots aren't listed here: too new. But follow the crowds and you spot them. Note that some of these singles places actually charge admission on certain days, usually weekends; we do not attempt to list which charge, or when, or to tell you why you should pay such a charge anyway—we don't know why.

First Avenue

The most famous singles strip is on First Ave. between 61st and 65th Sts. The first and one of the most well known of all is *Thank God It's Friday,* in its bright blue building at 61st St. Nearby is *Adam's Apple,* and one block north is *the* most famous singles bar, maybe in the world: *Maxwell's Plum,* which, surprisingly, is also an excellent restaurant; the two coexist in one space by the expedient of the bar being raised on a platform in the middle of the restaurant.

Skipping ten blocks to the north, there is a whole string of bars, each of which is wholly or partly a singles place: *Finnegan's Wake* (73rd St.); *September's* (75th St.) for the young; *Grass* (75th St.) for the possibly even younger; *Boodles* (at 77th St.) has a 30-ish customer; *Herlihy's* (at 77th also) is brasher than most; and *Samantha's* (78th) for somewhat more mature clientele.

Off First, toward Second Ave. on 79th St., is *Sugar Mill,* which has the loudest jukebox in town. As conversation is impossible, singles must converse by telepathy. Heats up late. On the other side of the street, and a little more toward Second Ave., is *Profiles,* a more sedate meeting place.

Second Avenue

Paxton's at 74th St., and *Hudson Bay* at 76th, are both pleasant, quiet neighborhood places. *Mad Hatter,* between 77th and 78th Sts., is less quiet, with a singles aspect; it is a favorite jock hangout, especially for rugby players. *Court Street,* between 80th and 81st Sts., has dancing later in the evenings. *O'Melia's* (81st St.) caters quietly to a more mature neighborhood crowd, as does *Red Blazer,* between 81st and 82nd Sts.; the latter has music, and is an old, if

BARS

somewhat staid, standby. *New York Boat Yard,* at 81st St., is for the younger set, while *Dorrian's Red Hand* (84th St.) and *Drake's Drum* (between 84th and 85th Streets) have been solid neighborhood standbys for years.

On 84th St. between Second and Third Aves. is *Brandy's,* a seedy-looking dive that is another survivor, with music "nitely," as they say. *Pedro's,* 251 E. 85th between Second and Third, looks even more downscale than Brandy's, but turns out to be quite a pleasant meeting place for Manhattan's Deep South contingent.

In the vicinity of the corner of Second Ave. and 88th St. stand three bars of special note. *Eric* has a slightly sinister decline-of-the-West feeling; live music in the evenings. *Elaine's,* across Second Ave., is fun if you are a nationally famous figure in the arts or politics. Otherwise, you'll be a lot happier across Second Ave. at *Rathbone's,* a rather jock-ish place run by a former British professional soccer player.

Third Avenue

Now we are on the Champs d'Élysée of the Upper East Side bar circuit (most of the places, incidentally, happen to be on the east side of the avenue). *Rusty's,* at 73rd St., and *Churchill's,* a few doors to the north, are both for a non-juvenile class of people. *J. G. Melon,* at 74th St., is likewise a nice but hardly madcap place. You can sit at the bar at *Bechet's,* up the block, and listen to live modern (progressive) jazz. *Harper,* between 74th and 75th Sts., is mostly a restaurant, but the bar scene is considered attractive by the sort of young or used-to-be young people who read *Vogue* or *GQ* magazines. And if Harper isn't smug enough for you, do try *Jim McMullen* between 76th and 77th for the ultimate in nervous Third Avenue quasi-chic. *Ravelled Sleave,* between 78th and 79th, is a long-established preserve for preppies of all ages; and a very pleasant place withal. This is the bar that a few years ago received a bequest from a finally departed regular, so that the surviving regulars could drink for free; we hear the fund has been depleted.

Willie's, at 81st St., is a no-nonsense neighborhood bar (and grill), whereas *Hoexter's Market* between 81st and 82nd Sts., as much a restaurant as it is a singles bar, is anything but no-nonsense, being a competitor of Jim McMullen's. (Both of the latter ask men to wear tie and jacket.) *Martell's,* on the corner of 83rd St., is one of the solidest all-purpose bars on the Upper East Side. There is a large restaurant as well, and tables outside in good weather. *Oren & Aretsky,* between 84th and 85th Sts., is another Jim McMullen look-alike, frequented by politicians and sports stars. And at 210 E. 86th St., between Third and Second Aves., is the huge underground complex—including singles action—*Wednesday's.*

Other Upper East Side bars are: *Peartree's,* First Ave. at 49th St., at the bottom of the Beekman Tower, where underemployed models act as waitresses; also a singles crowd, but later in the evenings. Up at the top of the building is the *Beekman Tower Bar,* a wonderful—and romantic—place for viewing the city at night. Across the street from Peartree's, on the other side of First Ave., is *St. John's,* which often has country and Western music later in the evenings.

Up First Ave. a bit, at 53rd St., is the *Mayfair,* a gathering place for the executives who make their homes in this very affluent part of the city.

ETHNIC BARS

The ones we recommend happen to be mostly of the Irish persuasion: *Donovan's Cafe,* 1604 Third Ave. at 90th St., has decor you'd expect to have found in Leadville, Colorado, in 1861, and on some nights the only customers will be a nice lady and her dog—but on other nights, especially weekends, it is a mob scene, with live music and lots of palaver. *The Green Derby,* 978 Second Ave. near 52nd St., makes an attempt to serve Guinness on tap—the right way. *Flanagan's,* First Ave. between 65th and 66th Sts., has a good, solid kind of person for trade, plus Irish music, especially on weekends. *The Eagle Tavern,* 355 W. 14th St., has country and Western, Irish and Scottish music on weekend evenings, and, every Wednesday evening, an open jam session. *John Barleycorn,* 209 E. 45th St., has Irish music. *Jim Brady's* and *Rosie O'Grady's* we've mentioned in the *Wall Street* section. Finally, a German neighborhood bar in Yorkville: The *Bavarian Inn,* on the south of 86th St. between Second and Third Aves.

Chances are that the bar you end up liking best isn't even listed by us. That's the way it is with New York City. Enjoy.

Attractions Near New York City

FIRE ISLAND AND THE HAMPTONS

"Out East" from Manhattan

by DENNIS STARIN

Shaped like a gigantic 1,723-square-mile fish, Long Island nudges Manhattan with its head and stretches its tail some 130 miles northeastward to Montauk Point. The western two-thirds of the island has increasingly become a bedroom community for New York City commuters, although a growing number of light industries has given the island's population of over seven million residents a sense of regional identification.

Of the four counties on Long Island, two are boroughs of New York City. Queens County is the borough of Queens and Kings County is the borough of Brooklyn. Between them they have more people than the entire city of Chicago. Nassau County—the center segment of Long Island—and the western half of Suffolk County are less citylike, with houses clustered lawn-to-lawn rather than wall-to-wall.

Fire Island National Seashore

Fire Island is a one-hour ride from New York City by car or train (twice that in heavy traffic); a half hour more by ferry. Passenger ferries to most Fire Island points leave from Bay Shore, Sayville, and Patchogue on Long Island. Unwinding on the ferry over is itself part of the Fire Island experience. The sand temperature of its 32-mile long ocean beach may climb to 120°F in summer; it has neither roads nor hills. Many of the few trees that grow there survive in a sunken forest, and it abounds with mosquitoes and poison ivy. And yet any good beach day may bring upwards of 30,000 visitors to its shores, in addition to the 15,000 residents who summer there. Clearly, Fire Island has its attractions, but the people who know it best are inclined to keep them secret. The island is actually a barrier beach between the Atlantic Ocean and Great South Bay. It is only a half mile wide at some places and as narrow as 200 yards at others. The highest point is at Davis Park—a mere 30 feet above sea level.

The fragile nature of its ecology has much to do with the protective attitude most islanders have about the place. But even more than this, perhaps, Fire Island represents a primitive retreat from the hectic pace of modern life where life has been stripped to the essentials and where commercialism is vigorously discouraged. Most Fire Island communities have no public restrooms or other such facilities—such as for changing clothes—and eating on the beaches is not allowed. Although a barefoot style prevails, the islanders can hardly be described as hut dwellers. Pole-mounted shanties coexist with million-dollar beach houses, as designer bikinis are as commonplace as cut-off jeans. The island supports over a dozen distinct communities, some clustered side by side, others separated by long stretches of beach. The social and age mix cuts across all lines. The communities of *Saltaire* and *Point o' Woods,* for example, are made up of older, wealthier and more conservative residents than those who inhabit *Davis Park.* While *Ocean Bay Park* has a reputation as being the island's singles center, *Ocean Beach* and *Seaview,* on the other hand, are family-oriented and have a large teen-age population. The ferry slip at Ocean Beach regularly disgorges tons of equipment brought over by day-trippers, even though the town has two supermarkets, ice-cream parlors, hardware stores, several restaurants and clothing boutiques, and other support services. The communities of *Cherry Grove* and *Fire Island Pines* are the home bases of a mixed, but predominantly gay, society from the New York theater, arts and fashion worlds. Lavish—and stunningly beautiful—homes, lavish parties, lavish food, and haute couture are the bywords there. An influx of singles at *Kismet* and *Davis Park* has brought about such summertime activities as wet tee-shirt contests, disco marathons, and nude sunbathing.

Throughout its history, Fire Island has suffered repeated devastations by storms, fire, slave-traders, and rum-runners. But none were as threatening to its continued existence as the invasion in the fifties and early sixties by real-estate developers intent on exploiting its resources for commercial gain. Efforts to protect the island from further development led to the establishment of the *Fire Island National Seashore* in 1964. At present, visitors can enjoy publicly owned facilities at *Robert Moses State Park* at the western end and at *Smith Point County Park* at the eastern end. Both parks are reached by toll bridges from the mainland. In addition, the National Park Service maintains facilities at *Sunken Forest, Sailors Haven, Watch Hill,* and *Smith Point West.*

Fire Island National Seashore is something more than the usual public beach. Here you have a chance to explore a scene formed by nature, rather than by man. The unspoiled seashore remains as essentially intact as it was when Isaac Stratford of Babylon set up a whaling station at Whalehouse Point in 1653. To help preserve this natural resource, visitors are given a number of "don'ts" regarding the disturbing of plant and animal life and are requested to keep off the fragile dunes. You may, however, enjoy surf fishing, swimming, strolling through Sunken Forest, or relaxing on an uncluttered section of beach. Guided nature walks are offered in summer and a park ranger gives talks for visiting groups at Watch Hill and Sailors Haven.

Facilities at Sailors Haven park include a marina, guarded swimming beach, ferry terminal, snack bar, visitor center with information and exhibits, picnic area, nature trail, restroom, change rooms and showers, pay phones, and dog walk area. Similar facilities are available at Watch Hill in addition to a 20-unit campground (reservations required). The Smith Point West facility features a small visitor center with information and exhibits, interpretive activities, and a nature trail.

Boating on Fire Island takes its character from shallow, breezy Great South Bay, and the most suitable boats are thus small, shoal-draft and capable of being beached or even carried home. Board boats like the Sunfish are extremely popular, and it seems likely that the new breed of Windsurfer-style sailboards will be even more so. For larger craft, most towns have marinas accessible to residents, but transient boats are discouraged, except in the two marinas operated for Fire Island National Seashore.

Hotel and guesthouse accommodations are available in a few communities. The facilities typically consist of room and bath with few amenities. On Fire Island the litterbug is considered Public Enemy No. 1. Local ordinances are strictly enforced.

Suffolk County

The eastern third of Long Island has retained miles of the unspoiled beaches, secluded coves and open spaces immortalized by its native bard, Walt Whitman. When New Yorkers speak about the island, they are usually referring to "out east"—a loosely defined area of farmlands, summer homes, and beach resorts situated along the north and south forks of the island's east end. Hoping to preserve the area's wetlands and open spaces from encroaching urban sprawl, east enders are making efforts to create a fifth county, "Paumanok," the Indian name of Long Island.

Organized in 1683, Suffolk County is one of New York State's ten original counties. More than 80 miles long and 20 miles wide, it encompasses the five west end towns of Huntington, Smithtown, Babylon, Islip, and Brookhaven, and the five east end towns of Riverhead, Southold, and Shelter Island on the north fork; Southampton and East Hampton on the south fork.

Southampton was settled in 1640 by a group of English colonists from Lynn, Massachusetts. When they arrived at North Sea Harbor, one of the pilgrim women is said to have exclaimed: "For conscience sake, we're on dry land!" The landing site became known as Conscience Point and is designated by a plaque mounted on a large boulder. With the help of the friendly Shinnecock Indians, the settlers planted their crops and soon reaped the harvests of land and sea. In those days the island was inhabited by 13 tribes whose territories extended from the lands of the Canarsies in the west to those of the Montauketts in the east. Today only descendants of the Shinnecocks survive. While their ancestors were known far and wide for the quality of their wampum beads, modern Shinnecocks are engaged in a number of occupations, including the growing of shellfish on a solar-powered sea farm. An annual Pow Wow featuring authentic Indian dancing, crafts, and food is held on their 400-acre reservation in Southampton during the Labor Day weekend and is open to the public. Throughout Long Island scores of Indian place names survive: *Sewánhaka* High School, Lake *Ronkónkoma,* the towns of *Massapéqua* and *Spéonk,* the *Níssequogue* River, *Nescónset* Highway, and *Masháshimuet* Park in Sag Harbor.

A Foodfaring People

Long Island is justly famous for its potatoes, ducks, and bay scallops. The first two are really foreign imports introduced to the new world in the last century. Potato farming had its start "up island" during the late 1800s, when Polish immigrants preferred to try their luck with the island's soil rather than brave Manhattan's teeming masses. After World War II, however, the housing boom gobbled up thousands of acres of prime farmland. At present the only remaining potato farms are on the east end, with Riverhead being both county seat and potato capital of Long Island. Surprising as it may seem, Suffolk is the leading agricultural county of New York State in dollar volume. And while the potato is still undisputed king, east end farmers grow sizable quantities of cauliflower, cabbage, strawberries, and Oriental vegetables for the Metropolitan market. In business for only a few years, the Hargrave Vineyards at Cutchogue, a short distance from Riverhead, has been producing a local vintage with much success. At an Eastport processing plant Long Island's famous ducklings are dispatched, plucked, frozen, and shipped throughout the country. The duck was introduced to Long Island in 1873 by a Sag Harbor sea captain who brought nine of them here from China. The birds took readily to their new surroundings and flourished. Today there is scarcely a restaurant that doesn't include the beautiful duckling on its menu. In fact, one Southampton restaurant, John Duck Jr., is named after the delectable bird and has likewise flourished since 1900.

Ask east enders which is their favorite time of year, and the answer is invariably: Fall. It is then when summer's hoards have dwindled to a precious few and when baymen take to their boats to dredge the Peconic Bay's nutrient-rich eelgrass beds for the prized bay scallop. At the many oyster festivals and old-fashioned clambakes held throughout the area during October, you can watch shuckers in action deftly opening shellfish with a flick of their knives. The tiny blue dots radiating along the outer edges of the scallop shell are actually eyes. Only the white adduct or muscle is eaten, however. Through careful management baymen and marine biologists have begun to revive the island's once-flourishing oyster and clam industry.

The Hamptons

No matter where he hails from, the first-time visitor out east is bound to experience a feeling of déja vù—that haunting suspicion of having encountered the place before. There is nothing mysterious about this, however, since the Hamptons and their residents—both the native-

Long Island Resort Areas

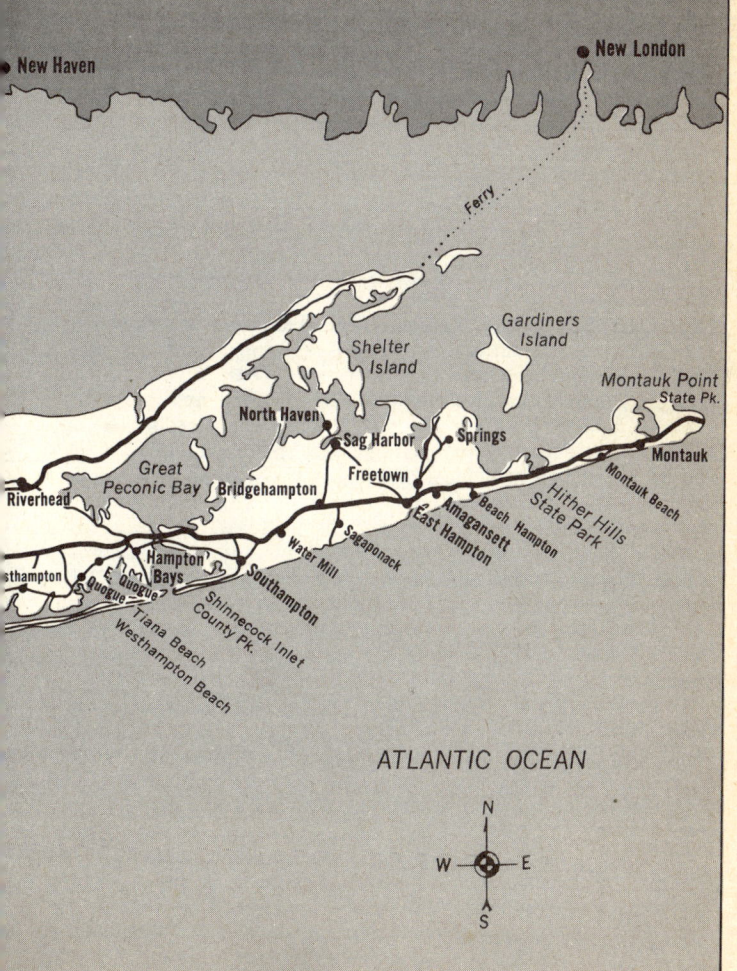

born descendants of the first settlers as well as more recent pilgrims—have been photographed, talked about and written about at great length. Even a partial listing of notable Hamptonites would include a good many stars and superstars of the literary, art, and theater worlds. The Hamptons are at once chic and sophisticated, while at the same time conservative and surprisingly naïve, depending, of course, on which part of the Hamptons you're talking about. The much-touted Hampton "look," therefore, is largely in the eyes of the beholder. There are "in" places and "out" places and a scorecard is sometimes needed to tell one from the other. An Amagansett disco that was packing them in a few summers ago unaccountably became "out" and you could have rolled the proverbial bowling ball the length of its bar without knocking over a single glass. Strangely enough, a former Southampton bowling alley was converted for use as a elaborate disco and is currently one of the area's most popular night spots. You're likely to find a best-selling author or two at Bobby Van's in Bridgehampton and will recognize one of your favorite movie stars on East Hampton's Newtown Lane. Déja vù encounters are a part of the Hampton scene. But chances are you have come out east not to meet celebrities, but to pursue the good life that has been attracting generations of east end pilgrims since the anonymous goodwife set foot on Conscience Point.

Not long after the Civil War the south fork was rediscovered by wealthy New Yorkers who found its ocean breezes, rolling farmlands, and quaint villages to be ideal watering places in which to spend their summers. Credit for the discovery must go as much to Walt Whitman's idyllic ballads extolling the virtues of this paradise regained as to the eastward expansion of the Long Island Railroad. The first summer people stayed in boardinghouses or roomed in private homes. Resort hotels soon followed. One of the earliest, the Howell House, was built in Westhampton Beach in 1866. The ravages of time, fire, and a disastrous hurricane in 1938 have left few examples of these early watering places.

The millionaires who came to Southampton and East Hampton built their summer homes on a grand scale, often importing not only marble, stone, and precious woods, but the skilled craftsmen who wrought them into regal showplaces. Throughout the older estate areas of both communities you can glimpse vistas of sprawling Tudor manors, splendid Victorian and Newport-style beach "cottages" and lavish villas, surrounded by magnificent gardens and emerald-green lawns.

While the real-estate boom has continued unabated, and condominiums often seen to sprout in the wake of the plow, there are still open stretches of farmland between ocean and woodland. From early to mid-June you can stop at a number of strawberry fields and pick your own. A month later will find acres of potatoes in snow-capped blossom, and all along the byways are the native charmers of blue asters, purple sumac, Queen Ann's lace, and the ubiquitous goldenrod. The colors and textures of land and sea are somehow intensified in the ever-changing light of the east end sky. This quality was discovered by generations of artists who came here for a summer of painting and remained for a lifetime. Approaching Southampton from the east via the old Montauk Highway, which becomes Hill Street in the village, you pass a cluster of ramshackle cottages almost hidden behind a jungle of wisteria. The place, now occupied by private residences, is known as the Art Village. It was here that William Merritt Chase founded the first summer art colony in the country back in 1892. Other painters soon followed, including Winslow Homer, Howard Russell Butler, and Charles Hawthorn (who later founded the Provincetown Art Colony). Many of Chase's works are in the permanent collection of the Parrish Art Museum on Jobs Lane. In the 1950s a second generation of painters, spearheaded by Jackson Pollock, settled in the Springs, a then secluded and entirely unfashionable section between East Hampton and Gardiner's Bay. His widow, Lee Krasner, lives and works there today, as do Willem deKooning, Balcomb Greene, Jimmy Ernst, and other noted artists. Major exhibits are held year round at Guild Hall in East Hampton and at summer galleries throughout the east end.

The Hamptons include all of the villages and hamlets within the townships of Southampton and East Hampton. In spite of some obvious similarities, each of the Hamptons has its own atmosphere and attractions. Westhampton Beach is the gateway to the Hamptons and is also the place to go for a shopping tour of interesting boutiques and specialty shops. Main Street is a broad shopping plaza punctuated by inviting alleyways where one can browse through art galleries and gift shops or pause for a light refreshment. By night, especially on frantic weekends, it is a mecca for under-40 singles. Several dance emporiums strike up the band as early as brunchtime on weekends, attracting a young and largely "preppy" crowd. The night spots open at various times, some dispensing with the usual cover charge before 10:00 P.M. But the action seldom begins before midnight, when the more popular establishments are jammed to capacity. At least a dozen disco clubs are situated along the Montauk Highway between Westhampton and points east. For the less energetic, Westhampton Beach has two cinemas, beach and tennis clubs, a golf course, and enough restaurants to suit every budget and taste.

Before dark you might want to take in one of the best shows in town. And it's for free. A drive along Dune Road will bring into focus an architectural kaleidoscope of houses ranging from stately homes of an earlier era to ultra-modern condominiums and fantastic geometric constructions that seem to defy the laws of gravity. Parking regulations are strictly enforced throughout the Hamptons. Daily and seasonal permits for beach areas are sold at most village offices and at some parking lots. By way of contrast, follow any of the tree-lined streets that meander through the nearby hamlets of Remensburg, Westhampton, and Quiogue. Nostalgia buffs will find the rose-covered cottages, picket fences, and authentically restored country farmhouses that have all but disappeared from the American scene. Don't miss the annual House and Garden tour through some of the area's finest homes. Other summer events of note are an outdoor art show, crafts show, and a mid-August flea market. Check the local papers for times and dates.

To the east are the quiet-as-clam villages of Quogue and East Quogue. Before continuing, a word about clams. We have it on the best authority that both *Quiogue* and *Quogue* are derived from the Indian word, *Quaquanantuck*—which refers to an area of soggy marshland that squishes underfoot. Such a place is the natural habitat of the round clam, known locally as a *quohog*.

Back on the mainland and to the north is Suffolk County Airport, which provides service for air taxis, executive jets, air charters, sightseeing trips, and general aviation.

As you continue east along the Sunrise Highway, or follow the parallel Route 27A (Old Montauk Highway) from Quogue through Hampton Bays, the flatlands and pine barrens give way to the Shinnecock Hills in slowly rising mounds. As the Sunrise crosses the Shinnecock Canal, you'll be met with a sweeping view of the Shinnecock Bay to the south and Peconic Bay to the north. East of the canal Route 27 is also marked County Road 39, but it is most often referred to as the North Highway or the Southampton Bypass. The canal represents both a physical and social dividing line between the heart of the Hamptons ahead and the neighboring towns to the west. The Shinnecock Hills played an important role in the development of Southhampton as a summer "colony"—a term still preferred to the more commercial implications of "resort." While today's Southampton millionaires take to the discos, restaurants, and tennis clubs for recreation, the founding colonists built private and exclusive clubs where they played the gentlemanly sport of golf. Across the highway from Southhampton College stands the magnificent clubhouse of the Shinnecock Golf Club, built in 1883 and considered the oldest in the country. A few miles behind it lies the National Golf Club, built several years later to rival the best clubs in Scotland and England.

Founded in 1963, Southampton College sprawls across 110 acres. Among its 33 buildings is a 254-year-old windmill. In addition to an extensive program of summer courses, workshops, seminars, camps for children, study and travel events, the college sponsors a number of cultural programs for students and area visitors. For some families with children, the summer program makes it possible to combine study and recreation. Prior arrangements must be made with the Residence Life Officer. The campus is regularly served by the Long Island Railroad, Hampton Jitney service from New York City and local villages, and Sunrise Coach Lines from East Hampton, Riverhead, and Greenport. In addition, the college runs a free shuttle bus service to the ocean beach and town every afternoon.

The Shinnecock Canal is also crossed by Route 27A just past Hampton Bays. Formerly called "Good Ground," Hampton Bays is an unpretentious fishing village, attracting families as well as singles and retired persons. Here you can rent or charter a boat, join an open party boat for a day, half-day, or night of bay fishing, or simply buy some fresh bait and try your luck canalside. One of the Hampton's largest discos, OBI East (Oak Beach Inn), lies a clam's throw from the canal. For many years this grand old establishment was known as the Canoe Place Inn and run as a fashionable resort hotel boasting a grand ballroom. During the duck shooting season Babe Ruth and other famous sports figures were frequent guests.

Southampton

Long recognized as one of the world's most fashionable summer resorts, Southampton has retained the patina of its Colonial heritage and the indomitable stamp of old money in the face of dramatic changes wrought by real-estate development and the march of progress. Its accessibility to New York via good roads, train and jitney bus service have combined to make Southampton a village for all seasons. It can boast of miles of open shoreline along the ocean and bays, well-known clubs, restaurants and shops, good schools, historic churches, a superb art museum, library and historical museum, and an excellent hospital. This very attractiveness, however, has also caused its remaining farmlands and white-elephant estates to fall victim to condominium sprawl.

The best way to explore the village is on foot. A walking-tour map detailing places of interest is available without charge at the Chamber of Commerce Building on Main Street. On Jobs Lane there are fashionable boutiques and art galleries along with a well-patronized thriftshop, eating places, and gourmet shops, and the beautiful Parrish Art Museum with its tree-shaded grounds and statuary. Herrick's hardware store and Hildreth's department store have been in business at the same Main Street location for well over a hundred years. Some of Long Island's most famous restaurants are in or near the village.

It's easy to miss the restored mill from which the neighboring village of Water Mill takes its name. As you enter the village on Route 27, make a sharp left turn onto Mill Pond Road opposite the Villa Maria estate. At the Old Water Mill Museum you will find an imposing array of Colonial hand tools, spinning wheels, looms and milling equipment; and if you happen to be there when Mrs. Barton McGuire, the museum director and resident miller, is at work, you can watch locally grown corn, wheat, and rye being ground into flour. The mill apparatus contains a pair of 2,400-pound grinding stones and is powered by a 1½-ton waterwheel fed by water from seven ponds north and west of the village. Classes in such old-fashioned crafts as potting, quilt and rug making, woodcarving, and early-American stenciling are taught in the museum throughout the summer. An annual crafts fair is held in mid-July.

Such descriptive street names as Butter Lane and Lumber Lane reflect Bridgehampton's ties with the land. This is still very much a farming community and its Main Street, like that of Water Mill, consists of a few shops, bars, and restaurants clustered along a stretch of Route 27. The village nevertheless supports six churches, a Community House (often used as a summer theater), a museum, library, and public school. Near the corner of Ocean Road at the far end of town you will find a lovely old windmill, which villagers hope to restore. The mill was actually built in Sag Harbor in 1820 and later moved to Bridgehampton. The road to the left of the War Memorial is the Bridgehampton–Sag Harbor Turnpike and was once a toll highway used to ship farming produce to the Port of Sag Harbor.

Sag Harbor National Historic District

Unlike its Hampton neighbors, Sag Harbor has always been a workingman's town. Built on industry rather than tourism, it has a hometown look and blue collar atmosphere that has attracted writers rather than painters to its shores. It was here that James Fenimore Cooper found inspiration for his sea tales, where John Steinbeck spent his last years, where Lanford Wilson writes his prize-winning plays, and novelist Velda Johnston creates her stories of romance and suspense. During the mid-19th century Sag Harbor ranked with New Bedford and Nantucket as a leading U.S. whaling port and is duly mentioned in *Moby Dick*. In the days of the tall ships Sag Harbor was a lusty and boisterous place. Its streets bustled with merchants, coopers, ships' chandlers, and sailors speaking a variety of languages. In 1845 there were 35 bars on Main Street alone, not to mention an untold number of brothels tucked away in a red-light district. Today there are still drinking men's bars that are suitably seedy and where the out-of-towner is not especially welcome. Back then, the rowdies were made to toe the line, however, since the majority of ships' masters, crewmen, and villagers were a

God-fearing lot. The well-known hymn tune "Jesus Saviour Pilot Me" was written by the Rev. Edward Hopper, minister at the Old Whalers Presbyterian Church (the one that lost its steeple in the hurricane of '38). Whaling voyages often lasted for years at a time and when an inbound ship was spied approaching the harbor, perhaps by an anxious wife or mother keeping watch from a widow's walk, it was the custom to run up a flag on the old Beebe windmill (the same mill that stands in Bridgehampton). The cry would go out: "Flag on the mill! Ship in the bay!"

Swashbuckling adventures were part of the local scene even before the whaling era. During the Revolutionary War the British fleet was anchored in Gardiner's Bay following their victory in the Battle of Long Island. In May 1777, a daring commando operation was carried out by a Col. Meigs and 130 Continentals who rowed across the Sound from Connecticut to Peconic Bay. From there they conducted a pre-dawn raid on the British garrison quartered on the site of the American Hotel on Main Street. The raiders set fire to 12 enemy ships, captured a number of Redcoats, and returned to the mainland without the loss of a single man.

A number of firsts: In 1789 Sag Harbor was declared the first U.S. Port of Entry in New York State. The first Custom House in the state was also here and can be inspected in restored condition at the corner of Main and Garden Streets. Long Island's first newspaper, the *Long Island Herald,* was published here in 1791. Its editor, David Frothingham, had the misfortune of backing Aaron Burr in his dispute with Alexander Hamilton, was arrested on a libel charge and disappeared under mysterious circumstances. Frothingham's wife continued publishing the paper for several years, no doubt becoming the first newspaperwoman in the United States.

With the California gold rush of 1849 and the drilling of the first oil well in Pennsylvania ten years later—reducing the need for whale oil—Sag Harbor's heyday came to an end. A number of light industries flourished for a while, but prosperity as the villagers had known was to be a thing of the past. Today, several light industries and the building trades provide employment for the whalers' descendants. The majority of young people, however, must seek their fortunes on distant shores as in the days of old. It is ironic that as the Hamptons developed into fashionable summer resorts, Sag Harbor declined into a virtual ghost town by the 1940s, since few could afford to make alterations to their century-old houses. The result, of course, is that today Sag Harbor homes can boast of a preserved and well-cared-for look instead of the simulated appearance so often found in historic restorations. Throughout the village you will find excellent examples of Colonial, Federal, Greek Revival, and Late Victorian styles. A walking-tour map is available at the Windmill Information Center on Long Wharf. House tours are conducted by the Friends of the Library several times a year, and a two-day Whalers Festival is held during the second weekend in June. Classes in sailing, scuba diving, and wind-surfing are conducted at Long Beach in nearby North Haven.

To reach the north fork from Sag Harbor, take Route 114 through North Haven to the Shelter Island ferry. Continue on Route 114 to the Shelter Island–Greenport ferry.

East Hampton and Montauk

East Hampton is reached via Route 114 from Sag Harbor or Route 27 from Bridgehampton. It is no idle boast that East Hampton has been described as "America's most beautiful village." At the intersection of Route 27 and Main Street you come upon a tree-shaded village green and lily pond that is Currier & Ives. In the background stands a venerable English-style country church and an ancient cemetery. Among its crumbling stones is one designating the resting place of Lion Gardiner, New York State's first English settler and Lord of Gardiner's Island. In the vicinity are two well-preserved homes, now run as museums, the Mulford Farm and the Home Sweet Home residence of composer John Howard Payne. Farther along Main Street you pass Guild Hall and the John Drew Summer Theater, the east end's cultural center. Across from it are the village newspaper office, library, and Clinton Academy museum. The shopping district lies along Main Street and Newtown Lane. East Hampton restaurants are plentiful and tend to be on the expensive side, and if restaurant reviews are to be relied on, price is not always an indication of quality. As an alternative you might try one of the many church suppers, benefit barbecues, or cocktail parties held throughout the summer, where food is usually abundant, prices reasonable, and may include entertainment and the chance to meet local celebrities. Check the newspapers for times and places. Past Newtown Lane Route 27 forks into North Main Street to the left of the village windmill. The remaining stretch of Route 27 goes to Amagansett and Montauk. North Main again forks into Three Mile Harbor Road and the Springs Fireplace Road. Both lead through miles of woodland and newer residential areas. According to local history, travelers to Gardiner's Island would light a signal fire at road's end to summon a boat from the island. The privately owned island is not open to the public. A number of good restaurants with reasonable prices can be found in the Three Mile Harbor area.

Amagansett has fully recovered from its status as the "in" place for swinging singles during the 1970s. Today it appears to attract a jogging crowd whose healthy good looks are an inducement to wholesome living. An interesting assortment of shops can be found in the Amagansett Square shopping mall, including a gallery devoted entirely to leather art. In spite of its tiny size the village boasts two museums: the Amelia Cottage and Carriage House on Route 27 and the East Hampton Town Marine Museum at Atlantic Avenue and Bluff Road (turn right at the Main Street flagpole). While marine buffs inspect whaling artifacts and displays of tides, navigational devices and vintage baymen's boats, children will delight in exploring a landbound outdoor fleet that includes the pilothouse of a real tugboat, a ship's hold, and the various nautical gear a sailor might use on board ship. Courses in wooden boat building are conducted several times a year.

A long stretch of road crosses the Napeague dunes before you reach the easternmost village of Montauk. Wild cranberries, beach plums and blueberries grow here in profusion. The road divides between a low road that follows the original Montauk Highway along the ocean, and a high road with an overlook where you can pause for breathtaking views of the Atlantic Ocean and Block Island Sound. Montauk is a place of rugged beauty where the emphasis is definitely on fishing. First-time visitors are surprised, however, at finding a seven-story city-style office building in the middle of town, awkwardly at odds with its surroundings. Vacant except for a real-estate office occupying the ground floor, it was built in 1927 as Carl Fisher's headquarters. Fisher was a wheeler-dealer millionaire who had hoped to repeat his earlier feat as builder of Miami Beach by transforming Montauk into a colossal summer resort. His plans included lavish estates and a deep-water port to accommodate ocean liners for his fellow millionaires, as well as 25-foot-wide lots to be sold to the working classes who would arrive by railroad. The great depression of 1929 put an end to his schemes, but not before he had erected the beautiful Montauk Manor on a spectacular hilltop setting. The Manor was run as a luxury hotel until well into the fifties. Since then it has stood like a white elephant, defying several attempts to convert it to condominium use. It was recently purchased by a young entrepreneur who plans to refurbish it and run it once again as a deluxe hotel. Barring another depression, he may yet succeed.

Montauk's most famous landmark, however, is the ancient lighthouse that has stood watch at land's end for 200 years. Its construction was authorized by George Washington in order to make the passage round the point less hazardous to navigation. Over the years the shoals around Montauk have become a graveyard for ships, which is also one of the reasons they provide some of the best fishing action along the entire East Coast. In summer the Montauk "fleet" swells to over 1,000 boats of every category. Charter boats carry sportsmen to the blue Atlantic for marlin, giant tuna, and swordfish, while party boats take anglers to the offshore haunts of blues, porgies, weaks, and flounder. Even during winter dedicated anglers brave mountainous seas for deep-water cod. Surfcasters will find plenty of action with stripers all along the Montauk shore. A number of sightseeing cruises, moonlight sails, and a passenger ferry to Block Island are available at the fishing docks. There are a number of good restaurants in the Westlake Drive area and prices are, for the most part, reasonable. Gosman's Dock is laid out along the lines of a New England village and includes an assortment of specialty shops, a retail fish market, outside clam bar, and waterfront restaurant. Oddly enough, Montauk had one of the earliest cattle ranches in the United States. Teddy Roosevelt also camped his Rough Riders here and you can still follow those early trails on horseback. Riding facilities are at Hidden Echoes Ranch and Deep Hollow Ranch.

The lighthouse is open for inspection by groups of 10 or more and includes a museum room filled with nautical artifacts and lighthouse lore. Admission is free, but since the facility is an active duty station of the United States Coast Guard, prior arrangements must be made. Write:

Commanding Officer: Light Station Montauk Point
P.O. Box 321
Montauk, NY 11954

PRACTICAL INFORMATION FOR LONG ISLAND

HOW TO GET THERE. This string of towns along the South Shore of Long Island begins with Westhampton, about 30 miles beyond Bay Shore. Then comes Westhampton Beach, Hampton Bays, Southampton, and East Hampton.

THE HAMPTONS

By car. From Manhattan and points west, take the Long Island Expressway (495) east to exit 68. Go south on William Floyd Parkway to Route 27. East on Sunrise Highway to the Hamptons and Montauk.

By air. *US Air* from major cities to Long Island-MacArthur Airport in Ronkonkoma. *East Hampton Aire* operates scheduled year-round air-taxi service between La Guardia Airport and East Hampton Airport. Tel. (516) 537–0560.

By train. Train service on the Long Island Railroad is frequent—at least on weekends—but it is often late and can be uncomfortable. From Manhattan fares range from $6.50 (Westhampton) to about $8.00 (East Hampton). Travel time is just over 2 hours for the former to almost 3 hours for the latter. There are also stations in Woodside, Queens, and downtown Brooklyn.

LONG ISLAND

By ferry. There is excellent and frequent service across Long Island Sound from Connecticut. Ferries from Bridgeport come into Port Jefferson; those from New London dock at Orient Point.

By bus. *Hampton Jitney* operates year-round coach and minibus service between East Side Manhattan and the Hamptons; also an airport connection in Queens with flights from JFK and La Guardia. Tel. (516) 537–3880, (516) 653–4659, (212) 895–1941.

FIRE ISLAND

By car. *Robert Moses State Park:* Southern State Pkwy east to exit 40. South on Robert Moses Causeway (toll). *Smith Point Park:* From Manhattan and points north, take the L.I. Expressway east to exit 68. South on William Floyd Pkwy to Smith Point Bridge (toll). From Brooklyn, Verrazano Bridge, points south, take Southern State Pkwy to exit 44 east. Sunrise Hwy to William Floyd Pkwy and Smith Point Bridge.

The drive to Bayshore, for example, from Manhattan can take anywhere from just over an hour to more than double that, depending on what time you leave. Long Island's culture is centered around the automobile and on summer weekends people take to the road early. On Friday nights it is even worse because New Yorkers are heading for their weekend retreats. Allow plenty of time.

Ferry service (passengers only) is provided from the towns of Bayshore, Sayville, and Patchogue, as follows:

Communities serviced:

Bayshore Terminal

Seaview
Ocean Bay Park
Ocean Beach
Kismet
Dunewood
Saltaire
Fair Harbor

Long Island Expwy east to Sagtikos Pkwy South; left lane exits onto Southern State Pkwy. Get off first exit: 5th Ave.- Bayshore, go south. Turn left on Main St., right on Maple St. (4th Ave.), follow to end.

Sayville Terminal

Cherry Grove
Fire Island Pines
Sailors Haven

Long Island Expwy east to Sagtikos Pkwy South; left lane exits onto Southern State Pkwy. Get off at Sunrise Hwy East exit, right off Sunrise onto Lakeland Ave. Go 2 miles to 2nd traffic light (Main St.), follow green and white signs to ferry terminal.

Sandspit Terminal (Patchogue)

Davis Park
Leja Beach
Ocean Ridge

Southern State Pkwy to exit 44 east. Sunrise Hwy to S. Ocean Ave. Turn right on S. Ocean to Maiden Lane/Brightwood St.

NEARBY ATTRACTIONS

Watch Hill

National Seashore Terminal (Patchogue)
Follow above directions to S. Ocean Ave.
Cross railroad tracks, turn right on
Division St. Pass the railroad station,
turn left on West Ave. The terminal is
behind the bowling alley.

By train. Take the Long Island Railroad to Bayshore, Sayville, or Patchogue. With the exception of the National Seashore Terminal, which is a short walk from the railroad station, a taxi is necessary to reach the ferry terminals. Train fare from Manhattan is about $5.00 and travel time is about 2 hours.

By air. *Watair Express, Inc.* operates seaplane service from the Marine Aviation Terminal in downtown Manhattan. Flying time is ½ hour. (516) 981–4634. Air taxis from other locations include *Gold Coast* (212) 885–1875, *Jersey City Seaplane* (201) 332–6105, *Pelham Airways* (212) 828–0420, and *Suburban Seaplane* (212) 895–6855.

TELEPHONE. The area code for Long Island (Nassau and Suffolk counties) is 516.

TOURIST INFORMATION SERVICES. *The Long Island Tourism Commission,* MacArthur Airport, Ronkonkoma, NY 11779. *Fire Island National Seashore,* 120 Laurel St., Patchogue, NY 11772. *Long Island State Park & Recreation Commission,* Belmont Lake State Park, Babylon, NY 11702. *Suffolk County Department of Parks, Recreation and Conservation,* Montauk Highway, West Sayville, NY 11796

HOW TO GET AROUND. Most of the Hamptons and Long Island South Shore communities facing Fire Island have telephone-ordered radio-taxi services—as do some Fire Island communitites. But the only efficient way to get around on Long Island—once you're at your destination—is by car. If you don't have one available, rent one.

Long Island's highways will get you the length of the island but most of them alternate between limited-access sections and double-duty stretches as the main streets of towns and villages. They usually have names as well as numbers, so asking directions may elicit a confusing, though well-intended answer. By all means, have a map along.

Towns on the South Shore are served directly by State 27A, called Merrick Road in the western half of the island, Montauk Highway in the eastern, a winding, busy thoroughfare. A bit to the north, but requiring less perseverance, is State 27, called Sunrise Highway. It runs as far out as Southhampton, then joins State 27A for the last lap to Montauk. The Southern State Parkway, with no consistent numerical designation, runs from Kennedy Airport to East Islip.

Down the center, you brave the Long Island Expressway from Manhattan to Riverhead. Thereafter, take State 25 to the north fork and Orient Point or State 24 southeast for a link-up in Hampton Bays with State 27 to Montauk.

STATE PARKS. Long Island has 21 state parks scattered along its north and south shores, and in between. *Jones Beach State Park,* in Wantagh, Nassau County, is one of the largest and most beautiful ocean parks on the East Coast. Its attractions include 5 miles of ocean beach, a 2-mile-long boardwalk, heated swimming, diving and wading pools, sit-down and fast-food restaurants, and scores of activities for children and adults. A spectacular Broadway show is featured at the Jones Beach Marine Theater throughout the summer. Facilities for use by handicapped persons are available at all L.I. state parks. *Captree* has both "open" and charter fishing boats. *Heckscher State Park* in East Islip, *Hither Hills,* near Montauk, and *Wildwood* at Wading River on the North Shore have campsites. Most parks have hiking trails, bridle paths, picnic areas, and refreshment stands. At the 160-acre *Montauk Downs State Park* facilities include a clubhouse, golf and tennis pro shop, locker rooms, restaurant, catering service, 18-hole golf course, driving range, 6 fast-dry tennis courts, swimming, diving and wading pools. Entry fees run from $1.50 to $2.00 per car. For further information and a full listing of camping and recreational facilities on the Island, contact: The Long Island State Park and Recreation Commission, Belmont Lake State Park, Babylon, NY 11702. *Fire Island National Seashore.* Marinas at Sailor's Haven and Watch Hill, nature walks at both. Bicycle trails and bike rentals at Watch Hill. New campsites at Watch Hill. Sunken Forest at Sailor's Haven is one of nature's wonders.

NATIONAL WILDLIFE REFUGES. Target Rock National Wildlife Refuge. Target Rock Road, Lloyd Neck, Huntington, NY 11743. This refuge serves as headquarters for the complex of refuges on Long Island and is located 15 miles east of New York City, 8 miles north of Huntington, off West Neck Road at the east end of the Lloyd Neck Peninsula. Established in 1970, this lovely 80-acre estate, donated to the Service by the Eberstadt family, will be a focal point for marine and ecological research, conservation education, and environmental interpretation. Warbler migrations coinciding with the peak of the rhododendron blooming season make this garden spot highly attractive in the third week of May. The area, due to its size, can be open only to limited public use and only for nature study purposes. A formal Environmental Education Program for students and teachers has developed at this site. Advance reservations are required for use of the interpretive trails because no more than 50 visitors can be accommodated at one time.

The following six refuges are under administration of Target Rock Refuge:

Amagansett National Wildlife Refuge. Located 4 miles east of East Hampton on Long Island, just off the Montauk Highway (Route 27) along Bluff Road. Established in 1968, it consists of 36 acres including 1,342 feet of barrier beach

350 NEARBY ATTRACTIONS

and the associated dune complex along the Atlantic. The property has special significance in the protection of a small segment of unspoiled beach and dunes. With interesting vegetation it has great value for environmental study of beach and duneland ecology. Public access is allowed along the shore for sport fishing, hiking and photography. A Special Use Permit is required for entrance into the fragile dunes.

Conscience Point National Wildlife Refuge. Near North Sea, Long Island (Suffolk County). Its 60 acres were bequeathed to the Service by the former owner in 1971. The area consists of open fields, meadows, woodlands, and about 15 acres of brackish marsh. It is an attractive area for nature study and is expected to be used in environmental education programs.

Morton National Wildlife Refuge. Located on Noyack Road, near the junction of Millstone Road, Long Island, off Route 27, between Little Peconic Bay and Noyack Bay. Donated in 1954 by Elizabeth Alexandra Morton, this 187-acre refuge serves as a resting area for waterfowl and shorebirds. A 2-mile trail to the north tip of Jessups Neck provides a delightful setting for nature study and photography. Interpretive facilities are available.

Oyster Bay National Wildlife Refuge. Located 12 miles east of New York City in Long Island Sound, adjacent to the town of Oyster Bay. Established in 1968, it comprises significant portions of the marsh and open bay areas of Mill Neck Creek, Oyster Bay, and Cold Spring Harbor. This 3,117-acre refuge is of special value in the protection and management of migratory birds and its preservation will be of value in the perpetuation of the existing ecology of the adjacent tidal wetlands and bay bottom. Portions of the area adjoining the refuge are used extensively for pleasure boating, fishing, swimming, waterfowl hunting, and commercial shellfishing. Access is limited.

Seatuck National Wildlife Refuge. Located near Islip, and established in 1968, this 10-acre refuge is subject to the life estate of the donors and is not open for public use. The area contains valuable habitat for migrating waterfowl, songbirds, shorebirds, and resident mammals. This refuge will serve as a valuable environmental studies site in future years.

Wertheim National Wildlife Refuge. In Brookhaven on Long Island. Established in 1947, it consists of 2,191 acres of brackish marsh, salt marsh, fresh meadows, and uplands. The Carmen River, recognized as a state scenic river, passes through the refuge. The area is a valuable waterfowl and shorebird habitat, containing one of the last natural esturine environments remaining on Long Island.

MUSEUMS. Amagansett: *Town Marine Museum.* Atlantic Ave. and Bluff Road. A see-and-touch museum with interesting and informative exhibits of marine life, fishing and whaling lore. Children's playground.

East Hampton: *"Home Sweet Home."* James Lane. Colonial saltbox, circa 1660, in which John Howard Payne composed his famous tune. The lovely Gardiner windmill (not open to public) stands next door, as does the *Mulford*

Farm. A companion saltbox filled with fine antiques including English Staffordshire china brought over by the original owner.

Sag Harbor: *Suffolk County Whaling Museum.* Main St. Collections of whaling artifacts, scrimshaw. The beautiful 1845 Greek Revival mansion was built by Minard Lefever. The building outshines the collections therein.

Southampton: *Parrish Art Museum.* Jobs Lane. Permanent collection of Renaissance art; sculpture garden with classical Roman and Greek statuary; an American art section changes exhibits frequently; one of the most beautiful museums anywhere.

Southold: *Indian Museum.* Bayview Road. Indian artifacts and archeological digs. Presently open Sunday afternoons only.

Riverhead: *Suffolk County Historical Society Museum.* Near County Center Bypass at W. Main St. Excellent collections of Indian artifacts and Colonial antiques. Changing exhibits feature various aspect of life in Southampton Town over the centuries.

Water Mill: *Old Water Mill Museum.* Old Mill Road near Rte. 27. The 1644 mill has been restored to working condition. Freshly milled flour and cornmeal can be purchased. Show-and-touch exhibits of looms, spinning wheels, farming implements, old American handtools. Gift shop.

West Sayville: *Suffolk Marine Museum.* West Ave. at State 27A. Permanent and changing displays depict the lives of South Shore baymen.

WHAT TO DO WITH THE CHILDREN. *Long Island Game Farm.* Manorville, L.I. Expressway, exit 70. An animal wonderland where children can walk among small animals that roam free. Sea lion shows, monkeys galore, snack bar, and picnic area.

Muller's City of Fun. Hampton Bays. Rte. 27A. A commercial fun city for kids, with rides, games.

Playground activities: Most Hampton towns offer programs from swimming and sailing lessons to arts-and-crafts projects. There are also roller-skating rinks in Hampton Bays and Southampton. Tutors and babysitters advertise in the local papers.

TOURS. The Long Island Railroad offers a variety of reasonably priced day-long tours. The tours leave from Penn Station, Brooklyn, or Long Island's Jamaica Station. Their "Around Long Island Tour" includes the train to Westhampton, a bus ride to Greenport, and ferry rides to Shelter Island and Sag Harbor, a visit to Montauk Point and return.

MUSIC. A *Bach Aria Festival* is held at the State University of New York at Stony Brook sometime in late June or early July. Call (516) 246–3511 for information. Summer theaters include *John Drew* at East Hampton, and the *Jones Beach Marine Theater*—the latter offering musical extravaganzas.

NEARBY ATTRACTIONS

SPORTS. *Swimming. Jones Beach State Park,* Wantagh Pkwy, where millions splash in the cool Atlantic surf or saltwater pools on hot summer days. *Hither Hills State Park,* Montauk, offers bathing, fishing, and picnicking. Superb *public beaches* at East Hampton, Fire Island, Patchogue, Quogue, Sayville, Shelter Island, Southampton, and Westhampton Beach, all on the Atlantic side. Most beaches on Long Island Sound are private.

Fishing, water sports and sailing. Charter boats and marina facilities available at many places in Montauk, Sag Harbor, and Shelter Island. The public dock in East Hampton provides excellent fishing. Unmatched saltwater fishing and freshwater angling at the Hamptons.

Golf. Bridgehampton, *Poxabogue Course,* 9 holes, greens fee $4–$4.50. Commack, *Commack Hills Course,* 18 holes, fee $6–$10.

HOTELS AND MOTELS

Sea Crest. *Deluxe.* Montauk Hwy, Napeague section. 48 units, all oceanfront. Heated pool, 2 tennis courts. One-week minimum stay during season. Deposit required.

Ocean Colony Motel & Tennis Club. *Expensive.* Montauk Hwy, Napeague section. 400-ft. private ocean beach; 2 pro tennis courts (free). Studios and suites with kitchenettes, 1- and 2-bedroom cottages. Pets accepted. Off-season rates April 15 to June 19 and September 11 to October 15.

Gansett Green Manor. *Moderate.* Box 799, Main St. Walking distance to ocean beaches and village; guest rooms, studios, and 1-bedroom efficiencies with kitchens; 1- and 2-bedroom cottages; laundromat; pets accepted conditionally. April 1 thru December 26.

The Mill Garth. *Moderate.* Windmill Lane. Complex of apartments and cottages in country garden setting; walking distance to ocean. All accommodations have kitchens, private entrance, and daily maid service. Open all year.

East Hampton

Holiday Acres Motel & Cottages. *Expensive.* Montauk Hwy. Motel efficiency units, 1- and 2-bedroom cottages; outdoor grills for each cottage, picnic tables. Off-season rates.

The Hunting Inn. *Expensive.* 94 Main St. Old World inn that dates back to 1699. Quiet location, spacious grounds, restaurant, cocktail lounge.

East Hampton House. *Deluxe.* Montauk Hwy, 1 mi. E. of village. Individual patios, heated pool. One-week minimum stay in season. Deposit required.

Hedge's House. *Deluxe.* Restored 18th-century inn. 14 guest rooms, each with private bath. En Brochette restaurant on premises. Outdoor dining patios.

Dutch Motel. *Moderate.* 488 Montauk Hwy. One- and 2-room efficiencies and apartments. Maid service, laundromat, cable TV, pool. Restaurant on premises. Open all year.

LONG ISLAND

Three Mile Harbor Inn. *Inexpensive.* Cottages with kitchenettes, sleeping 2 to 4 persons. Cocktail lounge, walking distance to Bay. Group rates available.

Listing of guesthouses in the East Hampton area is available at the East Hampton Chamber of Commerce, 74 Park Place, East Hampton, NY 11937.

Fire Island

Belvedere Hotel. *Expensive.* Bayview Walk, Cherry Grove (597-6448).
Beach Hotel. *Deluxe.* Main Walk, Cherry Grove (597-6600).
The Ice Palace. *Deluxe.* Cherry Grove. 80 rooms, restaurant, disco (597-6600).
Cherry Grove Inn. *Deluxe.* Lewis Walk, Cherry Grove (597-6162).
Clegg's Hotel. *Expensive.* Bay Walk, Ocean Beach (583-5399).
Dune Gate Hotel. *Deluxe.* Oak Walk, Kismet (583-8565).
Jerry's. *Deluxe.* 168 Cottage Walk. Ocean Beach (583-8870).
Flynn's Hotel. *Moderate.* Ocean Bay Park (583-5000).
Leja Beach Casino. *Moderate.* Davis Park. Rooms, restaurant, disco (597-6150).

Hampton Bays

Allen's Acres Resort Motel. *Moderate.* 62 motel and efficiencies. Private patios, 2 pools, coffee shop, cocktail lounge, and restaurant. Boating/fishing dock.

Hidden Cove Efficiency Motel. *Moderate.* 33A West Tiana Road. Kitchenette efficiencies, cable TV, pool, barbecues, recreation area, bike rentals, pool. Tennis nearby. Weekly, weekend, off-season rates. Open all year.

Sag Harbor

Baron's Cove Inn. *Deluxe.* Motel, marina and restaurant. All rooms with picture windows overlooking harbor. TV, pool, sundeck.

Whalers Motel. *Expensive.* Long Island Ave. 9 units on waterfront. Open April through November.

Shelter Island

Dering Harbor Inn. *Deluxe.* Winthrop Road, 2 blocks east of NY 114. 29 air-conditioned units, all overlooking the harbor. Some with fireplaces and some kitchenettes. Café, bar, entertainment, and dancing. Pool, tennis, and boat dock. Closed November through April.

Pridwin Hotel & Cottages. *Expensive.* Shore Road, 1½ miles west off NY 114. 40 hotel rooms and 11 cottages. Private patios and balconies. Private beach. Café, bar, entertainment, and dancing. Water sports and golf privileges. Hotel closed October through May.

NEARBY ATTRACTIONS

Southampton

The Sandpiper. *Deluxe.* North Hwy, Shinnecock Hills. Motel units, cottages, and efficiencies. Private beach, tennis, pool. Off-season rates. Open all year.

Southampton Inn. *Deluxe.* 91 Hill Street at First Neck Lane, 1 block west of State 27A. Luxury accommodations in Tudor-style inn. Tavern on premises. Tennis, pool, spa.

Squaw Island Resort. *Expensive.* Noyac Road. Family-style resort, private beach, playground, tennis, pool.

Hampton Heritage. *Moderate.* Route 27. Air-conditioned units, cable TV. Off-season rates. Open all year.

Montauk

Montauk has more than 78 motel facilities ranging from moderate to super-deluxe categories. Reservations are a must during the summer. Most motels offer off-season and special package rates after September 15th.

Montauk Yacht Club & Inn. *Deluxe.* Star Island Road, off West Lake Drive. A full-service Inn-Marina-Executive Conference Center and Spa complex on Lake Montauk. Two fine restaurants with music nightly. Indoor and outdoor pools.

Atlantic Terrace Motel. *Expensive.* Rte. 27. Family resort on the ocean. Heated pool, recreation room, and lounge. Continental breakfast is included.

Harborside Resort Motel. *Expensive.* West Lake Drive. 21 units with kitchenettes. 2 professional all-weather tennis courts. Barbecue area, pool, adjacent to marina. 1 mile from Montauk Downs Golf.

Westhampton Beach

Dune Deck. *Deluxe.* Dune Road. 86 rooms, pool, ocean beach, tennis courts. 20 percent discount on weekly rates. Breakfast and dinner included.

Westhampton Bath & Tennis Club & Resort. *Deluxe.* Dune Road. Luxurious bath and tennis club. Spacious rooms and suites. Restaurants, cocktail lounge, and coffee shop. Olympic-size pool and sauna, private beach and marina. 10 tennis courts.

NIGHT LIFE. The Hampton disco scene is without doubt the liveliest on the East Coast. Fire Island discos are unrivaled anywhere. Cover charges vary and may not apply until 10:00 P.M. Some are restaurant-discos, others disco-bars.

Fire Island

The Monster, Cherry Grove. *The Ice Palace,* Cherry Grove. *The Inn,* Kismet. *The Out,* Kismet. *Flynn's,* Ocean Bay Park, for singles.

Westhampton Beach Area

Scarlett's, Westhampton Beach. *Club Marakesh,* Westhampton Beach. *Neptune Beach Club,* Dune Road, East Quogue. *The Barge,* Dune Road, East Quogue. *The Mad Hatter,* Montauk Hwy, East Quogue.

Hampton Bays

La Plage, Foster Ave. *OBI East,* Off Sunrise Hwy, Exit 65 south at Montauk Hwy.

Southampton

Great Scott, Tuckahoe Lane and Rt 27. *LeMans,* intersection of Rtes. 27 & 27A. Fabulous disco in converted bowling alley. Celebrity hangout.

Water Mill

27 East Supper Club, Montauk Hwy.

Wainscott

The Swamp caters to a gay crowd.

East Hampton

Laffing Stock Dance Club, Three Mile Harbor Road.

DINING OUT

Amagansett

Ashley's. *Expensive.* Amagansett Square. N.Y. café-restaurant serving breakfast, lunch, and dinner. Indoor/outdoor dining.
Gordon's. *Deluxe.* Main St. Pretentious service, good food. By reservation only.
Lobsters Unlimited. *Moderate.* Main Street. Take-out seafood dinners.

Bridgehampton

Bobby Van's. *Expensive.* Montauk Hwy. Popular with the local literati.
H.S.F. (Hee Seung Fung). *Expensive.* Montauk Hwy. East end branch of famous N.Y. City Chinese eatery.
Candy Kitchen. *Moderate.* Montauk Hwy. Old-fashioned luncheonette, famous for its Sunday breakfast and homemade ice cream. The Hampton Jitney stops at its door.

East Hampton

Laundry Restaurant. *Deluxe.* Race Lane. Dinner nightly, lunch on weekends.
The Palm at the Huntting Inn. *Deluxe.* Main Street. East end branch of posh N.Y.C. restaurant. Closed Tuesdays.
1770 House. *Deluxe.* Main Street. Continental cuisine in elegantly restored home. Guest room available.
Georgette's. *Expensive.* Three Mile Harbor Road. Waterfront setting. Dinner only.
Lobster East. *Expensive.* Three Mile Harbor Road at Maidstone Village. Waterfront dining. No credit cards.
Buoy Restaurant. *Moderate.* Montauk Hwy east of village. Closed Wednesday.

Hampton Bays

Judge's. *Expensive.* North of Montauk Hwy on the canal.
Chart House. *Moderate.* On the canal.
Fish Net. *Moderate.* Montauk Hwy east of town. Good seafood. No credit cards.
Villa Paul. *Moderate.* Montauk Hwy. Italian-American cuisine.

Montauk

Gurney's Inn. *Deluxe.* Old Montauk Hwy east of village. Oceanfront dining in large resort-spa complex.
The Inn at Napeague. *Deluxe.* Montauk Hwy. Mediterranean specialities.
Gosman's Restaurant. *Expensive.* Westlake Drive overlooking Montauk Harbor. Indoor/outdoor dining in nautical setting. Dockside clam bar.
Gatsby's. *Moderate.* In-town ice-cream parlor and dessertery; family game room.
Kenny's Tipperary Inn. *Moderate.* Flamingo and Westlake Drive. Sidewalk café, entertainment nightly.
The Lobster Roll. *Moderate.* Montauk Hwy at Napeague. Simple but good. A popular place for lunch.

Sag Harbor

The House on Otter Pond. *Deluxe.* Jermain Ave. Continental menu; cabaret entertainment.
The Foxes. *Expensive.* Noyac Road. Good food, friendly atmosphere. A local favorite.
Long Wharf. *Expensive.* Indoor/outdoor dining with spectacular harbor view. Closed Wednesday. Calypso concerts on Sunday afternoons.
The Baykerry. *Moderate.* Bay Street across from Yacht Club. Vegetarian restaurant with imaginative specialties.

LONG ISLAND

The Paradise. *Moderate.* Main Street. Ice-cream parlor and family-style restaurant. Breakfast, lunch, dinner.

Southampton

Herb McCarthy's. *Expensive.* Bowden Square. A Southampton institution since 1938.

John Duck Jr. *Expensive.* Prospect & N. Main Sts. German-American cuisine and L.I. duck specialties.

Lobster Bill's. *Expensive.* North Sea Road at Conscience Point. Waterfront seafood restaurant.

Lobster Inn. *Expensive.* Sunrise Hwy at Rte. 27. Very crowded, especially on weekends.

Barrister's. *Moderate.* Main St. Popular with the brunch crowd.

Irene's. *Moderate.* Rte. 27 west of village. Chinese cuisine.

Westhampton Beach

Club Pierre. *Deluxe.* Beach Rd and Main St. Restaurant français.

Kruggerand. *Expensive.* Montauk Hwy and Seabreeze. Japanese cuisine.

Fire Island

The Copa. *Expensive.* Cherry Grove. Restaurant-disco; beach bar.

Matthews. *Expensive.* Ocean Beach.

The Monster, Cherry Grove.

The Inn, Kismet.

Le Dock, Fair Harbor.

Maguire's, Ocean Beach.

Leo's, Ocean Beach.

The Lemon Tree, Fire Island Pines.

WESTCHESTER AND THE HUDSON VALLEY

Majestic Homes on a Lordly River

"The Lordly Hudson" is one of the most magnificent and important rivers on earth. The scenic beauty of its Highlands rivals that of the Rhine. Its waters are the very heart's blood of the commerce that built the world's greatest metropolis. It was the highway that opened the West to settlement.

Near the Hudson's mouth, at Manhattan Island, the river is nearly a mile wide, both banks lined with piers at which liners, freighters, and tankers from countries around the world tie up. Great vessels bring goods from far away and sail up the river past the grand cliffs of the Palisades, to Albany and beyond, by way of the canals that reach to the Great Lakes and Canada. Yet as great rivers go, the Hudson is not long. It rises in a lonely pond high in the Adirondacks, and flows only 315 miles until it empties into New York Harbor. Without it, though, neither the city nor the state of New York would exist as we know them today.

From the days when the mighty Hudson was the only highway and settlements sponsored by the Dutch patroons outcropped its green banks, the Hudson River Valley has been a celebrated attraction. Along its shores occurred many important events during America's founding days. Historic sites are dotted along the banks and to the traveler it sometimes seems as if there isn't a town that doesn't have at least one old house to which the natives can point with pride as a place where George Washington once slept.

During the Revolutionary War, the Americans exerted their utmost efforts to retain control of the Hudson, both because it was a lifeline of supplies for them and because in British hands it would have been an open gateway to the interior. Battles and maneuvers took place almost continuously along its length, so it is quite possible that Washington really did sleep at most of the places that claim the distinction. A vital place was West Point, standing high upon the inside curve of a sharp bend in the river; cannon placed there could sweep the water in both directions. The Point was so vital that the rebellious colonists tried to block the river to British ships both there and a few miles below by stretching heavy iron chains from shore to shore. Some of the 300-pound links of those chains may still be seen in the museum of the U.S. Military Academy. The outcome of the war might have been different if Benedict Arnold had succeeded in his plot to surrender West Point to the British.

Progress Up the Hudson

Two early 19th-century events were of the greatest importance to the Hudson. The first occurred in 1807 when Robert Fulton steamed up the river from New York to Albany; the second in 1825 when Governor DeWitt Clinton opened the Erie Canal, stretching from the river at Albany to the Great Lakes at Buffalo. With the way to the entire northern part of the United States open, and with the means to move passengers and goods quickly and inexpensively, there was no stopping New York's growth. The picturesque sailing vessels vanished, but business and population boomed.

Art and literature took note of the Hudson. Washington Irving published his tales and a whole Hudson River School of artists began to paint the valley. Industry sprang up, especially along the East Bank, and Albany, Peekskill, and Tarrytown are listed among major U.S. ports to this day. And in the late 19th and early 20th centuries, more

NEARBY ATTRACTIONS

stately mansions, some of them literally palaces, were erected upon the hilltops.

More recently, bitter controversy has raged between environmentalists, who wish to preserve the natural splendor of the Hudson from further indignities, and those who would make continued use of its industrial and commercial potential, even at the expense of its scenery. Pollution has killed shad fishing, once a profitable local industry. Major attacks on the pollution problem have been made during the past decade, but there is still a long way to go.

Although drinking Hudson water or swimming in it at most places is not advisable, the pollution doesn't affect the sparkle of the river, the grandeur of the mountains, or the deep green of the wooded hills. It doesn't affect the fact that the Hudson River Valley, the Rhineland of America, is one of the world's most beautiful places.

In 1609, Henry Hudson and his crew were the valley's first admiring sightseers. Today, modern expressways like the Governor Thomas E. Dewey Thruway and Taconic State Parkway whisk travelers within easy reach of myriad historic sites and vacation attractions. In the Sleepy Hollow country around the Tappan Zee Bridge, according to legend, Dutch ghosts and goblins still wander on misty nights. You can visit Washington Irving's whimsically designed stone mansion Sunnyside; handsome Van Cortlandt Manor, its lawns and gardens appearing just as they did during the Revolution; and Philipsburg Manor and Gristmill, headquarters of Frederick Philipse's vast 18th-century landholding.

In an area rich in Revolutionary landmarks, history comes alive during drills and demonstrations at New Windsor Cantonment in Vails Gate, or at Miller Hill Restoration, with its diagrams and rails marking the progress of the 1776 Battle of White Plains. World-famous also are the United States Military Academy, clinging to a bluff above the river, the smart precision of the corps of cadets parading on the old grounds of West Point, and President Franklin D. Roosevelt's home, grave, and library at Hyde Park.

Awaiting sightseers elsewhere are such contrasting activities as a stroll through Oriental Gardens in North Salem, a ferris-wheel ride at Playland in Rye, mock battles of World War I aircraft in Rhinebeck, or tours of such extravagant mansions as Lyndhurst in Tarrytown, Olana in Hudson, and Boscobel in Garrison. The Hudson Valley also has a multitude of state parks where vacationers can enjoy swimming, boating, camping, and hiking.

HUDSON VALLEY

Westchester

Immediately above New York City, the area on both sides of the river is, as you might expect, largely suburban. It is here, in well-to-do Westchester County, that we will commence our journey through the Hudson Valley. On the map, Westchester looks rather like an athletic sock sitting upside down on the New York City line. It is bounded on the west by the Hudson and on the east by Long Island Sound and Connecticut. The squeezed-in "ankle" of the sock divides the county into what are usually called Upper and Lower Westchester.

The lower half of the county has a reputation that has not changed much during the last thirty or forty years. It is still regarded as a huge bedroom community for New York's business and financial tycoons. Tree-lined streets with houses set well back behind closely manicured lawns dominate much of this land; in many areas the towns are so built up that they run continuously into one another. Some of the richest people in the world live here. Scarsdale, along with half a dozen other communities from Greenwich to Beverly Hills, claims to be the wealthiest per capita town in the country. Other more modest communities are satisfied simply to cite some of their residents who are corporation presidents, members of old families, or millionaires.

Upper Westchester has an atmosphere that is somewhat more rural, and this section, more exurban than suburban, includes in its population some of the oldest names in the country and some of much newer luster, such as authors, publishers, and theatrical celebrities. In fact, as far as Westchesterites are concerned, even the Vanderbilts were once new here, snubbed at the time by older families who considered the old Commodore nothing but an ex-ferry boat captain. Nevertheless, the new people continue to come, and Westchester now crowds well over a million people into its 435 square miles.

What follows is a review of the main visitor attractions of Westchester and the Hudson Valley.

The Heart of the County

White Plains is the county seat of Westchester. In 1776, Washington outwitted a stronger and fresher force of British troops in the Battle of White Plains, re-enacted yearly in October. Here it was that the Declaration of Independence was adopted and the State of New York formally organized. The sightseer can visit Washington's headquarters in the Elijah Miller House and see demonstrations of colonial crafts, as well as various Revolutionary War relics.

NEARBY ATTRACTIONS

In Croton-on-Hudson, Van Cortlandt Manor, a restored 18th-century Dutch-English manor house on twenty acres of what was once an 86,000-acre estate, stands as one of New York's three Sleepy Hollow Country Restorations. Today it is the scene of demonstrations of spinning, weaving, and dyeing in early June, and of old crafts and country tasks in September, but once it was a welcome place for travelers to obtain food and lodging. The family entertained Franklin, Lafayette, von Steuben, and Rochambeau in the Manor House, now considered one of the most authentic extant restorations of early America.

East Bank of the Hudson

Take US 9 north along the Hudson to State 9D, and follow it past the Bear Mountain Bridge to Garrison. Here, be sure to visit Boscobel, one of the finest examples of Federal architecture in North America. High above the Hudson, this mansion commands a sweeping southward view of the majestic valley. Said to have been designed in 1805 by Robert Adam, it was scheduled for demolition in 1960. A local restoration society saved it, however, and moved it fifteen miles north to its present site.

Ahead on State 9D lies Beacon, a proud place that toots its own horn each June on Beacon Day, and lights up with fireworks and a big parade. Here, the Brett Homestead, built in 1709, has period furnishings and a formal garden. The Mount Beacon Incline Railway rises to where fires were lighted to warn Washington of the movements of British troops, giving the city its name. Fishkill, just north, is an oft-visited recreation center, with horseback riding and trap shooting in the summer, skiing and skating in the winter.

Vassar, Roosevelt, and Vanderbilt

State 9D joins US 9 at Wappingers Falls, and from there it's on to Poughkeepsie (pronounce it p-KIP-see), the habitat of Vassar girls (and boys) and the Smith Brothers of coughdrop fame. Poughkeepsie was state capital for a short while, and it was here that the Federal Constitution was ratified. Clinton House, containing historical pictures, Revolutionary War material, and antique furniture, served as headquarters for George Clinton when he served as New York's first governor.

A few miles further on is Hyde Park, with its National Shrine, the home of Franklin D. Roosevelt. Every year, thousands pay tribute to the late President who, with his wife, lies buried in a corner of the grounds. The house and library, containing many mementoes, photographs, and papers of FDR, are open to the public. Also in town is the

Ulrich Art Museum, with a permanent collection of seascapes and drawings by American artist Frederick Waugh.

Just up the road is the 700-acre estate of Frederick Vanderbilt, with its fifty-room mansion built in 1895 by noted architect Stanford White. A fine example of the ostentation of the 19th-century millionaires, it is rich in Italian Renaissance and rococo effects. Presently, it is administered as a National Historic Site, and contains many valuable furnishings and objets d'art. Still another plutocrat's palace is the Ogden Mills estate just up US 9 in Staatsburg, now a state park with two 9-hole golf courses. It, too, was remodeled into its present design in 1895, also by Stanford White.

In West Park, off of US 9W, is the 175-acre John Burroughs State Park. This area, known as "Slabsides," was the summer retreat of Burroughs (1837–1921), a leading naturalist-philosopher of his day. On Slabsides Day, the third Saturday in May and the first Saturday in October, tours are conducted through Burroughs' large log cabin where he lived and wrote during the summer.

Rhinebeck, a bit north along the river, is the home of the Old Rhinebeck Aerodrome, the world's largest collection of individually owned antique aeroplanes (up here, nobody says "airplanes"). On nice summer Sundays, there are aerial shows, and mock battles between the various World War I planes recapture the thrill of old-time flying.

Berkshire Gateway

Hudson, named after Henry, was once an important port, and the town just barely missed being named New York's capital years ago. Today it will interest fire buffs as the home of the American Museum of Fire Fighting, which has a large collection of pictures, trophies, flags, and equipment, including 18th-century hand pumpers and 19th-century horse-drawn steam pumpers. Just outside Hudson on US 9 is Olana, the estate of Hudson Valley artist Frederic Church. Created completely by Church, Olana is the total environment, designed as a work of art leaving nothing to chance. The state-owned Historic Site, built in Persian style, contains many fine Church paintings in its thirty-seven rooms. Situated on a hill commanding a spectacular view of the Hudson below, Olana was once described by its owner as "the center of the world."

Further on is Kinderhook, birthplace of President Martin Van Buren and site of an elegant Federal-style residence, the House of History, Benedict Arnold Inn, Ichabod Crane Schoolhouse, and the Van Alen Homestead, scene of *The Legend of Sleepy Hollow*. A little east, on State 66, is Old Chatham. The Shaker Museum here houses exhibits in a complex of six buildings to preserve and display the beauty and simplicity of the Shaker sect. Although there are few Shakers left today, an annual festival takes place in early August, and demonstrations of Shaker crafts are given every September.

West Bank of the Hudson

At this point, we are ready to cross the river to the west side and head back south.

Newburgh is rich in Revolutionary history. Here are headquarters used by Washington at the end of the Revolution when he created the Order of the Purple Heart, officially disbanded the Army, and announced the end of the war. Just outside the city, down State 32 in Vails Gate, is New Windsor Cantonment, a reconstructed army camp where Washington's men met, dined, and where he worshipped with his officers. Here, too, he dissuaded a group of officers who plotted a coup against the young Continental Congress. Guides here wear Revolutionary uniforms, and visitors enjoy picnicking. Outside here, on State 94, are the headquarters of Revolutionary War General Henry Knox, the heaviest man on Washington's staff.

Follow State 94 into Washingtonville for a visit to the Brotherhood Wineries, the oldest winery and largest wine cellar in the United States. A tour of the winery includes sampling of the finished product. Nearby, in Monroe, on State 208, the Museum Village in Orange County has a collection of authentic houses and items of antiquity, with an old country store selling penny candy the way it used to be.

Back to US 9W and West Point. The U.S. Military Academy is open to visitors, with its parades, battle monuments, museums, and other sights. The Storm King Highway, just above it, is one of the most scenic highways in the east, and a drive along that road will give a good indication of why the area held such strategic importance during the Revolution. Just south is Bear Mountain State Park, which has almost every facility for outdoor fun including a zoo, swimming pool, boating, ice skating, ski slopes and jumps, and an excellent restaurant.

Crossing the Hudson at the Tappan Zee Bridge, we arrive in Tarrytown, where the Rockefellers live at their sizable Pocantico Hills estate. In North Tarrytown, you'll find the Old Dutch Church of Sleepy Hollow, where Washington Irving is buried. The church itself dates from the 17th century.

Washington Irving Country

Just across the street from the church is a fascinating place, Phillipsburg Manor, which has recently undergone major renovation. This early 18th-century gristmill and trading center complex, once the headquarters of a 90,000-acre estate, has an operating water-powered mill and a two-story 17th-century stone house. Regular demonstrations of weaving, spinning, and candle-dipping are given.

Just below Tarrytown is Hastings-on-Hudson, on US 9 south through Dobbs Ferry and Irvington. Irvington boasts the unusual Sunnyside estate home of Washington Irving, whose tales of the Hudson River Valley have made the area familiar to millions. Hastings-on-Hudson is of interest to golfers, being the site of St. Andrews, the oldest golf club in America. The early members called themselves the "Apple Tree Gang" and were rugged individualists, if nothing else. Modern sports clothes not yet having been invented, they wore uniforms of their own design—pink coats and bright blue collars, with the club's monogram and the Cross of St. Andrew worked into the cloth in silver.

PRACTICAL INFORMATION FOR WESTCHESTER AND THE HUDSON RIVER VALLEY

HOW TO GET THERE. *By car:* The Governor Thomas E. Dewey Thruway, to the west of the Hudson River, and the Taconic State Parkway to the east are the fastest north-south routes through the Hudson River Valley. State Routes 9 West and 9 parallel the Thruway and the Taconic but run closer to the river, affording more interesting scenery at a slower pace. In Westchester County, I-95, also called the New England Thruway, runs near Long Island Sound through New Rochelle and Rye and on into Connecticut. The Boston Post Road (US 1) parallels the Thruway. Take the scenic Saw Mill River Parkway or the functional Major Deegan Expressway for the western part of Westchester; and the Bronx River Parkway or the Hutchinson River Parkway for points in between east and west. The Bronx River Parkway passes through Mount Vernon and Tuckahoe and into the Taconic State Parkway near Valhalla. I-87 travels north from the Major Deegan Expressway, crossing the Hudson River at the Tappan Zee Bridge. I-684 goes north-south from White Plains past Mount Kisco and Bedford Hills, leaving the county near Croton Falls.

By train: *ConRail* and *Amtrak* have service from New York City's Grand Central terminal to Westchester County and through the Hudson River Valley.

By air: *Air North, Command,* and *USAir* at Westchester County Airport in White Plains. *Command Airways* has commuter service to Dutchess County Airport in Poughkeepsie.

By bus: Poughkeepsie and Kingston are the primary bus depots in the Hudson River Valley, but most towns have scheduled, if less frequent, service. Among the bus lines serving the area are: *Adirondack Trailways, Hudson Transit* and *Mohawk*. *Greyhound* has service to White Plains in Westchester County. For specific schedule and fare information contact your nearest bus station on your travel agent.

TELEPHONE. The area code for Westchester and the Hudson Valley is 914.

TOURIST INFORMATION. Hudson River Valley Association, 150 White Plains Rd., Tarrytown, NY 10591, (914) 631-8702.

HUDSON VALLEY

CAMPING OUT. Hikers and backpackers may camp on any state-owned land in the Forest Preserve or State Reforestation Areas.

CAMPERS AND TRAILER TIPS. There are more than twenty organized camping areas in the Hudson Valley. A few of the larger ones are:

Taconic State Park, E of State 22 in the Copake Falls area, has 120 sites with swimming and fishing. No electrical or sewer hookups.

Brook-N-Wood, R.D. 1 in Elizaville, 12 mi. S of Hudson, has 100 sites, most of which have electricity and 20 have sewers. Swimming and fishing and the standard amenities of fireplaces and tables.

Harriman State Park, State 210 in Stony Point, has water sports on Lake Welch. No electric or sewer hookups. There are 220 sites here with tables and fireplaces.

Prices average about $5 per day for a site (state-owned campgrounds are slightly less), not including such extras as electric and sewer hookups. The booklet *I Love New York Camping* and the *Guide to Outdoor Recreation* provide full campground listings, as well as state *hunting* and *fishing* areas. They are available from The New York State Division of Tourism, 99 Washington Ave., Albany, NY 12245.

PARKS. *Mohansic State Park* in Yorktown Heights, State 121, offers all sorts of water sports on 100-acre Lake Mohansic, right along the Taconic State Parkway, while Peekskill's *Blue Mountain Reservation* has facilities for hiking and riding, as well as water sports. There is also a nature center at *Teatown Lake Reservation* center in Ossining.

Just east of Cold Spring on State 301 is *Clarence Fahnestock Memorial State Park,* whose lakes and ponds are very popular with residents of the area. Anglers will find plenty of trout and bass here, and the park also has a lot to offer devotees of skiing, camping, and soaking up nature's bounty.

James Baird Park in the Poughkeepsie area offers extensive recreational facilities, including an 18-hole golf course as well as roller-skating, archery, swimming, and a host of other amusements. In West Park, off US 9W is the 175-acre *John Burroughs State Park.* Between Hyde Park and Staatsburg is the *Margaret Lewis Norrie State Park,* which has beautiful camping and picnicking grounds and a yacht basin that is a docking haven for some of the largest and nicest pleasure craft cruising the Hudson River.

The *Taconic State Park* extends along the New York–Massachusetts border from Millertown through Copake to Hillsdale, a distance of over fifteen miles. Divided into two areas, its southern or Rudd Pond area has fishing, hiking, camping, and water sports during the summer, while its northen or Copake Falls area offers the same, plus cottage and cabin rentals. Both areas offer skiing and snowmobiling during the winter. Another attraction is the Catamount Ski Area in the Berkshire Mountain region. *Clermont State Park* in Tivoli was once part

NEARBY ATTRACTIONS

of the "Lower Manor" of the Livingston family estate. East of Tivoli, the *Lake Taghkanic State Park* features water sports and winter sports, as well as camping and picnic sites.

The *Marian Shrine* in Haverstraw overlooks the Hudson on 250 well-groomed acres. It possesses many inspirational and artistic treasures, and is America's most beautiful Rosary way. The Hudson area contains various facilities of the *Palisades Interstate Park,* a cooperative venture of the states of New York and New Jersey. Areas in Haverstraw, Nyack, Blauvelt, and Sparkill have colorful foliage and recreational facilities from swimming and golf to handball and hiking.

MUSEUMS. Beacon: *Madam Brett Homestead,* 50 Van Nydeck Ave. Historic home, formal garden, period furnishings. Hudson: *American Museum of Fire Fighting,* Harry Howard Ave. Most complete collection of fire fighting equipment in America. Monroe: *Museum Village in Orange County.* State 17, exit 129, 4 mi. W of Thruway Exit 16. 19th-century buildings housing Americana. Early crafts demonstrated. Newburgh: *Bethlehem Art Gallery,* Jackson Ave., ½ mi. N of State 94. Paintings, sculpture, tiles, ceramics. Old Chatham: *Shaker Museum,* off State 66. Festival first weekend of Aug. with products for sale, refreshments, picnic area. Staatsburg: *Mills Museum,* in Ogden & Ruth Livingston Mills State Park, State 9. Furnished 65-room French Renaissance mansion. Yonkers: *Hudson River Museum,* 511 Warburton Ave.

HISTORIC SITES. Bedford Village: *John Jay House,* State 22. Home of first Chief Justice of the U.S. Period furnishings. Croton-on-Hudson: *Van Cortlandt Manor Restoration,* US 9, 17th-century headquarters estate. Hyde Park: *Franklin D. Roosevelt Library,* National Historic Site, off US 9. Contains his books, papers and other mementos. *Vanderbilt Mansion National Site,* on US 9, north of Hyde Park. *Boscobel,* State 9D, Garrison. Restored 18th-century mansion in style of Robert Adam, famed Scottish architect. Period rooms, carriage house, garden. Irvington: *Sunnyside,* W of US 9 between Irvington and Tarrytown. Restored home of Washington Irving. Unusual design, period furnishings. Kinderhook: *House of History,* US 9. Birthplace of Martin Van Buren. *Van Alen House,* State 9H. Restored Dutch Colonial farmhouse with period furnishings. Newburgh: *Washington's Hqs.,* state-owned historic site. Liberty and Washington Sts. Adjacent is museum, arms, and equipment used in Revolution. New Rochelle: *Paine Memorials, Paine Cottage,* North and Paine Aves., Paine Memorial Bldg., 983 North Ave. Adjacent buildings contain Thomas Paine's personal effects. Poughkeepsie: *Clinton House,* 549 Main St., state-owned historic site. Stone Colonial house of first NY State governor. Period furnishings. Vails Gate: *New Windsor Cantonment,* Temple Hill Rd. Restored Revolutionary War winter camp. Museums of Colonial Freemasonry. *Knox Headquarters.* State-owned historic site, State 94; house of Revolutionary

HUDSON VALLEY

period. White Plains: *Washington's Headquarters* (1738), Virginia Rd. Used by Washington during Battle of White Plains. Original furniture.

HOTELS AND MOTELS are scattered everywhere. A few of the choice establishments in the Hudson Valley are listed, and you will find them all comfortable places to spend a night. Cost categories are comparisons between moderately priced rooms, double occupancy. Categories for this regions are: *Expensive,* $45 and above; *Moderate,* $35–44; *Inexpensive,* $34 and under. No accommodations here qualify as *Deluxe.* For a more complete explanation of categories, see *Facts at Your Fingertips* section.

ARMONK

Ramada Inn. *Expensive.* I–684 at exit 3. 100 rooms in Westchester Business Park, four miles from airport. Restaurant, cocktail lounge, entertainment, swimming pool.

BEAR MOUNTAIN

Bear Mountain Inn. *Moderate.* US 9W. Comfortable rooms in this rustic resort hotel within the state park. Dining room and cocktail lounge.

Morgan Overlook Lodge. *Moderate.* Also in the park. Secluded modern accommodations half mile from the main inn. Spring-fed pool, boating, and fishing.

BREWSTER

Heidi's. *Moderate.* State 22, 5 mi. N of town. There's a variety of large and comfortable rooms on spacious wooded grounds, coffee shop, pool, picnic and barbecue area.

CANAAN

Berkshire Spur. *Inexpensive.* State 22, at Thruway exit B3, 6 miles SE. In a scenic hillside location, it's convenient to Tanglewood. Features pool, coffee in rooms, café. Pets limited. Rates go up on Tanglewood weekends, with reservation deposit required.

Inn at the Shaker Mill Farm. *Moderate.* On Rt. 22. A restored Shaker Mill has been transformed into a wonderful inn. Modest rooms are set beside a waterfall in a woodland setting. Fine food.

Queechy Lake Motel. *Moderate.* Just off Rt. 295 on Queechy Lake. A beautiful setting high above the lovely lake. Large, commodious rooms. Pool and lakeside swimming.

CATSKILL

Friar Tuck Inn. *Expensive.* State 32, 8 mi. W. Well-furnished rooms in this modern inn done in medieval décor. Restaurant, nightclub. Indoor and outdoor pools. Health spa, tennis, driving range.

ELMSFORD

Holiday Inn. *Moderate.* State 119 at I-287. Seven-story version of the basic Holiday Inn, with lifeguard at heated pool. Restaurant and disco, nightly entertainment.

Saw Mill River. *Moderate.* 25 Valley Ave. (State 119) at Saw Mill River Parkway. Attractive rooms, houseeping units. Outdoor pool.

FISHKILL

Holiday Inn. *Moderate.* I-84 at US 9. Heated pool, bar and food service, wading pool, kennels, and restaurant highlight this nice motel. On weekends, the lounge has live music for dancing or listening.

HAWTHORNE

Hawthorne Circle Motor Inn. *Expensive.* State 9A, 1 mi. SW of town. Cozy motel with barbecue facilities, pool, restaurant for breakfast and lunch. On a forested hill, it has spacious grounds.

HILLSDALE

Swiss Hutte. *Moderate.* Off State 23, 3 mi. E of town. Inn and motel, with rates given for the inn. Rates higher at the motel. Two pools (one heated), café, tennis and putting green. Ice skating in winter; adjacent to Catamount Ski Area.

HYDE PARK

Dutch Patroon. *Moderate.* US 9, 1 mi. S of town. Handhewn beams and large gardens make this an attrative motel. Swimming pool. Restaurant adjacent.

Golden Manor Motel. *Moderate.* US 9, 2 mi. S. Across from FDR's home. Newly refurbished motel which includes some efficiency units. Heated pool and sauna.

KINGSTON

Ramada Inn. *Expensive.* State 28 at Thruway exit 19. Large and comfortable motel with restaurant and cocktail lounge, dancing and entertainment. Indoor heated pool.

HUDSON VALLEY

Howard Johnson's. *Moderate.* State 28 at Thruway exit 19. You'll find large, comfortable rooms at this convenient location. Heated pool, wading pool, with restaurant adjacent.

MOUNT KISCO

Holiday Inn. *Expensive.* Saw Mill River Parkway at Kisco Ave. exit. They have barber and beauty shops. Lifeguard at heated pool; wading pool, pets allowed. Coffee may be enjoyed in rooms, but there's also a full-scale restaurant.

NANUET

Sheraton Motor Inn. *Moderate.* State 59, 1 mi. E. Nicely furnished rooms and suites available. Pool. A reservation deposit is required.

NEWBURGH

Holiday Inn. *Moderate.* State 17K, ½ mi. W of Thruway exit 17. Yet another in a chain that is becoming a modern American tradition, the usual plus sauna.

Ramada Inn. *Moderate.* At 1055 Union Ave., not far from West Point. 115 rooms with telephones and color TV. Restaurant, nightly entertainment, outdoor heated pool.

NEW PALTZ

Mohonk Mountain House. *Expensive.* Large and attractive 300-room Victorian-type hotel set in a 2,500-acre estate surrounding Lake Mohonk. Housekeeping cottages available. Dining room, fine selection of sports, including tennis, horseback riding, and hiking.

Thunderbird. *Moderate.* State 299, ½ mi. E of Thruway exit 18. Nicely decorated rooms with an adjacent restaurant that claims to stay open all night. Continental breakfast available at the inn.

NYACK

Tappan Zee Town House. *Expensive.* Thruway exit 11. Modern hotel overlooking the Hudson. Restaurant, cocktail lounge. Heated pool. Golf and tennis privileges nearby for guests.

West Gate Motor Lodge. *Moderate.* State 59, 1 mi. W of Thruway exit 11. Attractive and nicely furnished rooms. Dining room and coffee shop. Lounge with dancing and entertainment.

PEEKSKILL

Peekskill Motor Inn. *Moderate.* State 35 at US 6, 9, 202. You get a view of the Hudson here. Restaurant, outdoor pool, and terrace.

NEARBY ATTRACTIONS

POUGHKEEPSIE

Po'keepsie. *Moderate.* US 9, 3 mi. S of downtown. A local favorite,

Best Western Red Bull Motor Inn. *Moderate.* 576 South Rd. Rte. 9. Newly renovated 160-room property, with swimming pool, patio, restaurant and lounge.

RHINEBECK

Beekman Arms. *Inexpensive.* State 308 at US 9. Old, historic inn, opened 1700, has a wonderful feeling about it. Coffee in rooms, pets limited, guests under 12 stay free.

SAUGERTIES

Howard Johnson's. *Moderate.* State 32 and 212, off Thruway exit 20. Motel has a café, sauna, indoor heated pool. Cribs and cots free, and there are even waterbeds in some rooms under that familiar orange roof.

TARRYTOWN

Hilton Inn. *Expensive.* US 9 at Thruway exit 9, 1 mi. S of town. King-sized beds, tasteful décor, and gardens. Weekend dancing, heated pool, pets allowed. Restaurant, coffee shop, cocktail lounge mean you can *stay* here.

TUXEDO PARK

Red Apple. *Moderate.* State 17, 3 mi. N of town. An important landmark of sorts to vacationers Catskills-bound, this pleasant spot, set back on a wooded hillside, has a heated pool, playground, and a good restaurant. Reservation deposit required.

WEST POINT

Hotel Thayer. *Moderate.* Lovely and historic hotel on the Academy grounds. Rooms overlook the Hudson. Restaurant, cocktail lounge. Family rooms for 3–4 persons and suites also available.

WHITE PLAINS

White Plains Hotel. *Expensive.* South Broadway and Lyon Place in town. Large attractive rooms with queen-size beds in this newly renovated hotel. Coffee shop, restaurant, lounge with live entertainment and dancing.

YONKERS

Holiday Inn. *Moderate.* 125 Tuckahoe Rd., ½ mi. W of Thruway exit 6. Outdoor and indoor pools, sauna. Pets are allowed. The rooms are comfortable and spacious.

YORKTOWN HEIGHTS

Yorktown Motor Lodge. *Moderate.* US 202, at Taconic State Parkway. Ideal acreage for the outdoor sports enthusiast. Mohansic State Park nearby. Pets allowed, two pools (one indoor heated), wading pool, dancing.

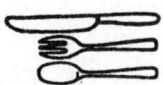

DINING OUT in Westchester and the Hudson Valley may bring you to a historic house in the middle of Washington Irving country, or a lookout over the Hudson itself. In eastern Westchester, perhaps you'll have a view of Long Island Sound. Restaurants listed here are but a tiny sampling of the many fine ones in the vicinity. For others, just drive down any main road.

Cost categories are comparisons between medium-priced meals from all the menus listed. In this wealthy region, the categories are as follows: *Deluxe*, $15.00 and higher; *Expensive*, $9.00 to $14.50; *Moderate*, $6.50 to $9.00; and *Inexpensive*, $6.00. Included in these prices are *hors d'eouvres* or soup, *entrée* and dessert. **Not included are drinks, tip, and tax.** A more complete explanation of restaurant categories may be found in the *Facts at Your Fingertips* section.

ARDSLEY

Water Wheel Inn. *Moderate.* State 9A, ½ mi. N of Thruway exit 7. Stroll in the garden, or sit on the patio before a meal of beef or duck prepared by excellent chefs. In summer, roof opens and you may dance under the sky. Jacket and tie required.

BEDFORD

La Crémaillère. *Deluxe.* Take exit 31 off Merritt Parkway, then go S on Banksville Rd. Building is classic Early American, but everything else is French, from wine cellar to service to cuisine with their own pastries. This is a place to go for a special night out. Jacket, tie, and reservations a must.

BREWSTER

Beau Sejour. *Deluxe.* State 22, 1 mi. N of town. Everything here is prepared in classic French tradition. The restaurant is set in the middle of an estate, on a wooded hilltop overlooking the lake. Authentic French dishes; specialties are bisques and *escaloppe de veau*. Jacket and tie required. Reservations necessary.

NEARBY ATTRACTIONS

CANAAN

Stony Kill Steak House. *Expensive.* State 295 at Thruway exit B3. Homemade bread complements basic American cuisine. The preparation and service are excellent. Open for lunch and dinner.

Inn at the Shaker Hill Farm. *Expensive.* State 22, New Lebanon. Unique dining experience inside a real old Shaker mill (built in 1824). Family-style service, but the informal atmosphere is half the charm. *Hors d'oeuvres,* drinks and dessert around a cozy fire. Good food with lots of *vin ordinaire.* Dinner.

Shuji's. *Expensive.* US 20 at State 22. Japanese cuisine served in a former baronial mansion. The fine food is served in *tatami* rooms (on the floor) upstairs, with conventional tables and chairs on the main level. *Sukiyaki, tempura, hibachi* cooking, and Oriental background music. Dinner only.

CARMEL

Dreamwold. *Deluxe.* Gypsy Trail Rd. Dine graciously here in a Tudor manor house that is set on 32 acres. Cocktails on the terrace; superb French cuisine in their intimate dining room; coffee and liqueurs in the drawing room. Jacket and tie required. Dinner only.

CATSKILL

Skyline. *Moderate.* State 23, ½ mi. E of town. Pleasant dining room on a hillside features a Continental-American menu, with seafood specialties.

CENTRAL VALLEY

Gasho of Japan. *Moderate.* State 32, 1 mi. N of town. The original timbers of a 15th-century Japanese Samurai warrior hideout have been reassembled with traditional rice rope and wood pegs. Tableside *hibachi* cooking. Oriental gardens.

COLD SPRING

Breakneck Lodge. *Moderate.* State 9D. Swiss-German and American entrées served in a chalet atmosphere with a Hudson River view. The staff is Luchow trained.

La Ruche. *Moderate.* US 9. Own pastries and French specialties. Music; jacket required. Dinner only.

CORNWALL-ON-HUDSON

Cornwall Inn. *Expensive.* State 218. French specialties, wine cellar, imported beer highlight this chef-owned restaurant.

HUDSON VALLEY

DOVER PLAINS

Old Drover's Tavern. *Expensive.* Old Drover's Inn Rd., ½ mi. E of State 22. Quaint 200-year-old building with original taproom and antique furnishings. Blackboard menu features game birds, curry. No tipping. 20% service charge. Jacket required.

ELMSFORD

La Stazione di Tony. *Moderate.* 15 Saw Mill River Rd. Dine here in a rustic inn that was once the town's old railroad station. Wide range of Italian specialties.

FISHKILL

Dutchess Manor. *Moderate.* State 9D, 3 mi. S of Beacon. Watch the Hudson roll on by as you enjoy variety of dishes in Continental style. Patio dining in summer.

GARRISON

Bird & Bottle. *Expensive.* State 301, 4 mi. NW. Before fireplace in winter, on terrace in summer, you'll be charmed by Early American setting, varied menu.

HARTSDALE

Auberge Argenteuil. *Deluxe.* 42 Healy Ave., off State 100. Paintings and antiques grace this fine establishment that specializes in French cooking. Luscious pastries. Dinner only.

HAWTHORNE

Taconic Brauhaus. *Moderate.* 15 Commerce St., off exit 5W from Taconic State Parkway. A great place for wurst and other Bavarian specialties. Their own pastries are dished up by waitresses attired in Bavarian costume. Jacket and tie required on weekend evenings.

NEARBY ATTRACTIONS

HILLSDALE

L'Hostellerie Bressane. *Deluxe.* State 22 at State 23. Antiques and 18th-century atmosphere, fine food. Cuisine is *haute* with prices to match. The wine list is excellent. Dinner only.

MARLBORO

Ship Lantern Inn. *Expensive.* US 9W. As nautical as it sounds, with captain's chairs, round tables, and displays of ship's models, circa 1799. The building itself dates back to the days of the Revolution. Fine food, with an extensive menu, offering specialties from "sea and stream" or "meat and fowl." For starters, try their Bloody Mariner.

MILLBROOK

Daniele's. *Expensive.* Franklin Ave. on US 44. Not for dieters, with its large portions, scrumptious pastries, and superb menu.

NEWBURGH

Beau Rivage. *Expensive.* 538 River Rd., 5 mi. N off US 9W. Soft music and Continental dishes make this an appealing restaurant within sight of the Hudson.

OSSINING

Dudley's. *Inexpensive.* 6 Rockledge Ave. Casual dining, with seafood and beef dishes chalk-written on a blackboard. In addition to lunch and dinner, they also serve a late supper.

PATTERSON

L'Auberge Bretonne. *Deluxe.* State 22. The chef here was once at the famous Stonehenge, so the food is *magnifique*. French provincial inn crammed with antiques, at the foothills of the Berkshires. Extensive menu of specially prepared Gallic dishes. Jacket and tie required.

PEEKSKILL

Monte Verde. *Inexpensive.* US 6, 202, 2 mi. N. Former Van Cortlandt mansion features Continental specialties, overlooks Hudson.

POUGHKEEPSIE

Treasure Chest. *Moderate.* US 9, 4 mi. S of the city. Inviting décor, pastries are features of a generally good menu in this mid-18th-century Dutch Colonial home.

POUND RIDGE

Emily Shaw's Inn. *Expensive.* State 137. Popular for both its inventive menus and physical charm. Fish specialties. Old-style English taproom is worth a visit. Dinner only.

PURDYS

The Box Tree. *Deluxe.* Junction State Routes 22 and 116. The service and the food are extra special here. Dining in one of two rooms that are replete with antiques, crystal, and paintings. The food is Parisian *haute cuisine*.

RHINEBECK

Beekman Arms. *Inexpensive.* US 9 at State 308. Tasty meals served in Colonial-style dining room, prime ribs specialty.

SOUTH SALEM

Horse 'n Hound. *Expensive.* Spring St. Game is the name of the game here in a 1735 inn that was once a stagecoach stop. Choose from the blackboard menu, then dine nicely on pheasant, venison, buffalo, or boar.

TAPPAN

Julio's. *Moderate.* 154 Washington St. Sumptuous north Italian cuisine served in a Colonial mansion where gaslight and candlelight add to the charm.

TARRYTOWN

Tappan Hill. *Expensive.* Highland Ave., 1 mi. No of Thruway exit 9. Mark Twain once owned this estate, but now it's home to fine duck and rock Cornish hen, served lovingly as you enjoy a view of the Hudson.

WHITE PLAINS

Sam's. *Expensive.* Gedney Way, off Mamaroneck Ave. Diners watch their meat cooking over a flaming grill, and, in the tradition of the former "Mayor of Gedney Way," superb steaks, roast beef, and spareribs are served.

Aphrodite. *Inexpensive.* 610 Hartsdale Ave. Seafood house done in Grecian décor. In addition to the fresh fish, Greek salads and desserts are served while bouzouki music plays in the background.

Bengal Tiger. *Inexpensive.* 140 E. Post Rd. East Indian fare served in a small storefront hideaway. Curries to taste and specially brewed teas, with haunting Indian music as accompaniment.

Maxl's. *Inexpensive.* N. Broadway. Bavarian atmosphere with the emphasis on game specialties. Everything from cream of venison soup to roast suckling pig served in their rathskeller. Music nightly.

YORKTOWN HEIGHTS

Ravetto's. *Expensive.* US 202, 4 mi. N of town. Fine Italian restaurant, with fettucini, scaloppini, and pheasant featured on an outstanding menu. Outdoor tables, jacket required, pleasant atmosphere. Dinner only.

THE CATSKILLS

Lively Resorts and Rustic Retreats

Onteora was the Indian name for the region, the "Land in the Sky," but with the tallest point just over four thousand feet, the Catskills are hardly the altitude champions of the Western world. In fact, they are not even mountains, really.

Over the years the Catskills became known simply as "The Mountains" because of the ethnic groups who discovered and sectioned off their own resorts retreats. It is the site of the German Alps Festival, complete with oompah bands and imported beer; and the stage for the National Polka Festival, an annual event, which brings dozens of bands from all over the country to keep things jumping for nine full days. But perhaps its most important claim to fame has been as the "Borscht Belt," where luxury fiefdoms like Grossinger's and the Concord served as training grounds for such stars as Milton Berle, Danny Kaye, Sid Caesar, Phil Silvers, and Eddie Fisher.

It isn't that the more famous resorts, with their all-inclusive environments are changing their styles; they're doing better than ever. But with horse trails, county fairs, camping areas, skiing, fishing, and historic sites and much more, vacationers are coming for the attractions alone. As for "The Mountains," their separate peaks are lofty ground between the valleys of a deeply dissected plateau, the peaks usually consisting of more or less continuous ranges. Lakes are few and small; large bodies of water like the Ashokan, Pepacton, Cannonsville, and Schoharie reservoirs are the results of dams. Forests cover hundreds of thousands of acres and sparkling streams flow through wild valleys and ravines.

Early settlers found plenty of deer, bear, wolves, and wildcats, and hunting is still a favorite pastime in season. Deer are plentiful and may be seen along the back roads in late evening and early morning. By day they are high up on the mountains or deep in the woods, doing their best to avoid the hunters. Bears and wildcats are still seen in the remoter sections—February 2 is "bear's day," not groundhog day, to local residents—and there are also fox, mink, woodchucks, raccoons, and porcupines. Pheasant and grouse abound in the vicinity.

In addition, there are hundreds of miles of trout streams, mainly the Esopus, Schoharie, Neversink, Beaver Kill, and Willowemoc, and the branches of the upper Delaware. The first two are the most popular, but little brooks feeding the big streams hold lots of fine fish. Lakes and reservoirs are full of bass and pickerel ready to put up a fight. And the Catskills are a favorite of photographers, artists, and birdwatchers, who flock here annually to capture nature with cameras, watercolors, and binoculars.

For those seeking a rustic vacation, many woodland tent and trailer sites are found in the Catskills. Quiet country inns in small villages offer the chance to enjoy the countryside, savor good food in a myriad of styles, and haunt back roads for antiques. Any time of the year is a good one for a Catskills vacation, as new facilities sprouting up all over are making this area one of the East's most popular ski centers, in a state which has more ski areas than any in the country. With luck, you might even hear the sound of wooden bowling balls echoing across the mountaintops during a summer thunderstorm. Legend has it that Henry Hudson and his crew return here every twenty years to visit the mountains they discovered.

The luxury resorts themselves have such extravagant features as private landing strips and year-round ice-skating, top name entertainment, and rooms with two baths deserve prominent mention. And over 50,000 permanent residents—farmers, builders, shopkeepers, plumbers, electricians—make their living largely from the resort business.

THE CATSKILLS

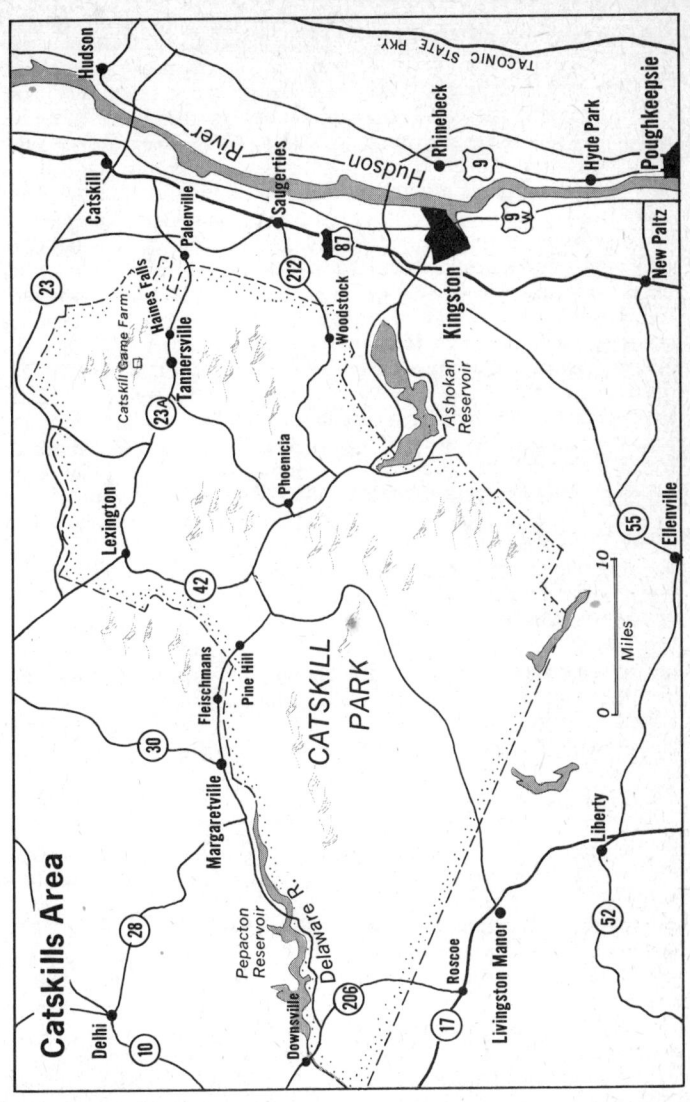

Most of the better-known Catskill hotels are self-contained city-resorts, and no guest need ever leave the premises for want of something to do. On the grounds are tennis courts, badminton, pitch-and-putt greens (some resorts have their own golf courses; the rest use public courses), baseball diamonds, outdoor and indoor swimming pools, archery, horseback riding, ice-skating rinks, toboggan runs, skiing, card rooms, recreation halls, nightclubs, hiking trails, and instruction in arts, crafts, painting, and dancing.

As an added feature, most resorts have day camps and night patrols. The day camp is a day-long recreational program for the small children, who are fetched at dawn, fed and entertained until after supper in separate areas which usually include small pools. At night, when the parents are at dinner or in the nightclub, the night patrol of counselors checks rooms to see that the children are safely asleep.

Grossinger's, fifteen miles northwest of the Concord, sits on a hilltop overlooking the town of Liberty, and has concrete walks and neatly spaced Tudor-style buildings—a suburban look—while in Kiamesha Lake the huge eleven-story Concord, with its mammoth lobby and dazzling chandeliers, has an urban flavor. Grossinger's, the older of the two, has been the subject of a book and the inspiration for a movie, and its fame is international.

But again, there are other places catering to every group, young and old alike. On side roads off State 17, there are many hotels and bungalow colonies priced to fit every pocketbook. Families often prefer the bungalows, which are less expensive and more informal, being without rigid meal schedules and entertainment. You can stop in a luxury resort, a highway motel, or a lean-to along a forest trail. You may come for the trout fishing, the mountain skiing, or just plain relaxation. Whether you stay for a weekend or twenty years like Rip Van Winkle, you are bound to have fond memories of your visit to the Catskills.

Kingston Into the Catskills

Entrances to the Catskills are many but a good one from New York City is over the Thruway to Kingston, where the Rondout joins the Hudson.

Kingston was the site of the first government of the State of New York. The State Senate met in a house that was already one hundred years old, but soon hightailed it out of town when British troops advanced on the city and burned it. Fortunately, the Senate House was not badly damaged, and it is one of the features of guided walking tours through the city during summer months. A separate Senate House Museum contains paintings, relics, and exhibits. Hurley, just below town on US 209, is the scene of an annual Stone House Day, when a

THE CATSKILLS

large number of privately owned stone houses—originals, not restorations or reproductions—are opened to the public. Visitors have an unusual opportunity to see historic homes whose distinctive architecture and furnishings are characteristic of Dutch influence in the New World.

At New Paltz, a few miles south on State 32, is an old Huguenot village with the original stone houses, remnant of the settlers who came in 1677. The Josiah Hasbrouck House features a bird sanctuary, as well as its own Federal architecture and period furnishings, and the Skytop Observation Tower at Lake Mohonk offers a view from close to two thousand feet. The Hudson Valley Winery, in nearby Milton on US 9W, displays wine-making arts, and offers wine tasting in a converted Early American railway station.

A short run to High Falls will take us to the Delaware & Hudson Canal Historical Society Museum, an interesting and worthwhile trip for anyone interested in the history of the canals that made the Empire State great. On State 213 in the area, between Rosendale and Rifton, is Perrine's Bridge, a covered bridge built in 1844 and recently restored. If you decide to see it, though, head back to Kingston afterwards, because we're going to take State 28—the Onteora Trail—west from there.

Five miles from Kingston, this road forks around the Ashokan Reservoir. It has an aerating spray of 1,600 nozzles and provides much of the water for New York City. Ashokan is the Indian word for "drinking water." Circling the reservoir, the grandeur of the Catskills becomes evident. On the north rise The Overlook, Mount Tobias, Mount Tremper, and others. Toward the west is Mount Pleasant, Panther Mountain, The Wittenberg, and in the distance the monarch of the peaks, Slide Mountain, highest of the Catskills. It is 4,180 feet, and is a short and easy climb via the trail from Winnisook Lake.

The Onteora Trail

Of all the roads entering the Catskills, few offer the attractions of the Onteora Trail, reaching from the Hudson Valley over the divide of the southern mountains to the East Branch of the Delaware River. An ancient Indian pathway for many miles, the trail runs beside streams bordering vast forests. No other road in the mountains leads to so much unspoiled natural charm.

Leaving Kingston by the Plank Road, the Onteora Trail crosses the Esopus and enters the mountains a few miles further on through Stony Hollow. From West Hurley, turn north on State 375 to Woodstock, the "Upstate Greenwich Village." It is like no other community in the Catskills. Incorporated in 1787, it remained a sleepy little village for more than a century until 1902, when Ralph Radcliffe Whitehead set up a home and handicraft community. The Art Students League of New York established a summer school a few years later. Since then, it has blossomed into an art colony.

Today, the town is a sophisticated community of artists, writers, music lovers, and stage folk. There are formal and informal art exhibitions, concerts, and indoor and outdoor theater presentations. Strolling about its curio shops and bazaars in informal dress, its inhabitants contribute to a free and easy atmosphere.

Farther along on State 28 is Phoenicia, summer resort and the trout-fishing capital of the Esopus and all the eastern slope. The town is also the scene of annual White Water Races on Esopus Creek, held early in June. The Catskills are becoming more and more popular with winter sports enthusiasts, too, and Phoenicia, at the southern portal of the picturesque Stony Clove, is, like nearby Fleischmanns, Shandaken, and Big Indian, a popular ski resort. The 688,660-acre Catskill State Park, a part of the huge Catskill Forest Preserve, is stretched over this area, with over 200 miles of marked hiking trails open to the public.

At Hunter, a few miles north on State Routes 214 and 23A, summer skiiing was introduced during the 1960s. The owners of the Hunter Mountain ski area had a plastic carpet installed on one of their smaller slopes. Although it is a far cry from a Bear Mountain incline, the slope drew praise from those who first used it, and is still popular. Palenville, twelve miles to the east, is the legendary home of Rip Van Winkle.

Back along the Onteora Trail, at Big Indian, a road turns left into the Woodland Valley. Woodland Creek flows beside the road, the forest all around, and there is a public rest site at the end of the valley. From here, leading up to the highest peak, begin the Slide Mountain Trails. Of this area, John Burroughs wrote: "Of all the retreats I have found among the Catskills, there is no other that possesses quite so many charms for me as this valley. It is so wild, so quiet and has such superb mountain views." On the highest elevation, white quartz and pebbles pave the trails, the result of erosion of the rock on Slide's summit.

Beginnings of Great Rivers

Slide Mountain is at about the center of the state park, which is spread over four counties in this area: Ulster, Greene, Delaware, and Sullivan. Almost all of the other notable Catskill summits are within the boundaries of the state park, too, and here also begin tributaries of three rivers: the Hudson, Delaware, and Mohawk.

North of the park, at Schoharie Reservoir and Gilboa Dam, can be seen remarkable natural wonders. Contractors excavating for the dam found a fossilized prehistoric forest, the oldest known in the world.

THE CATSKILLS

Hundreds of stumps and branches having fernlike foliage were unearthed. Geologists believe that this forest grew during the Devonian period of the earth's formation, some 200 million years ago. Near the dam is an interesting exhibit of the fossilized ferns that were the ancestors of our trees of today. Gilboa Dam now holds back 20 million gallons of water from Schoharie Creek, reversing its normal flow toward the Mohawk River and sending it instead southward to feed the Ashokan Reservoir.

From Hunter, State 23A goes to Prattsville, named after its founder, colorful industrialist Zadock Pratt. Shortly after he came to the area, he had amassed a fortune from a general store, and soon constructed his own village, building more than one hundred houses for new settlers. At one point, he operated a grist mill and a hat factory, as well as the largest tannery in the Catskills. Mountain neighbors called him "the most wonderful man the country ever produced."

Determined to preserve his name for posterity, old Zadock donated a public park to the village, named Pratt's Rocks, and had sculptors carve in them a bust of himself, his favorite dogs and horses, a bust of his son, a coat of arms, and a settee and armchair. The tannery was destroyed by flood, but you can still see Pratt's Rocks, as well as the Zadock Pratt Museum, which contains many items of Prattiana.

From here, State 23 heads east through winter ski center Windham until it reaches Cairo (pronounced KAY-row), ten miles west of Catskill. A zig and a zag to the north along State 32 will bring you to the Catskill Game Farm and its large collection of animals and birds. There is also a nearby picnic ground and children's amusement area. A replica Wild West town, Carson City, is also in the vicinity. Coxsackie, to the north, is the site of the Bronck House, a National Historic Landmark, which reflects three centuries of local history. The thirteen-sided "Freedom Barn," one of Greene County's most fascinating pioneer farms, is of particular interest.

Catskill is farther south along US 9W, a 300-year-old town retaining many ancient characteristics. An important port in the early 1800s, it was later a center of moonshining during Prohibition: local farmers turned out very good applejack and many gangsters vacationed there. Saugerties, a bit downriver, provided a background for James Fenimore Cooper's great character Natty Bumppo, and today holds an annual chrysanthemum festival in October.

Hunter, southwest of Cairo on State 23, is the scene in mid-July of an annual German Alps Festival, and in August is the stage for the National Polka Festival. West of Cairo, along State 145, is the town of East Durham, where two museums display exhibits of Indian relics, farming tools, railroad and military items, seashells, and butterflies.

Out west along State 23 is the attractive town of Stamford, home of a Maple Sugar Museum that displays old-time maple sugar manufacturing equipment. Above the town's maple-lined streets towers Mount Utsayantha. According to legend, beautiful Utsayantha, a Mohawk princess, fell in love with a Sioux brave, but was not allowed to marry him. She leaped into a lake and was drowned, and was buried on the summit of the mountain, where there is still a grave marker.

South of here is Roxbury, on State 30, home of John Burroughs. The drive along this road combines entrancing scenery with historic landmarks, and Burroughs' home, Woodchuck Lodge, is open when the family is in residence. A short distance beyond the home is his "Boyhood Rock," which now has a bronze tablet inscribed with a verse from his poem "Waiting." A rectangular stone wall in front of the rock marks his grave, near which bubbles a spring from which he used to drink.

Southern Catskills

State Routes 10 and 28 come together in Delhi, site of the Delaware County Historical Museum, where early farm tools and a country schoolhouse are visited in the restored 18th-century home of one Judge Gideon Frisbee. A little to the south is Downsville, which has a covered bridge built in 1854, and from which the Pepacton Reservoir and Bear Spring Forest Preserve are accessible. Below that is Livingston Manor, site of four covered bridges, junction of the Beaver Kill and Willowemoc Rivers, and our gateway to the southern Catskills.

Actually, there are a number of ways to approach the southern half of this region. State 17, the Quickway, is one, a fast direct drive through the Catskills, meeting the Thruway at Harriman. But the leisurely sightseer will start at Hancock and head south along State 97, the Hawk's Nest Drive. The Drive parallels the main body of the Delaware River, running high above the river's gorge and permitting spectacular views for almost its entire length. If twenty-three miles of scenery is enough for you, turn east at Callicoon onto State 17B, which will bring you into Monticello, the "Capital of the Mountains," where there are trotting races, antique auto shows, and an annual arts and crafts show on the courthouse green.

There's a lot more than Monticello in the Monticello area, however. Loch Sheldrake has a number of famous resorts, as well as the popular Big Vanilla ski slopes. Four trout ponds and a well-stocked fifteen-acre lake make for good fishing at Mountain Dale's Hey-Ru Trout Park, a private area where you don't need a license but pay by the pound for fish caught.

THE CATSKILLS

A bit east are Ellenville, Kerhonkson, and Mohonk Lake. The area is full of trout streams and fine resorts. Ellenville, on US 209, is the center of the Ulster County resort area, and has a few places in it frequently visited by tourists. One is Ice Caves Mountain, 2,255 feet above sea level, with a view of five states and a host of scenic nature trails and rock formations.

Kerhonkson deserves special mention, if only for its outstanding name, but it is also the site of the Merriman Dam, forming the Rondout Reservoir, an important part of the New York City water system. Mohonk Lake, an elegant resort in the Shawangunk Mountains, and nearby Lake Minnewaska, founded almost a century ago, are graced by natural wild gardens of glacier-polished rocks, delicately balanced boulders, wind-twisted pines, soft moss and mountain ferns, and bushes upon bushes of huckleberry, azalea, rhododendron, and laurel. It is a photographer's, as well as a vacationer's, dream come true.

Along the Delaware

Back along the Delaware, thirteen more miles of the Hawk's Nest Drive, almost all of it within sight of the river, brings you to Narrowsburg. Here are several interesting things to see, although most of them are open only during the summer. The Delaware River Model Railroad Exhibit offers electric trains in action. Fort Delaware, now the Musuem of the American Frontier, dramatizes life in the area between the French and Indian War and the American Revolution in its replica of a 1754 stockade. Snug Harbor is a collection of old country store furnishings and stock.

From Narrowsburg, the Drive leads to Barryville, where the Delaware River White Water Canoe Regatta is staged in August, as well as the Indian League of the Americas Powwow. Here also is the Eldred Preserve, a private fishing preserve and horseback riding area. From here, the road moves along to Port Jervis, where three states meet at one spot, and we move along with it. From here, US 6 and I–84 extend east into Middletown.

Middletown is the home of the Orange County State Fair, and the scene of an annual September Steer Roast held at the Fairgrounds. Middletown is also the home of the Empire State Railway Museum, no collection of miniatures but the real thing. It has an old-fashioned depot and an operating steam train, which offers rides in antique coaches, an observation car, and what is said to be the largest caboose in the U.S. The Middletown Savings Bank has a collection of 190 antique clocks.

From Middletown, it's a short run down the Quickway to Goshen, site of the oldest racetrack in America, which dates back to 1838, when trotters were raced under saddle. Harness races are still held there on Saturday afternoons during June and July. Nearby is the Hall of Fame of the Trotter, in a famous old stable. The museum contains records, Currier and Ives prints, paintings and statues, dioramas of famous horses and a library.

One more stop, Warwick, and we're back in the Hudson Valley and on our way again to the big city, New York. Warwick, pleasantly situated along a branch of the Wallkill River, has an interesting 1810 house with period furniture from Queen Anne to Duncan Phyfe, as well as an intriguing collection of sporting equipment, antique dolls, and flowering fruit trees. The Shingle House, a 1764 saltbox, has carriages and sleighs, plus interesting farm tools and machinery.

It is important to take off on your own, though, and not to rely on any one guided tour or set itinerary. Driving through the Catskills is a satisfying experience, with its mountain roads and clear streams, its deer and tall trees, and the traveler who follows his or her own instincts can't go wrong here. But an even better way to explore the area is on foot. Generations of visitors have found the Catskills a hiker's paradise, and in recent years the state has developed a network of trails with clear markers, open camps, and lean-tos.

During its run through New York State, the Appalachian Trail is a continuous marked footpath winding along a skyline route over the crest of the Catskill ranges. Hikers who traverse the Trail will find that pure mountain air is a treat for the lungs; that the sound of a rippling brook is a treat for the ears; that the gorgeous autumn hues of yellow, orange, and red are a treat for the eyes; that unique and unfamiliar scenes are a treat for the mind; and that in wilderness is the preservation of the world.

PRACTICAL INFORMATION FOR THE CATSKILLS

HOW TO GET THERE. *By car:* Take the George Washington Bridge out of Manhattan to I–80 westbound. Go north on Route 17 into the New York State Thruway. At exit 16 on the Thruway you rejoin Route 17, which will take you into Monticello and Liberty, the two main centers of the Catskills. It's limited-access highway all the way; travel time about 2½ hours. Exits 16–21 from the Thruway will also take you into the Catskills.

By bus: Adirondack Trailways has very complete coverage of the Catskills. Their main office is at 18 Pine Grove Ave., Kingston 12401. *Greyhound, Short Line (Hudson Transit),* and *Monticello Transit* also have service to the Catskills. A bus to Monticello is about $14.00 one way. Travel time is 2½ hours. Unless you have a specific destination and a way to get there from the bus terminal, you are better off driving.

TELEPHONE. The area code for the Catskills is 914.

TOURIST INFORMATION. Catskills Resort Association, Inc., 10 Hamilton Ave., Monticello, NY 12701.

CAMPING OUT. The state maintains lean-tos and marked trails throughout the Catskill Forest Preserve. The backpacker may, however, camp anywhere he likes in the Forest Preserve. Maps and information are available from the New York State Office of Parks and Recreation, Albany, NY 12238.

CAMPERS AND TRAILERS TIPS. *Catskill State Park,* small but picturesque, has a number of camping areas. For information write: New York State Office of Parks and Recreation. In addition, *KOA* runs private campgrounds in the Catskills.

MUSEUMS. Catskill: *The President's Wedding Museum.* Martin Van Buren, 8th U.S. president, was married here in 1807. Coxsackie: *Bronck House Museum,* on Pieter Bronck Rd., off Rte. 9W. Three centuries of local history, with the 13-sided barn the highlight. Delhi: *Delaware County Historical Association Museum,* Rte. 10, 2 miles N of town. Restored 1797 Frisbee House, plus "mini-village" attractions. Ellenville: *Ellenville Museum,* 126 Canal St. History of the Delaware and Hudson Canal, plus displays of pottery and glassware. Narrowsburg: *Fort Delaware,* Rte. 97. Museum of American Frontier. Prattsville: *Zadock Pratt Museum.* Rock carvings represent life of the founder of village.

HISTORIC SITES. Hurley: *Patentee Manor,* on Rte. 29. Restored 18th-century country mansion, now a National Historic Landmark. Kingston: *Senate House and Museum,* 312 Fair St. State-owned historic site. New Paltz: *Hasbrouck Memorial House,* Huguenot St. Houses owned by the Huguenot Historical Society. *Col. Josiah Hasbrouck House,* State 32, 4 mi. S, 12-room mansion with original furnishings. Roxbury: *Burroughs Memorials,* state-owned historic sites, in Memorial Field, 2 mi. west. Grave and "Boyhood Rock" of John Burroughs, his farmhouse birthplace and summer cottage, "Woodchuck Lodge," are nearby. Open when the family is in residence.

MUSIC. Hunter: *German Alps Festival* is held for two weeks in July. The *National Polka Festival* follows in August. Woodstock: Summer theater featuring musicals and drama. Also afternoon concerts on Sundays, June–September.

TOURS. Highmount: Belleayre Mountain Chairlift, State 28. Picnic area at summit.

WHAT TO DO WITH THE CHILDREN. Cairo: *Catskill Game Farm,* off State 32, between Cairo and Palenville. *Carson City,* State 32, between Cairo and Palenville. "Old Wild West Town," with picnic area.

SUMMER SPORTS. Outdoor activities that invite participation include golfing and hiking. There are beautiful courses everywhere. "Lone Path," beginning at High Tor State Park in the Catskills, challenges hikers.

Golf: Liberty, Grossinger's Hotel, a private course extending privileges to guests of hotels and motels, 18 holes; Sullivan County Course, 9 holes; Roscoe, Twin Village, 9 holes; Tennanah Lake, 18 holes; Windham, Windham Course, 18 holes.

Hiking: Slide Mountain, Catskill State Park.

Fishing: Phoenicia, trout fishing capital of the Catskills. Schoharie Creek through Catskill State Park.

Races: Monticello Raceway, at jct. State 17 and State 17B. Harness racing.

WINTER SPORTS. There are just too many areas to list them all. The New York State Division of Tourism makes available lists of *ski and snowmobile areas* throughout the state in their "I Love New York Skiing" brochure. A few of the popular ones in the Catskills are Belleayre (in Highmount), Big Vanilla (Woodridge), Holiday Mountain (Monticello), Hunter

THE CATSKILLS

Mountain (Hunter), Scotch Valley (Stamford), and Ski Minnewaska (Lake Minnewaska), open daily; and Highmount (in Highmount), open weekends. In addition, many other areas have *tobogganing*, *sleighing*, and *skating*.

HOTELS AND MOTELS are so plentiful and varied that you can stay anywhere you like in the Catskills. Choose from dude ranches with riding lessons, rudimentary lean-tos up in the mountains, simple conventional motels, state-owned camping grounds, commercial trailer parks, and some of the world's outstanding resorts with every possible recreation facility. The country's top entertainers appear nightly in the resorts' clubs.

Price categories for double-occupancy rooms in this region are: *Super Deluxe* over $70; *Deluxe*, $50–69; *Expensive*, $40–49; *Moderate*, $30–39; and *Inexpensive*, $29 and under. It's wise to call first to be sure the place you want to stay overnight accepts guests other than by the week. These rates are without meals, but most of the larger Catskill properties will quote rates that include at least two meals per day, at considerable savings. For a fuller explanation of price categories, refer to *Facts at Your Fingertips* section.

BARRYVILLE

Reber's. *Moderate.* State 55 at State 97. Bavarian-style architecture has provided large, comfortable rooms overlooking the Delaware River. Heated pool, barbershop. Pets are allowed.

DELHI

Buena Vista. *Inexpensive.* State 28, 1 mi. E. Relax in attractive, well-kept rooms. Pets are allowed, cribs are free, breakfast is available.

DEPOSIT

Hanson's. *Moderate.* Near exits 82, 83 from State 17. Luaus, barbecues, 9-hole golf course, pets allowed in cottages, water sports on Oquaga Lake, plenty more at this resort. Family-owned since 1919.

ELLENVILLE

Fallsview. *Deluxe.* Off US 209, 1½ mi. S of town. Accommodates 500 guests. Indoor and outdoor pools, health club. Championship golf course, tennis courts lighted for night play. Water sports on private lake, horseback riding, indoor skating rink, arcade for shopping. The dining emphasis is on Kosher dietary, but dozens of other choices available.

The Nevele. *Deluxe.* US 209, 1½ mi. S of town. Accommodates 900 guests. Pools, health club, tennis, racquetball, 18-hole golf course, playhouse, private lake, lawn games, sauna. Kosher-American menu.

NEARBY ATTRACTIONS

KERHONKSON

The Granit. *Deluxe.* US 44. Accommodations for over 800 guests in five-story hotel and annexes. Enjoy indoor ice-skating rink, indoor tennis, indoor and outdoor pools. 18-hole golf course, health club. Social director, teen programs; nightclub seats 1,500 people. Winter skiing. Kosher-American menu.

Pinegrove Ranch. *Expensive.* Cherrytown Rd. off US 209, 6 mi. NE of town. Rugged resort with riding, archery, skeet and trap shooting, golf privileges, tennis, winter sports, two pools, day camp for children.

KIAMESHA LAKE

The Concord. *Super Deluxe.* State 42, 2 mi. NE of State 17 exit 105B. Well, here it is, with accommodations for over 3,000 guests. One 9-hole golf course, two 18-hole courses, tennis, horseback riding, health club, sports director, world's largest artificial outdoor skating rink, skiing, enormous outdoor pool, indoor pool, sauna, fishing. Cocktail lounges, top entertainers, dance bands, social director, midweek and weekly rates available. Kosher dietary.

LAKE MINNEWASKA

Lake Minnewaska Mountain House. *Deluxe.* US 44, 12 mi. W of Thruway exit 18. Two main residential sections comprise this 3,500-acre resort in the beautiful Shawangunk Mountains west of New Paltz. Library, concerts, outdoor games, surry rides, horseback riding, lake swimming, sailboats, putting green, woodland walks, square dancing. Winter sports in scenic mountain setting with lakes, streams, and waterfalls. Reservations deposit required.

LIBERTY

Grossinger's. *Super Deluxe.* Just off State 17 exit 100. The original, and still the star in the Catskill crown, accommodates over 1,300 guests. Olympic-size pool, indoor pool, children's pool, putting green, 18-hole golf course, tennis, skiing, skating, tobogganing. Award-winning Kosher cuisine, 1,200-acre grounds, social director, top entertainment, dance orchestras, children's dining room. The complete year-round resort. Weekly rates available.

LIVINGSTON MANOR

Willowemoc. *Inexpensive.* Exit 96 from State 17. Hunting and fishing nearby, pets limited, coffee in rooms. Accommodations are comfortable.

LOCH SHELDRAKE

Brown's. *Deluxe.* State 52, 2 mi. W of the village. Over 500 rooms in more than a dozen buildings: new Palace building with super deluxe accommodations. Indoor and outdoor swimming pools, health club, tennis, jogging track, nearby

THE CATSKILLS

golf. Kosher dietary. Social director, top entertainers, dance bands keep things jumping. Midweek and weekly rates available.

MAPLECREST

The Sugar Maples Resort. *Moderate.* 1 mi. S on State 23. Large mountain resort hotel set on 100 acres. Dining room, music, and dancing. Heated Olympic pool, 15 tennis courts.

MIDDLETOWN

Middletown Motel. *Moderate.* 1 mi. E on State 17. Nice accommodations at the right price. Restaurant, cocktail lounge, swimming pool.

MONTICELLO

Kutscher's Country Club. *Deluxe.* Hurleyville Rd. 3 mi. N of State 17 exit 105B. Accommodations for 800 guests. 18-hole golf course, tennis courts, jogging track, indoor and outdoor pools, health club, day camp for children, boating and fishing, horseback riding. Kosher dietary. Social director, dance bands, teen program, day camp. Skiing, tobogganing, sleighing, indoor ice-skating, snowmobiles. Weekly rates.

Holiday Mountain Motor Lodge. *Moderate.* State 17 exit 109. Seasonal skiing and hunting attract many to this fine motel with a roaring fire in the lobby. Restaurant and cocktail lounge, pool, very nicely furnished rooms. Reservation deposit required, three-day minimum weekend stay, in summer season.

PURLING

Bavarian Manor. *Moderate.* 2 mi. S of Cairo off State 23. Cozy rooms in the Chalet or the main house. Alpine atmosphere on 110-acre estate. Pool, private lake, ski area.

SOUTH FALLSBURG

The Pines. *Deluxe.* Near exit 105B from State 17. Accomodations for 800 guests include 9-hole Robert Trent Jones golf course, indoor and outdoor pools, health club, indoor roller-skating and ice-skating, winter tobogganing and skiing. Kosher dietary. Social director, top entertainers, dance bands, teenage program, children's day camp. Mid-week, weekend, and weekly rates available.

STAMFORD

Red Carpet Motor Inn. *Inexpensive.* State 10 at State 23. Large, attractive rooms in two-story motel. Pets are allowed. There's a swimming pool. Coffee in rooms, café, dancing and entertainment.

NEARBY ATTRACTIONS

SWAN LAKE

Stevensville Country Club. *Deluxe.* State 55, 2 mi. S of State 17 exit 105B. Modern resort complex in rustic setting. Dining room, cocktail lounge, theater nightclub. Kosher dietary. Two pools, six tennis courts, 18-hole golf course, riding, roller-skating, sailing, boating, water-skiing, and fishing. Day camp and teen program. Mid-week, weekend, and weekly rates available.

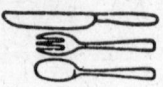

DINING OUT in the Catskills means eating in the hotel or motel to most travelers, but there are plenty of excellent independent restaurants, too. Old World atmosphere in many places will remind the seasoned traveler or the nostalgic new American of Bavaria, Holland, or wherever. Many of the hotels and resort hotels in the Catskills specialize in both Kosher and non-Kosher cuisine, with separate menus. Prices are for the lowest price meal on the menu unless a range is indicated. For a more complete explanation of restaurant categories see *Facts at Your Fingertips* section.

BARRYVILLE

Reber's. *Expensive.* State 97 at State 55. There's a jolly Bavarian atmosphere with waitresses in native costume to serve gourmet delights of German origin. Sauerbraten, Wiener schnitzel, and goulash are some of the specialties in this fine family-owned establishment hung with paintings.

MIDDLETOWN

Le Coq Hardi. *Expensive.* State 284. A delightful Belgian menu along with such specialties as duck à l'orange and frogs' legs. Dinner only. Reservations and jackets required.

PORT JERVIS

Flo-Jean. *Expensive.* US 6, 209. Lovely spot along the Delaware with a wide variety of excellently prepared dishes. Own baking tops the menu, with duckling and filet mignon especially good. At Delaware River Bridge.

ROSCOE

Antrim Lodge. *Expensive.* Highland Ave., just E of State 17. Steaks and ribs are very good at this locally popular spot. Fireplace and music make for a nice mood, too.

WOODSTOCK

Deanie's Towne Tavern. *Moderate.* State 212. Ribs, seafood, and home baking. A locally popular place, with music, pleasant ambience. Dinner only.

THE SARATOGA AREA

Horses; Healing Waters; Halls of Fame

Famed for its mineral springs, its horse racing, and its old hotels, Saratoga Springs stirs with anticipation in June, swings into preparatory activity early in July, and rushes headlong into the full tumult of its summer season in August. But in September the decline begins, and for most of the year Saratoga Springs is just another quiet upstate town. Not so, however, in the nearby village of Cooperstown, where its museums draw visitors, along with sportsmen, all year round.

Steeped in history, the Saratoga area presents a meeting place of America's proud past and promising future. Long stilled are the drums of war that sounded across Bemis Heights, east of Saratoga, where a ragtag collection of Continentals defeated the haughty British army in 1777 at the Battle of Saratoga and turned the tide of the American Revolution. The memories endure, though, and year-round residents and swarms of vacationers attest to the determination of the region to enjoy the best that both past and future have to offer.

The Battle of Saratoga

Along the Hudson River, where US 4 splits from State 32, is the Saratoga National Historical Park. Here, between the towns of Schuylerville and Stillwater, the victory of the American troops over the British stands out as the turning point of the seven-year struggle for American independence. It was here that General Horatio Gates and a ragged group of soldiers prevented British control of the strategic Hudson Valley, boosted American morale, and brought the recognition and assistance of France and Spain. The Visitors Center is open daily, and has a hilltop view of the battlefield, as well as a museum featuring exhibits, dioramas, and a twelve-minute film explaining the battle.

The park is crisscrossed with roads that enable the visitor to follow the battle action. The farmhouse that served as American headquarters is open, and there are many battle markers and monuments around the park, among them a granite monument, the famed "Monument to a Leg." It is at the site of a charge, that is credited with deciding the battle, led heroically by an officer suffering from a serious leg wound. The monument, depicting the left boot and epaulets of an American major general, bears an inscription recording the deeds, but omitting the name, of Benedict Arnold, hero at Saratoga, who later turned traitor. Another monument, a 154-foot granite shaft, marks the spot of Burgoyne's surrender. Its base has niches for statues of the four major American commanders. Statues of Gates, Schuyler, and Morgan are there. The fourth niche—Benedict Arnold's—is vacant!

Racing and Rejuvenation

Saratoga Springs, of course, displays a completely different ambience. For mid-Victorians it was the "Queen of the Spas," and thousands came here hoping to improve their health with the famous healing waters of its mineral springs. In summer, many thousands more, including the cream of society, came to enjoy the racing, gambling, and brillant social life. The most famous Saratoga gambler was Richard Canfield, and the casino which he operated from 1894 to 1907 was designed in part by Stanford White, and matched in costly elegance anything Europe had to offer. Bets of fantastic size were made there, and it was also there that Canfield invented the variety of solitaire which bears his name. Today, the casino is the home of the local historical society.

THE SARATOGA AREA

The Saratoga area is also the home of three American institutions. Pie à la mode is said to have been invented in the 1890s by a local schoolteacher. And in 1853, an irritated chef, responding to a diner's complaint that his fried potatoes were cut too thick, decided to get even by slicing some paper thin. *Voilà!*—potato chips! The third invention was Standard Time, conceived by Dr. Charles Dowd, who spent twenty years campaigning for it before it was adopted by the railroads in 1883. Prior to that, Americans everywhere had set their watches by the sun at noon locally, and railroad timetables used over six dozen different systems.

Today Saratoga is a quiet little town for most of the year, and it comes very much alive in summer. The state mineral baths and health clubs are always popular. Golfers can try their luck on the two state golf courses. There is thoroughbred racing in late July and August at the Saratoga Race Course, the nation's oldest thoroughbred track, and harness racing from April to November.

The Saratoga Perfoming Arts Center, summer home of the New York City Ballet and the Philadelphia Orchestra, has an amphitheater seating 5,100 persons, with lawn space for 10,000 more. A summer program has the dance during July, music during August, and a host of distinguished guest artists appearing from mid-June to mid-September.

There's more to do in Saratoga Springs, with Saratoga Lake offering fine swimming and boating, while some of the best fishing in the state is right here near Saratoga. There are amusement parks galore, too, and they have an appeal that spans the age groups. Trophies, prints, and other memorabilia of "the sport of kings" are to be found in the National Museum of Racing, and there are historical museums to be found both here and in nearby Ballston Spa. There is a Natural Historical Landmark in the vicinity—the Petrified Gardens—where the fossilized remains of insect and plant life are abundant on the reefs. The area also has a sundial museum, deer park, and a picnic area.

Speed-skating championships are held here, too, for although Saratoga Springs is mainly a summer recreation area, there is winter activity here for those who thrive on it. Skiing and snowmobiling areas are proliferating here, and rooms that used to be filled only during the summer months are now occupied by visitors during the winter months, too. There are horse shows during the summer; flower shows annually; yearly activities at the National Historical Park, and much more. All in all, the Saratoga area is a vacationer's delight.

Cooperstown's Museums

This small town called Cooperstown is one of the Empire State's premiere attractions. It is prettily set at the foot of Otsego Lake, a complete and delightful little village of great museums. First among them, of course, is the National Baseball Hall of Fame, wherein are enshrined the immortals of what is still America's national pastime. Here, in plaques and pictures, through displays and written material, are remembered the greats of the game, from Babe Ruth and Ty Cobb to Roberto Clemente and Mickey Mantle. Gloves worn, bats swung, and balls thrown by the stars of the major leagues are on exhibit, and visitors may stop in daily, except on Thanksgiving, Christmas, and New Year's Day.

One of the best times to come up is in early August. Then, the town swells to ten times its normal size as fans from all over, and many of the dignitaries of the game of baseball, travel to Doubleday Field for the annual Hall of Fame Game, in which a National League team and an American League team compete for the coveted Hall of Fame Cup. The day is made doubly unforgettable by the induction into these hallowed halls of newly elected members, chosen by the nation's baseball writers during the winter. If you can't make it then, the American Legion State Baseball Championships are held two weeks later.

Other fine in-town museums are Fenimore House, a real treasure with an extensive collection of American folk art, fine art, and James Fenimore Cooper memorabilia. (It was Cooper's father, Jude William Cooper, who founded the town in 1786.) The Farmers' Museum not only displays materials and equipment relating to agriculture, but has working craftsmen on hand to demonstrate the life and the ingenuity of a rural village of the late 18th century.

PRACTICAL INFORMATION FOR COOPERSTOWN AND THE SARATOGA AREA

HOW TO GET THERE. *By car:* Saratoga Springs lies 25 miles north of Albany on US 9. It is easily reached by taking I-90 from the east or west; I-87 from the north or south to the Capital and US 9 from there.

By air: The closest airport is Albany, which is served by *Air North, American, Braniff, Eastern, TWA,* and *USAir.*

By train: Amtrak's "Adirondack" stops at Saratoga Springs.

By bus: Via *Adirondack Trailways* or *Greyhound.*

TELEPHONE. The area code for the Saratoga Area is 518.

TOURIST INFORMATION. Brochures and information are available from: The New York State Division of Tourism, 99 Washington Ave., Albany NY 12245, and the Saratoga County Promotion Committee, 126 Woodlawn Ave., Saratoga Springs, NY 12866.

MUSEUMS AND GALLERIES. Ballston Spa: *Brookside.* Town's first hotel, now a historical museum. Cooperstown: The *Farmers' Museum.* Features displays dealing with the early life of the American farmer, complete with many actual tools. There are reconstructions of typical buildings of that time, and the infamous *Cardiff Giant,* a fake "prehistoric man," is also on display. *Fenimore House.* James Fenimore Cooper memorabilia, along with exhibits of American folk art. *National Baseball Hall of Fame and Museum.* A treasure house dedicated to the immortals of baseball. Saratoga: *Saratoga Historical Museum* and *Walworth Memorial Museum* in Congress Park. The place to find and trace the history of Saratoga Springs beginning with the Victorian era. *National Museum of Thoroughbred Racing.* Trophies, paintings, and racing mementos.

HISTORIC SITES. *Saratoga National Historical Park.* 12 miles east of Saratoga Springs, 28 miles north of Albany, at jct. of US 4 and State 32. Nine miles of roads around the park open daily, April-November. Visitors Center open all year. Schuylerville: *Schuyler House,* part of the National Historical Park. Country home of the Revolutionary War general.

NEARBY ATTRACTIONS

MUSIC. The New York City Ballet Company performs at the Saratoga Performing Arts Center during the month of July; The Philadelphia Orchestra in August, and there are guest performers in the summer from June through September.

SPORTS. Saratoga Springs is the scene of *thoroughbred racing* in August; *harness racing* April to November. The *Eastern States Speed-Skating Championships* are held in January. There are two 18-hole *golf* courses in Saratoga and one in Cooperstown. You'll find *tennis* courts at the Otesaga Hotel in Cooperstown and at the Gideon Putnam in Saratoga Springs. There are numerous *ski* resorts in the area, among them *Adirondack*, north of Saratoga Springs.

HOTELS AND MOTELS. Prices for accommodations in this area are in our *Moderate* range ($50–55 double, EP) all year, with the exception of the month of August when Saratoga Springs' rates are almost double. The two properties listed as *Deluxe* include two meals in their rate which runs $100–115 double.

COOPERSTOWN

Otesaga Hotel. *Deluxe.* Very attractive and outstanding Georgian-style resort hotel with many mementos of Cooperstown's historic past. Heated pool, 18-hole championship golf course, 2 tennis courts. Restaurant, cocktail lounge, dancing, and entertainment.

Cooper Inn. *Moderate.* Small, 32-room 19th-century mansion-turned-inn. All rooms with private bath. Open only from mid-May to mid-October. Guests have use of all facilities at Otesaga Hotel.

SARATOGA SPRINGS

Gideon Putnam. *Deluxe.* Lovely 136-room resort hotel and health spa set on 1,500 acres. Attractively decorated rooms and suites; memorable and specialized service. Restaurant and cocktail lounge. Mineral baths and all spa facilities. Three swimming pools, tennis courts, 27 holes of golf.

Best Western Playmore Farms. *Moderate.* Comfortable, family-style lodge with playground and swimming pool. Color TV in all rooms. No restaurant.

Holiday Inn. *Moderate.* 150-room motor hotel half mile from the downtown area. Facilities include heated pool, restaurant, lounge, entertainment, and color TV with Home Box Office.

Turf and Spa Motel. *Moderate.* Pleasant 42-room property located downtown. All rooms with refrigerators, color cable TV, telephone, and air conditioning. Swimming pool; restaurant across the way.

THE SARATOGA AREA

DINING OUT. You won't be disappointed with the food and atmosphere of the restaurants in this area. All the places recommended would be categorized *Moderate,* with mid-priced, full-course dinners costing between $10 and $12. Not included in the prices are drinks, tax, and tips. Restaurant categories are more fully outlined in the *Facts at Your Fingertips* section.

COOPERSTOWN

Sportsman's Tavern. *Expensive.* State 28, 3 mi. W of town. Trophies and pictures decorate this restaurant in the town where America's national pastime, the game of baseball, was born. Elaborate beef dishes and seafood are featured as well as their own breads. Cocktail lounge. Dinner only.

SARATOGA SPRINGS

Country Gentleman. US 9, 1 mi. S of town. Large dining room in an attractive dome-shaped restaurant that is set in verdant surroundings. Pleasant cocktail lounge with piano bar for pre-dinner relaxation and after-dinner dancing. House specialties are stuffed shrimp and prime ribs, but the menu is extensive. One of the few restaurants that will accept reservations during the August racing season. Jacket required. Open for dinner only.

Trade Winds. US 9, ½ mi. S of town. Nicely decorated dining room and pleasant music make this a fine place to dine. Jacket required. Menu is heavy on ribs and steaks; generous cocktails served in atmospheric lounge. Dinner only.

Ye Olde Wishing Well. US 9, 5 mi. N of town. Dine nicely in a 19th-century farmhouse that was built around the wishing well. Excellent American fare with a Continental touch.

THE ADIRONDACKS

A Spectacular Wilderness for All Seasons

New York State's North Country stretches across the upper reaches of the state from Lake Ontario and the St. Lawrence River to the Vermont border and Lake Champlain, from Quebec down to Saratoga, and takes in the vacationland known as the Adirondacks with its wealth of year-round rest and recreation.

The Adirondack Mountains present an interesting story. Although it may sometimes seem that every automobile in the country manages to end up on Adirondack highways every summer weekend, it is really only a very small part of the region that becomes crowded in season. The designation "in season" is itself quite inaccurate, in fact, since the Adirondacks are a year-round vacation paradise, with winter sports galore, beautifully verdant springtime, and some of the country's most exquisite fall foliage.

THE ADIRONDACKS

One of the major attractions of the Adirondacks is that they offer genuine isolation relatively near big cities, and there are many anglers and nature lovers who have a favorite spot here where they know there won't be another human being around for miles. The very vastness of the region swallows up not only the year-round residents, but the four or five times as many summer residents and visitors as well. The Adirondack Park, established in 1892, contains about 8,900 square miles, making it considerably larger than the entire state of Massachusetts. Of this, over 2,400,000 acres—an area larger than any of our national parks—is state-owned land which must, under the New York State Constitution, be kept forever wild, and never logged or otherwise despoiled.

The region is an outdoorsperson's Eden. Its spring-fed streams and lakes are crystal-clear and icy cold, and they are state-stocked with trout, perch, bass, and even salmon in a few places. The rolling hills and wooded mountains are ideal for hunting and hiking, with over five hundred miles of marked trail threading a number of exciting and scenic paths through the forest. There are excellent public camping grounds throughout the area and, needless to say, plenty of motels and restaurants in and around the popular resort centers. Many are open during the winter, too, for the Adirondacks have dozens of skiing and snowmobile areas a few hours' drive from New York City and Boston.

World's Oldest Mountains

Contrary to many people's impression, the Adirondacks are not part of the Appalachian chain, and although forty-two of them are over four thousand feet high—topped by Mt. Marcy at 5,344 feet—many are not very impressive to the eye, because they take off from a plateau more than 1,500 feet in altitude. Actually, the Adirondacks were taller than the Rockies when an upward thrust in the surface of the earth formed them millions of years ago. Today, however, the world's oldest mountains, they have been worn down to a more even contour by God and the centuries.

Few areas of the United States have been so involved with the discovery, settlement, battles, campaigns, and colonization of America as this one, and the thirteen counties totally or partially within the Adirondacks furnish a cross-section of the early history of this country. Because its two great lakes, Champlain and George, formed a natural highway north to south, the area was an arena of conflict for more than 200 years. Indians, French, British, and Americans fought up and down these lakes until the end of the War of 1812. Important naval battles were fought on Lake Champlain, both during that war and during the Revolution. Because the Colonists built their first warships there, the little village of Whitehall at the lake's southern end is still called the birthplace of the American Navy.

The Adirondacks were designated a National Historic Landmark by former Secretary of the Interior Stewart Udall, and New York State has placed its blue and gold markers on many sites where an important house or tavern stood, or where a significant military encounter took place. A historical oddity is that though the southern boundary of the Adirondack country is only about two hundred miles north of Manhattan, and though pioneers had been traveling up and down the lake valleys for more than two hundred years, the mountain area was little explored before the 1830s. The mountains were not even named until 1837, and explorers had crossed the continent and found the source of the Columbia River sixty years before the source of the Hudson was discovered.

Once opened up, however, the Adirondacks were quickly discovered by nature lovers, invalids, loggers, and society people, more or less in that order. A summer place near Saranac Lake was locally called the "Philosopher's Camp," because its visitors included Emerson, Lowell, and Agassiz. Joseph Bonaparte, Napoleon's older brother, built a house and lived for a time at Oxbow after his exile from Europe following Waterloo.

The loggers set up shop in the Adirondacks in force and by 1860 New York led the country in lumber production. However, conservationists protested until the Adirondack Forest Preserve was established in 1892. Today almost all of the timber that covers the region is second- or third-growth, and such logging as continues is done on private lands. Society moved in on unspoiled parts of the region late in the 19th century, and a hunting lodge in the Adirondacks soon became a necessary status symbol.

That sort of snobbery need hardly bother today's visitor who simply wants to enjoy the Adirondacks. It is a really pleasant region, with lots of places to enjoy the outdoors, many fine resorts and commercial amusements. The mean temperature is about ten degrees lower than that of New York City, though extremes of 105 degrees above and 52 degrees below zero have been recorded. The mountains abound in wildlife, and although game birds are few, 150 species of fine feathered friends have been seen there. Deer, foxes, wildcats, coyotes, beavers, skunks, raccoons, rabbits, and porcupines inhabit the forest, and black bear weighing as much as 532 pounds have been taken.

The Original Fish Story

As for fish, the first written record of the Adirondacks has a fish story. Champlain wrote in his journal that the Indians had told him of

THE ADIRONDACKS

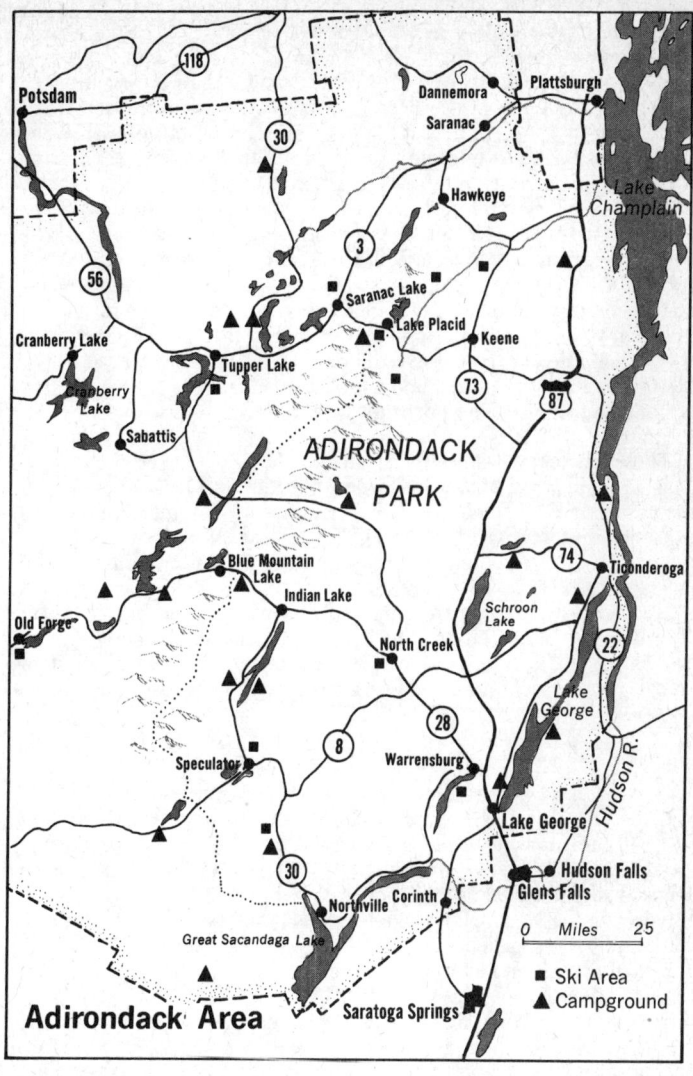

Adirondack Area

one called the chaousarou, which grew up to 10 feet long. "The extremity of its snout," he said, "is like that of a swine. The fish makes war upon all others in the lakes and rivers. When it wants to capture birds it swims along the rushes or reeds, where it puts its snout out of the water and keeps perfectly still, so that when the birds come and light upon its snout, supposing it to be only the stump of a tree, the fish adroitly closes it and pulls the birds by the feet down under the water." There is no guarantee that you'll be able to snag one of those, but perhaps you would be willing to settle for a creel full of fat trout.

Access to the Adirondacks is fast and direct. The Governor Thomas E. Dewey Thruway connects with the Adirondack Northway at Albany, and the latter takes you to Lake George at the southern boundary of the preserve. Before you get there, there are two points of interest at which you might enjoy stopping. State 197 turns east off the Northway a few miles to Fort Edward, where the Old Fort House shows historic exhibits, dioramas, and antiques in a 200-year-old former tavern and courthouse. The Fort Edward Center features workshops and exhibits by area artists.

Those art lovers whose tastes run to the Old Masters (and New Masters) will want to see the Hyde Collection in Glens Falls, which includes works by Rembrandt, Rubens, Picasso, Braque, and Renoir, to name only a few. Glens Falls also has skiing at West Mountain, with downhill and cross-country trails, as well as professional instruction. It is also the home of the Lake George Opera Festival, which presents opera in English during the summer. Nearby Lake Luzerne, west of Glen Falls on State 9N, is in the heart of the dude ranch country, and has rodeos and a fall festival featuring a white water derby, in addition to every variety of winter and summer sporting activity.

Lake George

As for Lake George itself, Father Isaac Jogues, a Jesuit missionary, was the first white man to see its shimmering blue waters. He arrived in 1646 and named it Lac du St. Sacrement—Lake of the Blessed Sacrament—but in 1775 its name was changed to honor the British king. Most of the islands they looked at then—there are more than one hundred in the 32-mile long lake—are today state-owned and available for camping and picnicking. Also open to the public is Lake George Beach, a $1 million facility with every amenity, which can accommodate 6,000 bathers along its sandy half-mile.

In and around the village are accommodations for 25,000 visitors, priced and styled to suit almost any purse or taste, although prices are higher during the height of the summer season. The village is bustling in summer, with strollers, shoppers, and automobiles jockeying for

THE ADIRONDACKS

space, while the lake buzzes with motorboats, and even planes. Visitors have a choice of numerous boat tours, speedboat rides, and moonlight cruises.

Historically minded sightseers will not want to miss Fort William Henry, a restored fort of the French and Indian War, which stands on a nineteen-acre plot in the village and commands the head of the lake. Rebuilt from original plans, it is a museum of Colonial America with mock military drills and demonstrations of musketball molding, and cannon and flintlock firing.

Just north of the village of Lake George is Warrensburg, where you are invited to drop in at the state-run fish hatchery, and where a flea market and antiques show is held in August. Along the west shore of the lake, along State 9N, is a succession of resort towns. One is Bolton Landing, with a park and beaches open to the public, and Time Town, where you can see a geodesic dome, take a space walk, or ride in an antique car.

Three Forts

State 9N continues and meets up with State 22 past the end of the lake at Ticonderoga, on Lake Champlain. Here is Fort Ticonderoga, made immortal to Americans on the 10th of May, 1775, when it was taken from the British by Ethan Allen and his Green Mountain Boys "in the name of Jehovah and the Continental Congress." Today, the fort has been restored and contains a museum. A nearby blockhouse, Fort Mount Hope, has also been restored, and features the ruins of a Colonial warship. Also in the vicinity is Mt. Defiance, where a toll road follows a British military trail to the summit for a spectacular panoramic view of the entire area. At Ticonderoga, you can take a ferry across Lake Champlain and back for a delightful scenic ride. The ferry service has been, with a single exception of five years during the American Revolution, in continuous operation since the earliest times.

Next town north is Crown Point, with typical village green of a small New England town, and a number of charming brick buildings. Nearby is the Crown Point Reservation, a National Historic Landmark, where the French built their southernmost outpost in 1731, and where the British later constructed a fort of their own. Visit the Penfield Homestead Museum for historic memorabilia of the iron industry here, and then take a tour through the ruins of the ironworks. The Champlain Lighthouse in the vicinity is a gift from the people of France. There are fishing, picnicking, and hiking trails through the ruins of an old iron works at Ironville down the road, home of Allen Penfield, the first to use an electromagnet to separate ores.

From here, the road follows the shores of Lake Champlain and gives a scenic drive with many views of Vermont's Green Mountains across the water. At Westport, the road turns inland to Elizabethtown. Here are three unusual attractions: the Adirondack Art Center, which is located in an old mill; the Adirondack Center Museum and Colonial Garden, which offers exhibits of forestry, mining, pioneer equipment, costumes, dolls, and a nature walk; and the Split Rock Falls Preserve, where the beauties of wildlife are lovingly cared for and saved for us all.

Ausable Chasm

US 9 brings the tourist north to one of the most exciting natural sights the region has to offer, Ausable Chasm. Opened in 1870, it is one of America's oldest organized attractions. Here the Ausable River plunges through a cut several hundred feet deep at some points and a mile and a half in length. There are spectacular waterfalls, rushing rapids, and massive rock formations carved into strange shapes by millions of years of erosion. The chasm can be explored on stairways, walks, and foot-bridges, and the trip ends with a magnificent boat ride "shooting" one of the safer rapids.

The chasm is at the border of the Adirondack Preserve, but the traveler may continue north of US 9 to Plattsburgh, site of an important victory over the British in the War of 1812. The town is the largest city in Clinton County, and has a number of spots of interest to vacationers. The Kent-Delord House Museum is one. An 18th-century home and British headquarters during the War of 1812, today it contains historical exhibits, and is furnished as it was when occupied by the Kent and Delord families, with china, glassware, silver, and furniture of the period.

At the northernmost tip of US 9 is Rouse's Point, the Canadian border crossing. The United States built Fort Montgomery just north of the town, only to discover too late that it was in Canadian territory. Being the sympathetic people that they are, the Canadians ceded us the few feet of land necessary to bring the fort home again. The fort became known as Ford Blunder, and its ruins are still there today.

Don't feel, though, that the entire scope of things to do in Clinton County consists of collections of antique furnishings, old forts, and interesting geological formations. There are golf courses here, miles of magnificent blue lake, yacht basins, sandy beaches, mountain trails, and ski slopes.

To continue exploring the Adirondacks, however, a good route is State 9N southwest from Ausable Chasm through Au Sable Forks (yes, the two are spelled differently) to Jay. This area could almost provide

THE ADIRONDACKS

enough material for a travel guide of its own, with Saranac Lake, Wilmington, and Lake Placid all in the vicinity. The most popular commercial attraction here, especially for children of all ages, is Santa's Workshop, in a town called North Pole.

Mountain Resorts

At Wilmington is Whiteface Mountain. Rising 4,867 feet, it is one of the most magnificent of the Adirondack peaks, and it is one of the most popular places to visit, winter or summer. A scenic eight-mile toll road rises almost to the summit, and from there you can continue by foot or by elevator. Chair lifts are also available, and as you may imagine, Whiteface Mountain is a skiing area. With six chair lifts, two lodges, and twenty-eight trails and slopes, it is one of the finest in the state.

State 86 west from Wilmington takes us to High Falls Gorge, one of America's most beautiful natural wonders. Carved by the Ausable River, it plummets seven hundred feet here in a series of falls. It may be seen on walks and bridges at important vantage points, while the woods, foliage, and pretty wildflowers add to the beauty in their season. The road continues to Lake Placid, where the Sterling-Alaska Fur and Game Farm is home to almost 1,000 animals. Children will like the llama rides and chimpanzee shows.

Lake Placid is a beautiful resort community sitting in a bowl surrounded by some of the Adirondacks' highest peaks. It has every imaginable facility for both winter and summer sports—and was chosen twice—in 1932 and 1980—as the site for the Winter Olympic Games. Unique among the facilities is the mile-long Olympic bobsled run on Mt. Van Hoevenberg, seven miles south of town along State 73. Heavy iron racing sleds rush down the mountainside at speeds of close to one hundred miles an hour, and climb twenty feet of glare ice on the curves. Visitors are taken down the run, too, but carefully supervised and at far lesser speeds.

Lake Placid is a year-round resort, and offers many other diversions, such as ice shows and games in winter, boat trips in summer. There is always something going on, be it the New York State Junior Ski Jumping Championships, an annual Winter Carnival, a cross-country race, the annual Ausable River Canoe Race, a bobsled competition, a golf tournament, a square dance festival, the yearly Summer Ski Jump, a horse show, summer ice-skating and ice-dancing competitions, swim meets, art shows. And, in September, they host the annual ice show at the Olympic Arena, an annual rowing regatta, and an AAU-certified marathon.

Near Lake Placid is the John Brown Farm, home of the noted abolitionist, a state-owned historic site. It is here that the body of the militant anti-slavery advocate, hanged in Harpers Ferry for his part in a raid to free slaves, lies a-mould'rin' in the grave. Throughout the Adirondack region are many marked sites denoting stations along the Underground Railroad, which served as an escape route for runaway slaves.

Lake Resorts

Saranac Lake lies ten miles west of Lake Placid along State 86, and here, too, can be found an abundance of sports facilities. In summer, there are concerts and fishing trips to be enjoyed. There is an annual Winter Carnival in Saranac Lake that has been held here every year since before the turn of the century. There are boat races on the Saranac River in July, an annual show and sale of antiques at the Town Hall, and an August Paint and Palette Festival.

From here, State 3 goes west to Tupper Lake, another popular resort, where a chair lift will take you on a three-thousand-foot ride to the summit of Big Tupper. Skiing is big at Big Tupper, of course, but hunting and fishing, boating and swimming, hiking and camping, and looking at the scenery all have their devotees. And Franklin County, in which Tupper Lake is located, considers itself to be the Snowmobile Capital of the Northeastern U.S.A.

Stick around for the June Water Carnival and forty-four-mile Flat Water Canoe Marathon between Long Lake and Tupper Lake, and then head south along State 30 to Blue Mountain Lake. The Adirondack Lakes Center for the Arts presents a summer program of concerts, films, exhibits, and classes. The Adirondack Museum, at the intersection of State Routes 30 and 28, is a superb place, which has twenty buildings and is outdoors as well as indoors. Its exhibits of paintings, maple sugaring, horse-drawn transportation, and tools, along with its dioramas of life in the 19th century, tell the story of humanity's relationship to the Adirondacks.

At this point, a decision confronts you; to turn east or west on State 28. Turning west would bring you to Old Forge, where there are plenty of snowmobile trails and a modern ski center; boat trips on the Fulton Chain of Lakes and the Moose River; the McCauley Chair Lift to give you a panoramic view; and the Enchanted Forest, a storybook land for children. Golf, camping, canoeing, and nature walks, tennis, fishing, beaches, and riding stables, hiking, art shows, hunting, and sailing are all enjoyed here, as well as many other activities. They even hold the New York State Fiddler's Championship here, at the Enchanted Forest during June.

THE ADIRONDACKS

Turning east takes you to North Creek, where they hold the annual Hudson River White Water Derby, and where you can tour the world's largest producing garnet mines and see the state gem being mined and processed. The Gore Mountain Chair Lift will take you on a one-hour, two-mile ride over the treetops during the summer, or start you on your way during the winter to the top of the more popular ski slopes in the state.

Just ahead lies the Tri-Lakes Area, embracing Friends, Loon, and Schroon Lakes. Here, off US 9 near Pottersville, is an unusual formation consisting of a natural stone bridge and caves. Grottoes, potholes, waterfalls, lighted caves, and stunning nature trails highlight this oft-visited attraction. Near Friends Lake is the famous Floating Rock, surrounded by Indian mounds, an old mica mine, and lots of scenic trails. Schroon Lake has an annual Winter Weekend in January, and summertime activities such as an Independence Day Festival, country fair, and hobby show.

PRACTICAL INFORMATION FOR THE ADIRONDACKS

HOW TO GET THERE. *By car:* Albany is the jumping-off point for the Adirondacks. I–87 (Adirondack Northway) goes through the eastern Adirondacks from Albany to Plattsburgh and across the Canadian border. State 30 (Adirondack Trail) travels north from I–90 at Amsterdam through the heart of the Forest Preserve. The Adirondacks may be reached by train, air, or bus; but you will need a car once you get there.

By train: Amtrak's "Adirdack" heads north right through the mountains, with several stops en route to Rouses Point at the Canadian border.

By air: Air North flies to Plattsburgh and Saranac Lake–Lake Placid.

By bus: Greyhound and *Adirondack Trailways* have service throughout the Adirondacks. New York to Lake Placid is $75.00 round trip. Travel time is about 6½ hours one way.

TELEPHONE. The area code for the Adirondacks is 518.

TOURIST INFORMATION. The Adirondack Park Association, Adirondack, NY 12808, will be happy to supply you with any information you might need.

CAMPING OUT. Backpackers may camp anywhere they like in the Adirondack Forest Preserve. The New York State Office of Parks and Recreation, Albany, NY 12238, has maps and brochures.

CAMPER AND TRAILER TIPS. New York's highest mountains tower over the hundreds of lakes that make the Adirondack Park one of the most scenic areas in the country. The area has over 130 campgrounds, and another forty or fifty are scattered through the Thousand Islands region. Official season is roughly mid-May through mid-September. Fees are $3 per person per day, $4 at improved campsites, which may be anything from sites with electric hookups to those with tent platforms or docking facilities. A maximum of six persons per campsite is permitted, with the exception of families made up of parents and their unmarried children. Permits, issued upon arrival, are renewed on a daily basis thereafter, depending upon availability of sites. Most private campgrounds encourage reservations, and a few require them. Several state parks require them, also. In July and August, campers are advised to make

THE ADIRONDACKS

reservations when possible. All state-owned, and some private, campgrounds have regulations about pets, and there are some that do not allow them at all. For more complete information, write to the New York State Office of Parks and Recreation.

MUSEUMS AND GALLERIES. Blue Mountain Lake: *Adirondack Museum.* State Routes 28N & 30, 1 mi. N. Indoor and outdoor museum. Exhibits relating to the history of Adirondacks. Elizabethtown: *Adirondack Center Museum and Colonial Garden.* State 9. Exhibits relating to the area. Glens Falls: *Hyde Collection.* 161 Warren St. Museum of Old Masters. Saranac Lake: *Dorothy Yepez Galleries.* Bloomingdale Rd. Changing exhibits. *Stevenson Cottage.* Robert Louis Stevenson literary shrine.

HISTORIC SITES. Fort Edward: *Old Fort House.* Historic exhibits. Lake Placid: *John Brown Farm.* State 73. Home and grave of the abolitionist. Lake George: *Fort William Henry.* A restored fort of the French and Indian War. Ticonderoga: *Fort Ticonderoga.* A museum and restored fort and dungeon.

TOURS. *Ausable Chasm:* State 9. Tour of gorge climaxed by boat ride through the "flume." Lake George: *Boat trips.* Daily sightseeing trips, speedboat rides and moonlight sails. Lake Placid: *Boat trips.* Several trips daily from George & Bliss dock. North Creek: *Garnet Mines Tour,* Gore Mt. off Rte. 28. Tour of open pit mine. Schroon Lake: *Frontier Town.* State 9, 8 mi. N. Western town. Rodeos, cavalry and wagon train re-enactments. Stagecoach, steam train rides. Tupper Lake: *Big Tupper Chair Lift.* State 30, 3 mi. south. Scenic 3,000-ft. ride to summit. Picnic area, snack bar, giftshop, hiking trails.

MUSIC. Bolton Landing: *Diamond Point Music Theater,* 10-week schedule of Broadway musicals begins late June. Glens Falls: *Lake George Opera Festival,* at Opera Festival Auditorium west of Northway exit 19. Opera productions in English, July-Aug. Lake Placid: *Opera Under the Stars,* in English, during the summer.

SUMMER SPORTS. Outdoor activities that invite public participation include golf and hiking. Beautiful courses are available everywhere, while "Long Path" challenges hikers. In the Adirondacks, it begins at Lake Placid.

NEARBY ATTRACTIONS

WINTER SPORTS. There are countless ski areas and snowmobile trails in the Adirondacks area. Whiteface Mountain, in Wilmington, a towering 4,867-foot beauty, has a famed vertical drop purported to be the highest in the East, over a dozen slopes, and three chair lifts.

Neighboring Lake Placid has all winter sports. Particularly noteworthy is the Mt. Van Hoevenberg Olympic Bobsled Run. The area is the scene of many winter carnivals, skating and skiing championships, and other sports competitions.

WHAT TO DO WITH THE CHILDREN. Lake George: *Animal Land.* State 9, 4 mi. south. *Gaslight Village.* State 9, 2 mi. south. Gay Nineties setting with silent movies, ice reviews, dozens of rides, and special shows. The *Cavalcade of Cars* is here, too, with priceless antique and classic automobiles on display. *Magic Forest.* State 9, 1 mi. south. *Storytown U.S.A.* State 9, 4 mi. south. Features Ghost Town, Jungle Land. Lake Placid: *Sterling-Alaska Fur and Game Farm.* State 86. Collection of game animals. Chimpanzee shows, llama and other rides. Wilmington: *Santa's Workshop.* On entrance to Whiteface Memorial Highway. Nativity pageant, puppet shows, rides.

HOTELS AND MOTELS of all sorts abound in New York's unique Adirondacks wilderness area, clustered around the lakes and mountains, or perched amidst landscaped tracts. Rustic inns, lodges, and cottages are ideal for family vacationing. Many accommodations on lakes provide canoes, rowboats, and sailboats. Cost categories for double occupancy rooms in this region are as follows: *Deluxe,* $50 and over; *Expensive,* $40–$49; *Moderate,* $30–$39; and *Inexpensive,* $29 and under. A fuller explanation of categories may be found in the *Facts at Your Fingertips* section.

BLUE MOUNTAIN LAKE

The Hedges. *Expensive.* State 28, 1 mi. W of the village. Informal resort, with rooms and cottages in woods at lakeside. Lake swimming, water sports, tennis, hiking, badminton.

Hemlock Hall. *Expensive.* 1 mi. N of State 28N. Rural setting, an ideal place for families. Activities range from nature walks to archery, water sports on private beach. A reservation deposit is required.

BOLTON LANDING

Sagamore. *Deluxe.* State 9N, ½ mi. E of town. Boat trips to Paradise Island, indoor and outdoor pools, health club, 18-hole golf course, tennis. Top entertainment, movies, open-air theater.

Melody Manor. *Expensive.* State 9N, 2 mi. S of town. Water sports, fishing, skiing, heated pool. Restaurant has an adjacent cocktail lounge.

THE ADIRONDACKS

Bonnie View. *Moderate.* State 9N. Motel and cottages, with private beach, heated pool, water sports, golf, lawn games. Evening barbecues, entertainment.

CANTON

University Inn. *Moderate.* State 11, 1 mi. E of downtown. Golf, tennis, winter sports adjacent. It's conveniently located next to the St. Lawrence University campus. Restaurant, cocktail bar, swimming pool.

DIAMOND POINT

Canoe Island Lodge. *Deluxe.* State 9N, ½ mi. N of town center. Lodge and cottages, with all the water sports, outdoor games, sandy beach. Three tennis courts. They hold barbecues on their own island. Wintertime has its share of sports, too.

GLENS FALLS

Queensbury Motel and Motor Inn. *Expensive.* 88 Ridge St. (State 9L) 160 air-conditioned and well-appointed rooms in a nicely restored, vine-covered building. Two restaurants, one with a garden view.

Sheraton Inn. *Expensive.* Aviation Road, Northway exit 19. Set in nice surroundings, 15 minutes from Lake George. Indoor pool, restaurant, lounge, entertainment nightly.

Landmark. *Moderate.* US 9, 5 mi. S of town. Well-kept lawns and small games court. The family will enjoy the pool and playground. Restaurant adjacent.

LAKE GEORGE

The Georgian. *Deluxe.* State 9N. Shoreside patio and nicely furnished rooms. Recreational opportunities include water sports, heated pool, tennis, and evening dancing. Restaurant and cocktail bar.

Roaring Brook Ranch and Tennis Resort. *Deluxe.* State 9N, 3 mi. S of town. You'll find very attractive rooms at this mountain retreat with large, well-kept grounds. Three pools, one indoor heated; tennis, golf, riding, water skiing. Three dining rooms, two lounges, nightly entertainment. Reservation deposit required.

Alpine Village. *Expensive.* State 9N, 1 mi. N of town. This is a lakeside resort with shaded grounds, rustic atmosphere and comfortable accommodations. You can play tennis, bask on the beach with lake swimming, or enjoy boating, canoes, fishing and water skiing. Dining room, cocktail lounge, entertainment.

Marine Village Resort Motel. *Expensive.* 350 Canada St. Rustic accommodations in village center. On the lake with spacious grounds, beach patio, snack bar.

Tahoe. *Expensive.* State 9N, 1 mi. N of town. Stunningly terraced lakefront grounds, with heated pool, private sand beach. Most rooms have balconies facing the lake. Pleasant poolside coffee shop.

Depe Dene. *Moderate.* State 9N, 3 mi. N. Well-run motel set among trees, with nice rooms and cottages on lakefront with beach, water sports. Restaurant adjacent.

LAKE LUZERNE

Hidden Valley. *Deluxe.* Off State 9N, 5½ mi. N. Dude ranch with just about every variety of leisure activity. Three tennis courts, swimming pool. Restaurant and cocktail lounge. Riding and instruction, cookouts, picnic rides. Skiing, snowmobiling, horse-drawn sleigh rides in winter.

LAKE PLACID

Mirror Lake Inn. *Deluxe.* 35 Mirror Lake Dr., just N of State 86. Large 75-room lakefront property on hillside, with fine view and large rooms. Heated pool, tennis, fishing, skiing and instruction. Health spa, fine dining. Accommodations in main lodge or in private cottages.

Placid Manor. *Deluxe.* Go 3 mi. W on State 86, ½ mi. N on Country Lane. Resort with lakeside setting, large comfortable rooms and cottages. Golf, tennis, fishing, boating, water skiing, lake swimming. Restaurant is complemented by barbecues, outdoor buffets, and box lunches.

Best Western Golden Arrow Motor Inn. *Expensive.* State 86. A complete resort on the lake, with a heated pool. There is boating, canoeing, fishing, lake swimming for summer fun. Restaurant is open 7:00 A.M. to 10:00 P.M.

Lakeside Motor Inn. *Expensive.* State 86. Spacious rooms and grounds on the lake, heated indoor and outdoor pools guarantee a happy stay. In summer, enjoy water sports; in winter, the guest lounge with fireplace.

Art Devlin's Olympic Motor Inn. *Moderate.* State 86 at State 73. Pleasant and well-kept rooms, gorgeous mountain view, many rooms with patio or balcony. Heated pool and playground. Restaurant nearby.

Holiday Inn. *Moderate.* One Olympic Dr. On State 86. Adjacent to Olympic Arena. Nice setting overlooking the lake. Restaurant, bar. Tennis, indoor pool, and sauna.

LONG LAKE

Long Lake. *Inexpensive.* Just off State 30. Pleasant cottages and motel rooms on the lake. Private beach affords water sports and lake swimming.

Shamrock. *Inexpensive.* State 30, 1 mi. S of town. Lakefront grounds. Private beach and marina, water sports, playground. Pets are limited. You can have coffee in your room.

MALONE

View. *Inexpensive.* State 11, 1 mi. W of town. Comfortable rooms, well-maintained grounds, in a favorite winter sports area. Heated pool, pets allowed. Reservation deposit required.

THE ADIRONDACKS

NORTH CREEK

Valhaus. *Moderate.* Just off State 28, ½ mi. S. Large rooms, pleasant setting at the foot of Gore Mountain. Continental breakfast is available. There's good hunting and fishing in the vicinity.

OLD FORGE

The Mohawk. *Expensive.* Off State 28, 8 mi. N of town. This is a family-style resort hotel, with private sand beach and all water sports. Golf, tennis, outdoor games. Barbecues; planned entertainment includes movies, dancing. Dining room, cocktail lounge, live entertainment. On Fourth Lake.

The Forge. *Moderate.* Just off State 28. Spacious, terraced grounds overlooking lake. Nice rooms, swimming pool, convenient to tennis and golf and restaurants.

PLATTSBURGH

Howard Johnson's Motor Lodge. *Moderate.* Exit 37 off I-87. Relaxed atmosphere, with heated pool, sauna, game room, and two restaurants.

Pioneer. *Inexpensive.* US 9, 4 mi. N of town. A small grove of evergreens is the setting for this excellent motel. Playground, pets allowed.

ROUSES POINT

The Anchorage Motor Inn. *Inexpensive.* 164 Lake St., State 9B. Cozy historic inn on Lake Champlain. Swimming, restaurant, and lounge. Golf nearby.

SARANAC LAKE

Saranac Inn & Country Club. *Expensive.* 10 air-conditioned rooms, all overlooking the 18-hole championship golf course. Restaurant and cocktail lounge. Pro shop.

Saranac Hotel. *Inexpensive.* 101 Main St. Older, established hotel in town's center. Excellent restaurant operated by Paul Smith's College.

SCHROON LAKE

Frontier Town. *Moderate.* US 9 at Northway exit 29. Open April through October only, it has lake swimming, playground. Restaurant and cafeteria.

TUPPER LAKE

Shaheen's. *Moderate.* State 30, ½ mi. E of town. Has 35 units, some air-conditioned. Heated pool, restaurant adjacent.

Tupper Lake. *Inexpensive.* State 30, ½ mi. E of town. Friendly motel has well-kept rooms. Heated pool. They'll insist on a reservation deposit.

NEARBY ATTRACTIONS

WILMINGTON

Hungry Trout Motel. *Moderate.* State 86, 2 mi. SW of town. Nicely situated on the Ausable River, with landscaped grounds and fine mountain view, pleasant rooms. Pool, playground, fishing nearby. Attractive and excellent restaurant on premises.

Ledge Rock. *Moderate.* Placid Rd. (State 86), 2 mi. S of town. Barbecue areas for eating, large pleasant rooms for sleeping. Large heated pool, playground, pets allowed. A favorite of the ski crowd. Deposit required for reservations.

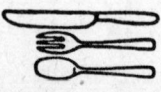

DINING OUT in the Adirondacks can include French cuisine at one of the resort centers or a good old American hamburger at one of the plain, but good, roadhouses sprinkled throughout the region. Many ethnic cuisines are represented, too. For other worthwhile restaurants, check hotel listings.

Establishments are categorized according to the price of a dinner from the middle range of their menus. For this region, the categories are: *Deluxe*, $15 and above; *Expensive*, $10–$12; *Moderate*, $7–$10; and *Inexpensive*, below $7. Included are *hors d'oeuvres* or soup, *entrée* and dessert. Not included are drinks, tax, and tip. For a more complete discussion of price categories, turn to the *Facts at Your Fingertips* section.

BOONVILLE

Hulbert House. *Expensive.* Main St. (State 12). Dine in a 19th-century inn, pleasantly restored, while listening to soothing music. Sauerbraten, ribs and lamb are the specialties.

CROWN POINT

St. Frederic Hotel. *Moderate.* Downtown. Shrimp, steak, and lobster, plus their own baking. Children's plates. Entertainment on weekends.

GLENS FALLS

Red Coach Grill. *Expensive.* US 9, 4 mi. N of town. The ambience is pleasant with soft music. Fine steaks and ribs, shrimp and lobster are served. Dinner only.

Blacksmith Shop. *Inexpensive.* Howard Johnson's, ½ mi. W of US 9, at Northway exit 19. Steaks and salad bar, period, but done very well and in a nice atmosphere. Dinner only.

HAGUE

Indian Kettles. *Expensive.* State 9N, 2 mi. N of town. Unusual seafood, own baking and desserts to tickle your taste buds, while you dine outdoors in a rustic setting overlooking the lake.

JAY

Tirolerland. *Moderate.* State 9N, ½ mi. N of town. Outdoor tables with a view of the mountains. Appropriate Swiss décor and lively atmosphere. Traditional German dishes include pigs' knuckles and Wiener schnitzel. Own pastries.

LAKE GEORGE.

The Georgian Terrace Room. *Deluxe.* US 9, ½ mi. N of town. Convenient to the lake, you will find an attractive view from your table near the window. French and American cuisine, all first-rate. Cocktails, some patio dining.

Le Chalet Français. *Deluxe.* Go 15 mi. N on US 9, then 6 mi. W on SR 418 from Warrensburg. If you can plan ahead for a real dining treat, this out-of-the-way place is worth the effort. Superb cuisine, leisurely dining in a charming atmosphere. Meals individually planned and prepared. Their own pastries are alone worth the price of admission. Jacket required. Reservations necessary. Dinner only.

Dino's Montcalm. *Expensive.* US 9, 1 mi. S of town. A relaxing spot for shish kebab, many gourmet chicken and seafood creations. They do their own baking. Reservations recommended in season. Locally popular. Dinner only.

Bavarian House. *Moderate.* Lake Shore Dr. State 9N, 2 mi. N of town. Noted for German dishes and beer served in a Black Forest dining room. Well-prepared menu features sauerbraten, Wiener schnitzel, prime ribs.

Ridge Terrace. *Moderate.* US 9, 1 mi. S of town. Dine in a rustic log cabin on lovely grounds, and enjoy good German and American cooking. Salad bar, meat cooked on the open hearth, cocktails served. Reservations recommended.

LAKE LUZERNE

The Hitching Post. *Moderate.* 3112 Lake Ave. State 9N, 5 mi. N of town. Specialties change daily, but the baked stuffed shrimp is always good in this pleasant log building. Dancing and entertainment in season. Dinner only.

LAKE PLACID

Marcy. *Expensive.* State 86. An impressive place overlooking the lake, where the diner can enjoy personal attention and the utmost in American and European cuisine. Dancing and entertainment nightly.

Steak and Stinger. *Expensive.* 15 Cascade Rd. (State 73), E of town. Very good food in rustic surroundings. Old-time newspaper menu features shrimp, scallops, lobster, juicy steaks. Salad bar and their own baking. Dinner only.

MALONE

Crossroads. *Expensive.* US 11, 10 mi. W of town. Attractive décor in this locally popular eating spot. Menu features steak and ribs, own rolls and pastries. Dinner only.

OLD FORGE

Knotty Pine Tavern. *Moderate.* State 28, 1 mi. S. Informal rustic atmosphere. Tasty menu has chicken, steaks, seafood, own baking. Soft music completes the scene and provides for an enjoyable evening. Dinner only.

PLATTSBURGH

Royal Savage Inn. *Expensive.* Lakeshore Rd. US 9, 5 mi. S of town. Historic items from the early days of the area provide a charming décor, while the country store features many items of interest. Steak and seafood specialties liven up the menu. Own baking, cocktails served.

POTSDAM

Town House. *Moderate.* 38 Market St. (State 56). This pleasant downtown dining establishment has a large selection of well-prepared dishes. Seafood and prime ribs top the menu and the breads and pies are their own. Cocktails served.

SPECULATOR

Zeiser's. *Expensive.* State 30. Background music and elegant décor in the heart of the Adirondacks. Continental menu, cocktails served. Dinner only.

WILMINGTON

The Hungry Trout. *Expensive.* State 86, 2 mi. SW. Collection of antiques sets off this Victorian dining room. After cocktails, try the wild game, or a more conventional prime ribs dinner. Their great location gives a scenic view of Whiteface Mountain and the Ausable River. Lunch not served.

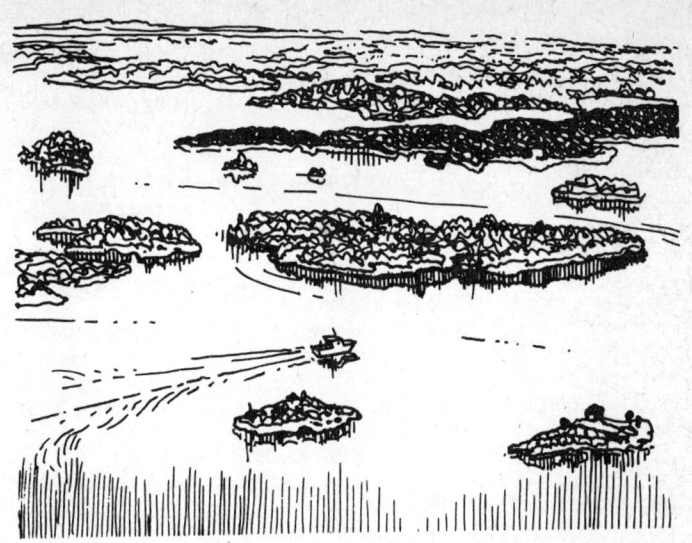

THE THOUSAND ISLANDS

Excursions to the Summer Isles

The name Thousand Islands is no exaggeration. In fact, there are more than eighteen hundred of them, some mere points of rock, some large enough for an entire village. Most of the islands can accommodate a home or summer camp, and there are several old stone houses and mansions on them. With the U.S.–Canada border running to and fro down the St. Lawrence, many of the Thousand Islands are not even in this country.

Along the Seaway

Cape Vincent is the point where the waters of Lake Ontario flow into the St. Lawrence. Here are a state-owned aquarium, the ruins of an old fort, the Tibbits Point Lighthouse (which can be seen for 14 miles), and a fisheries station of the State Department of Conservation.

The stretch of the St. Lawrence between Cape Vincent and Ogdensburg is an angler's delight, with bass, pickerel, pike, and muskellunge all ready to give you a run for your money. Fishing isn't the only water activity around; there's lots of swimming, too, and scenic boat tours of the islands on the sightseeing vessels that depart frequently from many of the towns along the river. Gourmets will want to take the opportunity to sample the local "shore dinner." Come dinnertime, the party goes ashore on a convenient island and the guide whips up a meal from whatever luck has brought your way.

Whether one goes up river or down from Cape Vincent, State 12E runs along the southern shore to Clayton, where there are two museums to interest sightseers. The Thousand Islands Museum displays local memorabilia, and the Shipyard Museum has a collection of antique power boats and outboard motors.

Alexandria Bay is a bit farther up the shore, along State 12. Here, the Thousand Islands Bridge, from which motorists can see two hundred of the islands, is part of a seven-mile span of uniquely beautiful scenery between "E Pluribus Unum" and "Maple Leaf Country."

Here also, on Heart Island, is Boldt Castle, a German-style castle planned by a wealthy hotel owner for his wife, and left uncompleted upon her death in 1902 after an expenditure of over $2 million. The grieving widower just left it there, and it stands today, eerie, vacant, and full of crates of the marble and rare woods that were to have been installed.

State Rtes. 12 and 37 extend north to Ogdensburg, where there is a museum of great interest to western fans. The Frederic Remington Art Memorial, housed in an 1809 mansion, contains the largest single collection of the noted artist's paintings, bronzes, and sketches of the Old West. There is also a re-creation of his last studio. The town itself, an important crossing-point into Canada, is over 225 years old, and northern New York's oldest settlement.

Our journey comes to an end at Massena, the power plant and shipping center of the North Country. This is the place to see the famed St. Lawrence Seaway at its most spectacular. The city is the site of the third-largest electricity-generating complex in North America, but it is the Seaway itself which is most fascinating to watch. From Robert Moses State Park, on Barnhart Island, and from St. Lawrence State Park, on the same island, some of the locks and other engineering marvels of the Seaway are visible. From there you can see the great Moses-Saunders Power Dam. From a nearby visitors' grandstand, you can watch the Dwight D. Eisenhower Lock as it raises or lowers seagoing ships ninety feet.

PRACTICAL INFORMATION FOR THE THOUSAND ISLANDS

HOW TO GET THERE: *By car:* Take I–81 north through Syracuse or State 12 from Utica. I–81 crosses the St. Lawrence to Canada at Wellesley Island. State 12 runs along the St. Lawrence on the American side from the toll bridge at Wellesley Island to Morristown where it joins State 37 heading north to Cornwall.

By air: Massena, Ogdensburg, and Watertown, in the Thousand Islands area, are served by *Air North.*

By bus: Greyhound and *Adirondack Trailways* have service throughout the area.

TELEPHONE. The area code for the Thousand Islands area is 315.

TOURIST INFORMATION. The Thousand Islands International Council, Box 429, Alexandria Bay, NY 13607.

MUSEUMS. Clayton: *The Thousand Islands Museum.* Riverside Dr. Interesting displays of Indian lore and local memorabilia. *The Shipyard Museum.* Mary St. Collection of antique power boats and outboard motors.

TOURS. Alexandria Bay: *Boat trips.* Hourly schedule May through September. *Boldt Castle.* On Heart Island. Most tour boats stop here. Natural Bridge: *Natural Bridge Caverns.* A ¼-mile boat trip on the Indian River, which flows undergound. *Seaway and Power Development Bus Tour.* Guided tour covers locks, Robert Moses State Park, New York State Power Authority Building, and power dam.

SPORTS. *Golf* at any of 10 courses in the Thousand Islands, among them, the 9-hole Alexandria Bay Municipal Course. *Skiing* at Dry Hill, Watertown. Three slopes and trails, two lifts. *Cross-country* skiing at Wellesley Island Nature Center Trails. *Ice-fishing* on the St. Lawrence River.

NEARBY ATTRACTIONS

HOTELS AND MOTELS. Accommodations at Alexandria Bay are open only from May to October. Prices are at their highest at all properties from mid-June until Labor Day. Hotels and motels in nearby Ogdensburg and Watertown are open all year round. Cost categories for double occupancy room are as follows: *Deluxe,* $50 and over; *Expensive* $40–$49; *Moderate,* $30–$39.

ALEXANDRIA BAY

Thousand Islands Resort. *Deluxe.* Wellesley Island, 5 mi. N of exit 50 from I-81. This secluded woodland resort features an 18-hole championship golf course, tennis, heated pool, yacht basin, all water sports. Spacious rooms, dining room with river view, and terrace for outdoor dining. Dancing and entertainment. Accommodations are in the main clubhouse or in surrounding cottages.

Capt. Thomson's Motor Lodge. *Expensive.* Just off jct. of State 12 and State 26. On the shore of the St. Lawrence River, it offers exciting views of the Thousand Islands and Boldt Castle. Heated pool, boat dockage.

Pine Tree Point Club. *Expensive.* State 12, 1 mi. NE of town. A 40-acre estate on the St. Lawrence. Main building has beautiful, natural-wood-paneled rooms, individual heat, picture windows with river or forest view. The cliffs and chalet guests have private balconies overlooking the river. Heated pool, excellent dining, cocktail lounge and entertainment.

Alexandria Motel. *Moderate.* State 26, 1 mi. E of town. 38 quiet rooms which look onto landscaped grounds. Coffee shop, swimming pool, nice for families.

Edgewood Resort. *Moderate.* Historic summer resort on the shore of the St. Lawrence. Accommodations in small cottage units or in modern motel rooms. Dining room and lounge. Heated pool, water sports.

OGDENSBURG

Quality Inn-Gran View. *Moderate.* State 37, 3 mi. W of town. 48 attractive rooms, each with private balconies, from which are visible the river and the distant falls. Restaurant, cocktail lounge, heated pool and patio.

WATERTOWN

Holiday Inn. *Moderate.* 300 Washington St. Typical of the chain, with large rooms, restaurant, coffee shop, and lounge with entertainment.

Ramada Inn. *Moderate.* 6300 Arsenal Rd. 149 air-conditioned rooms with color TV. Heated pool, restaurant, cocktail lounge, entertainment.

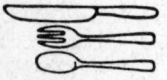

DINING OUT. This is the area for fine seafood, nicely served along the St. Lawrence River. For this region, our categories are *Expensive,* $10–$12; *Moderate,* $7–$10. Included are appetizers or soup, *entrée,* and dessert. Not included are drinks, tax, and tip.

ALEXANDRIA BAY

Cavallario's Steak House. *Expensive.* 24 Church St. (State 26). Food served and cooked extremely well. Specialties are steaks, lobster, Italian dishes. Their own baking and live entertainment add to the good time. Dinner only.

Edgewood Restaurant. *Expensive.* States 12 and 26, ½ mile S of town. Nice dining in attractive rooms that overlook the water. Seafood specialties, homemade desserts.

Old World Inn. *Moderate.* Pine Tree Point Rd., 1 mi. NE of State 12. Continental menu with the emphasis on *entrées flambé,* and their own pastries.

MASSENA

The Village Inn. *Expensive.* On State Rte. 37B. Well-prepared food served in a delightful country setting. Enjoy seafood, duckling, and their homemade desserts.

THE NIAGARA FRONTIER

Roaring Falls on a Peaceful Border

The Niagara Frontier, a vacation destination for millions every year, has a lot more to it than just Niagara Falls. This is not to imply that the Falls are merely sound and fury; it is simply to point out that in the region are also two of the Great Lakes, a number of splendid art galleries and museums, rich rolling farmlands on which are found some of America's finest orchards and vineyards, and many quaint cobblestone structures reminiscent of an era when the Niagara Frontier was the very frontier of the nation itself.

Still, the Falls, called by many "the eighth wonder of the world" and by Oscar Wilde "the second greatest disappointment in a young bride's life," are the area's top attraction; it is to see and hear their rushing waters that sightseers and newlyweds journey from all over the globe.

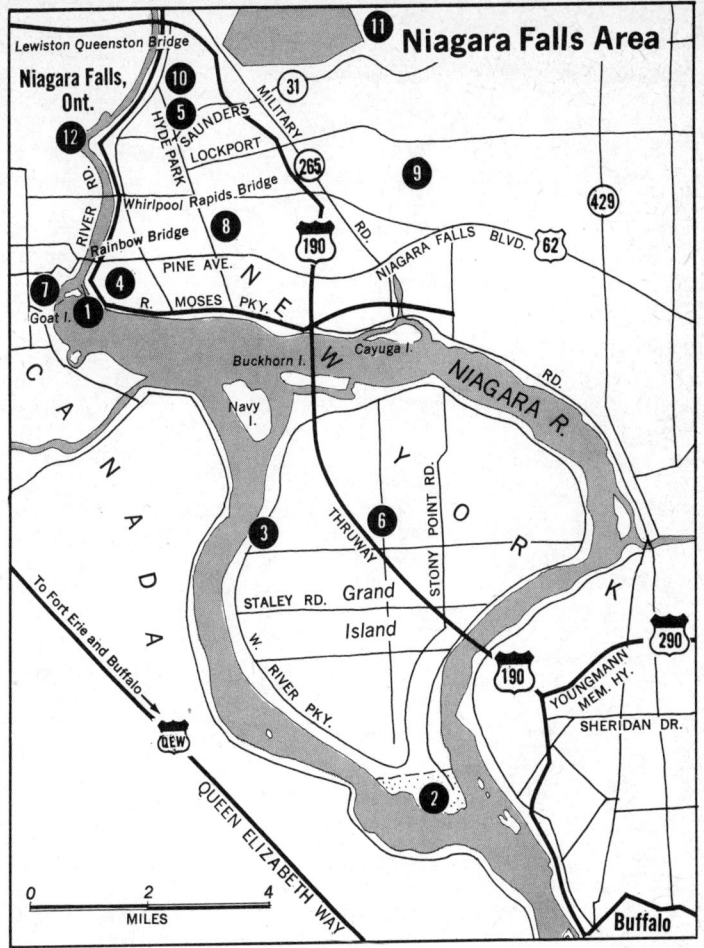

Points of Interest

1) American Falls
2) Beaver Island State Park
3) Big Six Mile Creek Marine State Park
4) Convention Center
5) Devils Hole State Park
6) Fantasy Island
7) Horseshoe Falls
8) Hyde Park Stadium
9) Niagara Falls International Airport
10) Niagara University
11) Tuscarora Indian Reservation
12) Whirlpool State Park

NEARBY ATTRACTIONS

Here, then, is where we shall begin, in an area which was for many centuries the domain of the Indian. Native Americans regarded the Falls as a sacred shrine, and heard in the waters' thundering roar the voices of their gods. In 1678, Father Louis Hennepin, a French missionary, became the first European to visit and describe the Falls, and a couple of centuries later they fell victim for a while to exploiters interested only in a fast buck. However, they are now under joint ownership of the U.S. and Canada, with the State of New York and the Province of Ontario cooperating to preserve and improve the surroundings of this great natural wonder. The Empire State fulfills its public charge through its administration of the State Reservation at Niagara, established in 1885 as the first New York State Park. One dramatic improvement on the New York side was the Robert Moses Niagara Parkway, which connects with the Thruway and parallels the river from Grand Island north to Youngstown.

The Three Falls

In its thirty-six-mile run from Lake Erie to Lake Ontario, the Niagara River (in reality an inland strait) drops 326 feet, more than half of it in a single plunge—Niagara Falls. Actually, there are three falls: the American Falls, 182 feet high and 1,075 feet wide; the Canadian (Horseshoe) Falls, 176 feet high and 2,100 feet wide; and the more modest Bridal Veil Falls. The Falls were originally six miles downstream, but as the cascading waters bring rocks crashing down to the bottom, the Falls continue to retreat. Although the Niagara River was rerouted for a while in 1969 to study the problem, the Falls have been turned on again now, and are once more moving upstream at a rate of about a foot per year.

But don't worry, the Falls aren't expected to reach Buffalo for another 130,000 years or so, and you have plenty of time left to see them while they're still at Niagara. This is just as well, because Niagara Falls deserves more exploration than a few short hours' visit allows. They should be seen from below, by day and by night—they are illuminated at night—from both sides of the river and from right in the middle. Lest you think we are suggesting you traverse the Falls in a barrel, let us remind you of Goat Island, between the American and Canadian Falls, and accessible by a bridge from the American side. Parking lots operated by the Niagara State Park Commission are the best place to leave your car if you want to see the Falls up close.

What makes Niagara unique among the waterfalls of the world is that you can stand next to it, descend to the bottom, and even ride almost into its curtain of falling water. To see Niagara Falls close up, start on the U.S. side. The crests of the three falls are all beautifully visible from Prospect Point, where most visitors catch their first sight of the Falls. An observation tower here has an elevator which one can take for a panoramic view of the entire scene from a hundred feet up. Next comes Goat Island, in the middle of the river, a seventy-acre park where you can stroll along the very edge of the Falls. Luna Island can be reached from here by a footbridge, and overlooks the Bridal Veil Falls.

If your time is limited, try a "Viewmobile" ride. These sightseeing cars circulate around the principal points of interest, and you can get on and off as fancy dictates. The Viewmobile visits Goat Island, whence you may embark upon a helicopter flight and survey the Falls and surrounding area from above. And try to see the Falls after dark, when they are very colorfully lighted up—it is an entirely different spectacle.

One of the most magnificent views is from the bottom looking up, and there are many ways to go about securing this unforgettable experience. The Prospect Point Observation Tower elevators descend into the gorge below. From here, visitors may opt for an even closer look; they can board the *Maid of the Mist* and approach to within yards of the Falls. From here, also, giant rafts depart regularly on a White Water Tour through downriver rapids. Another elevator on Goat Island takes visitors to the Gorge Walkway, which ends under Terrapin Point below Horseshoe Falls, or to the Cave of the Winds, where yellow-slickered explorers trek across the base of Bridal Veil Falls.

The Canadian Side

It is simple for U.S. and Canadian citizens to cross the river and pass through customs and immigration with a minimum of formalities. Queen Victoria Park on the Ontario side is a well-groomed expanse of arboreal greenery and bright flowers. Although one cannot get as close to the Falls on the Canadian side, it offers the highest panoramic towers. The Seagram Tower, rising 525 feet above Horseshoe Falls, has seven glass-enclosed floors; the Oneida Tower, at the end of the Rainbow Bridge, offers a view from a height of 450 feet; and the Niagara International Center, which features exhibits of science, industry, and government, operates the "Skylon," an observation tower that rises 775 feet above the river and has a revolving dining room at the top. There is also a Canadian landing at which you may board the *Maid of the Mist*, and from April to October there is an elevator and tunnel to the water's edge—the Niagara Daredevil Gallery—at 4330 River Road. The Table Rock Scenic Tunnels (enter at Table Rock House), an alternative, are open all year. In 1950, the U.S. and Canada became signatories to a treaty designed to preserve the beauty of the Falls and to enable each country to use the energy generated by the Falls to create

NEARBY ATTRACTIONS

two large power projects: the Robert Moses Niagara Power Plant on the New York side, and the Sir Adam Beck Power Station on the Ontario side. Both are open year-round to visitors. Maps, models, and films explain the development and operation of the hydro-electric facility. There is an unusual horticultural clock in the Canadian project, and murals by Thomas Hart Benton grace the American building.

Outside Niagara Falls, stop and visit the dolphins at Marine Land and Game Farm (7657 Portage Road South). If weather permits you'll be able to enjoy the whale show, which stars a killer whale.

There are a number of state parks along the Niagara River which are worth a visit, most notably the two just downriver of the Falls, Devil's Hole State Park and Whirlpool State Park. The former, 4½ miles north of the Falls, was the site in 1763 of a bloody massacre by members of the Seneca tribe, while the latter consists of 109 acres on a bluff adjacent to the turbulent Whirlpool rapids. These and the other state parks of the Niagara Frontier offer a wide range of attractions, from bathing to camping, colorful foliage to winter sports, and hiking to picnicking.

Along the Canadian side of the river between Niagara-on-the-Lake and Fort Erie to the south (across the river from Buffalo) is the Niagara Parkway, one of the world's prettiest drives. There are numerous charming parks all along the drive, and everything is maintained in the best condition.

Old Fort Erie, with its drawbridge, moat and cannon, guards the town of the same name twenty miles south of Niagara Falls. Fort Erie also offers some of the best thoroughbred racing in Ontario. Crystal Beach on Lake Erie is a beachside carnival town; shrieks of laughter from its Comet Coaster riders can be heard for miles.

Around the Falls

In addition to the Falls themselves, there are several other attractions in the area. The Aquarium of Niagara Falls, U.S.A., is the world's first inland "oceanarium," and performing dolphins and eels, sharks, octopi, and deadly piranha are some of the exotic fauna on display. Aoudads, peacocks, and yaks are some of the 150 species to be seen at the fifteen-acre Oppenheim Zoo. The Schoellkopf Geological Museum offers a history of the Falls that covers 500 billion years, using exhibits, displays, and audio/visual techniques. And don't miss Niagara's Wax Museum of History, where you can see life-size wax figures, as well as some of the barrels and balls in which people have tried to go over the falls.

The river enters Lake Ontario fourteen miles north of the Falls, at Youngstown, where stands Old Fort Niagara, important in the exploration of the territory and in armed conflicts through the War of

THE NIAGARA FRONTIER

1812. The French built it (in 1679), the British captured in (in 1759 and again in 1813), and you ought to visit it. There is a military museum, and pageants are staged for the public during the summer months. Just south is Our Lady of Fatima Shrine, a fifteen-acre outdoor cathedral under the supervision of Barnabite Fathers, where pilgrims may walk over beautifully maintained grounds with over ninety life-sized marble statues of saints. In nearby Lewiston, the 170-acre Artpark is an interesting blend of culture at work. A modern indoor-outdoor theater is the stage for opera, ballet, and drama companies, while the land along the River Gorge is the perfect setting for arts and craft shows. There are also nature walks and picnic grounds on the property.

Children will enjoy a visit to Grand Island, in the middle of the Niagara River, between Niagara Falls and Buffalo. It features Fantasy Island, where one admission price includes everything from animal and circus shows to rides and an authentic Western Town.

PRACTICAL INFORMATION FOR THE NIAGARA FRONTIER

HOW TO GET THERE. *By car:* Buffalo is on I–90, the Governor Thomas E. Dewey Thruway. From Buffalo take I–190 to Niagara Falls.

By air: American, Eastern, TWA, United Airlines, and *USAir* service Buffalo.

By Bus: Buffalo and Niagara Falls are served by *Blue Bird, Canada Coach, Trailways* and *Greyhound,* among others.

By train: Buffalo is on *Amtrak's* "Niagara Rainbow" route.

TELEPHONE. The area code for the Niagara Falls area is 716.

TOURIST INFORMATION. The Niagara Falls Convention & Visitors Bureau, 300 Fourth St., Niagara Falls, NY 14303. Buffalo's Area Convention and Tourism Division, 115 Delaware Ave., Buffalo, NY 14202.

MUSEUMS AND GALLERIES. Buffalo: *Albright-Knox Art Gallery.* 1285 Elmwood Ave., in Delaware Park. Outstanding contemporary collection. *Buffalo & Erie County Historical Society.* 25 Nottingham Court. Indian, pioneer and early craft exhibits. *Buffalo Museum of Science.* Humboldt Pkwy. Exhibits of astronomy, botany, zoology, geology and the natural sciences. The museum's Kellogg Observatory is well worth a visit. Niagara: *Niagara's Wax Museum of History.* 333 Prospect St. Wax figures, displays. *Schoellkopf Geological Museum.* Robert Moses Pkwy. Exhibits and displays trace the geological history of the Falls.

TOURS. Lewiston: *Artpark.* All the arts on display on 170 verdant acres. *Cave of the Winds.* Trip from Goat Island down elevator to base of Falls. *Helicopter Ride. Maid of the Mist.* Boat ride almost into the Horseshoe Falls. Fee includes use of raingear. *Observation Tower.* Elevator also descends to the gorge. *Niagara Power Project.* Lewiston Rd., State 104, 4 mi. N. *Power Vista.* Observation Bldg., animated models, films. Balcony views of U.S. and Canadian Falls.

THE NIAGARA FRONTIER

SPORTS. *Golf:* Batavia: Terry Hills, 9-hole course. Buffalo: Delaware Park, 18-hole course. South Park, 9-hole course. Grand Island: Beaver Island, 18-hole course. Niagara Falls: Hyde Park, three courses, 18 holes.

Harness racing: Buffalo Raceway in Hamburg, December–July.

Skiing: Frost Ridge (in Le Roy), Glenwood Acres (Glenwood), Honey Hill (Warsaw), Kissing Bridge (Glenwood).

SPECTATOR SPORTS. Buffalo Bills of National Football League. Buffalo Sabres of National Hockey League. Many colleges engage in varsity athletics.

WHAT TO DO WITH THE CHILDREN. Buffalo: *Delaware Park Zoo. Children's Zoo.* Grand Island: *Fantasy Island.* Thruway Exit N–19. Children's amusement park, Western Town, *Animal Kingdom,* rides and playground. Niagara Falls: *Oppenheim Zoo.* Niagara Falls Blvd.

TRAVELING INTO CANADA. Although the traveler will generally have little or no difficulty crossing the international border between Canada and the United States, there are a couple of important points that should be mentioned.

If an American motorist is involved in an automobile accident in Canada, he or she may be required to produce proof of adequate liability insurance coverage valid in Canada. In the event of inability to produce such proof, local police may be authorized to detain the motorist until such proof can be obtained. This particularly annoying eventuality can be easily avoided, however. Motorist planning to enter Canada can obtain from their insurance agents a certificate stating that they have liability insurance coverage that is valid in Canada and of sufficient limits to be in compliance with Canadian regulations.

Travelers may have difficulty attempting to bring pets across the international border. In some instances, a pet can be taken from the United States into Canada but not allowed to return to the United States without its owner having to go through lots of time-consuming formalities. Travelers with pets should have accurate information concerning their pets' vaccination and immunization records, and should make sure before crossing the border that their pets will be allowed to return.

Travelers who are not citizens of the United States or Canada may be required to present their passports at the border and if they are in the U.S. on a visa they should be absolutely sure that that visa is a multiple-entry visa that will allow them to re-enter the U.S. from Canada.

NEARBY ATTRACTIONS

CUSTOMS PROCEDURES. Customs regulations between the United States and Canada are among the most liberal in the world. Passing from one country to the other is usually a simple matter of presenting some valid and acceptable form of identification and answering a few simple questions about where you were born, where you live, why you are visiting Canada, and how long you will stay.

The identification need not be a passport, although this is certainly acceptable. You can also use a driver's licence, birth certificate, draft card, Social Security card, certificate of naturalization, or resident alien ("green") card.

The entry procedure for citizens of Great Britain, Australia, and New Zealand is similarly simple.

Canada allows British and American guests to bring their cars (for less than 6 months), boats or canoes, rifles and shotguns (but not handguns or automatic weapons) and 200 rounds of ammunition, cameras, radios, sports equipment, and typewriters into the country without paying any duty. Sometimes they will require a deposit for trailers and household equipment, but these are refundable when you cross back over the border. (This is to guarantee that you do not sell these items in Canada for a profit.) Needless to say, you may bring clothing, personal items, and any professional tools or equipment you need (if you work in Canada) without charge or restriction. It is also a good idea to carry your medical insurance and insurance for boats, vehicles, and personal luggage.

Some items are restricted, however. You need the contract for a rented car. And, if you are going to return home and leave behind a car you rented in the States, you have to fill out an E29B customs form. Tobacco is limited to 200 cigarettes, 50 cigars, and 2 pounds of pipe tobacco. Alcohol is limited to 40 ounces or 2 dozen 12-ounce bottles of beer. Dogs, for hunting or pets, are duty-free, but you must bring a certificate from a veterinary inspector to prove that the dog has no communicable diseases. (Cats may enter without restriction.) Plants of all kinds must be examined at the customs station to preclude the entry of destructive insects.

Most important, Canadian officials are diligent in pursuing smugglers of narcotics and other illegal items.

Americans returning to the United States after at least 48 hours in Canada may take with them personal articles worth up to $300 without paying duty, but they may claim this privilege only once every 31 days. Part of this merchandise may be 100 cigars, one quart of liquor, and 200 cigarettes. Exemptions may be pooled and claimed by a family. One warning: an oral declaration is usually sufficient, but you may be required to fill out customs declaration forms. And, just in case, pack for your return trip in a manner that will facilitate inspection of newly bought merchandise, and keep sales slips handy. That way, if the customs officials want to see your purchases, you won't be delayed unnecessarily.

For Americans who stay less than 48 hours there is a limitation of $25 on imported goods; if your purchases come to over $25, you will have to pay duty on everything. The exemption may include 10 cigars, 50 cigarettes, 8 ounces of tobacco, 4 ounces of alcohol, or 4 ounces of perfume made with alcohol. (If you

THE NIAGARA FRONTIER

include the perfume, you may not include the tobacco products or alcohol.) And you may not pool the items for a family claim.

You can save yourself a lot of trouble by sending gifts to the United States at intervals during your stay in Canada. Such packages are duty-free if the contents are worth less than $25 and you do not send more than one such package a day. Be sure to write "Unsolicited gift, valued under $25" prominently on the package to guarantee duty-free treatment by American customs officials. These packages and the value of their contents are over and above the $300 limit at the border and need not be declared when returning home.

MONEY. The Canadian dollar, like the U.S. dollar, is divided into 100 cents, and coins and bills exist in the same denominations as in the U.S.—*i.e.*, 1¢, 5¢, 10¢, etc.; $1, $2, $5, $10, etc.

Actual exchange rates fluctuate from day to day but the Canadian dollar is usually worth about 85 U.S. cents and about 45 British pence. In order to get the most for your money, convert it before you leave home. Waiting until you get to Canada can create problems. The banks, which are open only from 10:00 A.M. to 5:00 P.M. Monday through Friday, are usually not prepared to exchange foreign currency, and even if you find one that will, it is not always convenient to go to a bank. Furthermore, hotels, stores, and restaurants may offer something less than the best rate. The best policy is to find the nearest Deak Limited foreign exchange office. (There are Deak bureaus at 555 Howe Street, Vancouver; 10 King Street East and 55 Bloor Street West, Toronto; and 1155 Sherbrooke Street West, Montréal.)

There are no restrictions on the amount of money you may bring into or take out of Canada. Both Canadians and foreign visitors may convert money from Canadian tender to another currency or from a foreign currency to Canadian dollars as often as they want, in amounts as great as they want, either inside or outside Canada.

HOTELS AND MOTELS in the Niagara Frontier are geared to the needs of vacation travelers, and many in Buffalo cater to the needs of business people as well. Most newer motels have swimming pools and play areas. Many at Niagara Falls are within sight and sound of the Falls themselves.

Cost categories for double-occupancy rooms in the region are: *Deluxe*, $55 and above; *Expensive*, $40–$54; *Moderate*, $31–$39; and *Inexpensive*, $30 and below. For a more complete explanation of categories, refer to the *Facts at Your Fingertips* section.

BUFFALO

The Buffalo Hilton. *Deluxe.* On Church St. at the waterfront downtown. With 500 rooms, this is the city's largest. Extensive recreational facilities include

NEARBY ATTRACTIONS

6 indoor tennis courts, health club, and swimming pool. Continental restaurant and lounge bar.

Buffalo Marriott. *Deluxe.* 1340 Millersport Hwy. Opened in the spring of 1981, this 340-room property is located in the Buffalo suburb of Amherst, 5 miles from the International Airport. Elegant dining in their Panache Restaurant, evening entertainment in their lounge. Indoor/outdoor connected swimming pool, sauna, giftshop.

Lord Amherst. *Expensive.* State 5 at Thruway exit 50, 5 mi. E of the city. It has a heated pool with sundeck. This is a convenient and sumptuous stopover where you can avoid most of the jet-noise. Restaurant, cocktail lounge.

Statler Hotel. *Expensive.* 107 Delaware Ave., at Niagara Sq. Excellent facilities in the center of town. Barber, beautician, drugstore. Pets allowed. Restaurant, cocktail lounge.

Holiday Inn. *Moderate.* 620 Delaware Ave. (State 384). Comfortable downtown motel, with pets allowed, guests under 12 free, heated pool. Restaurant, cocktail lounge.

NIAGARA FALLS (U.S.)

Niagara Hilton. *Deluxe.* Fall and Third Sts., 3 blocks E. Superb accommodations, restaurants, cocktail lounges, entertainment. Heated pool and sauna.

Holiday Inn–Grand Island. *Deluxe.* Resort hotel overlooking the Niagara River. Tennis, golf available. Indoor and outdoor pools, sauna. Restaurant and cocktail lounge.

Holiday Inn. *Expensive.* 114 Buffalo Ave. (US 114). In downtown area near the Falls, it has a heated pool, kennels. Restaurant, cocktail lounge, as usual in this chain. Reservation deposit required for later-than-4:00 P.M. arrival in season.

Ramada Inn. *Expensive.* 401 Buffalo Ave. (State 384). View of upper rapids. Outdoor dining at restaurant. You'll find a heated pool and plenty of very nice rooms. Reservation deposit required for later-than-4:00 P.M. arrival.

Red Jacket Inn. *Expensive.* 7001 Buffalo Ave., State 324. Modern high-rise hotel on the banks of the Niagara River. Dining room, lounge, heated pool.

Howard Johnson's. *Moderate.* 454 Main St. (US 104). Downtown, with view of Falls. Indoor heated pool, sauna. Restaurant, bar. Also 6505 Pine Ave.

Niagara Falls actually boasts more than 3,000 rooms in the area on the American side, including several downtown motels. There are also scores of motels at modest prices located along US 62 between Niagara Falls and Buffalo. In addition, the Canadian side offers numerous accommodations. Most facilities have a summer rate and an off-season rate.

NIAGARA FALLS (CANADA)

Old Stone Inn. *Expensive.* A 1904 flour mill, now a quiet, luxurious, sunken baths retreat. Outdoor pool, licensed dining room with antique furniture.

Sheraton Brock Motor Inn. *Moderate–Expensive.* A popular place to stay, with an outdoor pool, golf, babysitting services, licensed dining room and TV in its 264 air-conditioned rooms.

THE NIAGARA FRONTIER

Michael's Inn. *Inexpensive–Expensive.* Overlooks Niagara Gorge and Rainbow Bridge. Pubs on the premises are popular. Its 110 rooms have air conditioning and TV, and there's an indoor pool.

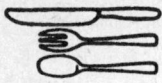 **DINING OUT** in the Niagara Frontier, and especially around Buffalo and Niagara Falls, often means eating at a hotel or motel. There are, however, many good independent restaurants you may sample if you desire. Medium-priced full-course dinners at the restaurants listed occupy only two categories: *Expensive,* $9–$12; and *Moderate,* $6–$8.50. Included are *hors d'oeuvres* or soup, *entrée* and dessert. **Not included are drinks, tax and tip.** A more explicit discussion of restaurant categories is found in the *Facts at Your Fingertips* section.

BUFFALO

The Cloister. *Expensive.* 472 Delaware Ave., 5 blocks N of town. Lovely atmosphere and excellent food indoors; cocktails served in a lush garden area. Jacket required.

Gepetto's. *Expensive.* 3902 Maple Rd., off State 62. Italian-American cuisine served in a maritime setting. A small but special place to dine.

Red Mill Inn. *Moderate.* In Williamsville, 11 mi. NE of the city. Charming inn built more than a century ago, with steak and seafood specialties. Also has railroad cars for dining and a caboose for cocktails.

Royal Knight. *Moderate.* 3485 Delaware Ave. (State 384) in Kenmore. Background music creates a pleasant atmosphere for dining on American favorites like prime rib, chicken, or pork chops.

LEWISTON

Riverside Inn. *Moderate.* 115 S. Water St. A selection of dining rooms in this old home that is set on a bluff above the Niagara River gorge. Steak and seafood, along with such house specialties as chicken breasts in whiskey sauce and duck in orange sauce.

LOCKPORT

Quarterboard. *Moderate.* 274 Gooding St., off State 78. This relaxed dining spot features steaks and seafood specialties.

NIAGARA FALLS (U.S.)

John's Flaming Hearth. *Expensive.* 1965 Military Rd., 6 mi. NE of downtown. The menu is limited, but what they do they do well. Steak and lobster specialties, interesting desserts. Locally popular dining room.

J.P. Morgan's Shopping, Eating, and Drinking Establishment. *Expensive.* Third St. and Rainbow Mall. Excellent seafood and prime ribs. Unique spot, with indoor dining terraces and a New York-style deli.

The Crown and Anchor. *Moderate.* 2901 Pine Ave. Hearty portions of good Italian-American cuisine.

The Speakeasy Restaurant and Cabaret. *Moderate.* 1919 Whirlpool St. Generous American fare. Disco dancing nightly; entertainment weekends.

NIAGARA FALLS (CANADA)

Falls Manor. *Moderate.* Barnboard panelling, broasted chicken, steak, homemade pies. No license.

Betty's. *Moderate.* In Chippawa. This is no-nonsense, no-frills, dependably good home cooking. Steak or turkey dinners, real whipped cream in the desserts. Licensed.

THE JERSEY SHORE AND ATLANTIC CITY

by JOHN MAXYMUK

One of New Jersey's largest industries is tourism, and its main attraction is the 125-mile eastern coastline that stretches from Sandy Hook to Cape May, the Jersey Shore. Diversified recreation is what makes the shore so appealing: it offers boardwalks, amusement parks, beaches, facilities for surf- and deep-sea fishing, swimming, boating, bird sanctuaries, wildlife refuges, historical landmarks and exciting nightlife—particularly in Atlantic City's gambling casinos.

The entire shore is located within a few hours' drive from New York City. To start the tour from the north, take the Garden State Parkway to exit 117 onto Route 36 and head toward Sandy Hook. An exhilarating bird's-eye view of both the Atlantic Ocean and Sandy Hook is available along Ocean Drive in Atlantic Highlands. The well-named Highlands were the setting for James Fennimore Cooper's 19th-century novel *Water Witch*.

The Sandy Hook peninsula arches back toward New York and is divided into two sections. The northern section houses a government installation including Fort Hancock, headquarters for the 52nd Artillery Brigade. Sandy Hook's strategic military importance dates to the pre-Revolutionary days of the Colonies and derives from the fact that the Hook extends into New York Harbor. Whoever controlled Sandy Hook could easily intercept anyone headed for New York.

While the northern section is closed to the public, the southern section is a 460-acre National Park, part of the Gateway National Recreation Area. Originally popular among Indians as a hunting and fishing preserve as well as for its varied vegetation of beach plums, hackberry, holly trees, and even some cactus, Sandy Hook was first purchased by English Colonist Richard Hartshorne for 13 shillings in 1678. It now attracts 30 to 50 million visitors annually.

Besides the wilds, Sandy Hook's public beaches permit both bathing and surf fishing, and the park has picnic tables. Though not open to the public, the Sandy Hook Lighthouse is also on the grounds. It was built at the water's edge in 1762, but since then approximately 1,000 feet of shoreline has accumulated in front of it through tidal action. The beacon is the oldest continuously lit lighthouse in the nation.

On the way back to the mainland, make a stop at Navesink Twin Lights on Beacon Hill off Route 36. A massive fortress-like structure which you can tour, this lighthouse was built in 1862 (on the site where a previous lighthouse had been built in 1828), and in clear weather affords an unhampered view of the distant New York skyline. In the summer, a marine museum is also open on the grounds.

Traveling south, you'll come upon Long Branch, which has been a forerunner to Atlantic City in two aspects: from the 1870s to the 1890s Long Branch was the nation's leading recreational resort, and in the same time period it featured casino gambling.

The whole idea of summer-resort housing rentals is said to have begun in 1788 in Long Branch when Philadelphian Elliston Perot rented a Long Branch mansion for the summer. Soon others saw the choice business opportunity and began to buy property to rent out in the summer. At that time, Long Branch catered to the elite of Philadelphia and vied with Cape May for their resort trade. Long Branch was known then (and perhaps admired) for its modest bathing rules, one sex in the water at a time.

By the time President U.S. Grant became a frequent visitor after 1868, the town had loosened up quite a bit. Long Branch became

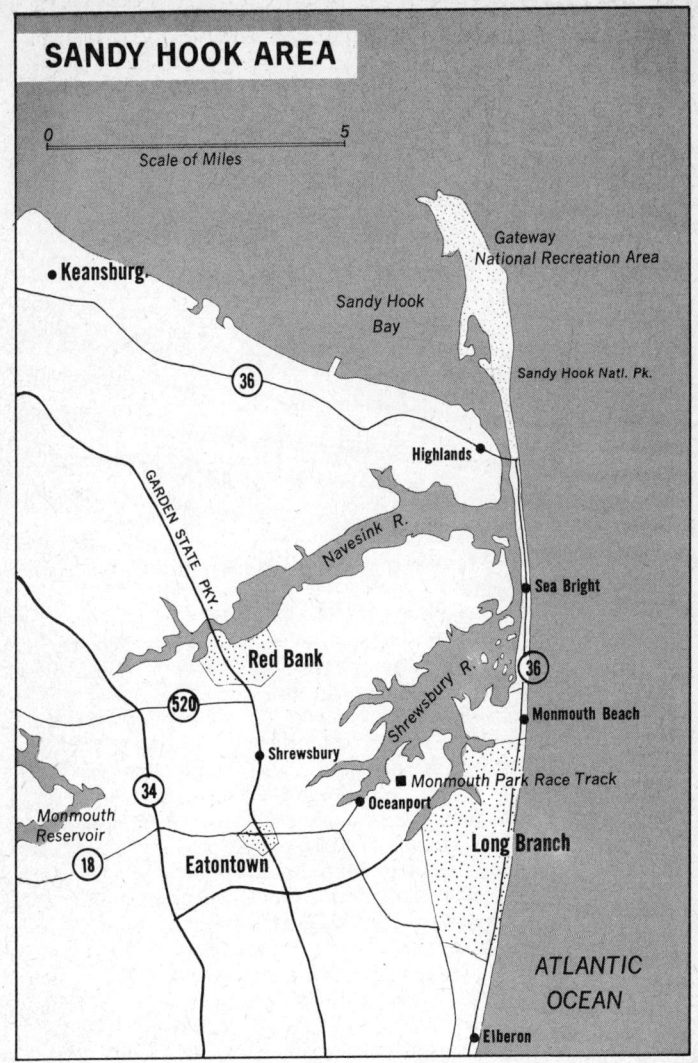

known for its gold-domed gambling casinos (gentlemen only) during this country's Gilded Age. Such New York personalities as Diamond Jim Brady, Lily Langtry, and Lillian Russell were frequent visitors, as well as Presidents Hayes, Harrison and Garfield (who was brought to Long Branch to die after having been shot). Much later President Wilson also visited here.

In some casinos there was gambling even on Sundays until 1894, when Congressman James A. Bradley spearheaded a reform movement and gambling was abolished.

Although Long Branch's salad days are long past, it is still a pleasant resort. It has seven miles of ocean front with five beaches along two miles of boardwalk. In addition to the boardwalk amusements and ocean bathing, Long Branch also has the longest fishing pier on the East Coast (800 feet), open around the clock.

Asbury Park gives the impression of not only the carnival-come-to-town, but of the carnival-become-the-town. Asbury Park is the image of Atlantic City in the 1960s, on the decline, but still attracting people who "knew it when." It was founded in 1870 by the aforementioned Congressman Bradley and named after Methodist Bishop Francis Asbury. Although first termed "Bradley's Folly," because it was then mostly briars, the venture was a rapid success.

Asbury Park's appeal doesn't seem to change: rides for the kids, amusements for teenagers, games of chance, novelty stores, sweetshops, music, and a convention hall. You still walk the mile-long boardwalk, play on the beach, and swim in the ocean (there are locker facilities available at both the Fourth Avenue Bathing Pavilion and the Eighth Avenue Bathhouse).

Entertainment is booked year-round in Convention Hall, which is on the boardwalk and seats 3,500. Band concerts are held every Thursday night from June through August outdoors at the Fifth Avenue Pavilion. Through music the area has achieved a certain amount of new fame in recent years, as contemporary popular musicians Bruce Springsteen as well as Southside Johnny and the Asbury Jukes surfaced in area bars.

Asbury Park holds special appeal to fishermen because of the three freshwater lakes within its boundaries. Not only can local fishermen fish from the beach and from deep-sea boats, as at most resorts, but in Asbury Park freshwater fishing is a viable option.

The neighboring community of Ocean Grove is a small religious resort which used to be notorious for its strict blue laws. Until 1979, not only was there no swimming permitted on Sundays, but there were no automobiles allowed within town limits on the Sabbath. All cars had to be parked outside the front gates of the city from midnight Saturday to midnight Sunday.

THE JERSEY SHORE

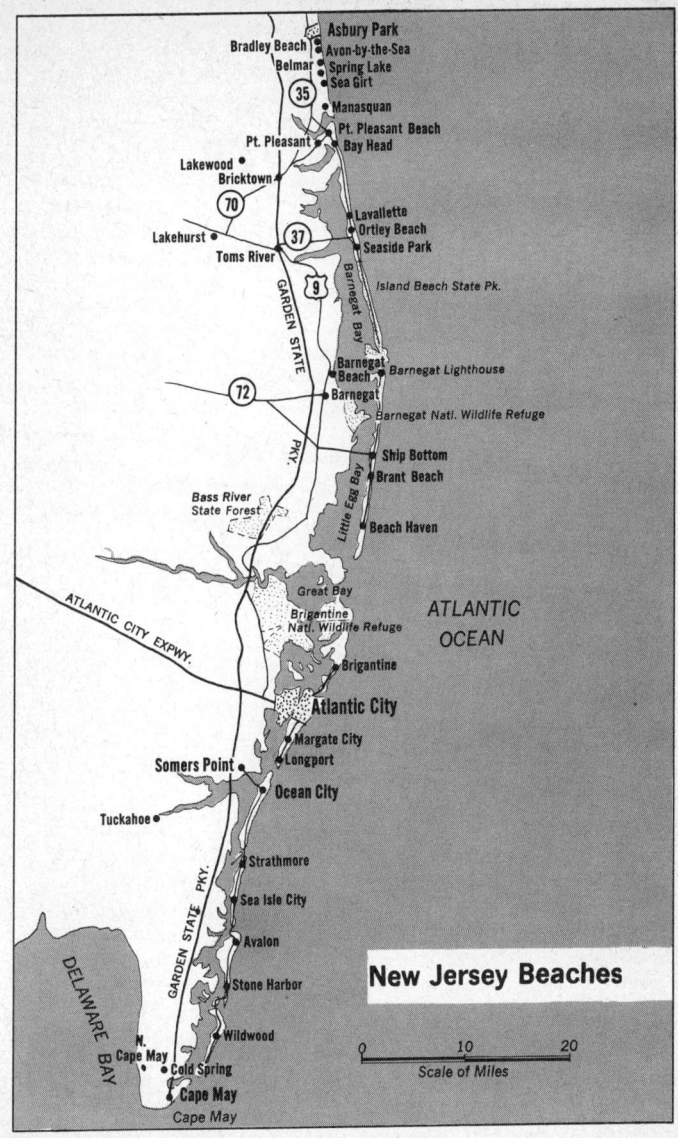

The gates are always open now, but this is still a quiet seaside town filled by Victorian-era boardinghouses surrounding the massive wooden Great Auditorium built in 1869 and still the center of the town's activities. Ocean Grove is where Woody Allen shot most of his 1980 feature film, *Stardust Memories.*

Although still far from being densely populated, Ocean County is one of the fastest growing counties in New Jersey, increasing its population by five times since 1950. To get an idea of what it once was like, you can visit two large parks. Near Lakewood on the mainland off Route 88 is Ocean County Park, one of the largest county parks in the state. Formerly the park's 575 acres of pine groves belonged to John D. Rockefeller, Sr., as a vacation estate. Its vast grounds—on which picnicking is permitted—are impressive and well kept.

Back on the shore is Island Beach State Park, 2,694 acres of remote long-stretching dunes. The state purchased this land in 1953 and opened the park six years later. The park offers the chance to see a natural barrier beach in near-pristine condition. As well as dune grass, briar, and ivy, you'll find beach plum and other rare vegetation covering this "island" (it hasn't been an island since the Cranberry Inlet closed in 1812). There are a few beach houses and parking lots in one area, in addition to picnic tables. The northern section of the park is devoted to guided nature trails. The central section features several beaches where swimming is allowed and lifeguards are on duty. The southern third is for birds and fishermen.

There is only one way to reach Long Beach Island by land—via the Route 72 causeway—and this says something about the resort's style. If you're looking for big-city excitement on your vacation, don't look here. Appropriate to the Philadelphia Quakers who founded it, Long Beach Island offers simpler pleasures. The various towns are virtually indistinguishable. There is no boardwalk, but there is an abundance of clean beaches, boating, sailing, fishing, and bathing.

Both powerboats and sailboats speckle Little Egg Harbor and Barnegat Bay surrounding the island as well as the Atlantic Ocean. The fishing is excellent, both in the bay and in the ocean. You can troll for tuna, bonito, and bluefish, or deep-sea fish for mackerel, porgy, and sea bass, or catch striped bass and weakfish both in the bay and in the surf.

At the northernmost point of the island is the "Grand Old Champion of the Tides," the Barnegat Light State Park. More affectionately known as "Old Barney," the light is on 13 acres of unsoiled and unspoiled beach that has facilities for picnicking, jetty fishing, and bathing. The lighthouse was originally built in 1858 by General George G. Meade, later a hero at Gettysburg. Thanks to regular maintenance and the structure's durability, the beacon is still in good condition. The walls are 10 feet thick at the base and taper toward the top of the

THE JERSEY SHORE

172-foot structure. From the top you have an excellent view of Barnegat Shoals, the scene of more than 200 shipwrecks. There is an admission charge.

On the way to Atlantic City, two stops are worthwhile: the Historic Towne of Smithville and the Brigantine National Wildlife Refuge. Smithville is located 12 miles north of Atlantic City on Route 9 and is a meticulous restoration of a typical 18th-century southern New Jersey town. Many of the town's buildings have been moved to Smithville from their original South Jersey sites. There are a number of fine inns at which to eat, 30 specialty shops, and many preserved historical buildings to stroll through. The Smithville Inn was originally built in 1787 by James Baremore and used as a one-room stagecoach stop for many years. The shops feature everything from antiques and reproduction furniture to tasty baked goods. The "Old Village" of restored historical buildings transports you to an authentic Colonial atmosphere. By the pond is a 170-year-old grist mill, and on the pond are the popular swan boats, which you can rent.

Another mile south on Route 9 will bring you to the Brigantine National Wildlife Refuge, a coastal sanctuary mostly for birds. Established in 1939, the refuge has over 20,000 acres of preserved tidal marshes, barrier beaches, and wooded areas. Fall and spring are the best times to visit because of the migratory habits of the birds along the Atlantic Flyway, but even at other times you might see snow geese, black ducks, skimmers, and expatriated Canada geese, gulls, terns, brants, and rails. There are well-marked wildlife trails amid the marshy and wooded acreage. There is some hunting in season. Admission is free.

Atlantic City

The greatest tourist attraction on the shore is of course Atlantic City, the aging "Queen of Resorts." Having adopted casino gambling by referendum in 1976, the resort is in a period of transition. Once a sparking jewel on the water, Atlantic City had declined so formidably in the 1960s and '70s that some referred to it as "Newark by the Sea." The injection of the casinos has given the town new life and spirit. "Casino City" will never be what Atlantic City was, but in undergoing its change it is becoming something equally rich.

Until the 1850s, Atlantic City was known as Leeds Point after its first landholder, Jeremiah Leeds. It was then a small community of fishermen, for the most part. In 1852 Dr. Jonathan Pitney and others were able to convince the Camden and Atlantic Railroad to charter a line to transport bog iron from the nearby Pine Barrens to the cities and

NEARBY ATTRACTIONS

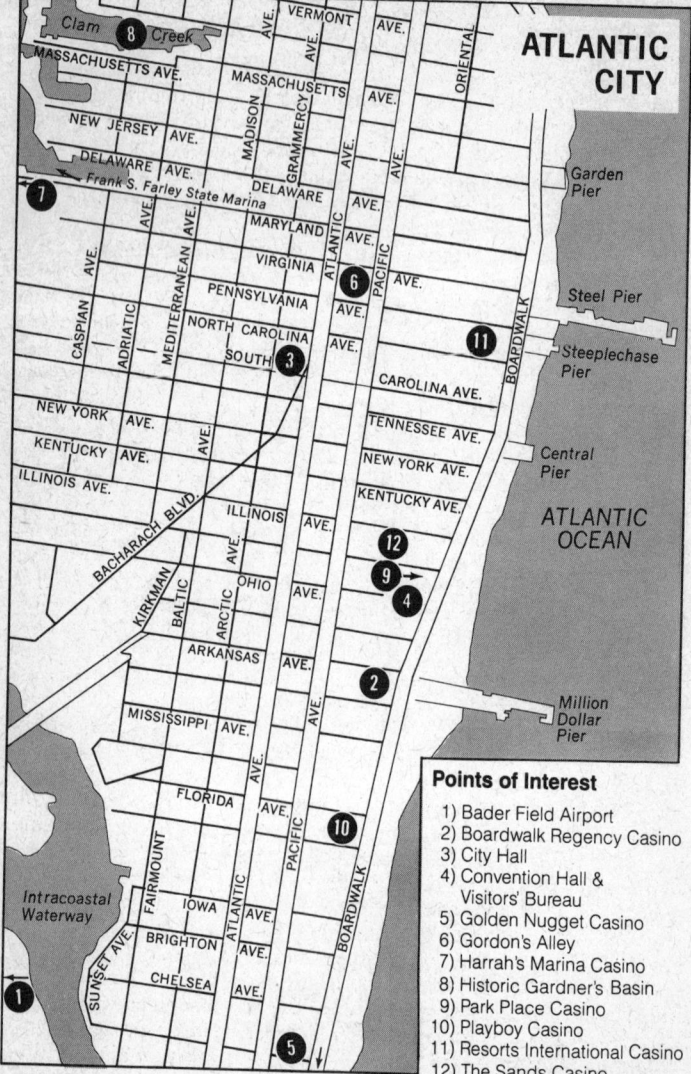

Points of Interest

1) Bader Field Airport
2) Boardwalk Regency Casino
3) City Hall
4) Convention Hall & Visitors' Bureau
5) Golden Nugget Casino
6) Gordon's Alley
7) Harrah's Marina Casino
8) Historic Gardner's Basin
9) Park Place Casino
10) Playboy Casino
11) Resorts International Casino
12) The Sands Casino

THE JERSEY SHORE

to promote the shore as a fisherman's haven. In 1854, Leeds Point was incorporated as Atlantic City, and in July of that year the first trains started arriving.

Not too long after a regular trade began, boardinghouse owner Charles McGlade decided to upgrade his house (installing wallpaper, comfortable beds, and stuffed chairs) in order to attract women. Heretofore women had not been interested in coming to the shore and staying in white-washed fishermen's shacks. As McGlade's idea quickly proved successful, other hotelmen followed suit and the resort was born.

In 1870, local businessmen began to clamor about the popularity of beach strolling among the tenants, and the subsequent damage done to expensive hotel carpets from the tenants tracking the beach sand in. A portable boardwalk was devised. Built in eight-foot sections and taken down at the end of the season, it was the first boardwalk the world had seen. Since that time the Boardwalk has been rebuilt five times, each time higher and larger. The present walk was built in 1939 and is six and a half miles long. People flocked to walk the boards, and Atlantic City was fully launched.

In 1881, Colonel Howard built the first Boardwalk pier, but both it and a subsequent one were destroyed by natural disasters. Even though the idea of piers was derided as "Howard's folly," soon there were five piers extending into the sea: the Million Dollar, Central, Steeplechase, Steel, and Garden Piers. Each offered its own combination of rides, amusements, shows and attractions. The Steel Pier became famous as "The Showplace of the Nation," consistently signing the biggest names in show business, be they Harry James, Frank Sinatra, or Fats Waller.

In an effort to extend the summer season to one week beyond Labor Day, an enterprising promoter hit upon the idea of a beauty pageant in 1921. Over sixty years later, the Miss America Pageant is going stronger than ever, still attracting a large national television audience each September.

So many firsts, largests and general oddities have occurred in the "World's Playground." The first postcard in 1895. The origin of salt-water taffy in the 1800s. The long-suffering high-diving horse on the Steel Pier. The term "airport," coined in 1919 at the opening of what is now the world's oldest commercial airfield, Atlantic City Airport. Boardwalk entrepreneur Captain John Young's Italian villa residence right on the Boardwalk, Number 1 Atlantic Ocean. And this is only a short selection.

The hotel district was built up along the Boardwalk, and it featured a magnificent string of hotels, each built grander, more elaborately and ornate than the last. Most of them are gone now. The Dennis grew from a two-room cottage in 1860 to an enormous 450-room hotel in this century. The Marlborough-Blenheim was the first poured-concrete hotel in the country; the process was supervised by its inventor Thomas Edison. (It has been torn down to make way for Bally's Park Place Casino.) The 634-room Ambassador was demolished. The 14-story, twin-domed triumph of Moorish architecture, the Traymore, was dynamited. The St. Charles, The Breakers, and others . . . all gone. Only the Chalfonte-Haddon Hall, remodeled into Resorts International Hotel Casino, and the Claridge, remodeled into Del Webb's proposed casino, remain.

Times were tough on the shore just as they were everywhere else during the Depression. In 1941, the island was filled with soldiers preparing to go overseas, and resort business declined. In the post-war period the recreation trade was good and Atlantic City prospered, but the fall was rapid in the developing jet-travel era of the '60s and '70s. Legalized gambling was seen as the salvation.

Resorts International was the first casino to open in May 1978, and things started to turn around again. In the next three years, six more casinos opened: Caesar's Boardwalk Regency, Bally's Park Place, The Sands, Golden Nugget, Harrah's, and Playboy. The Tropicana and Del Webb's Claridge are due to open at press time. The increase in visitors has been remarkable; the crowds have returned and the city is struggling to keep pace. Once again there is nightlife in Atlantic City, and now it's year-round.

And there are other things to do besides gambling. Gordon's Alley is an imaginatively designed Old World mini-mall in a somewhat run-down section uptown. It features small, sophisticated shops and free parking. Gardner's Basin at the Inlet section of town is a re-creation of a 19th-century maritime village. There are large ships, small craft, a marine mammal rescue center, and a saltwater aquarium as well as shops, exhibits, and a restaurant. There is a slight admission charge. Lastly, you might visit the Atlantic City Historical Museum on the Garden Pier, look at the sundry memorabilia and imagine what Atlantic City must have been like.

South Along the Shore

The most interesting way to travel south from Atlantic City is to take the Ocean Drive, 40 scenic miles along the coast over six connecting toll (30 cents) bridges. Just follow Atlantic Avenue through Atlantic City and its neighboring exclusive suburbs on Absecon Island: Ventnor, Margate, and Longport. Margate is perhaps the most well-known due to its cluster of popular summer-season bayside bars which cater mostly to a college-age crowd.

THE JERSEY SHORE

Also in Margate is Lucy the Elephant, a National Landmark. She was originally built in 1881 by a real-estate promoter to attract business, and had two sister pachyderms: one on Coney Island which burned down in 1896, and one in Cape May that was torn down in 1899. Lucy is six stories high, 38 feet long, and 80 feet around. She was a hotel attraction as well as a tavern before she fell into a state of drastic disrepair in the 1960s. She has since been entirely restored and moved two blocks from the original site. For a slight admission charge you can tour her—climb up the inside of her legs, peek out her eyes and stand in her howdah overlooking the ocean.

After leaving Longport, start looking for signs reading "Flight of the Gull"; they will direct you along Ocean Drive into Cape May County. Cape May County is noted for its clean sand, fun boardwalks, and marinas, as well as being rumored as having more *Mayflower* descendants than any other county in the United States.

Over the first bridge you'll come to Ocean City, "America's Greatest Family Resort." Ocean City is the dry town by the water. There is no liquor, beer, or wine sold within its limits. Founded in 1879 as a Methodist resort by three ministers, the Lake Brothers, Ocean City forbids alcohol in its original charter and continues to uphold that spirit.

Eight-mile-long Ocean City's appeal lies in its small-town atmosphere and in its small but active beaches. On the two-and-a-half-mile boardwalk are arcades, shops, candy stores, and eateries. Throughout the summer free concerts are put on nightly by the Ocean City Orchestra on the Music Pier at Moorlyn Terrace. There is also charter-boat fishing, as well as excellent surf casting and plenty of pleasure boating along the very accessible inland waterways.

Ocean City sponsors a number of imaginative events. On the Saturday nearest to August 1, each year for 25 years crowds have flocked to the bayside of the island to watch "A Night in Venice," a parade of brightly decorated boats along the bay. Bayfront houses join in with their own strewn lights. Other recreational activities range from crab races to beauty pageants.

And if you want to buy alcoholic beverages or down a drink in a tavern, just take the Ninth Street Bridge to the causeway to Somers Point. Somers Point has nightlife for everyone, loud raucous bars for the younger crowd, and fine dining for others.

If you continue to follow Ocean Drive southward, you next come to Sea Isle City. Sea Isle is a picturesque fishing village, alive with on-the-water pleasures upon its docks and lagoons.

Avalon is the next town, less developed than the others along the drive. It has a small boardwalk and lovely sand dunes. On the same island, Stone Harbor is known for its mélange of sparkling waterways highly conducive to boating. At its southern end is the Stone Harbor Bird Sanctuary, the only heronry in the United States sponsored by and located within a municipality. Established in 1947, the 21-acre sanctuary is populated by many species of herons: American egret, snowy egret, cattle egret, Louisiana heron, black-crowned night heron, and green heron. The only non-herons are the glossy ibises, which first arrived here in 1958.

Over the next bridge are the Wildwoods. They were originally named for the area's lush vegetation, but most of that has been replaced by a dense covering of motels in this very popular resort. Along with Atlantic City and Asbury Park, Wildwood offers probably the most exciting night life down the shoreline. Atlantic City has the casinos, but Wildwood and Asbury Park have the honky-tonk bars. This is in addition to its beautiful wide beaches, its excellent facilities for fishing, boating, and sailing, and its two-and-a-half-mile-long boardwalk packed with rides, games, and excitement.

More sedate, but no less interesting, is Cape May, at the southern tip of New Jersey. One of the oldest seashore resorts on the East Coast, Cape May's attraction is primarily the past. The town is filled with Victorian-era architecture, particularly in the Victorian village section of town. The upkeep on all that "gingerbread" alone is staggering. Cape May reached its peak before the Civil War, when it attracted a mix of federal officials and wealthy Southern planters to its six gambling casinos. While that era is long gone, the town is still deservedly popular and well maintained.

Besides going to Fisherman's Wharf to eat and Washington Street Mall to shop, you'll also want to explore Cape May's fine beaches. Along them you may find some semiprecious stones known as "Cape May Diamonds." Actually weathered quartz pebbles, these "diamonds" come in different shades and colors and vary from the size of a pea to that of a walnut. Some colorless ones resemble diamonds. When wet, they're bright and clear, but they dull upon drying. Cut and polished, they're sometimes set in rings, necklaces, and bracelets.

On the southernmost tip of the shore is Cape May Point, where the Atlantic Ocean meets the Delaware Bay. Here you can take the Cape May–Lewes Ferry to Delaware and cross the gateway to the South.

ATLANTIC CITY

PRACTICAL INFORMATION FOR ATLANTIC CITY

HOW TO GET THERE FROM NEW YORK. *By car:* The easiest way is to get on the New Jersey Turnpike and follow it to the Garden State Parkway. To get to Atlantic City, take exit 38A, and take the Atlantic City Expressway, a toll road, into the city. But parking fees in Atlantic City are exorbitant.

By air: There is regular air service from Philadelphia to Atlantic City on *Allegheny Airlines*. There is also service available from the Newark and New York City airports.

By bus: You can leave the driving to someone else either by conventional bus line runs from Port Authority to the Atlantic City Bus Terminal (the trip takes 2½ hours and costs about $16.00 round trip) or you can reserve a seat on a special Atlantic City bus package. These packages take you right to the door of a specific casino and are run through collaboration of the casinos and different bus companies. You'll get round-trip transportation, a free gift (usually a box of saltwater taffy), and either a meal or eight to ten dollars in quarters. Contact: *Domenico Tours,* (212) 732–0274; *Greyhound,* (212) 594–2000; *Harran Transportation,* (212) 343–6060; *Casser Tours,* (212) 840–6500, and *Trailways,* (212) 563–9432.

TELEPHONE. The area code for Atlantic City is 609.

TOURIST INFORMATION. Contact the Visitors Bureau, 2300 Pacific Ave., Atlantic City, NJ 08401.

CASINOS. Atlantic City has staked so much of its future on the success of casino gambling that it's not unusual for even long-time residents to refer to their hometown as "Casino City." Whether the casinos will help alleviate many of Atlantic City's urban problems remains to be seen, but the fact that casinos attract visitors is undeniable (13 million in 1980). Although they all draw customers, each has its own individuality and style.

Resorts International on North Carolina Ave. is the largest and oldest. It opened in May 1978 in the remodeled Chalfonte-Haddon Hall, has 819 rooms and plans to more than double that. Its casino is the largest at 60,000 square feet, and it has more slot machines, lounges, and restaurants than any of the others. It draws the biggest names in show business for its shows and features good, exciting live music in all its lounges. It has top-flight eateries including French, Italian, and Japanese restaurants, as well as an oyster bar, a coffee shop, and a fairly priced buffet. The lobby is very small and the casino is always crowded, but as Frank Sinatra says, "Resorts runs a classy saloon."

Caesar's Boardwalk Regency on Arkansas Avenue opened in June 1979. The casino is the third largest, with 48,600 square feet, and the hotel has 506 rooms. The style is flashy and decorative. There are five restaurants, three lounges, and a number of shops on the second floor. Caesar's also signs the biggest name performers to appear in its theater and offers live entertainment in its lounges (though usually more pedestrian than the music in Resorts' lounges). The finest of its many restaurants is the Palm Court. Their gourmet menu features French Provincial dishes and seafood. This casino is also usually crowded, but there are always places to sit and rest.

Bally's Park Place on Park Place opened December 1979. Outside, the building's smooth curves are easy on the eye, while inside two towering escalators flanked by cascading waterfalls rivet your attention. The casino is spacious (60,000 square feet), elegant, and active. Billy's Pub is the only lounge, but it's large and comfortable. There are a handful of restaurants. Bally's does not book star attractions, though; instead they put together revues of varying quality.

The Sands (formerly The Brighton) on Indiana Avenue and Brighton Park is the only casino not on the water, being a block from the Boardwalk. It was the first casino built completely from scratch, and opened in 1980. The casino floor is the smallest in town, 32,000 square feet, and it has about half the slot machines and blackjack tables as Resorts or Bally's. The idea was to attract the high rollers, those who gamble regularly for high stakes. It has not been as successful as hoped in this regard, or in regard to entertainment, where its big splashy revue folded and was replaced by a lounge act. The Brighton Restaurant has been highly recommended, however, and the casino has been taken over by new management.

Golden Nugget on Boston Avenue and the Boardwalk also opened in 1980. Going to the Nugget is like attending a costume party. The $131 million newly constructed building is designed along Victorian lines with an abundance of brass and marble. There are 80 custom-made chandeliers, gold flaking on the walls, and 50,000 square yards of ceramic tile. Each of the hotel's 520 rooms has a view of the ocean. The casino has 40,000 square feet, and every employee is dressed in costume: doormen are in livery, security guards are fancy-Dan Western marshalls, and the cocktail waitresses are dance hall girls wearing less than a sneeze. There's a fine gourmet restaurant and an excellent buffet. Golden Nugget is ostentatious and overblown, and the taped ragtime Muzak becomes annoying, but it shouldn't be missed.

Harrah's Marina Hotel Casino is a $2.50 cab ride away from the others. It's located on the inlet, and opened in 1980. The design is modern and attractive. The casino is open and bright, with upstairs windows looking out on the water. The restaurants are good and the breakfast and dinner buffets are wonderful. Lounge acts are frequently very good. Always on display are vehicles from Harrah's enormous collection of antique automobiles. Parking for your non-antique auto is free.

ATLANTIC CITY

Playboy at Florida on the Boardwalk opened in the spring of 1981. The casino is on three levels, all overlooking the ocean. All of the games are played on each level. Of course the main attraction to this popular new casino has been the Playboy Bunnies—some of whom are dealers and some of whom are cocktail waitresses. Although Golden Nuggets wear equally skimpy costumes, the Playboy Bunnies seem to hold a particular mystique over casino goers.

Del Webb's Claridge and **The Tropicana** are *scheduled* to open some time after we have gone to press.

NIGHT LIFE. Atlantic City's main reason for being is its night life, but the casinos aren't the only such game in town. There are many fun nightspots for spending either a relaxing or exciting evening.

To hear quiet but contemporary music, try *Camillo's* on 114 South Carolina Ave. It features a cool and comfortable atmosphere with brick walls and dark tables. There's light gourmet dining and fresh fruit drinks as well as live jazz. At *The Last Resort* at South Carolina and the Boardwalk, live entertainment (again mostly jazz) is the main attraction. *TK's Café* at 3426 Atlantic is open 24 hours a day, seven days a week. It has a bar and a stage both upstairs and down. Upstairs there are dance parties while downstairs features swing, folk and mellow music. Casual dress.

If you want to party heartier visit *Little John's,* a bar-restaurant in a converted stone church once slated for demolition, at Tennessee and Pacific Avenues. There's dancing nightly and a cover charge. *The Lido* at 3006 Atlantic Ave. also has dancing nightly, in addition to late-night snacks and a delightful happy hour. For disco-dancing, there's the *Chez Paree* at New York and the Boardwalk. Atlantic City's foremost disco features flashing lights, continuous 16-minute disco cuts and a heavy cover charge.

Just to go and talk and have a good time, there's *The Easy Street Pub* at 30 S. Florida Ave. It has a casually elegant atmosphere and has fast become a favorite meeting place in town. Lastly, there's *The Irish Pub* on St. James Place and the Boardwalk. A friendly, joyous, old-time party atmosphere enlivens this very Irish pub. Irish music on weekends.

OUTDOOR SPORTS. Like so many shore areas, Atlantic City allows for good *fishing* and lots of it. There are party, charter boats, and rowboats. You can fish from the beach and off piers, bridges, or jetties. There is also good crabbing. Trolling for game fishing, you may catch bluefish, marlin, or tuna. Deep-sea fishing you may snag flounder, mackerel, porgy, or weakfish. In the Inlet and Bay are crab, flounder, bass, and weakfish. The best place to head for charter, party, or simple fishing boats is the *Frank S. Farley Marina* at the Absecon Inlet between Huron and Maryland Aves.

As for *tennis* and *golf,* there is an abundance of courts and country clubs in the immediate vicinity. The country clubs are all off of the island however.

NEARBY ATTRACTIONS

AMUSEMENT CENTERS. The best and most convenient places to take the kids for amusements are the Boardwalk piers. The *Million Dollar Pier* at Arkansas Ave., *Central Pier* at Tennessee Ave., and the *Steeplechase Pier* at Pennsylvania Ave. are all open and offer rides, games, and exhibits. A number of casinos such as *Golden Nugget* and *Harrah's* have game rooms which are filled with the latest and most popular arcade games.

In Brigantine, a popular summer attraction for kids of all ages is *The Brigantine Castle,* a dark and spooky haunted castle. Be forewarned that the castle is very dark and can be quite unsettling, so it's not recommended for the very young.

HOTELS AND MOTELS. In general, Atlantic City's places to stay are the most expensive along the typically expensive Jersey shore. Yet they are filled, particularly during the summer season, so make plans and reservations well in advance.

Since casino hotels are covered in their own section above, they are not included here. However, the accommodations there are uniformly *Deluxe.*

Double-occupancy rates are categorized as follows: *Deluxe,* $60 and higher; *Expensive,* $50–$60; *Moderate,* $40–$50; and *Inexpensive,* below $40. For a more complete explanation of categories, see *Facts at Your Fingertips* at the front of this guide.

Bala Motel. *Expensive–Deluxe.* 110 S. Illinois Ave. Pool. Restaurant. 348-0151.

Best Western Inn of Atlantic City. *Expensive–Deluxe.* Indiana and Pacific. Rooftop pool. Restaurant. 348-9175.

The Deauville Hotel and Motor Inn. *Expensive–Deluxe.* Brighton Ave. and the Boardwalk. Pool, sauna, restaurant. Seasonal rates. 344-1251.

Seaside Hotel and Motor Inn. *Expensive–Deluxe.* Pennsylvania Ave. and the Boardwalk. Pool, restaurant. Seasonal rates. 340-3000.

Lafayette Motor Inn. *Moderate–Expensive.* 111 S. North Carolina Ave. Pool, restaurant, cafeteria. 345-3251.

Midtown Motor Inn. *Moderate–Expensive.* Indiana and Pacific Aves. Two pools. Coachman Restaurant and Lounge. 348-3031.

St. Moritz. *Moderate–Expensive.* 134 S. Virginia Ave. Efficiencies available. 344-7186.

World International. *Moderate–Expensive.* 110 Pennsylvania Ave. Pool, restaurant, movies, bingo, fishing. 344-1151.

Atlantic City Barbizon. *Moderate.* North Carolina Ave. Pool, air-conditioned. 348-0134.

Mt. Royal. *Moderate.* S. Park Place. Pool, restaurant, coffee shop. 344-7021.

ATLANTIC CITY

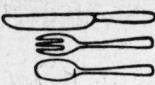

DINING OUT. Atlantic City does not lack for excellent places to eat, particularly since the casinos brought new life to the town. Again, the casinos are considered under their own heading and are not included here.

Price categories may be interpreted as follows: *Deluxe*, $12.50 and above; *Expensive*, $10.00–$12.50; *Moderate*, $6.50–$10.00; and *Inexpensive*, below $6.50. These costs include appetizer, main course, and dessert; they do not include drinks, tip, or tax. For a more complete explanation of categories, consult *Facts at Your Fingertips* at the front of this guide.

The Knife and Fork Inn. *Expensive–Deluxe.* Albany and Atlantic Aves. Seafood and meat dishes. Baking on premises. Jacket required. 344-1133.

Orsatti's. *Expensive–Deluxe.* Raleigh Ave. and the Boardwalk. Italian specialties and seafood. Bar. Dinner dancing. Jacket preferred. 344-7671.

Abe's Oyster House. *Expensive.* 2031 Atlantic Ave. Seafood specialties. Liquor. Since 1926. 344-7701.

Flying Cloud Café. *Expensive.* Historic Gardner's Basin. Seafood smorgasbord. Entertainment, dancing. 348-3290.

The Front Porch. *Expensive.* 132 S. New York Ave. French food. Light and airy atmosphere on the second-story porch. 345-1917.

Le Grand Fromage. *Expensive.* 25 Gordon's Alley. French *nouvelle cuisine*. Seafood and meat dinners. Baking on premises. 347-2743.

Margate Fishery and Captain's Gallery. *Moderate.* 125 Douglas Ave. Continental-American cuisine. Fine seafood. 822-6100.

12 South. *Moderate.* 12 S. Indiana Ave. Sophisticated sandwich house. Pleasant, comfortable atmosphere. Bar. Dinner menu. 344-1112.

Los Amigos. *Inexpensive–Moderate.* 1926 Atlantic Ave. Mexican food. Mexican atmosphere. Bar. Late-night snacks. 344-2293.

The White House Sub Shop. *Inexpensive.* Mississippi and Arctic Aves. A local landmark and still making the best hoagies along the shore. Autographed photos of athletes and entertainers adorn the walls. 345-1564.

PRACTICAL INFORMATION FOR THE JERSEY SHORE

HOW TO GET AROUND. *By air:* Newark Airport is a major international air terminal. It is served by most domestic major airlines. Other smaller airfields are at Atlantic City, Teterboro, Caldwell, Morristown, Monmouth County, Princeton, and Trenton.

By Bus: The Jersey Shore: Stretching more than half the length of New Jersey—from Lower New York Bay to the mouth of the Delaware River—are the hundreds of towns collectively called the Jersey Shore. There is bus service to almost every dot along "the Shore." Asbury Park is 1 hour and 40 minutes from the Port Authority Bus Terminal ($10.00 round trip). Point Pleasant is 2¼ hours away ($11.10 round trip). Seaside Heights is 2½ hours ($12.20). Cape May is 4 hours, 10 minutes away ($21.70). *Transport of New Jersey, Atlantic City Transportation Co., Asbury Park–New York Transit, Boro Buses, Greyhound, Trailways, Domenico Bus Service,* and the *New York-Keansburg-Long Branch Bus* companies all offer commuter, charter, and special tour service within the state. For information about bus travel to and within New Jersey, contact the Port Authority Bus Terminal at 8th Avenue and 41st St., New York City. Tel. (212) 466–7000.

By car: The most common way of reaching any of these places is by car, however. Take the Lincoln Tunnel out of New York City. Follow Route 3 to the New Jersey Turnpike southbound. At exit 11 pick up the Garden State Parkway. The Jersey Shore begins just a few miles south and continues for about 125 miles. Pick your spot and bring along plenty of quarters for the frequent toll booths on the Parkway.

TELEPHONE. The area code for the Jersey Shore is 609.

TOURIST INFORMATION. *State Promotion Office,* N.J. Department of Labor and Industry, P.O. Box 400, Trenton 08625. *New Jersey Dept. of Conservation & Economic Development,* Box 1889, Trenton; *Visitors Bureau,* 2300 Pacific Ave., Atlantic City 08401; the *Cape May County Dept. of Public Affairs,* Box 365, Old Court House, Cape May Court House 08204; and *Ocean County Bureau of Public Relations,* Court House Square, Toms River 08753.

THE JERSEY SHORE

BEACHES. Sun-soaked beaches are the primary draw of the Jersey Shore. Although for the past few years shore sunbathers have had to pay to get on most of the beaches along the whole shoreline, the crowds continue to come. Beach tags are necessary at every beach on the shore aside from those in Atlantic City and the Wildwoods. Tags may be purchased from the local municipality. Generally, for the season they cost around $3.50 if purchased before Memorial Day and $5.00–$7.00 if bought later. Weekly tags usually run from $2.00–$2.50.

New Jersey offers quality beaches to fit a wide variety of tastes. Long Beach Island beaches are not wide, but their jetties and dunes are picturesque, and since there's no boardwalk, these beaches present a more natural appearance. They are also among the best surfing beaches in the state.

Atlantic City beaches are completely different. They're free and filled with hubbub, being the world's oldest and wildest Boardwalk. They cater largely to a day-tourist trade. On the same island, Ventnor and Margate are much more sedate. They offer wide family beaches which are closed to regular traffic.

Ocean City beaches are small but popular, a bit rowdy, and next to a fun boardwalk. The surfing is good here, too. The Wildwoods are free and are well known for their wide white-sand beaches. The beaches in Wildwood Crest in particular are very pleasant and quiet because there is only a walking boardwalk with no stores. All the way to the south, Cape May offers big, clean, wide beaches attractively dotted with rocks. Contact the New Jersey Division of Travel and Tourism, CN 384, Trenton, NJ 08625, for a free beach guide.

CAMPING OUT. One could tour all of New Jersey and camp for the whole trip either at public or private campgrounds. The most consistently nice places to stay near the shore are a handful of state parks not too far from the beaches. *Allaire State Park* in Farmingdale envelops the richly historic Village of Allaire, a Revolutionary-period restored bog-iron community. In the surrounding 3,000-acre park there are picnic tables, tent sites, riding trails, and canoeing.

Part of the *Pine Barrens* (the largest unspoiled woodland in the Northeast), *Bass River State Forest* is 9,400 acres of woods in New Gretna. There are 187 campsites as well as swimming, boating, and fishing on *Lake Absegami*. *Wharton State Forest* is 100,000 acres, also in South Jersey's Pine Barrens. Wharton can accommodate 1,600 visitors and offers swimming, fishing, and canoeing in and on its plethora of streams. Also amongst the Pines is another historic bog-iron town, *Batsto*, which also features mansion exhibits and craft demonstrations. The 11,000-acre *Belleplain State Forest* in Woodbine has 193 campsites and also offers facilities for swimming, boating, and fishing.

For a free guide to New Jersey's campgrounds, contact the New Jersey Division of Travel and Tourism, CN 384, Trenton, NJ 08625.

NEARBY ATTRACTIONS

FISHING. Traditionally, fishing in New Jersey is second only to the beaches for shore recreation. By the sea there are four ways to go after the fishes. The least productive and least expensive method is surf fishing. Most beaches along the shore permit surf fishing after lifeguards go off duty, though jetties, piers, and bridges are often more lively. *Weakfish, flounder,* and *striped bass* are all catchable. Renting a small boat and fishing or crabbing in the shore's many inlets and bays is another relatively inexpensive option. Rentals are usually motor boats, and rods and reels can also be rented. The four- to six-person boats generally range from $18 to $30 for a full day. *Flounder, weakfish,* and *bluefish* abound in the bays.

Party boats are a third choice available almost everywhere. It's simple; just pay from $15 to $30 for a full-day trip, get on board with the others, and an experienced captain will take you to where the fish are biting. Fish vary according to season, but *weakfish, drum, flounder, bluefish,* and *mackerel* are among the most populous. Charter boats are for high rollers only. You and the rest of your party of six to twelve can expect to pay at least $200 to be chauffeured about the water to fish for whatever you wish. Tackle is supplied and often there will be a mate aboard for general assistance.

Information on shore fishing can be obtained from the Division of Fish and Game, New Jersey Department of Environmental Protection, Trenton, NJ 08625. No license is required for saltwater fishing.

AMUSEMENT CENTERS. Aside from the games and rides provided on so many boardwalks along the shore such as in Asbury Park, Wildwood, and of course Atlantic City, the biggest and most exciting place to take the children is *Six Flags Great Adventure* in Jackson. A high admission charge is the one drawback to this $100,000,000 project open only in the summer. There are two parts to Great Adventure: an enormous amusement park with games, rides, attractions, and live shows, and a 450-acre safari. The drive through safari is the highlight of the park. Over 2,000 exotic animals and birds can be seen virtually in their natural habitats. It is possible to pay admission only to the amusement park if you're short on money or time.

HOTELS AND MOTELS. All along the popular shore resort areas the visitor is a captive audience and room rates are usually high and at times exorbitant. Accommodations are generally of standard quality, but remember that you'll be spending most of your time outside the room.

Double-occupancy rates are categorized as follows: *Deluxe,* $60 and higher; *Expensive,* $50–$60; *Moderate,* $40–$50; and *Inexpensive,* below $40. For a more complete explanation of categories see *Facts at Your Fingertips* at the front of this guide.

THE JERSEY SHORE

ASBURY PARK

Betsy Ross Motel. *Inexpensive.* At junction of Rtes. 66 and 33, Neptune. Pool, air-conditioned. (201) 922-1920.

Howard Johnson's Motor Lodge. *Expensive.* Asbury Park Circle, Neptune. Pool, restaurant adjacent, pets. (201) 776-9000.

LONG BEACH ISLAND

Engleside Efficiency Motel. *Expensive-Deluxe.* 30 Engleside Ave., Beach Haven. Oceanfront. Efficiencies available. Pool. 492-1251.

Mariner Motor Inn. *Expensive.* Bay Ave. and 33rd St., Beach Haven. Gardens. Pool, refrigerators. Seasonal. 492-1235.

Quarter Deck Inn. *Moderate.* 351 W. 9th. Ship bottom. Pool, some efficiencies. Seasonal rates. 494-9055.

The Seashell Motel. *Moderate.* Centre and Atlantic Aves., Beach Haven. Pool, restaurant. Seasonal rates. 492-4611.

OCEAN CITY

The Flanders. *Deluxe.* 11th St. and the Boardwalk. American Plan in summer. Social program. Three pools, tennis, golf. 399-1000.

Port-o-Call Hotel and Motor Inn. *Expensive-Deluxe.* 1510 Boardwalk. Efficiencies available. Pool, sauna, dining room. 399-8812.

The Forum Motor Inn. *Moderate-Expensive.* 8th St. and Ocean Ave. Pool, coffee shop, refrigerators. 399-8700.

Harbor House Motor Inn. *Moderate-Expensive.* 2nd and Bay Aves. Bayfront. Pool, marina, fishing, coffee shop. 399-8585.

Sting Ray Motor Inn. *Moderate-Expensive.* 1280 Boardwalk. Pool, restaurant. Seasonal. 399-8555.

CAPE MAY

Cape May is deservedly famous for its guesthouses, large Victorian-era homes which are used as boardinghouses. They are comfortable and unique places to spend a vacation and are no more expensive than hotels (they're often cheaper). Some, like *The Queen Victoria* on Ocean Street, include large country breakfasts in the room rate. Others, like the *Holly House* on Jackson Street, don't serve meals, but are less expensive while retaining the Victorian atmosphere. A list of Cape May's guesthouses can be easily obtained by writing the Cape May County Department of Public Affairs, Box 365, Old Court House, Cape May, NJ 08204. If you prefer modern accommodations, they are also available.

Atlas Motor Inn. *Deluxe.* Beach Drive and Madison Ave. Pool, sauna, efficiencies, restaurant with cocktails and entertainment. Toll-free tel.: from New York (800) 257-8513; from New Jersey (800) 642-3766.

NEARBY ATTRACTIONS

La Mer Motor Inn. *Expensive.* Beach and Pittsburgh Aves. Pool, restaurant, playground, efficiencies available. 884-2200.

The Buckingham. *Moderate-Expensive.* 1111 Beach Drive. Sun deck, refrigerators. Efficiencies and weekly apartments available. 884-4073.

The Patterson. *Moderate-Expensive.* Broadway and Grant Aves. Refrigerators. Efficiencies and Colonial-style apartments available. 884-4187.

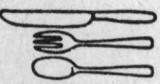

DINING OUT. Being right on the water, most of the best restaurants along the shore serve good, fresh seafood. In southern Jersey, good authentic Italian dishes are also common. Prices run fairly reasonable.

Price categories may be interpreted as follows: *Deluxe*, $12.50 and above; *Expensive*, $10.00-$12.50; *Moderate*, $6.50-$10.00; and *Inexpensive*, below $6.50. These costs include appetizer, main course, and dessert; they do not include drinks, tip, or tax. A more complete explanation of the categories can be found in *Facts at Your Fingertips* at the front of this guide.

LONG BEACH ISLAND

Morrison's. *Moderate-Expensive.* 2nd Ave., Beach Haven. Seafood. Dining overlooking the bay. 492-5111.

The Port-O'-Call. *Moderate-Expensive.* Engleside and Bay Aves., Beach Haven. Traditional seaside atmosphere. Meat, seafood, salad bar. Bar. 492-0715.

The Village Pub. *Moderate.* Centre St. and Bay Ave., Beach Haven. Italian and American dishes. Bar. 492-0192.

The Owl Tree Tavern. *Inexpensive.* 80th St. and the Boulevard, Harvey Cedars. Bar atmosphere. Late-night snacks. Entertainment. 494-8191.

OCEAN CITY/SOMERS POINT

The Culinary Garden. *Expensive.* 841 Central Ave. Ocean City. Beef, seafood, and New York deli sandwiches. Informal. 399-3330.

The Salt Box. *Expensive.* 1046 Asbury Ave., Ocean City. Seafood and French cuisine. Comfortable atmosphere in an old converted house. 399-9219.

Daniel's. *Moderate-Expensive.* 234 Shore Rd., Somers Point. Prime rib, steak, seafood. Bar. 927-4117.

Dorothy's Olde World Cuisine. *Moderate-Expensive.* 406 14th St., Ocean City. European and American dishes. Small and cozy. 398-3482.

Gregory's. *Moderate-Expensive.* 900 Shore Rd., Somers Point. Broiled seafood. Big Sunday brunch. Bar. 927-6665.

Mac's. *Moderate-Expensive.* 908 Shore Rd., Somers Point. Steaks, chops, seafood and Italian. Bar. 927-2759.

Watson's Restaurant. *Moderate-Expensive.* 9th and Ocean Aves., Ocean City. Traditionally popular. Seafood, meat dishes. 399-3482.

CAPE MAY

The Lobster House. *Expensive.* Fisherman's Wharf. Cocktail lounge on a fishing schooner; dance floor on the dock. Seafood of course. 884–8296.

The Mad Hatter Restaurant. (at the Carroll Villa Hotel). *Expensive.* 19 Jackson St. Sumptuous gourmet dining. Outdoor Victorian atmosphere. 884–5970.

Top of the Marq. *Expensive.* 501 Beach Drive. Beef, seafood. Baking on premises. Formal. View of Atlantic Ocean from six flights up. Seasonal. 884–3431.

The Merion Inn. *Moderate.* 106 Decatur St. Seafood, fresh fruit pies, "make your own" relishes. 884–8363.

The Pilot House. *Inexpensive.* 142 Decatur St. Seafood. Lunches and dinners. Bar. 884–3449.

The Ugly Mug. *Inexpensive.* 426 Washington St. Mall. Jumbo sandwiches. Dinners. Entertainment. Bar. Warm atmosphere. 884–3459.

PRACTICAL INFORMATION FOR THE NEW JERSEY MEADOWLANDS

THE MEADOWLANDS. The opening of the Meadowlands Sports Complex (Route 3, East Rutherford, off Routes 3, 17, 20 and Turnpike exit 16W) has revolutionized spectator sports in New Jersey. There is *night trotting* or *thoroughbred racing* all year. The Stadium holds more than 70,000 spectators and has halls where fancy balls are held. The Cosmos *professional soccer* team has drawn crowds of more than 72,000. The Giants *professional football* team uses it as its home field. The new Brendan Byrne Arena is used for special sporting events, concert performances, and other kinds of shows.

HOW TO GET THERE. To get there by car take the Lincoln Tunnel and go west on Route 3. You can't miss it. There is also bus service from the Port Authority Bus Terminal every 20 minutes; $1.40 each way.

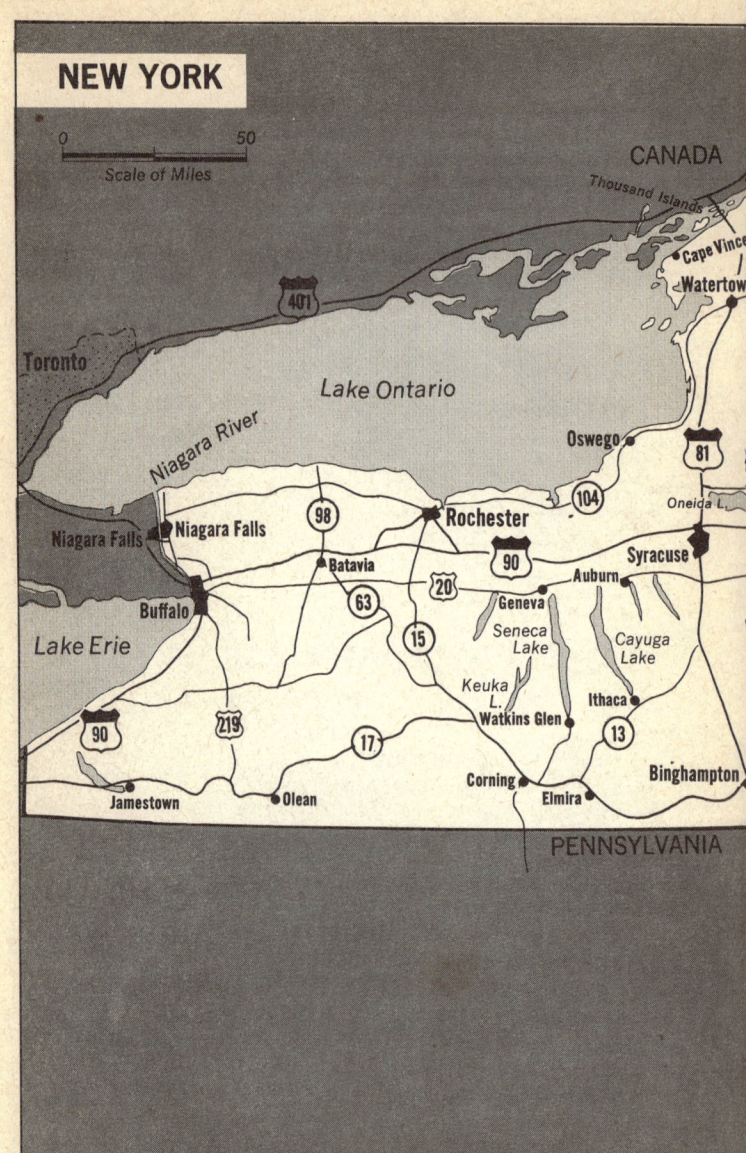

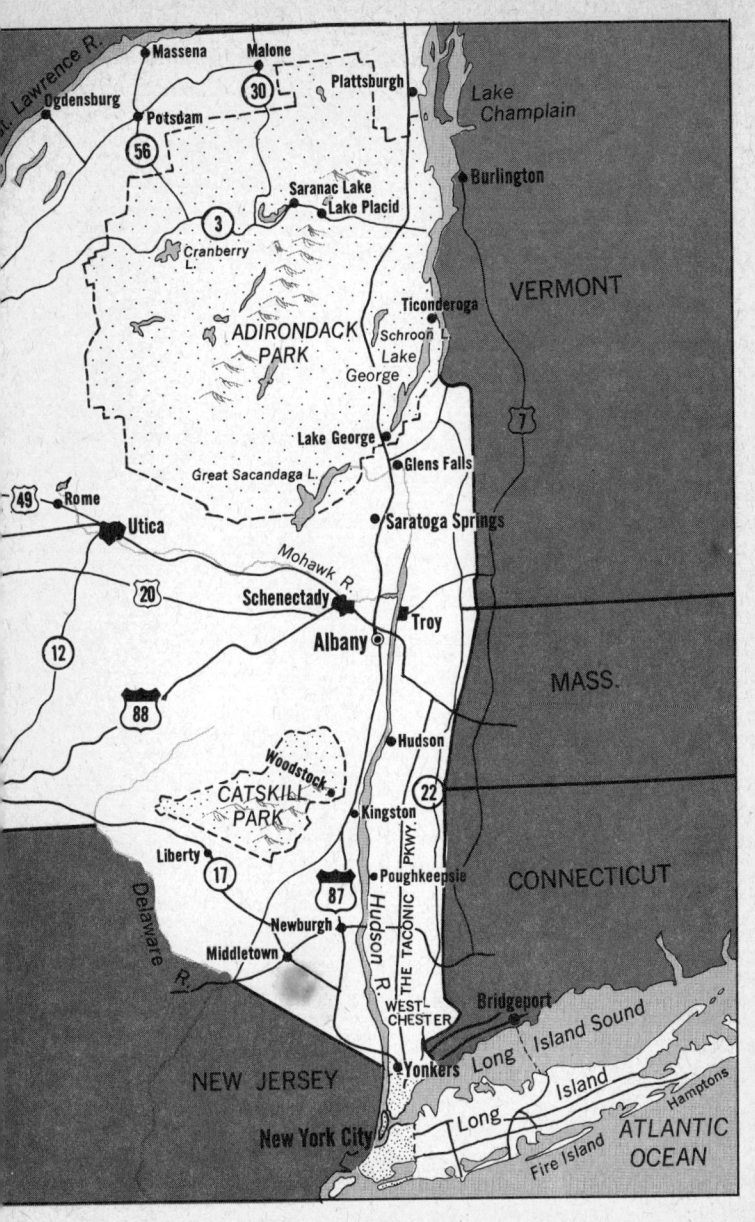

INDEX

The Index is divided as follows:
General Information
New York City
New York State, Jersey Shore and Atlantic City

(The letters H and R indicate Hotel and Restaurant listings.)

GENERAL INFORMATION
Auto travel & driving laws 25-6
British visitors information 20-1
Camping & trailers 26-7, 34, 35
Climate 40
Conversion tables 38-39
Costs 23-5
Drinking laws 31
Emergencies 39
Farm vacations & guest ranches 34
Handicapped travelers 38
Holidays 39
Hotels & motels 27-30
Hours of business 32
Information sources 22
Local time 32
Mail 32
Packing & clothing 22-3
Pets 23
Religious worship 31
Restaurants 30-1
Seasonal events 32-3
Senior citizens 37-8
Sports 32, 35
State parks 35-6
Students 37-8
Tipping 36-7
Trip planning 19-20

NEW YORK CITY
American Indian-Heye Foundation 109-10
American Museum of Natural History 104-5, 190, plan 191-2
American Numismatic Society 110
Aquarium 119
Avenue of the Americas (6th Avenue) 90-2

Babysitting services 169
Bars 318-28
Battery Park 51, 55-6, 163
Beaches 167-9
Beekman Place 98-9
Botanic Garden (Brooklyn) 118, 166
Botanical Garden (Bronx) 124, 165-6
Bowery, The 68
Broadway 88-90
Bronx, The 121-5
Brooklyn 116-20
Brooklyn Heights 116-7
Brooklyn Museum 118, 210-1
Bryant Park 90

Cabarets & floor shows 312-4
Cafés & coffee houses 305-6
Carnegie Hall 92
Central Park 100-01, 161-3
Chelsea 80-2
Children's entertainment 169-72
Chinatown 65-6
City Hall 64-5
Cloisters, The 110, 193, plan 194
Columbus Circle 92
Coney Island 119, 167-8
Customs House 56

Dance 218-20
Discos 314-5
Dyckman House 111

East Village 78-9
Ellis Island 55
Empire State Bldg. 86, 126

Federal Hall 60-1
Fifth Avenue 83-6
Flushing 121
Fort Tryon Park 110-1
Fraunces Tavern 58-9
Free events 156-8
Frick Collection 105-6, 195, plan 196

Gambling 180
Gardens 165-7
Gramercy Park 79-80
Greenwich Village 70-8, map 72
Guggenheim Museum 108, 195-6

Hayden Planetarium 105
Historic sites 180-5

INDEX

Historical Society 104, 206-7
Hotels & motels 130-42

Information sources 50, 151-2
Inwood Park 111

Jamaica Bay Wildlife Refuge 120
Jazz 308-10
Jewish Museum 109, 197
Jones Beach 168

Libraries 185-9
Lincoln Center 101-4, 126, 214-5
"Little Church Around the Corner" 80
"Little Italy" 69
Lower East Side 68-9

Manhattan 49-111
    key to street numbers 147
Maps
    Central Park 162
    Chinatown 67
    Greenwich Village 72
    Lincoln Center 102
    Little Italy 67
    Lower Manhattan 57
    Manhattan 44-5
    Midtown Manhattan 84-5
    Night life areas 320-1
    Shopping areas 228-9, 238
    SoHo 67
    United Nations 96
    Upper East Side 107
    Upper West Side 103
    see also individual entries
Metropolitan Museum of Art 106-8, 197-203, maps 198-201
Morris-Jumel Mansion 110
Movies 212-4
Museum of American Folk Art 203
Museum of Modern Art 92, 204-6
Museum of the City of New York 108, 203-4
Museums 189-212
Music 214-8

Night Life 306-18

Parks 161-5
Plymouth Church 117-8
Pop/Rock 311-2
Prospect Park 119, 163
Public Library 185-7, 207

Queens 120-1

Radio City Music Hall 91
Recommended reading 152-3
Restaurants 251-306
    general information 251-6
    Manhattan 256-300
    other boroughs 300-4
Richmondtown 114-5
Riverside Church 109
Riverside Drive 109
Rockefeller Center 92-4, 126
Roosevelt Island 97

St. John the Divine 109
St. Patrick's Cathedral 94
St. Paul's Chapel 62-3
Seasonal events 153-6
Sheepshead Bay 119-20
Shopping 224-51, maps 228-9, 238
Sightseeing 49, 125-8, 158-60
SoHo 70
South Street Seaport 59, 127
Sports 172-80
Staten Island 112-6
Statue of Liberty 52-5, 126
Stock Exchange 60

Telephones 142
Theatre 220-4
Times Square 88-90
Tours 158-60
Transportation
    in New York 142-51
        airports 150
        auto 143-9
        bus 149
        subway 142-3
        taxis 150-1
    to New York 129-30
Trinity Church 61-2
Turtle Bay 98-9

United Nations 95-7, 126-7

Van Cortlandt Park & House 122-3

Wall Street 60-1
Washington Square 73-4, 163
Whitney Museum of American Art 106, 207-8
World Trade Center 63-4, 126

Zoos
    Bronx 124-5, 164-5
    Central Park 101

INDEX

NEW YORK STATE, JERSEY SHORE & ATLANTIC CITY

(N.J.) indicates New Jersey listings

Adirondack Mts. 402-11
Alexandria Bay 422, H424, R425
Amagansett 344-5, H352, R355
Ardsley R373
Armonk H369
Asbury Park (N.J.) 442, H459
Ashokan Reservoir 383
Atlantic City (N.J.) 445-8, H454, R455, map 446
Atlantic Highlands (N.J.) 440
Ausable Chasm 408

Ballston Spa 397
Barnegat Light State Park (N.J.) 444-5
Barryville 387, H391, R394
Beaches (N.J.) 457
Beacon 362
Bear Mt. State Park 364, H369
Bedford R373
Blue Mt. Lake 410, H414
Bolton Landing H414-5
Boonville R418
Brewster H369, R373
Bridgehampton 342, R355
Brigantine Natl. Wildlife Refuge (N.J.) 445
Buffalo H435-6, R437

Camping & trailers
  Adirondacks 412-3
  Catskills 389
  Jersey Shore 457
  Westchester & Hudson Valley 367
Canaan H369, R374
Canada (travel to)
  Customs 434-5
  Currency 435
  Regulations 433
Canton H415
Cape May (N.J.) 450, H459-60, R461
Cape Vincent 421-2
Carmel R374
Casinos (Atlantic City) 451-3
Catskill 385, H370, R374
Catskill State Park 384

Catskills, The 379-88
Central Valley R374
Children's entertainment
  Adirondacks 414
  Catskills 390
  Fire Island & Hamptons 351
  Niagara Frontier 433
Clayton 422
Cold Spring R374
Cooperstown 398, H400, R401
Cornwall-on-Hudson R374
Croton-on-Hudson 362
Crown Point 407, R418

Delhi 386, H391
Deposit H391
Diamond Point H415
Dover Plains R375

East Hampton 344, H352-3, R356
Eastchester R375
Elizabethtown 408
Ellenville 387, H391
Elmsford H370, R375

Fire Island 332-4, H353, R357
Fire Island Natl. Seashore 333
Fishkill 362, H370, R375
Fort Edward 406
Fort Erie (Ontario) 430
Fort William Henry 407
Friends Lake 411

Garrison 362, R375
Glens Falls 406, H415, R418
Goshen 387-8
Grand Island 431

Hague R419
Hampton Bays 341, H353, R356
Hartsdale R375
Hastings-on-Hudson 365
Hawthorne H370, R375
High Falls 383
High Falls Gorge 409
Hillsdale H370, R376
Historic sites
  Adirondacks 413
  Catskills 390
  Saratoga area 399
  Westchester & Hudson Valley 368-9
Hotels & motels
  Adirondacks 414-8

INDEX

Atlantic City 454
Catskills 391-4
Fire Island & Hamptons 352-4
Jersey Shore 458-60
Niagara Frontier 435-7
Saratoga area 400
Thousand Islands 424
Westchester & Hudson Valley
  369-73
Hudson 363
Hunter 384, 385
Hyde Park 362-3, H370

Information sources
  Adirondacks 412
  Atlantic City 451
  Catskills 389
  Fire Island & Hamptons 348
  Jersey Shore 456
  Niagara Frontier 432, 433-5
  Saratoga area 399
  Thousand Islands 423
  Westchester & Hudson Valley
    366
Irvington 365
Island Beach State Park (N.J.) 444

Jay R419

Kerhonkson 387, H392
Kiamesha Lake H392
Kinderhook 363
Kingston 382-3, H370-1

Lake Champlain 403-4, 407-8
Lake George 403, 406-7, H415-6,
  R419
Lake Luzerne 406, H416, R419
Lake Minnewaska 387, H392
Lake Placid 109-10, H416, R419-20
Lewiston 431, R437
Liberty H392
Livingston Manor 386, H392
Loch Sheldrake H392-3
Lockport R437
Long Beach Island (N.J.) 444,
  H459, R460
Long Branch (N.J.) 440-2
Long Lake H416

Malone H416, R420
Maplecrest 393
Maps
  Adirondacks 405

Atlantic City 441
Catskills 381
Fire Island & Hamptons 336-7
Jersey Shore 443
New York State 463-4
Niagara Frontier 427
Margate (N.J.) 448-9
Marlboro R376
Massena 422, R425
Meadowlands (N.J.) 461
Middletown 387, H393, R394
Millbrook R376
Mohonk Lake 387
Monroe 364
Montauk 345-6, H354, R356
Monticello 386, H393
Mount Kisco H371
Museums & galleries
  Adirondacks 413
  Catskills 389-90
  Fire Island & Hamptons 350-1
  Niagara Frontier 432
  Saratoga area 399
  Thousand Islands 423
  Westchester & Hudson Valley
    368
Music
  Adirondacks 413
  Catskills 390
  Fire Island & Hamptons 351
  Saratoga area 400

Nanuet H371
Narrowsburg 387
National Wildlife Refuges
  Fire Island & Hamptons 349-50
  Jersey Shore 445
New Paltz 383, H371
Newburgh 364, H371, R376
Niagara Falls (U.S. & Canada)
  426-30, H436-7, R437-8
Nightlife
  Atlantic City 453
  Fire Island & Hamptons 354-5
North Creek 411, H417
Nyack H371

Ocean City (N.J.) 449, H459, R460
Ocean Grove (N.J.) 442-4
Ogdensburg 422, H424
Old Chatham 363-4
Old Forge 410, H417, R420

Palisades Interstate Park 368

INDEX

Patterson R376
Peekskill H371, R376
Phoenicia 384
Plattsburgh 408, H417, R420
Port Jervis R394
Potsdam R420
Pottersville 411
Poughkeepsie 362, H372, R377
Pound Ridge R377
Prattsville 385
Purdys R377
Purling H393

Quogue 340

Restaurants
  Adirondacks 418-20
  Atlantic City 455
  Catskills 394
  Fire Island & Hamptons 355-7
  Jersey Shore 460-1
  Niagara Frontier 437-8
  Saratoga area 401
  Thousand Islands 424-5
  Westchester & Hudson Valley 373-8
Rhinebeck 363, H372, R377
Roscoe R394
Rouse's Point 408, H417
Roxbury 386

Sag Harbor 342-4, H353, R356-7
St. Lawrence Seaway 422
Sandy Hook (N.J.) 439-40, map 441
Saranac Lake 410, H417
Saratoga Natl. Historical Park 396
Saratoga Springs 395-7, H400, R401
Saugerties H372
Schoharie Reservoir 384-5
Schroon Lake 411, H417
Shelter Island H353
Smithville (N.J.) 445
Somers Point (N.J.) 449, R460
South Fallsburg H393
South Salem R377
Southampton 334, 340-1, H354, R357
Speculator R420
Sports
  Adirondacks 413-4
  Atlantic City 453
  Catskills 390-1
  Fire Island & Hamptons 352
  Jersey Shore 458
  Niagara Frontier 433
  Saratoga area 400
  Thousand Islands 423
Stamford 386, H393
State Parks
  Fire Island & Hamptons 349
  Westchester & Hudson Valley 367-8
Stone Harbor (N.J.) 449-50
Swan Lake H394

Taconic State Park 367
Tappan R377
Tarrytown 364-5, H372, R377
Thousand Islands 421-2
Ticonderoga 407
Tours
  Adirondacks 413
  Catskills 390
  Fire Island & Hamptons 351
  Niagara Frontier 432
  Thousand Islands 423
Transportation
  Adirondacks 412
  Atlantic City 451
  Catskills 389
  Fire Island & Hamptons 346-8, 348-9
  Jersey Shore 456
  Niagara Frontier 432
  Saratoga area 399
  Thousand Islands 423
  Westchester & Hudson Valley 366
Tupper Lake 410, H417
Tuxedo Park H372

Warwick 388
Water Mill 341-2
Watertown H424
West Point 359, 364, H372
Westhampton Beach 339-40, H354, R357
White Plains 361, H372, R377-8
Whiteface Mt. 409
Wildwood (N.J.) 450
Wilmington 409, H418, R420
Woodstock 383-4, R394

Yonkers H373
Yorktown Heights H373, R378
Youngstown 430-1